The Aga Khan Rural Support Programme

A Journey through Grassroots Development

The Aga Khan Rural Support Programme

A Journey through Grassroots Development

SHOAIB SULTAN KHAN

OXFORD
UNIVERSITY PRESS

OXFORD
UNIVERSITY PRESS

Great Clarendon Street, Oxford OX2 6DP

Oxford University Press is a department of the University of Oxford.
It furthers the University's objective of excellence in research, scholarship,
and education by publishing worldwide in

Oxford New York

Auckland Cape Town Dar es Salaam Hong Kong Karachi
Kuala Lumpur Madrid Melbourne Mexico City Nairobi
New Delhi Shanghai Taipei Toronto

with offices in

Argentina Austria Brazil Chile Czech Republic France Greece
Guatemala Hungary Italy Japan Poland Portugal Singapore
South Korea Switzerland Turkey Ukraine Vietnam

Oxford is a registered trade mark of Oxford University Press
in the UK and in certain other countries

© Oxford University Press 2009

The moral rights of the author have been asserted

First published 2009

All rights reserved. No part of this publication may be reproduced, translated,
stored in a retrieval system, or transmitted, in any form or by any means,
without the prior permission in writing of Oxford University Press.
Enquiries concerning reproduction should be sent to
Oxford University Press at the address below.

This book is sold subject to the condition that it shall not, by way
of trade or otherwise, be lent, re-sold, hired out or otherwise circulated
without the publisher's prior consent in any form of binding or cover
other than that in which it is published and without a similar condition
including this condition being imposed on the subsequent purchaser.

ISBN 978-0-19-547668-2

Typeset in Times
Printed in Pakistan by
Kagzi Printers, Karachi.
Published by
Ameena Saiyid, Oxford University Press
No. 38, Sector 15, Korangi Industrial Area, PO Box 8214
Karachi-74900, Pakistan.

Dedicated to

My grandfather (Late) Sultan Ahmad Beg

My wife Musarrat

My daughters
Roohi, Afshan, Shelley

and

Falaknaz who left this world in 1988
with our grandson Shan and granddaughter Pareesa

My granddaughters Sarah, Zahra and Ayesha

My grandson Amil

My great granddaughters Zehra and Merziyeh

My sons-in-law (Late) Peter Metcalfe, and Tim and Patrick

Afshan's friend Philip

and

My grandson-in-law Hasan

Contents

Acronyms	ix
Preface	xiii

Section I: Origins and Early Experiences

1. An Autobiographical Introduction	3
2. The Daudzai Project	24
3. The Personal Diary of a UN Consultant in Japan	41
4. Letters from Sri Lanka—The Mahaweli Ganga Project	85
5. Transition from the Civil Service to the Aga Khan Foundation	161

Section II: AKRSP

6. His Highness the Aga Khan's Vision of AKRSP	171
7. My Introduction to AKRSP	176
8. The AKRSP: Goals and Operating Principles	208
9. Programme Impact and the Numbers Game	232
10. Partners in Development	257
11. Community Mobilization at AKRSP	278
12. Women, Equity and Economic Justice	325
13. New Management Paradigm	332
14. Dr Akhtar Hameed Khan	350

Section III: Scaling Up and Replication

15. Scaling Up by the Government	369
16. A Case Study of Advocacy with the Government	389
17. SAPAP and Andhra Pradesh	400

List of Appendices	414
Index	473

Acronyms

AC	Assistant Commissioner
ADG	Assistant Director General
ADP	Annual Development Programme
AK	Aga Khan
AKES	Aga Khan Education Services
AKF	Aga Khan Foundation
AKHS	Aga Khan Health Services
AKRSP	Aga Khan Rural Support Programme
AKU	Aga Khan University
AJK	Azad Jammu & Kashmir
BCCI	Bank of Credit & Commerce International
BD	Basic Democracy
CIDA	Canadian International Development Agency
CDWP	Central Development Working Party
CEO	Chief Executive Officer
CSP	Civil Service of Pakistan
CRPs	Community Resource Persons
DC	Deputy Commissioner
DFID	Department for International Development
DJ	Diamond Jubilee of Aga Khan III
DG	Director General
DMG	District Management Group
DMLA	Deputy Martial Law Administrator
DSP	Director Special Programmes
DPO	District Programme Officer
EAD	Economic Affairs Division
ECNEC	Executive Committee of the National Economic Council
FIA	Federal Investigating Agency
FAO	Food & Agriculture Organization
FCNA	Force Commander Northern Areas
FEC	Foreign Exchange Component
GBHP	Ghazi Brotha Hydro Project
GBTI	Ghazi Brotha Taraqiati Idara

ACRONYMS

GM	General Manager
GVM	Gram Vikas Mandal
HBL	Habib Bank Limited
HRD	Human Resource Development
HRDI	Human Resource Development Institute
IDA	International Development Agency
IFAD	International Fund for Agricultural Development
IPS	Investment Promotion Services
IRDP	Integrated Rural Development Programme
ISSB	Inter Services Selection Board
KKH	Karakorum Highway
KAF	Konrad Adenaure Foundation
LB&RD	Local Bodies & Rural Development
MER	Monitoring, Evaluation & Research
MG	Management Group
MLA	Martial Law Administrator
MNA	Member National Assembly
MPA	Member Provincial Assembly
MTDF	Medium Term Development Framework
NAC	Northern Areas Council
NATCO	Northern Areas Transport Corporation
NAWO	Northern Areas Works Organization
NFR	Note for Record
NIPA	National Institute of Public Administration
N-IRM	NRSP Institute of Rural Management
NORAD	Norwegian Agency for Development
NRSP	National Rural Support Programme
NWFP	North West Frontier Province
OED	Operations Evaluation Department of the World Bank
OPP	Orangi Pilot Project
ODA	Overseas Development Authority
PARD	Pakistan Academy for Rural Development
PFS	Pakistan Foreign Service
PIMS	Pakistan Institute of Medical Sciences
PRSPr	Poverty Reduction Strategy Paper
PRSP	Punjab Rural Support Programme
PC-I	Planning Commission Form-I
PPI	Productive Physical Infrastructure
PPP	Plant Protection & Production
PPM	Programme Planning Meeting

PSO	Personal Staff Officer
PTDC	Pakistan Tourism Development Corporation
PWP	Peoples Works Programme
PM	Prime Minister
PWD	Public Works Department
RSPN	Rural Support Programmes Network
SRSC	Sarhad Rural Support Corporation
SRSP	Sarhad Rural Support Programme
SG	Secretary General
SRSO	Sindh Rural Support Organization
SMELC	Social Mobilization Experimentation & Learning Centre
SAARC	South Asian Association for Regional Cooperation
SO	Social Organizer
SOU	Social Organization Unit
SDC	Swiss Development Corporation
UC	Union Council
UNCRD	United Nations Centre for Regional Development
UNICEF	United Nations Children Fund
UNDP	United Nations Development Programme
USAID	United States Agency for International Development
VDC	Village Development Committees
VO	Village Organization
WAPDA	Water & Power Development Authority
WID	Women in Development
WO	Women Organization

Preface

In 1978 at Nagoya, Japan, I gave a presentation on the Daudzai Project at the United Nations Centre for Regional Development (UNCRD). In the audience was Prof. R.P. Misra of the Institute of Development Studies, Mysore, India. He came to me at the conclusion of the session and urged me to write down my experiences at Daudzai in order to share them with others. I responded, 'Who would be interested in reading the book? Besides, who would print and publish it?' Professor Misra persuaded me to leave that to him. I should only concern myself with producing the manuscript, he said, and he would take care of the rest. Accordingly, during my stay at UNCRD, with the help of Hiroko Okada, one of the secretaries at the Centre, I produced the draft of the book *Rural Development in Pakistan* and mailed it to Mysore. True to his word Professor Misra got the book printed and published by Vikas, a well-known printer and publisher of India. But for Professor Misra's initiative, I don't think the book would have seen the light of day.

In 1992 in Paris, in a seminar organized by the World Bank, after I had made a presentation on the Aga Khan Rural Support Programme (AKRSP), one of the participants came to me and said that I should be confined to an island and asked to write my experiences in implementing the AKRSP. Subsequently, Prof. Mahmood Hasan Khan of Simon Fraser University persuaded me to co-author a book on the AKRSP which was published by Greenwood of USA.

My full time employment in implementing the AKRSP followed by my full engagement in the South Asia Poverty Alleviation Programme (SAPAP) between 1994–2002 and thereafter, the tremendous demands of the ten Rural Support Programmes (RSPs) which had federated in a network, the Rural Support Programmes Network (RSPN), hardly gave me time to think about writing a book on the AKRSP.

Suddenly in 2006, out of the blue, I received an email from Fayyaz Baqir in London, who, having come across my Notes for the Record (NFRs) on the AKRSP, spanning the entire twelve years of my involvement with the programme, at the Akhtar Hameed Khan Resource Centre of NRSP Institute of Rural Management, suggested that they were excellent material for a book. He also enclosed a three-page outline of topics on which he wanted me to give lectures which could be transcribed to fill the blanks in and complement the NFRs. Sitting in London, surrounded by the entire family including grandchildren and great-granddaughters, I started writing my thoughts on each of the topics identified by Fayyaz. I was amazed at the recollections of the happenings of the past when I started to pen these down; even with very selective filtrations the personal recollections spread over a hundred pages.

Fayyaz Baqir has with great dexterity integrated the NFRs with my recollections, besides giving headings to the NFRs and editing and arranging them in an order that achieves a coherent and continuous flow. I am profoundly indebted to Fayyaz, without whose initiative and perseverance I doubt if I would ever have been able to cast the NFRs into the form of a book.

The NFRs which I did not write myself were authored by members of the Management Group of AKRSP. Prominent among those were Tariq Husain, Feroz Shah, Hasan Naqvi, Maliha Hussein, Izhar Hunzai, Nabeel Anjum Malik, Zahoor Alam, Amenah Azam Ali, Khaleel Tetlay, Zahir Meghji, Anis Dani, Najma Siddiqi, Masoodul Mulk, Shandana Khan, Shahida Jaffrey, Syed Mutahir Shah and others. Fayyaz selected those NFRs which threw light on the concept, approach and methodology of the AKRSP besides including all the NFRs which I had personally written. I am grateful to all those who wrote the NFRs, which proved to be a rich resource for this book.

Ultimately, it fell to the lot of Dr Virginia of NRSP to give the material its present shape. She worked hard and long before achieving a coherent and readable document. I am greatly indebted to her for editing, re-arranging chapters and organizing the material into a book for the consideration of publishers.

The editors at OUP gave sparkle to the manuscript by their excellent editing and my heartfelt gratitude to Ameena Saiyid OBE for accepting the manuscript for publication.

Finally, I must express my appreciation for Abdul Rauf's hard work, ably assisted by Mansoor Abid, in typing and retyping the draft. I am grateful also to the RSPN and N-IRM for their support in publication of this book, and indebted to Shahid Hussain for reading the manuscript and giving useful advice.

His Highness inspecting the newly constructed irrigation channel at Teru below Shandur Pass
Courtesy: Karim Jan

A dialogue with villagers on the project site
Courtesy: Karim Jan

Akhtar Hameed Khan with villagers in Chaprote Valley, Nagar
Courtesy: Karim Jan

Village Organization Shahtote members explaining their land development plan at the site
Courtesy: Karim Jan

First dialogue at Sherqilla, Punyal Valley
Courtesy: Karim Jan

Rahul Gandhi with the author in the Vision Workshop, UP, India, July 2008
Courtesy: Rajiv Gandhi Memorial Trust

Rahul Gandhi with the author and some participants of the Vision Workshop, UP, India, July 2008
Courtesy: Rajiv Gandhi Memorial Trust

Section I
Origins and Early Experiences

1
An Autobiographical Introduction

In 1992, as a recipient of the Magsaysay award, I was told that my life history was of some interest, and Professor Rushbrook of Arizona University had been commissioned by the Magsaysay Award Foundation to glean the interesting facets of my life through a long interview. This initiative made me think that it might be a good idea to give my own perceptions and insights on the factors that have influenced my life and moulded my future.

I have but faint recollections of my childhood. I was part of a large household and I seemed to have had a special place in everybody's heart. There were three other boys in my age group, all of them two or three years older than me. One was my own elder brother Sohail Sultan and the other two were my maternal uncles Rafat Sultan and Waseem Abbas. There were a large number of girls in the family, some older and some younger than I, but they were all my seniors in relationship—mostly aunts and hardly any cousins. My mother always seemed a bit lost in her thoughts and a bit sad, but I was too young to understand the reason for her sadness.

I vividly recall my mother's mini gramophone on which she played records only one third the size of normal records. I have tried to jog the memories of people about this gramophone but no one recollects anything about it nor where it went.

My mother died in childbirth when I was three years old. I even heard it said at times that I had jumped on her, causing the problem that led to her death. I don't know what, in fact, happened. All I remember is that one day I saw her being carried away from the house on a bed, and that I accompanied the crowd that took her. I have no other recollection except that my mother's younger sister once told me that I brought tears to everyone's eyes when in the evening I insisted on going to bring Mother home. I used to call her *Baji*, which means elder sister, and had never looked upon her as my mother. Nor did she behave towards me as one. To me she was as distant or as close as everyone else in the house.

The patriarch of the house was my maternal grandfather and the matriarch his elder sister. All our needs were met through them and no one else mattered.

The mystery of my mother's sadness slowly revealed itself to me nearly six years after my mother's death, when my father approached me to intercede on his behalf with the matriarch (she was universally called *Bubu*) of the family, to forgive him. I innocently told her to do so, because I neither knew this stranger nor why he was making this request and in any case I felt a bit important that I was being asked for help by an adult and saw no harm in making the request. However, I was told off very firmly by *Bubu*, who said that that this was none of my business. I let the matter rest there.

I was very happy with my life for I was living like a prince. All my needs were taken care of. I was loved by everyone. I recollect the arrival of a brand new chocolate-coloured Ford convertible when it was driven in through the huge front gates by a cousin (universally known as *Baba*) of my grandfather's. I also recollect how the old green convertible had started giving trouble and had to be pushed more often than not. I remember going out for drives in the convertible and sometimes even camping out in the countryside with the entire family.

My childhood days at Shahjehanpur (probably founded by the Mughal Emperor Shahjehan), a district of northern India in the province of UP (now the state of Uttar Pradesh), came to an end with Grandfather's transfer to Dehra Doon. Besides the convertible and the forays into the countryside, sometimes for hunting, I have memories of the reception celebrating the Silver Jubilee of George V in 1935. I remember also watching the vernacular version of the film *Hamlet*. I ran away from the cinema house when the ghosts wearing long white robes appeared. It took me a long time to shake off the reputation of being a coward who should not be taken to movies that featured ghosts.

My grandfather was one of those magnanimous souls who loved being surrounded by as many people as possible. Besides his direct family, that is, his sons and daughters and their children, he insisted on having his sisters and their children, his cousins and friends also live with him. This normally meant a household of thirty to forty persons and a large number of servants. Some of them had been there since before I was born and they knew how to keep young people in their proper places. Once when I failed to greet one of them I was reprimanded and told to mind my manners. Servant or not, it was age which determined who was to greet whom first. The lesson was never lost on me.

Before Grandfather could settle into his new post I was sent off with some members of the family to our ancestral village. I had no idea at that time where my father came from. Later on I learned that he came from a village called Pharia in the same district as my grandfather's and in fact was my grandfather's sister's son. My paternal grandfather died before I was born at Moradabad.

No one remembers the exact date of my birth but I was considered lucky for my father, who got a job as Chief Executive Officer of Moradabad Municipality immediately after I was born. Since he got that post in June 1931, I must have been born around that date. My father retired from the same post on attaining superannuation. I was shocked to see that his starting salary was the same as mine in CSP in 1955!

The village I was sent to, known as Muslim Patti, was that of my maternal grandfather. The six months I spent at Muslim Patti, when I was about five years old, were perhaps my only exposure to purely rustic life. I also started my education in the local mosque, where a rather well built and fat religious teacher (who used to lead the prayers in the mosque) very kindly taught me to write the Urdu alphabet on a wooden slate.

My fear of the unknown and of ghosts played havoc with me. Especially after sunset, my imagination used to run wild and I would conjure up figures of demons and their spouses all over the place. One of the girls came to know this weakness of mine and took full advantage, playing all kinds of pranks and tormenting me. I never tried to find out who she was later in my life, but she was the most vivacious girl that I have ever come across. She even made up a teasing limerick she would recite as soon as she caught sight of me.

I used to love going out in the fields and remaining outdoors. I found the rounding up of the animals in the evening, especially the bulls, particularly fascinating. The making of *gur* (unrefined sugar) from sugarcane used to hold me spellbound for hours. I used to love sucking sugarcane, and still do. However, my little idyllic world encountered its first disaster when one afternoon I was subjected to the Muslim religious ritual of circumcision and for weeks afterwards had to suffer the inconvenience and pain.

Dehra Doon has been compared to Paradise and it was indeed a beautiful place. One day all four of us children began our formal education. A few months earlier a female relative of the same age and I had already been initiated into religious education. I must say that I hated studies. Dehra Doon was famous for its two schools: The Doon School and Colonel Brown's School. The other three aspirants were too old for either school but Colonel Brown's was prepared to accept me. However, the family elders, and here the decisive voice was that of my mother's elder brother, decided that all four should go to the same school. So, we were all admitted in the American Presbyterian Mission High School, of which an American, Dr Ewing, was the Principal. This was the year 1938, so I must have been around seven. However, when the time came to go to school, I refused to go and wept so hard that my grandfather decided I was too young and that school could be postponed for another year.

Soon it was 1939 and I had to go to school. Judging from my performance my uncle Shoukat Sultan thought it prudent to give me a two-year cushion for failing examinations. His own son Mahmood Sultan, like my elder brother Sohail Sultan, was a marine captain for nearly two decades before becoming an internationally acclaimed insurance executive. His concern and affection for me are quite extraordinary. Contrary to all expectations I sailed through my exams, obtaining a master's degree in 1953 before I was twenty.

School was a torture for me and I used to look forward to holidays and pray for rainy days. My maths teacher was especially unhappy with me. One day he brought the headmaster to the class to complain against me. I was trembling with the fear that I was going to be expelled. However, when the headmaster asked who I was and was told that I was the grandson of Mr Sultan Ahmad Beg, the city magistrate and political agent for Afghan refugees,[1] he left the class without a word. That was the first and last time that I was ever reported for lack of interest in studies.

By all accounts my education was patchy. I went to no less than six secondary and high schools (Dehra Doon, Bulandshahr, Karvi, Hamirpur and Kheri) before obtaining my high school certificate in first division with distinction in arithmetic—a feat my old maths teacher would have found hard to believe.

The golden period of my life was now coming to an end. My guardian, who, from the day of my birth, had taken care of me, had now to let me loose in the world. Under his protection I had savoured a luxurious life, albeit governed by principles, and characterized by magnanimity and hospitality. Day in and day out I had observed the art of administration and management, and had participated in out-door life at its best. I was a proficient rider and hunter and driving was my mania. I had learnt to camp out for prolonged periods. This was my life and I could not imagine leading another.

Somehow I had come to believe that studying humanities, rather than the sciences, would best equip me to follow the career of my choice. A number of people advised me against it but I stood steadfast. My objective was to take the competitive examination in order to get into the Civil Service.

The time had now come to break away from the world of pomp and ceremony. Nor could I continue to live in mansions like the house in Hamirpur, which used to be the residence of the Maratha governors in the olden days. That house had a one square mile compound, in which one of my grandfather's predecessors had shot a leopard and my uncle had shot a hyena. You could hear the partridges and see the peacocks dancing from the veranda of that house. The compound was bounded on one side by the river Jumna, infested with crocodiles which one could often see basking on the sandbars. My fear of those crocodiles meant that to this day I have not learnt to swim.

The tiger shoots of Lakhimpur Kheri with, at times, thirty to forty elephants trying to bring the tiger into the open, were exciting beyond words. The episode of the eleven feet two inches long tiger shot by my grandfather but accredited by him to the chief guest, his cousin Sir Iqbal Ahmad, chief justice of the Allahabad High Court, is still vivid in my mind. So is the magical grandeur of the princely states where we often accompanied my grandfather, especially when the British governor was visiting.

Despite all this splendour, the collector's first responsibility was to the people. Whether at headquarters or on tour, work came first. Adjudicating cases and meeting visitors had precedence over all else. I used to love reading the daily Situation Reports or the Collector's Who's Who in the district and then the judgments. I would marvel at my grandfather's ease in churning out judgment after judgment, immediately after hearing the cases. In my later life I tried hard to emulate those qualities. I recall with pride his principled stand against the Commissioner, Mr Nethersole, who used to boast that he was Nethersole to his friends but Leathersole to his enemies. Grandfather stood by his principles and Nethersole could not harm him.

My father, who had taken a second wife even before my mother had died, had by now rehabilitated himself with the family. Since my grandfather was now on the verge of retirement and because I did not want to study in the local college at Azamgarh (although it was a renowned college, founded by one of our great ancestors Allama Shibli Nomani), Grandfather gave me the option to go and study at Moradabad as my father strongly desired that I should spend some time with him. I came to Moradabad like a stranger and throughout the two years I stayed with my father, ours was a very formal relationship. My stepmother went out of her way to make me feel at home and my other brothers and sisters were absolutely angelic and charming. However, there was such a tremendous contrast between my earlier life and this one that the nostalgia for the past never left me for a moment. It was then that a wonderful thing happened, turning my dreams into reality. A most beautiful person gave me the love and sustenance I was in search of, and a most exciting phase of my life commenced.

In two years I had passed the higher secondary examination from the Moradabad Government Intermediate College and my heart was set on going to Lucknow University for higher education. My elder brother had pursued an undergraduate degree course there before being selected through an all-India examination for entrance to the mercantile marine training ship Dufferin. His example was later emulated by a large number of family members, including his son, who now commands a ship of his own.

I wanted to follow in the footsteps of my grandfather who had a master's degree in English Literature, but my History teacher in high school had taught his subject so well that I decided to change to History. However, English remained one of my favourite subjects and for my graduate studies I studied both English and History. As fate would have it, I would eventually agree to my wife's insistence that I take English for my master's degree. She felt that historians tend to become argumentative: her experience was with her father, who had a doctorate in history from London University.

The decision about where I should go for higher studies was referred to my grandfather. The question of expense for my schooling was a consideration now that he had retired. Grandfather had already distributed the commuted portion of his pension, including a share for me. The balance was just enough to maintain him. But these considerations were not going to deter him. He asked me where I wanted to study. I replied 'Lucknow' and Lucknow it was. Father had to pay the expenses but I never took a penny more than was absolutely necessary. Grandfather would often ask if I needed any money but I always told him I had enough, which was a fact. I had more than a thousand rupees in my post office account, half of which had been given to me by Father (from his poker winnings, it was rumoured) five years before I had gone to stay with him in Moradabad and the balance came from my grandfather's commuted pension. People knew I had this money and I gave it away as loans to needy relatives. I never got the money back nor was I ever in such a dire financial situation as to ask for repayment.

I wrote to my grandfather in 1950, asking my favourite aunt to deliver the letter to him at an opportune moment. In the letter I had sought his permission to marry. Grandfather's reply was a bombshell. The only other occasion I can remember him losing his temper with me was when I was very young and used to cry at night for no rhyme or reason, with everyone helplessly trying to quieten me. Suddenly one night I heard grandfather shouting at me to be quiet. That was the last time anyone heard me cry at night.

Since my childhood there had been talk of my marrying my mother's younger sister's daughter. I had nothing against the girl, but having resolved not to repeat my mother's experience, I was determined to marry only for love. Besides, I was only in the second year of a five-year graduate studies programme. My grandfather wrote that I should go to the grave of my mother and ask her whether I should marry or study. It was shattering but I was determined. Although permission was given, no one attended the wedding. My elder brother, however, made it a point to visit us a couple of days later.

Shortly after, when I not only completed my education but obtained a first division and a university gold medal in his favourite subject, English Literature, I was able to win over my grandfather. I remember once he was discussing literature with someone and observed that unlike others who liked Shakespeare very much, his favourite was Shelley. Shelley became my favourite too from that day and I not only read Shelley and enjoyed him but also named my youngest daughter after him. My grandfather received my wife Musarrat with open arms when I took her to him before migrating to Pakistan. Grandfather had been offered the post of chairman of Pakistan's Federal Public Service

Commission but had declined the offer, much to the regret of many younger members of the family, who thought that this would be their gateway to good jobs in Pakistan.

Grandfather wished us happiness. He knew that my wife's parents were living in Peshawar and that her father originally came from Dera Ismail Khan in the NWFP. He was overjoyed when I sent him the telegram informing him about my selection in the Civil Service of Pakistan and telling him that as part of my training I was going to Cambridge for a year. I was determined that on my return I would persuade my grandfather to come and live with me, but that was not to be. One day while at Cambridge I received a letter from my uncle informing me that my grandfather had passed away. My role model and my benefactor par excellence was no more.

The most flattering compliment I ever received was from my elder brother, at the end of his last visit to the Northern Areas in 1985. He said that his visit reminded him of the time we used to spend with our grandfather.

I could not have chosen a better partner for life than Musarrat. She has given me love, courage and support of every kind when I needed it. During my university days she made no demands on me except to ride my bicycle. Despite having a baby to look after she allowed me to fully concentrate on my studies. She even saved money from her own pocket money and gave it to me. I tried my hand at a part-time job as the manager of a treadle press for nearly a year. I had no need to make ends meet, but did it for the sake of experience and to prove my *bona fides* as a hardworking and conscientious person. A mutual friend of my and Musarrat's grandfathers', Mr Reyaz Ahmed Khan, offered us a room in his cottage when he heard about our problem of accommodation. This was a touching offer which he forced us to accept. He kept us there for nearly a year. I can never forget his kindness and generosity, but then he belonged to the same group of people as my grandfather.

My master's degree came in very handy in Pakistan as there were no dearth of openings for lecturers in English; but I wanted the position only as a stepping stone for my main goal: the Civil Service. Jahanzeb College in Swat offered the best choice and I accepted it. I made my intentions known to the ruler of Swat (the Wali Sahib) who very graciously gave me a written undertaking, without the knowledge of the principal of the college, that in case of my selection to the Civil Service I would be released from the service of the college.

Musarrat had by then (1953) given birth to our second daughter. In Swat things were so cheap that we could afford to have two maids and a cook. Musarrat was settling down to our life and did not in the least share my enthusiasm for the Civil Service, yet she left no stone unturned in helping me achieve my goal. She left me alone in the house to prepare for the competitive examination, which I took in 1954. However, I failed to get one of the top positions in the examination because of a poor performance in the *viva voce* (I got 119 marks out of 300). Ten years later, when posted as deputy director of the Civil Service Academy, I was mollified to read the expatriate director of the Academy, Mr Burgess's remark that the *viva* marks did not do justice either to my personality or to my capabilities. With the position I got on the basis of the exam I was entitled to get into the Civil Service only on the quota reserved for the NWFP. Musarrat saw to it that her husband got his due. Holding a domicile certificate was not enough; it had to be proved that I had roots in the province. A good samaritan in the person of an under secretary in the Establishment Division of the Government of Pakistan, Mr Rasheed Ahmad from the province of Punjab, saw to it that a refugee was not deprived of his rights in the newly created state and kept Musarrat posted with developments behind the scene. Musarrat found the best person to testify to my status. She went to Dr Khan Sahib, who was a minister in the federal cabinet and explained the case to him. Someone sitting there pointed out to Dr Khan Sahib that Musarrat was the daughter of Dr Abdur Rahim, his arch rival in politics. The great Khan said that 'politics is politics but he is also my friend and besides, this is a genuine case'.

I was playing tennis in the college courts, quite oblivious to the game that Musarrat was engaged in, when a telegram was delivered to me informing me of my selection in the Civil Service. A few years later, in what was then East Pakistan, I was saddened to read about the stabbing to death of Dr Khan Sahib in Lahore.

Life at the Civil Service Academy was a new experience but I loved the rigour and discipline enforced by Mr Burgess. The director made it very clear that getting into the Civil Service of Pakistan did not mean that you were the best or that everyone should bow to you in deference. He insisted that unless you proved yourself clearly and demonstrably superior no one was going to accept you as a leader. He also underlined the importance of integrity and impartiality in public service. He used to say that your moral fibre would be tested only very rarely and if you gave in and buckled under on that odd occasion, the fact that on hundreds of other occasions you had acted correctly would be of no significance.

He also made us keep diaries and observe and record in them everything of consequence. He used to read each diary and make copious comments. Over time I noticed a change in the way I started taking note of my surroundings and observing things. I became analytical and constructive. I have found diaries a most powerful training tool.

The posting in 1957 to the eastern wing of Pakistan came as a surprise to many of us because it had been rumoured that the chief minister of East Pakistan wanted only officers from his Wing to be posted to his province. With Mr Huseyn Shaheed Suhrawardy as the prime minister it was taken for granted that he would accept the recommendation of his political party's chief minister. However, Mr Suhrawardy had different views on the matter and when the summary was put to him for a decision he ordered that all East Pakistanis should be posted to West Pakistan and all West Pakistanis to East Pakistan. The only exception was the people selected for the NWFP list. I had always wanted to be in the NWFP list but my Pashto was not proficient enough. Later on in my career I got postings to Kohat and Peshawar districts, as well as to the health, education and social welfare departments as secretary, and to the Pakistan Academy for Rural Development as director.

After my return from Cambridge I went to Kushtia (in the then East Pakistan) in September 1957 to take over as assistant magistrate and collector with the power to sentence a person found guilty of an offence to a simple imprisonment of one month and a fine of Rs 1,000 or both. On arrival I found that the offices were closed for 23 days for *puja* holidays. I cursed myself for not listening to Musarrat, and complying to the letter with my orders to report for duty immediately without taking any 'joining time'. No one in Karachi had bothered to find out that in those days everything in Bengal used to shut down for nearly a month during the *puja* festival.

Since there was no residential accommodation earmarked for the post I was holding, I was lodged at the Ganges-Kobadak Project inspection bungalow. Under the rules I could stay there only for 30 days at a stretch. When I received a notice to vacate the room at the end of the month I was furious. My pride had been hurt. How dare a lowly functionary with the rank of a sub-engineer treat a CSP officer in this manner! I mentioned this to one of the engineers who was also staying in the bungalow and expressed my intention of teaching this person a lesson by hauling him up under some pretext of the Criminal Procedure Code. My engineer friend looked appalled and said that he did not expect such a reaction from me, which was more in keeping with the mentality of a police SHO. I felt ashamed and never forgot this reprimand.

I was given my first independent charge of Brahmanbaria subdivision. Mr Taffuzal Ali of the Muslim League came from the subdivision and announced a public rally in his hometown, Quasba. The local president of the Awami League (the party in power) decided to disrupt the meeting and humiliate the ex-federal minister. I tried to reason with the Awami Leaguers, asking them to hold their meeting either on a different day or at a different place, because Mr Ali had publicised his meeting prior to their announcement. However, the Awami Leaguers were adamant. I instructed the police to stop the Awami Leaguers from disrupting the meeting. The local president of the Awami League, Mr Abdul Bari, a member of the Bar, complained against me to the Chief Minister, Mr Ataur Rehman, and sought my transfer to some other place. The chief minister declined to accede to the request, telling him that if what he was saying was true then at the next place I would be likely to put up even more resistance to the Awami League.

A few days later, while I was expecting a visit by no less than four ministers of the provincial government, an early morning telephone call from the collector informed me that martial law had been imposed and the provincial government had been dismissed. That day in the office I sent for Mr Bari and reassured him that I had nothing against him, and if he had any apprehensions in this regard I would like to allay them right away. I stayed on in Brahmanbaria for another two years and Mr Bari and I remained the best of friends.

The Laxmipur border skirmish between India and Pakistan happened during my tenure as SDO of Brahmanbaria. One day the Indians established themselves on a spur, which according to us was well inside Pakistan. Since the border between the countries was in the process of being finally demarcated, this occupation was likely to give an advantage to the Indians. According to established practice such disputes had first to be resolved by the civilian authorities. We held a meeting on the disputed site in which my collector and I represented the Pakistan side and the deputy commissioner of Agartala (a Colonel Butalia) came from the other side with a number of officers. The meeting ended in failure because the Indians refused to budge from the positions they had taken. They had already moved a good number of armed personnel and set up tents on the site.

Major Mohammad Tufail was the wing commander of the East Pakistan Rifles detachment at Akhora, a railway junction for trains to Sylhet, Chittagong and Dacca (now Dhaka) and about ten miles away from Brahmanbaria with no road link. I often used to visit Major Tufail and he would do the same. He was a very kindly and fatherly sort of person and despite the difference in our ages we got along very well. Very often Major Sahib would baby-sit my two daughters, allowing Musarrat and I to have time to ourselves. Sometimes, if it got too late and we had missed the train connection, we used to spend the night at his bungalow. A few days after the abortive meeting with the Indians I happened to visit Major Tufail and found an emissary from Dacca closeted with him. After his departure I could sense that there was something bothering Major Sahib. I could not believe my ears when he told me that he had received instructions to throw out the Indians without firing a shot. I said 'I am sure you are not going to do anything of the kind because I have been to the site and the Indians are armed to the teeth'. He agreed, but said this was such a small operation that if he did not succeed he would not be able to live it down. On the other hand if he did succeed it hardly mattered. We talked about many things. He was not happy about the imposition of martial law, saying this was not the job of the army. That night he did not ask me to spend the night at his bungalow and made the railway power trolley available to me to return to Brahmanbaria.

The next morning I received a telephone call from Akhora informing me that Major Tufail and Subedar Major Sarwar had been injured in action at Laxmipur. True to his orders, Major Tufail is said to have divided his company of soldiers into two, one under his own command and the other under the subedar major, and demanded that the Indians surrender. The Indians opened fire with light machine guns, felling the commanders of both columns in their first bursts. Tufail fell but went on commanding, even capturing the Indian major who commanded the Border Force. Later on, at the time of handing him back to the Indian authorities, the Indian major told me that but for Major Tufail he would have been killed. Major Tufail had told his troops that the Indian major would be more useful alive than dead.

Tufail and Sarwar died of excessive bleeding because it took more than twelve hours to take them by train to the Comilla Combined

Military Hospital. That afternoon I saw a seaplane landing at Akhora Lake bringing senior army officers, and I wondered why the plane could not have been sent in the morning to evacuate the casualties and save precious lives. Tufail was decorated with the *Nishan-e-Haider*, Pakistan's highest military award and Sarwar with the *Sitara-e-Jurat*. As I had known both of them I was asked to commemorate their heroic deed, which seemed to be in the class of the charge of the Light Brigade. I had a marble tablet fixed at the Laxmipur spot saying 'Here the heroes fought, fell, crawled and commanded'. The people of Brahmanbaria rose magnificently to the occasion, raising over Rs 200,000 to construct a Tufail Memorial Health Dispensary at Akhora. They also instituted an annual Tufail Memorial Football Tournament. The way my family and I mourned his death led some people to think that Tufail was a close relative of mine. They hardly realized that although he was from Burewala in Punjab he was more than a relation to me. Musarrat used to call him Clark Gable and he would innocently ask who this man was. Much later, I was happy to see in Gilgit the house where Major Tufail used to live in the 1950s as commandant of the Scouts, named Tufail House.

I got the most warm and loving treatment from the people of Bengal whether it was Bakargunj, Kushtia, Brahmanbaria, Mymensingh or Dhaka. Bengal's most precious gift to me was my third daughter who was born during this period. The value of the gift became even more apparent when I lost her thirty years later.

In late 1961 I was posted back to West Pakistan. We took the boat from Chittagong to Karachi, covering the journey in seven days with a brief stop-over at Colombo. I could not have known then that I would return to Sri Lanka seventeen years later to live in elephant country.

I wanted a posting to Hazara but the Chief Secretary posted me to Kohat instead, saying that I would have problems in Hazara as it was the then President's district. Even in Kohat I only lasted a year-and-a-half. During the Basic Democracies and presidential elections of 1964–65 all kinds of pressure was brought to bear, especially by political ministers. On one occasion when one of the ministers said to me in public that the president was unhappy with me, I thought he was referring to the local Muslim League president but he said he meant the president of Pakistan. I retorted that as a civil servant I served during the pleasure of the president and if he was unhappy with me I was prepared to resign. This put the minister entirely on the defensive and he retracted his remark. Since all this happened in public at the

Kohat circuit bungalow, one of the national English dailies carried the whole episode with a four column title 'Ministries on the Hunt'. My service batch mate and Musarrat's cousin Humayun read the news in the United States, where he was pursuing a doctoral degree, and wrote me a letter saying how proud of me he was. I was, of course, very happy to receive the compliment.

The elections to Basic Democracies[2] were followed by the presidential elections. One of the requirements was an address by the presidential candidates to the newly elected Basic Democrats canvassing for their votes. On the appointed day all the members were transported to Peshawar. President Ayub's address was to be followed by that of Ms Fatima Jinnah. Having sent the members a day earlier I reached Peshawar on the morning of the appointed day. I found an urgent message from the Commissioner, Mr Masroor Hasan Khan, waiting for me. He was always extremely indulgent and kind to me. As soon as I met him he told me that without asking me he had informed the governor that I had refused to comply with the wishes of the authorities to ask the Basic Democrats of my district to stage a walkout when Miss Jinnah stood up to address them. He said that all my other colleagues—Ijlal Haider Zaidi, Kunwar Idris, Salim Abbas Jilani and Jamil Ahmed—had been asked the night before to take part in the walkout and had flatly refused. I was very touched by the commissioner's confidence in my integrity. The members from the Districts and Agencies of Peshawar, Kohat, Mardan, Mohmand and Khyber remained seated even when strong winds blew the *pandal* down during Miss Jinnah's speech.

Three weeks prior to the elections to the national and provincial assemblies the governor of West Pakistan, the Nawab of Kalabagh, visited Peshawar to meet all the deputy commissioners and political agents separately. When my turn came Nawab Sahib came directly to the point, telling me that the president of Pakistan had been informed that if I were to remain the deputy commissioner the Muslim League candidate in Kohat would lose the election. The president had, therefore, desired my assurance of the success of the official Muslim League candidate in the national assembly election. I protested that I had no way to predict the results of an election held by secret ballot and said I could give no such assurance. I was totally stunned when Nawab Sahib responded by saying he was proud of me. He then offered me the choice of any district in Punjab because in the NWFP he had to abide by the president's wishes. I submitted that I did not want to cause any more problems for him and would prefer a posting in the federal government. The Nawab's feudal streak was touched. Admonishing me not to worry about his problems, he agreed to speak to the establishment secretary on my behalf. Two weeks before the elections I got my transfer orders to the federal government. The Establishment Secretary, Mr M. Azfar, who was my father's class fellow at university, asked me what I had done to cause the Nawab to praise me so highly. Within a couple of weeks I got the best posting imaginable—deputy director of the Civil Service Academy. From 1965 to 1969 I came in close contact with no less than 175 probationers of the civil and foreign services who have been my lifelong friends the world over.

During this period I also had a lengthy attachment with the Royal Institute of Public Administration, London. In their final report on my work they said they would very much like to have me join their staff. During my visit to UK our fourth daughter was born. I named her Shelley.

On return from London, having specialized in the art of training, I was looking forward to a long stay at the academy. Instead, less than a year later I was being considered for a posting in the field. On my protest the posting was changed and I was made secretary to one of the committees set up to look into the cases of officers accused of malpractice. The committee was headed by a High Court Judge. On reporting for duty the judge's private secretary advised me to report to the establishment division instead. There I was told that the judge was not sure if I would feel comfortable looking at cases of my civil service colleagues, and therefore, he had requested a non-CSP officer to be posted as secretary of the committee. In my heart of hearts I was most grateful to the judge for this solicitude but I could not take this aspersion on my integrity lying down. I wrote a letter of protest to the cabinet-cum-establishment secretary requesting an inquiry into the matter to enable me to establish my *bona fides*. In reply I got posted to another committee of the same type. I simply refused to take notice of these orders. In the meanwhile, my dear friend the late Nasrum Minallah (then secretary to the governor) arranged my posting as secretary to the Government of West Pakistan, Services and General Administration Department, on a very strong protest to Nasr by Musarrat, for notifying my posting as deputy commissioner of Lyallpur, without consulting me or more specifically her.

By now my attitude towards politicians had matured somewhat and the initial assumption that whatever the minister said amounted to interference gave way to a more rational approach. Now I could admit that my refusal to transfer a *patwari*[3] because the provincial revenue minister asked for it but accepting a similar request of a friend, was not a matter of principle. In fact, what I was prepared to do for a friend, a relative or a senior colleague, I should also be prepared to do for a politician. One day Colonel Qayyum (Military Adviser to the Governor) walked into my office at the West Pakistan secretariat and said that he had been wanting to meet me since he had read the intelligence reports on happenings in Kohat during the last elections, in which I had figured very prominently. A few days later he returned and showed me a list of officers who were going to be retired under the now infamous '303 list'. Many of the names I knew personally and vouchsafed for their integrity but the colonel was unmoved and said that the names had been given by my own service colleagues. I could not believe it.

Qayyum remained a very good and sincere friend of mine till his last days and tolerated almost all of my indiscretions. Once, as military adviser to the governor of NWFP, he wanted me to order the arrest of a lawyer whom I did not wish to arrest. On his refusal to send a written order, I issued the arrest order in the name of the provincial government. This was thrown out of court the next day. Qayyum was furious but did not do anything against me. In fact, he always went out of his way to help me whenever I landed into trouble. When trumped-up charges pertaining to subversive activities were being investigated against me for my work at the Pakistan Academy for Rural Development in the Daudzai area, Qayyum used his good offices with General Jilani of the ISI to get an impartial report on the factual position. For many people Qayyum was a controversial figure, but I always found him a very sincere friend.

The dismemberment of One Unit brought me back to the NWFP. I was tipped as secretary, health, education and social welfare department but as a last minute adjustment I accepted the post of deputy commissioner, Peshawar, which I relinquished in 1971 when my friend Ijlal handed over as commissioner, Peshawar. I had a perfect working relationship with Ijlal, which I knew would not be possible with any other person.

As deputy commissioner of Peshawar I came in close contact with the NWFP politicians, all of whom I found extremely cooperative and helpful, and above all, thorough gentlemen. The only exception was

Khan Abdul Qayyum Khan whom I never met but only spoke to once on the phone, when he tried to browbeat me into refusing permission to the National Awami Party (NAP) to hold a Pakistan Day procession. Qayyum Khan feared large scale bloodshed if the two processions came face to face. Since the Muslim League had announced their plans before the NAP released theirs, they felt that the NAP was deliberately provoking a confrontation.

On the whole, I had very smooth sailing with the NWFP politicians and all of them are still my very good friends, irrespective of party affiliations. I was received with utmost hospitality when I called on Khan Abdul Wali Khan at Shahibagh and was warmly invited to spend weekends there to get away from the pressures of Peshawar. When Fida Mohammad was governor and I requested an interview, I was promptly invited to lunch at the governor's house. Ajmal Khattak was very candid on the procession issue and told me not to feel bad about it because the Muslim Leaguers were always trying to prove that the NAP is anti-Pakistan. He said 'At least your refusal has given us a propaganda value and shown them in their true colours so everyone can see that they do not want NAP to be seen to be associated with Pakistan Day'.

Khan Abdul Qayyum Khan's defeat at the hands of young Hayat Sherpao in 1970 really let loose his anger against me. Speeches were made at Chowk Yadgar testifying to the fact that the DC got votes cast in favour of Sherpao. The fact was that a NAP-PPP alliance was unbeatable. All that the DC ensured was that there was no bogus polling of votes, especially at women's polling booths.

The landlord-tenant dispute in the Hashtnagar area was another sensitive issue in the District. At the very outset I had a clear understanding with the late Afzal Bangash that he would not do anything unlawful provided I would ensure legal rights to tenants. I tried to resolve the issue through landlord-tenant committees, which in some places worked very well but there was so much misunderstanding and distrust of each other that a very long time was needed to build real bridges, and unfortunately, I had to leave the district too soon.

I espoused a policy of issuing arms licenses liberally for the simple reason that everyone in the NWFP was armed and most of the crimes were committed with unlicensed arms. Most of the people in power failed to appreciate the policy and when I had issued over 10,000 licenses in less than a year a whispering campaign got around that I was building a private army. But no one in the government interfered with my powers or ever asked me why I was doing this. On the two weekly *mulaqat* (open meeting) days, despite the hundred chairs provided on the lawns of the DC's house, the queue of arms applicants used to extend right up to the governor's house.

On relinquishing the post of deputy commissioner in 1971 I was assigned to the Department of Health, Education and Social Welfare, for which I had originally been tipped. However, my sense of the ethical way to proceed required that I wait until Abdul Ali Khan himself asked me to come and take over. Humayun, who by now had a PhD and was secretary to the NWFP government, called to ask why I was not taking charge of my new post. No sooner had I told him the reason than Abdul Ali Khan rang up to ask me to take over.

East Pakistan was already in turmoil. On the day that the national assembly was to be convened and President Yahya was to make a special announcement, we received a message that the president had decided to come to Peshawar. Everyone was wondering why he wanted to visit Peshawar on such a fateful day. President Yahya and his entourage arrived in two helicopters accompanied by, amongst others, the managing director of the Standard Bank. On their arrival the mystery was solved: the president wanted to see the progress of the house he was constructing in the Peshawar Cantonment area.

The situation in East Pakistan began to go from bad to worse. One day news was brought that the martial law authorities had decided to post officers with East Pakistan experience to that Wing, to stem the worsening situation. I thought the proposal simply preposterous and decided to act immediately. I spoke to Musarrat and she was even more vehement about my not having anything to do with such a scheme. I went to see the Chief Secretary, Mr Ejaz Naik, and informed him of my intention to resign from the CSP before the establishment division issued orders transferring me to an immoral administration in East Pakistan. I informed him that I had enjoyed some of my happiest moments with the people there and could not imagine myself part of a repressive regime. Mr Naik advised me to wait until the orders were received, although he agreed with my reasoning that it might then be too late and the government might decline to accept my resignation. He took my written resignation, saying that if he did not succeed in stopping my transfer orders he would hand in my resignation, prior to the orders being issued. I was extremely touched by his kindness and concern and his attitude that he was doing this not as a favour to me but because he did not want the government to lose a good officer.

Thereafter Mr Naik apprised the governor of the situation, urging him to take up the matter with the personal staff officer (PSO) to the president. The governor was rebuffed by the PSO General Peerzada, who told him that the provincial governments were not going to be consulted in this matter. Mr Naik relayed the information to me and I went to see the Governor, General K.M. Azhar, to thank him for his effort and to take his leave prior to my leaving government service. General Azhar was very kind and greatly regretted both my decision and his inability to do anything. A few days later I received a telephone call from General Bachhu Karim of the president's office, informing me that my name had been taken off the list of officers being considered for posting to East Pakistan. I still wonder what Mr Naik did with my letter of resignation.

An important stage in a CSP officer's career in those days was the promotion to the scale of joint secretary to the federal government which was equivalent to the post of the commissioner of a division in the field. I got my promotion orders with my posting as commissioner Karachi in November 1971. It was a brief but eventful posting. Within a fortnight of my arrival in Karachi, Musarrat developed a heart problem while packing our belongings in Peshawar. No sooner had we overcome that crisis and brought Musarrat to Karachi than the war between Pakistan and India broke out. Kunwar Idris was my deputy commissioner and we thought it prudent to involve the elected MNAs and MPAs of Karachi in the war effort. The elected members, who had been cooling their heels for over a year since elections, greatly welcomed the initiative and proved a great source of strength to the Karachi administration in those difficult days.

Karachi was so unprotected and so much at the mercy of the Indian bombers that at times the 'all clear' siren could not be sounded for hours at a time. This obviously created a lot of panic and there was a great exodus of people from Karachi. In army parlance Karachi had the defence protection of a fortress. I suggested to the local fortress commander that it might be a good idea for an army regiment to do a route march on the main streets of Karachi to restore people's confidence, since rumours were afoot that Karachi was totally unprotected. The brigadier thought this was a good idea but said he could do this only after a week because just then he had no troops at all.

The war came to an end and the PPP government took over. The next day I had gone to see off the governor who was going to

Islamabad, probably for the last time as governor, when I was asked to take a call from the President's House. I went to the VIP lounge telephone kiosk and found Hafeez Peerzada on the line. He conveyed the president's desire to arrest five prominent citizens, some of whom I knew personally. I argued that the PPP had been in the forefront of citizen's rights and asked him on what charges would it be possible to issue legal orders of arrest. I reminded him that I had no original powers to order an arrest and said I would have to ask the deputy commissioner, who would also ask the reason for the order. Then I had a sudden brainwave and told him to ask the Ministry of Interior, which had original jurisdiction in the matter, to carry out the arrests. I thought I had settled the matter but Peerzada again rang up at one in the morning to enquire what had been done. I told him that I thought I had already explained my position and there was nothing that I could do. Whatever little I knew of Kunwar Idris I was sure he would never issue an order unless there were good grounds for doing so. Otherwise, what justification would he have to defend his orders in the superior courts? I got Mr Peerzada off my back but at four in the morning the provincial home secretary woke me to enquire why I was being difficult. I told him politely that I simply found no justification in asking my deputy commissioner to issue invalid orders. The provincial home department issued the order and sent it directly to the deputy commissioner for compliance. Throughout this episode I was reminded of Burgess's golden words: 'It is only rarely that you will be put to the test and if you fail it you are no good'.

Despite my first brush with the new government my relations with the provincial government remained very cordial. The new governor, Mr Mumtaz Bhutto, was very kind to me and consulted me on many matters, especially with regard to ethnic problems. He seemed to agree with many of the suggestions I made, such as initiatives for greater interaction between different groups, but when he put forward these proposals to others he apparently did not get the required approval. He also very kindly offered me another posting in the Sindh province when the decision was taken to abolish the post of commissioners in the province. Once the decision to abolish the post of commissioner, Karachi had been taken, I did not wish to cling to the appointment. I, therefore, issued an order declaring myself *functus officio*. The provincial government was not amused and ordered me to withdraw the order, so I continued as a lame duck commissioner for another month. I thus had the privilege of being the last commissioner of Karachi. The post was, of course, revived after three years.

My friend Hayat Sherpao, who was now governor of NWFP, arranged my posting as Director, Pakistan Academy for Rural Development (PARD), Peshawar: thus affording me an opportunity to implement the Daudzai Project under the tutelage of Akhtar Hameed Khan on the pattern of the Comilla Project. This had lasted a little over three years when fate took me to Japan in search of new pastures.

NOTES

1. The followers of King Amanullah who had been deposed by the British.
2. The system of local government introduced by Field Marshal President Ayub Khan in 1959.
3. The lowest revenue department functionary.

2

The Daudzai Project[1]

THE STORY OF A PILOT PROJECT APPROACH

In early 1972, when the prime minister of Pakistan (then president) decided to launch an Integrated Rural Development Programme (IRDP) to improve the 'quality of life' in the rural areas of the country, the different provincial governments set about implementing the central government's directive. In the NWFP the government decided to adopt a pilot project approach and five IRDP projects were initiated under the project directorship of different agencies such as the agriculture, cooperatives, irrigation and general administration departments. The Pakistan Academy for Rural Development, located in Peshawar and catering to all four provinces, had experimentation and research among its main functions, in addition to training the officers of the nation building departments of the four provinces.

In the field of research the academy endeavoured to develop viable models of rural development, which could be replicated all over the country. Thus, when the government of the NWFP asked the academy to take up one of the IRDP pilot projects, it accepted the offer with this objective in mind. In the course of time the NWFP government accepted the Daudzai model as potentially the most successful and decided to expand it in the whole province.

Search for a Viable Unit of Development Administration

The academy researchers initially set out to determine the physical boundaries of the project area. In this connection they kept in view the following principles of development administration: (1) provision of services in both the public and the private sectors, fully coordinated and supported with adequate supplies; (2) upgrading the skills of the rural population to enable people to make the best use of the services being provided; (3) integration of the public agencies such as development departments with elected local councils.

Existing Pattern of Administration

The academy researchers understood the existing pattern of administration as a legacy from the British days. It had emerged in its present shape over a period of about a hundred years. They found it to be a law-and-order oriented administration with emphasis on revenue collection. It was certainly not 'development' oriented. It was also not fair to blame the colonial administrators for devising an administrative set-up which best suited their needs and which was efficient from the law-and-order and revenue collection points of view. However, after Independence, the same administrative pattern was geared to development needs. No wonder it did not produce the desired results. Another phenomenon which came to the attention of the academy researchers was the fact that since Independence there had been tremendous expansion at the higher levels of administration such as those of the central and provincial governments. Over the years a highly sophisticated planning apparatus has been developed in the country but this expansion had hardly affected the administration at the district level and achieved next to nothing below the district level. The British wanted to establish the imperial peace (*Pax Britannica*) and they did so by taking the law-and-order administration right down to the grassroots, i.e. the police station, level. The British wanted to collect revenue and they extended the revenue department right down to the village level. They were at best only marginally interested in development; therefore, none of the development departments were expanded in the same way as the police and revenue departments.

The first concern of the academy researchers was to determine a viable unit for the purposes of provision of services. In the existing pattern of administration the services did not filter down below the subdivision (*tehsil*) level, and the subdivision was an unmanageable unit for either provision of services or for integration of development departments with local councils (as was apparent in the 'Basic Democracies' days) and of course it was hopelessly unwieldy for upgrading skills.

The Peshawar subdivision is nearly 500 square miles in area and has a population of about 500,000. The other subdivisions of the country would be the same in area and population, a little more in area and less in population or vice versa. The fact was that a subdivision could not be a viable unit of development administration because there was no organization at the grassroots to implement the often very good plans that have been devised.

Having concluded that administration had to be devolved and that the subdivision was too remote a level for meaningful Integrated Rural Development (IRD), the academy researchers discovered that the existing jurisdiction of the police station could very well be converted into a viable unit for development administration. Herein they found an area which was not only compact and manageable but, in 99 cases out of a 100, would have infrastructure facilities, if any existed in the rural areas, centred at the police station headquarters. If there was a school or a health dispensary or a veterinary dispensary, or if there were any roads these were usually at the police station (*thana*) level. When the academy researchers collected data relating to Daudzai thana they found there was an area of 79.5 square miles covering 89 villages, with a population of 96,196 (1972 Census).

There are six police stations in the Peshawar subdivision and approximately 105 in the NWFP. These have an average of about 140 square miles in area and a population of 50,000 for the six settled districts. Except for Balochistan, where the area might be too large and the population too small, the conclusion that a police station jurisdiction was a viable unit of development administration would be applicable to all provinces. Thus, the jurisdiction of a police station, which had the advantage of being an established unit of administration (though being used purely for the purpose of law-and-order) proved viable for the provision of services and even more viable for upgrading the skills of the rural population. No village would be more than a day's return journey from the headquarters of this unit.

Another advantage of selecting a pre-existing unit of administration was lessening the chances of political bickering and bureaucratic highhandedness. The task which the academy had undertaken was to convert the police station, which for over a hundred years had stood as a symbol of law-and-order, into a symbol of development. We renamed this symbol of development the '*Markaz*'. It was to become the administrative centre of an IRD project area and became the base of operations for IRDP.

The Markaz: A Symbol of Development

In late April 1972, when the academy selected the jurisdiction of Daudzai police station for its IRDP area (Markaz), it found that except for the agriculture, police and revenue departments no other department had expanded to the grassroots since Independence. The organization of the agriculture department meant that its impact was minimal. The agriculture assistant, posted at police station headquarters in the case of Daudzai, had more than 34,000 acres of cropped area and nearly 19,000 landowners to deal with. In the first place, therefore, the academy set out to persuade the departments to expand to the Markaz level. The departments of health, education, animal husbandry, co-operatives, forestry and irrigation agreed to do so. The revenue department was persuaded to decentralise its records and to establish a revenue record room at the Markaz level under a *Naib-Tehsildar* (assistant revenue officer). This meant the dispersal of the naib-tehsildars who had previously been located at the tehsil headquarters. At the insistence of the agriculture department the number of agriculture assistants was increased from one to eight in the Daudzai police station.

A project manager was appointed to integrate and coordinate the activities of the development departments, which had expanded to the Markaz level. The project manager belonged to the local government department. This was done intentionally to avoid establishing a new department of integrated rural development. This was because integrated rural development, in the eyes of the academy researchers, meant the expansion of the existing departments to the Markaz level and organizing the rural people for the purpose of upgrading their skills to enable them to make the best use of the services provided at the Markaz. It was not meant to be the creation of a 'super department'.

Inadequacy of the Departments

After nearly 8 to 10 months of survey research by the Daudzai functionaries a considerable number of problems came to the surface. The rural population was in need of a hundred and one things and the Markaz functionaries could do nothing. The people's lands were deteriorating, becoming waterlogged and affected by salinity; the irrigation system was falling apart; villages were threatened by floods and erosion. There was lack of communication about marketing, which caused indescribable hardship in obtaining consumer goods, medical attendance and education. With the best of intentions and with goodwill from the departments, the Markaz functionaries were getting nowhere. Farmers were in need of fertilizers. They were in need of pesticides. They were in need of extension education. However, even eight agriculture assistants were incapable of doing much to change the situation. The absence of skills in the rural population made the inadequacy of the department even more pronounced. The departments were so organized that they could not do much for the rural population. The Markaz functionaries were becoming more and more frustrated every day and the academy researchers had to take a close look at the situation in the Markaz and come up with proposals to rectify it.

Establishment of Development Units

The survey research carried out by the Markaz functionaries determined that the people's first priorities in the Daudzai area were land development, water management and communications. The reliance of the Markaz on the provincial Public Works Department (Irrigation Branch) did not produce the desired results, not because the department was not willing to help, but simply because it was not organized so as to be able to help the Markaz in preparing the necessary blueprints for development. In a little less than a year, the department produced only two blueprints for the Markaz, whereas the Markaz functionaries and the rural people wanted many more and thought that even more were needed. It was, therefore, decided to establish an Engineering Unit with a qualified engineer and supporting staff at the Markaz level.

Since it was also evident that without organizing the people it would neither be possible to identify the problems nor to execute the work if and when the blueprints were ready, a Co-operative Unit was also inducted at the Markaz level. This Unit initially comprised two co-operative organizers. In the case of Daudzai, we converted two of the existing agriculture assistants *ad hoc* to co-operative organizers after suitable training.

The establishment of the development units proved a very wise investment and within six to nine months a development plan in Daudzai emerged which consisted of nearly two hundred blueprints, complete with cost estimates.

The academy learned two very important lessons from this exercise: first, that the rural people are in the best position to identify their needs because they have been living in the villages for generations and no one else is more sensitive or alive to their needs. Second, it was found that they were also capable of suggesting solutions to their problems which at best needed to be given technical shape after they had been examined by a technician such as the engineer. In this regard the academy noted with interest that the development plan prepared for the Daudzai area by the Markaz functionaries in the early days of the Markaz, without consulting the people, had nothing in common with the development plan which emerged through the efforts of the development units in consultation with the people.

Another lesson which was learned was that, at the micro-level, the needs of one village very often differ from those of another, and unless and until an intensive survey research is undertaken by development units, a meaningful development plan of an area cannot be prepared. The preparation of the development plan for the Daudzai area reflected the intensity of development required for the rural areas. For years we had talked and thought of rural development by self-help. In Daudzai it was apparent that to leave the development to the rural population on the basis of self-help would be no more than untenable hope and in fact it would add to the frustration and disappointment with the government already felt by the rural people.

Methodology of Development Units

It is interesting to note that in many cases the development units at Daudzai were confronted with villagers' problems, the solutions to which were given the highest priority. Without first getting their particular problems solved, the villagers were not prepared to accept or even listen to any other type of assistance or extension advice. In one case, for instance, when the Markaz functionaries offered inputs for better agricultural production such as fertilizers and seeds, the people demanded that land development works and land protection works be undertaken before they would be willing to accept the inputs. In another village, the seemingly uninformed rural people demanded that the sand-dunes which had blocked their irrigation channel for many years should be dealt with, before they could be motivated for any other projects. The Daudzai development units had many such encounters; they learned the hard way what people demanded, and that what they demanded was the right thing. For months the engineers and the co-operative organizers had to live the life of gypsies, moving from one village to another.

The picture that emerged in Daudzai was alarming. Of the total cultivated area of 34,408 acres, including 28,985 acres of irrigated land, more than 29,000 acres were damaged and deteriorating fast. The land was subject to floods, scouring, erosion, water-logging and salinity, drought and inadequate irrigation. This had resulted in only 47 per cent cropping intensity for *Rabi* (winter crop) and only 74 per cent cropping intensity for *Kharif* (summer) crops. An area which was capable of over 200 per cent cropping intensity had only 121 per cent cropping intensity. In cost effectiveness terms this would mean land development (at 5 to 7 million rupees) resulting in a 12–15 million rupees income every year, at a modest return of Rs 500/acre.

Organizing People

It was obvious to the academy researchers that a massive land development programme was necessary for restoring lands in the Daudzai area to their original richness. It was also evident that land development was not possible without organizing the people. The Chinese experience in this regard had many lessons to teach. The Comilla Experiment (in Bangladesh)[2] was another model before us. The Markaz functionaries found that it was possible to organize people around the solution of problems which the people thought to be their principal priorities. Thus problem-centred organizations were the first ones to emerge in the Daudzai area.

These organizations were initially used to execute the land development work and subsequently for extension education and to maintain the work carried out in the villages. They would ultimately be useful for developing representative leadership. Right from the beginning, based on Raiffesen's principles of co-operation, the Markaz insisted on these organizations meeting weekly and on depositing savings regularly. Each organization met as a general body every week and thus the defect from which the traditional co-operatives in the country suffered, i.e. the dominance of the executive committee, was done away with. These organizations varied in membership from as few as 20 members to as many as 150. However, they represented interest groups in the villages, and primarily comprised the 'small' men. Although there was no bar against the 'bigger' man becoming a member of the organization, he found the rigours of the organization, i.e. weekly meetings and weekly deposits, a little too much and apparently of no use to him. Once people were organized, the Daudzai Markaz functionaries became more effective.

Working of the Village Organizations

(a) Works Programme: The People's Works Programme was very useful for carrying out land development works through the project committees nominated by all the concerned village organizations. The technical supervision was provided by the Markaz engineer and his staff but the task of the paymaster was left to the village organization itself through the project committee. The elimination of the contractor from the scene not only resulted in upgrading the skills of the local rural labour (because the project committees engaged local labour) but also resulted in quality work at much less cost because the village organizations, through their weekly meetings, proved effective watchdogs on the project committees. The village organization thus had a sense of involvement in the completion of the work, which, on completion, came to be looked upon as the property and asset of the whole village organization. The villagers, in this process, learned how to maintain muster-rolls, how to keep accounts and how to maintain the works when they were completed.

Invariably, the works were completed at less than the cost estimated by the engineer. In the beginning the organization used to demand that the money thus saved should only be spent within their village. However, very soon they learned the philosophy of the programme and were convinced that there were many other benefits which were accruing to them because of their having organized themselves. They also learned the hard way that the organizations that did not fulfil the role of partners in development failed to move forward.

(b) Development—A Partnership: Through the village organizations it was put forward to the villagers that development was a partnership between government and the people. The government would only help the villagers if they were prepared to fulfil certain obligations, i.e. to organize themselves, to hold weekly meetings, to adopt improved methods of cultivation, etc., recommended by the agriculture experts of the department. In this manner, the agriculture assistant who had previously felt completely at a loss had now focused on those model farmers who cultivated their own land and were permanent residents of the villages. Whatever they learned at the Markaz from the agriculture experts they applied in their fields and reported at the weekly meetings of their organizations. Thus, in the course of time, they would become the extension agents who would then teach improved methods of cultivation to other members of their village organizations.

Two years after the model had initially been implemented Daudzai Markaz started the sprayers programme. It was found that the sprayers and *Beldars* (ploughmen) of the agriculture department were very few in number and could not reach every village. It was, therefore, decided to train the village model farmers in handling and using the sprayers. After being taught the correct techniques the organizations were encouraged to buy their own sprayers for which credit was made available to them. Now (six months later) over fifteen village organizations have their own sprayers and it is hoped that in course of time each organization will have one to protect their crops from pests.

Similarly, soil testing kits are being demonstrated to the model farmers and it is expected that the organizations will own their own soil testing kits. The interest the agriculture extension programme evoked in Daudzai is apparent from the fact that in November 1974 about 87 per cent of the managers and the model farmers of the organizations attended the fortnightly training at the Markaz.

(c) Health Programme: At the time of the inauguration of Daudzai Markaz it was found that there was only one health dispensary with two visiting dispensers under a compounder (para-pharmacist) for the Daudzai area, which has a population of over 96,000. With the organization of people, the medical technician at the Markaz prepared first-aid boxes, each containing medicines worth Rs 250 and suitable for treatment of 15 to 20 simple diseases. The village organizations were requested to nominate their village *Pesh-Imam* (religious leader) for first-aid training by the medical technician. After some training, which continued every fortnight, the medical technician handed over the box to the Imams, with a price-list showing how much they were to charge for each medicine so that their stocks could be replenished at suitable intervals with this money. The experiment was initiated only in November 1974 in four organizations. However, on demand from other organizations, it was extended to fifteen. This is, in a way, an adoption of the Chinese 'Bare-Foot Doctors' programme. The Imam was chosen because the villagers also have faith in his healing power through prayers. The idea was that with sufficient training and experience, the Imam would be able to treat more diseases and also provide the referral service for patients suffering from serious diseases.

(d) Other Programmes: Programmes for women, youth and in the field of education will soon be initiated. As soon as people get organized and village organizations come into existence, a forum for technicians and experts becomes available. In Daudzai more than 50 of the 103 or so villages have been organized.

Almost all the villages are now ripe for organization and as soon as the Markaz is in a position to do so, i.e. has the services to offer, these villages will be organized. It is expected to cover the whole Markaz area in the next six months.

Creation of Rural Cadres

The Markaz was fully geared to upgrading the skills of the rural population, and was steadily creating rural cadres of co-operative managers, model farmers, Imam-compounders, etc. The cadre of co-operative managers now had persons among its ranks acting as co-operative organizers themselves. We had enlisted the services of managers to make their village organizations function as a nucleus for unorganized villages. The experiment proved very successful and selected co-operative managers in turn took up the organization of 3 to 5 unorganized villages within a distance of 1 to $1^{1}/_{2}$ miles from their home village. The number of manager-organizers is likely to increase and it is expected that this proliferation will also take place in other rural cadres.

The Role of Departments

The history of rural development administration in Pakistan is replete with instances in which many a good programme was sacrificed on the altar of departmental jealousies. In Daudzai, when the departments expanded to the Markaz it was decided by the secretaries' committee of the provincial government of the NWFP that the project manager, who would be an employee of the local government department, should be the co-coordinator of all the departments at the Markaz level. The committee, on the recommendation of the academy, had decided that: (1) the jurisdiction of the line departments would cease at Markaz level and departments would deal with their functionaries only through the project manager; (2) the project manager would be the drawing and disbursing finance officer for all the Markaz functionaries; (3) the project manager would initiate the annual confidential reports on all the Markaz functionaries and: (4) the project manager would be the leave-sanctioning authority for casual leave and the recommending authority for the earned leave for all Markaz functionaries.

To our great discomfiture, we found that the powers meant nothing to the departments and the decision of the secretaries' committee was no more than a piece of paper. The departments, who had been well entrenched for the last hundred years or so, felt their position threatened and were, therefore, out to destroy this 'monster' of integrated rural development which they felt would otherwise destroy them. We learned the hard way that we wanted only two things from the departments: (1) to expand to the Markaz level and (2) to upgrade the skills of rural population and help in creating rural cadres.

For these two things the academy researchers decided that no powers were required for the project manager. The departments (and we discussed this with them individually) were very happy, in fact very keen, to expand to the Markaz level. They were not very clear about their role as teachers in creating rural cadres, but they had no serious objection to performing this role. It was, therefore, decided that each department would expand to the Markaz level on the pattern of the Daudzai project and the departmental representatives would be directly under the control of their respective departments from where they would continue to receive salary, etc. However, the departments agreed to make the contingent expenditure such as travelling allowance, available to their Markaz functionaries, either by placing the funds at their disposal or earmarking the funds separately for their use. Co-ordination, if any, would be carried out by the project manager, not in his capacity of project manager but ultimately in his capacity as secretary of the Markaz Council, as and when it was inducted.

To ensure that the departmental experts were available to the project manager for carrying out the training programme of the rural cadres, a training allowance was fixed for each class taken by the departmental experts. The training funds were controlled by the project manager. Through this simple device the co-operation of the departmental functionaries was obtained by the project manager. The system worked extremely well at Daudzai.

Conclusions

To sum up, integrated rural development as evolved at the Daudzai Project meant:

1. Establishment of a base of operations in a viable unit of development administration in Pakistan. This viable unit of development administration could easily be co-existent with the jurisdiction of the existing police stations in the country.
2. Expansion of the departments, especially the basic needs departments such as local government (project manager, project engineer, co-operative organizer), agriculture (extension and plant protection), animal husbandry, forestry, co-operatives, health, education, revenue, police, WAPDA, small industries, to the Markaz level.
3. Survey research of the area for preparation of a development plan, in consultation with the rural people.
4. Organizing people for land development works, for building up equity capital, for agricultural extension and for the creation of rural cadres.
5. Use of the Markaz as a training and development centre.
6. Two-tier co-operative organization, i.e. primary village co-operatives federated in a Markaz federation to serve as a central bank for the credit needs of small farmers.
7. To expand health and education programmes as the villages became better organized.
8. To add gradually other processing industries at the Markaz, with emphasis on the growth and expansion of the co-operative sector financed and controlled by the small farmers through their organizations federated at the Markaz.
9. To integrate development departments with local councils as and when local council elections were held.

Devolution of Power and the Daudzai Experience

Daudzai, like the Comilla Thana Training and Development Centre (TTDC) or in India, the Block or Mandal, was an attempt to revamp the law-and-order-and-revenue based colonial administration inherited from the British into a Development Administration (DA).

The first requirement for a DA is a viable unit of administration. Akhtar Hameed Khan demonstrated through TTDC that neither the district, the tehsil or subdivision or the taluka was a viable unit for the DA. It was the thana. DA envisages the provision of services and supplies easily accessible to the people. District and subdivision, tehsil or taluka headquarters are too far removed from the village or the *mandi* towns now emerging through urbanization.

The 2001 Devolution Plan does not address the issue of creating a viable unit for development administration. At best it only attempts to improve the management and administration at the district and tehsil levels for services and supplies, both of which are inaccessible and far removed from the grassroots. In Bangladesh and most of the states in India, they have at least created a viable unit for the development administration to revamp the colonial administration.

Akhtar Hameed Khan used to identify three essential infrastructures for DA: administrative, political and socio-economic. The administrative infrastructure comprises the entire government setup, from the grassroots to the federal level. Here he used to identify the vacuum below the tehsil level. Neither the departments nor the government supplies reached the people with the exception of a few like the police and the revenue departments. There was need for all so-called 'nation building' or line departments to be devolved like the police or revenue departments with the hub at the thana level.

The political infrastructure comprises all the elected bodies from union council to the national assembly. The devolution plan has mainly concentrated on the political infrastructure and tried to empower it by transferring many of the powers from the administrative infrastructure. This simple shift of power, and that too in a half-hearted fashion, does not ensure access to services and supplies to the grassroots.

The socio-economic infrastructure comprises people's involvement at the grassroots in decision-making and empowering them for economic and social development. This entails harnessing the potential of the people by organizing them and requiring them to fulfil the obligations for their development. It enables the grassroots to enter into development partnerships with government, local councils, donors, commercial and private development agencies and NGOs on equal terms.

The Independent South Asia Commission on Poverty Alleviation set up by the SAARC heads of state in 1991 had come to the conclusion that socio-economic infrastructure should be the centrepiece of all poverty alleviation strategies of the governments of South Asia. The commission had also concluded that socio-economic infrastructure (SEI) is neither within the mandate nor the capacity of the existing government departments, ministries or corporations. SEI can only be implemented by independent and autonomous support organizations which should be fully funded by the governments of South Asia. The commission quoted the example of the National Rural Support Programme (NRSP), which had received an endowment fund from the government of Pakistan in 1992. The commission had recommended the countrywide replication of these organizations, with governments taking the lead role in providing resources. This recommendation was endorsed at the 1993 SAARC Summit in Dhaka.

Over the last twenty-four years, the RSPs have been endeavouring to foster the SEI countrywide, without which massive allocations of resources by government of Pakistan for poverty reduction would not have the desired results because those resources would neither filter down to the grassroots nor could be accessed by them.

The Mid-Term Development Framework (2005–2010) based on Pakistan's Poverty Reduction Strategy Paper (PRSP) has, for the first time, recognized the importance of SEI and the prime minister took a personal decision to make US$120 million available for SEI between 2007 and 2009.

Guy Hunter's Ten Propositions Based on the Daudzai Experience[3]

Based on the Daudzai experience, Professor Guy Hunter at the Overseas Development Institute (ODI) gave several very practical field illustrations of a number of propositions about agricultural administration for small farmers in a study published in 1976. These confirmed the tentative conclusions reached by the Reading University ODI research carried on over the last six years. The ten propositions he attached to the report are given below, since they may be of wider interest.

(A) Administration

Proposition 1. The largest area over which detailed contact, assistance, village-level programming and investment can be exercised is one covering about 10 x 10 miles, with a population of 40,000–70,000.

Note: Obviously the relation area-population depends on density. Area is more important than population (access by farmers to centre, and by staff to villages). This area is roughly a *Thana* (Pakistan, Bangladesh), a smallish *Block* (India) or a sub-district (much of tropical Africa).

Proposition 2. The departments most actively involved must have trained personnel stationed at this level, with adequate discretion.

Proposition 3. A coordinating officer is necessary at this level.

Note: Compare Area Coordinators (Special Rural Development Programme, Kenya): Block Development Officers (India). In this report, it was found impossible and unnecessary for the coordinating officer to have command and disciplinary power over officers of departments; but an administrative technique is needed to give him some leverage. The arrangements by which co-ordination at field level *and* adequate senior technical supervision from specialized departments are both ensured constitute a problem which is still not satisfactorily analyzed.

(B) Survey and Diagnosis

Proposition 4. No village programme should be initiated before a preliminary survey and discussion with farmers, leading to diagnosis of priority action, has been carried out. An engineer, as well as an agronomist, is almost certainly needed at this stage, building up later to 'a development unit' of mixed skills.

Note: The question of the depth of the survey and time taken by it, the number of skilled personnel needed for it, and the extent to which each village may need separate attention is very difficult. ODI is doing further research on this.

(C) Investment

Proposition 5. Land or water development and other, often minor, investment is almost always needed *before* a successful production programme can be launched. (See Section: 'Methodology of Development Units'.)[4]

(D) Farmer Groupings

Proposition 6. (a) Farmer groups should be built around the situation of specific problems to be agreed by farmers, or around a specific facility. (b) Groups should initially be quite small—20 to 150 persons in this case—and need not be standard 'co-operatives'. Some administrative innovation will be needed to define the corporate character of such groups and to settle the necessary-rules for their action. (c) They should be composed mainly, but not exclusively, of small farmers. (d) The *whole* group should meet regularly and frequently. If an executive committee is appointed, it should be under constant scrutiny from the whole group meetings.

Proposition 7. Cadres for group organization and management can be created, after a year or two of working, from among the membership of the small groups. The people themselves are thus slowly relieving the bureaucracy of multiple jobs.

(E) Training

Note: No proposition on this subject. The report refers to regular training for 'model farmers'. A question both of terminology and of meaning arises here. 'Model Farmers', 'Master Farmers' and 'Progressive Farmers' are terms that have often been used to indicate farmers who have been picked, either directly or indirectly, by the extension or administration officers, partly so that their farms can be used for demonstrations, and partly as contacts through whom the diffusion of information or instruction can be made. Since they have often proved to be the bigger and better-educated farmers, this system has often been criticized (not conducive to small farmer development, etc.).

There are shades of difference in the ways in which selected farmers in the village may be used. In Comilla, a young and energetic farmer was made 'manager' for the small co-operative group, and visited the Rural Academy regularly for training: he had a definite managerial role.

Again, in some states of India (notably UP) *Gram Sahayaks* were appointed, who were really part-time agents for the official Village Level Worker (*Gram Sewak*), and in consequence followed the official package policy. Another system, used by the SORADEP (French-aided) project in Ethiopia, with some similarity to the *animateur* system widely used in Francophone Africa, consisted of the selection *by the village* of a farmer, or even a man without a full-time farm who, after three weeks' initial training, was used partly as an assistant extension officer and paid a salary. He had organizing, rather than technical, duties and acted partly as a clerk or secretary to a group of 20 to 100 farmers, recording performance, forwarding requests and problems, and relaying information, amongst other tasks.

Obviously, there is a distinction to be made here between 'farmer training centres', where groups of ordinary farmers come in for short residential courses, and the training of rural cadres, paid or unpaid, who act as organizers, demonstrators, or supplementary extension officers.

(F) Financing and Credit

Proposition 8. While initial 'task or facility-oriented' groups are often not large enough to manage a major credit programme, in early stages loans can be made administratively to these small and mutually responsible groups. Later, a federation of groups at a rather higher (thana) level may be absolutely necessary.

Proposition 9. Weekly savings and group responsibility are of high importance in building finance.

Proposition 10. Commercial banks are not effective pioneers of credit to small farmers, seldom having sufficient flexibility or knowledgeable staff. At a later stage, where considerable funds pass through the thana-level organization or co-operative, banks can be of great assistance.

NOTES

1. Based on a case study by Shoaib Sultan Khan, *Agricultural Administration* (3), 1976. Applied Science Publishers Ltd. England.
2. The Works of Akhtar Hameed Khan (Volumes 1, 2 and 3). *Development of a Rural Community: Rural Works and the Comilla Cooperative*. Bangladesh Academy for Rural Development, Kotbari, Comilla. 1983.
3. Guy Hunter. *The Daudzai Project: Some Practical Implications for Agricultural Administration* (2). Overseas Development Institute, London. Agricultural Administration (3) (1976). Applied Science Publishers Ltd. 1976.
4. The Lilongwe Project (Malawi) was in fact called the 'Lilongwe Land Development Programme'.

3

The Personal Diary of a UN Consultant in Japan

My friends Zaki Azam and Mohammad Ahmad of the Asian Development Bank (ADB) of Manila, having read my 'travelogue' of the overland journey from London to Peshawar in 1977, urged me to keep a diary while in Japan. My permanent host in Manila, Mr Rasheed Khan, Executive Director of the ADB, also lent his support to the idea. However, I did not give the suggestion a second thought. However, after a three week stay in Nagoya—the headquarters of the United Nations Centre for Regional Development (UNCRD) and my place of work for the next few months—the idea of following in the footsteps of my mentor in rural development, Dr Akhtar Hameed Khan, crossed my mind. He had also kept a diary (later published) during one of his sojourns in the United States.

After this *apologia* and pinning of blame on Zaki and Mohammad Ahmad as the prime movers for the effort, I must acknowledge that everyone I spoke to before going to Japan unnerved me by pointing out the numerous difficulties I would encounter. The one redeeming feature, some people conceded, was that the Japanese on the whole were a friendly people.

First Impressions

3-30 September 1978

I was, therefore, pleasantly surprised when, from the moment I arrived at Narita International Airport from Manila, I felt completely at home in Japan. There were forms available in English. Changing dollars into Yen was equally smooth. Only at the Immigration did I sense that the officer was a little flustered. Later, I came to learn from the administrative officer UNCRD, Mr Kawashima, when he saw my passport, that on my visa 'good for multiple visits' the officer had, by mistake, stamped 'used' and then written alongside in Japanese that the 'used stamp' had been put by mistake and the visa was valid for multiple visits during the full duration of my mission in Japan.

As I had to fly to Nagoya, I hired a porter and headed for the domestic terminal. At the check-in counter, I was told that the flight did not fly from Narita but from Hanneda, the other Tokyo airport. Luckily I got a seat on a flight from Narita for Nagoya.

Since I wanted to phone Ashraf Kazi, Counsellor at the Pakistan Embassy, who had also recently arrived, I headed for the telephones. It caused me some consternation to find the telephone directories printed in Japanese only. However, I found a Japanese girl using the phone who helped me.

A recorded message informed me that the Embassy was closed (it was a Sunday) and that in case of urgency, I could call another number. I dialled that number and the gentleman informed me that Ashraf had arrived but was staying in a hotel and that since the Embassy would be closed for the next four days because of the festival of *Eid,* I should try again after that period. This was all rather heartening. So far I had not encountered any insurmountable problems despite some difficult situations like the change of flight from Narita to Nagoya and obtaining the Pakistan embassy's phone number. On the food front, I found an excellent hamburger and a hot cup of tea.

The airport atmosphere did not give any indication of having been the scene of a pitched battle which made world headlines only a couple of months ago.[1] Of course, the security arrangements were in full force and each ingress to the airport was well guarded. Narita is a beautiful airport equipped with all modern facilities, shopping arcades, escalators and very broad runways.

As I had arrived a couple of hours earlier than expected, I did not expect anybody from UNCRD to meet me till it was time for the flight from Hanneda. Hence I rang up UNCRD and Mr Kawashima told me that they had no information about the flight I would be taking as they did not receive the cable I had asked UNDP Dhaka to send them. However, a room had been booked for me at the New Plaza hotel and that I could easily get there by taxi. Accordingly I hired a taxi and was in the hotel in less than half an hour. However, at the hotel the receptionist communicated to me that my room was booked in Nagoya Plaza, another hotel owned by the same management. Mr Ashraf of the

Pakistan Planning Commission, who had been to Nagoya recently, had informed me that the New Plaza was the better of the two hotels, I therefore, insisted on staying there. When the receptionist did not understand my objection, I asked him to ring up Mr Kawashima who informed me that the room was booked at Nagoya Plaza because it was cheaper by 1,000 Yen. I told him that I would prefer to stay at the New Plaza and since I was going to stay for six months, the management should give me more concession than what they were already giving members of the UNCRD team. This exchange resulted in a further concession of 400 Yen.

I found the hotel room a little congested but it had almost all the amenities. As the snack bars were closed on Sunday, however, I was directed by the receptionist to go to a Chinese restaurant close to the Nagoya Plaza hotel. I happened to go in the opposite direction and entered the first restaurant I saw to enquire about the Nagoya Plaza hotel. Since they did not know where it was, I had dinner in that very restaurant. There were two girls having dinner in the same area as I. After I had started my dinner, I noticed that one of the girls whispered something to the butler, who then brought a cigarette lighter with the restaurant crest on it and presented it to me with the compliments of the management. When I had nearly finished dinner, the same butler came to me and said, 'The ladies want you to join them'. The remark of my friend's wife at Islamabad 'Shabbu! Be careful of the Japanese women; they are very sweet and very fast!' flashed through my mind. I moved over to the girls' table and there discovered that the butler was really the owner of the restaurant and the girl was the cashier, who was entertaining one of her girl friends. Although I am always very polite and nice (much to the annoyance of my wife) to the fair sex, I seldom find them alluring unless they are strikingly beautiful (by my own standard of beauty). Thirty years ago, I found one such woman and married her; she had already set too high a standard of beauty for me to allow room for waywardness. Anyway I found this a good introduction to Japanese individuals and thought of cultivating the acquaintance of this girl. However, despite my efforts to get acquainted with her, I did not meet her again. So much for my friend's wife's observations, who probably read too much into discovering the photograph of a Japanese girl in her husband's briefcase, after a visit to Japan. Japanese girls are sweet indeed, but fast, indeed not. On the streets of Japan I have not seen any of those amorous scenes that one observes in Europe or the States. I have seldom seen Japanese couples walking hand in hand in public. The Japanese standard of morality is certainly high.

About the Japanese attitude towards foreigners, I was greatly impressed when, upon my asking a garage attendant the way to the hotel, he took out a car and drove me to the hotel because it was drizzling. Nagoya underground ('subway' in Japan) railway stations have beautiful shopping arcades and it was in a labyrinth of these arcades that I lost my way and headed out in a different direction. On another occasion, when I asked a man about the bus to Imaike hospital, he directed me to a girl who understood a little bit of English. She not only pointed out the right bus, but while boarding the bus, gave me a 100 Yen coupon and despite my protestations refused to accept payment for it. Again at Imaike, I could not find the bus stop for my hotel. Ultimately a kindly person walked to the stop with me.

Japan is a country where Pakistanis are comfortable and even prosperous. I met one Pakistani who is doing extremely well and owns three cars, a Mercury Monarch, a Toyota Century and a British car. He explained to me that the managing director of a company is expected to own a foreign manufactured car, otherwise his solvency is doubted. The Toyota, he explained, was necessary if one was dealing with the Toyota company because they do not allow any other make of car to enter their factory area. The three cars, according to him, were a status symbol for facilitating business dealings and for impressing the neighbours. I had to accept his word because it was his eleventh year in Japan and he is married to a Japanese woman.

On the food front, again contrary to the predictions of the prophets of doom, I experienced no problem either in regard to quality or price. My friend Ralph Diaz, who was instrumental in getting me the consultancy in Japan, introduced me to Chinese, Japanese and 'mixed' cuisine. I found all of them most palatable and wholesome. Haruo Nagamine with whom I am directly working at the Centre, introduced me to the famous Japanese dish *shabu shabu*, which was indeed exotic and delicious. It consists of wafer-thin layers of beef which you dip in boiling water for a minute and then in a specially prepared sauce. It is eaten with a lot of salad and other accompaniments. Kentucky Fried Chicken and McDonald's hamburgers are also available.

I was having some problem with breakfast because even the most frugal Japanese breakfast consists of a slice of bread almost two inches thick, buttered and smeared with jam. I had to ask the waitress to reduce the width of the slice. However, one day when I ventured out to the Sakae shopping centre, I found everything available in big departmental stores which remain open even on Sundays. I made purchases of teabags, sugar, coffee-mate and rusk type bread to solve my breakfast problem, and incidentally achieved considerable savings on these meals. Later I extended this practice to dinner also, gaining the twofold advantage of not having to dress for dinner after returning from work, and keeping my weight under control.

A skin rash which I had neglected in Pakistan suddenly erupted in Nagoya and I sought the assistance of the UNDP Administrative Officer. He made an evening appointment with the doctor at a local hospital. The hospital was very clean and the receptionist very efficient. The doctor, Dr Kawahara, a very pleasant and helpful person prescribed an ointment which proved quite effective. I was also given a registration card by the hospital for future use. So on the health front, I was now fully conversant with the procedure to follow, but I did miss the British national health service where once registered on arrival, you got the finest health care, free.

My introduction to travel by the underground railway, the subway, was quite accidental. I had not even tried to travel by the subway because all the signs were in Japanese and I thought it would be impossible to decipher the system. One day when I had walked down to the Nagoya station I ran into Roy Kelly, who also worked at the UNCRD. Roy has been in Japan for the last fifteen years and speaks fluent Japanese. His parents are missionaries and have lived in Japan for a long time. Roy showed me how to use the subway system.

A few days after my joining the UNCRD, a Vietnamese man also joined the Centre as a Research Associate. NguYen Tri Dong (pronounced Yong) and I had lunch together a couple of times and became friends. He is a doctoral research student and has been away from his country for the last ten years. He hopes to complete his research in the next two years and then return home. His wife is at the Tokyo University doing doctoral research in bio-chemistry. Dong usually goes away on weekends to Tokyo, but one weekend his wife came to Nagoya instead. We went together to visit the shrine and the botanical gardens. Mrs Dong's Indian friend Miss Rama, who is working for her doctoral degree at Kyoto University, also came with us. The Dongs are emphatically patriotic and are looking forward to returning to their country on completion of their education. Meeting the mild and sweet Dongs, I wondered at the steely determination of the Vietnamese which humbled a super-power.

Dong told me that this was his given name and his surname was NguYen Tri which appeared first. The Vietnamese always write their surname first and given name last. Miss Rama is a South Indian and now settled in New Delhi. She hopes to return next March after completing her research. Her major is Philosophy.

The Nagoya shrine was re-built in 1892 but the original dated back to the ancient period. People come to this shrine, throw a coin or two inside and clap their hands once or twice and bow down for a few moments in meditation. The botanical garden is also the zoo. Dong was quite amused by the antics of the penguins. One of them kept walking on the ridge apparently pondering whether to jump into the pond below. Dong wanted it to jump. I thought she was only indulging in brinkmanship and would not jump. I suggested a wager to Dong. He was still undecided when the bird jumped—much to my relief and Dong's annoyance.

The last day of September was a Sunday. I usually get up late on weekends. In the beginning when I used to hang up the 'do not disturb' sign, the hotel maid would knock at 1100 hours but after a week she started leaving the fresh linen etc., outside my door and would come back around 1300 hours to clean the room and make the bed. On weekends I combined breakfast and lunch, so one Sunday I went to have a brunch of Kentucky Chicken. I was surprised to see a procession on the street shouting slogans. On reaching the main Sakae shopping centre, I found other processions parading on both sides of the street. Luckily, I met a man who knew English and was quite amused by all this activity. He told me the protesters were Communists, demonstrating against war and America. When I asked why this date was significant he replied laughingly. 'Don't you think it is a fine day for this type of activity?' At the same place I saw Japanese police, who are usually conspicuous by their absence. There was one helping the lady traffic warden control traffic and there were two police vehicles at the end of the procession. I found the law-abiding Japanese citizens quite amazing. Japanese traffic is most orderly and even the people in the demonstration observe the traffic rules, unlike our countries where demonstrations take precedence over all traffic.

My introduction to the international telephone dialling system took place within hours of my arrival at Nagoya. The KDD (international telephone and telegraph office) is only a few blocks away from my hotel. Since my wife, four daughters and two grandchildren are in London, I surprised them by calling them from Nagoya. On my eldest daughter's birthday on 26 September, I booked a personal call. Roohi was overwhelmed on the other side and broke into tears on hearing my voice. I had made her very happy by making this call. Being the eldest, she has been taking care of the family for the last two years. Although in terms of distance I have come farther away from my family but in fact I feel much closer to them from Japan than I used to feel from Pakistan. Here I can pick up the telephone anytime and talk to them, whereas from Pakistan it used to take hours and there was the operator in between.

One other very good thing about Japan is the total absence of the custom of tipping. You are not expected to tip either at a hotel, or a restaurant. Nor do railway or airport porters, or taxi drivers expect you to pay them over and above the charge for their services. The first time I left a tip for the waiter at a restaurant, he came running after me, thinking that I had forgotten my change.

October 1978

I had attended the 34th annual session of the ESCAP (UN Economic and Social Commission for Asia and the Pacific) as representative of the International Planned Parenthood Federation in my capacity as Chairman of the Training, Research and Evaluation Committee of the Family Planning Association of Pakistan. During the session, the Population Division of the ESCAP had invited me to give a short seminar on the integration of family planning activities in other development programmes. As a sequel to that seminar, I had received an invitation from them in Pakistan to attend a proposed workshop on the subject at Bangkok in October. In the meanwhile, since I had come to Japan, I informed the ESCAP that I would be unable to attend the workshop from Pakistan. However, to my great surprise, Japan Airlines called to say that they had received a PTA (Pre-travel Authorization) to enable me to travel to Bangkok and back, from Nagoya. Haruo Nagamine very generously agreed to my attending the workshop. Later on I had to ask him to allow me to visit Sri Lanka also, because UNICEF wanted me there for a couple of days. Fortunately, this could all be done without much disruption of the work at the centre because of three holidays between 2 and 10 October.

The flight from Nagoya to Bangkok stopped at Hong Kong, where Minhaj Hussain, Consul General of Pakistan, and my friend Meraj Hussain, his younger brother, had very kindly come to receive me at the airport. Meraj put me up at his house in a room which had an impressive view. The Merajes looked after me extremely well and showed me the whole of Hong Kong; but for them my visit could not have been so enjoyable.

On the return trip I had to take a flight from Hong Kong to Osaka and as it was too late to get a train to Nagoya I had to spend the night at a hotel. The next morning on entering the railway platform for a train to Nagoya, I saw a big signboard in English which said, 'Shinkansen'. I was looking forward to travelling on this famous Japanese 'bullet train'. It seemed to me that the train was not moving very fast and when after nearly 15 minutes it began to slow down I started entertaining grave doubts about the reputation of the Shinkansen. I thought that, like our trains in Pakistan, this was also subject to unscheduled stops and mechanical problems. However, the stop turned out to be Kyoto station—the famous old capital of Japan, a top tourist attraction—and the train left after stopping for only two minutes or so.

Exactly an hour and ten minutes after leaving Osaka, the train stopped at Nagoya—a distance of nearly 200 kilometres. I was surprised and greatly impressed. It was like travelling in a jet where you don't feel the speed. I had covered a distance of over 125 miles and travelled from one hotel room to another in only two hours. The Japanese are rightly proud of their Shinkansen.

Shinkansen trains come in two types: one, which travels non-stop from one big city to the other, and the other type which makes a few stops. Thus the former type covers the Nagoya-Tokyo distance in two hours, the latter in three hours.

Like railways, the telecommunications system in Japan is also partially in the public and partially in the private sector. The KDD from where I make telephone calls to London, is privately owned but the internal telephone and postal system is in the public sector. Instead of the familiar public telephone booths, except at railway stations, airports etc., one finds telephones kept on high stools outside shops or inside departmental stores. These are privately owned and authorized by the telephone department for public use on the usual coin-box system. At closing time the shopkeepers lock up their shops, leaving these telephones with their stands outside.

My friend and colleague Haruo Nagamine invited the group working with him at the centre to a day's outing, with stops at his apartment, a nearby museum and a Chinese restaurant. The 'task force' working on the study dealing with identification of basic needs comprises Lea

Serano from the Philippines, Chung from Korea, Achutta from India, Oya and Hosaka from Japan. Haruo is the Co-ordinator and I the Adviser. Oya was in Sri Lanka and did not come. Haruo's secretary Hirako Okada, who also acts as my secretary, came to my hotel to guide us to Haruo's place. I have found her to be very efficient and pleasant. She is able to type page after page of my atrocious writing without making a single mistake.

On our arrival we were welcomed by Haruo and his eleven-year-old daughter at the museum—a private collection of 17th and 18th century scrolls and porcelain donated to a Trust. There was also a 2-storey 'tea house' where we were treated to the 'tea ceremony' complete in the minutest detail. Since the actual tearoom could accommodate only four persons, one group had to wait. We took off our shoes and waited in the entrance. After a while we were taken upstairs by a very grave looking man dressed in a suit and sporting a small beard, who requested us to wait in the guest rooms. The rooms had *sitalpati* type of bamboo mats on the floors and no other furniture. We sat down cross-legged on the floor. After a little while we were invited downstairs. I wanted Hirako to enter the room first but the gentleman with the beard beckoned to me. Hirako whispered to me that the main guest is supposed to be invited in first—the principle of 'ladies first' does not operate in the tearoom. The entrance to the tearoom was through two doors, one leading to a small alley and the other to the actual tearoom. The guest is supposed to open the sliding door to the tearoom and enter, bowing. Haruo was already sitting there and motioned me to sit in a corner of the room. You are supposed to sit in the same posture as Muslims do while offering their prayers.

The small room was 'L' shaped. One of its sides was slightly raised and was adorned with a painting, a flowerpot and a tea container. The mistress of ceremonies was seated in the alcove with another lady (all attendants of the ceremony were dressed in *kimonos*, which are the formal dress) who was preparing the tea under her guidance. The tea was served with great ceremony in two-hundred-year-old bowls. The tea itself is a frothy green liquid to be taken in three to three and a half sips. When the bowl is placed before you, it is ensured that the decorative part is facing you and while sipping the tea you are supposed to give the bowl a little turn so that the decorative part is not facing your lips. Before the tea we were served with Japanese cakes—one each on a leaf-like utensil. This is supposed to intensify the taste of the tea. I found the tea quite palatable and had two cups after being assured that it is not in bad form to ask for a second bowl. There were at least five to six ladies in attendance—two in the tearoom and three or four in the adjoining anteroom which had a sliding door connecting it to the tearoom.

There were two long pipes with a container for tobacco kept in a tray in the middle of the room. This, we were told, signified that the ceremony was informal. On finishing the tea we had to go out of the door walking backwards. I wondered what a formal ceremony would be like, if this was supposed to be informal. It was certainly one of my most exotic and dream-like experiences in Japan. One can never imagine what a Japanese tea-ceremony is like unless one experiences it. Thanks to Haruo it was all especially arranged for us. The Japanese are quite overwhelmingly hospitable.

From the tea-house we walked over to Haruo's flat. Housing is probably the most expensive and most inadequate facility in Japan. Haruo's flat has four bedrooms and a dining-sitting room, all compressed into a very small space and costing a princely sum. Mrs Nagamine had left the hospital and come home to meet us. She had hurt her ankle while climbing a mountain and had been hospitalised for treatment. They have two sons and a daughter. The younger children gave a charming violin performance. The eldest, who is a bit of a rebel against parental authority, has a very inquisitive and innovative mind and is a non-conformist, a circumstance which seems to cause Haruo some anxiety. On being asked what he would like to do when he grew up, he said that he was interested in becoming a sound engineer. He then confided to his father that, on second thought, he would like to become a critic of pornographic literature. I suggested that he had better keep to the first profession. I assured Haruo that every family has a child like his son and he shouldn't worry too much. Such children seem to look after themselves pretty well given some understanding and encouragement. We were served excellent tea and pastries at the Nagamine household.

It is a custom in Japan to take gifts of flowers or sweets on being invited to someone's house. A reciprocal gift is given and not considered bad form, unlike in some other countries. After tea and a delightful time at Haruo's flat, we went to the nearby Chinese restaurant and were treated to a sumptuous meal there.

Another Japanese practice which I found impressive is that the staff of a restaurant greet customers cordially on their arrival and bid them a warm farewell when they leave. At first I was a little flustered by such cheerful attention from the waiters and waitresses on entering or leaving their restaurant, but later it began to sound like a warm and friendly gesture. Another thing which I have noticed in Japan is that it is probably the only country where the first words you hear (or utter) on picking up the telephone are not 'hello' but '*mushai mushay*' which possibly mean the same thing as hello.

One night when I was lying in bed, the peace of the night was shattered by a loud sound. It was followed by the sound of a number of cars stopping or slowing down. On looking out of the front window I saw a car with its front smashed, resting against a pole almost directly beneath my room. Another badly damaged car—a Toyota Starlet sports—stood some distance away in the middle of the road. Close to the Starlet, I was horrified to see a man lying motionless.

I was indignant when I saw that no one from the crowd that had gathered bothered to help the injured man. I was disgusted with the Japanese at this exhibition of callousness. Getting dressed quickly I went downstairs and was relieved to see that the man was alive and conscious, though lying in a pool of blood. People were waiting for the ambulance to arrive. That was when I remembered the first aid instruction that in case of accidents the injured person should not be handled by untrained individuals if expert help is quickly available. Ultimately a police car and then the ambulance arrived. In the meanwhile a sizeable crowd had assembled and a number of motorists kept stopping and getting down from their cars—after proper parking—and coming to the scene of the accident. There were also quite a few hotel inmates in slippers and some only in pyjamas, wandering around the place. I was distressed to see some people from the crowd even cracking jokes and laughing at the whole thing. I am sure they had been berating the foolhardiness of the motorist who had collided at the traffic lights because, obviously, he had disregarded the traffic signals, and hence did not deserve any sympathy.

Soon the police took control of the situation. Suitable fluorescent signs were displayed, cordoning off the area where the accident took place; the injured man had already been rushed to the hospital and the crowd confined to the pavement. The traffic flow was smoothly re-regulated. When I returned to my room I realized that the whole episode had taken only 20 minutes. A few minutes later I saw a policeman sweeping the glass off the road and the two damaged cars parked along the curb, and I wondered when the police in our country would become so effective, efficient and conscientious.

On one Sunday Dong rang up to ask if I would like to join him for lunch. We went to the Chinese restaurant on the top of the 25 storey Tokai Bank building. This is the best Chinese restaurant I have come across anywhere. The prices are reasonable and you get an impressive view of Nagoya. On the same floor of the building in another corner is an exclusive club where Honjo, Director of the Centre, had once taken me. The food there is ridiculously cheap and good, though I am sure the entrance and monthly subscription must be proportionately high. One such club is very close to my hotel. It is called the Red Horse Club and has a brass plaque outside with a long quotation in English — one could easily mistake it for a pub in England.

The Nagoya festival was being celebrated. We could see the procession from the Tokai building as it moved through the Sakae shopping area. Dong and I went down after lunch to see it close up. The procession had many bands and floats. Because of the rain, all the 'kimono girls' were sitting inside the truck with the driver, and their seats by the float were covered with polythene covers — must have been bitterly disappointing for the girls, yet they kept waving cheerfully from behind the windscreen. The festival is an annual event and ends in the selection of Nagoya's Kimono Girl of the year. Honjo had told me that these girls spend as much as $500 and more to buy a kimono just for the day. It made me wonder if the switchover to western dress by the Japanese women is more because of the expensiveness of the kimono than the American influence.

A number of people in Pakistan had asked me to make enquiries about purchasing reconditioned cars for them in Japan. I had asked the Pakistani businessman, Mr Zafarullah Khan, who had been resident at Nagoya for the last eleven years and was also dealing in export of second-hand cars, to get me information relating to price, availability of cars etc. On my return from Bangkok I rang up his house and his father answered my call. I was shocked to learn that Zafarullah Khan had died in an accident a week earlier.

Zafarullah Khan had been very well-spoken of by all the Pakistanis I met in Nagoya. In fact it was people like him who had built a good image of the country in Japan. However, unscrupulous Pakistanis have already started tarnishing the image of their country and their countrymen in the eyes of the Japanese.

One Sunday I got up very late and by the time I left the hotel it was well past lunchtime. I headed for the nearby Kentucky Chicken snack bar, which was unusually crowded, and had some lunch. The weather was very pleasant, like November in Islamabad or Peshawar and I had an urge to go and sit in a park. London in this respect is peerless because there is always a park within a stone's throw. The only park near my hotel is the central park, which to my great wonder, has been built (there is a lot of masonry work) literally before my eyes. Big trees and plants have been transplanted. Beneath the central park is, of course, Nagoya's speciality — a big underground shopping arcade.

While sauntering along, I came upon a street in the heart of the Sakae shopping area which had a very festive look. There were no vehicles and people were walking in the middle of the road. Youngsters were roller skating, and at intervals, in front of big shops and departmental stores, chairs with sun umbrellas were placed right on the road. For some time I could not make out what it was all about. I walked from one end of the street to the other and thought the street was perhaps closed to vehicular traffic on an experimental basis. People were really enjoying themselves. Later on I learned that every Sunday the street was closed for sixteen hours and reserved exclusively for pedestrians. People were making full use of this facility and really enjoying themselves. Besides the kids on the roller skates, there were youngsters engaged in yoga. A photographer was taking photographs, while his assistant handed leaflets to the client. In many cases, especially if they were girls, the reading of the pamphlet would cause a lot of amusement and even refusal to be photographed, whereas some elderly people had no hesitation in getting themselves photographed. I could not muster the courage to find out what it was all about, so it remained a mystery.

Sometimes not knowing the culture and the language can lead to complete misinterpretation of a situation. This once happened to me when I saw a stunning newsflash on the TV. On the screen was a man in a car surrounded by people with pickaxes and stones. Then the car was on fire and the people were breaking open the windscreen with their stones and pickaxes, and dragging the man out. To me it looked just like a lynching scene from a Western movie. I was surprised to find no mention of the incident in the morning newspapers next day. Later I learned that it was not a lynching, but just the reverse: the man had locked himself in the car and after seven hours of refusing to come out had set fire to the back seat. Then the bystanders had broken open the car and dragged him out. As for me, the episode taught me not to jump to conclusions.

One day I sat on one of the chairs lying alongside a store in the middle of the road and basked in the delightful sunshine for over an hour. Observing the passers-by, I found it interesting to note that while the Japanese women seemed to be dressed in the most modern and stylish French fashions, the Japanese males continued to wear the narrow bottom trousers.

I had a standing invitation from Ashraf Kazi, Counsellor Pakistan Embassy, to stay with him in Tokyo. Ashraf belonged to one of the first batches that came to the Civil Service Academy during my tenure there. Being very handsome and endowed with charming manners, Ashraf has been a favourite of everyone in my family.

My Vietnamese friend Dong, who goes to Tokyo every weekend, was my travelling companion on the Shinkansen. This journey was not as smooth as my first journey from Osaka and on the way to the restaurant car I could feel the speed of the train and had to hold on to the seat handles. I saw the speedometer registering 210 km per hour and the meter showed 300 km as the maximum speed.

Ashraf has a very spacious flat, unlike the usual Japanese accommodation. Although I had met Mrs Ashraf (Abida) once or twice before I knew her only slightly. I met his two lovely daughters—Nilufer and Maha—for the first time. Unfortunately the weather on the last weekend of October instead of yielding an autumn-blue sky was too wet and murky. However we went off to climb the Tokyo tower, which is higher than Eiffel and yet, as proudly declared in the brochure, 3,000 tons lighter, thereby proving the superiority of Japanese steel. Nevertheless, the Eiffel tower is peerless in grandeur, while the Tokyo tower looks too slender. Usually one can get a magnificent view of Tokyo from the tower but unfortunately the murky weather on the occasion precluded this. However, the claim about its height was amply proved when on reaching the top stage, we found snowflakes drifting by the viewing windows. Ashraf looked at me in disbelief when I pointed out the flakes to him. I found Tokyo city like any other big city. However, I was pleasantly surprised to find it spacious and open, unlike the impression one carried in one's mind about what the most populous city in the world would look like.

My visit coincided with Ashraf's first formal dinner party at his home since his arrival in Tokyo. His guests included the Russian Counsellor and Mrs Kamarasky, the recently dismissed Afghan Counsellor and Mrs Sadullah Ghonssey, the Indian Counsellor and Mrs Ram, a Pakistani gentleman with his Chinese wife, an Australian diplomat and his wife, and a few others. I found Mr Kamarasky and Dr Ghonssey very interesting to talk to. The Russian had been studying Japanese language and culture for the 28 years he had been at the Russian Embassy in Tokyo, intermittently, since 1959. I was most impressed by his knowledge of Japan and the deep study he had made of the Shinto shrines and Japanese architecture and history. He expressed the view that the Japanese have the great quality of assimilating outside influences and 'Japanising' them instead of fighting or resisting external onslaughts — whether on their culture or religion.

As a case in point he mentioned the Buddhist phenomenon, which took a uniquely Japanese form in Japan. He also underlined the place of consensus in the Japanese way of life. He said 'Believe it or not the attack on Pearl Harbour was launched only after a consensus had been obtained from the government, business and commercial as well as other groups'. Everything from the smallest family enterprise to the giant commercial organizations in Japan functions on consensus. The Russian also touched on the Sino-Japanese treaty and was critical of the fact that, although in the case of China the Japanese have agreed to leave the resolution of certain pertinacious disputes to the future generations, they do not appear to adopt the same attitude towards Russia. I was greatly impressed by Professor Kamarasky's candid and insightful assessments. For a Russian he was very frank and open.

The recent changeover in Afghanistan resulted in Dr Ghonssey's taking up a professorial assignment in Tokyo. He was of the view that Russians had literally taken over control of his country and the Afghan diplomatic service and the Foreign Office were being systematically disintegrated. He was very bitter against the Russians and his wife had murder in her eyes for them. Ashraf and I sat on, discussing the Haiku, the form of Japanese poetry in which ideas and thoughts must be expressed in no more than seventeen syllables. I was impressed by Ashraf's immersion in Japanese culture — probably the only way to understand a country and its people.

I found Abida a perfect hostess. Despite the pressure of the party, she kept her composure and seemed to be attending to everything without once losing her temper or getting cross about anything — so usual for ladies in such a situation. Although I did hear Ashraf raising his voice at the children when he seemed to be getting late for his courtesy call on Admiral Sharif, who landed in Tokyo at a few hour's notice on a weekend, but Abida took everything calmly and in her stride. I was most impressed by the quiet, unruffled way in which she attended to everything, including her children. She sounded very genuine and warm in inviting me to visit them again. Ashraf's little daughter Maha is a real fiery petrel. I was quite amused by her fluency in abuses when provoked, obviously picked up from the maidservant.

Suzukisan, the embassy driver, who had waited for a good part of the day at the hotel for the Admiral on a Sunday, was somewhat mollified when I assured him that there was only one Admiral in Pakistan and he had to be shown special consideration even at the cost of grave inconvenience to others.

Back in Nagoya, I was greatly touched when the bus driver allowed me to have a free ride in the bus because he had no change for the 1,000 Yen note I offered him. Back home I would have been either refused entry into the bus or asked to produce the required change from anywhere.

November 1978

My acceptance of the invitation to attend an ESCAP meeting in November, prior to coming to Nagoya, took me to Bangkok again, this time via Manila where I once again enjoyed Rasheed and Nighat's hospitality. In Bangkok I met Sudarshan, my University class-fellow, after more than 25 years. She is now married to my university friend Amarnath Varma, who is working as an ESCAP consultant. Meeting with Sudarshan brought back memories of yesteryear. When I complimented her on preserving her youthful looks, she chided me for becoming very bold. It reminded me how correct and careful I used to be towards her. In those days friendship with a coed really made one feel very self-important. I knew a lot of boys who wanted to be friends with Sudarshan but she hardly encouraged any of them.

Another person I met after nearly seventeen years was my friend Sultanuz Zaman, and his wife. We had joined the Civil Service together and in 1961 when Sultan was getting married, I, as the owner of the only tomato red Opel Rekord in Dacca (now Dhaka), drove the bridegroom to the bride's house and brought the couple back to the groom's house. Sultan is now Chief of the Agriculture Division at ESCAP from Bangladesh. The Sultans are a most hospitable and charming couple.

Since the cost of a haircut in Nagoya was nearly $10, I thought of having the haircut at the Bangkok airport barber's salon. No sooner had my hair been trimmed than I was laid flat on the chair with my head in the washbasin, ostensibly for a shampoo. But simultaneously with the shampooing, while my face was covered with a towel, a girl started massaging my legs with a machine and another began to give me a manicure; the massage continued even after the shampoo was over. The girl doing the massage asked me if I was feeling hot, whispering the question in my ear, which incidentally had also been cleaned with cotton wool. She followed up her question with the pleading that she was very good. It was all said with such innocence and abruptness that it left me completely speechless. It appeared that the cost of the massage depended on the time spent in the barber's chair. Finally when I did wrest myself away from the barber's chair, despite the girl's protests, the cost was $11 for the haircut, shampoo, massage, manicure and cleaning of the ears!

Back in Japan, Dr Dilawar Ali Khan from Pakistan, while coming to attend a seminar at UNCRD also brought my suitcase containing winter clothes. In order to do so he had to leave his own behind. I was greatly touched by his kind gesture, especially as Nagoya's weather is turning colder day by day and I would have surely frozen without the warm clothes. Buying clothes in Japan is simply out of the question because they are so expensive. This also brings to my mind the most expensive dinner to which we were entertained along with some members of the UNCRD advisory council. It was a *shabu shabu* dinner followed with melon and ice-cream. The food was superb.

The visit to Kyoto was made possible through the courtesy of Shoukat Ali from Mirpur (Azad Kashmir) who asked his friend Mr Kamura to drive us to Kyoto. The research fellows from India (Achutta) and Korea (Chung) also came along. The Japanese expressway is a four-lane road and far inferior to British or European motorways. It took us nearly an hour and a half to reach the outskirts of Kyoto.

Sunday seemed to be a bad day for a visit to Kyoto, which is the star tourist attraction, being the old capital of Japan and the only city which, at the behest of the Smithsonian Foundation, was saved from American bombing during the Second World War. We visited the Ohara and the silver temples and bought postcards of the golden temple. The temples and the miniature gardens are beautiful. The Japanese practice Buddhism and some also observe the old religion, namely Shintu. However, I didn't find much difference between the Buddhist and Shintu temples except that the latter do not have Buddha's images.

Since we were unable to find parking space at the temples, we left the car at the first park we came across. The park was full of beautiful Japanese maples. This time of the year, at the advent of autumn, the green leaves turn red, yellow, burnt orange-a range of lovely colours. The scene defies description. The whole forest of maples appears to come alive with hues and colours—just before the leaves fall—and await the winter snow. This was one of the most beautiful natural scenes I have ever seen.

A cable car took us to the top of the hill in two stages, giving us a magnificent view all along the way. However, it was quite surprising to note that fare was charged separately at both ends—for going up and coming down. However, I must say that I noted some students walking down the hill on the way back.

I was very keen to see the old city of Kyoto because the main streets that we had been motoring along were newly constructed. Kitamura, therefore, took us away from the main thoroughfare and we walked through lanes no more than two yards wide—reminding me of the *galis* of Peshawar city—with houses in the old style. It was peaceful and serene, away from the hustle and bustle of modern life. There were beautiful canals lined with weeping willows along the roads. It was enchanting. The Japanese appear to be quite fond of weeping willows because even in Nagoya, the streets, wherever possible are lined with them. I was grateful to Kitamura for showing us the real Kyoto. We returned late in the evening.

November was a busy month at the UNCRD, with two international seminars and the annual meeting of the UNCRD advisory council taking place. I could hardly find time to write my diary. However I met a number of experts and world-renowned people like Friedman, Benjamin Higgins, Keith Griffins, and Bhalla and Misra from India. Guy Hunter came to attend our Expert Group meeting. I was quite pleased at Dr Misra's (Director of Institute of Development Studies, University of Mysore) suggestion that I should write a book on the Daudzai experience. He said he had a publisher who would be interested in it. I just wondered what people in Pakistan are going to say to a book being published in India on an experience in Pakistan. Guy as usual was a real asset to the group's meeting. I found the South Korean team of Professors Choe and Choe very amiable and accomplished. It was indeed a pleasure to meet again Shahid Latif—my probationer at one time. He was representing Bangladesh, a job he did ably.

December 1978

The visit of the experts' group to the Matsuzaka beef country was indeed illuminating. This is a city of over 100,000 persons, situated about 90 km from Nagoya. We took a privately-run train service and I was pleasantly surprised to get a bottle of cold milk and a buttered roll at the Nagoya station for the princely sum of 120 Yen (65 cents). The mayor and the city officers met us and gave a briefing on agriculture in the vicinity. We were told that on the whole, no more than 26 per cent of the household income, on average, came from agriculture. The officers were of the view that farmers holding less than 0.5 hectares, who constitute nearly 30 per cent of all landholders, should give up agriculture. This was also the trend. There has been a decrease of 40 per cent in full farming activity amongst the landowners of less than 2 hectares, whereas there has been an increase in households owning over 2.5 hectares. The sale of land, which was taboo in the past, is now being resorted to and households are selling out in order to move from agriculture to full time industrial employment. The crops grown are rice, vegetables, mushrooms, strawberry and lettuce. Rice is planted in April and harvested in September.

The most startling piece of information for me was that the cropping intensity, generally all over Japan, was only 110 per cent. I had believed all along that the Japanese farmer was a highly intensive cultivator and produced more than two or three crops, meeting all his requirements from agricultural income. Here on the other hand I saw a situation in which most of them not only got less than 26 per cent of their income from land but also that they did not use the land intensively. Guy Hunter agreed with me fully when I mentioned to him that this was a waste of a precious resource. He was also perplexed at this phenomenon because the climate in England is somewhat similar to Japan, yet the land there is not allowed to lie fallow for six months in a year. I tried to probe this question with Oya and Yogo at the UNCRD. Oya, a Research Associate at the Centre, is a farmer's son and he explained that in his childhood they used to get a minimum of two crops from the land but it was really hard work—getting up early at five on a winter morning to dig up the potatoes and so on. With an assured high price for rice (almost six times the international price) from the government, and more lucrative industrial employment in the winter months, people have tended to prefer winter employment and leaving land fallow. Yogo, an agricultural engineer attributed the issue to the economics of the co-operative: he thought that the co-operatives stifle individual initiative: unless everyone decided to grow a second crop, the few who want to can't do so, because the marketing outlet is only through the cooperative. He added that there is a need to let the land lie fallow to retain productivity. Whatever the reasons may be, the fact remains that whereas in other countries we think of increasing incomes by increasing cropping intensity, Japan is not exploiting this resource. Indeed because of comparatively lower returns and higher labour input, there is a definite trend towards moving away from agriculture. The city officials vehemently rebutted the suggestion that agriculture might totally disappear from Japan by the turn of the twenty-first century, as the farmers are being offered exorbitant prices for converting agricultural land to industrial purposes.

Matsuzaka is famous for its beef. I had tasted some of it at *shabu shabu* joints. We were told that one of the animals fetched as much as $20,000 last year. We saw one that had already been booked for $10,000. Besides being kept on a special diet, these animals are constantly massaged — some say with beer — so as to produce quality beef.

The co-operative organization is very strong. All persons owning a minimum of 0.1 hectares and engaged for 90 days in a year in farming are members of the co-operative. The co-operative goes into all types of commercial ventures such as super-markets, super-highway motels and cold-storage. I was reminded of the activities undertaken by the Kotwali Thana Central Co-operative Association in Bangladesh (KTCCA) — dairy farming, cold storage, processing industries. The only difference is that there are thousands of such co-operatives in Japan, whereas we could not fully nurture even one KTCCA. The *markaz* federation in Pakistan is being opposed tooth and nail by the co-operative department. I wonder when we will learn, and from whom. Or are we never going to learn these things to enable our poor farmers to get out of poverty?

We also visited two farmers, identified by the experts as a large farmer (one family owned 7 ha.) and the target group farmer (owning 1 ha.). The contrast between the two establishments was obvious. The big farmer had a spacious house — much larger than the standard Japanese home. He could seat 25 people in his room. He served us coffee and delicious oranges. The farm was full of machinery and vehicles and had two beef cattle. The poor farmer had none of these things, although his house had almost all the amenities of life — the toilet was outside the house and had a hole for a lavatory. The village was beautiful, though as Guy remarked at the Matsuzaka railway station when I asked him how he found the countryside: 'I have yet to find the countryside.'

The weekend following the conclusion of the experts' group meeting, my friend Ralph Diaz invited me over to spend a weekend at his house. Ralph's family has gone to the Philippines to prepare their house at Manila, as Ralph is planning to leave UNCRD after nearly six years. Ralph is one of the very few people I have met who understands the intricacies of micro-level development; and no wonder that he does, with his background of working in the backward areas of Italy, the Israeli *kibbutz* and academic institutions of West Germany. Ralph lives in a rambling place, big by Japanese standards, in a most secluded area on the outskirts of Nagoya. The house is like an eagle's nest hidden away from prying eyes. The other houseguest was Somkiat, an Assistant Professor from a university in Thailand, who is engaged in writing a book on rural development at UNCRD. We had a most enjoyable weekend. Ralph is a very generous and hospitable host. The first night he took us for a steak dinner at a posh restaurant. The next morning we persuaded him to buy things from the market which he did from a nearby cooperative of the farmers at 30 per cent cheaper prices, and I showed my expertise at making an omelette and salad dressing. We also visited the nearby forest park which is indeed most beautiful. Ralph also took me to a place where bonsai (miniature trees) were on display and sale. Some of the trees were really a wonder.

We also drove around the new housing estate of nearly 80,000 inhabitants, with an extensive shopping centre. Ralph told us that most of the population of the new estate comprised young couples with the result that the estate administration was faced with problems such as a bumper crop of babies, throwing the planned facilities, for a diversified population age-wise, in total disarray.

On the basis of two-and-a-half days leave earned every month, I was sanctioned nine days annual leave and Ashraf was able to buy an inexpensive round-trip ticket to London for me. Since Musarrat likes gems and pearls, I had no difficulty in deciding what to take for her. For my three elder daughters also I bought white pearl necklaces and for the youngest daughter and the two grandchildren I got Seiko watches. In fact I got so carried away by the spectrum of watches that I not only bought watches for the children but could not resist buying beautiful and cute looking ring-watches for the whole family. Unlike

Pakistan the wholesalers in Japan also sell to individual customers and there was great price variation between goods sold at wholesale markets and at the departmental stores.

While walking down to office, I was surprised to see an old man urinating on the pavement. Nobody, of course, took any notice. To me the man appeared feeble and sick. The care of the old is an acute problem in Japan because of the cramped accommodation in houses. Old people have to be moved out to old people's homes. Since the opening of the central park, I have also noticed an odd couple kissing in public, an unusual sight in Japan.

Although the majority of the people in Japan are Buddhist and 25 December is not a public holiday, New Year is celebrated with great enthusiasm. There is a buying spree with Christmas and New Year sale in every departmental store and most of the shops. All establishments close down from 28 December to 3 January. At the UNCRD, the building which houses the Centre, is locked for three days and as the UN does not recognize these holidays, the staff is forced to take compulsory leave for the period.

One morning Ralph announced that there had been a theft in his house. It happened in the week following our stay. Nothing much was taken except some of the Christmas gifts that Ralph had bought for his family. Ralph suspected that some boys from the nearby orphanage were involved. The matter was reported to the police. In Japan the police operate at a micro-level and this is why the policemen and women are usually seen on bicycles. They are required to know almost all the permanent inhabitants of the area under their custody; hence outsiders visiting their areas immediately come to their notice. Three days later Ralph announced that all the things had been recovered and the chief of police himself brought the things to Ralph's house and offered profuse apologies for the inconvenience caused.

The director of UNCRD, Honjo, is an affectionate and fatherly personality. He invited me to a crab dinner. I had not known that crabmeat is so delicious. It was one of the best white meats I had ever tasted. After the New Year's UNCRD staff party on 26 December, Mr and Mrs Honjo, an extremely hospitable and pleasant couple, invited me to join the young crowd whom they were taking to a disco. Honjo had never been to a disco and he wanted to have the experience. While entering the disco, I had noticed hundreds of half finished bottles of whisky lying stacked on shelves. I understood its significance at the time of leaving the disco when Honjo also deposited his less than half finished bottle for safe custody, to be used on his next visit, if ever. The atmosphere at the disco was like that of any other disco except that in the dance area, multi-coloured lights were being flashed from beneath the floor, which created a rather weird atmosphere.

O. M. Mathur and Mrs Mathur, the Indian couple at the UNCRD, have always gone out of their way to make me feel at home, and at the slightest pretext they invite me over for meals to their flat, which is in the same building as the Honjos. When Mathur recently decided to buy a car, the dealer asked him to produce evidence to show that he has parking space for the car. A prospective buyer who has no parking may hire a garage but no one can buy a car in Japan unless he can provide parking for the vehicle.

I was pleasantly surprised to get a call from Tokyo and to find it was my elder brother on the line. Being a mercantile marine captain, he had come to Japan in connection with purchase of ships for his company. He paid me a visit at Nagoya. His visit coincided with the visit of the Ashrafs from Tokyo. We took the same flight on Friday, 29 December. He was bound for Karachi and I for London.

To take the flight out from Narita International Airport, I left for Tokyo. The Ashrafs, as usual, were very hospitable and arranged for my journey to Narita. On the way, Katusan, the embassy driver, informed me that in Japan, besides the diplomats, only the Emperor and the press cars fly flags. He was quite agitated that day because a famous actor who lived near his house had committed suicide because of debts he could not repay.

In Japan there still exists an examination system like the British 11+ examination, the results of which determine the future educational careers of boys and girls. There have been cases of suicide among young students who have failed to make the grade in this examination. I wonder why the educational authorities in Japan have not looked at the British experience where 11+ examinations have now been discarded.

The flight over China presented a most unusual phenomenon. The ground below appeared absolutely flat and of a dirty white hue—almost as though it was cemented. While landing at Peking, where the temperature was -6° Centigrade, it became apparent that everything was frozen solid. The villages consisted of structures that resembled dormitories. I was later told that they were all fitted with the type of stoves, which are called 'Quetta stoves' in Pakistan. At the airport our passports were taken away before deplaning and then the passengers were allowed to go where they wanted. Unlike other airports, there were no separate immigration and customs enclosures for the transit passengers. The Chinese take pride in showing things as they are. There is not the slightest attempt at whitewashing.

Because of a heavy snowfall, mine was one of the last flights to land in London. It snowed heavily at night and due to union trouble, flights were disrupted the following day. For the first time, I directly experienced the effect of union action in England when I had to queue up for more than an hour to get petrol. The two weeks in London passed in the blink of an eye. I read out my diary to Musarrat and to my daughter Monchu and they liked it very much. Later on, as an afterthought, my wife teased me about the girl in the restaurant. I must say she is very understanding about these things, unlike many other wives. I was glad to see the family in fine fettle. Roohi had become a permanent employee of the British Civil Service and her two children were really vivacious and endearing. Sarah became very attached to me. Afshan's exhibits for her postgraduate degree in graphics from the University of London showed real talent and a high degree of professionalism of which any father would be proud. I was very happy that she had made such good use of her time in London. Monchu as usual was the most amiable and lovable and seemed very steady in her studies for the diploma in business studies from Harrow College. And Shelley, the darling of her daddy, and the youngest of the daughters, exuded pure happiness at seeing me. I felt a sharp pang of separation when I was bidding them goodbye.

January 1979

Due to a delay the flight landed at Narita on Monday morning instead of the previous night, as Narita closes down at 2300 hours. The countryside from Narita to Tokyo was covered with snow, which must have fallen during the first two weeks of the new year. The airline crew, through whose courtesy I was using their transport, dropped me at the Tokyo Hilton. I took a taxi to Ashraf's flat and after lunch left for the Shinkansen station. After a 40-hour journey from London, I dozed on the Shinkansen. From Tuesday evening a peculiar thing happened to me and I could not sleep a wink till the early hours of Saturday when I slept for nearly ten hours. I had only heard of the jet-lag but never experienced it before. I must say that except for some anxiety about not sleeping it left no adverse effect.

There are quite a few departures from UNCRD scheduled in the near future, including mine. This has prompted a spate of dinners and parties. The one tradition which I like at UNCRD is the practice of dining impromptu one evening with the person who is leaving. This is an occasion on which the maximum number of UNCRD staff members are present, and everyone goes 'dutch'. Dong is the prime mover of most of these valedictory impromptu parties. Mike Douglas was leaving UNCRD after a nearly two-year stay. He confided to me that he was getting married to a Japanese girl before leaving for East Anglia University in the UK. I was quite touched by another member of the staff at UNCRD in the accounts section, Terao Kazuhiko, when he came and told me that he would like me to know that he was planning to get married in March. Later on at Mike's dinner, his *fiancée* also came and he said he wanted me to meet her. She was a beautiful Japanese girl and I complimented Tero on his choice.

In Japan the custom is to add the word 'san' at the end of a person's name, irrespective of sex, and also irrespective of whether you address the person by his/her first name or surname. The word changes to 'chan' in case of children and to persons you want to show affection to. Thus I am now usually addressed as 'Khansan'.

Haruo Nagamine called me over to his house and his wife treated me to a most sumptuous *sukiyaki* dinner. This was the first time I tasted *sukiyaki* and so I owed my introduction to it as well as to *shabu shabu* to Haruo. The only difference I found between the two was that unlike *shabu shabu*, to make sukiyaki, food such as beef and vegetables were fried in a skillet in very little oil. It was a delicious meal. The Japanese are quite innovative and versatile in their food. Most exotic food items such as seaweeds and mushrooms were discovered during the war out of sheer necessity but now these are delicacies. In Tokyo I had also found a very good Indian food restaurant to which I was introduced by Nasim from the Embassy.

Haruo showed me the pack of New Year's cards he had received. These usually consist of plain white cards (obtained from the post office) with New Year's greetings printed on them. The sender usually rubber stamps his address on the card he is sending out. It seems to be only a way of keeping in touch with others by notifying them of one's address once a year. Haruo also showed me some cards which merely gave the information that because of a death in the family the sender would not be posting a New Year's card. The objective of intimating one's whereabouts as well as announcing a bereavement is thus achieved. No wonder that each Japanese receives hundreds of cards. The Post Office encourages the purchase of their cards by assigning numbers to cards. Subsequently some of these win prizes at a national draw.

Ralph Diaz again took me to his house to spend a weekend. Surprisingly, it has been a very mild winter in Nagoya. Ralph drove me around the countryside and also took me to Seto, famous for its ceramics. I had a most enjoyable time. I had always found the Sakae area choked with taxis whenever I passed that way at night. Ralph explained that most Japanese men do not go straight home in the evening. Instead, they make a detour through drinking places, night-clubs and cabarets, mostly at company expense since expense accounts can be debited towards tax exemption. Most companies are quite liberal in this respect.

Although Japanese girls work before marriage it is looked down upon to work after marriage. The trend seems to be changing now and nearly 30 per cent of the married women work. Overall, the Japanese housewife is more domesticated than her Western counterpart. Many of them suffer from social and psychological problems. They live in big cities, in cramped houses and lack gainful employment. Their husbands are away at work all day, leaving early and returning late because of distances and the detour mentioned earlier.

My stay in Japan was almost coming to an end. Yogo, the UNCRD Agriculture and Rural Development expert, suggested that I might like to visit some of the places to which a study tour for the forthcoming UNCRD training course was being arranged. On Monday morning of the last week of my stay, Oya, Research Associate at UNCRD, came to fetch me from the hotel. On the way to Gifu, we picked up Kanno, another recently recruited UNCRD research assistant. Kanno belongs to the House Building Finance Corporation of Japan. Unlike in Pakistan, the Japanese Corporation undertakes the actual construction of housing estates and another institution which issues credit to private individuals for building houses. The Pakistan HBFC only issues credit.

In fact, Kanno lives in one of the housing estates built by the Corporation. There are still over 1,000 flats lying vacant in the estate, contrary to the expectations of the Corporation. It is an estate built on the outskirts of Nagoya by almost levelling little hillocks and mounds. I teased Kanno that at this rate very soon most of the mounds and hills would disappear from Japan. Gifu is the adjoining prefecture to Aichi, in which Nagoya is situated. Our first visit was to Gifu Agricultural College. Although education here is totally subsidized, the competition for vacancies at the college is only 1.25 candidates for each place. The college gives practical training in agricultural farming including livestock, and is more a vocational institution than a traditional one. In fact it is an attempt on the part of the Japanese authorities to keep Japanese agriculture alive. Agriculture demands more hard work and gives less return compared to industry, so no wonder the Japanese farmer and his children are turning away from agriculture.

I was a little disappointed to see the condition of the farm that was attached to the college. Although 27 acres in area, which is very large in terms of Japanese land holdings, the farm was running at a loss. I had hoped to see better performance of the public sector in Japan but it seems the public sector is the same all over the world, whether it is Japan or Pakistan. The cost per student, for a two-year farm management course, comes to 1.85 million Yen to the prefecture. It is a heavy investment but it is worth the effort to save Japanese agriculture. Ninety per cent of the students do take up farming, according to the college authorities.

Our next visit was to Ena, where we visited the Tono Dairy Farm Cooperative Federation of four primary societies, which in turn had federated 32 primary societies. This is one of the cooperatives under the Ena multipurpose Cooperative Federation with a total membership of 3,000 formal (0.3 ha or more) and 3,000 quasi-formal members. One hundred per cent of the eligible members were within the Federation's membership. The Ena Federation had specialised in Associations pertaining to rice, broilers, hog-raising, beef-cattle, milk and horticulture. The organizational structure in Japan is at its acme. The visit to Gifu Livestock Prefectural Corporation took us to the real interior of the countryside. The Corporation purchases young heifers (3 months old) at Yen 37,000 and sells them 21 to 23 months later at Yen 370,000 on a no-profit no-loss basis. This farmland has been developed in collaboration with the national government, which has another 38 such farm pasture lands in the country run by the Farmland Development Agency. We were very proudly informed by the director of the Gifu farm that his was the only one not operating at a loss. He showed us his three Australian dogs, in proper pay of the Prefecture to guard the animals. The drive back was interesting and enjoyable. We drove on the road skirting along the hill at an elevation, while down below we were passing by one town after the other including Tajimi, famous for its ceramics. I thanked Oya for a most illuminating and beautiful outing.

Towards the end of my nearly six-month stay in Japan the impression that overshadowed all others was the characteristics of the people that inhabit the land of the rising sun. Honjo, Haruo, Kawashima, Yogo, Oya, Hosaka, Hirako, Kando, Muto, Torie, Hasegewa, Masako, Jurko, Tutsumi, Takayama, Hirano, Teramura and numerous others were people I met inside UNCRD. There were others such as Kitamura and the hotel staff whom I met outside the organization. Dong, though a Vietnamese, contributed greatly to my understanding of the Japanese people and so did Roy Kelly. Of course to Ralph Diaz, I owe my visit to Japan and the many pleasant days I spent there.

I found that the Japanese, as a people, impressed me greatly. There is a basic minimum standard of courtesy which every Japanese man or woman, irrespective of his acquaintance with you, extends to every foreigner. To win over a Japanese person's confidence is an extremely difficult and tortuous process. By nature he appears to be suspicious and nervous (being conditioned to homogeneity) of foreigners and it takes a long time before he opens his heart to you. But, despite his inherent reserve, he never makes you feel uncomfortable nor is he ever discourteous. However, once you win his confidence, he is all on your side and nothing will shake his confidence in you. On the whole the Japanese are the most organized, civic minded, law abiding and courteous people I have seen anywhere in the world.

JAPAN REVISITED

January 1993

The last time I visited Japan I kept a diary, at the behest of some of my friends in Manila. Unfortunately, two of those friends, Mohammad Ahmad and Tariq Jaffrey are now no more in this world and so also the friend whose wife had warned me against the fast women of Japan. Since February 1979, when I left Japan, I spent four years in Sri Lanka, where I also kept a diary. In December 1982, I returned to Pakistan to initiate and implement the Aga Khan Foundation's rural development programme—AKRSP. I started keeping a diary in Gilgit, but the pressure of work did not allow me to continue after the initial few days. However, I did write many 'Notes for the Record' of my visits and meetings, along with a monthly record of my daily activities. This material would provide enough food for thought if I ever sit down to record my impressions of the ten years that I spent in Gilgit.

The tragedy of my daughter and her two children's death in a gas suffocation episode, in our own house at Islamabad, on 20 December 1988, made me see this world in a different light. Its insignificance was brought home to me in the most brutal way imaginable. My daughter left us forever but she did not go away without leaving a priceless gift for me. She took away all worldly worries from me. They pale into insignificance in the backdrop of what has happened to my family. Nothing gives me pain and nothing seems worth striving for, except, perhaps, making this world a little more happy and comfortable for others. I have marvelled, like Keats, at the capacity of the human heart to suffer misery and have come to the conclusion that if my heart could bear this loss there is nothing more to worry about. The omens which used to cause concern (one for sorrow and two for joy) have no place in my scheme of things now.

When I received my old friend Haruo Nagamine's letter inviting me to accept a visiting Fellowship, for a year at the Nagoya University's Graduate School of International Development (GSID) I was thrilled by the prospect. However, I knew a year would be too long to stay away from the programme, though I might be able to manage six months. Yet even six months seemed too long to my employers. Furthermore, the decision of the prime minister of Pakistan, in the meanwhile, to replicate AKRSP countrywide made my visit to Nagoya even more doubtful. However, I was determined not to let down my old friend, who had already obtained six months' funding from the University authorities. It would have been a pity to let it lapse. I persuaded the AKRSP board of directors to allow me to go to Nagoya for three months, which they did subject to approval by the AKF Board; in other words, by His Highness the Aga Khan. Fortunately, His Highness, during our meeting at Aiglemont in October, told me that I could go to Nagoya.

Having crossed all these hurdles I had now to face the opposition of my wife. Musarrat had initially jumped at the idea of going to Japan, but her indifferent health made it quite clear that she could not accompany me. With great difficulty, she agreed to my going to Nagoya only for one month. I was trying to figure out how to resolve the issue, when in the meeting of the AKRSP Board, 5 February was fixed for the consideration of the report of the AKRSP strategic development committee. I was asked to make myself available and the Board agreed to pay my fare to Nagoya and back. I breathed a sigh of relief that at least one obstacle was removed. I had still to plan the strategy for returning to Nagoya. But I knew that ultimately, Musarrat would agree to whatever was in my best interest.

Just before I was to leave, a note came from the Planning Division informing me that the prime minister wished me to be present at the briefing on the Social Action Programme (SAP) likely to be held in the next few days. I kept my fingers crossed, hoping that the date would be prior to my flight to Japan on 4 January. Fortunately, the briefing was fixed for 30 December, but was then postponed *sine die*, and the finance minister told me that it was likely to be in March.

At last, despite all these hurdles, 4 January arrived and Musarrat saw me off at the Islamabad Airport where I boarded the PIA flight to Tokyo. Thirteen hours later, the flight had arrived at Narita airport. There followed a 40 minute flight from Tokyo to Nagoya. It was a welcome change to be offered hot soup, instead of cold drink, tea or coffee, during this short flight.

I was very pleased to see Haruo at the airport. The drive from the airport to the international residence of Nagoya University took about half an hour. My accommodation there was an apartment comprising a bed-sitter, kitchen and bathroom. It was almost six times larger than my previous room at the New Plaza hotel. Haruo had very thoughtfully purchased a few things for my breakfast and borrowed for me some cutlery and crockery from the office.

The next morning Haruo came to take me to the University, which was hardly a five-minute walk from the International Residence. The Graduate School for International Development (GSID) is the latest addition to Nagoya University's Hashigayama campus. It is a small, brand new building, and is the only housing in the Administrative block. Most of the faculty is housed in other buildings. I have been given a room in the School of Economics, where Haruo was a professor before he moved to GSID, of which he is a founding member.

I was introduced to the administrative staff, as well as to the dean of the school. As a Visiting Fellow I have been given the status of professor and the amenities have accordingly been extended to me. My neighbour is an assistant professor who looks after the affairs of the foreign students. Haruo introduced me to her, and Matsuura was most helpful in getting my bank account opened and my shopping done. I am now fully fortified to look after the apartment and chores such as cooking, laundry and cleaning. I was marvelling at the transformation: in Pakistan I needed servants for each of these activities, and here I was managing everything from making the bed, vacuum cleaning, washing clothes, drying and ironing them to going shopping on foot to a market two km away and preparing my own breakfast and dinner. I could not believe that I could do all this and with such ease. Haruo also solved my problem of the plugs for Japanese sockets for my laptop and the shaver, by asking one of his students, Kanako Suzuki, to take me to the foreigners' market. In Japan, deviation has no place and causes tremendous problems, and unless you know how to go about it, you simply end up moving in circles.

The Hashigayama campus is very compact and functional and caters to over ten thousand students and four thousand teachers and university staff. The two landmarks are the library and the rather drab, concrete Toyota auditorium. The campus has a number of eating places, from cheap cafeterias to more expensive restaurants and two Co-ops, where almost all necessities of a student's daily life can be had. Haruo has introduced me to almost all the fare available on the campus, including a tiny eating place in the School of Economics itself, to be resorted to during stormy weather. Thanks to Haruo, I have met quite a few members of the GSID faculty at luncheons, who are all extremely nice and helpful. One of them, a Ph.D. from Chicago, hearing about the lack of linen and crockery etc. in the apartment, very kindly sent me quite a few things the next day.

I have had discussions with Haruo to chalk out my work plan and he agreed with my idea of working on a book, of which one chapter could focus on the concept and the operational principles of rural development, as distilled through my experience of implementing rural development programmes in different locations of the world.

Three weeks have gone by and I have hardly found the time to attend to the diary. Today is the beginning of the third weekend. The last weekend was an extended one, because Friday was a public holiday. It was, in fact, what the British call the 'debutante day'. All the Japanese girls who turn 20 celebrate the day and it is dedicated to them. Unfortunately, for the first time in twenty years, it happened to be a rainy day. Hence, not many girls were to be seen, yet some still braved the weather in their kimonos. Japan is not the same as I found it almost fourteen years earlier. One can see the same signs of decadence that one sees in the western societies. I am reminded of what Professor Galbraith said in 1978, during his visit to Japan. When asked to give his impressions of his visit, he observed that the people of Japan appear apprehensive that this prosperity is not going to last. It seems that his appraisal was not too far from the truth. Japan does not exude that confidence and *panache* that was noticeable the last time I was there. I wonder if it is the change of area, because last time I was living in Sakae, but the place seems run down, as if people no more worry about cleanliness, as they used to in the past. The International Residence is a magnificent building, but its upkeep leaves much to be desired. This is also true of the University buildings and its toilets and the computer rooms. No one bothers to remove the dust from the machines, although these are constantly in use. I was surprised to see squatting type toilets in the university buildings. The change in Japanese behaviour is also quite perceptible. There is no more that enthusiastic 'hie', which was the hallmark of Japanese women. You seldom hear it now. The dress is almost westernized. In restaurants, the fork and spoon have dethroned the chopsticks, unless it's a restaurant serving only Japanese cuisine, in the Japanese style.

The language is still holding sway, and one hardly comes across English speaking Japanese, but many more people than before understand English. Yet the basic characteristics of the people are unchanged. When I asked someone in Motoyama to tell me the way to the subway, he was unable to explain in English, but insisted on taking me to the subway entrance, although this was in the opposite direction to where he was going. There is still no system of tips and in restaurants and taxis you only pay what is written on the menu or displayed on the meter.

My main worry has been my walks. In Islamabad, the one hour climb on 'trail no. 3' had almost become a ritual with me in the early mornings, since I gave up jogging after Manchu's departure, and afternoon walks to her grave, because they took the whole evening. So I compromised, by resorting to a morning hike and going to Manchu in the afternoons by car. I had not realized that in Japan, I would have to follow a very strict regimen, as far as office hours were concerned. I had imagined that since most of my work would consist of writing, I would keep my own hours; I was shocked to learn that you may be a professor but the rules demand that you should be seen to have put in forty hours a week and to ensure this you are required to sign a register, every morning at 0830 and stay in your office room till 1700 hours. On my first visit to GSID I was promptly shown the register and my room in the School of Economics. When Haruo suggested I may sign the register, in the School of Economics, as I would be sitting there, the response was a polite no. The GSID staff wanted to make sure that they saw my face every morning at 08.30 hours. But I had my revenge on them when one day I found that none of the office staff had arrived and the office door was locked. I am sure this must have caused quite a bit of consternation. Haruo had already warned me not to come before nine or nine thirty, as no one would be there. I know that the professors do not come early, unless they have a class. Anyway it is quite convenient for me to be early. Now with that kind of regimentation, I hardly get any time on weekdays to go for walks. On the first Saturday, therefore, I ventured out to explore my walking trail. I had been told that there was the Higashiyama Park in the vicinity, but it was more of a zoo and children's fun-fair than a park for walks, and you had to pay to enter it.

The walk I took, going along the road, did take me to Higashiyama Park and when I thought I had lost my way, I came out near the university campus. I was quite pleased with my discovery because I had walked for nearly one hour and forty-five minutes. The next day I was bolder and explored another road on the same route and didn't get lost. The next weekend, I ventured into a rather lonely looking park, which had some features of 'trail no. 3'. I was very pleased with this discovery and now I feel that I have discovered a reasonable walking trail, which will give me enough exercise on weekends. At times I did feel a little frightened of all the lonely places I was venturing into, but this fear was totally unfounded. The Japanese, especially the youth, are extremely well behaved and you don't see the kind of rowdiness you find in the West.

On the weekend following my arrival, Haruo came with his daughter, to take me out for dinner. Ryoko is almost Shelley's age and is doing her Master's in Development at the GSID. Her course is different from the one Haruo teaches. The GSID has two concurrent Master's courses, with about 24 students in each course. Haruo is very pleased at Ryoko's full recovery from a very serious automobile hit and run accident in Delhi, which caused her head injuries. Haruo's eldest son, who had told us last time that he wanted to be a critic of pornographic literature, is now married and lives in Tokyo. His second son is studying for a Doctoral degree at one of the national universities.

Life at the International Residence has fallen into a routine, without much ado. On weekdays, after a bread, butter, marmalade and tea breakfast, I am off to the university or more specifically to room 330, in the School of Economics, via GSID. I have lunch at the university. Sometimes, when Haruo is free, he rings up and we eat together. Twice, so far, I was befriended by strangers, who came and sat at the same table as mine. One of them happened to be a Singaporian, who had studied in Japan, and was now teaching there. Coincidentally, he is also attached to GSID. He seemed a very friendly sort and gave me his address and telephone number. At one of the lunches, Haruo had introduced me to another foreigner, a Burmese, who after his studies in Japan had started teaching. But foreigners are not allowed to stay for more than three years at national universities. This is why Dr Maung Maung Lwin, although he had taken his Doctorate from Nagoya University, was now transferring himself to a private university, which, besides offering him a full Professorship, was prepared to keep him for as long as he wished to stay. There are 95 national and 35 private universities in Japan.

On the second occasion, the three gentlemen who came and sat at my table were professors from Tokyo and Osaka Universities. They had come to attend a symposium of scientists. The professor of physics, from Tokyo University, knew Prof. Salam and spoke very highly of him. Professor Takao Koda had spent nearly 25 years in the United States.

In Japan people prefer to be known by their first names, as some surnames, like Khan in Pakistan, are so common that without the first name it would be hard to place the individual. I did not realize that Watanabe, Kato and some others were in that category of surnames. I had always thought that our Eimi Watanabe of UNICEF (now a representative in India) had a distinctive surname. A student in GSID whose surname is Watanabe insisted on being called by her first name, Keiko.

The first snowfall in Nagoya had been predicted by the weatherman as a fifty-fifty probability. Although the morning was sunny and bright, in deference to the weatherman's forecast I picked up the umbrella and sure enough before noon the snow came. I had to brave the biting cold wind and occasional flakes of snow while going for lunch to the restaurant on the hill. By the late afternoon almost a blizzard was blowing. By the time we had finished dinner at GSID everything was blanketed in snow. The snow had stopped when I made my way to the International Residence, a five-minute walk, and everything looked heavenly and pure white. It was a scene they crave in England for

Christmas. The trees and ornamental plants looked even more beautiful covered with snow. The ground had become somewhat treacherous for treading, though it was still not difficult to walk. The next day the snow started melting and by the evening all traces of snow had disappeared. But it did usher a cold blast of weather into Nagoya, in an otherwise rather warm winter.

As I had not thanked Prof. Arayama (the Chicago Ph.D.) who had very kindly sent me quite a few things, I gave him a call to invite him to lunch. He regretted his inability to accept because of another luncheon engagement. However a few minutes later he came to invite me to lunch with an American Professor. Dr Tweeten was from Ohio State University and his discipline was agricultural economics. He had been to Pakistan twice and knew Prof. Naqvi of PIDE very well, with whom he said he loved to discuss Islamic economics. Professor Tweeten was quite an opinionated academic and when he came to know that rural development was my field, he declared that the textbook on rural development he had written in 1976 was still being used. He had, of course, not heard of Dr Akhtar Hameed Khan and did not know any of the Americans who had either been associated with rural development academies or had worked in Pakistan. Nevertheless, he was quite a good conversationalist. When I asked him if he agreed with what Galbraith had said in 1978 about Japan, he fully agreed that so long as Japan was trying to catch up with the West, it was easy. But having caught up, it is most difficult to go beyond. He felt that like the US, Japan will also have to turn to the service sector for Asia and unlike the productive sector it is far more difficult to make inroads in this sector.

Even after Husain Wali had installed a computer in my Chinar Inn suite, I did not go near it for months, although I had also acquired a laptop in the meantime. It was only a few weeks before I was due to leave for Japan that I realized that it was either now or never. Husain Wali had always said that for me the most important use of the computer would be the ability to carry a lot of documentation abroad while on tour, and the facility when at home to be able to review materials and documents easily. I only realized the importance of what he was saying when the material I wanted to carry to Japan weighed hundreds of kilos, which could easily have been transferred on no more than a dozen discs. I had to perforce leave the material behind for Rauf to transfer onto floppy disks. At last the day came when Anis sent one of his staff to initiate me into the mysteries of the laptop. In all I took three lessons before I was on my way to Japan. However, the saying that 'a little knowledge is a dangerous thing' was brought home to me when, one day, being stuck on something very minor, I resorted to the corrective told to me by Anis once and the consequence was disastrous. The laptop stopped working and all efforts, including summons to the local Toshiba man, came to naught. In Japan they do not use DOS 4.0. Deviation has no place in Japan. Fortunately I had all my work copied on floppies and the GSID had a spare laptop, which Professors Ezaki and Osada personally delivered to me. I was most touched by their solicitude and am indebted to Haruo for suggesting that I contact them. Although it happened only two weeks before I was due to leave, without the laptop I was feeling totally immobilised.

I have almost finished my contractual obligation of writing a thirty page paper on the theoretical framework and operational principles of rural development, as laid down in my contract with the President of the Nagoya University, before I leave for Pakistan on 2 February to attend the meeting of the Strategic Development Committee of the AKRSP at Karachi. I have also given one of the three lectures which Haruo wanted me to deliver. The next two are scheduled for 17 February and 18 March. As already agreed with Haruo, I will devote the rest of the time to preparing the draft of the proposed book, which would include the paper already finished in draft form. In addition, on Haruo's request I have so far reviewed three theses, written by students to fulfil the requirement for their Master's degree. I have also been giving tutorials to one student on the subject of her Master's thesis. It has been altogether a very refreshing and stimulating experience. The university environment is a world in itself and I have found it a very happy and enjoyable one, so far.

Suddenly the telephone extension in my room rang. It seldom does because except for Haruo hardly anybody calls me on the extension. The person on the other side was my good old Vietnamese friend NugYen Tri Dong. He had come to know about my arrival from Haruo. Dong promised to get in touch again. I was, therefore, pleasantly surprised to see him getting down from his car, while I was taking out the rubbish. Dong had not changed much except that age had slightly matured his boyish looks. A Vietnamese couple is also staying at the Residence and Dong invited them also to lunch and took us to a nearby Chinese restaurant, which had excellent decor and food. The Vietnamese couple were just as mild and pleasant mannered as I had found Dong, nearly fifteen years ago.

I showed Dong what I had written about him in my diary, when I had first met him. Reading about his wife Yen, Dong explained that following the defection of a Vietnamese trainee from UNCRD, Dong became a prime suspect in the eyes of the Vietnam government and Yen's family also came under a lot of pressure, so much so that the family decided to emigrate to Australia. They wanted Dong to migrate also. As he did not want to do so it ended in their separation.

Dong is now married to a Japanese. I was quite surprised when I asked his wife what I should bring from Pakistan and she showed me a disc of Nusrat Fateh Ali Khan. She works in a Japanese advertising agency. Dong is living in a posh locality of Nagoya in a brand new block of apartments. But the whole of his flat could easily fit into the room of my International Residence apartment. However, the flat was furnished with every amenity. We sat at the dining table and the food was served to us from the portable stove placed on the table. It was something of the same type that I had tasted at the students' dinner at GSID. Considering that Dong had hardly given any advance notice of my visit, Mrs Dong had managed to prepare an excellent dinner. Dong showed me a video, made by the Japanese TV, on the work he is doing in Vietnam. He has opened vocational training schools with donations of second hand sewing machines reconditioned in Japan, and introduced computers into Vietnamese schools. He is now planning to set up an institute for the social and economic development of Vietnam. He wants me to be one of the honorary Directors of the Institute. I was very impressed by Dong's enthusiasm to do as much as he could for his country.

He was quite taken by the idea of an AKRSP type non-profit joint stock company to undertake development. He said it was very difficult for the Vietnam government to understand that any other agency besides the government can undertake development. Business and commercial activities are looked down upon. I invited Dong to come to Pakistan and see for himself how he could undertake such an initiative.

The International Residence is an eight-storey building with three wings: A, B and C. Of its inmates, I have so far made the acquaintance of two Indians (Dr Ashwani Kumar Roy and Brahm Pal Singh), an American, a Romanian and the Vietnamese couple to whom Dong introduced me the other day.

The telephone has proved to be a boon. I talk to Musarrat every alternate day and feel close to my near and dear ones, whether they are in Islamabad or in London.

Visit to Yamagishi Village, March 1993

I wanted to visit a rural area of Japan and on Prof. Nagamine's suggestion I agreed to accompany a group which included some GSID students, on a trip scheduled for Sunday and Monday the 7 and 8 March 1993.

Since I was not sure what would be available at the village, as a precautionary measure I had packed almost everything including a towel. This meant that unlike the members of the group who were happily treading along with nothing to carry except very light bags I had a rather substantial weight to cart along. The others very kindly offered help but I deserved to carry my own burden as a penalty for my excessive caution. As soon as we got off the bus the rain and hail started falling. On top of all this we seemed to be groping for the way. In fact, there was only one main road so there was no question of our going astray but Gotosan wanted to be sure that the village was not on one of the side roads. I must state here that without the guidance of the students Gotosan and Akisan the journey would not have been so smooth. The little mix up at the end wasted no more than a few minutes of our time and very soon we were at the Yamagashi village reception centre. This reminded me of the AKRSP visitors' centre in Gilgit.

We were soon joined by Mr Hashiguchi and Ms Tokaya, who introduced themselves as the guide and the interpreter, respectively. Tokayasan informed us that she had an American husband. Since the reception room was crowded, Hashiguchisan suggested that we shift to another place. This turned out to be Room 304 of the dormitory, which Gotosan and I were to occupy for the night. This was the typical Japanese-style room with sliding doors and cushions on the matted floor. The room was very comfortably heated. We soon settled down on our cushions and I sat next to Tokayasan since Inbal is quite proficient in Japanese.

Speaking in Japanese, Hashiguchisan explained that Yamagashi was a friendly village inhabited by 700 adults and 800 children. No one needs money in this village because all their requirements are met from the common stores and everyone is at liberty to draw from the stores whatever he needs. The food is available in the different cafeterias and things bought from outside are paid for from the common fund.

Inbal explained that in the *kibbutz* in Israel also there is communal living but there is a limit on how much you can consume or spend and that is regulated through a system of coupons. Of course, some common services like food in cafeteria, school facilities, laundry and barbershop are available to everyone whenever needed, but other goods have to be paid for through coupons. Hashiguchisan wondered why you need coupons when there is unlimited access to money available according to your needs. He said that Yamagishi's basic tenet is 'Truth' but if a principle formulated on the interpretation of truth at a given time does not work it is changed because the thinking might change the truth. The process through which this is attained is called *kensan*. There is no leader in Yamagishi. Everyone has a role or a job. 'My job is to meet the visitors, to guide them and take them to the appropriate persons', he said. To our question 'Without leaders how do 1,500 souls do *kensan*?' he replied that there are jobs and departments and each group can *kensan* whenever they feel the need. The idea is that through *kensan* all people should think together. There might be ten *kensan* a day. The meetings may be of many types on different subjects. Any person can summon a *kensan* of his group if he feels the need for it. There is a *kensan* every morning for every job.

Hashiguchisan explained:

> I joined Yamagishi because I understood it to be a new way of thinking in finding the truth, but the way of thinking might change and with that the truth. We seek it all the time to make people happy because true happiness has to be unconditional and we try to seek what makes people happy. Is it money, girlfriend, wife, family, house? What is it? Money was the most important thing to me previously. A friend told me about the YG one-week workshop. I attended the workshop. It was not religion. I could see myself in the past. I was destined to get the top job but YG was offering something different—unconditional, complete happiness. The workshop taught me one lesson, not to get angry. Now I don't try but I don't get angry. Not being angry is the natural state.
>
> How is the world going to develop if there is no competition? At YG there is no competition but we always work and search for better things — new methods, new technology, new tools. Because we are happy we want to make more happiness. Everyone in YG makes 100 per cent use of his or her capabilities without competing and without any fear of loss of job or expectation of reward. In the paradise camp for children we don't admonish

or flatter children for lapses or gains. We don't judge them by their achievements but by the effort they are putting in.

In a kibbutz the thinking is that people can be happy only if they live there. How do people living outside YG live happily? People in YG are happy because of changes in their thinking and the way of looking at the world. So one can be happy wherever one may live so long as his thinking is YG. The border is not outside but inside yourself.

Tokayasan said that she lived in an urban city but her mind was bound by the YG rules.

In everything there is a way of thinking. For example instead of making money from the production of YG agricultural fields or cows or chicken or pigs, the YG thinking is to deliver food to so many hundreds or thousands of people and to make them happy. If people say YG products are good, that is our objective: not making high profits.

On the question of the evolution of YG we were informed that about forty years ago a big typhoon hit Japan destroying all crops, yet the rice fields of Mr Yamagishi remained unaffected. His chickens were easy going and did not stink. Animals, human beings and nature seemed to be living in perfect harmony in Yamagishisan's farm. The government people were impressed and propagated Yamagishisan's techniques. His chickens spread all over Japan but people bred them with his methods in order to make money which made Yamagishisan unhappy and he thought of YG and how to make the world happier. He started one-week workshops on YG. He died but people who wanted to be happy got together and these villages became Yamagishi villages. No one has forced them. There are about forty of these villages in Japan and others in Switzerland, Australia and Brazil.

The *kensan* is practised at all levels in all departments and in all spheres of human life. Through *kensan* an effort is made to find the best way and it is only put forth as a suggestion to the people who decide how to implement it or reject it or modify it. All decisions are made through *kensan*.

Inbal wanted to know the status of writers, poets and artists because in the kibbutz, which was based mainly on agricultural activities such people had no place. In YG there is no problem with such persons. They have their own jobs which are considered as valuable as other jobs. There is no distinction in terms of importance of one job and the other because all jobs contribute to human happiness. Inbal said that in case of the kibbutz it has not worked out this way. The objective was to make a purist society based on socialism but spiritually they try to be one with Judaism. It worked well with a small number of groups, especially the farming communities, but when people from urban areas, who were dissatisfied with their lives, opted for the kibbutz, problems arose. Then the people who were born and raised in the kibbutz wanted everything out of it as their right.

In YG everyone has equal rights irrespective of the job he is doing or the area he comes from. There is no dislike in their hearts. Anyone's problem is everyone's problem. They are all trying to find the truth. Hashiguchi's 17-year-old son wants to cultivate sweet potatoes on an 8 ha. plot, not to make money but to make people happy when they eat his sweet potatoes. He was an urban child and used to behave like one. Farming is a good way for the young to learn for themselves. Children coming from cities are very self-centred but they have to learn that unless they work with others things don't happen. If someone has more knowledge that does not mean that he is better: it is a simple case of his knowledge being used more.

Inbal observed that the kibbutz tried to make a communal experiment successful and in Pakistan AKRSP is trying to eradicate poverty and have a better standard of living. YG is different. It wants to cure the sickness of urban life. YG is not saying that urban life is bad. It does not deny other ways of life. It tries to find the true way, the happiest way. Everyone wants to go for happiness but one needs to know what real happiness is and if one can find that everyone can be happy; that is what YG is trying to find out. We are eating good food and that is making us happy while there are other countries where there is no food. How can YG arrange food for them and thus spread happiness? Our children go to the neighbours and spread manure on their fields. Our neighbours now call on our children to spread manure and now the kids want to go to Africa to do so. The children are looking 100 years beyond. They are interested in forestry. They want the trees to grow for future generations. Here at YG we recycle everything. There is no concept of garbage. Everything is used and reused.

At six in the evening we broke up and had a delicious repast of YG farm produce to which Gotosan did full justice. We admired his foresight when we got our next meal at ten in the morning, which again was very sumptuous and nutritious. After the meal we had a *kensan* with a group of people including a Swiss person, who has been staying at YG for the last five years and intends to live there all his life. There was also a Nigerian who was visiting from Osaka, as well as half a dozen other Japanese. The discussion was held both in Japanese and English. Before the *kensan* we had visited the final day function of a children's paradise workshop. I was asked to give my impressions of the function. I said I was impressed by the self-confidence, discipline and deference to elders shown by the children. In the West, with self-confidence the youth tend to become aggressive and there is little respect for age. It was good to see YG instilling and preserving traditional values because Japan was now at the pinnacle of its industrial development like the West, in the past. The West has degenerated into a decadent society because it failed to preserve its traditional values. I quoted to them the Chinese Nobel Laureate who, after living for 15 years in the USA, felt that American society has been destroyed because the family has been destroyed. The challenge for the Japanese is how to preserve the family without denying equal rights and privileges to women. YG seemed to be showing the way. Hence I was very optimistic that the Japanese will be able to tide over the transformation.

Gotosan and Akisan wondered about the replicablity of YG and the impact of the workshops on children in the long run who do not get the same kind of exposure as the children studying in the YG academy. The Nigerian highlighted the heterogeneity of society in most of the third world countries and the difficulty of implementing a YG type of concept in such a society. The others spoke about their experiences and their feelings about YG. Gotosan raised the larger issue of development and the impatience with long term strategies. I explained that there is no short cut and one cannot circumvent the process. Unfortunately, the developing countries, in their search for short term solutions, end up in increasing the problem. In South Asia alone there are over 400 million people living below the poverty line. Without a long term commitment to eradicate poverty the problem cannot be eliminated. However, it does not mean that short term measures for alleviating unemployment and increasing production should not be simultaneously taken in hand. But the decision to adopt only the latter measures to the exclusion of the long term solutions would fail to achieve the objective of poverty eradication.

I was introduced for the first time to the Japanese bath, which was most welcome after a long day. The toilets were of the recycling type as nothing was wasted at Yamagashi. I slept soundly on the floor in the Japanese style and had to be woken up the next morning. Gotosan was an excellent roommate. I did not even notice his presence in the room.

The day began at seven on Monday, 8 March 1993. It was biting cold. A few minutes earlier it had snowed and hail and rain kept falling intermittently the whole morning. Hashiguchisan drove us through the different sections and departments including the 16 ha. vegetable plot cultivated by the students. The animals indeed appeared very calm and relaxed and the people, whether those at the cowshed or students at the vegetable packing depot, seemed to be busy in their work without any control or supervision being exercised on them. Everything was modernized and the most sophisticated techniques of management seemed to be in operation. The YG Academy was established only nine years ago and had over 1,200 residential students, two thirds of whom came from outside. There was even a fruit processing plant directly linked to a Brazilian village with a 10,000 hectare orange plantation, exporting the produce in a concentrate form to YG.

At the end of the field trip we again sat down for a *kensan*. I said what had impressed me most was the corporate structure of YG. 'You have created a company which is as efficient and as productive as a highly successful multi-national. Yet you follow none of their principles of incentives and competition. Your corporate structure is without a hierarchy. There is no system of productivity rewards and there is no hiring and firing. There are no managers, no supervisors and no controllers. Every worker is an equal shareholder and an equal partner. No one is more important than the other. All jobs are of equal significance. This, in my view, is your singular achievement. Even Tolstoy and Gandhi were afraid that if the village adopted modern methods it would lose its innocence and purity. You have shown that you can retain all your values despite adopting the most modern technological advances.'

By now we were hungry, Inbal especially, who could not resist asking 'Why do you go to work in the morning on an empty stomach?' It was a simple question of training your system to have only two meals a day: one at ten in the morning and the other at five in the evening.

The final *kensan* took place after the brunch in which Hashiguchisan, on Inbal's inquiry, expressed pleasure at having spent time with us because he learnt about so many new things like the kibbutz and he would like to do so more often. The purpose of making everybody happy is like a phase. He suddenly realized that he wants to do *kensan* with people like us. Giving his impressions Gotosan said that initially he had thought that YG was a different world: separate from the other world like the kibbutz. Now he felt that YG is not a separate community. It is in people's minds. People can have the same thought whether they are in the village or outside. People say they are happy from the heart. YG knows no boundaries. YG is in everybody's heart. Giving my final impressions I said that YG is like Utopia, which normally is considered unattainable, but YG has tried to demonstrate that Utopia can be achieved in this world.

Before the expiry of my consultancy assignment with UNCRD in 1979, UNICEF Sri Lanka offered me a long term assignment as Social Development Consultant to the Mahaweli Ganga Project. I could not believe my luck because the Mahaweli Ganga Development Project was tailor-made for implementing the social mobilization strategy. A few eyebrows were raised in Colombo, both at the headquarters of the Mahaweli Authority and the UNICEF Country Office, when I proposed living at the project site in the Kalawewa area where 27,000 families were being settled in elephant country infested with cobras and wild animals. My decision to live in the wild paid great dividends including a full page coverage of my work in *Newsweek* entitled 'A Man Named Khan'.

NOTE

1. The protest was about the building of the airport.

4

Letters from Sri Lanka—The Mahaweli Ganga Project

Handungama Circuit Bungalow
Galnewa, Mahaweli
2 March 1979

...You have always been complaining about the shortness and stereotyped nature of my letters. Today I have decided to write you a different kind of letter. I can only make my letters interesting by sharing my work and experiences in them. I hope you will enjoy reading these letters.

When I landed at Colombo from Nagoya I felt, as I wrote to you at that time, as if I had come from a world of fantasy to a world of reality. Coming to Galnewa in the Mahaweli area, I realised that this is the real world and not Colombo—which is only an imitation of westernised cities. This real world is the world of the majority of the people living in the developing countries. The journey from Colombo took nearly four hours because both the driver and I were new to the area and we were trying to locate a brand new township, established only seven months earlier....Only a few years ago, it was a beautiful teak forest and the abode of wild elephants. The poor elephants have now been pushed out. No wonder there is an uproar from wildlife conservationists, asking what is going to happen to the 500 elephants when the Mahaweli project is completed.

The Mahaweli Ganga Project, besides producing electricity, will ultimately bring 900,000 acres of land under irrigation. Sri Lanka has at present only three times that acreage under paddy cultivation and has to spend a huge amount of foreign exchange on importing rice. Bringing new land under paddy cultivation will solve the food problem. It was originally planned to complete this project in phases over thirty years. However, the present government has decided to telescope the work to five to six years.

You will be surprised to know that Sri Lankans are fiercely democratic. There are two political parties, the United National Party and the Sri Lanka Freedom Party: neither has ever been elected to office for two consecutive terms. The voter turnout is over 80 per cent, perhaps because the rate of literacy in this country is over 80 per cent as compared to 25 per cent in Pakistan.

The Sri Lankans are basically very polite people, and exhibit none of the brashness that you find in inhabitants of the subcontinent. The difference between rich and poor in this country is also much less compared to the other countries in the region. The civil service in Sri Lanka is indeed poor—in terms of salary, office accommodation, residences, other fringe benefits, but there is an absence of total poverty. You don't come across beggars and people in rags. Sri Lanka remained under colonial and foreign rule since 1506 unlike India which came under British domination much later—almost three hundred years later.

On the fringe of the Mahaweli area is the ancient Buddhist city of Anuradhapura. Ninety-four per cent of the population in Sri Lanka is Buddhist and the Anuradhapura area is full of Buddhist relics and temples and enormous statues of the Buddha.

When I arrived here on Wednesday afternoon, I found that the room reserved for the Chairman of the Mahaweli Development Board had been allotted to me. Not only that, there was furious activity going on—the whole room was being repainted and redone, complete with fly-proofing. I was most touched by this warm welcome. The office of the Resident Project Manager (RPM) is about a mile away from the Circuit Bungalow. The RPM is from the Ceylon Administrative Service and joined the Project only a fortnight ago. Previously the Deputy Resident Project Manager (Operations and Maintenance), an engineer, had been looking after the project. In view of the slow progress on the social side, it was decided to have a full time RPM—a generalist administrator. The RPM (Mr Karunatillake) was at Cambridge in 1975-76. Can you believe that he used to live just opposite my college (Selwyn). He went to Wolfson, which is one of the new colleges. Another college which has come up since we left Cambridge in 1957, is the Churchill College. The RPM is a very nice person and showed real pleasure at my arrival. As you know my main work in rural development has been the provision of government services to rural people and creating a capability and capacity, especially among the rural poor, to gain access to the services being provided and utilise them effectively. In the absence of access capability, the services are either siphoned off or fully utilised by the rich. The RPM has kindly agreed to get all his deputies—Agriculture Extension, Engineering & Community Development—to attend a discussion with me next Monday.

This morning, as the jeep was delayed, I decided to walk to the office. It was cloudy and the scenery all around was beautiful. It is hilly with small mounds of lush green. The '*maha*' paddy crop (like our spring *Rabi* crop) will be harvested late this month or early next month. I walked to the office to the cooing of doves and chirping of birds. It is a long time since I have taken such a walk. It made me forget the world of fantasy. I wish you were here to share with me this bounty of nature.

Some times I do envy you though, especially when I want to hug my children.

* * *

Handungama Circuit Bungalow
Galnewa, Mahaweli, Sri Lanka
6 March 1979

...You must have got my earliest letter by now. Please do write how you found it. Here is another one in the same style. I hope you enjoy reading it.

I will be returning to Colombo tomorrow and will ring you up from there. I am anxiously waiting for your letter. I do hope at least one is waiting for me there. Your letters are as naughty and tantalising as they can get. Sometimes they don't show up for days together and then suddenly make their appearance in doubles.

As time proceeds I am meeting the other officers of the project. The Resident Project Manager (RPM) has three deputies (DRPM), of whom the DRPM Community Development is my main contact in the project. The other two deal with agriculture and engineering. Mr Jayawickrama, the DRPM for community development, has been working here since 1976. He has kindly offered me any assistance I require. The DRPM Agriculture, Mr Sam Alwis, is a seasoned agriculture expert who spent a year in Japan also and is the most experienced project member. Mr Weerasooriya, the DRPM Engineering, joined the project only a month ago. It was a wise step on the part of the government to have changed the previous engineer who was Acting RPM for the last one year. He would have found it difficult to adjust himself to the role of the deputy after having remained the chief. He is a quiet man and quite young. I also met another Sri Lankan who dropped in at the circuit bungalow to have his lunch. His manner and brashness were strikingly different from the general run of Sri Lankans. The reason was not too difficult to discover. After barely a few minutes' conversation he declared with a superior air that he had been living in the UK for the last twelve years and had returned only two months back. His specialisation was agricultural engineering.

To make him more responsive, I tactfully put across to him that I was glad to know that the RPM had been to my old university in the UK. It came as a surprise to him that the RPM had been to Cambridge. After the initial diffidence the news caused him, he appeared to be a nice person.

On Tuesday afternoon, the RPM informed me that due to an emergency he had to rush to his hometown, Kandy, which is about 47 miles from here. His wife was about to give birth. You might remember the film 'The Bridge on the River Kwai', which had many scenes shot on location in Kandy. When the RPM returned he brought the news that his wife had had twins. I offered my felicitations.

To post a letter I go to the post office, which is housed in a small, beautiful building. Considering that the place is only seven months old I was impressed by the amount of activity.

I had my first exposure to the rural people on Saturday. Surprisingly enough it was through the courtesy of the Family Planning Association of Sri Lanka. You must be thinking that these people have not left me alone even here. What to say of these people here, even the Family Planning Association of Pakistan has again elected me to the Chairmanship of their Training Research and Evaluation Committee in absentia, although I had informed them that I was likely to remain out of Pakistan for quite a few years. Now don't jump to conclusions. It is only that they cannot find a suitable replacement.

To come back to my village visit: the RPM thought it would be a good idea if I went along with the FP team because it was going to a Muslim village called Nelliyagama. The Lankans are linguistically divided in two, the Sinhalese and the Tamils. The Tamils are originally from India. Most of the Muslims are also Tamil speakers. A few years ago there were bitter riots between the two factions. Most of the Tamils are Hindus and the Sinhalese are Buddhists. An agreement was reached with India envisaging the return of nearly 300,000 Tamils to India. Sri Lanka has a total population of around fourteen million. In area, size and population, it is like the North West Frontier Province (including tribal areas) of Pakistan.

Nelliyagama is a *purana* (old) village. In the project area 'new villages' are those settled since 1946. Some, like Galnewa, are being settled now. The total population of the project area, including both new and *purana* villages is around 230,000. There are more than 300 *purana* villages. The total area under cultivation will ultimately be 106,000 acres. At present 72,000 acres are under development and being cleared of the jungle. Surprisingly, the Mahaweli Project is aiming to achieve revival of an old settlement. A few hundred years ago there was a thriving population in the area. Sri Lankans call the area a dry zone but the rainfall here is around 75 inches annually. You can imagine the extent of rainfall in comparison to the Peshawar valley where the rainfall is less than 30 inches a year. This area is as beautiful and green as Abbottabad and it is equally hilly. The valley is adorned with terraced paddy fields bordered with forests and distant blue hills.

The rainy season extends from September to March, covering the *Maha* crop season. For the *Yala* crop (April to August), irrigation was done through storage tanks because torrential rain falls during two to three months. The ancient rulers called them 'tanks' but they are huge reservoirs like the Mangla lake or Tarbela lake in Pakistan. The project area takes its name after the Kalawewa tank: when I came to Galnewa the tank seemed as large as the sea. The population tended to migrate to the thriving coastal towns—first founded by the Portuguese, then the Dutch. It was only the British who occupied the whole island. By then the ancient tank irrigation system had eroded, and forests had grown and taken over the paddy fields.

Through Mahaweli these lands are being reclaimed and people from other areas being resettled there. Each settler family gets 2.5 acres of paddy land and 0.5 acre of highland, enough for a homestead and a kitchen garden. The tanks are being rehabilitated. By building dams on the Mahaweli Ganga river and through a system of canals, water is being transferred from one tank to the other. A main canal has been dug from the Kalawewa tank and two branch canals have been dug out from this main canal to irrigate the project area. The main canal itself finally joins another tank, meaning that the water surplus to the two branch channels is stored in the other tank. From this tank also, another main canal, with branch canals, is dug. Thus an interconnected and cohesive irrigation system has been planned, in addition to rehabilitation of the old tanks. I do hope you don't find these details too cumbersome but to understand the ecology of the area, these details are important.

Look how much I have digressed, and I had wanted to tell you about my first village visit. This 200-year-old Muslim village consists of 85 families. There were about 26 adults and half a dozen minors present when the meeting started in the school shed. The school was closed because it was Saturday. My interpreter was a young man named Naseer whose sister had married someone from this village. He lived at Matale district town. Naseer informed me that the people had collected at 8 am, the given time for the meeting, but since we were 90 minutes late they had gone away. He added that the people were afraid that they were going to be injected against bearing children.

The distribution of young and old in the group was equal. The leadership appeared to be in the hands of a young man although the old traditional leaders were also there and tried their best to exert their influence. The village seemed to be very well organized, with a mosque committee consisting of 20 members and a score of office bearers. One young leader was the head of the committee and his brother was the *Pesh Imam* of the mosque. He asked some nasty questions of our friends from the Family Planning Association. First, he had them on the run by saying that God had taken the responsibility for feeding everyone born in this world. Secondly, he wanted to know whether family planning was only for Muslims or for Buddhists and Hindus also. The implications of the questions were quite significant and showed deep mistrust of the government. When my turn came to speak, I made it clear that I was not connected with the Family Planning Programme. I also said that I would come again, if they would let me, to discuss with them and mutually try to find solutions to rural poverty. There was a resounding yes to this proposition and I was warmly asked to come again.

In the afternoon we had an important visitor, Mr Panditratne, who is not only Chairman of the Mahaweli Development Authority but also President of the political party in power. The organization of the Mahaweli project is, to say the least, a little complex. There is the Mahaweli Development Authority—the supreme body, with two national ministries: the Ministry of Mahaweli Development with whom I am attached, and the Ministry of Lands and Lands Settlement. Then comes the Mahaweli Development Board. I was told that the Ministry of Lands and Lands Development had opposed my consultancy but the Minister had over-ruled them. I had an occasion to see the Minister today when he came to receive a gift of tractors from USAID and to open a newly constructed bridge. He is very young and his name is Mr Gamini Dissanayeke. With Mr Panditratne was the Additional Secretary of the Ministry of Lands and Lands Development, Mr de Silva. From my point of view in community development he seemed to be the most important person. He had come to approve the annual programme. I got an agreement from him that the programme would remain flexible and could be changed without much ado, because it was only between him and the RPM. I think I will have to work on him to get government backing for the programme.

Today being Sunday, I woke up late, though not so much as you do. I was up by 0900 hours but lazed in bed till 1200 hours and skipped breakfast which is normally a papaya or a piece of bread with butter and jam. The circuit bungalow cook is very efficient. He prepares the food of his own choice except that I have told him to be careful in adding chillies. The lunch consists of rice and a wide choice of dishes with a plateful of pappadums. The dinner is strictly western.

Today I took a stroll. Very close to the circuit bungalow is a rivulet—almost a picnic spot. The causeway on it is under construction because the new bridge, built last November, was washed away by the first floods—the PWD is the same all over the sub-continent. Just in front of the circuit bungalow is a big expanse of rocks. I climbed over it just to see what was beyond it and saw green paddy fields and brushwood.

* * *

Handungama Circuit Bungalow
Galnewa (Mahaweli),
Sri Lanka
18 March 1979

...Last night I woke up in the middle of the night and suddenly my sleepy-open eyes caught sight of the most luminous and big star, through the Venetian blind covered glass-window of the room. The thought came to me that this star must be twinkling in London also. I felt a sudden nearness to you. This was the morning star. I never knew it was so big and bright.

I posted you a letter from Colombo on the 13th, as I was leaving for Mahaweli. Your letter of 16 March had reached me by then. I wonder when the next one will come. I had asked my Secretary to redirect here all the letters received until the 27th, because after that date I will be returning to Colombo. As I wrote you in my last letter, I will, *Insha'llah*, ring you up on the 5th or 6th of April at the same time as I rang you last time (between 10 and 12 in the morning, London time). How is Shelley darling? I have bought a card for her and will post it to her soon.

On my return from Colombo last Tuesday, which was a holiday — *poyaday* (the full moon day) I saw quite a few elephants walking on the roadside. The driver told me that the elephants were doing *parahera*: a sort of an offering to Lord Buddha, by undertaking this journey of about 3-5 miles round trip. On the way we stopped at Dambulla and saw the Rock Temple. It is a marvellous temple consisting of five caves. Inside the caves are huge reclining statues of Buddha carved out of living rock, and hundreds of seated and standing Buddhas. Most of them were painted in gold by the ancient kings. The Rock Temple dates back to the first century BC but quite a few statues were added by later kings. The pity is that it is a strenuous half a mile climb on barren rock before one reaches the temple. I have taken quite a few photographs and will send those over to you when the prints come.

The most beautiful thing that I have seen so far in Sri Lanka is the 39 feet high statue of Buddha at Aukana, which is just about a mile, as the crow flies, from the Circuit bungalow. I cannot tell you what a beautiful image it is. People say it looks marvellous at sunrise. The statue was carved on the orders of King Dhattusana in the 5th century AD. This is the same king who constructed the Kalawewa tank (100,000 acre feet of water), and in celebration and thanksgiving built the statue near the tank.

I find my room in Colombo really comfortable. It overlooks the stately town hall on the right and the big park on the left. The service is also very good. There is an old man named Anthony, assisted by a young man who is the keeper and the cook of the guesthouse. He is very efficient and prompt. He also washes my clothes and irons them. I am lucky in this respect because the chowkidar at the Handungama

Circuit Bungalow is also very efficient and prompt. He prepares excellent food and also does the washing for me. I wonder if you will like the two places. I am sure you will.

Before leaving for Colombo I had to attend a meeting in the Anuradhapura District called by the Minister for Mahaweli development and attended by all the district officers including the Deputy Commissioner who is called the Government Agent (GA). The meeting was an exact replica of the District Council meetings I used to hold as Deputy Commissioner of Kohat between 1963 and 1965, except that here I was one of the spectators. The problems were the same — complaints from politicians about the inefficiency and lack of attention from the government's departments and officials, and the government servants' stock explanations about lack of resources and staff. Even the District Minister, who is supposed to be the political head of the district, complained to the Central Minister about the lack of response from the officials. I thought that, as the head of the District, he should share the responsibility.

One thing, though, is different in the Lankan situation. Here the government servants are at the beck and call of the politicians. The system works well because the politicians know that they are answerable to the people, who will not tolerate excuses when the elections are held. India and Sri Lanka are outstanding examples of the fact that in the ultimate analysis it is democracy which pays and not authoritarian rule or dictatorship. Also, as I mentioned earlier, the standard of living and the social amenities and facilities available to Sri Lankans are much better than many countries in the region.

As the cultivation season for the Yala crop (April to August) is approaching fast, the project staff is in the midst of making the necessary preparations: issuing irrigation water; the harvesting and threshing of the standing Maha (September to March) crop; the availability of tractors and so on. Water is issued to the farmers from the branch canal on a turnout basis — each turnout area covers an average of 40 acres of land owned by 15 farmers. Those farmers are responsible for distributing the water amongst themselves. The engineer complained that the farmers near the turnout 'head' used up all the water and left little or none for those at the 'tail' end. I suggested to the Resident Project Manager that the farmers be organized on a 'turnout' basis. The RPM did not pay much attention to my proposal because the other officials were suggesting that a small committee be appointed to manage the distribution of water. I told the RPM that this would not work unless we had representatives of each 'turnout' on the committee. I stressed representation because selection of anyone from the group without the group's confidence in the person would not ensure equitable distribution of water. In the evening some of the farmers had been called to discuss the matter. They spoke in Sinhalese so I could not understand them but after the meeting the RPM said to me 'You almost prophesied what should be done because the farmers made the same suggestion'.

I was very pleased. The RPM, who in his heart was convinced that this was the best way to proceed, immediately issued instructions on these lines. The meeting of farmers was attended by the Additional General Manager and Additional Secretary of the Government of Sri Lanka in the Ministry of Lands and Lands Development, Mr Chandranandan de Silva. This was the Ministry, as I wrote to you earlier, which had opposed my consultancy. I knew that their opposition was based on lack of knowledge about my work. In Sri Lanka, I mean Colombo, I had tried to call on the secretary and the additional secretary of the ministry but although they agreed to meet me, I waited for more than an hour in their offices but they could not see me as they were called away by the minister. However, Mr de Silva promised to have dinner with me at Handungama Circuit Bungalow on his visit to Galnewa on Friday the 5th.

Mr Silva arrived from Colombo at 1500 hours. First he met the officials for nearly two and a half hours. Since I did not know the schedule of the meeting and since I saw the farmers standing outside, peering through the open windows of the meeting hall I thought that this exclusion of the people whose welfare was involved must be typical of the bureaucratic approach. However, I was mollified to see them ushered in after a two and half hour wait and also served tea like the officials. I was introduced and then the farmer who had wanted the farmers to be organized on a 'turnout' basis asked Mr De Silva, on behalf of the farmers, to allow me to speak. Mr Silva asked me to speak for five minutes: of course I had no intention of speaking any longer, because I was going to speak in English and someone had to translate. I addressed them thus. 'My name is Shoaib Khan and I am from Pakistan. For the last twenty-five years I have been working in the field and trying to banish poverty. I have been to many countries to see how those countries succeeded in alleviating poverty. Before coming here I was in Japan where 99 per cent of the people are Buddhists (90 per cent of Sri Lankans are also Buddhists) and fifty years ago they were also as poor as you are today. But now the Japanese farmer produces 200 bushels of rice per acre (Sri Lankans produce from 30 to 80 bushels of paddy). This they have achieved through a close partnership between farmers and government. Would you like me to come to your hamlets and discuss with you how to improve your income and finish poverty from your villages?'

There was an instantaneous 'Yes' and clapping from the farmers. I had been introduced to them but I was very surprised when one of them spoke to me in English[1] after the meeting and said 'You must come to us alone and not with the officials, then we will tell you everything'. Of course I had no intention of doing any such thing, but this typifies the hostility that exists between the officials and the farmers.

* * *

Handungama Circuit Bungalow
Galnewa, Sri Lanka
22 March 1979

...Your letter of 4 March, arrived here yesterday. This is my fourth letter from Galnewa. As discussed on telephone last time, you should plan to come to Karachi or Islamabad around the first of May and *Inshallah* I will reach there on the 3rd of May. For Manchu's marriage, I will manage to come again for a week in July. Anyway this can be finalised in May when I am in Pakistan.

In the last letter I had mentioned my dinner invitation to Mr de Silva, Additional Secretary of the Ministry of Lands and Lands Development. I also invited the RPM and his three Deputies. I did not complete the story about Mr de Silva's visit as the last letter was getting too long and I was afraid it might bore you. I have still to know your reaction to these prosaic letters of mine.

After the two meetings at Galnewa, which is only about a mile away, we all arrived at Handungama Circuit Bungalow at about 19:30 hours. Mr Alwis the DRPM Agriculture could not join us. I saw Palpulla—the gentleman who has just returned after living in Croydon for 12 years—at the bungalow, so I invited him to join us. The Circuit Bungalow table can only accommodate six persons so it was just as well that we were only six. I had left the menu to Nandasiri, the cook-cum-chowkidar of the bungalow. He had about a six-course dinner ready. Everyone liked it.

Looking at my room Mr de Silva remarked that he was reminded of his Cambridge days. It transpired that he had also been to Wolfson—the same college to which the RPM had been—opposite Selwyn. I think all these things may have helped the Ministry to change their views about the consultancy and about me. However, that remains to be seen. The truth will come out when the extension of the consultancy will come up for consideration later in the year.

The RPM has become very responsive to me after realising that my proposal was the same as that of the farmers. He invited me to attend a meeting of the farmers in the Kandalama Scheme, which was begun in 1954. Six hundred and sixty farmers were settled here on lots of five acres each—three for paddy and two acres of highland for a homestead and kitchen garden. The meeting was called near Dambulla at a government production farm, with about 100 farmers present. The RPM proposed 20 March as the date of beginning to issue the irrigation water and 10 May as the last date of sowing the Yala crop. The farmers were not yet ready for harvesting and threshing the Maha crop, so they wanted those dates extended. The discussion continued for about two hours and at last a consensus was reached on that the release of the first irrigation water would begin on 1 April and end on 15 May. I was very pleased with the outcome of this meeting and the way the RPM had conducted it. After making his suggestion he spoke very little and allowed others, especially the farmers, to speak. Community consensus is a great thing because in the end when one of the farmers wanted to reopen the issue after a consensus had been reached the others simply walked out and the man realised that his was a lone voice. If officials would only begin to involve the farmers in discussions affecting them, most of the problems would not arise and the officials would not be subjected to unnecessary criticism. Let us hope we succeed in developing a model in the project area for others to follow.

I had written in my last letter about the great statue of Buddha. In a book on Sri Lanka given to me by UNICEF Representative Paul Ignatieff, I learned that there was another statue of Buddha nearby. My Sinhalese counterpart Jayawickrema had promised to take me there on Sunday afternoon. He wanted to come in the morning but I told him to come later because of my habit of getting up late on Sunday mornings. The campus in which the circuit bungalow is situated has only one other house in which the head clerk of the office lives—Tannekoon.

The statue, situated about four miles away at Reswelira, is carved out of a rock and stands 39 feet in height without the pedestal. It is very majestic but the Awkana Buddha is a sheer beauty. Legend has it that this statue was carved by the disciples of the sculptor who carved the Awkana Buddha. There are also caves and Buddha images around the Raswelira Buddha. Mahaweli is at the centre of a triangle of Buddhist temples covering an area of nearly 100 by 50 miles with Anuradhapura, Pollunurwa and Kandy at the three corners.

* * *

Handungama Circuit Bungalow
Galnewa, Sri Lanka
29 March 1979

...Your letter of 8 March reached me here. So you did get my first letter from here. So you want me to write only one such letter a month. Well this is the fifth letter I am writing and this is only the fourth week. I don't think I can now stop writing these long letters, now that you have promised to publish them. Do you really find them interesting? Do write honestly. In fact, you should start writing long letters to me also—your stories, your impressions about anything, the little details of what happens in the house, so that I would feel as if I was present on those occasions.

I have been quite upset these last few days. The news from Pakistan has been depressing. I never liked Bhutto but I would never like him to hang. It may be a catastrophe for the country—it would further alienate the Sindhis. Let us hope and pray for the best. The trouble on the Afghan border also does not augur well. I don't know where our rulers will take the country. Anyway you shouldn't worry about these things. I mention them because in the solitude of this place it was becoming too much and I had to get it off my chest. How are you now?

So you want to know about Dr Eimi Watanabe. She is one of the programme officers at UNICEF Colombo. I think I had better tell you about the UNICEF office in Colombo. As I wrote to you earlier, the head of UNICEF in Colombo, who is the UNICEF Representative in Sri Lanka and the Maldives islands, is Mr Paul Ignatieff, a Canadian. His wife Catherine is a Scot. They have two children. They are a very hospitable couple and whenever I am in Colombo, they invite me to their house. Under the Representative, there are Programme Officers and Assistant Programme Officers. Dr Eimi Watanabe is in charge of Planning. There is a lady doctor Dr Hiranthi who is in charge of the Health Programme. She is the wife of a leading Sri Lankan surgeon. Then there is a water section (drinking water) which is under the charge of Mrs Marty Rajendran. She is American and married to a Sri Lankan. Amongst the Assistant Programme Officers, there is an Englishman, Rupert, a Welshman, Martin, and an American, Cliff, besides Bjorn who is Norwegian and Sena who is Sri Lankan. The Finance Section is headed by a Sri Lankan, Mrs Rohini de Silva. Her husband is in the National and Grindlays Bank, Colombo. Most of the Secretaries are wives of well placed Sri Lankans, such as army colonels and company executives. I think this is enough for the present. When I go to Colombo I will write more about them, if you so desire.

The other day I was invited to dinner at the Kalawewa Rest House. Kalawewa is a 1,500 year old tank, almost 20 square miles in area. There are a lot of stories about this tank. One is about a man who was in charge of opening the sluice gates when too much rain fell. It is said that the watchman kept an earthen pot outside his hut—if the rain filled the pot he would rush down to the tank to open the sluice gates to prevent the water breaching the 3 mile long [protection] *bund* and flooding the tank. One night, a group of monks passing by the hut put a stick in the pot and created a hole in it. Subsequently the rains poured but the pot did not fill and the poor watchman only learned that the pot had a hole when the bund had breached. In remorse the man jumped into the breach and was drowned. A spot on the bund commemorates the event.

During dinner, we heard the trumpeting of elephants from the other side of the water where they occupy the small piece of jungle still to be colonized. A group of about six or seven elephants are said to have become trapped in this small area of jungle. Efforts are now afoot to save them: the plan is to take the herd to the sanctuary about 40 miles away. One of the officers told me that on the other side of the project elephants sometimes take a dip in the irrigation channel.

Another dinner which I attended this week was hosted by probationers of the Ceylon Administrative Service, who are under training for one month in the Mahaweli Project. The dinner brought back memories of the Civil Service Academy in Lahore. The party continued until 02.00 hours when speeches were made and I drove back ten miles to my Circuit Bungalow. A brand new Fiat-18 has been delivered to me as my official car along with a driver.

This week I attended a number of Cultivation Committee meetings in different parts of the project area. I also addressed two of the meetings at the RPM's request. I was very pleased with the reaction of the farmers. They really liked it and clapped heartily. I speak through an interpreter but I have started learning Sinhalese which has many words in common with Sanskrit and Hindi.

The cultivation committees were first set up under the Paddy Lands Act in 1958. This was the first attempt by the government in Sri Lanka to give leadership to the farmers. However some non-cultivators also managed to get elected to these committees. The last government abolished this election system and nominated its party workers to these committees. Then, when the present government came to power in 1977, it abolished the cultivation committees altogether.

One of the functions of the previous committees was to determine the land preparation period, irrigation issues and harvesting dates. The present *ad hoc* committees are determining the cropping performance for the coming Yala crop. Fortunately these gatherings are no longer small committees: between 50 and 100 farmers attend the meetings. The conduct of business is strictly democratic and no decisions are imposed. When a consensus is reached after lengthy discussion, often lasting over two hours, a resolution (duly seconded) is moved by the farmers and carried unanimously. Since all the farmers are literate, they sign their names, and the proposer and seconder also sign. I have been greatly impressed by these meetings. The RPM conducts them in a most detailed and democratic way and everyone has the opportunity to be heard. It only needs to be made into a permanent arrangement instead of being *ad hoc*.

My first big break came when I held a meeting of the 75 field officers of Project Regions III and IV. I had a very detailed discussion with them. First I identified the problems being faced by the officers. These included the distribution of water by farmers amongst farmers; maintenance of field drains by the farmers; solution to problems pertaining to land and irrigation by government officers. Other issues included extension education, training farmers and their leaders in agricultural practices by government officers, and the organization of an input-delivery system. Yet other issues discussed were the organization of religious, cultural and sports programmes; programmes for women, youth and children, and health education, nutrition, and maternal and neonatal health. The officers agreed that these were indeed the most significant set of problems to be addressed.

The project area is divided into parcels of about 35 acres, each with 12-15 farmers. Without organizing the farmers of each turnout, the officers can never hope to solve their problems. My proposals in this regard were accepted in their entirety. I discussed these for nearly three hours because I wanted the Field Officers to understand and accept them, although the RPM had given me the authority to impose these decisions. A programme of activities for organizing the farmers at the turnout level has been drawn up. At the RPM's request I drew up the minutes of the meeting. He did not attend the meeting but he accepted the minutes *in toto* and in fact asked his other deputies to lend full support. I am very pleased at his response and more so at the response of the field officers, because they have started coming to me asking my advice and inviting me to accompany them on their village visits. It is exciting.

The other events here last week included a meeting of Sri Lanka Mahila Samity. This is like APWA (All Pakistan Women's Association) of Pakistan. The office bearers of this Samity had come from Colombo. They addressed a gathering of about 50 women at the nearby Agriculture Training Centre at Bulnewa. Most of the settlers in the Project area are young but there is an old population of about 70,000 people also. About 23,500 settler families will ultimately be brought into the area by 1980. The Samity succeeded in registering two branch Samities and received applications from three others.

There is a fairly well developed school system in the Project area. I was particularly impressed by the design of school buildings, which are covered sheds, open on all sides, ideally suited for the climate here. There are no thefts of school furniture or equipment.

I had another visitor from Colombo—Mr Dantonaryan, Assistant General Manager of the Mahaweli Development Board. He is an engineer and a very pleasant person. I invited him to dinner at the Circuit Bungalow and we had a very interesting and useful discussion.

* * *

Handungama Circuit Bungalow
Galnewa, Sri Lanka
15 April 1979

...I am back at Galnewa. Yesterday was the Sinhala and Tamil New Year and a period of festivities. Today while driving from Colombo, I came across village fairs, cycle races, and almost everybody on the street in their Sunday best. This is one occasion which both Sinhalese and Tamils celebrate together. Otherwise there is quite a bit of tension between the two communities, often leading to bloody riots. The Sinhalese are Buddhists and the Tamils are Hindus who came to Sri Lanka about two thousand years ago from South India. The Tamils number about three million out of a total of about 14 million. Some of the Tamil leaders are openly demanding a separate state in the northern Sri Lankan province of Jaffna, to be renamed Elam. Unlike in Pakistan, no one has put these people behind bars. They go on propagating their ideas and the government counters it with their own political campaign. The political tolerance in Sri Lanka is worthy of the highest praise and a model for others to follow. There are Tamil Muslims also but they are staunchly in favour of a united Sri Lanka. Recently some leading Hindus also broke away from the separatists and joined the government.

In one of your letters you wrote that it seems from my letters that I have gone back to Bengal. Well this place is not exactly Bengal but I have certainly gone back to my SDO days. My work, my office, the atmosphere and the environment are indeed no different. For the first time I am living in a place which is a good twelve miles away from the nearest town, Kekirawa. This town is also one tenth of the size of my first subdivision, Brahambaria in Bengal. That place had two cinemas and a club and was a cultural centre of art, dancing and music. You know how much you contributed to the advancement of the cultural life of Brahmanbaria. I still remember the pseudonymous letter I received after you had taken the role of Mira in a dance drama. The Mullahs were furious—the SDO's wife, a Muslim, adopting the role of Mira—it was blasphemy of the highest order. You laughed it away but I could not, and had reluctantly to curb your artistic talents.

I was saying that here, there is no habitation for miles around. Galnewa, the brand new town about one mile away, reminds me of Western movies, with its broad dusty roads and few buildings with big signboards. Except for the bar and the saloon of the Westerns, the bank, post office and shops are all there.

Despite all this I seem to discover a new world everyday. The two tall narrow windows of my room reveal a new world to me. I have begun to notice things I had never noticed before and am discovering new avenues of pleasure and enjoyment. I wrote to you how I often gaze at the stars from these windows while lying in bed. In the mornings I am often visited by a long, black-tailed bird. The other day I watched a sparrow bathing in dust for quite some time. In the brushwood beyond, a rabbit was hopping. The other day I was quite amused and touched to see a dog and a cat playing together and literally embracing each other. It was a most tender scene. You must be thinking that I am becoming a poet. I also saw a bird called the emerald dove—it is indeed as beautiful as its name.

And now, back to business. I was delighted at the response of the farmers when I went, at the request of one of the field officers, to organize the farmers in turnout groups. Farmers from four turnout areas were present. One of them complained that someone had broken their turnout sluice gate so he was not getting water. On enquiry it transpired that there were only 10 farmers in that turnout area and since 8 were getting water they were not bothered about the other two. Ultimately the farmers were convinced that the government could do nothing in the matter unless the ten farmers got together and followed the rules. I made it very clear to them that if the water was not reaching the sluice gate it was the responsibility of the government but within the turnout area the responsibility rested solely with the farmers. It was agreed that, in consultation with others, each turnout would nominate one farmer to discuss the methodology of organizing farmers.

I was quite taken aback when one farmer said that their yields were low because the top soil from the fields had been washed away. On enquiry from the engineers in charge of land preparation I found this to be true. They expressed their inability to do anything about this because the donors had ordained that a particular type of tractor, called the tyne-tiller, should be used in land preparation and had had hundreds of these tillers imported into the country. Akhtar Hameed Khan always used to say that the World Bank is a great 'disruptionist' and they often destroy projects. This seems to be a case in point. However, I raised the issue at Colombo and it seems that some notice is being taken. A World Bank team is visiting the project next week. Let us see what they have to say.

In Colombo I had very useful meetings with the Secretary, Ministry of Plan Implementation, Dr Wikrama Weerasooriya. He was the one who got the opposition to my consultancy vetoed by the Minister, who happens to be his brother-in-law. Dr Weerasooriya is a fine gentleman and really makes you feel comfortable. He shows genuine concern for you and takes steps to make you as much at home as possible. I was greatly impressed by his kindness.

My meeting with the General Manager of the Mahaweli Development Board was equally fruitful. I explained to him the training programme that I had drawn up for the project staff and the farmer leaders. He liked it very much and as Paul Ignatieff had already agreed to provide the funding—amounting to five hundred thousand Sri Lankan rupees—the General Manager undertook to get the proposals cleared by the Board in their next meeting. I was very pleased with this and a few other things. Paul, who is very perceptive and has a very dynamic approach, completely agreed with my approach and, being a great tactician, took all possible steps to see the proposals through. He had a meeting arranged in his room with all the Programme Officers and Assistant Programme Officers.

Eimi Watanabe is away in China these days, Marty Rajendern has given birth to a baby girl and is presently confined, Martin Griffith was away from town, and Rupert has gone to Sweden to get his rig for drilling water wells. So Hiranthi, Sena and Cliff were present. Paul especially wanted the Sri Lankans to react to the approach. Fortunately they were there. The discussion with them was very enlightening. They generally agreed with the idea.

Since Dr Weerasooriya had asked me to comment on the UNFPA (population people) proposals for assistance to Mahaweli, Paul arranged a meeting with the UNFPA Coordinator Alex Marshall.

I have really been impressed by the feasibility study carried out by the Board and the French firm of consultants called Sogreah about the project pertaining to Area 'H' of the Mahaweli Development. However, it seems that no one has bothered to read the study, and proposals for undertaking umpteen new studies are being mooted every day. In fact the last UNDP mission made recommendations to undertake studies which would require 8,000 man-months of national experts' time and about 3,000 man-months' of expatriate experts. These studies will only tell you what to do in the Mahaweli area, whereas a lot of lessons can be learnt from this 'H' area and the past studies. Alec Marshall also wanted to fund a new study and to draw up a training programme for staff and farmers. When I explained to him what I had already done and what studies were already available he agreed with me entirely. Unfortunately he was going on two months' home leave but he promised to support me to the hilt. Paul had in the beginning withheld the circulation of my paper containing the strategy and an overview of the Sogreah study. Now he decided to send it to Dr Weerasooriya.

There is another Pakistani UN expert in Sri Lanka, Dr Mushtaq Hussain. He is a very nice person and often takes me out to different places in and around Colombo. The Pakistan ambassador had twice invited me to his house, so I decided to make a courtesy call. I had a most terrible time. He took pains to justify Bhutto's execution and I could see that he was speaking in his master's voice. ambassadors are expected to represent the people of the country also but unfortunately some of our ambassadors consider themselves the personal employees of the rulers in power and pose themselves as 'more loyal than Caesar'.

In my last letter I wrote to you how the Ignatieffs take care of me when I am in Colombo. This time Paul invited me to spend the weekend with him in the hill country. So on Friday we drove to a tea estate called Aisalaby near Banderwela, about 130 miles east of Colombo. A German couple with their two children and the Ignatieffs with two children and their daughter Nicky's friend Vanessa made up the party. The tea estate bungalow is indeed perfection itself—beautiful natural scenery, homely comfort, excellent cuisine and room service and all this at a princely charge of 3.5 Pounds per day! I offered to pay Paul, but he would not allow me to do so but for my information said that the charge is only $7.50 per day. I almost believed that it could be $750 per day; the place is so idyllic. I was really surprised when he clarified it was seven dollars fifty cents only. I am sure you would love the place. It is somewhat like Nathiagali's Government House—all surrounded by tea gardens. This is one place in Sri Lanka where I would like Manchu to spend part of her honeymoon.

I think this letter is getting too long. I am enclosing a cutting from the newspaper showing wild elephants being driven from the Project area to the nearby game sanctuary. I will leave the description of the fortress of Sigriya, which I visited on the first Sunday of the month, for a later occasion.

* * *

Handungama Circuit Bungalow
Galnewa, Sri Lanka
25 April 1979

...In my last letter I wrote to you about my visit to the tea-estates of Bandarwela. I had a chance to talk to one of the tea pluckers at the Aisalaby Estate. I found him waiting at the crossroads with two loads of freshly picked tea leaves. To my good fortune, he spoke English. Normally tea-pluckers are women but on the Aisalaby Estate, the work force consists of 50 men, each responsible for two acres. Paul Ignatieff had informed me that it was owned by a foreigner named Bostack. Unfortunately for him, when the last government was contemplating nationalizing the tea plantations, he incorporated his estate, thinking that companies would not be nationalized. This proved a big mistake because he lost all but 50 acres of his estate: otherwise he could have saved 50 acres per member of his family. However, he seems to be doing pretty well even with 50 acres. He has a poultry farm also. The tea plucker earns eight cents per pound of plucked tealeaves. The maximum he can pluck in a day is four loads of 45 lbs. each. Thus on an average he makes Rs 350 to Rs 400 per month. This one pound of tea leaves sells in the market for 1,200 cents. Of course you have to take into consideration the cost of planting, treating the tea leaves (which reduces their weight also), packing and marketing. Still, the plucker deserves a better deal than what he is getting at present.

Now, about my visit to Sigriya. It is a huge flat-topped rock, almost 600 feet high. King Kassyapa, the son of King Dhatusena who built the big Kalewawa tank at the heart of the Project I am working on, killed his father to deprive his elder brother of the throne. This happened about 1,500 years ago. Although he committed patricide, he later proved himself a great builder and an artist. He built himself a palace on the top of the rock and designed beautiful gardens on the grounds with geometric precision. It is enthralling to see everything from the top of the rock. On the top there are big tanks for water storage and even a grandiose swimming pool with steps chiselled in the rock. On the way up there are beautiful platforms with thrones carved out of the rocks, and midway, on a sheer bluff, is a beautiful art gallery protected by a ledge of rock. Tourists can only go up to it through a steel staircase and can view the frescoes from a long steel platform protected by an iron mesh railing. Even after 1,500 years, the paintings are very clean and bright, although a few years ago some vandals covered the paintings with a thick coat of paint. Most of the paintings have been restored to their original beauty. It is amazing to consider how these rocks were painted, as there is no place to climb or to stand. Maybe they were more ingenious than the present generation and without any modern machinery, could accomplish things which we cannot do today. Below the rocks on which the frescoes are painted is a long shining glass wall on which calligraphy and poems are inscribed. The last portion of the rock is only accessible through the mouth of a huge lion—each nail of the lion's paw is equal to the size of a full grown man. The last climb is very steep and difficult. Legend has it that the king used to ride a horse to the palace on top of the rock. No one has been able to find that secret passage, although the legend seems plausible because it is really a very strenuous climb and must have been more so for a king in those days.

The Sinhala New Year is celebrated with great fervour. The office was totally deserted on Monday and actually people did not show up until Wednesday. One day I was pleasantly surprised to see Ken Lyvers of USAID Islamabad at Galnewa. It is indeed a small world. Ken has been posted to Sri Lanka USAID, and had come to the Project area in connection with problems of water management. I was very happy to see such a close friend. I am sure he will be a great help. Another very good person that I met this week was Mr Kapila Wimladharma, the newly appointed Additional General Manager (Operations) of the Mahaweli Development Board. In him, at last, I found someone in the government of Sri Lanka, who has the time and patience for the programme I am doing, and takes a real interest in it. We had detailed discussions during which he evinced his keen interest in the project. Fortunately for me, he is the main person in the Board concerned with my work. I am really very happy at this turn of events.

The World Bank team along with British, Canadian and American representatives visited the Project Area this month. The British representative was very happy to meet me and remarked to the Chairman of the Mahaweli Development Board that he had been greatly encouraged to hear what was being accomplished and planned in the realm of community development. The RPM had invited me to have lunch with the team and thereafter I stayed with them and other officials of the Board till late at night. Today being Sunday, I stayed late in bed. In the afternoon of the next day we went out for a drive and in the evening met the RPM to discuss the World Bank visit.

Yesterday I visited Kandy, which is about a two hour drive from Galnewa. I had meetings at the Peradeniya University. You might recollect Brian Seneweratne who was with me at Cambridge in 1956–57. Until two years ago he was a Professor of Medicine at Peradeniya University. Now he has migrated to Australia. It would have been great to meet him after nearly 22 years. Kandy is indeed a beautiful place surrounded by hills with a lake in the middle. It almost reminds me of Naini Tal in India. On one side of the lake is the famous tooth relic temple of Buddha. The relic is shown ceremoniously in the evening at 1900 hours. Forty-five minutes prior to the showing drummers go into action and it all creates an atmosphere full of sanctity and splendour. There is a long queue for viewing the relic. The relic itself is encased in a huge 'hill' of golden caskets, with the smallest containing the tooth of Buddha. However, only the outside casket is visible to the viewer.

The Perideniya University campus is perhaps one of the most beautiful campuses in the world. Next to it is the Botanical Gardens—very beautiful and soothing and patterned on the Kew gardens. I am sure you would love to see Kandy. On the return journey I visited the Polgolla, Baotenire and Noaga power station and weirs, which are all part of the Mahaweli Development Project.

I was due to leave for Colombo on the 27th but have received a telegram stating that the minister wants to see me on the 26th, at 19.00 hours, in the Ministry of Plan Implementation. I am now due to leave tomorrow morning for Colombo. I shall ring you up from there....

* * *

Handungama Circuit Bungalow
Galnewa, Sri Lanka
9 July 1979

...The last letter I wrote you in English was on 25 April. Since then I have been to Pakistan twice and you have been in Pakistan from 6 May. My last trip to Pakistan, in retrospect, looks to me like a very pleasant dream. Manchu's marriage was one of the most beautiful events of my life....But this last visit has totally upset my resolve and concentration. I suddenly feel that I can't live without you and the children. Galnewa, where I used to keep myself very busy in work, seems a lonely place now. I arrived here on the first hoping to get busy in work but the first few days were bleak.

Getting no letters from you since May has created a vacuum. No doubt you have been busy and we have been talking on telephone but I still wait for your letters because I can read these again and again whenever I feel lonely. You must not stop writing letters.

I had concluded my last letter by saying that I had received a telegram to attend a meeting in Colombo at 1900 hours on 26 April. I was under the impression that this was to be a meeting with the minister. However, on arrival in Colombo, I rang up the minister concerned and was told that the meeting had been called by the secretary of the ministry of plan implementation and it was at 16.00 hours. The meeting turned out to be a meeting on the UN Fund for Family Planning Activities for the Mahaweli area. I had given my comments informally on the UNFPA proposals at the request of the Secretary. I had not realised then that these comments would be made public. I was more concerned because the UNFPA proposals were those of my new friend Kapila Wimladharma. Fortunately Kapila accepted my proposals and I must say that the secretary of plan implementation not only said that he agreed with my views but even sent me a letter saying so. Anyway this was just by the way.

The expected meeting with the minister took place today (9 July) at the Kalawewa Circuit Bungalow. It came about by chance. Unfortunately the RPM's 84-year-old father had died and I had gone to Kandy to attend his funeral. The chairman of the Mahaweli Development Board informed me there that the minister was visiting Kalawewa and Galnewa the next morning and would greatly appreciate my being there if it did not interfere with my weekend plans. It certainly did because I had planned to drive on after the funeral from Kandy to Nawrelliya hill station and spend the full-moon holiday there. However the call of duty got the better of me and I returned to Galnewa that night.

The minister was due at 0900 hours. He did not turn up until 1200 noon and he came in a bus with twenty other people. It transpired that in order to debunk criticism that nothing was being done in Mahaweli 'H' Project, the minister had decided to bring a busload of members of parliament and pressmen from Colombo to let them have a look at the project. In a brief session I explained to him what I was doing and how the project officers were being trained to first organize farmers in turnout groups and then train their leaders. The minister was so impressed that, after the briefing by project officials, he asked me to give a briefing about my work and proposals. It generated quite a bit of interest and a lot of questions were asked. The minister apparently felt very pleased and thanked me many times. He especially called me to be photographed with him and promised to give me any support I required. He also said that he would come for three or four days another time to have discussions with me. I am feeling very pleased at his support. I must say, although young in age, the minister is very mature, extremely polite and courteous. He is the first important politician to recognize my work.

There has been a stream of visitors also during the last seven days, all because of the training course I organized at the beginning of the last month, just before I went on leave to Pakistan for Manchu's marriage. This was the first course for the project staff. Besides the chairman and the general manager, five secretaries to the government of Sri Lanka also came and addressed the trainees. On my return to Colombo, Eimi Watanabe asked me to make a presentation on the Mahaweli Project to programme officers for nearly all the foreign and United Nations aid agencies stationed in Sri Lanka. As a sequel to this presentation, people have been coming all the way from Colombo to see me at Galnewa—a Dutch sociologist, British water management experts and institution specialists amongst others. I enjoy meeting the visitors as it breaks the monotony of the routine work. The visitors often either lend support and reinforce my line of thinking or I come across new ideas in our discussions. The Dutch sociologist especially encouraged me because he had been to the project six months earlier and was very positive about the progress made in organizing and training farmers to upgrade their managerial and productive skills.

The minister's visit was splashed in the papers. One of the papers gave prominent coverage to my utterances and relegated the minister to the inside page. However, the minister seems quite happy because the other day when I met the secretary, ministry of plan implementation (who by the way is the brother-in-law of the minister), he remarked 'Shoaib! you seem to be blazing a trail in Mahaweli'. When I mumbled that the minister was too generous, he countered that he had himself been to the area last Sunday along with *Newsweek* columnist Vittachi and he personally got the impression that I was highly acceptable to the area. In fact, Eimi Watanabe went to the extent of saying that she would like to come to the area and to spend a few days as my apprentice. Well! I am writing all this not to impress you, because that I never can, but just to make you happy to learn that the work is being recognized and everyone concerned is encouraging me in the endeavour.

Otherwise you know fully well that I am never carried away by these things. I know that this is only the beginning and much remains to be done, requiring a lot of patience, hard work and optimism.

We had a two-day training course for the officers on the settlement side. It went very well, with over 50 officers attending. The general manager also came, to inaugurate it. The direct effect of the first course held in June was to commission the village training centres, which had been lying unused. In fact the officers of one of the four regions held a brief ceremony to inaugurate the centre and called all the field officers and emphasized the need for cooperation and coordination amongst them all to achieve the objectives of the project.

I arrived in Colombo on the evening of the 14th, a fortnight after I had left. Perhaps I had written you from Nagoya about the Welshman and his Italian wife. On his way back to England, Richard Broyd stopped over in Sri Lanka and spent a couple of days in the Mahaweli area also. He came back with me to Colombo and left for London two nights later. His father has a farm in Wales very near Abrysthwithe where, in 1974 you might remember, we spent a week. Maybe next time when we are both together in England, you might like to pay a visit to his farm.

I attended a meeting of the National Steering Committee which evaluates the implementation of the UNICEF programme in the country. In the UNICEF office a controversy is raging over whether I should be required to do the work of a programme officer also, which means assuming full responsibility for implementation of UNICEF projects in the Mahaweli area, including procuring supplies and budgetary responsibility. The opponents to this suggestion say that my time as a consultant is too valuable to be spent on routine work. I have taken a neutral stance and would leave it to the representative to decide the matter. Of course, on my own, I would not offer to do the routine work but if asked to do it, I know it won't pose any great difficulty.

I am keenly awaiting the arrival of Manchu, Shelley and Afshan.

* * *

45A, Alexandra Place
Colombo, Sri Lanka
28 July 1979

...In my last letter I wrote to you about the minister's visit and my week in Colombo. I returned from Galnewa last evening. On the way I was thinking that July is not only my official month of birth, it also is the month in which I started my working career, to be precise on 13 July in Jehanzeb College, Saidu Sharif, Swat State in the North West Frontier of Pakistan. On 13 July this year, I complete twenty-six years of my working life. In 26 years the United Nations is now my third employer—the first being the ruler of Swat and the second the government of Pakistan. Technically, I continue to be an employee of the government of Pakistan and deputed from there to the United Nations.

The week at Galnewa was uneventful except for the arrival of two visitors from Colombo and the start of the first follow-up course for the project Range and Regional level officers. The two visitors, Hammond Rust and Russ Cromer, were from USAID. They were interested in water management because USAID is planning a $10 million assistance programme to rehabilitate the Galoya irrigation scheme in the south of the island. I explained to them how we are trying to organize 'turnout groups' of farmers for water management in project area 'H' of Mahaweli Development Project. After lengthy discussions I met them in the evening at the Kalawewa Circuit Bungalow. There Rust confided that after hearing me and seeing what is being done here, he felt that USAID was just going to waste its $10 million because it was concentrating on rehabilitating the irrigation infrastructure but had no provision for human organization. Then he turned round and said 'Shoaib Sultan, people like you don't grow on trees and without your perception and vision it would not be easy to do this'. Then he jokingly asked if I would divide my time between 'H' Area and Galoya. I said 'Of course, with the greatest pleasure, if you think it worthwhile and the results in 'H' Area are encouraging'.

The follow-up course (a sequel to the first foundation course held in early June) met my expectations. It was attended by almost all of the regional and range level officers. Not all the project level officers—the RPM and DRPMs—could attend. I thought this was just as well because it gave me more time to concentrate on the issues relevant to organizing and training farmer leaders. I was also happy to see the field-level officers speaking their minds. They even aired their disappointment at the absence of some of the project level officers. Slowly I am getting to know the inter and intra-unit jealousies. The agriculture DRPM does not seem to be on the same wave-length as his regional and range-level officers. There is a definite communication gap. Similarly the CD and WM units in the region don't seem to be getting on too well. But I was happy that these things were brought out in the course. At least remedial action could be set in motion, which I hope would lead to improvement. The comparative performance of the different regions, reflected in their regional reports, also had a very positive effect. I am sure this impact would be visible in the next course, scheduled for 30–31 August.

I went back to Galnewa after a three-day stay in Colombo and returned to Colombo early in the morning of 5 August. On the way to Colombo, I made a detour via Kandy to see the world famous Perahera. This is a religious procession in which hundreds of gaily decorated elephants take part, as well as many dance troupes and drummers. The main temple elephant, which is a big tusker, carries on its back, separately encased in a golden lion, the tooth relic of Buddha. Kandy is famous for the sacred tooth relic temple. Legend says that the tooth was brought to Sri Lanka hidden in the hair of an Indian princess. The Perahera is a big event and tourists from all over the world flock to Kandy. The hoteliers take full advantage of the situation and increase their charges four or five times. A seat on the Perahera route costs anything from Rs 100 to Rs 500. The event started this year on 30 July. Besides elephants there were many dance troupes and drummers. It lasted for an hour and a half. On the full moon day it will last three hours, I am told. The biggest Perahera will take place on the full moon day, which is a public holiday.

Last week in Galnewa there was an interesting group of five Englishmen visiting the Mahaweli Project. Since UNICEF was looking after them they brought a letter for me, but as I had not received firm information about their programme I had made no arrangements, except to mention that a group of students was likely to visit. On the basis of the letter, they were able to get accommodation at Maha Illuppallama Circuit Bungalow, situated at the Agricultural Research Farm. The project officers looked after them until my arrival.

I met them on the morning of the third day of their visit. Although they were all travelling under the aegis of Kings College, Taunton was the only one of them associated with that college. He had studied at

Oxford, which he rather apologetically told me on learning that I had studied at Cambridge, and was now going to teach history at Kings College. One of them had just completed his first year at Cambridge so I asked him how much Cambridge had changed since I was there in 1956–57. The other three were agricultural engineering students. I took them to a farmer leaders' training session which had begun the previous week and also to the project officers' and a farmer's house. They were very pleased with their visit and later wrote me a letter of thanks.

They also said they had been totally misled, by an American whom they had met at the Circuit Bungalow, about the situation in the project and about Sri Lankans. I knew that this American was trying to run an experimental farm in 'H' area from Kandy and was totally disillusioned. I was glad that the visitors got a balanced view.

The farmer leaders' training programme got off to a good start last week. I attended all the four sessions, over four days, and was happy to note almost 90 to 95 per cent attendance. The project officers also did all the right things. The future programme was also firmed up. I had mentioned earlier the non-cooperation between the community development staff and the water management engineers. Since this was openly discussed in the follow-up course, as expected, the situation dramatically improved. As the engineer in charge of the project took a personal interest and also attended one of the farmers' training sessions, the field level engineers were found present on all the four days. The other regions will start training from 6 August. The spirit of coordination and cooperation exhibited in one region took the shape of joint written instructions issued to field officers by the regional heads of the agriculture, water management and community development units. If we are able to sustain this spirit, the success of the programme is assured.

A very interesting thing happened in a meeting of the socio-economic research committee attended by professors and research scholars at the Kalawewa Circuit Bungalow. After I had presented the programme and proposals about the project, one of the scholars (with a doctorate) commented that all the assumptions I was making were wrong and hence the programme was bound to fail. I was completely taken aback but fortunately the DRPM (WM), the RPM and others rebutted him. When Kapila Wimladharma, the Additional General Manager, further questioned him about the basis of his comments, he had little to say. After the meeting I spoke to him and offered to discuss the matter fully. He was very attentive and I do hope that I set him rethinking about his comments. Fortunately, there was a farmers' training session in a village a few miles away and I invited them to visit the place to see the farmers in action. Out of 62 farmer leaders, 57 were present and showed great interest in the programme.

I am so excited at the prospect of Manchu and Shelley arriving on the 9th.

* * *

Handungama Circuit Bungalow
Galnewa, Sri Lanka
19 September 1979

…I waited for your letter but in vain. Manchu and Shelley came and went away. It was as if they had never come. I am once again left to my solitude but the enchanting days I spent with them have left sweet memories. On 14 August, I threw a dinner party to celebrate Manchu and Shelley's arrival in Sri Lanka. I had invited almost everyone from the UNICEF Offices as well as my friends in the Sri Lankan government — Dr Weerasooriya, Secretary Ministry of Plan Implementation, Dr Abeygunawardena, General Manager Mahaweli; Kapila Wimladharma and the Additional General Manager Mahaweli. My friends Dr Mushtaq Hussain, Mr Allauddin and Kamran Niaz from the embassy also came. Almost sixty people attended the party. Everything was arranged by my landlord Dr Chandrakirti, as I had to go to Galnewa on the 13th and returned only a few hours before the dinner. Manchu and Shelley arranged the house. We had invited the three Russian tenants in the house to the party also. The party was a great success. Manchu and Shelley had arranged some music by getting the landlord's teenage sons to bring the music system. Shelley made everybody dance. Everyone thoroughly enjoyed the party.

Later, I made my first visit to the hill country, with Manchu and Shelley. We spent two days at Nawarelleyia, a tea plantation 6,000 feet above sea level. We stayed at the house of the Regional Manager of the State Plantation Corporation as paying guests. It was a most delightful stay. The atmosphere in the tea estates is like what must have been in the early part of the century during the colonial regime. The tea estate superintendent is looked upon by the workers as a demigod. They almost tremble and shiver in his presence, as most of the workers are Tamils of Indian origin, awaiting repatriation to India. They have no sense of security. Their plight is indeed awful. Although they get enough money as wages and have a decent place to live in, this sense of insecurity and the autocratic behaviour of the estate superintendents must play havoc with their minds. This is indeed a very ugly aspect of a very beautiful countryside. I also visited a tea estate where only Sinhalese labour was employed. This is a post Independence plantation; shabby and ill kept but the people are happier. I wondered whether the regimentation and authoritarian rule in the old estates was worth the suffering it caused to the workers.

We drove from Nawarelleyia to Kandy and then on to my project area. It is a beautiful drive. The road meanders along beautifully pruned tea bushes and it looks as though the hills have been covered with a thick pile of green carpet. Paul Ignatieff also visited the project area during this period. This was his first visit since my arrival in the area. He seemed visibly pleased with what he saw, especially the farmer leaders' training sessions. Indeed, later on he wrote a very nice letter to me greatly commending the work I am doing in the project area. I took Manchu and Shelley to the Wilpattu National Park where we saw two leopards and a number of other animals. We visited the old city of Anuradhapura also and spent a night at the Anuradhapura Rest House. Yes, Shelley and Manchu climbed the Sigriya Rock also.

On our return to Colombo we celebrated *Eid*. My secretary, who is a Muslim, took me for Eid prayers to the Zahira College mosque. It was a brief affair because after the prayers most of the people left without waiting to hear the *Khutba* (sermon). The ambassador had invited us to a reception where, besides the resident Pakistani community, I also met Mohsin [a Police Service of Pakistan officer] and his wife. They were returning from Japan and were guests of the ambassador.

From the reception, I took Manchu and Shelley directly to the Bentuta Beach Hotel, about 40 miles from Colombo, where UNICEF was holding a workshop with the managers and assistant regional managers of the tea estates. Since the nationalization of the tea estates by the previous government, all the estates are managed by two corporations: the State and Janata. Although there is a lot of criticism of the way estates are being run since nationalization, no deterioration was visible. I gathered that the lot of the workers had certainly improved since the government take-over. Sena Ganawatte from UNICEF, who had organized the seminar, asked me to make a presentation and also to preside over the concluding session. Like the 'turnout' in Mahaweli, I identified the 'gang' in the estates for launching production programmes to improve the workers' standard of living. The idea was greatly appreciated and Sena was so pleased with the reaction of the managers to my presentation that he came and said to me that he was really proud of me.

Several important visitors came to the project area last month. Mr Clarence Long, the Chairman of the US Senate Foreign Aid Sub-Committee was the first visitor. Mr Long came by helicopter and immediately struck me as a man who knew precisely what he wanted to see and do and no one could persuade him into anything else. His main interest lay in meeting and talking to the farmers. Although I had informed the project staff of this, the higher authorities had over-ruled them and no farmers' meeting was arranged. Since Congressman Long's desire was clearly to meet the farmers, I asked one of the community development officers to assemble as many farmer leaders as possible at the Galnewa training centre to meet the congressman. We took about an hour to reach the centre. By then about twenty farmers were there. The congressman had a long talk with them. I knew where his interest lay because he showed impatience with the very short briefing I gave about the farmers' training programme. However, after listening to the farmers and having visited some of their homes and driven through the area earlier, the congressman declared that this was his best visit in 56 countries. The congressman expressed the view that this project appeared to be really benefitting the majority of the farmers unlike other projects which only benefit a few, and mostly the better off ones. The general manager, who was accompanying the congressman, told me that the minister had been very keen that the congressman meet me. In fact the general manager told me that the minister said that the general manager should have taken me in the helicopter by which the congressman came to the area. The Congressman was escorted by the minister for culture.

Congressman Long's visit went off pretty well except at the USAID water management farm. Our friend George Kernim, who, as I wrote you earlier, lives in Kandy and controls the farm remotely, told the Congressman that the MDB officials did not want him to give the demonstration of land levelling by buffaloes. This rather pricked the congressman who concluded that since the MDB wants tractors in aid, they were stopping George from giving this demonstration. In fact, although the farm had been in existence for the last 12 months, George was trying the buffaloes for the first time. It was Sam Alwis, the DRPM for agriculture, who had cautioned him against the demonstration. Sam is also opposed to tractors. The incident caused a bit of a diplomatic ripple. The minister tried to explain the situation and stated that George was doing the buffalo demonstration on a plot of land which had already been levelled by tractor and that the MDB needed tractors not for land preparation and levelling but for jungle clearing and secondary growth. Unwittingly, George Kernim had created a situation which left Sam Alwis furious.

Another incident of the same strain appeared when Dame Judith Hart, the Overseas Development Minister in the UK Labour Government, left the official vehicle and the president of UNP (the ruling party) who is also chairman of MDA, and came and sat in my little Fiat, saying that she wanted to talk to me about farmers' organizations. It left me embarrassed and project officers sheepish. I had no choice but to drive her around the project area for three hours.

Two parliamentary groups also visited the project area in the last month. One, from Europe, was escorted by the Chairman of the MDB. The other included Dr (Mrs) Nafis Sadiq, the daughter of the late Mr Shoaib (Finance Minister of Pakistan), now in UNFPA. Since their helicopter did not land where the RPM was waiting for them, they came straight to the Bulnewa community centre where I was conducting a training course for project officials. The chairman was quite pleased and remarked that he had brought the group on an appropriate day. The second inter-parliamentary group made us wait for four hours in the Kalawewa Circuit Bungalow before showing up. There were many questions asked. While departing, the lady MP from UK Mrs Beadley remarked to me 'Yours is a very satisfying job. I wish I had a job like this'.

It seems that Dame Judith Hard told the consultants, Huntings Technical Services of UK, that 'according to Mr Khan the 'H' area organization is quite sound and no further experimentation is required'. Huntings, who wants to be different just for the sake of being so, did not like it and told the Dame, 'You should not believe everything that Mr Khan says'. Huntings, especially their expert Mr Hugh Arundale mentioned that they are trying an approach different from UNICEF. In actual fact, it is not so because they have also agreed to the organization of the farmers in turnout groups which is really the sole basis of my work here. However Paul Ignatieff is feeling quite piqued at this.

Paul's meeting with the Huntings experts, Mr Brian Duncan and ODM Coordinator Mr Frank Dunhill has not been much help. I attended a meeting in one of the experimental areas Huntings have taken up on the 'H' area, as the RPM wanted me to go with him. I found their attitude rather rigid. The RPM rightly decided to do everything in their experimental area strictly according to their wishes. Five of their experts attended the meeting. I had not met any of them earlier. As most of the new settlers in Huntings' experimental area are from the Minister's constituency, no one is prepared to take any chances. The Huntings team is preparing land at a cost of Rs 10,000 per acre. In 'H' area it was prepared by the farmers at Rs 800 per acre and is being done at Rs 1,000 by the MDB Agricultural Engineering unit. Huntings do not probably appreciate this but their attitude is not at all liked by the field officers. However, since UK is giving 100 million pounds, no one from the MDB wants to contradict the Huntings team. When I asked the AGM, he told me candidly, 'We will accept all their proposals to get the money but will do what we consider most appropriate.'

The other day I met Professor Mirral from the Netherlands who is collaborating with the Geography Department of the University of Colombo in running a diploma course in rural development. I was reminded of our project at the Pakistan Academy for Rural Development at Peshawar, which organized a similar diploma course in collaboration with the University of Peshawar.

I had better finish this letter now. It has become so lengthy that it will take you ages to read. Also, my handwriting is not too readable. After Manchu's departure, Shelley and I again came to the project area and since she was so happy at the village at Habrana (about 20 miles from my office in the project area), we stayed there again. Shelley became really popular in the hotel and was friendly with everyone there—the receptionists, the butler, the bearers, the boutique attendants and the gem-shop Manager. Another staff member from UNICEF was also visiting the project area during this period. He is a Norwegian called Bjorn Vaseth, recently married to a French girl, Odille. Probably I wrote to you earlier how Bjorn was very forlorn because his girlfriend had gone away to France. She came back two months ago and married Bjorn. She is rather daring in her clothes but is a very nice person. Shelley got on very well with her and when Shelley went to say goodbye to her in Colombo, she made her stay for dinner. Bjorn is our information officer and a very talented young man. He always reminds me of our Norwegian friend Frederick Barth who came to Swat in 1953 and later met us at Cambridge. In fact Bjorn is his student.

* * *

Handungama Circuit Bungalow
Galnewa, Sri Lanka
8 October 1979

...You must have got my letter of 19 September 1979. I wrote to you about the difference of opinion between me and the British firm of consultants called Huntings Technical Services. While I was at Galnewa, one of them, Mr Hugh Arundale met Paul and Eimi Watanabe and explained to them the work he was doing and tried to clarify his misconceptions about my programme. When I returned to Colombo, Mr Arundale also came to see me and realized that there was really no conflict in what I was doing and his proposed management organization. I explained to him that since he was proposing a manager for 500 acres instead of for 5,000 acres as at present, naturally his organization would be more effective, provided the government could afford such an expensive structure. To my mind the crucial thing was the farmers' organization in turnout groups because in the absence of farmer organizations even his proposed management organization would come to naught despite intensive staffing. Probably I did make an impression on him because a few days later he came again with Brian Jones and requested me to help Huntings in organizing farmers in their experimental area. I was, of course, delighted with the change in attitude.

I was very happy this morning when the unit manager of block 404 and another Huntings expert came to my office in Galnewa to fix a date for my visit to the Huntings area to organize farmers. I was really amazed by how they could have missed the argument I was making that with farmers' organizations even the existing setup in 'H' area could be made to work. They kept on emphasizing changes in administrative structure and the intensification of staffing, although all the time they were claiming that their proposed setup would have fewer staff.

Another visitor last month was Mr M.R. Khan from Bangladesh who, after seeing what I was doing here, remarked that he would recommend a similar programme for the UNICEF-assisted programme in Sirajganj. I was really amused that what I had learnt from Comilla was going back to Bangladesh via Sri Lanka. I never thought that people could get so prejudiced that they could not see things clearly. The principles evolved at Comilla [Bangladesh] were applicable to Daudzai [Pakistan] and now to Mahaweli.

Dr Eimi Watanabe, who is leaving for Burma at the end of the month, paid her final visit to the project along with Mrs Pat Allaidiwa, of the Ministry of Planning and Finance. They saw the farmers' training. I am sorry at Dr Watanabe's leaving Colombo. She had a big hand in getting me here and was one of my greatest supporters. She publicized my work everywhere, both in national and international circles. In fact, in Paul Ignatieff and Eimi Watanabe, I had found tremendous support for my work. Fortunately Paul is still there. He is very considerate and solicitous. He has ensured the extension of my contract to 30 April 1981 which amongst other things has entitled me to certain financial benefits also such as the freight for the car. Otherwise on less than a two-year contract one doesn't get the freight.

A group of Sri Lankan MPs, accompanied by the Deputy Minister Mr Matthews, also paid a visit to the 'H' area. This visit was part of a programme to acquaint the MPs with the Mahaweli Project. I gave them a briefing at the Community Centre. I have found another friend in Mr Denis Fernando, the Director of Planning of the Ministry of Mahaweli Development. He is a great advocate of investing in local people's abilities. He is a little brash in stating his point of view but I like him.

The second set of MPs came on the 13 October. I met them at the Kalawewa Circuit Bungalow and on Denis Fernando's and the RPM's request accompanied them in the mini-bus. The MPs did not get out of the vans at the community training centre; instead, I gave a commentary on the vehicle's public address system. The MPs left the bus at the newly settled block in H4 where displaced persons from Kotmale whose lands are going under the reservoir have been settled. Unfortunately the settlers had been without water for the last three days and complained to the MPs about it. The MPs were naturally agitated. At the end of the tour, lunch had been arranged at a place where the Minister of Mahaweli Development had also come. The Kotmale settlers come from the minister's home district. He was very annoyed and after the MPs had left, wanted to visit the area. He asked me to accompany him in the jeep. He expressed great displeasure with the local officers and even threatened to send one home. He was also annoyed with the RPM although that area is not directly under him. It all happened because one foolish officer did nothing even after being told by the settlers about water scarcity. The supervisory staff failed to respond to this basic need.

The H4 area is a classic example of a small place where an army of government functionaries has been inducted: there are literally scores of officers to look after a group of 100 settlers, but each section (construction, settlement and management) is going their own way. The settler has to go from pillar to post for everything. The minister called me over on Sunday and took me on another round of visits with the Kotmale settlers. I could take his leave only after he had entertained me to lunch.

The minister arrived a week later to perform the opening ceremony of the newly constructed right bank canal, which will irrigate H4 and H5: a total of 40,000 acres. This canal has been completed ahead of the schedule. The opening ceremony consisted of a *Pirith* religious ceremony beginning the night before the actual opening of sluice gates. I went to the religious ceremony but finding the beginning of the ceremony still an hour or two away, I made my way to the Kalawewa Circuit Bungalow. On arrival there, I was told by the MDB General Manager that the minister had been enquiring about me and someone had been sent to call me. The following day, after the opening ceremony and lunch, when I took leave of the minister, he asked me to see him at Colombo. Consequently I saw him there on 30 October. As he was very busy in his office, he asked me to see him the same evening at his house. Since his last visit to Kalawewa and the Kotmale settlers incident, a lot of commotion has taken place. The minister has decided to transfer the Resident Project Manager and appoint a man of his choice. In my meeting with him, he explained the reasons for this action. I only mentioned to him the hard work done by the RPM and the minister assured me that he was going to give him another good appointment at Colombo, but he did not consider him suitable for RPM's post because, in his view, the RPM lacked initiative and drive and he wanted a tea plantation superintendent to be the new RPM. I met the proposed new man for the first time when the minister brought him along to the opening ceremony.

The next time I met Mr Rohan Wijenaike, the RPM-designate, he was in the room of the Chairman MDB, who had asked me to see him in connection with organization of farmers in the H4 area. The chairman also called over the deputy general manager (marketing and credit) and agreed to my proposal to have a two-tier system of cooperatives in the H4 area—primary cooperatives consisting of turnout groups and a Federation at the Block level with two representatives each from the turnout cooperative. We also discussed the management organization and the chairman asked me to submit a proposal in consultation with Mr Wijenaike. On my way to Galnewa this time, I spent a night with Mr Wijenaike at his tea-estate near Kandy and was pleased to find that we agreed with each other. He agreed with my suggestion that instead of changing the management system, we should concentrate on organizing the farmers because once the farmers got organized, the services become effective and the management system more responsive to the farmers' needs. Without the farmers being organized, the management system can never be effective and will at best benefit only a few.

The other visitors to Kalawewa included an FAO/WHO team of nutrition experts, namely Drs. Payne and Pradillo. I took them to a farmer cultivation committee meeting. Dr Radosavich of USAID also briefly visited the area. He is engaged in drawing up legislation for water management in Sri Lanka, especially the Galoya Irrigation scheme which is being rehabilitated by USAID at a cost of $10 million.

I had a long luncheon discussion with my friend Kapila Wimladharma who was very agitated at the Kotmale settlers incident and felt that the whole thing was set up by the construction people to malign and discredit the Settlement Division. I tried to explain to him that the incident could be traced to the negligence of a settlement division functionary and there was no use blaming anyone else. I do hope Kapila understood. The incident has created really bad feelings between the two MDB Divisions and will adversely affect the work in the field unless remedial action is taken. Since the chairman is an engineer, the others think he did not protect the settlement officers before the minister. The chairman aptly observed that someone has to protect the settlers and he adopted an attitude which to his mind, was in the best interest of the settlers.

On 24 October UN Day was observed with great fervour. Almost the whole of Colombo came to attend the function at the Bandranaike Memorial International Conference Hall. This was followed by a get-together at UNDP offices, where I again met Professor Scarlet

Epstein, my CSP probationer Akbar's tutor. She is an anthropologist and is visiting Colombo in connection with a seminar.

* * *

Colombo
17 November 1979

...I returned yesterday from Galnewa to find out from Manchu's letter that she is still in Paris. I was under the impression that she was now in London as mentioned by Roohi. Hence I had sent her birthday greetings cable to London on 14 November. I rang her up last night in Paris and she was indeed overjoyed. Before that she had been sulking, thinking I had forgotten her birthday. I am keenly awaiting Afshan's arrival tonight.

This morning Jerry, Allauddin Chacha's son, rang up. He has come with the Pakistani golf team. I will be seeing him this evening. Nawab Saeed Khan, Tariq's cousin, is also here these days with my friend Mr Allauddin. They paid a visit to my project area, stayed there for a couple of days and returned with me yesterday. The rains have started now and the weather has improved in Colombo. There is less humidity and it is very pleasant. By the time you come it will get even better.

The visitors to the project in the first half of November included a group of MPs, Professor Epstein, the World Bank team and a few others. This time the largest group of MPs came, 17 in all. Most them were district ministers and were escorted by the deputy minister of Mahaweli. A team of media men also covered their visit. I was able to make some good contacts amongst the media people for Afshan. They were very enthusiastic about her working and helping them when I told them that she has a postgraduate diploma in graphics from the University of London. The ministry is bringing out a magazine on the pattern of the German magazine *Scala*. I hope Afshan finds it worthwhile to associate herself with the magazine. A girl by the name of Sharda is in charge of the magazine section. The MPs' visit this time went quite smoothly. I gave them a briefing in the bus as well as at the Bulnewa Community Training Centre.

Akbar's tutor Professor Epstein paid a visit the following day along with one Mrs Watt. Professor Epstein is quite an opinionated lady and too hasty to jump to conclusions. She has indeed a lot of ideas but so have many others. I told her that if she really wanted her ideas to be put in practice, then she should implement them herself. No one else is going to do it for her. However, I like her enthusiasm. This has prompted her to write to Paul [Ignatieff] that Shoaib has very little assistance and inadequate resources and these should be provided to him especially for the Mahaweli women's programme.

The World Bank team was on its biannual visit and was headed by Mr Stan Baker. Last May when we had met he had asked me what I was doing. I had told him that when he had the time, I would explain it to him. He had said that he would find the time. I did not hear from him again but then I received a radio message from Colombo asking me to be available to meet the team on Friday morning, 8 November. Fortunately it turned out to be a farmers' training day. A day earlier when I had gone to see the training at Bulnewa, I had found a large number of farmers present. On Friday about 58 of the 62 farmers came. The World Bank team spent about three hours there and were very favourably impressed, especially their agriculture expert Mr Andrew Seager. After they had seen the training, I gave a short briefing. The previous day the Canadian member of the team, Mr Saaltink, had especially asked me to emphasize that administrative efficiency improved through turnout groups of farmers. The Additional General Manager (Engineering) told me later that my short briefing had really taught him something new. The World Bank team was especially interested in the fact that I had made the existing administrative structure work instead of suggesting a new one. The team had earlier visited the Huntings experiment in Block 404 and violently disagreed with the proposed structure which had excluded the ministry of agriculture. Mr Baker, the WB team's leader, expressed great admiration for the work being done by me and especially thanked me for helping the World Bank which has put in $19 million in the project, almost 50 per cent of the foreign exchange cost. The total cost of the project is $100 million. The balance in foreign exchange is being provided by the Canadian, British and American governments.

After the team's visit the GM invited me to Colombo to attend the dinner being given in honour of the bank by the chairman. At the dinner on Saturday, I met Mr Sivananam and the secretary of the ministry. He was quite sorry at the RPM's transfer. After dinner, the chairman asked me to remain and later in front of his staff declared that 'Khan is one of us, he is not a foreign expatriate'. Later, he told me that our people do not accept everything that foreigners say but in your case, there has been immediate acceptance. I felt very pleased at this compliment.

Another member of the World Bank Team, Mr Seager, found my work very interesting and entirely agreed with the strategy. We had three sessions together and he concurred with my proposal to strengthen the range level and abolish the field level. I had not expected such quick response.

Amongst the new visitors, Mr John Presswood has recently come to the area as an agriculture extension expert. He is based at Anuradhapura and has been brought to Sri Lanka by the British government for two years. I spoke with him, and I think he could be of great help with the training programme. The RPM-designate, Mr Wijenaike also came, along with another planter Mr Jayawardene, to attend the third Foundation course. I had already told Karunatilleke, the RPM, about their visit. Karu is now reconciled to going away because the minister wants somebody who is always in contact with him. He had told Karu also to get in touch with him if there was any problem. Of course being the correct type of civil servant that Karu is, he could never muster the courage to go to the minister over the head of his superiors. I was happy to see that Karu adopted a very positive attitude towards the visitors and did not show any feelings of resentment about his removal.

Dr (Mrs) Hiranthi Wijemanne, with whom I share my office in Colombo, also came to the project for the health volunteers' training, as did Dr Walter Patrick and Dr Perera of the Health Education Bureau. In Dr Patrick I have found another strong supporter of my programme and we are planning to integrate the health volunteers and the farmer leaders' training programmes.

Prof. Weber of the Asian Institute of Technology (AIT) in Bangkok and Dr Singh of UNDP Dacca who had been invited to Colombo by the Agrarian Research and Training Institute to organize a training course for Mahaweli community development officers, were indeed surprised to learn about the farmers' and project officers' training programme that I had organized in the 'H' Area. Professor Weber commented that this was a much more comprehensive programme than what he had in mind. I welcomed the collaboration with Agricultural Research and Training Institute (ARTI) and AIT in this field. As a follow-up, ARTI research officers paid visits to Kalawewa area to observe the farmer leaders' training sessions as well as the project officers' follow-up course.

Professor Weber made no secret of his annoyance at not having been briefed on the subject. It was only by chance, when he called on the

GM Dr Abeyganawardena, that the latter gave him the portfolio which I had given him, containing all the training material on the 'H' Area.

The ARTI invited me to give a talk on the work I am doing in the 'H' Area at their weekly study circle meeting. After the talk, the Director Dr Subhasingha graciously commented that he understood clearly for the first time the meaning of the 'H' System and the position of the other systems in the Mahaweli development project area.

Another interesting and important visitor to the project in November was Mr Gamini Irrigala, who had raised a political storm with his controversial book *The Truth About Mahaweli*. Now he has joined the ministry as a consultant. I found him a very alert and intelligent man with a quick grasp of issues. I was delighted at his positive reaction to the farmers' training programme. I again met him briefly when he came to Kalawewa with the minister during Christmas. On the minister's observation that the farmers should not become grumblers, as he had noticed in his meeting with a group of farmer leaders, I said to the minister that unless the demands and difficulties of the farmers are attended to, little else could be expected from them. I had noticed a deep apathy building in the Regional and Range level staff, at the lack of action by the project-level officers to the farmers' demands. I thought that the RPM should realize this, especially now that the minister had decided to retain him in the project under Wijenaike. The minister reacted very positively and wanted action taken immediately on the farmers' demands. Mr Irrigola wanted to know the reason for the delay and I told him that the project had been stagnant for the last two months, with the news of the RPM's transfer. It was also the case that priority had been given to other work, rather than to the farmers' training and attending to the needs identified in those training sessions.

I explained to the minister that there was now a forum of 1,290 farmer leaders. If project level officers were to maintain contact with them through the training sessions held fortnightly, most of the farmers' needs could be met. I explained that the farmers' unresolved needs and demands were accumulating and if this state of affairs continued, the farmers would lose confidence in these organizations. I was keen to invite the minister and Mr Irrigola to the project officers' sixth follow-up course which was then in session but the RPM had especially requested me not to do so because of the absence of the DRPMs. In actual fact only one DRPM was absent and the attendance of officers was also quite normal. I felt sorry to have missed this opportunity to expose the minister to the training course. The officers would have also felt encouraged by the minister's presence. I am sure there will be another opportunity.

Mr Hopper, Vice President of the World Bank, met me briefly. We talked in the jeep because I had to rush back to Colombo. He evinced a keen interest and especially wanted me to meet the World Bank sociologist Miss Anna Quandt. A fortnight later she arrived at Galnewa to see me and Miss Dissanayake. Later I learnt that Miss Dissanayake was the minister's sister. I had an interesting discussion with Miss Quandt. She showed keen interest in my approach, especially in upgrading the farmers' human skills and unifying them, as against the common solution of unifying the management system.

UNDP Colombo was quite appalled at Paul Ignatieff's proposal that I should work at the operational level in the 'H' Area. As time passed, I could discern a change in their attitude: from their original stance of wanting feasibility studies requiring 1,200 man-years to be undertaken for the Mahaweli Project they had started to take an interest in the work UNICEF was doing in the 'H' Area. Their programme officer, Ms Broiker, along with two Australian ladies came to Kalawewa to see the farmers' training programme. The farmer leaders are now taking an active role in their work, in organizing women and in identifying needs. The latter include a training programme for women in agricultural extension and a vocational training programme for young girls whose education has been disrupted.

The Norwegian Aid people NORAD (Mr Engibrigsten) especially requested me to assist them in their Hambantota integrated project. With Paul's concurrence, I attended a meeting of the project committee where I explained the 'H' Area situation and the relevance of the Mahaweli experience to their project. The committee members were very interested and the chairman (local government agent) especially requested me to attend the next meeting. I suggested that they also pay a visit to 'H' Area to see things for themselves.

The Mahaweli Project is passing through a phase where a lot of reorganization is being discussed and a new relationship is being forged between the Mahaweli Development Authority and the Mahaweli Development Board. Of late I have been very impressed at the ideas floated by the Chairman MDB, Mr Ladduwehetty. He asked me to write a paper on the Kalawewa administrative structure and responded to my suggestions at length in a letter containing some very pragmatic ideas.

The latest visitor to 'H' Area in this regard was Mr Wickramaratne, the newly appointed Working Director of the MDA. I spent a whole day with him and was very pleased when he asked me to assist the MDA in organizing the farmers' training programme in H5, the MDA's experimental area. This was of special interest to me because I had so far had no meaningful contact with the MDA. Two of the H5 officers also attended the sixth follow-up course.

Another group I met accidentally included Mr Siva Bandara, Additional General Manager (Information) and Dr Colin McKay who are engaged in bringing out a monthly and a quarterly publication (in English) on the Mahaweli Project. At their request I took them to a farmers' training session also. The RPM thought they were a team from NBC TV and that I had invited them. He apologized for having misunderstood. The next time Dr McKay wanted to come, I specifically asked him to ask the MDB to inform the RPM, in order to avoid any misunderstanding.

Things had been going on so smoothly that it was almost too good to be true. Sure enough, I got a sudden jolt when at the end of the sixth follow-up course in late December, one of the regional level officers wanted to have a word with me. I was astonished at what he told me about what the senior officers were saying: whether, prior to Mr Khan's programme, nothing had been done? If this was so then what had they all been doing 'scrapping accounts'. The regional officer who was asked this question in Colombo replied as follows: 'A lot had been done before, and a lot is being done now, with the assistance of Mr Khan. It is true that prior attempts to organize farmers did not succeed and Mr Khan showed us the way.' He did not know the reason for the negative queries; nor could he say who was responsible for them.

Luckily for me the whole mystery was unravelled by the General Manager MDB, Dr Abey Gunawardena, when I called on him on my next visit to Colombo. He asked me if it was true that I had been spending very few days in Galnewa of late. I informed him that on average over the last three months, I had spent 16 days a month at Galnewa, whereas the UNICEF working days for the period averaged no more than 20 days a month. Then he explained to me that this was all started by an interested officer in Colombo, who had seen a World Bank *aide memoire* which greatly praised the farmers' training programme and had dubbed it 'Mr Khan's programme'. He went on to say that this officer, who considers himself an expert in the field, was incensed at the World Bank's observation[2] and started this adverse propaganda. However, he assured me that he would protect my position and ensure that the programme is continued.

I was quite upset at this development, as this was something I wanted to avoid at all costs, having learnt a bitter lesson at Daudzai. It also brought to mind Tariq Siddiqi's advice in Pakistan last June that before I cause jealousies, I should get out of the project. I have done everything possible but still to no avail. Anyway, I met the officer concerned, who incidentally had been a great supporter of the programme and tried to mend fences. I don't know how far I have succeeded in this but our relationship is now not as free and frank as it used to be. To further heighten the situation, the minister, while giving a briefing to the AID Administrator, publicly praised me and this praise was broadcast on the national news. Rohan and Jayantha, the tea planters who have taken over as coordinators in 'H' Area also told me that the minister is fully aware of this incident. I thanked God for this understanding on the part of the policy makers. However, I am now determined to be even more careful. I cannot afford to take any chances with my work.

My meeting in Colombo with Mr Wickramaratne proved to be very productive. Earlier I had called on Mr Sivananam, Secretary Mahaweli Ministry and he had also advised me to see Mr Wickramaratne for developing programmes for Systems 'B' and 'C'. Mr Wickramaratne not only supported my approach, terming it the only grassroots programme he had seen in the Mahaweli area, he also asked for my views on the UNFPA/FAO women's programme, on which I have sent him my comments. He has already written to the Board that this project should be executed by UNICEF since they are already involved in social development of the 'H' Area. I am very happy at forging these links with the Mahaweli Authority. I have already organized a foundation course for their staff in 'H5' area, which was greatly appreciated by their project manager and I hope to organize follow-up courses on the same lines as H1, H2, H7 and H9.

Things are settling down and Karunatillike the RPM is again regaining his poise and confidence, thanks in part to Rohan and Jayantha who are providing him the necessary back-up support. At Rohan's initiative, RPM Karunaratne has also agreed to organize a training programme soon. Their training centre in Block 404 was opened by the Minister on 1 January and we are hoping to inaugurate the foundation course for the RPM Tambutegama's staff there on 12 February 1980.

The UNICEF staff visit from the Colombo office, planned since last October, materialized on 30 January, coinciding with the project staff training programme. I was very pleased that the staff enjoyed their visit to Mahaweli.

The farewell party for Sam Alwis (DRPM Agriculture) was a late night affair at Kalawewa CB. I never realized that there was so much musical talent amongst the project officers. Sam has been transferred to Colombo as Director of Training, with the Agriculture Development Authority. He had been in this area for the last five years and is going to be greatly missed. He is a real gentleman and is extremely knowledgeable about the 'H' Area.

The other visitors to the project included Dr Paire (a Sri Lankan) from the UN Social Development Institute in Manila, along with Mr Dissanayake of the School of Social Work, Colombo. A team from Peradiniya University, headed by the Dean of agriculture, also visited the area at the behest of the minister. I also met the team and suggested that they take up a range for their work instead of a hamlet which they were thinking of adopting. This seems preferable because the range is the lowest administrative tier where services have been organized.

The Sri Lankan ambassadors to China, USA and Italy also visited the project area. The latter two came on a brief visit to the training centre also when the 7th follow-up course was in session. They were accompanied by the GM.

Musarrat has been visiting the project and since her arrival on 24 November 1979, has spent about 33 days in the project area.

The training programme has been extended to areas H4 and H5. When I met Mr Wickramaratne in Colombo, he suggested that I now shift to system 'C' where a training centre is being set up at Grindarkotte. Originally the Huntings were planning to set up a national centre there, but they later decided to change it to a development centre. Earlier in February Mr Frank Dunhill brought Cecil Fonseka, Director-designate of the Centre, to have a talk with me. Subsequently he requested me to meet I.K. Weerawardena, Project Manager-designate of system C to discuss the training programme. After the meeting Mr Dunhill asked me to help organize training courses for the project officers as well as farmers. I.K. Weerawardena evinced real interest in my work and eagerly sought my help. I was very pleased with this development because this ensured the expansion and continuity of the programme started in the 'H' Area. I was also happy to see Frank Dunhill sympathetic to the training programme I had been doing in 'H' Area and wanting to adopt it for system 'C'. Even regarding the administrative structure, he was now open to discussion and prepared to accommodate the ministry of agriculture.

The foundation course for H^4 was inaugurated by the general manager and was well attended by the project staff. Because of Musarrat's impending departure from Sri Lanka, I spent most of the days in Colombo and returned to Galnewa only on 24th after she flew off to Karachi on 21 February.

Prof. Guy Hunter and Mrs Hunter arrived on the 19th from Coimbatore and after spending a few days in Colombo came to Galnewa via Kandy. Guy had detailed discussions with all levels of the project staff and visited both the Kalawewa and Tambuttegama areas. He also addressed the eighth follow-up course. He fully endorsed my strategy of organizing farmers in turnout groups but cautioned against undue haste in federating them in hamlet organizations. He also expressed his apprehension about using community and development staff for input delivery. In his view this was a commercial and management activity and it would not be fair to blame the CD for not doing it. In fact they had no control over the resources in this case and should not be held responsible for such a situation. He rightly pointed out that the agriculture extension staff would put full blame on the CD. As to who should be responsible for this, he thought it should be someone who had control over the distribution system, to make the inputs available.

I was very happy to see Rohan and Jayantha back. While sitting with them at Kalawewa CB, we heard the trumpeting of elephants across the water from H^9 area, which persisted for quite some time and almost sounded like the call of animals in pain. It happened exactly on the day I completed one year at Galnewa (28 February).

I decided that it was time now, one year after I had begun to work, for the UNICEF Representative Paul Ignatieff to meet the people in government and hear from them about the expansion of my work in other systems. Despite his busy schedule, Paul called on the Secretary Mahaweli Ministry, Chairman MDB, General Manager MDB, Secretary Ministry of Plan Implementation and the Executive Director of the Mahaweli Authority. At Paul's suggestion we met with the UN Resident Representative also. The meetings, held in the first week of March, proved very fruitful, especially with Mr Wickramaratne, the Executive Director. He expressed his interest in the UNICEF programmes and wanted me to formulate proposals immediately for training newly recruited staff in system 'C'. I did so within a fortnight, and he accepted them in their entirety. In fact, he came all the way to MDB to meet me and then took me to the ministry to discuss the details with the Project Manager I.K. Weerawardena, and the Project Coordinator, Austin Perera. I found both of them extremely pleasant fellows. In no time, we were able to work out a detailed plan, which I followed up with the training schedule. A few days later we finalized a plan to hold the course from 5–28 May. It was very gratifying for me indeed.

Back in 'H' area, however, things got a little muddled up with the RPM, Mr Karunatilleke, showing some reservations towards the programme. So long as he did not oppose it, things carried on smoothly, but once his reservations began to filter down to the regional and range level officers, I became quite apprehensive. Rohan Wijenaike tried to reason with the RPM, when it transpired that the RPM was smarting about my having said to the minister last November that the farmers' complaints identified in the training sessions were not being attended to, which resulted in the farmers being dissatisfied. Since these complaints were usually reflected in the recommendations of the follow-up courses, the RPM criticized the follow-up courses and wanted the monitoring and progress reviews to be excluded from these courses, and the content limited to theoretical training. I tried to explain to him (i) that these were job-specific and problem-oriented training sessions and (ii) that the follow-up course was also a monitoring and evaluation mechanism. However, he seems to have developed a mental block to all arguments and suggestions. I told the minister bluntly that the chairman and the GM may be with me but if he was not, the programme had no chance of success.

In view of the RPM's attitude and the fact that the training in H4 and H5 and system C has also become my responsibility, I have decided to carry out an evaluation of the training done so far in the Kalwewa area and then submit a detailed paper with recommendations and suggestions about the future course of the training programme in the Kalawela area, based on the findings of the evaluation. In fact the GM and the secretary, ministry of plan implementation had also suggested (during Paul's visit with them) that an evaluation of the programme be carried out.

I am quite amazed and distressed at the similarities between what happened in Daudzai [Pakistan] and what is happening here. The only difference, to my good fortune, is that the people higher up and lower down agree with me and it is only a couple of people at the lower policy level and the project operational level who seem to be at loggerheads with the programme. When the Additional GM, Mr Wimaladharma spoke at the end of the first follow-up course in H4, many of the things he said were in sharp contrast to what he had said a few months earlier at the fourth H4 area follow-up course. The World Bank observations really brought out that there had been no improvement because of the farmer leaders' training programme. This caused quite a bit of consternation amongst the regional and range level officers, as they came to discuss it with me and openly told me that they did not agree with what Mr Wimaladharma was saying. What bothered them was that even the RPM seemed to share his views and was reported to have remarked that the farmers come only because of the ten rupees they were given to attend the training sessions. The regional officers retorted that if this was so then the attendance should have been 100 per cent and not 70 per cent. I tried to reassure them and urged them to rely on their own conscience and on what the farmers felt about the programme. However, I knew very well that this was of little comfort to them. They are on the horns of a dilemma: on one side is a programme which they genuinely believe to be good and effective, and on the other are their two superiors (the RPM and the Additional GM), who seem to have reservations about the programme. The Additional GM has even berated them for the interest they have been taking in the programme. They wanted me to show them the way but I could only preach patience and hope for the best.

On one of his visits to the Republic of Maldives Paul Ignatieff had promised the president that he would persuade UNICEF to help in the social development of the islands. As a sequel to this promise, Paul sent me off to the capital, Male. I spent nearly a week there, including a visit to one of the islands. The Maldives is unique in that it consists of over 200 inhabited islands. The largest island (Male) is about one square mile in area. A group of islands form an atoll, geologically described as a collapsed volcano. I have never seen such beautiful shades of sea as I saw in the Maldives.

I discovered the most self-reliant rural community in the islands. There is no bureaucratic set-up. One of the islanders is appointed as the island chief, and the island community is responsible for the development and social and welfare needs of the islanders. The central government at Male pays precious little attention, except that its representative, the atoll chief, pays occasional visits and sees that law and order is maintained. I considered the situation in the Maldives ideal for a 'diagnostic survey' to help the islanders meet their needs themselves. Outside intervention is needed only in the form of some resources which are beyond the reach of the islanders. Accordingly, I proposed a strategy and was delighted to hear from Richard Bridle, our liaison officer in Male, that the government would accept it. Considering that in the beginning, the National Planning Agency, in particular their World Bank Consultant, Dr Ali Soleman, took me to be a social worker rather than a social planner, I was very happy with the news. I was most impressed by young Richard, who started with a sceptical attitude about the whole project and grasped the fundamentals of the strategy I was proposing so expertly and so quickly that the discussion paper he prepared at the end of my visit was a lucid, well-argued and complete document from my point of view.

In Male I also ran into Baz Muhammad Khan, who knew me from Peshawar and is now the manager of the Habib Bank in Male. We visited a tourist island, one of previously 200 uninhabited islands which have been converted into tourist resorts. The island reminded me of the Village at Habarana, near Kalawewa. The airport is located on an island exclusively used for that purpose, about a 15-minute boat ride from Male. Male is nothing but a concrete jungle. The housing is like that in Afghanistan's capital, Kabul, minus the greenery and with no elbow room. The guest house in which I was staying, was only 20 paces away from the jetty. The National Planning Agency office was another 50 yards away. All the government ministries were housed in a row on the water-front. Each ministry consisted of two rooms on the ground floor and two at the top, except for the big ministries like fisheries and foreign affairs. Of course, the most imposing and the biggest building belonged to national security, but a typical ministry is headed by a minister, assisted by a director or an Under-Secretary and no one else. It is really a make-believe world.

On my return from Male, I went straight to Galnewa where Tariq Farooqi, the UNICEF auditor from New York visited me. He proved a very pleasant person and delightful company. Tariq had formerly belonged to the Pakistan audit and accounts service. Everyone was pleasantly surprised to find him so understanding and helpful.

Two groups from the water workshop organized by UNICEF New York visited Mahaweli. I was very happy to meet Martin Bayer and Paul Biron once again. One member of the group, who was the UNICEF representative in one of the Latin American countries, came up to me after the visit to the area and said, 'Nowhere have I seen

UNICEF funds more properly utilized'. However, I was quite irked at the questioning of the UNICEF regional office man from Delhi about the project funding and the circumstances leading to the acceptance of the project by UNICEF.

The other group was the UNFPA needs mission headed by Julia Henderson, the former Secretary General of the International Planned Parenthood Federation (IPPF). Julia and I recognized each other immediately, as I had served as a resource person to IPPF in 1976. The coordinator in Colombo had especially requested me to meet this group. One of the members of the group, Mrs Abdullah said to me after the field visit that this was the only project they had so far seen in Sri Lanka that had a genuine element of community participation.

Immediately on the heels of these groups came a group of Nepalese development officers at the behest of ARTI (Appropriate Rural Technology Institute). Since all these groups had expressed the desire to meet me and see the project, the RPM thought that I was inviting them all to visit. I tried to make it clear to the RPM that the UNFPA needs mission was sponsored by the ministry of plan implementation and the Nepalese by the ARTI. I don't know if I succeeded. The ARTI research officers in the group told me that AIT Bangkok, which had been invited to organize a training programme in System 'H' after seeing our programme, had observed that it was very comprehensive and there was no need for another one in the immediate future.

Katherine, Paul's wife, had mentioned before I left for Male that she might come with friends to explore the ruins of Ritigala. Paul, Katherine and their two children and a friend arrived on the last Saturday of March. For the first time since I had got it my car broke down so I reached Kalawewa CB by taking a lift in one of the transport vans. Paul felt very concerned and said that if not a Range Rover (which I had jokingly asked him to order for me during his last visit) at least a more reliable mode of transport was certainly needed.

The next morning we set out to discover Ritigala. I vaguely recalled having seen a signpost showing the direction to Ritigala on the Habarana-Anuradhapura Road. Paul was quite sceptical about the whole venture but Katherine, fortified with maps and guidebooks, was determined to find it. Luckily my hunch proved correct and we found the signpost intact. As we proceeded on the road (really only a narrow track) leading to Ritigala we started having doubts about the direction. We finally accosted a herdsman minding his cattle. To my great surprise and delight, he left his herd and got into the car to take us to the ruins. Sure enough we found the place. We also discovered the signpost, which should have been on the track, lying safely in the keeper's office. Without the herdsman, we could not have found the place so easily.

There was a paved path up to the hilltop. We were told by the local guide that these were the ruins of royal abodes. However, on checking up the details, it transpired that these were monasteries and only monks used to live there, not Queen Amika as we had been told.

Last week Paul showed me his assessment of my work for the last 12 months. He had graded me outstanding from A to Z except in regard to punctuality in attending office and meetings. He told me that when he said 'B' for this column instead of 'A', Priya Coomaraswamy, his Secretary looked at him in disbelief while taking the dictation. Paul told her that he had to say 'B' somewhere otherwise the people in New York would not believe the report. Under the UN system of staff assessment, a copy of the report is given to the staff member concerned. Paul has been so generous, understanding and supportive of my work that it really came as a shock to me when he confided in me that he was due to leave on transfer for New York in July. I considered this no less than a catastrophe for the programme. Paul did not agree with me and tried to reason from every possible angle that it would not be so. He may be proved correct but I know very well from my past experience that support of the type that Paul gave me is critical for the success of such programmes. I am reminded of the situation where an expert of the calibre of Akhtar Hameed Khan found himself totally helpless when I had left Daudzai on a six-month visit abroad. It seemed to me that Paul is playing the role I was playing in relation to Akhtar Hameed Khan and Daudzai.

The General Manager, Dr Abeygunawardena, who has been a great supporter of my work informed me that the minister was visiting Galnewa on 10 April 1980 to participate in the Sinhala New Year celebrations and it would be nice if I was there. I had been planning to return to Colombo on the 8th after my presentation on 'community participation' to the UNICEF staff. I had come to Colombo on 31 March—the day Paul returned to Colombo from Galnewa after inaugurating the day care centre. Three weeks later the roof of the centre (made of coconut branches, collapsed. I thanked God that it did not happen on the day of the inauguration when it was packed with small children. There appears to have been a technical flaw, because the roofs of all other centres also came down. Fortunately, this happened before any of them was opened. Since these were designed by the DRPM (WM), a quiet and reserved man, everyone seems to be taking malicious pleasure at this happening. However, Athula is quite unruffled and is getting the roofs repaired. I have impressed upon him the need for doing this urgently to stop the gossip.

I don't know what Paul's reaction will be when I tell him that the centre he inaugurated, has collapsed, but the most humorous thing was that I received a protest from the department of probation and childcare (through UNICEF) that they were not invited to the opening ceremony. I think they will thank their stars for this when they learn of the latest happening.

The minister came and the New Year's function was a great success. It all happened so spontaneously that everyone enjoyed it, despite some mismanagement. I have always been impressed by the dedication and devotion of the large number of people working at all levels of the project. If they fail at times, it is because either it is beyond them or they just do not know how to do it. I have still to come across a single case of intentional dereliction of duty.

Rohan Wijenaike told me that the minister expected me at the Kalwewa Circuit Bungalow in the evening, I returned from there late at night with the invitation to join him at breakfast also. The following morning, with the RPM present, he asked me when my contract would end. I replied that it had another year to run. He asked me to tell him when to write for an extension because I had to complete the project. I wondered if Rohan had reported my earlier conversation with the RPM, in which I had told him that I did not want to be an obstacle in his way. I was there to help him and not to be a nuisance to him. Perhaps the minister thought this the appropriate occasion to let the RPM know that he wanted me to stay. The minister has really been very kind and supportive of my work. The RPM is indeed a bundle of complexes and impossible to get along with in matters where he seems to have developed mental blocks.

The training programme for system 'C' commenced on 5 May 1980 at Bulnewa community training centre. It was inaugurated by Mr Panditratne, Director General of the Mahaweli Authority and the Chairman of the ruling political party. I had always been in dread of him because I never got the chance to explain the work I was doing except in a very hurried fashion. Being from the 'old school' he has some fixed ideas, but when he said that his main concern was to train all the farmers, because it is they who produce, I knew that our objectives were the same.

At lunch he said that, although he did not believe in dealing only with leaders, he was making this concession to me and the World Bank, and agreeing to 'turnout groups' and their leaders. I explained to him that the farmer leaders were selected as a means of communication with the rest of the farmers, because with the present staffing intensity each range-level officer had to deal with nearly 1,000 farmers. Since the authority had now appointed a unit manager to deal with only 200 farmers, it might be possible for him to be directly in contact with all of them but at the Block level, it is only with their leaders (2 per turnout) that the experts of the different disciplines would be able to interact. Later M. Wikramratne also raised this issue and expressed the director general's anxiety in this regard. I assured him that there was no conceptual difference. Rather, it was a technique which could easily be adapted to the new management system. Frank Dunhill, who had also come for the inauguration, spoke highly of the design of the training programme and the concept of follow-up courses in system 'C'. I was very pleased when I thanked Mr Panditratne for coming to inaugurate the course and he put his arm around my shoulders in response.

The next morning, at Wikramaratne's suggestion, he visited the farmer leaders' training session at Kallankuttiya. I was later told that the visit had gone well and the farmers had exhibited great discipline and intelligence. A Canadian team with Mr Saaltink also came and sat through part of my lecture.

Mahe Wikramaratne has been hinting that I move to system 'C'. Even Mr Panditrane mentioned over lunch that it was not good to stay in one place too long and I should come to Grindarkotte (the HQ of system 'C'). He pointedly said that he was sure the RPM would not object. I thought in my heart that he would be quite happy. Last week the RPM had invited the Principal of the School of Social Work, Mr Dudley Dissanayake, to organize or reorganize the training programme. Mr Dissanayake came and talked to the project officers and at my invitation with me also but the RPM did not consider it advisable to discuss this reorganization with Mr Dissanayake in my presence. Last Sunday, when I raised the issue, he said 'Well, you and Dissanayake can decide about the programme'. Everyone else told me that if I withdrew from the programme, the training would come to an end. I also knew that all the work done so far would come to naught, but I have not yet decided what steps to take.

Fortunately the review has been completed and it could be the pertinent document to raise the issues for discussion and to obtain a decision by the policy makers, provided they have the time and inclination. Jayantha Jayweardena told me that Rohan Wijenaike had already brought the matter to the notice of the General Manager and that he might come next week to discuss it with the RPM. I know it will not come to anything because the RPM has a closed mind and no one can persuade him to change his thinking on the matter. The worst example of it was when at the last training session, he stopped discussion on whether training of farmers should be continued in H9, after the take-over of the Ceylon Tobacco Company because in his view this was a management issue. He has sent written instructions that management and monitoring matters should not be discussed in the follow-up courses.

At Paul Ignatieff's behest, I had prepared and submitted my proposals concerning the expansion of the Mahaweli project. Paul had insisted that I include an extension of the consultancy for the next three years. Last Thursday Alex Marshall of UNFPA rang up Paul and came over to discuss their project for Mahaweli with UNICEF collaboration. Last month, UNFPA consultant Dr Loquian had visited me and we met later in Galnewa. We discussed the areas where UNFPA could come in. I was especially interested in their assistance for farmer leaders' training as UNICEF appeared a little diffident to put in half a million dollars into this activity. I was, therefore, very happy to see Dr Loquians' proposals which included the farmer leaders' training component. Paul was also pleased at UNFPA's intention of putting in nearly one and a half million dollars in the next three years. We met again on Saturday in Alex's office. After that meeting Paul asked Mahazent, the UNICEF Programme Officer who had succeeded Eimi Watanabe, to forward to New York the expanded project outline I had prepared. Of the total $3.5 million I had projected 1.5 million were likely to be put in by UNFPA. For the balance would they like a fresh noting for the 1981 Board, or possibly funding from the general reserve from which the on-going project was funded. I was gratified at this development.

Richard Bridle, his wife Clare and Afshan came last week. He was on a short visit from Male and wanted to discuss the terms of reference for the Consultant for the Maldives. The Government of Maldives had given him the go-ahead on the lines of the proposals we had made while I was there.

I considered this an appropriate time to inform the GM about the RPM's attitude towards training. The review I had undertaken was now complete and I had already given a draft copy to the GM. I rang him up, ostensibly to discuss our forthcoming visit to South Korea, and he invited me to visit him at his home. He referred to the work being done by the RPM and asked my view in the matter. I told him about the latest situation regarding the training programme and my lack of rapport with the RPM. Dr Abeygunawardena was a little taken aback but he said that the turnout leaders had even complained to the Chairman that they were going to resign as no action was being taken on their complaints. He offered to speak again to the RPM. I told him that nothing would come of it because I had already tried every possible way with him but to no avail. I pointed out that my intention in saying this was simply to keep him up to date with these developments so he did not learn of the matter through a third source. I had always held the GM in great esteem and I considered it my obligation to tell him about the factual position.

The promotion of Weerakoddy, one of the community development officers, to Assistant General Manager of Training, was ordered by the GM at my request yet the RPM did not convey the orders to him; nor did he implement the promotion. Instead he was trying to keep Weerakoddy as his DRPM. Fortunately Weerakoddy did not agree and, at Rohan's initiative, he will now be under Rohan as the Incharge of the Training Unit. Things appear to be brightening up now, just as I was growing dismayed about the prospects of the training programme in the Kalawewa area.

On the other hand, the training of system 'C' project officers has been proceeding very smoothly. The second follow-up course for H4 was also a great success and with the setting up of the training unit, I am confident that the programme will get a great impetus in the H4 area. The programme in H5 is already proceeding smoothly.

The other day I received a message from the GM requesting me to meet the Director General, Mr Panditratne, on Saturday 17 May in his office (in Colombo) at 0830 hours. In any case I was planning to return to Colombo on Friday. It seems that my assessment of Mr Panditratne's last visit, when he came to inaugurate the system 'C' training course, was accurate: he had found something worthwhile in the training programme I had begun in System 'H'.

The purpose of the meeting Mr Panditratne had called and to which I was invited was to discuss the concept of building plans of the proposed development centre at Grindra Kotte in system 'C'. Mahe Wikramaratne asked me what I thought of the plans and later confided that he wanted me to be fully associated with it, so that the Centre did not develop into an 'extension of the Sussex Institute of Development Studies'.

The training programme for system 'C' proceeded smoothly and ended on 28 May 1980. The consensus was that the programme had been a resounding success. The project manager I.K. Weerawardena went so far as to say that he had received offers to organize training programmes for system 'C' from several institutions, including one from Bangkok in collaboration with the Agricultural Research and Training Institute (ARTI), Colombo. He said he had found the UNICEF consultant's approach to be most suitable and decided to ask him to organize the training programme. He expressed the hope that there would be greater collaboration with UNICEF and welcomed my offer to arrange follow-up courses. I am quite pleased at the way the course went; being the first long course, I had been concerned about its impact. This course has helped me in establishing good rapport with the Authority, its officials and the field level officers of system 'C'. The quality of this relationship is extremely crucial for the success of a programme like the one I want to implement there. I am feeling elated that I have lived up to Mahe Wikramaratne's expectations and not let him down. He had been the prime mover in getting me involved in system 'C'.

The Review finally came out. I was pleased at its presentation. Paul Ignatieff commended me on the report. In my meeting with Mahe Wickramaratne, I told him about my problems with the RPM. Mahe responded that he thought the RPM was rather narrow-minded and lacking in calibre and could be made to behave if admonished by people in authority. He offered to raise the issue with the chairman and GM in his next meeting. In the meanwhile, I had found that the RPM was planning a training programme with the principal of the School of Social Work and had asked the training officer, Mr Welikela, to set up the programme for the next follow-up course. As I was away with system 'C' trainees, Welikela could not discuss it with me. The RPM, knowing full well that I was not there, wanted it done immediately. On my return Welikela told me that the RPM wanted one day (of the training course) to be allocated to the principal and one day to the normal course. As the RPM had already notified me in writing that from the 1st of May, he would like the programme changed, I told Welikela that I did not want anything to do with the training of the staff until the RPM clarified exactly what he wanted. Perhaps all this was conveyed to him.

Most probably the GM in Colombo also had a word with him because on his return from there, he was a changed person. He came to my room and requested a discussion on the training programme later in the day. Fortunately Rohan also came along. We found his attitude quite different from what we had seen when in our earlier discussions. Now he professed that training was entirely my domain and would continue the way I wanted it. He even solicited a message for me for the next course, as I told him that I might be away in Korea. I simply marvelled at the spinelessness and *naiveté* of the man. Although, I had no illusion that he would give any real support to the programme, this would at least help clear the confusion in the minds of other officers who did not know which way to go.

The trip to South Korea was a unique experience. As the minister wished Rohan to attend the seminar in place of the GM, almost at the last minute, frantic cables and calls had to be made to Bangkok and Korea. Fortunately, Rohan's clearance came through and he was able to follow me a day later. What I saw in the rural areas of Korea strengthened my resolve in the principles of rural development I had learnt from Akhtar Hameed Khan and had followed at Daudzai and in Mahaweli. Here was a situation where a Daudzai or a Comilla project had been extended and replicated countrywide with tremendous results. What we saw was almost a carbon copy of what Akhtar Hameed Khan had been advocating. Coincidentally, I was quite pleased to get a report from Akhtar Hameed Khan in Karachi about his involvement in an urban project at Orangi (Township).

The study seminar had been organized by Steve Umemoto in collaboration with the UNICEF Korea office. I was quite amused when Steve introduced me in the working committee to Elizabeth Preble from the New York office. She appeared a bit aloof in the beginning but turned out to be a very warm and nice person. I was quite pleased to make her acquaintance.

The seminar proved to be unique in many ways. The first two days at a Local Administration Training Institute included work from 0600 to 2200 hours including a two kilometre jog in the morning and near-military regimentation in the dormitory where I shared the room with

Steve, Rohan, Park Lee, Housey and another person. Having been elected leader of the room in my absence, I had to present the others for room inspection at night. At the close of the session, I made a speech which was greatly appreciated by the hosts and by my fellow colleagues especially Kitachai from Thailand who almost condemned me as Director of LATI. At most of the places, Rohan and I had to share rooms and I must say Rohan proved an excellent companion and roommate. The Governor of Suwan gave us a dinner and by public acclaim, I had to make another speech which was unanimously applauded because I told them that what they had achieved in rural agriculture could not have been accomplished without full community participation and that is what impressed us most and not their buildings, which any government could build.

I had persuaded Steve to form a South Asian group with Sri Lanka, Nepal and Bangladesh for preparation of the report. Ashraf and Quddus from Sylhet and Comilla proved great friends and so did Pitambar from Nepal. We were able to finalize our report two days in advance which meant we had more leisure at the end of the study seminar. On my return I stopped over at Nagoya and Manila.

My return from Korea found me at loggerheads with my colleagues at the UNICEF office in Colombo. My daughter Afshan, who is very friendly with Mahzent, expressed her apprehensions at the misgivings expressed by the people at UNICEF about expanding the Mahaweli project. Although I knew about the reservations of other programme officers, I dismissed Afshan's apprehensions as unfounded. I could understand Marty's reaction, as she is a very difficult person to get along with but I was surprised at Martin's attitude especially when Mahzent showed me his comments on the UNFPA project. I decided to meet him directly, a move which proved very fruitful and Martin suggested that I should circulate a note to other programme officers. He also confirmed my views about Marty and gave me some background on her attitudes.

On 18 July 1980, the first meeting of the review committee was to be held, to consider the expansion of the programme through 1981–83. I suggested to Mahzent that we hold a meeting of the Programme Officers prior to the meeting of the review committee. In Mahzent's and Paul's absence, the meeting was a complete fiasco. Marty not only opposed the expansion of the day care centres but also insinuated that the approach I had advocated had no backing from the Mahaweli authorities. I had called on Mahe Wickramaratne and at his suggestion met Gudamunne, Secretary-General of the Authority, who was going to be the chairman of the review committee. Since Lalit did not know the background, I briefed him. Although, I had sensed a certain aloofness earlier, after the meeting I felt satisfied with his understanding of the situation. I had already briefed the GM of the MDB who had promised to attend the meeting.

Mr Gudamunne had suggested that, in consultation with Mahe, I should arrange a course in group dynamics in collaboration with the Institute of Management for officers of the level of RPM, so as to enable them to understand the approach I was advocating, and to help them understand that farmers' complaints should not be understood as criticism. I sincerely thought that he had a good point.

Dr Hiranhthi Wijemanne, after meeting Mrs De Silva, the DGM of settler studies, had written a confidential note for record, expressing great dismay at the views of Mrs Silva and the RPM about the accounting system. Being the wife of an additional secretary, Mrs Silva wields much greater influence and power than a person of her status would normally have. I knew that she had been completely biased by Kapila, as she and he used to share an office. Her attitude towards all my work had been negative and all my attempts to explain my position had always fallen on deaf ears. Hence, I was quite happy when the Authority became the *de facto* power and I felt I would not have to reckon with Mrs Silva anymore.

Unfortunately, my judgement proved totally wrong. In the meeting on the 18th, Mr Gudamunne took exactly the same line as Mrs Silva. In fact, from the beginning he gave me the cold shoulder and cut me out when I tried to speak and brushed aside my suggestion to circulate the revised agenda and the working paper prepared for the meeting. Later, the working paper was circulated when detailed proposals were taken up.

While taking up the proposals he skipped over the consultancy and when Dr Abeygunawardena specifically took it up, saying that he must narrate what had been done and why the consultancy must be continued, Mr Gudamunne said that he was negotiating with UNDP to have a consultancy and research cell in the Authority. On Paul's clarification about the UNICEF consultancy, Mr Gudamunne said he was not discussing personalities. Later on he modified his statement to say that 'Mr Khan can be in the proposed research cell'. He also referred to the report of the School of Social Work which was opposed to setting up the day care centres. I knew that Mr Gudamunne had been extensively briefed and he had chosen to accept their version and go along with them.

I felt very disappointed and realized why the letter relating to my extension, written at Mahe's behest, had elicited no response for over a month. Mahe had told me that he had passed it on to Mr Gudamunne. Mahe could not attend the meeting because he was away in Washington. Paul Ignatieff was also very concerned but dismissed my suggestions to pull me out of Mahaweli. When he came to Kalawewa with Liv Ullmann he said to me 'You have such powerful friends: misuse them.' I had avoided doing this so far but Rohan insisted that I should stay on and meet the minister on Monday when he was due to come to Kalawewa. I had to send a radio message to I.K. Weerawardena to postpone the course for system 'C' to Tuesday.

When Professor Ted Scudder, whom I had briefly met at Colombo, came to Kalawewa, I had three long sessions with him. I mentioned to him how the minister had bracketed my name with him while talking to Director AID and Radio Sri Lanka broadcasted this comment. The discussions with Professor Scudder were very frank and fruitful. As he is the supervising professor for Kapila Wimladharma's doctoral studies, he knew Kapila's version which, in brief, appeared to be that Kapila had thought of turnout groups back in the 1970s while doing the feasibility study for system 'H' and yet all the credit had been taken by me. I told Ted (as he insisted on my calling him) that my proposal for training, wherein the turnout group was conceived, was submitted on 21 March 1979 whereas I met Kapila for the first time in April. The feasibility study for system 'H' had no mention of the organization of farmers at turnout level. I think the professor was convinced that I did not plagiarize Kapila's idea. However, he advised me to get out of the Kalawewa area in view of the RPM's hostility and to concentrate on H5 and system 'C'. His advice was almost the same as Tariq's; that I should get out as soon as I started exciting jealousy.

When Professor Scudder praised my approach and the work done so far in organizing and training the farmers, I asked him the reason for lack of understanding on the part of the RPM. His diagnosis was that being a very religious and highly conservative man, the RPM could not appreciate this approach and was wedded to conventional and traditional approaches. I think Ted was right.

One of the most glamorous visitors to the Mahaweli project system 'H' was the world famous Norwegian actress Liv Ullmann. She came by helicopter escorted by Paul Ignatieff and the minister for Colombo hospitals. The party also included her friend from Yugoslavia, Mr Drajon Babic, and Mr and Mrs Ling of UNICEF, New York. As her helicopter landed forty minutes earlier than scheduled I arrived to find Paul helping her onto a Ceylon Transport bus, which was passing by on its way from Galnewa to Kekirawa. This was the first time that I also got into a CTB bus.

I was quite nervous, having little experience of dealing with visitors like Miss Ullmann. But one look at her rid me of all my misgivings—there was no artificiality and no *hauteur*. She appeared so natural that it put me completely at ease. She came earlier than scheduled and left 90 minutes later than scheduled. During this period she visited a school, a woman health volunteer, a day care centre, the Bulnewa community training centre, a hand pump well, the water treatment plant at Galnewa, and finally the Aukana Buddha. She was very perceptive and a born actress. At the school she was so natural that she established perfect rapport with the children without knowing a word of their language. I had seldom witnessed a more moving scene. At the community training centre, she was most impressed by the unity and organization among the farmers, which she said was lacking even amongst farmers in Norway. At the well pump, she instinctively put her feet under the water to wash the dust away. In this she reminded me of Musarrat.

We were travelling in the UNICEF bus. Being the tour guide, I was sitting just behind Miss Ullmann who had chosen to sit in the front seat. After the school visit, she observed that language barriers can make it so difficult to communicate. I responded by saying that what she did at the school could not have been conveyed by any number of spoken words. She seemed quite pleased. After visiting the community training centre and meeting the farmers, she turned round to me and said 'this must all be very satisfying to you.' I nodded in agreement.

We were already behind schedule. A big stone got stuck between the bus tires but fortunately it was quickly dislodged with a jack. Banda had prepared a fabulous lunch. Paul and the Minister, Dr Attapattu, whom I had met two years ago on my way to Nagoya, made short speeches. Liv Ullmann also made a brief speech and recalled the last lines of the play *Diary of Anne Frank* in which she acted when she was eighteen (now she is forty but looks much younger), saying that human beings everywhere have goodness in them whatever they may do.

The minister did not come to Kalawewa on Monday, 28 July 1980. His younger brother, who had been to the US for treatment for a heart condition, had died there and the minister went to Colombo to receive his body. I proceeded to system 'C' to conduct the postponed training course for the project officers at Mahiyangana. To my surprise and pleasure Rohan and Jayntha also joined me at the Circuit Bungalow that night. The follow-up course went very well. I was also very pleased to see the progress made by the project staff in implementing the worker-settlers scheme. The potential settlers had responded to the challenge in a most positive manner, and the groups were well organized by the group leaders.

I was also greatly impressed by the rapport forged by the Project Manager, I.K. Weerawardena, with the settlers and his staff. There appeared to be complete harmony and understanding, unlike the situation in the Kalawewa area.

Before leaving for Mahiyangana, I received a radio message asking me to attend a meeting at the Authority on the 29th at which the proposals for extending the UNICEF Project were being reconsidered. I had no desire to attend another meeting there after the treatment meted out to me by Mr Gudamunne at the last meeting. Fortunately, as the date coincided with the system 'C' training course, I sent a radio message regretting my inability to attend the meeting.

On my return to Colombo I found the situation confused and dismal. Paul tried to rationalize it but I knew it was nothing but personal jealousy and a vindictive attitude on the part of some people, and that Lalit Goodamunne was playing into their hands. Still, at Paul Ignatieff's insistence I went with him to see Lalit again. The final outcome of this discussion was that I should write a position paper on the comprehensive training programme for the Mahaweli project. Paul was also toying with the idea of postponing my leave and getting something finalized regarding the training programme, because in the meeting on the 29th, while all other proposals were accepted, the consultancy and training proposals were deferred. Paul was keen that during his forthcoming visit to New York he should be able to put forward the government's request to the New York headquarters. However, even Paul was reconciled to letting things drift for the time being and asked me to return from leave before his departure on 29 September.

Paul left for the Maldives and I listlessly prepared the position paper, which I knew nobody would read. In fact, however, it turned out to be a useful exercise. I presented it to Mr Jayawardene of the Authority, as asked by Lalit. He, of course, had no comment to make on the paper and agreed with almost everything, but was reluctant to accept anything without Lalit's approval. Martin Griffiths of UNICEF who had gone along with me to discuss the training proposals with Jayawardene, tried to get some sort of commitment from him but without success. I must say that Martin has been a real source of strength to me and a genuine supporter of my work.

A day after the minister's brother was cremated, Rohan rang me up to say that he had met the minister and spoken to him about the whole matter. The minister was apparently very distressed and asked to see me. The following day I met him at his residence in the morning and explained the whole situation to him, supported by relevant letters accepting the training programme and its extension to system 'C'. I pointedly stated to him that Lalit's attitude had not only belittled my position in the eyes of my UNICEF colleagues, it had depicted me as having fed everyone wrong information regarding the UNICEF programme in the Mahaweli area and my consultancy. I requested him to clarify whether or not I was needed. If not, it would be much better to inform UNICEF of that fact. The minister reacted very strongly and said 'This is my Ministry. What I say will be done. I have already told you that I want you to continue and complete the project. Who are they to say otherwise?' He also asked me to ask Paul to see him immediately on his return from the Maldives. He also promised to send for Lalit and speak to him as I requested him to win over Lalit to the programme, in the interest of the project. On Paul's return I mentioned what the minister had said. He did not seem very hopeful but promised to see him. I took the flight on Thursday the 7 August for London via Karachi on annual leave.

In London, Felicia (Mahzent's secretary) sent me a photocopy of the request made by Lalit to UNICEF through the External Resources Division for the extension of the programme from 1981 through 1983, including the consultancy and the training programmes. A specific request was also made for the extension of my contract for another two years. True to his word the minister had taken immediate and effective action. I knew even before I left Colombo that he had already spoken to Lalit and Mahe Wickramaratne because the latter had told me so on the phone. On my return to Colombo, when I attended the reception to bid farewell to Paul and to welcome the newly arrived representative Dr (Mrs) Hoda Badran, Lalit came and greeted me very warmly and said all that had happened in the past should be forgotten, and now we should look ahead.

When I thanked him for the letter requesting that my contract be extended he said that he had taken the initiative of asking for two years instead of one. Later, the minister confirmed this fact. Obviously, he was under the impression that they had agreed only to one year. He was happy to learn that the programme has been extended to three years. I must say the real credit goes to Rohan Wijenaike who raised the issue in the strongest possible terms with the minister at the first available opportunity. But for Rohan's initiative the matter would have dragged on and caused more unpleasantness and unhappiness. On return, at Rohan's behest, he and I went and thanked the minister. I also paid a courtesy call on Lalit and I must say he was very polite and warm.

The visit to London was like a very happy and pleasant dream; it passed in a flash. I was back and not even aware I had been away. All that is left of it is an acute and recurrent melancholy that reminds me that something precious has been left behind.

The forty-seven days that I spent with Musarrat surrounded by Roohi, Afshan, Manchu, Shelley and three grandchildren Sarah, Amil and Zeeshan seem too happy and too good to be real. Suddenly, from the solitude of Galnewa, I had been transported to a different world. On the return journey in the aeroplane, when suddenly I looked at my watch, which showed a quarter to four GMT, I felt a sudden stab at my heart thinking that today my child would have to take a bus home from school. Tariq Farooqui, our auditor at the New York headquarters had seen my lonely existence on his last visit to Mahaweli and had vowed to do something to take me out of it. When he met me in London on his return from home leave, he mentioned an opening in Egypt. He wanted me to write to the newly appointed UNICEF Representative (Mr Krueger) but I thought it better to wait for Mr Krueger to ask for my services if he so wished. I was, therefore, surprised to learn from Paul Ignatieff that the NY Headquarters had already asked for my transfer to Cairo. The proposal would have taken effect but for Paul's resistance and the opposition of the newly appointed UNICEF Representative to Sri Lanka, Dr (Mrs) Hoda Badran. Both Paul and Hoda Badran agreed to let me go to Cairo early next year and see how things might work out. Dr Badran (an Egyptian) was even contemplating the idea of my providing consultancy services to both places.

Paul left on the 1 October 1980. Apparently he was very pleased with the government's decision to extend the Mahaweli project. Even before NY headquarters could respond to the extension request, Paul had talked the Swiss government into channelling US$135,000 in aid to the Mahaweli project to cover the consultancy and the farmer leaders' training for 1981. He was planning to stop in Berne on his way to New York to finalize the proposal and had already received clearance from the NY Headquarters by phone. The amount of support and help Paul gave me in my work was indeed incredible. His commitment to the approach I had adopted in the project was complete and unshakable. He was a great source of strength. His going away has saddened me beyond measure. Although, the new representative appears a very genuine person and has promised me complete support in my work, I know I am going to miss Paul. His concern and solicitude for me were always spontaneous and unreserved. I indeed wish him the best of everything and will ever feel indebted to him for his kindness and consideration.

The visit to Galnewa after a gap of two months was pleasant. Progress was visible all around. The World Bank mission had come in my absence but in their report they mentioned me by name twice, commending the good work done in the farmer leaders' training and the settler participation in the development effort. I was also pleased to note that Weerakoody and Welikela had kept the torch of training burning, and had organized most of the planned follow-up courses. The situation in H5 appeared to be very encouraging indeed. The farmer leaders training in Kalawewa area also went smoothly and successfully despite the gap in follow-up courses for project staff. However, the situation in H4 appears a little disheartening. I hope things will improve after the next Training Committee meeting.

The follow-up course for system 'C' was held on 9 October and went very well. Frank Dunhill of ODA attended, as did Rohan Wijenaike, and Jayantha. I.K. Weerawardena took a keen interest in the programme. At his behest the course has now been extended to two days. Concerning the third course, arranged for 12 and 13 November, I could only marvel at the contrast between the positive attitude of I.K. and the negative attitude of Karunatillike. Rohan told me the other day that Karunatillike complained that I was obstructing him from doing his work. He is so mistaken! After Professor Scudder's advice, I have left his area alone and am concentrating in H4, H5 and system 'C'. There is no doubt that I do not like his lack of support for the training programme but I do not have to instigate Rohan against him. If Rohan has formed any opinion about Karunatillike's work, it is based on Rohan's personal observation. After all Rohan is also resident in the area and is an intelligent person.

It is nearly five months since I have written anything about the happenings behind the scene as a backdrop of my consultancy. A lot of changes have taken place, the most far-reaching being the taking over of the project management by the Mahaweli Authority. Rohan has been appointed the Resident Project Manager and Jayantha the Additional RPM. This has indeed greatly facilitated my work. Rohan is so perceptive and supportive of the initiatives I have proposed that it gives me a great feeling of confidence about attaining the goals and objectives. The tenor and texture of the follow-up courses and the farmer leaders' training has changed in a very positive way. Rohan attends the courses himself, which makes all the difference to the attitude of the field officers. In the H4 area, I have started going to the farmer leaders' training sessions and holding discussions with them. These sessions have proved very effective and useful. In this process I have discovered a very able aide in the DRPM, Culson Gunnawardena. He has the potential to become a strong pillar of the training programme in System 'H'. I was happy when he agreed to accept the additional charge of AGM (Training), as the post had become vacant when Weerakoddy left.

The training unit at Medagama is also taking shape and will very soon be fully effective. It will serve as the focal point for training in all the three sub-systems: the Kalawewa area (H1, H2, H7 and H9), Thambuttegama (H4) and Nochiyagama (H5).

Paul's departure had left me depressed and rather unsure of the future of my work. It was, therefore, a very pleasant development to learn that the new Representative Dr (Mrs) Hoda Badran, fully supports the approach I was implementing in the Mahaweli project. I knew I would not feel certain about this, however, until she had seen the project. I had developed admiration for her because she had opposed my transfer from Sri Lanka to Egypt and now, solely on the basis of discussions and written material, she was committed to supporting my work.

Fortunately, she decided to visit the project in view of her impending participation in the seminar on 'Integration of Community Participation Approaches in Country Programmes' in New York. I had also been invited. She came for a day long visit and was totally won over. She liked the approach of linking the productive and social sectors and of making economic need the entry point for community involvement. She visited a hamlet to assess the need for a day care centre and was distressed to learn about the death of a child while the parents were working in the paddy field. She was also greatly impressed by the attitude of the project staff towards UNICEF. Rohan and Jayantha convinced her of the government's abiding interest in the programmes started by UNICEF.

Hoda visited the project again along with Mr Dave Haxton, the UNICEF Regional Director from New Delhi. Mr Haxton had made a few uncharitable comments on the Annual Report, which had evoked a rather indignant rejoinder from Hoda. The visit was understandably charged with a little tension. After the visit, Mr Haxton was full of praise and mentioned to me that the Annual Report did not truly reflect the innovative work being done here. Hoda was impressed to see that her suggestion to use video equipment for training had been put into practice by Rohan. In fact, he showed Mr Haxton's visit to the area on the VCR at the training centre, immediately when it concluded. I was very pleased that the visit helped in mending the fences between the Country and the Regional offices.

Hoda paid her third visit in six months in connection with the organization of an orientation course for Hambantota District officers on the request of NORAD. We had detailed discussions on many issues. I found a complete identity of ideas and, I must say, I felt very reassured about the future of my work in Sri Lanka. Hoda wants me to get involved more and more in other areas, especially in the Maldives. With this in view, she issued an office order designating me as Senior Project Officer (Social Development) instead of Mahaweli Consultant and also nominated me to the Office Management group. She offered me another two-year contract and persuaded me to stay on till I get an assignment in New York. When I suggested that the contract be for two and a half years, to coincide with the completion of five years in UNICEF, thereby entitling me to a pension, Hoda thought that this might give New York the impression that I planned to leave after that, so she said she would recommend a four year contract to coincide with the programming cycle.

The big news of the year for me was V. Tarzie Vittachi's article in *Newsweek* of 5 January 1981 entitled 'A Man Named Khan'.[3] I learned about it by chance at Karachi while returning from New York to Colombo. My friend Air Commodore Alahdad's son Mozzam, who had come to meet me, casually asked if I had seen the article since I was the subject. Someone later produced a copy of *Newsweek*. I had met Tarzie in New York at a reception in the headquarters office. Tarzie has joined UNICEF as Deputy Executive Director and had visited the

Mahaweli project in 1989. I found Tarzie's article overwhelming. It was the best tribute that I could have hoped for after the two years' work and the hardships I had subjected myself to—above all, separation from my loved ones, not to speak of hazards such as snakes, and midnight journeys on deserted roads through the jungle.

Tarzie paid a second visit to the project in the first week of January 1981, immediately after writing the article. He went away very pleased with what he had seen. He was accompanied by the secretary general of the House of Parliament of Sri Lanka. Tarzie's article evoked a news story in Pakistan's national daily, *The Muslim,* titled 'The Mysterious Mr Khan of *Newsweek*'. I have still to see that article.

My visit to New York resulted in another article on my work in the *UNICEF News Bulletin.* Jack Ling, Chief of the Information Section, asked his information aides to interview me. However, the last word on the subject had already been written by V. Tarzie Vittachi.

The visit to New York in December 1980 to attend a seminar organized by Mary Hollesteiner of the people's participation section, though not so satisfying in terms of seminar participation, proved a boon in many other respects. One was the meeting with Mr Heyward, Senior Deputy Executive Director, UNICEF at lunch. When I received his invitation I assumed that everyone at the seminar would be present. I was surprised to learn that it was a private lunch with Mr Heyward in the main UN Building. When I thanked him for the invitation he replied 'everyone wants Shoaib Khan, so I wanted to see the man.' During lunch, I was amazed at his understanding of the principles of community involvement. When he asked me 'Why is it that only Khans do this type of work?' I knew that he had met Akhtar Hameed Khan and had even visited Comilla. He questioned me in minute detail about the Mahaweli project and the activities I was undertaking there, including the linkages I had forged between farmers and government functionaries. When I asked him if he thought that UNICEF would be interested in trying this approach in other countries, he said 'How do we find 50 Shoaib Khans?' I replied this could be done by exposing interested UNICEF personnel to the approach. On logistics, I answered him that a group of ten officers, after 3-months' training, orientation and exposure to the approach, could initiate projects based on community involvement.

Earlier, when I had met Tariq Farooqui, he had mentioned that I was being considered for a posting in the Middle East and that Mr Heyward probably wished to size me up in this regard. Tariq himself was being tipped for a post in Beirut and was very keen that I come along with him. I wasn't too enthusiastic about Beirut. I did not show it but I was relieved to learn subsequently that Tariq's posting had fallen through. Later, over dinner in his home, I complained to his wife Nasreen about Tariq's decision to go to Beirut and advised Nasreen to stop him from making such decisions. In Nasreen I found a very pleasant and charming personality. Tariq and Nasreen make an ideal couple.

I was quite surprised to learn that Mr Heyward had followed up on our luncheon discussion. Hoda told me that New York had telexed to enquire if Colombo could organize a 10-day seminar to further explore my proposal. Hoda had suggested early 1982 for the purpose, in line with the programme plan. Due to the country programming exercise Hoda suggested early next year for the purpose.

The seminar on 'Integration of community participation approaches into country programmes' was a bit of a disappointment from my perspective. This was my first exposure to an exclusive UNICEF staff seminar to which representatives and programme officers, all experts in the subject, had been invited. I found they had little inclination to learn about innovative approaches. There was more of an 'I know it all' attitude. I found my interaction with group participants a little frustrating: although most of the things essential for community involvement were identified, the prioritization of the essentials was, I thought, rather lopsided.

The visit to New York also gave me an opportunity to meet Paul and Katherine Ignatieff again. Paul appeared a little lost but was putting up a brave front. He was as kind and solicitous as ever. I will, of course, always remain indebted to him for the help and support he gave me in my work in Sri Lanka.

I also ran into Shoukat Fareed (one of my trainee probationers at the Civil Service Academy in Pakistan, now a Counsellor at the UN) and Iqbal Riza. Iqbal Riza had been the Deputy Director at the Academy with me and had resigned from the Foreign Service during Bhutto's regime. Shoukat also invited me over for dinner. He told me that Mrs Zaki was in New York with her brother Mr Koirala, a former Prime Minister of Nepal, but I could not meet her as she was in the hospital attending to her brother.

On the way back to Sri Lanka I stopped in Pakistan and visited Peshawar to arrange a field visit to the Daudzai project for some Sri Lankan officers. Fortunately, Akhtar Hameed Khan was also in Peshawar. He invited me to visit his urban project at Orangi in Karachi.

We were indeed very pleased to see each other again. I made him promise to come to Sri Lanka. Since Hoda had floated the idea of inviting eminent people in different fields of specialization to interact with the staff, I have now sent a letter to Khan Sahib requesting him to come to the Mahaweli project for three weeks in May or June next year as well as to help in the Maldives country programming exercise. I am keenly awaiting his reply.

The visitors included Dr Herman Steni (visiting Colombo), and Mr H. Ghassami and Mr and Mrs Jun Rose (visiting the project area) as well as Tarzie Vittachi who came in the first week of the year. Dr Steni spoke about the reorganization of UNICEF and took note of my point that reorganization should not detract from the flexibility and innovative and creative initiatives made possible and encouraged under the existing set-up. I had met Dr Steni in 1979 and he had greatly encouraged me in what I was trying to do in Mahaweli. He was equally positive this time and was only sorry that he could not visit the project area. Mr Ghassami is the Chief Advisor on Nutrition at New York. He came to the project with Hiranthi. Mr Jun Rose, the latest visitor, is a UNICEF consultant on publications and a close associate of Tarzie Vittachi. He had changed his flight schedule to London to visit Mahaweli system 'H' after reading the material I gave him pertaining to the project. After the visit he remarked that he had found it worthwhile to cancel and change his original schedule.

The minister also visited the project area but I hardly had a chance to talk to him. Maybe he now gets so much information about the project through Rohan that he feels he is well-informed about the developments. I mentioned this lack of communication to Jayantha and he dismissed it as insignificant. What I perceive to be a diffident attitude in Sri Lankans sometimes bothers me. Sometimes they act so coldly and distantly that one wonders if anything is the matter. Of course, the minister has never done so and he always greets me very politely but sometimes the others even fail to do that.

I haven't written my diary for a long time—so long that I have almost lost track of the time. Let me pick up the thread from where I left it. Mr Heyward, on his retirement from the post of Senior Deputy Executive Director, stopped over in Sri Lanka on way to Australia and visited the project. He spent two days in the project with his wife Elizabeth and held detailed discussions with me. On his return to Colombo he wrote to his successor, Mrs Catley Carlson, reviving his proposal for training UNICEF personnel in community participation, along the lines of the strategy being used in System 'H'. I was quite pleased to see an internal Memo circulated by Catley Carlson with the subject heading 'Seminar on Community Participation: Expertise of Mr Khan'. She went on to state how the impressive work done by Mr Khan has been commended by Dr Richard Jolly (UNICEF's Deputy Executive Director) and now by Mr Heyward, and recommended steps to replicate [my] skills within and outside UNICEF. Mr Charles Egger, another old giant of UNICEF, followed Mr Heyward a few months later. He too, after retirement, found the project very interesting, and in fact, he joined the UN community meeting. In his observations, he spoke highly of the strategy and uniqueness of the approach and recommended that the executive director visit the project. He even mentioned my future and suggested to the director of the Personnel Division that I be considered as a candidate for a core appointment to pre-empt my leaving the organization.

The most recent visitor to the project was Mr Kunio Waki, Chief of the Asia Section from headquarters. He left his impressions in the form of a note and described the project as one of the few successful projects UNICEF was assisting in Asia. He also commended the strategy and considered its achievements indisputable.

In the background of these reactions and comments, the attitude of the Mahaweli Authority bosses has been anything but understandable. During the last few months I have again and again been reminded of my friend Tariq's advice: 'Get out of the project as soon as you feel that you are causing jealousy'. I almost felt and sometimes still feel that perhaps I have reached that point. It all began with Rohan Wijenaike's transfer from the project. On my return from home leave in January, I found the atmosphere totally changed. I had no doubt that Rohan and Mahe Wickramarathne, Executive Director of the Mahaweli Authority of Sri Lanka were on a collision course. I had cautioned Rohan many a time but to no avail. Mahe had told me that on the basis of my work I had carved a place for myself. I did not need anybody's support and I should not try to court anyone. He hinted that there were people much closer and nearer to the Minister than Rohan. I thanked him for his advice but did my best to convince him that I was not courting anyone's support: I had dealings with everyone and these were strictly in the interest of the project. I had no other axe to grind. Anyway, I tried my very best to take whatever precautions I could to dispel any impression about my being partisan to anyone. This I did despite the fact that Rohan always went all out to support UNICEF assisted activities even after the areas of jurisdiction were separately demarcated between Jayantha (H1, H2, 7 and 9), Rohan (H4), and Samarasinghe (H5).

Rohan applied himself with real vigour and gusto to the programmes in his area. He attended farmer trainings, organized the officers' training, gave an impetus to the protected wells programme with hand pumps, and actively supported the day care centres and women's programmes. Despite all this, I know that in the past a bone of contention had been my suggesting his name for a study tour. Hence this time when an offer came for participation in a conference on regional development in Japan, I wrote to Lalit Godamunne and even personally requested him to participate in the conference. It was he who told Rohan about the conference and got approval from the Director General for himself and Rohan to attend.

My request to Akhtar Hameed Khan to pay a visit to the project materialized in October 1981. As a sequel to his visit, I sent a proposal to the Secretary General about the need for organizing turnout groups with greater vigour and the importance of a policy directive to this effect. I learned later that, in a meeting at the head office, when Mahe propagated the formation of hamlet organizations, Rohan opposed it tooth and nail and propounded the formation only of turnout groups. This hardened Mahe's attitude towards turnout groups. Although, he had taken a flexible attitude in a circular issued in early February 1982, he issued a very rigid circular in April almost negating formation of any groups other than at the hamlet level. The circular also mentioned that foreign consultants are suggesting organization of turnout groups which is logistically not feasible. I wrote him a long note, since his latest circular was endorsed to me, explaining the need for turnout groups, thereby giving economy of scale to the settlers. I explained that despite the heavy investments in physical and administrative infrastructures, the settler starts with the big disadvantage of a subsistence holding. Then he suffers from many handicaps and has to be helped to overcome these by pooling of resources, the re-division of labour, investments, and marketing.

It happened that during this period the World Bank review mission made its bi-annual visit accompanied by Mahe. Dr Abeygunawardena, whom I had met earlier in the week, had mentioned that the Canadians, Pan and Saaltink, who had always supported my work and were indeed instrumental in getting the funding to the extent of US$1.5 million from CIDA, also wanted me to meet the Mission. I also wanted to show them the video film we had prepared on UNICEF-assisted activities in System 'H'. I got a message that the team would visit Medagama although later on I learnt that Mahe wasn't too keen on this visit. Pan also took me aside on arrival at Medagama and mentioned that there seemed to be some disillusionment with the turnout groups especially because during the recent drought the turnout leaders proved of no help and took the law into their own hands. I explained to him that his was a very unjustified criticism against the farmer leaders.

First of all, in a crisis when the wrong political decision was taken to deprive a whole area of water in order to save another area, the natural reaction was 'let us all hang together'. Why should one group be sacrificed to save another? Second, if the turnout groups had been effectively organized, which has not happened in the absence of a policy directive, the situation would not have taken this ugly turn in which nearly 1,000 settlers sat in agitation till the sluice gates of the left bank canal were opened. Ultimately, when people make up their mind about something it is very difficult to make them see reason. Pan's warning was correct. At the lunch at Mahailluppallama, Mahe literally accused me of corrupting project officers, of channelling all assistance to the RPM instead of to children, and of meddling in internal affairs. I thought he was joking but he seemed very serious.

The Mission leader, Mr Stan Baker, in the meanwhile came up and asked Mahe if there were any proposals to change the existing pattern of training farmer leaders and if so he would like to express the Mission's concern because the Mission has been impressed by the work so far done in this field with UNICEF assistance. I explained to him that there appeared to be need for clarification of certain issues and, if Mahe would agree, I would do so on my next visit to Colombo.

On my next visit, when I called Mahe, he told me that he was very busy with the Mission but could see me later in the afternoon. He came one hour late from the meeting for the appointment and thereafter kept me waiting for another hour. I could not understand what he was trying to prove, but I waited patiently. I did not want to give him the satisfaction of angering me. When we met, he explained that he was not unwilling to meet me more frequently (I had earlier asked him for more frequent meetings) but that I could see he had no time. With regard to his comments, I explained to him how UNICEF has assisted in system 'H' and how 60 per cent of the budget was expended on equipment directly ordered by UNICEF and the balance on day care centres, training allowances of 3,000 farmer leaders, workshops for 300 project officers, training of 900 health volunteers and so on. In the light of this information, I wanted to know the basis of his comments. He said that he would accept what I had said unless it was proved to the contrary in the probe he was undertaking.

I did get a (rather rude) letter immediately after the meeting in reply to mine explaining the need for turnout groups. In this letter the decision of the MASL to organize hamlet associations was urged and I was categorically asked if I would be willing to support the MASL policy in this regard. Of course, I replied, without even showing it to Hoda, that UNICEF always worked in accordance with the policy of the government and there was no question of my doing the contrary. Mahe had circulated this letter to all RPMs. Obviously there was considerable consternation amongst my friends and well wishers in the project who took exception to the contents and language of the letter. I tried to mollify them and made light of the whole affair. Indeed, I was hurt but Hoda's attitude and stance in the matter stopped me from taking any rash action. She made me feel that I was really wanted by UNICEF and that she was determined to take a stand with MASL if they tried to interfere in any way. The matter has rested since then. I have started totally ignoring the MASL, especially after I asked for an interview with Mr Panditratne, Director General and he directed me to see Mr Lalit Godamunne. The work goes on. In fact, the monthly review meetings under Torry Jayweardena have become fairly effective and a good forum for monitoring the progress of activities. Whereas in the past I was fully involved in implementing activities, now I am in a position to ask as to why certain things were not progressing. Decisions taken every month are now reviewed and a sense of responsibility is being engendered in the project as well as headquarters staff. It is no longer my sole responsibility to chase after things.

On his visit to Sri Lanka in 1981, Akhtar Hameed Khan had urged me to accept the Aga Khan Foundation's offer to initiate a rural development programme in the Northern Areas of Pakistan. I had at that point not received the offer. In any case I was not mentally prepared to go back to Pakistan after the horrendous experience I had had at Daudzai. Before the end of his stay in Sri Lanka, Akhtar Hameed Khan had changed his mind about my going to the Northern Areas and asked me to come to Karachi to work with him. I showed my willingness, provided my services could be obtained on deputation from UNICEF. Akhtar Hameed Khan appreciated my point of view and agreed to ask the BCCI (Bank of Credit and Commerce International), which was funding the Orangi Pilot Project in Karachi, to secure my services from UNICEF. The President of the Foundation, Mr Hasan Abedi, interviewed me in Karachi in June 1982 along with Akhtar Hameed Khan, and made the request to the Executive Director of UNICEF. He expressed his inability to second the services of an international employee to his home country but agreed to release me for three years to be treated as a break in service with UNICEF. Hoda was totally opposed to this arrangement and Akhtar Hameed Khan also felt that this was not in my best interest, as I would lose the UN umbrella.

In April 1982, I received a letter from the Director of Special Programmes of the AKF, Mr Robert d'Arcy Shaw, enquiring about my interest in working for the AKF in Pakistan. My response was on similar lines as to Akhtar Hameed Khan. A few months later, Hoda informed me of a telephone call from UNICEF headquarters conveying orders of my deputation to the AKF. Bob Shaw, whom I had met at Islamabad in 1978, when he was Ford Foundation representative in Pakistan, came to visit me at Mahaweli, after my confirmation as General Manager by the Board of Directors of the Aga Khan Rural Support Programme (AKRSP). I had by this time made a short visit to Gilgit, the proposed headquarters of the AKRSP. I developed an instant rapport with Bob and was most impressed by the depth of his support for the kind of work I was doing. In the meanwhile, I received frantic calls from the headquarters of BCCI in London to come for a meeting with Mr Abedi. On my visit to London for a haemorrhoids operation I visited him at the BCCI office. He made me an offer for a job based in London. When I expressed my inability to accept, in view of my commitment to the AKF, I was given an appointment letter to be effective after the completion of one year with the AKF. I wondered what Akhtar Hameed Khan must have told them about me. On my return from London, I relinquished my post with UNICEF in Sri Lanka on 30 November 1982 and the following day, in Karachi, I joined the Aga Khan Foundation.

NOTES

1. 90 per cent of Sri Lankan farmers are literate, many of them in English also.
2. Stan Baker's mission which visited Kalawewa in November.
3. See Appendix 1.

5

Transition from the Civil Service to the Aga Khan Foundation

The abolition of the post of Commissioner, Karachi in 1972, by the newly inducted provincial government of Sindh, offered me the opportunity to request a posting to the Pakistan Academy for Rural Development (PARD) at Peshawar. No sooner had I taken up my new assignment than Dr Akhtar Hameed Khan visited me. Looking at the Daudzai Markaz Pilot Project of the Integrated Rural Development Programme (IRDP) of which he was the author, he observed that 'Daudzai is like an island of sincerity in a sea of hypocrisy'. He used to lament that, like an architect's plan, he had presented IRDP but the government, instead of implementing the entire design, had decided only to build the dome without the foundations or the walls. To my good fortune, Akhtar Hameed Khan even gave up his teaching assignment at Michigan State University and came to live at the Academy in Peshawar to help me implement the Daudzai Project. The NWFP government accepted Daudzai as the 'mother project' of IRDP for replication in the entire province and by 1975 had drawn up plans to cover all the 110 thanas of the province.

As PARD was a national institution, the director was mandated to disseminate the Academy's knowledge and experiments to other parts of Pakistan. It was at this juncture that my friend and service batch mate Dr Tariq Siddiqi, having blatantly, with no justifiable reason been dismissed from the CSP, accepted my invitation to visit me and accompany me on my trip to the Northern Areas. We took the Kaghan route and entered the Northern Areas via the Babusar Pass joining the under-construction Karakoram Highway (KKH) just beyond Chilas. It was a memorable experience.

We encountered thousands of Chinese working on the road, along with Pakistanis on separate sections of the road. Whereas we would always see Pakistanis being supervised, we never saw the Chinese being ordered about by any supervisor and at times we saw a lone Chinese worker trying to finish his assigned portion of the job even late at night. At times we had to wait for hours before the rocky mountainside could be blown up and cleared to allow vehicles to pass. It was a hazardous and time-consuming journey but in Tariq's company it was a great learning experience. Tariq would encourage me to break the journey by the Indus riverbank, and we would sleep on cots under the sky by wayside restaurants. On reaching Danyore, on the outskirts of Gilgit, we came across women with their distinctive headgear and we knew we were in the heart of Central Asia. We went right up to Gulmit where, to our great dismay, we found that the 'Friendship Bridge' had been sunk under tons and tons of debris and an avalanche. The substitute was a boat bridge. At the Hunza Rest House, I felt as if we were perched on a cliff. Our return journey from Gilgit to Battagram took us more than 72 hours and I cannot forget our entrance in the Pattan valley at night which was the epicentre of the 1974 earthquake. It was a moonlit night and we seemed to be entrapped in a prison surrounded by high black rocks. Sleeping on the hotel terrace which hung over the Indus, I felt I was in a strange and forbidding world. The moonlit view of Nanga Parbat, which we had experienced earlier at Jaglote, now seemed like a mirage.

My meetings with the Resident Commissioner, Development Commissioner, NAs and Deputy Commissioner, Gilgit, besides the Assistant Director, Local Government and Rural Development Department, and the Assistant Commissioner, Hunza, were very productive and they evinced keen interest in the Daudzai strategy and methodology of development. To my mind, with nearly 95 per cent small landowners, the social mobilization strategy would have an immediate impact on their livelihood. On return I sent my note for record (NFR) to the Resident Commissioner NAs for implementation of a social mobilization strategy in the Northern Areas. I had no inkling at the time that seven years later, I would get the opportunity to implement the strategy myself in the Northern Areas.

On return to Peshawar from the NAs, I was intrigued by my friend the Development Commissioner of NWFP, Masoodur Rauf's query about whether Tariq Siddiqi had gone with me on the tour. On my insisting to be told the reason behind his query, Masoodur Rauf confided how the chief secretary was summoned by the establishment secretary and confronted with the transcript of a telephone conversation which he had with the Commissioner, Lahore expressing indignation and serious criticism of the orders dismissing Tariq Siddiqi. The establishment secretary gave friendly advice to the chief secretary not to deny the contents of his telephone conversation when confronted by the PM as intelligence agencies had taped the conversation and passed the transcript on to the PM. I understood the purport of this message when shortly afterwards, on my return from the NAs, I was made an officer-on-special duty (OSD) and asked to report to the establishment division. At the behest of the Chief Minister, NWFP through one of the provincial ministers, Abdul Raziq, who had visited Daudzai and greatly appreciated it, the establishment secretary granted me an interview and when I asked him the reason for my appointment as OSD, his response was that the government was unhappy with me. I protested and said 'Why doesn't the government hang me then?' he retorted 'Yes, we will hang you' and followed it by asking whether Tariq Siddiqi had visited me. It was a long interview and I came away with the impression that I had fully clarified my position with the establishment secretary. However, a week after my interview, a Federal Investigation Agency (FIA) team appeared at the Academy making all kinds of enquiries but refused to see me although I was still living in the director's house since my next posting was under consideration.

Very late one night, an assistant director of the FIA came to see me. He was very polite and courteous and said that everyone in the Frontier Province was aware of my reputation, since I had served the province since 1963 as deputy commissioner, Kohat and Peshawar, and as secretary, department of Health, Education and Social Welfare, as well as director of PARD. He felt I was the best person to answer the charges levied against me although he was under strict orders from the team of four officers headed by a deputy inspector general of police not to make any contact with me. However, the director FIA, Mohsin, had given special instructions that no injustice should be done.

The charge sheet was an anonymous letter containing more than twenty allegations, which were baseless and had not an iota of truth. These included the accusation that Tariq and I went to the NAs to hatch a conspiracy to overthrow the government; that Daudzai was a hotbed of conspiracies against the government, being a National Awami Party area; that my daughter's father-in-law was the owner of the *Manchester Guardian* which was anti-Pakistan; that I was an agent of both the CIA and KGB because both the Americans and the Russians used to visit me; that I had invited Akhtar Hameed Khan, who openly instigated Sindhi participants of training courses at the Academy to make

Sindhudesh; that I had smuggled a Mercedes car from Kabul and sold it in the black market and so on and so forth.

I explained to the kindly officer the falsehood of the allegations. How could Tariq and I hatch a conspiracy and with whom and with what and what for? A delegation of villagers of Daudzai went on their own to the PM in Rawalpindi and pleaded for the cancellation of my transfer order. I had nothing to do with it. They never even informed me about their intentions. My daughter was indeed married to an Englishman but her father-in-law was a businessman and had no connection with the *Manchester Guardian*. PARD was set up with American assistance and very often the Director of USAID and the Representative of the Ford Foundation used to visit the Academy and many of them became my good friends but I had nothing to do with the CIA. The only Russian whom I ever met at PARD was a Russian girl studying at Punjab University who came to spend a fortnight at the Academy to study the Academy's programmes. Akhtar Hameed Khan had already written to the chief secretary explaining the absurdity of the charge leveled against him. As to the smuggling of the Mercedes car, I happened to be traveling from London to Pakistan and as my friend Dil Jan was the minister at our embassy in Kabul, I broke my journey there, arriving by Ariana Afghan Airlines and returning to Peshawar by road. Dil Jan's Mercedes needed to be serviced and he very kindly offered me a lift in the car which his driver was taking to Peshawar for service. So much for 'smuggling and selling the Mercedes in the black market'.

I enjoyed my time as OSD. For the first time in twenty years of service, I was being paid for remaining on forced leave. However, it all came to an end one day when I got a phone call from the establishment division to report immediately to Mr Roedad Khan, who was heading a commission in addition to his normal duties of being a federal secretary in charge of a ministry. I enquired what the hurry was and said I needed time to pack up and shift my residence from Peshawar to Islamabad. The special secretary establishment was a bit nonplussed because here I was being offered a posting and instead of jumping to rejoin, I was asking for time. Anyway, he agreed to let me settle the matter in consultation with Roedad Khan, who readily acceded to my request.

A few years later, in 1978, when Ejaz Naik asked me to join the service in the cabinet division, he pointed to a cupboard in his room which bore the letters 'NGO' written on top of it. He asked me to take all the files from the cupboard and to send them to the concerned sections. He had no idea why his predecessor was keeping the files; the letters NGO stood for 'Not to Go Out'.

Among those files, I found some pertaining to the enquiry against me, and the file relating to Tariq's dismissal. In the latter the PM had passed the orders on the summary recommending Tariq's dismissal, as 'Such persons have no place in the service of Pakistan'. The inquiry committee in my case exonerated me of all the allegations leveled against me but the DG, FIA, while sending the report to the establishment secretary, wrote in the covering letter that, while he was serving as IG Police, NWFP, complaints were made to him against the Deputy Commissioner Shoaib Sultan for his leftist leanings in the landlord–tenant dispute raging in Charsadda at that time. He further added that the chief secretary used to complain about Mrs Shoaib as being very vocal in criticizing the government. I have no idea why the DG, FIA, whom I thought was my well wisher, should have felt the need to write what he wrote in his covering letter.

Meanwhile, Daudzai withered away. I ran from pillar to post trying to enlist the support of my perceived powerful friends in government. They all showed their helplessness, only offering their support to me personally to rehabilitate me in my career which I always politely declined. Daudzai taught me how important the champions of a cause are. Ejaz Naik as Chief Secretary was followed by Nasrum Minallah who said to Akhtar Hameed Khan that Shoaib was the chief secretary in terms of implementing the IRDP in the NWFP on the pattern of Daudzai; Ijlal Haider Zaidi as commissioner who would endow Daudzai with all the resources it needed, and above all, Hayat Muhammad Khan Sherpao as senior Minister. Gradually each one of them left the scene and with Hayat's death in a bomb blast and Nasrum Minallah's transfer, Daudzai lost all its champions.

I was heartbroken and shaken. In the CSP if your *bona fides* are established, even your wrong actions are condoned. Everyone from top to bottom supports you. I had never imagined that I would ever be taken to task for doing the right things. My faith in the service was snuffed out. I decided to leave the service at the first available opportunity. By now I thought I had established some kind of a reputation in community development and I should not have any difficulty in finding an overseas assignment. My first shock was the establishment division's refusal to forward my application for any foreign post that I applied for. I could not afford to resign from service and apply. This was the case not only for posts abroad but even within the country. When Dr Afzal asked me to take a semester in the Masters Course in Public Administration at the Quaid-e-Azam University, the establishment division refused to give permission although I had already started teaching as Dr Afzal had promised to get the permission. Dr Akhtar Hameed Khan tried to get me over to Michigan State University but even he did not succeed. I spent a few months with Roedad Khan's Commission followed by a posting in the ministry of Local Government and Rural Development but I kept on looking for avenues to go abroad, and in disgust, took six months' leave but to no avail. The nearest I came to getting an assignment was with UNICEF Indonesia. I even went for an interview and the government of Indonesia liked my CV but were not impressed by the profile of development in Pakistan. They preferred an advisor from South Korea.

On return from leave, I found Ejaz Naik as cabinet and establishment secretary and he asked me to join the cabinet division. I frankly informed him of my intentions to serve abroad after my Daudzai debacle. He promised not to stand in my way if any such opportunity came my way. It was during this period that Dr Ishrat Husain, whom I had known from his days as a probationer in the Civil Service Academy, visited me at the cabinet division and mentioned to me an opening at the UN Centre for Regional Development (UNCRD) Nagoya, Japan. He also wrote a letter to Dr Ralph Diaz at the Centre enclosing my CV. Promptly came the response from UNCRD offering me initially a six months consultancy. As government servants were prohibited from accepting direct offers of consultancies or service contracts, Ejaz Naik treated the UNCRD offer as an offer to cabinet division and nominated me against the offer.

In August 1978, I left for Japan where I would eventually build up a close friendship with Dr Haruo Nagamine, to whom I was assigned to advise on the UNCRD Project MPCRD relating to applied research programmes on planning methodologies. Before the expiry of my consultancy assignment, UNICEF Sri Lanka offered me a long term assignment as social development consultant to the Mahaweli Ganga Project. Haruo was not very happy at my leaving UNCRD and in 1993 invited me again as a visiting professor for a semester at the newly established Centre for International Development of Nagoya University of which he was a founding professor.

TRANSITION FROM THE CIVIL SERVICE

In October 1982, Bob Shaw invited me to Karachi to have lunch with the Aga Khan Foundation (Pakistan) and visit Gilgit. The lunch was an interview because a couple of hours before, Bob rang me up to brief me about the type of questions I should expect from the members of the AKF(P) Board. He was not taking any chances. I had no idea who else the Board had interviewed that day for the post of General Manager, Aga Khan Rural Support Programme (AKRSP).

Bob and I flew to Gilgit. This was my second visit to the Northern Areas. I called on the Commissioner Jamil Haider Shah who offered all possible support from the NA administration to the new programme. I stayed in Room No. 8 of the Chinar Inn, little realizing that it would become my constant abode for the next twelve years and continue to be my residence in Gilgit till to date. Our return journey by air never materialized because the flight turned back from Nanga Parbat. The Gilgit airport was most primitive with tin shed security boxes for entrance to the plane. Bob negotiated a taxi for our return. This taxi ride was the fastest journey I ever did on the Karakorum Highway. We left the PTDC Motel at midday and in ten hours the taxi drove into the porch of the hotel in Islamabad to drop Bob off.

I had still heard nothing from UNICEF when one morning the UNICEF Representative Hoda Badran gave me the news of a telephone call she had received from Deputy Executive Director Catley Carlson in New York. The news was of my secondment for three years to the AKF. I left Colombo on 30 November and joined AKF on 1 December 1982 as General Manager, AKRSP. The impossible had been made possible. I was coming back to Pakistan to resurrect Daudzai. The protective umbrella I had sought was in place. UNICEF had agreed to post an international civil servant in his home country. Of course, this could never have happened without Akhtar Hameed Khan's blessings and Bob Shaw's perseverance.

There was another hurdle to be overcome. I was still on deputation to UNICEF from the government of Pakistan. This was the end of my 28 years of association with government service; a service which began with a letter of appointment signed by the then Establishment Secretary, Government of Pakistan Sir Eric Franklin 'Your Most Obedient Servant'.

Section II
AKRSP

6

His Highness the Aga Khan's Vision of AKRSP

MEETINGS WITH HIS HIGHNESS

I first met His Highness on the lawns of the Commissioner's House at Peshawar at a lunch hosted by the Commissioner Masrur Hasan Khan in 1964. However, it was Musarrat who had the privilege of sitting at the table with His Highness. She recounts how he asked her about the most beautiful place she had seen and when she replied 'Switzerland', His Highness described the beauty of the Northern Areas. She did not know at that time that nearly twenty years later, her husband would be asked by His Highness to implement his rural development programme there.

My second meeting with His Highness took place at Karachi when, in early 1972, as the commissioner of Karachi, I had the privilege of receiving and seeing him off at the airport. While his jet was being refueled we spent a couple of hours in the VIP Lounge and he told me all about his plans to establish the Aga Khan University which he had been planning for the previous twelve years.

In 1983, soon after I had taken over as the General Manager of AKRSP, I was requested by Mr Ramzan Merchant, Chairman of the AKRSP Board of Directors, to drive to Islamabad from Gilgit, as bad weather prevented His Highness from travelling there. With the help of some slides I explained to His Highness the strategy of the AKRSP. He assured me of his full support to the programme and said that I should feel free to approach him directly if I ever needed any help. Such *carte blanche* support by him, in the presence of the AKRSP Chairman, meant that AKRSP never created a situation where I needed to invoke His Highness's intercession. His Highness emphasized the geo-political importance of the Northern Areas and Chitral and observed that he and his grandfather had initiated many development programmes in the area over many years. He noted that these were mostly in Ismaili populated areas although non-sectarian in nature and predominantly in health and education, thereby benefiting the entire population. To avoid fostering 'islands' of prosperity, His Highness wished to develop the entire region with an economic programme. His Highness asked me to enter into development partnerships with every community in the region, provided (i) the Northern Areas administration supported the initiative, (ii) the elected political leaders of the area wanted it, and above all, the local religious leaders were not opposed to it.

He was true to his word about supporting me when I extended AKRSP to Baltistan. I had done so at the request of Commissioner Jamil Haider Shah, on the insistence of the Chairman of the Baltistan District Council, Nashad, and with the approval of the local Shia divine Allama Ghulam Mohammad. The AKRSP Board thought I had exceeded my mandate, but His Highness silenced every opposition by observing that he was under the impression that the programme had been extended there long ago. When a villager in Barkulti, on one of His Highness's earlier visits to AKRSP, had implored His Highness to continue AKRSP for a long time, His Highness had responded that as long as people benefited from it, AKRSP would continue.

In another meeting in Islamabad attended by the AKF and AKHS, AKES, AKRSP and many other national and international professionals connected with the Aga Khan Network, His Highness was asked how long, in his view, AKRSP would take to achieve its objectives. He answered that he would be satisfied if, in 25 years, AKRSP brought about a change in the economic standard of living of the people of the region.

I was asked to make a presentation on AKRSP in this meeting and when I apologized to His Highness that he had already heard much of what I had to present, His Highness graciously observed that a good lesson needs to be heard again and again. Such was the support of the founder of AKRSP to the programme and to me personally.

I was invited to join His Highness in mid-1983 on his visit to the Oxfam office in London, and to give a presentation on AKRSP. At the conclusion of the meeting, the Director of Oxfam observed that he had hoped to get a donation from His Highness for Oxfam but after hearing about AKRSP, Oxfam would like to collaborate with the programme in its assault on poverty. In due course Oxfam made a donation of GBP 30,000 to AKRSP. This generosity also opened avenues for AKRSP to seek funding from the British government: that assistance continues today.

The interest that His Highness took in AKRSP was a great source of encouragement and inspiration to everyone in AKRSP—from the drivers to the General Manager. During my 12-year stay with AKRSP, His Highness visited the Northern Areas four times and despite *Imamat* (religious) and other official obligations, always found the time for AKRSP.

On his first visit to a VO, I noticed the local Intelligence Officer walking ahead of us and I introduced him to His Highness, complaining that the officer thought that AKRSP was inciting a revolution. His Highness said to the officer 'Yes, it is a revolution but a development revolution'.

I always rewarded good VOs/WOs by including them in His Highness's itinerary but the most satisfying event of this kind occurred when His Highness visited Broshal in Nagar. No one had ever imagined inviting His Highness to visit them, as they were strict followers of Imam Khomeini. The reception His Highness received was spontaneous and overwhelming. The people of Nagar took great pride in narrating what they had achieved through collaboration with the AKRSP. They proudly displayed their newly acquired tractor and I requested His Highness to take the driver's seat on the tractor, remembering AKF Geneva's request for some photo opportunities. His Highness graciously got into the tractor and jokingly observed 'I will now negotiate the remuneration for driving this machine'. In Chitral, in meetings of Sunni VOs, His Highness would willingly go to the rostrum to speak to the audience, unlike in the Ismaili areas where he always spoke from where he was seated. Once in the Ismaili area His Highness asked me where should he speak from and I pointed to the rostrum which he did without the slightest hesitation. However, late at night I got a phone call from the president of the Council angrily demanding that I see him immediately so that I would not commit such a *faux pas* in future. The president was staying two miles from the Chitral Scouts Mess where I was spending the night. Fortunately, the AKRSP Chairman Ramzan Merchant was also staying there. He told me to relax as this could be discussed in the morning.

The visit to a far off VO near Broghil took much longer than the time indicated in the programme, and I saw His Highness looking at his watch and at me. I thought the best option was not to look at him again until we reached the VO. It was extremely cold. Fortunately, His

Highness's beautifully cut overcoat was produced from somewhere. He insisted on going up to the channel which the VO members had constructed with AKRSP assistance. He was also presented with a yak which he later asked me to look after. I passed on this responsibility to the VO, and His Highness's yak became quite famous in the area.

On the way from Chitral to Gilgit, His Highness stopped over in Phander Valley where VO Terru had constructed an irrigation channel high up on the hillside to bring 200 acres of land under irrigation for forestry. A large number of people from Karachi were also in the party. His Highness looked at the channel, which was pretty high, and asked me if we could climb there. I wondered how he was going to do it, little realizing that he was an excellent skier. So the entire party started climbing up. Slowly the people from Karachi started dropping off one by one. I saw His Highness using the skiers' technique of climbing and finally we reached the top with VO office bearers and Hussain Wali. His Highness looked down from the channel and with a chuckle to me pointed to all the Karachi-ites left behind standing below at different places.

In my fifty-four years of working life, I had three major benefactors: the Government of Pakistan, the United Nations (UNICEF and UNDP) and the Aga Khan Foundation. The vision and long term perspective of His Highness and the personal interest he took in my work remains unequalled. I have been invited many times to Aiglemont (the Aga Khan's headquarters) where His Highness would spend hours discussing the programme strategy and its future course of action. I never had any difficulty in getting His Highness's approval and support to whatever I wanted to do. Bob Shaw and Bill Spoelberch were a very good conduit for me to His Highness; especially Bill who was very close to His Highness. Bill's retirement from the post of General Manager AKF, proved a great setback to me, compounded by Bob Shaw's diversion of focus from AKRSP to AKF.

His Highness's interest in my personal welfare was unbelievable. When, in 1988, tragedy struck, resulting in the death of my twenty-nine-year-old daughter and her two children, His Highness flew Musarrat and me to Aiglemont and personally consoled us. He spoke of the trust his grandfather had bestowed on him and compared it to the trust I was entrusted with—the welfare of 100,000 families of the Northern Areas and Chitral. He asked me to ask myself what my daughter would have liked me to do if she was alive. His Highness assured me she would have never liked me to give up what I was doing.

Musarrat and I were greatly touched by His Highness's compassion and empathy and were consoled beyond measure.

Though not directly connected with the programme, even Prince Amyn Aga Khan always praised the work AKRSP was doing. On one of his visits to the Northern Areas, he told me he had never seen as much greenery in the Northern Areas as he saw now. Prince Amyn sends me Seasons Greetings every year despite the letter I wrote him in acknowledgement that since the 1988 tragedy, I have not been able to bring myself to send greeting cards on Eid or Christmas/New Year.

In 1992, the Prime Minister Nawaz Sharif wrote a letter to His Highness requesting my services to oversee the evolution of the National Rural Support Programme (NRSP). His Highness only agreed to transfer my headquarters from Gilgit to Islamabad, but insisted on my continued association with the AKRSP. In 1994, when the UNDP approached me to replicate AKRSP throughout South Asia, by becoming Senior Adviser to the South Asia Poverty Alleviation Programme (SAPAP), I knew I could not do so without His Highness's blessing. I requested Bill to get me an appointment which he very kindly did and His Highness agreed to see me at his house in Paris.

When my daughter Shelley, whose husband Tim Le Breton was doing MBA at Insead, living near Paris, drove me to the address and asked a policeman about the street the policeman asked 'Why do you want to go there, there is only one house on that street?'

His Highness listened to me and expressed his happiness that the AKRSP had succeeded in its second objective of developing a replicable model of rural development. However, he still wanted my continued association with the AKRSP, and AKF agreed to my release to UNDP only on condition that 10 per cent of my time would still be allocated to the AKRSP. UNDP gladly agreed to this. The feeling of being wanted has always been a tremendous source of inspiration to me. I left AKRSP in August 1994 with a heavy heart because I knew I would never again have an employer like His Highness the Aga Khan to inspire and encourage me in my work.

7

My Introduction to AKRSP

TERRA INCOGNITA

On 30 November 1982, I flew to Karachi and took over as General Manager, Aga Khan Rural Support Programme (AKRSP) the next day. It was a new world for me. From government and the United Nations, I was stepping into a private sector international organization to work with its national branch, the Aga Khan Foundation (AKF) Pakistan, which in turn claimed AKRSP as one of its projects. I was an employee of the AKF Geneva, working for AKRSP which was a special project of AKF and totally funded by Geneva. It all looked very complicated and complex but I was determined to give it my best. The Chairman AKF, Pakistan, Mr Ramzan Merchant and the Chief Executive Officer Mr Hakim Feerasta made me feel most welcome and assured me of all support.

In Islamabad the local AKF office under Brigadier Shafi had a couple of rooms for visitors and I toyed with the idea of getting one of these rooms for Musarrat till I could make more permanent arrangements for her stay in Islamabad. She was making the biggest sacrifice. She knew she could not live in Gilgit all by herself but she did not object to my taking the new assignment. Three of our daughters were in London and one was in Peshawar with her husband who was serving in the Pakistan Air Force. I was distressed when Hakim rang me up to say that the rooms at AKF Islamabad were for visitors and I should not entertain any idea of bringing my wife there. I was quite surprised because I had not even asked for it. I was only thinking aloud.

For nearly six years Musarrat shifted from one apartment to another in Islamabad until we got our own house vacated in 1988. By an inexplicable twist of fate, less than two months after moving into the house, the greatest tragedy of our lives occurred when my daughter Falaknaz and her two children died due to suffocation caused by a gas

MY INTRODUCTION TO AKRSP

leak (see appendix 2). Musarrat did not give up and did not stop me from doing what I was doing. She took the entire burden on herself which sent her into a coma for ten days. Thereafter, for six weeks, the Pakistan Institute of Medical Sciences (PIMS) was our home. The miracle makers of PIMS not only brought Musarrat out of the coma; they revived her heart twice. Dr Shaukat Malik and his team of doctors snatched Musarrat from the jaws of death. PIMS for us proved to be the best hospital in the world. There is a saying that behind every successful man is a woman. I do not know about others but in my case it is more than true. My four daughters always made me feel proud of what I was doing because they took so much pride in their father's work.

To go back to my first days with the AKRSP, when I stepped out of the Pakistan International Airlines jumbo jet into the chill of the Islamabad evening, I realized that the tropical, humid climate of Sri Lanka which I had got so used to was now a thing of the past. The drive to the Aga Khan Foundation office-cum-guest house in Islamabad slowly made me believe that I was not on a visit from abroad, as had been the case in the past four years, but was now on a more extended stay. The guesthouse, though located on Margalla Road and part of a beautiful house, was furnished in a spartan style and was extremely cold at night. There being no satisfactory arrangements for messing in the guesthouse, it was just as well that I only eat lunch. The night was cold and the chowkidar outrageously apprehensive that I might suffocate if the gas heater developed problems thus the window next to the gas heater was kept open. To make things worse, the WC in the attached bathroom was not functioning hence I had to go to the next room, which had a functioning bathroom but no heater.

In the morning I had to go to the Central Board of Revenue (CBR) to attend to some official errands including tax exemption on my salary and emoluments being paid in foreign exchange. I was astonished when I looked at the tax assessment. Since I was not liable to pay taxes, the Aga Khan Foundation was liable not only to pay income tax on my net salary but also tax on the tax they were paying on my behalf. However, my friend Mr Fazlur Rehman, Chairman of the CBR held out the hope that the tax over tax might be exempted. As always he very generously acceded to my request to grant exemption from customs duty on the equipment being imported by the Aga Khan Foundation for the AKRSP. Tariq Siddiqi (now Additional Secretary, O&M Division) had also been called by Fazalbhai to join us at tea. If I were asked to list my sincerest friends, Tariq would figure very prominently on that list.

Before leaving the CBR, we called on Reyaz Naqvi, whose kindness I always remember. Way back in the mid-1960s, without any introduction, he went out of his way to help me in clearing my Mercedes Benz, which I had brought with me on my return from England. To go to the CBR and not to meet Sherazi would be sacrilege. A more charming, gentlemanly and sincere person and a wonderfully dependable friend it would be difficult to find.

Tariq, as usual, had accepted a dinner invitation on my behalf without ascertaining my programme. I had to take the afternoon flight to Peshawar for the few hours I could squeeze out of my busy schedule to see my daughter Manchu, and then return by the evening flight to be able to catch the 6 a.m. flight to Gilgit. I felt quite bad about it because the dinner was given by no other than Mr M. Azfar, my Chief Secretary in East Pakistan and Establishment Secretary in the Federal Government. He was a class-fellow of my father's and had always treated me with the utmost kindness and consideration. I made my apologies the next morning to him since the Gilgit flight was cancelled. He was extremely gracious and did not mind my behaviour in the least.

I had heard rumblings about the inappropriateness of my secondment by UNICEF to the Aga Khan Foundation while being on deputation from the Government of Pakistan to the UN. In fact, I had already written to Ijlal Haider Zaidi, the Establishment Secretary, from Sri Lanka, seeking his advice about severing my link with the government of Pakistan, although the government had generously agreed to my deputation till the end of October 1983.

I did not want my friend Ijlal to be embarrassed in anyway. He has always been very affectionate and sympathetic towards me. I knew the part he had played in getting my transfer orders to East Pakistan in 1971 cancelled when I had submitted my resignation. I was also indebted to him for getting my name approved for the post of additional secretary to the government while I was still on deputation outside the country. Hence, when I met him at his Islamabad office and offered to seek retirement from the government, he was obviously pleased. Indeed, so were all my other friends when they learnt that UNICEF had offered me long-term employment. The only person who tried to dissuade me from leaving the civil service was Kunwar Idris. My acquaintance with him dated back to 1958 when he came to my sub-

MY INTRODUCTION TO AKRSP

division as a civil service probationer. Since then our friendship had grown into a warm and close association. He and I truly rejoice in each other's success. His protest, therefore, caused me the only pang in severing my twenty-seven years association with the government. It obviously meant cutting the professional bond, however tenuous, with people like Idris. I could no longer claim to be part of that club.

It was symptomatic of the working of the government that my letter of retirement was drafted by Dr Zafar Altaf, once my probationer at the Civil Service Academy and now deputy secretary in the establishment division. I must say that I could not have drafted the letter with such feeling and verve as Zafar did.

Tariq had invited a few of my friends and batch mates to a lunch at the Holiday Inn. In his office, on the way to the lunch, I met Pedro (Jamilur Rehman Khan) who was proudly showing the letter from the University of Oxford asking him to supplicate himself for conferment of the degree of D. Phil. I thought this was a remarkable achievement on Jamil's part.

Ibrahim and Khalid came to the lunch and were later joined by Allauddin Bhai who was desperately looking for a foreign assignment. Nigar was also present at the lunch and young Bilal, to whom both Tariq and Nigar are deeply attached, also showed up. There was also a chance meeting with Mr A. H. Kardar and Ashraf Kazi. I was delighted to see Ashraf after our 1978 encounter in Japan.

Journey to the Northern Areas

In December 1982 I made my first journey to Gilgit to initiate the AKRSP. I was accompanied by Tariq Husain, fresh from Chicago where he had studied economics. He had been recruited by Bob Shaw as the Programme Economist. The flight to Gilgit was cancelled due to bad weather and we were told there was no certainty that it would go the next day. Sometimes it doesn't go for weeks. The reason is that the Nanga Parbat peak is nearly 5,000 feet higher than the maximum altitude of the Fokker plane. If there are clouds in the valley around the peak and the pilot cannot see the peak, the flight has to be aborted. Whether the flight is to be continued can only be known once the Fokker reaches the vicinity of the peak. If it is clear and the plane can continue, a bell is rung at Gilgit airport, announcing the likely arrival of the flight. Having heard all these stories, which proved to be absolutely true, Tariq Husain and I returned to the AKF office.

We saw a jeep parked in the driveway of the office. We learned from the Office Manager Shafqat Hussain, who always went out of his way to be helpful, that the jeep was meant to go to Chitral but because of the closure of the Lowari Pass, which would open only in May, it had been parked in the AKF office. When I asked if we could borrow the jeep to go to Gilgit, instructions were sought from Karachi and permission given. Like novices in the game, we started late in the day.

Luckily Tariq Husain proved a competent and safe driver on the 600 km drive up the Karakoram Highway. Since I had undergone an operation only three weeks before in London, Tariq Siddiqi sternly ordered me not to drive, otherwise he would come with me. I assured him that I had no such intention.

The drive up to Abbottabad in the brand new Toyota landcruiser was uneventful except that, when stopping for tea at Hasanabdal, I was rather amused by a painting in the restaurant with the caption *Zindigi Sari to Kati Ishq Butan Main Momin—Akhri Waqt Main Kya Khak Musalman Haungay*' (Your whole life has been spent in loving idols, Momin what will you do becoming a Muslim in your last days?). In this age of Islamisation this rather bold statement in a wayside restaurant situated in an area known for its orthodoxy and religious fervour, restored the confidence of the heretics.

At Abbottabad Tariq stopped at his house and introduced me to his mother who has been a private medical practitioner, and his younger brother. Tariq's father is a retired colonel of the Pakistan army and was currently visiting his lands in Shikarpur, Sindh. I tried to check by phone with the commissioner the state of the KKH. He was out but his personal assistant told me that a few days back they had been informed about the closure of the road by a landslide but he assured me that it must have been cleared by now. Since it was almost eight in the evening, I enquired about possible places for a night's stay on the way. He advised me to stop over at the Batagram PWD resthouse, which was usually vacant.

To our great discomfiture, when we reached Batagram at eleven that night, the resthouse was fully occupied, not by touring officials but by the local public works department officer and the overseer. I felt like reporting the overseer to the government of the NWFP who showed scant concern for two helpless travellers in the cold and dark midnight. We retraced our steps to where a board indicated the Rural Works Resthouse. The *chowkidar* of the resthouse claimed to be sick and refused to come out. Someone else opened the door and informed us that there was no bedding. Our hearts sank, but there was no alternative but to stay there. It was the coldest night I had ever endured. For the first time in my life, I slept with my gloves on. Fortunately I had my thick woollen dressing gown with me but despite that I was extremely cold all night. I remembered tropical Sri Lanka and wondered where I had landed myself.

At last the long cold winter night came to an end. There was no question of getting breakfast or even a cup of tea at the Batagram resthouse. We drove up to Besham and found a place which produced a first class breakfast.

My spirits began to lift and I bought some fruit for the way. Suddenly I remembered that I did not even possess a radio or cassette player, as I had presented my old one to my driver at Colombo. When I found Tariq buying transistor cells from one of the shops, I decided to buy a cassette recorder. At the first stop I found one, larger in size than what I was used to, but being desperate I almost bought it. However, I realised that it was a used item. I cursed and called the shop-keeper a cheat, an allegation which he boldly refuted. Luckily at the next shop, I found a Sanyo cassette recorder which was exactly the same type as the one I had first bought at Hong Kong and again at Male in Maldives. I bought it and felt very pleased that now I was well fortified for the lonely evenings at Gilgit. I remembered how I used to cling to it in Mahaweli and what solace it used to give me.

Luckily the Karakoram Highway was passable all the way to Gilgit. We stopped at Dassu (Comilla), the headquarters of Kohistan District, and met the Deputy Commissioner, Mr Salim Khan and the Assistant Commissioner. We reached Gilgit by sunset and I moved into a room of the Pakistan Tourism Development Corporation (PTDC) motel which, compared to the Galnewa Circuit Bungalow, was luxurious. I must acknowledge with gratitude, however, that I spent the last two years of my stay in Mahaweli in a specially constructed cottage in the Handungama Circuit House compound, fully furnished and tastefully decorated by Christine, Jayantha's wife. Since the arrival of Rohan and Jayantha in system H, I was pampered in every possible way by the project managers and the field staff to compensate for the lack of enthusiasm and warmth at Colombo for my work. But the Chinar Inn grew on me and even after ten years, remains my permanent abode in the Northern Areas. I am grateful to my friend Abdul Qayum Khan, who, during his tenure as MD PTDC, converted my two rooms into a beautiful suite and made it into a haven for me. He issued a circular giving me the same privileges as enjoyed by Justice Cornelius at the PTDC Hotel Falettis in Lahore.

By late afternoon the next day we reached the Chinar Inn in Gilgit. I had no idea at that time that in the next twelve years I would traverse the Karakorum Highway no less than 80 times, with each journey taking no less than 12 hours. Once it took more than 36 hours because of a landslide, not on the KKH but between Thakot and Batagram.

I assembled my team on the morning of 8 December at the Chinar Inn. Fortunately Feroz Shah and M.H. Naqvi, whom Bob had recruited on my recommendation from the Pakistan Academy for Rural Development as Programme Specialists in Human Resource Development and Natural Resource Management, had also arrived in Gilgit. We four were then joined by two local people, Tawallad Shah and Mohammad Yar who were managing AKF's Farm Information Centre from a shop in the main bazaar of Gilgit. AKRSP literally had its beginning with the opening of a shop.

However, the place was too small for all of us to sit down and at this juncture Ali Dad, who was managing a social sector project of the AKF, offered his office, located in a small house in a *mohallah* at the back of the bazaar street. All five of us huddled around a kerosene heater (Gilgit was -8c) to plan the future strategy and methodology of AKRSP. Gilgit was a sleepy little town with hardly any facilities. Electricity was more often conspicuous by its absence and even when it was available the voltage was so low that we had to augment it with candles. Later on one of my enterprising drivers found a gaslight as a bedside lamp for me. On one of my visits to the United States, my cousin Azad had given me a rechargeable torch. It proved a real boon for me here. Gilgit taught me the value of the little things in life which otherwise we take for granted. Light of any kind, Japanese kerosene heaters, hot water in the tap or in buckets were the luxuries we craved. Mahaweli was elephant country and primitive but Gilgit was unimaginably harsh, difficult, risky and total wilderness. How I survived those early years, traveling on jeep tracks inches away from sudden death day in and day out, is a mystery for me. I used to call the AKRSP drivers 'precision drivers'. Sher Ali, Mir Ahmad, Ibrahim, Jalil and Naib Khan, my personal drivers, took care of me in a way which belies description.

In 1985, our daredevil helicopter pilot braved a snowstorm below Shandur Pass near Phandar. Hussain Wali, who had forewarned me of

MY INTRODUCTION TO AKRSP

the risk of the pilot losing control in a 'whiteout', now advised me to jump. Fortunately I did not because down below was a frozen river. The helicopter crashed, falling onto its left side. I fell out on top of the others. Two of the AKRSP drivers walked twelve miles in the snow to reach us. The Army Puma came twenty-four hours later to pick us up from the crash site.

Once while driving up from Gupis to Phandar, the local Deputy Superintendent of Police Nazrab asked if he could accompany me. A few miles up on the road, I saw a distraught woman sitting on the road. On enquiry she pointed to the river. The jeep she and her family were traveling in was in the river with dead bodies floating around. I felt totally numb looking at the scene. To my great surprise, in a flash, I saw Nazrab hurtling down the slope of the river bank and rescuing whomever he could. He was soon joined by others and many precious lives were saved although quite a few died. I was glad that on my recommendation, endorsed by the Commissioner of the Northern Areas, Nazrab was awarded the *Tamgha-e-Shujaat* (Award for Bravery) by the President of Pakistan. In a strange coincidence, Nazrab had come to my office in Gilgit a few weeks earlier and said that he had seen the Imam in his dream. The Imam had advised him to see me and that was the reason why he had come to see me. I thanked him for his visit: what else could I say?

The mountainous Northern Areas were totally unlike any terrain I was accustomed to. In the first few months I was there, the four non-local staff, including myself, in the management group used to drive the jeep ourselves so we did not have to sit in the back. Our first trip to Hunza, a journey of some four hours, negotiating the jeep track from Karimabad to Aliabad had me sweating in December. The suspension bridges were a nightmare as was one particular stretch of the Gilgit–Ghizar road, which seemed to be hanging with no support. We always sighed with relief and even thought of issuing medals for bravery for crossing some sections of that bit of road.

On my first visit to the Gujal valley, about 80 miles from Gilgit I was shown a small, innocuous funnel of rock jutting over the KKH, which I was told was the 'snout' of an annual avalanche, which used to block the KKH between Hunza and Gujal for days. Once, while I was having a dialogue with villagers at Ghulkin, someone whispered to me that the avalanche had started and the road was blocked.

On another occasion a few years later, I missed the avalanche by a few seconds as the entire area in front of my jeep became clouded with snow sprayed by the avalanche at Shishkat. It was indeed a narrow escape. A few miles before the Shishkat avalanche site, someone pointed out a harmless *nullah* (stream) crossing the KKH. A few weeks later my borrowed jeep dropped me at Passu and while returning got stuck in the same nullah. The driver, a new one appointed on the recommendation of the chairman of the District Council, abandoned the vehicle and ran for his life. Next morning the jeep was a hundred feet below the road, covered in mudflow, and was being dragged up with the help of hundreds of villagers. I could not believe my eyes. It was the same jeep which had given me such faithful service. I saw its lights on, as if pleading to me with its eyes for rescue and help. I learnt the lesson never to hire a driver who did not have a proven track record.

Unlike during my service in the government or with the United Nations, this was the first time I was left to fend for myself. Everything had to be built from scratch. Finding a suitable place as a base of operations for AKRSP was the first priority. The Commissioner, Jamil Haider Shah, went out of his way to allow AKRSP to take over the Northern Areas Transport Company (NATCO) office as he had already asked NATCO to shift from their existing premises which was running at a great loss. The building was a private house with a compound and NATCO seemed to be using it as a *godown* (warehouse). On my visit I found only one person in the office who introduced himself as the finance manager of the company. The building was in a poor state of repair. NATCO promised to make it available to us as soon as possible as the Commissioner's orders had to be complied with immediately.

The Management Group (MG) had a meeting and dispatched Alidad to Karachi with a list of furniture and office equipment. By 1 January 1983, AKRSP had started functioning from Babar Road where it still has its headquarters. With the landlord's permission a block housing the Visitors Centre and Library was designed and constructed under the supervision of Hussain Wali. After the first evaluation of AKRSP, and looking at the number of visitors, the World Bank suggested setting up a visitors centre to meet the pressure of work. Shahida Jaffrey made the Visitors Centre a place we were all proud of, and which greatly impressed the visitors

Having established the base of operations for AKRSP in physical terms at Babar Road, the challenge was now to recruit people to fill the two vacant positions of the management group, namely engineering and finance, and hire the support staff. For finance I offered the position to Mutabiat, the finance manager of NATCO and never regretted the selection. For engineering, I explained the job requirements to Hussain Wali. He responded that this was not an engineer's function. Hussain Wali had served as chief engineer, Northern Areas Public Works Department and was currently the Project Engineer of the Kohistan Development Authority. I persuaded Hussain Wali to join AKRSP because I needed the highest expertise to find engineering solutions to the problems faced at the grassroots. I had decided that in the MG, there would be no differentiation in salaries between local and non-local people and that every MG member would get the basic salary of Rs 15,000 p.m. There being no income tax in the Northern Areas (NAs), this was to be the take home pay. I suspect initially that Hussain Wali was only attracted by the salary, and not so much by the work. But in due course, he proved the best person for the job and when time came for me to leave AKRSP in 1992, in my view there was no better person to take over the General Manager's position than Hussain Wali. His death saddened me beyond measure.[1] The MG had now four non-local and two local staff members. However, there was no woman in the MG.

On one of my visits to Islamabad, Musarrat identified Maliha Hussein and strongly recommended her candidature for employment in the AKRSP. Maliha was a member of the Pakistan Foreign Service (PFS) and was greatly dismayed by General Ziaul Haq's decision that no unmarried PFS girl should be posted in Pakistani missions abroad. Maliha had decided to resign. On return to Gilgit, I asked Tariq, our programme economist, to meet Maliha on his next visit to Islamabad and let me have a report on Maliha's suitability for a job in AKRSP. Tariq as usual was non-committal but I needed a woman MG member and Musarrat's recommendation was too important to be disregarded. I offered Maliha the job as the head of the women in development (WID) section. Maliha brought credit and distinction to the work she did. Tariq and Maliha got married and eventually I lost both of them though not before they had made matchless and abiding contributions to the progress of AKRSP.

The recruitment of support staff posed a twofold problem: first there were hardly any trained stenographers available in the market, and when I did offer the job of my personal assistant (PA) to one individual, it raised shock waves right up to Karachi. I was accused of poaching staff of other AKF projects by offering them higher salaries. I solved the issue by getting my PA from PARD to work in AKRSP. Twenty-four years later he is still with me. Rauf joined UNDP after AKRSP and is now in the Rural Support Programmes Network (RSPN) managing the Chairman's Office. Alidad, Mohammad Yar and Tawallud Shah all got absorbed in AKRSP. We had no shortage of excellent drivers, peons and administrative staff. Sulaiman was always there day and night whenever I decided to visit my office. Shakoor was the handyman and a jack-of-all- trades. He was a doer. I was sorry to hear about his death and so also of Alidad. Ali Yar looked after transport.

However, the backbone of AKRSP was the field staff manning the Social Organization Units (SOUs) comprising social organizers, engineers and specialists in agriculture, forestry, animal husbandry and allied areas. The social organizer was my eyes and ears. Initially I imported field staff from PARD, including Mutahir, Sartaj, Ikram and Ghulam Habib. They had worked in Daudzai and IRDP (Integrated Rural Development Programme) in NWFP since 1972. This small band grew into a large cadre, now extending from Pakistan to Tajikistan. In the words of Dr Akhtar Hameed Khan, social organizers had to work like gypsies, constantly on the move in villages of their area, and they had to work like primary school teachers in the same place for a lifetime.

To ensure that the MG, the field staff and above all the organized communities, such as village organizations (VOs) and women's organizations (WOs), moved in the same direction, I instituted the system of programme planning meetings (PPMs), something I had learnt from UNICEF. All members of the MG met every week. There was a monthly meeting of the MG and field staff followed by a monthly conference of VO/WO managers and presidents in which the MG and SOUs participated. For the first ten years, I never missed these events.

I read all the available books on the Northern Areas and found Mr Baig's Bookshop a treasure trove and G. M. Baig himself a walking encyclopedia about local traditions and customs. On His Highness the Aga Khan's first visit, when I mentioned to Her Highness Begum Aga Khan the book *Continents in Collision,* which I had bought from Baig Sahib's Bookshop, she could not believe it as she had not been able to find the book anywhere in France. She was keen to see it and I sent it to her. The next day the book was returned with a note of thanks by Her Highness saying she would try again to search for the book on her return. When I showed the note to Musarrat she retorted she couldn't believe I could be so dumb and asked me to present it to Her Highness.

MY INTRODUCTION TO AKRSP

Next day at the airport, I took the book with me but Musarrat had already told her that I had brought the book for her. Before I could reach Her Highness, she came running to me asking me where the book was. To have a bookshop like this in Gilgit was incredible. But the bookshop was only a reflection of the personality of Baig Sahib. I was shocked to learn of his death in a Fokker crash. He was indeed an institution.

The books proved to be a great source of understanding the history of the area. The book I presented to Begum Aga Khan told me precisely where the continental plates had collided in a gorge located near Chalt. I even persuaded Hussain Wali to put up a plaque on the rock announcing 'Here the Continents Collided'. I also discovered the grave of Heyward, the English explorer, in the cemetery next to the PWD Rest House. Heyward was murdered in Yasin Valley on his way to Darkut at the behest of the Maharaja of Kashmir, and having a premonition of his death, had left footprints on the route he was travelling. An arrow engraved on one of the rocks beyond Yasin, pointing to Darkut, can still be seen. I would never have noticed the wedding cake type pillar across the Hunza river between Ganesh and Gulmit commemorating Lord Kitchener's journey to Mintaka in the footsteps of Lord Curzon. The two of them used to try to upstage one another.

The image of geese flying over Srikul Lake the whole night on the Pamir Steppes in winter for fear of getting frozen in the water were indelible descriptions. Sartaj Aziz's book on China was fascinating and most reassuring about the strategy AKRSP planned to follow. The immortal words of Francis Younghusband in his book *The Heart of a Continent* summed up the unique environment and the people of the area:[2]

> I lay down on the ground and gazed and gazed upon the scene, muttering to myself deep thankfulness that to me it had been [given] to see such glory. Here was no disappointment—no trace of disillusionment. What I had so ardently longed to see was now spread out before me. Where I had reached no white man had ever reached before. And there before me were peaks of 26,000 feet, and in one case 28,000 feet, in height, rising above a valley bottom only 12,000 feet above sea level. For mountain majesty and sheer sublimity that scene could hardly be excelled. And austere thought it was it did not repel—it just enthralled me. This world was more wonderful by far than I had ever known before. And I seemed to grow greater myself from the mere fact of having seen it. Having once seen that, how could I ever be little again.

However, my real education lay in the dialogues I had with the people. Dialogues and field visits taught me the most about the area and the people. In the first 55 days, I had held 55 dialogues traversing all the valleys in Phandar, Gupis, Yasin, Chattorkhand, Ishkoman, Punyal, Gakuch, Juglote, Hanochal, Danyore, Haramosh, Chalt, Bar, Nagar, Hunza, Hispar, Gujal and Misgar. Some journeys required a back-breaking nine to ten hour drive. No wonder when Guy Hunter visited me he observed 'This is not a rural development programme. It is a heroic programme'. Without these overland journeys, I would have never understood the lie of the land or the conditions under which people lived. The terrain was awesome, the weather biting and cold and the roads dangerous but the people were welcoming and warm hearted and incredibly strong and determined. Every valley I visited had something new to tell me and teach me.

The visit to the forbidden land of Nagar, to meet followers of Imam Khomeni, in the darkness of the night accompanied with Agha Yahya, who proved a true well wisher of AKRSP, was a singular experience. It was there that for the first time I was introduced to the local bread, *phiti,* which in later years was declared by a Hungarian bread expert to be one of the most delicious breads in the world. Further up, beyond Nagar, in Gujal valley, the sheer dimensions of cathedral spire-like peaks and massive fan-like alluvial plains gave the impression that the earth was born here. The valley beyond Phandar looked like a massively scaled up Hyde Park with the Serpentine twenty miles long. Passu and its people, diehard mountaineers, many of whom had climbed K2 and Nanga Parbat, were similarly impressive. The frozen springs by the roadside and the glaciers, coming one after the other and breathing cold air like giants and demons left no doubt in the mind that this was a different world. An awesome world. A beautiful world. A fascinating world. My twelve years in this world were beyond my wildest dreams.

Being the new boy on the block, it was my duty to win the goodwill and cooperation of all and sundry. This included the civil administration headed by the Commissioner, the army divisional headquarters under the Force Commander Northern Areas (FCNA) of the rank of a major general, the NAs Council and the District Councils of elected members, the Ismaili *Jamaat* and the Shia and Sunni leadership. By a strange coincidence, I got involved in a Shia-Ismaili dispute over a *Jamaat Khana* and an *Imam Bargah* in Ganesh. The Ismailis were furious that the administration was siding with the Shias as they held them

MY INTRODUCTION TO AKRSP

responsible for the trouble. I knew the Commissioner Jamil Haider Shah very well and strongly challenged this view, offering to arrange a meeting with him. I spoke to Jamil, who readily agreed to meet the Ismaili leadership led by the Chairman of the Hunza Council, Ghulam Mohammad and the matter was resolved amicably in consultation with the Shia leadership. When Agha Yayha saw me at the meeting he remarked 'we didn't know you do this also.'

Because of Jamil the civil administration were most helpful and cooperative but I knew the departmental heads resented us, especially when comparisons were made between the excellent work being done by AKRSP and the departmental outputs. I made every attempt and gave strict instructions to the AKRSP staff to be on their best behaviour when dealing with government officials. During my 12-year stay, there were eight Heads of the NA administration. Even the designation of the post changed, from Commissioner to resident commissioner to chief commissioner and then to chief secretary. All of them were very kind and helpful to me and without the support and indulgence of people like Jamil Haider Shah, Khalid Ahmad, Captain Abdul Qayyum, Afzal Kahut, Shakil Durrani and Mahmood Khan, AKRSP would not have had such smooth sailing. The programme owes a great debt of gratitude to them and I cannot thank them enough for their kindness and consideration towards me.

The FCNA, though not directly involved with AKRSP, always lent us a helping hand. Major General Safdar Ali Khan always went out of his way to help us and to publicise AKRSP. During General Aslam Beg's tenure as COAS, when on his first visit to the NAs, he sent a special message to meet him at lunch. Everyone wondered about my relationship with him. But with the army I had to tread very carefully.

Even with General Safdar, I once got on the wrong side. I invited him to inaugurate the Sust Channel tunnel, to which he readily agreed. It so happened that the same day Mr Ejaz Naik, Secretary General, Economic Affairs Division made a programme to visit the NAs and AKRSP. I naively invited him also to attend the inaugural ceremony. Early morning on the appointed day, I got a call from the FCNA HQs that the General regretted his inability to come as he has some other pressing engagement. I rang up his staff officer who asked me, 'How could the General come when you have also invited the Secretary General EAD?' I tried to assure him he just happened to be here, saying that the general was the chief guest and the people were waiting for him. The personal staff officer did not budge and I made hasty arrangements for Mr Naik to visit the project after the inauguration and with great difficulty persuaded the general to keep the appointment which he did. The general always praised the project sky high everywhere.

The elected leaders of the Northern Areas Council (NAC) and the Chairman District Councils were of the view initially that AKRSP should act according to their wishes and advice. They were an important segment of society and I very much wanted their goodwill and cooperation for AKRSP. I made it a point to invite the elected leaders to my dialogues with the community. In one case, when the chairman of the District Council Gilgit insisted that a village in Gakuch desired to have a different project than what AKRSP had identified, I persuaded him to come to the village with me and hear for himself what the priority project of more than 75 per cent of the households was. The VO assured the Chairman Mr Latif that their first priority was the project they had identified in the dialogue with AKRSP. However, if the chairman was willing to finance an additional project then they would welcome the second project also. After this incident, Chairman Latif became AKRSP's great supporter and personally went to many dialogues, especially the one to Hanuchal which is a living monument to the expertise and determination of the people. In Chitral, the Chairman of the District Council, Shahzada Mohiuddin, after having a few dialogues, started holding the dialogues himself which was a big relief to me, as he didn't need any interpreter. The Chairman Baltistan District Council Nashad placed the entire development budget of each Union Council at the disposal of AKRSP to entice me to initiate the programme in Baltistan—a totally non-Ismaili district. The NAC members started placing the grant money at their disposal for development work at the disposal of AKRSP for implementation of projects in their village of choice according to the AKRSP methodology. Of course, the NAC members from Diamir would come and express the wish that they could invite AKRSP, but they were afraid of opposition by religious zealots. Ultimately the Astore subdivision of Diamir District separated themselves and persuaded me to initiate the programme where Shias and Sunnis alike joined hands to make a request for the programme.

One day I was very happy to receive the Pesh Imam of the Sunni Idgah (mosque) who asked me if the programme was only for Ismailis. I responded that AKRSP would enter into a development partnership with any community irrespective of sect, if they were willing to accept AKRSP's terms of partnership. The Pesh Imam saw nothing objectionable in the terms of partnership and we organized the community in the vicinity of the Idgah. I was told that some priests from Kohistan came to Molvi Gul Sher and remonstrated against his link with AKRSP. He countered by asking them how come they have used the KKH which has been constructed by people who do not even believe in God (*i.e.* the Chinese). I never went to any religious leader myself but always welcomed them if they wanted to see me and explained and clarified the working of AKRSP. In some places, they remained unconvinced and despite my being a born Sunni felt that I had sold my soul.

Once I took Akhtar Hameed Khan to a diehard Sunni area and he narrated how Emperor Aurganzeb had refused to reward his teacher because the education he gave did not equip him to fight the foreigners whose technology was far superior to that of the Mughals. Akhtar Hameed Khan exhorted that if the Sunnis did not take advantage of the modern education and technology AKRSP is offering them, they would be left far behind like the Mughals were left far behind the foreigners.

AKRSP succeeded in bringing about a tremendous change and improvement in many of the backward areas with the exception of a few. Darel and Tangir in Diamir did not budge. Surprisingly enough the present Speaker of NAC, Malik Miskeen from Diamir, is now trying his best to get an AKRSP type programme started in the two valleys and regularly visits me.

AKRSP held its first dialogue on 15 December 1982 in village Japuka of Punyal valley. Hussain Wali had stipulated that the Village Organization (VO) would take three months to complete its Productive Physical Infrastructure, but it was finished in six weeks for the simple reason that the VO 'man days' were 12 hours and not eight, and the average manpower used per day was not 40 but 100 or even more. The work had been done strictly according to the specifications and no land compensation was claimed for the land used for the link road. The NA PWD had built a bridge across the river but the village, which was more than a couple of miles in length, had no link road running through it. A 'jeepable' road was the dire need. Hussain Wali had devised a formula for the cost estimate, including wages for unskilled work at a negotiated rate so that in the name of self help day labourers did not have to do *begaar* (free, usually involuntary, labour). The VO was entirely responsible for implementation and maintenance of the work done. Payments were in four instalments on the basis of output, irrespective of the details of how it was done in terms of labour employed and cost of material purchased, so long as the quality was the same or better as indicated in the cost estimate. Irrespective of the fact that the Japuka link road was completed six weeks in advance, AKRSP made the full payment to the VO according to the estimates.

The example of the Japuka link road spread like wildfire. Overnight AKRSP was in the sellers' market instead of the buyers' market. Instead of the AKRSP MG going and exhorting villagers to hold dialogues with them, the villagers started coming to AKRSP requesting dialogues in their villages. The credibility of AKRSP was established and people began to have faith in what AKRSP was saying. Soon AKRSP built up a reputation for strictly abiding by the terms of partnership signed with VO or WO.

I made it abundantly clear to the staff that, as in the commercial world, the client is always right. In AKRSP the villager was to be treated with the utmost courtesy and consideration. I issued strict orders that when the VO members visited AKRSP they should never be kept waiting. I set an example, requiring to be informed of the arrival of anyone wanting to see me, even if I was in a meeting. In the initial years, the VO/WO loan applications had to be approved by the general manager personally and I did my best to ensure that no VO manager or president coming to get loan approval should be subjected to any delay or inconvenience. If I saw any member of a VO or WO waiting anywhere in the AKRSP premises I made it a point to enquire the nature of his or her business.

In case of a complaint by a VO or WO against any functionary of AKRSP, the functionary had to respond to the complaint in public in a VO/WO meeting. These steps established a high sense of accountability in the staff. A complaint by a VO membership against a AKRSP staff member, publicly voiced and proved, meant there was no place for the staff member in AKRSP. I made it a practice to deal with such complaints personally. It worked both ways. I never received a superfluous complaint from a VO or WO and the AKRSP staff were well aware of the consequences of any misdemeanor, especially corruption, on their part. In Daudzai, Akhtar Hameed Khan had asked me to put up boards in all the Daudzai offices, declaring that this was not a programme for thieves. Everyone in AKRSP was aware that *bona fide* mistakes would always be acknowledged as such, but that theft,

MY INTRODUCTION TO AKRSP 193

graft and corruption would never be condoned. I prided myself on hardly ever receiving complaints of corruption, although the staff handled millions of rupees as grants for 'productive physical infrastructures', the savings of VO and WO members and loans made to them. Many a time, due to lack of banking facilities, our staff had to carry and handle large amounts of cash but during my twelve years in AKRSP, except for one social organizer, I never had to take action for corruption against any AKRSP staff member from the drivers to members of the MG.

I was very pleased when the World Bank, in its first assessment of AKRSP in 1987, highlighted the primacy and sovereignty of the VOs and WOs established by AKRSP. It also lauded the process approach of AKRSP against the traditional 'blueprint' approach followed by most of the World Bank funded rural development projects. It observed that 'the first four years of AKRSP were the missed four years' in most of the Rural Development Projects worldwide.

The corporate culture of AKRSP envisaged listening to villagers, treating them as equals, sitting on the ground with them instead of on chairs and sofas and never, never accepting food and drink while on AKRSP dialogues or other business.

I had a lot of difficulty in enforcing the rule about accepting food and drink. The villagers were the most vehement opponents and said it was against the local traditions of hospitality and an insult to them as hosts. My reasoning was straightforward, however. AKRSP was there to reduce poverty and not to impoverish them by being their guests every time the staff visited them, which was going to be very frequently. I used to narrate to them the story of how the Chinese man in charge of the KKH construction force refused to accept a gift of apricots from a local person, saying if he accepted it, there were 25,000 Chinese working in his command and not a single apricot would be left on the trees belonging to the people.

This issue came to a head when, on one of my first visits to Chitral, accompanied by the commissioner, the deputy commissioner, the Commandant of Chitral Scouts and other officials, I found a lavish feast laid on by the local Khan at the venue of the dialogue. I held the dialogue but refused to partake of the feast. The other officials followed suit. The Commissioner Shamsher Ali Khan, who had been my probationer at the Civil Service Academy, fully shared my point of view but the local Khan and the deputy commissioner were furious. However, the message of the incident was publicized widely and I was overheard the president assured him that he had been following the same approach.

The dialogues were the key to the success of AKRSP. They not only helped in fostering community organizations like VOs and WOs, they also facilitated those organizations in identifying honest and competent 'activists' as managers and presidents. They also provided feedback to AKRSP about the institutional maturity of the VOs/WOs. For me personally the dialogues were the main training and orientation tool for the members of the MG and the field staff. On my initial 300 dialogues I made it a point to take the entire MG with me. This helped greatly in clarifying the nuances of the Conceptual Package. This was coupled with writing of a Note for the Record (NFR) on each dialogue and a daily diary of activities by each Social Organizer (SO). Every month I would read the diaries and make comments on the documentation and the observations of the SOs. It was a two-way communication. The diaries told me a lot about what was happening in the field and the SOs learnt a lot about the strengths and weaknesses of their approach. It soon became quite clear to the MG and the field staff that the success of AKRSP depended on three essentials:

i) The willingness of the community to enter into a development partnership with AKRSP could only be ascertained if at least 75 per cent of the households in a community agreed to organize, hold regular meetings and generate savings.

ii) The presence of a competent and honest activist in the form of a manager or a president who understood the AKRSP vision and was successful in disseminating it to the general membership, and

iii) dedication and strict adherence to the conceptual package of AKRSP by the staff of AKRSP, especially the Social Organizers with full support from the MG.

I was often criticized by the MG for giving too much importance to the SOs, but I knew they were my eyes and ears and they were the regular frontline contact with the communities. I also knew that any delinquency on their part was bound to have an adverse impact on the programme. The SO's success lay in helping communities in identifying a genuine and competent Activist to lead them. Behind every successful VO/WO, there was an Activist. If the Activist became dishonest or stopped taking an interest in the affairs of the organization, the VO/WO invariably became dormant. No amount of effort on the part of the programme staff could revive the VO/WO. In this connection Passu VO comes to my mind. There, mountaineer Ghulam Mohammad was the driving force. Then he opened a hotel and lost interest in the VO. I took Akhtar Hameed Khan to Passu and we spent two nights there, exhorting VO members to fulfill their terms of partnership. Nothing happened, despite empty promises, for three years until another genuine and honest activist emerged and took on the responsibility of leading the VO. In a short time Passu was back on the rails and fulfilled all the promises they had made to AKRSP. A large majority of the activists were teachers or retired army personnel. They were indeed the real social capital of the community.

The programme approach was straightforward and simple. It was based on the assumption that there is tremendous potential in people, even the poorest, and they are willing to do whatever is within their capacity to improve their situation not only individually but also collectively. In the dialogues, when I used to be asked 'what is the limit of AKRSP support', my response was always 'what is your limit?' Whatever the community was capable of doing, AKRSP would support it to achieve that. In one of our initial dialogues in a predominantly Shia village, the assembled villagers identified a bridge on the river Hunza connecting them with KKH as their priority project and said to me 'Please request Sir Aga Khan to build a bridge for us'. An Ismaili sitting next to me whispered in my ear 'why don't they ask Imam Khomeni to do it for them'? However, the matter was amicably settled when it was realized that construction and maintenance of the bridge was beyond the expertise, capacity and knowledge of the community. For such projects, AKRSP could only act as their lobbyist with government and convey their request to the Northern Areas Public Works Department.

The same argument held when communities identified school or health facilities as their priorities. The question of whether they could meet the recurrent cost of such projects used to bring home to them the challenge of undertaking such projects. At one of the dialogues, the community berated me for not giving priority to education without which, they admonished me, I would not have been the GM of AKRSP and talking to them. I explained that AKRSP was not a 'super department' and that it could not do each and every thing. Its niche was to harness the potential of the people and to help in unleashing it. There was no government department with this mandate but there were departments for health, education and many other disciplines whose mandate was to undertake those activities in accordance with allocation of resources dedicated for these purposes.

Akhtar Hameed Khan used to advise that engineers and other subject matter specialists should be persuaded initially to graft on existing local expertise and knowledge instead of introducing innovations. The soundness of this advice was beautifully demonstrated in the case of Sust where, against the AKRSP Engineering Section's proposal for construction of the *khul* alongside the mountain, the VO decided to tunnel the hillock—nearly half a mile. On my refusal to accept their proposal—on Hussain Wali's advice—the villagers were crestfallen. However, a month later the VO President Subedar Aziz came to Gilgit and requested me to revisit Sust with Hussain Wali. I promised to do so and on arrival on the appointed date, the VO members made Hussain Wali and I climb to the top of the hillock and literally lowered us 150 feet to the mouth of a tunnel 6 feet high, 3 feet wide and already 200 feet long. Hussain Wali had this great quality of not being rigid. He accepted the viewpoint of the VO and advised me to approve the Rs 300,000 the VO wanted to complete the tunnel and to construct the *khul* (irrigation channel) to bring nearly 5,000 *kanals* (625 acres) of new land under irrigation. It took the 64 households of Sust sixteen months to complete the channel-tunnel. I still remember receiving a telephone call from Sub. Aziz late one evening at the Chinar Inn. He was calling from Sust on a faulty telephone line to inform me that the two halves of the tunnel (one from each side) had met in the centre. Sust became one of the wonders of AKRSP and a favourite with visitors, including His Highness the Aga Khan, President Leghari and President Musharraf. Sust taught me, and more so our engineers, not to underrate the expertise of the local people. On my last visit to Sust, I saw a tablet with the names of 17 men who had worked on the project and were now dead. I said a silent prayer to the courage and determination of these brave people.

A similar project was carried out in Hanuchal where District Council Chairman Latif had taken me after our joint visit to Gakuch. Hanuchal took four years to complete but the people never gave up. It was my favourite project for visitors to let them experience the potential of the people. The VO President Abdullah Malang was a born leader and a gifted poet. Anyone who had visited Hanuchal was prepared to believe any achievement of AKRSP. When the first World Bank Evaluation team visited the area in 1987, Dr Donaldson remarked this was AKRSP's 'softening up' approach even for the diehard critic. Shipusan in Buni valley, Chitral used to have a similar effect on visitors. When Secretary General EAD Ejaz Naik visited Shahtote and saw the condition of the people, he felt they were cavemen. Shahtote left an impression on his mind persuading him to open up a bilateral funding window for NGOs despite opposition from the ministry.

The two siphon irrigation projects at Prawvak Chitral and Sonikot Gilgit constructed by VOs which the Canadian Development Counsellor (who was an engineer) declared incredible and had serious doubts about their sustainability even after 20 years are as functional today as at the time of construction.

Hussain Wali built the first micro hydel (*i.e.* hydro-electric project) at Gulmit in 1984 to light the hotel of Raja Bahadar Khan and followed it up with a micro-hydel at village Shahtote. Slowly the micro-hydels multiplied and the local technician from Shahtote was extensively used by Hussain Wali for installing new ones. But it was Masood ul Mulk in Chitral who took the micro-hydel programme to its zenith, covering hundreds of villages. The World Bank said that Chitral had the highest concentration of micro-hydels anywhere in the world by 2000. The micro-hydels of Chitral received the Ashden Award in 2005 and the Global Development Network Award for the most innovative project in 2006. Looking back at the Gulmit plant, I had never visualized it would have such great potential.

Productive Physical Infrastructure (PPI) was an investment in organization and a VO was entitled to only one PPI. During my stay as GM AKRSP I made only one exception in the case of village Hamaran in Bagrote valley. Accompanied by Fayyaz Baqir, I had gone to visit the village, when I discovered that the only way to reach the village was to go through a deep ravine with near vertical slopes. I do not know how I managed to negotiate the slopes and I wondered how the people of Hamaran managed to get across the ravine, especially women during emergencies. Although Hamaran VO had already been given a grant for a *khul* which they had completed, as a special case I sanctioned a bridge also over the ravine for Hamaran.

The only case where we were duped by the villagers in identifying a PPI was village Jutal where they identified a *khul* and fooled our engineering section into believing that the source of water for the *khul* was sufficient. Later it transpired that the construction of the *khul* was to get proprietary rights to the land commanded by the *khul* under the

Natore (newly broken land) Rules of government. The water at the source was only enough for the existing *khul* and they had only diverted that water for a few days to hoodwink our SO and engineers. Anyway the ghost *khul* did benefit the villagers by securing them property rights to a vast tract of land.

Programme Achievements

- According to the people who had been familiar with the Northern Areas prior to the advent of AKRSP, changes in the thinking and behaviour of the people appeared to be the most striking achievement of AKRSP.
- The organization of nearly 90 per cent of the households in the VOs and WOs enabled everyone to participate in decision making about their own development. Fostering a large cadre of activists from amongst the grassroots organizations as the 'social capital' of the community proved to be the key to the success of the programme. This cadre acted as the service providers for the members of the VOs and WOs.
- AKRSP ushered in genuine democracy at the grassroots level through the process of community participation. This was in contrast to representative participation, where one person used to speak on behalf of 1,000 households. Now 90 per cent of the households had a say in their economic development. The process also resulted in political education: currently 70 per cent of the elected members of the District and Union Councils are former VO/WO Activists and many of the Northern Areas Council members are also former Activists.
- Generation of their own capital through savings amounting to hundreds of millions of rupees. Capital is power. In the case of Women's Organizations, savings gave women a new kind of empowerment. Some VOs excelled in savings, accumulating more than ten million rupees. Savings also enabled easy access to credit and built the capacity of VOs/WOs to manage VO Banking.
- Land development through PPIs made the biggest contribution in increasing household incomes and promoting large scale forestry, fodder cultivation and planting of orchards.
- Unlike the clamour for equal distribution of funds amongst villages as in the case of Union Council and Local Bodies and Rural Development Department funds, the VOs/WOs learnt to be satisfied

with funds according to their identified needs and their capacity. Although the average cost of PPI was US$10,000 (Rs 150,000 exchange rate of 1983), in some cases the VOs needed and received as little as Rs 50,000 while others received as much as three million rupees, but there never was any dispute amongst VOs/WOs on this account.

- AKRSP succeeded in banishing the contractors and replacing them with VOs/WOs and putting full responsibility for maintenance onto the communities for the projects they implemented. This method persuaded the VOs/WOs to take full ownership of the projects.
- Organized VOs/WOs eagerly adopted technological packages in every field especially NRM and livestock improvement. French cherries, California apples and Heifer Project breed of animals became household names. The processing of fruits, especially apricots, reached new heights seeking markets abroad and down country.
- Conservation of environment and wildlife was given great importance and currently all villages in the NAs and Chitral participate with the government Wildlife Department in a trophy hunting programme. In the Bar valley, where it all started in 1985, the ibex population had more than doubled, according to a scientific survey done by the Wildlife Department expert Mr Ashiq Ali. AKRSP also helped Dr Anisur Rahman (CEO of the Himalayan Wildlife Foundation) in his efforts to protect the Deosai brown bear.
- The framework of grassroots institutions persuaded the government to channel local development through the VOs and WOs. In 1990, when floods and mudflows destroyed many irrigation channels (*khul*s), the prime minister placed 50 million rupees at the disposal of AKRSP to rehabilitate the damaged infrastructure through the VOs and/WOs.
- The linkage of VOs/WOs and their clusters, called Local Support Organizations (LSOs), with government departments, donors, NGOs and other development agencies is now an established practice. The linkage with the Aga Khan Health Services (AKHS), spearheaded by Steve Rasmussen (the CEO of AKHS), brought about a revolutionary change, especially in non-Ismaili areas like Nagar. Similarly, the Aga Khan Education Services (AKES) took full advantage of the VOs/WOs in implementing their programmes.

Learning how to learn

AKRSP was established to learn from its own experience. Several important lessons emerged over the first 45 months, and resulted in alterations in programme direction. In particular, agricultural technology suitable for the area was originally thought to be readily available: in practice, the micro variations within the project area and the differences from the rest of Pakistan were underestimated. This has led to much greater emphasis on adaptive research and to a change in training courses. Similarly, experience has shown that much staff time and funding have had to be devoted to land development after new land is opened through a PPI irrigation channel. Marketing was initially felt to be a question of cooperative collection and sale of surplus products that were otherwise being wasted: it has proved to be far more complicated, since there are few wasted surpluses of quality, direct selling by VOs to wholesalers in distant markets has proved risky and occasionally unprofitable. Marketing also needs to begin with the identification of potential demand, working back to quality products to meet the demand. In the women's programme, initial ideas for PPIs have foundered on socio-economic realities, and a different approach is now being tried. Finally, the expansion into Baltistan District occurred several years before originally anticipated, as a result of strong pressure from local people. This has involved very considerable staff time and expense.

The most lasting effect of AKRSP's efforts so far has been the spread of an idea: the conviction that villagers can manage their resources collectively and control their own future is beginning to acquire currency among the villagers of Gilgit District. This idea needs to be translated increasingly into concrete projects that will sustain the VOs into the future.

The project area contains threats to stability and sustainability, and there are major issues concerning optimal resource management, especially in relationship between crops, forestry and livestock. These will be the subjects of special attention in Second Phase programming. The limited experience of AKRSP and the UNDP/FAO project indicates the potential availability of a wide spectrum of new crops, varieties and breeds that could be used in the Northern Areas if attention is paid to ecological variation in the region.

In its first 45 months, AKRSP has shown considerable flexibility in making course corrections, instituting remedial measures, and strengthening weak mechanisms whenever it has been confronted with negative experiences. Such resilience will become even more important in the future in designing robust technology and institutions that will prosper into the twenty-first century.

Nurturing Local Talent. One of my greatest achievements was nurturing local talent. I had arrived in 1982 with a team of professionals, all from down-country (*i.e.* other parts of Pakistan). When I left in 1994, over 95 per cent of the 400 staff were from the Northern Areas and Chitral and many of them had acquired educational qualifications from abroad under AKRSP's donor-funded training and education programme in Canada, the UK and Norway. I was happiest when I handed over the reins of AKRSP to Hussain Wali and am happier now that Izhar Ali Hunzai, who came as an intern in 1985 and comes from Hunza, is the general manager. On my visit to Tajikistan to attend a seminar a few months ago, I was most pleasantly surprised to be received at the Kabul airport by ex-AKRSP staff Dr Farman Ali, Manzoor Hussain, Darjat and Safdar Ali and at Dushanbe by Khalil Tetlay. The AKRSP trained staff is now spread all over Rural Support Programmes in Pakistan with Masoodul Mulk heading the Sarhad Rural Support Programme, Rashid Bajwa as the CEO of the National Rural Support Programme, and Shandana Khan as the CEO of the Rural Support Programmes Network.

The Donors

AKRSP was His Highness the Aga Khan's idea. It was given concrete shape by Robert d'Arcy Shaw, Director Special Programmes AKF and nurtured by Bill de Spoelberch, General Manager AKF Geneva. J.P. Naz as the finance manager of AKF always ensured the smooth flow of funds to AKRSP.

The first donor to visit AKRSP was John Martin from the Canadian International Development Agency (CIDA). His visit was sponsored by Nazeer Ladhani, the CEO of the Aga Khan Foundation Canada. John was very perceptive and greatly appreciated what AKRSP was doing. AKRSP forged a long partnership with CIDA and I personally made many visits to Canada, making presentations on AKRSP in Calgary, Vancouver, Toronto and Ottawa. I was very happy when Margaret Catley Carlson who, in 1982, as Deputy Executive Director of UNICEF, had conveyed approval of my deputation from UNICEF to AKF, took over as President of CIDA. My contact with Margaret has continued even till recently through the Global Water Partnership. CIDA today remains a steadfast supporter of AKRSP.

Oxfam opened up a bilateral window of funds for AKRSP through ODA (Overseas Development Agency) and later on through the Department for International Development (DFID). The first tranche of funding from ODA for AKRSP's Chitral Programme was approved, I am told, only after Foreign Secretary Douglas Hurd had given a certificate that the funds were not going to be used for Pakistan's nuclear programme. This was a long term partnership and when replications of AKRSP started happening in Pakistan, DFID funded the establishment of the Rural Support Programmes Network (RSPN) in 2000 mainly through the effort of Steve Jones. Sir Nicholas Barrington, British High Commissioner in Pakistan, was a true believer in AKRSP.

I have already mentioned how the Netherlands Ambassador Von Geen's visit to Baltistan in 1985 resulted in opening up a bilateral window for NGOs with assistance from the then Secretary General EAD Ejaz Naik. The Dutch assistance to Baltistan continued for a long time.

AKRSP's contact with the Norwegians was through the good offices of the IUCN, whose Country Director, Aban Markar, channeled NORAD (Norwegian Agency for Development) assistance to AKRSP for a forestry project in 1987. This subsequently resulted in a long term relationship between NORAD and AKRSP in Natural Resource Management, with a great deal of technical assistance from NORAGRIC.

Initially, the German assistance to AKRSP was for Human Resource Development through the Konrad Adenauer Foundation's Halbach but a visit to AKRSP by Ambassador Vestring resulted in GTZ[3] funding AKRSP's Astore Programme for five years. The Vestrings were my personal friends, so much so that my youngest daughter Shelley's wedding reception was held on the lawns of the ambassador's residence.

AKF (USA), under Iqbal Noor Ali, arranged presentations on AKRSP at all the major universities, including Harvard and Princeton, Berkeley, Johns Hopkins, Los Angeles and the World Bank and so also AKF (UK) which also organized a joint programme of presentations on AKRSP Pakistan and India to different *Jamaats* in the UK.

There were many other donors besides, of course, the Federal and Northern Areas and NWFP governments which supported AKRSP.

The World Bank

Although the World Bank was not a donor of AKRSP, the decision by its Operations Evaluation Department (OED) to carry out the first assessment of AKRSP in 1987 proved to be one of the most important landmarks in introducing AKRSP globally.

It was a stroke of genius on the part of Bob Shaw to have persuaded all the donors to have one evaluation acceptable to all and to have enlisted OED's agreement to do it, because OED had never previously assessed a project or programme which had not been funded by the Bank.

The World Bank assessment strongly reinforced the AKRSP strategy and methodology and applauded my personal qualities of leadership, management, dedication and setting a personal example for the staff to follow. I was told Dr Graham Donaldson asked the Bank to recommend my name for the King Leopold Development Prize and the two finalists for the prize were myself and the Indian Institute of Agricultural Research (IIAR). Finally the IIAR won but I was greatly touched by the review team's assessment report and what they said about me. It proved a great source of encouragement and inspiration to me. As of 2006, OED has carried out four evaluations of AKRSP.

However, the most memorable moment during my tenure as the GM of AKRSP was the day when I offered to resign because I felt some of my staff members (not the MG) had lost confidence in me and openly challenged my decision pertaining to annual salary adjustments in 1991. I had my nameplate removed from outside my office and my personal documents and things put in a carton when an entire group of VO activists, who had come to Gilgit for a training course, appeared in front of my office and announced they would not let me go. They said they no longer needed the staff and were capable of managing VO/WO affairs themselves. But they still needed my guidance and support and for them that was more important than any help or support the staff could give them. I was most touched and the recalcitrant staff learnt their lesson.

The only other occasion when I had to face some opposition was a few years earlier, when a few persons forced themselves into my office and I walked out because they were most unreasonable and not prepared to listen to anything unless their demand for promotion of a local boy of their area was met. They refused to leave my office, at which point I left. They went away but a few days later, when the Canadian High Commissioner was visiting AKRSP, they staged a protest with placards denouncing me and asking the High Commissioner to talk to them. I conveyed their demand to the ambassador who readily agreed to meet them. After listening to their complaint that I was wasting donor money, he assured them personally that AKRSP does not waste money and the proof was not only frequent visits of the High Commission and CIDA staff to AKRSP, but also his present visit. He told them emphatically that CIDA was very satisfied with the way AKRSP was using the funds.

Documentation and Knowledge Management

The inclusion of the monitoring, evaluation and research (MER) section, on equal terms with institution building, engineering, natural resource management, human resource development and finance, proved of immense value to AKRSP. The MER section under Tariq Husain fulfilled the important functions of continuous monitoring, course corrections and documenting all the programme activities, besides issuing quarterly and annual progress reports. Visitors to AKRSP, especially review teams and appraisal missions, used to be overwhelmed by the documentation provided to them on AKRSP.

In addition, the audio-visual section of AKRSP, set up by the Pakistan Academy for Rural Development audio-visual expert Mohammad Sadiq and ably supported by Karim Jan, ensured the video recording of all the dialogues I held and audio recordings of all the dialogues held by Social Organizers. The video, audio and photographic documentation of AKRSP since its inception is of immense value in tracing the history of the development of AKRSP.

UNICEF had commissioned a Canadian film crew to make a film on the work I did in the Mahaweli Ganga Project in Sri Lanka. Bob Shaw saw the film and contacted the same crew to make the first film capturing the beginnings of AKRSP. The film, titled 'Valleys in Transition' was shot in 1983, within the first six months of AKRSP's establishment. The film was so well made that no amount of oral description could have had the same effect. We used it extensively for introducing AKRSP and mobilizing resources. A second film entitled 'First Harvest' was made by the same crew at the end of ten years of

AKRSP and the two films are a most moving depiction of the achievements of AKRSP.

Of all the academics and visitors to AKRSP, Prof. Mahmood Hasan Khan of Simon Fraser University, Canada took the keenest interest from a researcher's angle. Mahmood Hasan Khan was and is known for his blunt, outspoken and highly critical attitude. I found him extremely honest, with an intellectual rigour seldom seen in Pakistan. Above all, I found him to have an open mind with no rigidity of views. Encouraged by Akhtar Hameed Khan, Mahmood Hasan Khan first visited AKRSP in 1987 and within five years wrote the first book on AKRSP. He generously included my name as a co-author. The book was published in the United States. Akhtar Hameed Khan used to say you need a historian to write whatever is being done, otherwise it is like the saying 'the peacock danced in the jungle but who saw it'. Mahmood Hasan Khan not only wrote on AKRSP, he has become the veritable historian of the RSP movement in Pakistan and has been a regular visitor to RSPs all over Pakistan. Unlike other senior researchers, he supervises the fieldwork himself, spending weeks and months in the desert of Thar, the hills of Balochistan or the mountains of Azad Kashmir.

NOTES

1. My posthumous tribute to Hussain Wali is attached as Appendix 6.
2. *The Heart of a Continent*, 1896.
3. *Deutsche Gesellschaft fur Technische Zusammenarbeit*.

8

The AKRSP: Goals and Operating Principles

RURAL DEVELOPMENT AND ECONOMIC JUSTICE

The concern has sometimes been raised that the AKRSP strategy would perpetuate the gulf between the haves and have-nots. I have argued that AKRSP is aiming to help subsistence farmers rise above the level of mere subsistence and become commercial farmers. If this goal is achieved it does not matter that the well-to-do farmer become richer, because this would not be at the cost of the small farmers. AKRSP is an economic rather than political programme. It is in fact an alternative both to the North American Agricultural Development Model based on private ownership of large land holdings and the Socialist model premised on collective ownership. AKRSP is fostering Village Organizations to develop into small scale entrepreneurs and thereby, ensure social justice and equitable distribution of the fruits of development.

Rural poverty and community organization: debating methods and goals[1]

Mr Sartaj Aziz (former federal minister) explained that of the 4.3 million agriculturists in Pakistan, 7 per cent owned 41 per cent of the land and were responsible for 65 per cent of all agricultural production. Ninety per cent of all government subsidies to the agricultural sector go to that seven per cent. There was, therefore, an urgent need to both increase the productivity of the 93 per cent of agriculturists and to achieve growth with social justice. Organizing the small-holders is a pre-condition for achieving these objectives. On agricultural credit, the *quantum* of the increase from 100 crores[2] to 1,600 crores of the production loans have benefitted only 6 per cent of the agriculturists.

I explained the importance of a credit programme based on savings and the importance of Village Organizations in creating accessibility for small farmers. Mr Sartaj Aziz contended that the problems of urbanization could only be solved through rural development. Economic and other opportunities need to be increased and a system of incentive put in place in the rural sector. I explained the components of the Comilla approach, and the principles on which it was based, pointing out how the World Bank had destroyed the Thana Irrigation Programme which had 36,000 water-users' groups, by introducing large tube-wells. In regard to maximising production, Mr Sartaj Aziz pointed to large-scale 'neutral' technological package and the need to create access to this package for small holders. I then explained the dynamics of group organization and the role played by an activist in organising an interest group. Mr Sartaj Aziz hoped that the lessons learnt in Gilgit would help in organizing the rural small holders of Pakistan.

Collective Management. The most striking achievement of the five VOs is their decision to stop free grazing which has resulted in their getting an additional crop of maize, millet and buckwheat. They have been able to increase the number of animals because the additional crop is used as fodder. One person after another has told me they have doubled or quadrupled their livestock holdings. If this is true, we are indeed at the threshold of a big break-through. Free grazing is resorted to so that animals do not starve. However, this cluster of 5 VOs has shown that by prohibiting free grazing, the VOs also increased yields so much that the people can afford to raise more animals. I have asked Syed Mutahir Shah (the DPO) to make in an in-depth study of the package developing at this place for its expansion elsewhere. I urge the District Programme Officer to spare no effort in finding out the impact of this decision by the VOs.

Criteria for determining different levels of collective management. I explained that the highest level of collective management will be the most sustainable and long-lasting. Suppose that one VO decides to get its irrigation channel (or newly developed forest, pasture or orchard land) maintained or planted and irrigated, by sending members in rotation to do the job, and the other VO pays people to do the work. The latter (hiring and paying people) would be a higher level of collective management because there is an element of sustainability and division of labour. Instead of each VO member contributing labour to do the same type of job, the VO assigns the work to a few members, thus freeing others to pursue their own productive work and pay only a fraction of their earnings to the paid employees. It also provides employment to the poorer members. The former method is also prone to conflict, if people shirk their responsibility, whereas the latter is less likely to produce conflicts. Collective management can take many shapes and forms but we should be clear about how effective and sustainable it is. We should always try to foster the highest level of collective management, while remembering that any level of collective management is better than no collective management.

AKRSP Board of Directors[3]

I was quite intrigued at the structure of AKRSP. This was the first time I had learnt that a rural development programme could also be implemented under the 1984 Companies Ordinance. I had always thought the purview of the Ordinance only extended to commercial and profit making ventures. AKRSP was registered as a not-for-profit joint stock Company sponsored by a minimum of 7 Directors whose personal liability did not extend beyond Rs 1,000. The Ordinance gave the Board of Directors full financial and administrative powers to manage the affairs of the Company or, in the case of AKRSP, a programme. Although the Directors are elected for three years, they are eligible for re-election and in case of AKRSP without any limit on the number of terms. Once elected, the Directors can continue unless they choose to resign or commit an indiscretion which comes within the purview of disqualification as laid down in the Articles and Memorandum of Association of the Company. In case of AKRSP, the directors also call the Annual General Meeting (AGM) of the company which elects the directors.

Thus the success of a not-for-profit company lies in the initial choice of the sponsors of the company as first directors. It is on their integrity, expertise and wisdom that the success of the company depends. It is they who hire or fire the chief executive of the organization. AKRSP had the added advantage of the patronage of His Highness the Aga Khan. The AKRSP Board had representatives from AKF Geneva, the Aga Khan Education Services, the Aga Khan Health Services and a few others, besides some eminent personalities including Ejaz Naik. During my entire tenure, the late Ramzan Merchant was the Chairman of the Board, although the membership of the Board was partially changed every three years. I have had the privilege of beginning as an *ex-officio* director and remaining a director until the present.

In the initial stages, I had to face some difficulties when the chairman, probably on the working pattern of other AKF Service Institutions, felt that I should seek financial and administrative approval for all expenditures and appointments. My point of view was that once the Board had approved the budget, the financial and administrative powers should be vested in the GM, with the exception of those which the Board had specifically decided to retain. Sometimes I felt frustrated and impatient when some Directors would display a lack of understanding in approving some proposals, but each time a visit to the field by the Directors used to greatly help in their better understanding. Of course one of my greatest advantages was that AKF Geneva was always prepared to act as a shield or as a promoter when I needed their help or support.

The only exception was in one case when they thought that my proposal to start Village Banking was a retrograde step in promoting micro finance. It was ironic because when, in 1983, I had asked for the Board's permission to take a Rs 250,000 wholesale line of credit from Habib Bank Limited, to initiate a micro-credit programme, AKF Geneva had fully supported me, although the Board, including the Chairman felt that this money would never come back. The Village Banking episode was the only situation when I had decided to leave AKRSP if the Board overruled me. I took my Management Group into confidence and they fully supported me.

The original Strategy Paper on which AKF Geneva had secured His Highness's approval to set up AKRSP (at an annual recurring cost of US$600,000) was very broad-based and provided a framework with immense possibilities. I had learnt from Akhtar Hameed Khan that the essentials of small-farmer development comprise: (1) Administrative Infrastructure (2) Productive Physical Infrastructure (PPI) and (3) Socio-economic infrastructure. The original strategy paper made no provision for the socio-economic infrastructure and envisaged that a small team of highly qualified experts in disciplines such as management, institution building, engineering, natural resource management, monitoring, evaluation and research and financial administration would be enough to achieve the twin objectives of AKRSP. Those were (i) doubling the income of the one million people of Northern Areas and Chitral in ten years and (ii) in the process developing a replicable model of rural development.

AKRSP initiated its operations in the District of Gilgit which had a population of about 250,000 including over 30,000 residing in the Township. AKRSP's first challenge was how to reach 30,000 plus households spread over a number of valleys. The Management Group (MG) drafted an operational plan to achieve the objective of doubling incomes. The revised plan, submitted to the Board within three months of AKRSP's inauguration, stipulated setting up field Social Organization Units (SOUs) to implement the framework of the conceptual package of AKRSP. This consisted of:

i) organizing rural men and women to facilitate unleashing of their potential and leadership;
ii) upgrading the human skills of the rural poor; and
iii) motivating the rural poor to generate their own capital through savings.

The 'organized rural poor' in village and women's organizations (VOs and WOs) were the missing infrastructure in the original AKRSP Strategy Paper. The Board accepted the approach submitted by the MG and sanctioned the requisite budget with full administrative and financial delegation of powers to the GM. This caused a bit of concern amongst the nominees on the Board of other highly-centralised AK network institutions for which all decisions were taken in Karachi instead of Gilgit.

AKRSP was the trail-blazer in decentralizing and delegating administrative and financial powers from Karachi to the Northern Areas. However, the local directors on the AKRSP Board also took some time to understand that in management matters, they had as much or as little say as the other directors. Their physical presence in the Northern Areas did not mean a license to interfere in administrative and management affairs of the Programme. On the whole the Board functioned extremely smoothly, fully backed by AKF Geneva and even the donors, who played an effective role in interpreting the Management Group's proposals and intentions before the Board.

AKRSP was approved for registration by the Board of the Aga Khan Foundation (AKF) in November 1981. The proposal to set up the AKRSP was based on the recommendations of the Aga Khan Foundation Team of Experts which visited the Northern Areas in July

1981. Two documents, 'The Report of the Experts Group' and the 'Proposal for a Rural Development Programme in the Northern Areas of Pakistan' prepared for the Aga Khan Foundation (Pakistan) contain detailed information relating to the land and people of the region including the administrative set up.[4]

AKRSP Premises and Objectives

1. The establishment in 1982 of the AKRSP as a private, non-profit company to serve as a catalyst for rural development in a particular area of northern Pakistan was based on five premises:

(i) that the government's capacity to effect the stimulation of development in the Northern Areas is limited by shortage of funds and staff as well as by the relatively slow response of government agencies;
(ii) that local opportunities and initiative for development exist throughout the region but are hindered in their realization by lack of effective local organizations, skills, technology appropriate to local conditions, capital and a working infrastructure;
(iii) that special attention needs to be paid to the long-term environmental impact of development activities because of the fragile nature of the ecology of the region and because of its significance for the rest of the country. Local people, subjected to the pressure of poverty, are unlikely to be able to take full account of these considerations, while government activities are undertaken principally within the framework of short-term plans and budgets;
(iv) that a wide range of donor agencies (multilateral and bilateral, government and private) have funds and technologies available for Pakistan, but often experience difficulty in finding properly prepared projects on which to use these resources; and
(v) that a small, private and flexible organization (staffed by Pakistanis of the highest caliber) can achieve a great deal in drawing together the aspects mentioned above and in acting as a 'development entrepreneur' to make strategic interventions to promote local initiative and to mobilize outside resources to assist in that process.

2. The broad objective of AKRSP was set as increasing the capacity of local people in the project area to make use of opportunities for

improving their welfare and to overcome the problems they faced. It was intended that AKRSP should promote development in an equitable and sustainable manner in the project area. In the first instance, the project area was defined as Gilgit District: this was subsequently expanded to embrace Chitral District and then Baltistan District: the three Districts are referred to as the 'the Northern Areas', an inaccurate but convenient term. During its first few years, AKRSP was expected to focus its development efforts on income-generating activities, though the possibility that it might later expand into social sector activities was not excluded.

3. It is important to recognize that AKRSP was conceived from the outset as a self-liquidating organization. That is, it was expected to function for approximately 10 years, leaving in place a set of local institutions and skills that would facilitate continued progress towards the AKRSP objective. By the time this transition had occurred, it was hoped that AKRSP would have contributed substantially to at least doubling the *per capita* income in the project area, with, at worst, no significant increase in income disparities.

4. In order to achieve its broad objective, AKRSP was expected to fulfil the following six functions:

(i) to organize local people to meet common needs and to provide or obtain services in a cost-effective manner;
(ii) to train local people in a range of managerial and practical skills;
(iii) to seek to introduce new activities and technologies to enhance incomes;
(iv) to assist in the identification and preparation of development projects and in the mobilization of resources for these projects from the public and private sectors;
(v) to work to develop a strategy for optimal long-term use of available natural resources at a high level of productivity; and
(vi) to undertake technical and socio-economic research, where necessary, to support the previous functions and to measure progress towards them.

5. In all these functions, AKRSP was expected to complement and supplement the activities of government and other agencies, rather than to duplicate or replicate them. This meant that AKRSP should

coordinate its programme closely with other agencies, relying on their resources wherever possible, seeking to function at a different level (*i.e.* directly at the village level), and working in fields in which AKRSP could develop special strengths stemming from its private nature.

6. These premises, objectives and functions of AKRSP were established before the organization began its work. Its specific approach, methodology and programme were deliberately left vague, to be determined by the company's management when selected, and to be refined in the light of actual experience in the field. The most important of the principles on which AKRSP operates are:

(i) that small farmers in isolated communities require a village organization (VO) to promote increase in productivity, since an organization allows small farmers to overcome the disadvantages of small scale;

(ii) that these VOs can increase equity among rural families if steps are taken to ensure that control is not gained by one section of the community (*e.g.* through supervision by a high level body and by ensuring that all members of the village regularly attend and participate in meetings);

(iii) that VOs are an efficient, effective and equitable mechanism, because of the genuine participation they promote, for disseminating technical innovation, distributing services (inputs, marketing, credit etc.) to promote agricultural production and encouraging initiatives and planning by the villagers;

(iv) that villagers can most effectively be organized on a permanent basis around productive, rather than social sector activities in the first instance;

(v) that an effective entry point for the organization of villagers is a productive physical infrastructure (PPI) project which can both raise agricultural productivity for the majority of households and serve as an opportunity for villagers to learn and exercise skills in collective management;

(vi) that, in order to have the PPI projects implemented quickly and efficiently, without exploitation within the village, and as a contribution to the poverty problem, village labour employed in the PPI projects should be paid;

(vii) that regular savings, however small, are an essential part of the discipline of collective management and serve as the basis for long-term development through the creation of capital which can be used as collateral for loans;

(viii) that numerous members of the VOs can quickly and cheaply be given specific skills (both managerial and technical) which make the VOs effective, provide readily available and cost-effective services for all small farmers and for which other villagers are prepared to pay; and

(ix) that VOs, formed in accordance with these principles, can be encouraged and taught simple techniques to take responsibility for long-term, sustainable development of the resources at their disposal.

7. From these principles, it will be clear that AKRSP regards the establishment of effective VOs as the key to successful development of the Northern Areas. In order to achieve this goal, the VOs enter into a formal partnership with AKRSP, under which the latter is prepared to offer technical and financial assistance in the form of programmes. These programmes include:

(i) the development of organization skills and discipline;
(ii) the first PPI project;
(iii) land development and longer-term resource management planning;
(iv) agriculture and livestock development;
(v) savings and credit;
(vi) marketing;
(vii) women's development; and
(viii) monitoring, evaluation and research (both socio-economic and technical).

Socio-Economic Situation in Gilgit

The programme's object was to improve the quality of life of nearly 100,000 families of small farmers comprising a million people living in more than 1,200 villages spread over an area of 70,000 sq. km. of the most difficult terrain in the world.[5] As recommended by the AKF Team and approved by the AKF Board, AKRSP initially concentrated

THE AKRSP: GOALS AND OPERATING PRINCIPLES

its activities on Gilgit district. A glance at the situation in Gilgit in 1983 will give a clear idea of the challenges faced by AKRSP.

The Population. There were 200,000 people and 160 villages in Gilgit in 1983. There were 66,940 men, 60,340 women and 72,780 children. The small population was scattered over a vast mountain area including some of the most inhospitable and inaccessible locations. The economy was very fragile and the small farms owned by the majority of the households provided a very narrow income base. Eighty five per cent of the work force were engaged in agriculture and only 15 per cent of the workers were employed in non-agricultural occupations.

Table 1: Estimates of population (1983)

Aggregates	Orders of magnitude
Children (under 15)	72,780
Men	66,940
Women	60,340
Total population (say)	200,000
No. of households	24,000
No. of villages	160

Physical Capital

(a) Land. Analysis of land use pattern revealed that 35 per cent land was cultivated and 49 per cent uncultivated. Uncultivated land consisted of land that was cultivable (14 per cent) and land that was not (35 per cent). An average household cultivated 12.3 *kanals*[6] of lands and allocated 2.7 *kanals* for orchard, 2.8 *kanals* for forest and kept 17.2 *kanals* uncultivated.

Table 2: Agricultural land and its uses

Aggregate	Kanals	per cent
Cultivated land	295,000	35
Orchard	65,000	8
Forest	66,000	8
Uncultivated land	414,000	49

(b) **Other agricultural assets.** Agricultural machines and implements were conspicuous by their isolated presence. For instance, there were reported to be only two threshers in Ishkoman Tehsil. Although, no systematic data were collected, the ownership of tractors seemed to be concentrated in Gilgit sub-division, with Hunza probably in second place. The tractors were used mainly for transporting freight along jeep roads. As for farm implements, the only ones to be found were the traditional ones. A livestock census showed that there were 49,000 cows, 18,000 bullocks, 110,000 sheep, 173,000 goats and 61,000 poultry birds in the district in 1982.

(c) **Non-agricultural physical capital.** The principal item in this category was the household dwelling unit. This was almost invariably a *kutcha* (mud-brick) house of variable proportions. It was impossible to ascertain the average size of a dwelling unit and the area on which it is built. Another difficult item to estimate was the quantity of movable assets per household — this includes furniture and jewellery.

Investment: The Addition to Wealth

(a) **Land.** Two types of profitable activities were identified; increasing the available cultivated area (land development) and increasing the productivity of existing cultivated land (productivity investment). Land development could be accomplished by providing irrigation water to barren land where this was technically possible. Productivity investment involved the introduction of increased and reliable supply of inputs such as water, fertilizer and improved seeds for use on existing land. As indicated above, the average amount of uncultivated land per household was 17.2 *kanals*. Of this, villagers reported an average of 4.9 *kanals* of land that could be developed. In Gilgit District, on the assumption that the price of land would increase by the same percentage as the increase in cultivated land *i.e.* 40 per cent of all the land that can be developed (117,600 *kanals*) was in fact developed, the price of cultivated land would increase to Rs 5,360/- per *kanal*. It was estimated that the net benefit of all land development projects would come to more than Rs 439 million or Rs 18, 326 per household. The constraint in land development was lack of capital that could be borrowed by villagers and invested in expectation of a profitable return. Another constraint was the farmer's inability to use inputs for increased productivity which emanated from his inability to take out 'production loans'. In addition, there was also the institutional constraint—a delivery system and a marketing chain, for example, from fertiliser factories down-country to villages on remote mountain tops.

(b) Livestock. Considering the environment of the district and the failure of species imported from outside the region, there seemed to be little to be gained from the introduction of 'more productive' livestock. Species that were more productive elsewhere also required larger amounts of feed and other inputs than could be obtained locally. In the foreseeable future, increases in the value of livestock seemed to depend on increasing the availability of fodder and pastures. The major source of such increases had to be additions to cultivated land, as discussed above.

Human Capital: Opportunities and Constraints

As noted above, crop yields in Gilgit matched those in Pakistan, even though modern inputs were not available in the district. This is testimony to the ability of Gilgit villagers to farm the land as efficiently as existing constraints would allow. However, once modern inputs became available, the cultural practices of farmers there would have to change, to obtain maximum returns from investments in physical inputs. However, given the existing structure of markets and incentives, the returns to extension education appeared to be very small. It is no coincidence, therefore, that extension appeared nowhere on the lists of priorities obtained in 53 villages during the AKRSP Diagnostic Survey conducted in 1983. The situation would change dramatically once modern inputs favoured by the villagers were introduced in the region, since extension and the use of modern inputs are complementary activities in agricultural production. International evidence suggests that investments in extension pay for themselves many times over. At the time, however, there existed no agency for imparting extension education at the village level in Gilgit District.

Needs and Problems

In the equation of social progress and agricultural development, one important but often overlooked factor is the inspired, voluntary and organized endeavour of the farmers to enter into an effective working relationship with the government or programme authorities. Organising farmers to participate in agricultural and rural development, and helping build an appropriate institutional framework through which technical and other forms of assistance can be channelled, as well as fostering and strengthening the national development programme at the grassroots levels, should constitute the main objective of a coordinated approach to agricultural development in rural areas.

The ability and willingness to respond to the innovation of methods and techniques of agricultural production are closely tied with three factors: ways of organizing the farmers, the level of their technical know-how and the social and cultural context. It is essential, therefore, to regard investment in people to be as important as the financial economic investment in large-scale agricultural projects.

The distinction between the VOs built up 'from below' and the statutory bodies created by the government from above is very critical. The VOs have to be conceived in terms of new, local-level organizations as a means of social promotion to gradually create a class of enlightened and responsible farmers who understand the benefits and the implications of agricultural development. They will also be able to manage their own affairs and be willing to pull their weight in the development effort.

The VOs have to be conceived in terms of new structures and new organizational patterns which can bring all the functions together into a new syndicate encompassing all of the farmers' agricultural, social and commercial needs, and avoiding any functional or area overlapping. The chief objective of the VOs should be the promotion of human and social development.

Improvement to the irrigation systems, better water distribution and control, land development, provision of better marketing and transport facilities, inputs such as fertilizers and agro-chemicals and the supply of agricultural credit—all of which are expected to be the regular functions of the VOs—require a combination of local organization and administrative infrastructure backed with financial support. The solution, therefore, is to create a single, multi-purpose organization—the VO—to cover all aspects of the social, economic and institutional life at the village level, within reasonable reach of the farmer in the geographical as well as social, economic and institutional senses.

Objectives. The ultimate aim of the programme was to develop an innovative and replicable model with a small NGO acting as a catalyst for rural development. The NGO would work with local people to identify and appraise project opportunities, to develop local skills and organizations, and to promote the provision of needed services for tackling the problems of high mountain valley areas.

The Approach

Strategy Options[7]

The **North American capitalist model** drives small farmers out of the agriculture sector but provides alternative means of livelihood and creates large land holdings. In America today, only 2.7 per cent of the population is engaged in agriculture.[8] In contrast, in the Northern Areas 95 per cent of the population is engaged in agriculture, the average holding per family is less than 2 hectares and the majority of the persons who leave agriculture end up in the slums of Karachi with a tiny minority being absorbed in the service or the business sector.

The **Socialist model** does not admit of private ownership and is, therefore, not in consonance with state policy. Its effectiveness as a way of life and as a means for achieving higher productivity in agriculture is a moot point.

The **Raiffeisen model**, which has its origins in the mid-19th century Europe, admits of private ownership as well as making small farmers highly productive and helps them to rise above the level of subsistence. This 'credit union' model has the greatest relevance to the Northern Areas.

The Methodology

An offer of developmental partnership to villagers is known as a Terms of Partnership. It makes AKRSP assistance and collaboration dependent on villagers fulfilling their three-fold obligation to (i) organization and collective management, (ii) generation of their own capital through savings and (iii) upgrade skills in the AKRSP human resource development programme. On acceptance of these terms of partnership, a process known as a diagnostic survey begins: comprising a series of dialogues with VOs, initiated to identify the villagers' needs and aspirations. This resulted in the evolution of a developmental package.

The AKRSP approach is based on the following seven principles:

1. Although the selection of the most appropriate level for agricultural and rural development would have to be determined by each region, taking into consideration the particular conditions operating, some considerations that could objectively determine this process would include; (i) its coverage of an area viable enough to allow the provision of essential services and upgrading of managerial and productive skills of the rural poor through group action to assist in the mobilization of resources for activating a locally inspired development programme; (ii) the ability of the programme to facilitate direct and indirect participation in the planned development process; (iii) its coincidence with the lowest level of the administrative hierarchy; and (iv) its ability to link up with primary growth centres and markets.

Bringing the rural poor into an organized fold seems to be the key to ameliorating their economic and social problems because it is only as a group that the villagers are able to articulate problems and evolve solutions; only through organizations and collective responsibility can credit be made available to the small farmers. Agricultural knowledge can be made available more quickly and in a more relevant form with a VO. Investment becomes possible through individual savings in a cooperative society and the resulting capital accumulation. In this way funds are made available and controlled by the VOs. Administrative innovations are needed to define the corporate character of such groups and to determine the rules for their action.

2. The emphasis of agricultural and rural development should be on projects to increase production and thereby raise incomes. Social welfare programmes should be deferred to a later date or to concerned national government departments/ministries. There are general and specific reasons for this, namely, welfare services must be commensurate with incomes and what people can afford. Therefore, they must follow rather than precede income levels. This is borne out by the fact that the additional patronage from large landowners or the government, which has traditionally been schools and dispensaries, does not break the vicious circle of poverty.

THE AKRSP: GOALS AND OPERATING PRINCIPLES

3. A steady guaranteed level of funding, at whatever level possible, for implementing local level plans is of critical importance. Sudden reductions in funds have a disillusioning effect on the VOs and a devastating effect on staff and saps people's belief in the programme.

4. Creation of rural cadres for group organization and management has to be vigorously pursued with a view to people themselves slowly relieving the bureaucracy of multiple jobs. The development of VOs is by far the most direct, face to face expression of democracy and of the needs and demands of the people themselves on matters which are of most direct concern to their village with the federation of organizations serving as a democratic organization on the economic and technical side to look after their interests such as credit needs, establishment of processing industries and marketing.

5. Given that local plan formulation cannot be undertaken in a vacuum, it would appear that this process should integrate into it the means whereby adjustments and modifications can be made to national, regional and sectoral planning guidelines while working within the framework of available resources. This would ultimately lead to a developmental scenario at the local level consistent with the specific needs of the people, growth potential of the area and budgetary allocations available.

6. Training, research and evaluation are important. Given the varying environments obtaining in the region, training programmes will have to be district-specific in nature. Similarly, the first requirement is not research but records—a data—a time series of acreage, yields, investment etc. Without good records evaluation will be extremely difficult and benefit-cost of project impossible to ascertain. Beyond this, research would be needed on the level and sources of farm incomes and off farm employment and in incomes at village level. At a higher level, there will be a need in the initial years of the programme for more experienced economic, social and administrative research on the strategies and performance of local development including administrative and management methods within the programme. The universities may be able to play a major role here provided they are willing to tackle operational research designed to give answers to policy issues. The need for continuous monitoring and evaluation envisages the desirability of a commitment in favour of rigorous and

continuous internal evaluation with a clear definition of accurate indicators to measure progress. Development of simplified systems of monitoring and evaluating rural projects with the participation of local functionaries and local people would be pertinent.

7. Whereas the role of traditional local councils is acknowledged in the field of inter-village planning, raising of taxation and coordination with development departments, their effectiveness or competence to undertake economic development or infrastructure planning, implementation and maintenance of projects at village level is questionable. Experts have come down quite firmly against entrusting the development process too much to these highly unequal democratic (selected) bodies in the early stage. The formation of disciplined groups i.e. VOs in which the weaker sections are the majority, proves more viable for economic and agricultural development of each village. Along with the local councils structure, the formation of VOs is, therefore, of prime importance for ameliorating the condition of the rural masses.

THE AKRSP PROGRAMMING CYCLE

Box 1: AKRSP Programming Cycle

Diagnostic Survey
Project identification, preparation and appraisal through village dialogues.

i- Identification: First Dialogue
Explanation of AKRSP methods and objectives.
Identification of productive rural projects.
 General Manager
 Villagers
 Management Group

ii- Preparation: Second Dialogue
Feasibility of Physical Infrastructure Works or Social & Economic Infrastructure Scheme.
Preparation of blue print or objective plan
Cost Estimation.
 Prog. Sr. Engineer or Prog. Sr. Agric., with Prog.Trg. Specialist and villagers

iii- Appraisal: Third Dialogue
Explanation of Terms of Partnership.
Acceptance/rejection of Terms of Partnership.
Assessment of Range of Benefits of
Project/Scheme, Implying Acceptance or Rejection.
 General Manager
 Villagers
 Management Group

THE AKRSP: GOALS AND OPERATING PRINCIPLES

Implementation	
Base-line Survey for Evaluation.	Prog. Economist
Execution of project/scheme	Village Organs.
Monitoring, Training and Supervision of VOs.	Management Group
Completion	
Management of project/scheme including maintenance, monitoring and evaluation.	VO with Prog. Trg. Specialist
Post-project survey for evaluation.	Programme Economist
Long-term evaluation of persistence of results.	Management Group

Programme activities of AKRSP generally followed the pattern outlined in the AKRSP Programming Cycle. Like project cycles everywhere, the APC covered five broad phases of activity: identification, preparation, appraisal, implementation and completion (Box 1). The progress in each activity, and in the particular steps it involves, is summarised in the Programme Activity Status Table (Box 2), which is updated at the end of each month.

Box 2: Specimen of Programme Activity Status Table

Number of villages in which activity has been completed as of 31 December 1982/31 January 1983.

	SUB-DIV HUNZA	NAGAR	GILGIT	PUNYAL GUPIS DISTT.		
				Ishkoman	Yasin	Gilgit
Total No. of villages	30	22	30	32	43	157
Programme Activity	No. of Villages Covered					
Identification						
1. Explanation of AKRSP methods and objectives	2/6	0/4	9/12	13/13	0/18	24/55
2. Identification of Productive Rural Projects	2/8	0/4	9/10	13/13	0/18	24/53

Preparation						
1. Feasibility of Physical works or Socio and Economic Infrastructure Schemes	0/2	0/0	0/3	0/5	0/0	0/10
2. Preparation of blueprints or objective plans	0/0	0/0	0/3	0/0	0/0	0/3
3. Cost Estimation (Provisional)	0/2	0/0	0/3	0/5	0/0	0/10
Appraisal						
1. Explanation of Terms of Partnership	0/6	0/0	0/3	0/13	0/0	0/22
2. Acceptance of Terms of Partnership	0/6	0/0	0/1	0/13	0/0	0/20

The Diagnostic Survey[9]

The distinguishing feature of AKRSP as a development agency was the belief and experience of its Management Group that a self-sustaining development process in the countryside could only be built on the skills, wealth and organization of village residents. In practice, this philosophy means that every step of the first three phases of activity— identification, preparation and appraisal—proceeds through a series of interactive dialogues between villagers and AKRSP. Together, the first three phases of programme activity constitute the Diagnostic Survey.

The diagnostic survey starts with a visit by the MG to a village whose residents have agreed to meet with AKRSP staff. Within exactly 55 days of the arrival of the first member of the MG in Gilgit, residents of 55 villages in the district had heard the General Manager (GM) explain the Objectives and Methods of AKRSP. The extent of coverage, so far, includes villages in all five of Gilgit's Sub-divisions, and in eight of its nine Tehsils. The audiences with whom the AKRSP MG initiated a dialogue on development, ranged in size from 10 to 250, and in composition from village farmers to the Chairmen of Union Councils, Members of Northern Areas Council and office-holders of

Ismaili Regional Councils. The result of this first dialogue was the identification of 132 development schemes by the residents of 53 villages.

The identification of productive rural projects is followed in the APC by the initiation of the second series of dialogues. The first step involves a preliminary Feasibility Survey of identified schemes. Supervisory responsibility for this technical assessment rests with the Programme Senior Engineer or Programme Senior Agriculturist. Responsibility in the field devolves on the Social Organization Unit (SOU), comprising a Social Organizer (SO), a sub-engineer and an agriculturist. This unit works with informed village residents to assess the feasibility of proposed projects and to obtain data on the prices of locally available inputs/material. The preliminary survey was completed for 84 physical works projects in 34 villages. Reports on these projects were submitted to the Programme Senior Engineer who drew up provisional cost estimates for 32 projects in 10 villages. Detailed blueprints were also prepared for the projects.

While some physical works projects were being prepared by the technical staff, the Programme Training Specialist and the three SOs he supervised initiated the third series of dialogues. In the process, they visited 22 villages to explore the Terms of Partnership that would characterise the relationship of AKRSP to village residents. On behalf of AKRSP, these terms of partnership are explained as general principles of rural development that have proved successful elsewhere in the world. In turn, the villagers could demonstrate their acceptance of these principles by spelling out precisely the manner in which they would organize to plan, implement, manage and maintain specific projects that involve physical works, skill development and the creation of equity capital over time. To date the Terms of Partnership have been defined to the satisfaction of AKRSP and village residents in 20 villages. Thus, 20 broad-based VOs had been formed whose members were all the beneficiaries of proposed AKRSP-sponsored projects. The beneficiaries will meet together as a general body two to four times a month to cooperate on issues of common interest. This will lay the foundation on which to build the pillars of development that will serve villagers and the generations to come. The formation of VOs is followed by an assessment of project benefits conducted by concerned members of the Management Group. This completes the Diagnostic Survey.

Implementation. After consultative planning, programme activity enters the implementation phase. The VO undertakes the EXECUTION of the scheme. Concurrently with execution, a BASE-LINE SURVEY for evaluation is conducted under the supervision of the Programme Economist. When the implementation phase begins the VOs begin to follow a pre-established schedule of weekly or fortnightly meetings. The records of these meetings, together with the personal participation of the SOU members, provide information that enables the MONITORING of specific schemes by members of the MG. The VO meetings are also the medium through which MG members and the personnel they supervise impart TRAINING AND SUPERVISION to village residents. Both monitoring and training and supervision are ongoing activities that follow an interactive process focussed on improved management of the village economy.

Completion. Once a specific scheme has been executed, the responsibility for its MANAGEMENT is completely vested in the VO: villagers become responsible for all aspects of managing the scheme they had identified, helped to plan and executed. A POST-PROJECT SURVEY for evaluation is carried out under the Programme Economist's supervision. The continuous monitoring of VOs and the ongoing processes of training and supervision, together with specific surveys, provide the MG with the information it needs for a LONG-TERM EVALUATION of sustainability of results.

Monitoring and Evaluation

(a) **Monitoring** is a management function. It is an internal programme activity, an integral part of day-to-day decision-making. MONITORING entails the collection and collation of information, the routing of information through reporting channels to specific lines of management, and the managerial assessment of this information with respect to particular programme objectives. Thus, monitoring enables the management to conduct an ON-GOING EVALUATION of programme activities. This on-going evaluation is MANAGEMENT RESPONSE for course-correction through direct channels of supervision.

Monitoring is thus one of the responsibilities of each member of the MG. The role of the Programme Economist in the monitoring unit is to work with professional colleagues in the following ways:

(i) to identify specific and general objectives, and to develop indicators against which to measure progress towards these objectives;
(ii) to collect and analyse information flowing from various lines of management;
(iii) to collate and analyse data from beneficiaries of AKRSP-sponsored projects to supplement available records;
(iv) to prepare reports that highlight the findings of various analyses;
(v) to prepare option papers of general interest to the MG; and
(vi) to develop and maintain various data series as an aid to later evaluation.

(b) Evaluation is the assessment of impact with respect to expectations. It is not necessarily an integral component of management, though it relies on the monitoring system of a programme for much of the required data. Evaluation involves more than simple quantification of changes in the project area: it attempts to identify influences exogenous to the project in order to isolate effects specific to the project. The evaluation exercise assesses both intended and unintended impacts, and helps draw lessons for further improvements or similar projects elsewhere.

The methods of evaluation used by the Programme Economist are the standard analytical tools together with the procedures of econometric testing. The database for project-specific evaluation is built on the base-line and post-project surveys. Activity-specific (or sector-specific) evaluation will be based on household panel surveys designed in modules. Four sectors will be subjected to particular scrutiny: demography and human capital, income and labour supply, land use and agricultural production, and livestock and non-land production. Finally, general and specific objectives will be stated as refutable hypotheses and tested with reference to separate and pooled time series and cross-sectional data.

Conventional Rural Development and AKRSP

A clear description of methodology did not mean smooth sailing. The programme dynamics was very well described in a discussion with Mr Addleton of the World Bank who said that he had heard a lot about AKRSP and was interested to know of any problems that proved more difficult than imagined a few years ago. The GM answered that the most difficult task was conveying the vision of a self-sustaining institution to the villagers. Unless they understood the vision, they would simply not organize. Many a time they would take on just one of the components, for instance the PPI, whose completion they considered to be the end. AKRSP would then have to persuade them that this was just the beginning and there was much more that had to be achieved. The only encouraging thing was that if we went to 20 villages we would immediately come across a few people who would understand and would share the vision. These men and women provided the local leadership. We could then refer to these VOs to spur others onwards. The development of package, in the fields of agriculture, livestock and marketing were the most difficult.[10]

Dr Donaldson of the World Bank referred to the elements of personal leadership and to the dedication with which the AKRSP staff had carried out the work on 'jeepable donkey tracks'.[11] He noted in particular the Management Group's emphasis on a clear cut economic model and the importance of the KKH in farmers getting high returns on their investments. In his view the AKRSP strategy was the reverse of what the Bank had been doing. As he noted, there is an immediate cash flow need right from the beginning and without this basic investment it is not possible to achieve rural development in the vacuum.

Villagers' Response.[12] The sound approach followed by the programme led to outstanding results. In terms of organization, 90 per cent of rural households in Gilgit got organized in five years. The entire VOs accumulated over Rs 72 million as their savings in the Programme area.

NOTES

1. Note For the Record: Panel discussion at the National Defence College, Rawalpindi, 1 August 1988.
2. One crore = 10 million.
3. 7 December 2006.
4. AKRSP Strategy Paper, 1983.
5. NFR—Outline of Briefing on AKRSP.
6. 8 *kanals* = 1 acre, 20 *kanals* = 1 hectare.
7. NFR—Outline of Briefing on AKRSP, 1983.
8. *The Economist*.
9. The Diagnostic Survey, *Strategy Paper*, 1983.

10. NFR—The group was shown 'The Changing Valleys', 12 April 1988.
11. NFR—Shoaib Sultan Khan Visit to Geneva, 16-17 February 1988.
12. NFR—Presentation on AKRSP for Prime Minister of Pakistan, Mohtarma Benazir Bhutto, 13 April 1989.

9

Programme Impact and the Numbers Game

ACCOUNTABILITY

Self accountability and self monitoring were ingrained in the design of AKRSP from the beginning. Akhtar Hameed Khan observed that one of the major reasons for the failure of the cooperative movement was the lack of accounting. He had tackled this by having one accountant for every 5 villages. It was decided that the AKRSP should have one accountant at each cluster, appointed from the cluster, trained by AKRSP and paid by the people. Akhtar Hameed Khan also enquired whether the cluster activists were being overpaid. Hussain Wali said that, at present, this activist was being paid from the service charges levied on the medium-term loans. Hussain Wali felt that the cluster functionary worked during the whole month. Akhtar Hameed Khan wound up the day's discussion by saying that the AKRSP policy had to take into account two levels of functionaries: one at the cluster and the other at the village level.

Self Accountability at the VO Level

The GM asked about a project that would become a permanent source of income for the people of Sildhi. Haji Mehboob Ali, the manager of VO Sildhi, noted that they were dependent on snow melt for irrigation. An irrigation channel could be constructed that would take water from the river. He further added that all had an equal share in the barren land of 2,500 *kanals*. The GM noted that the SOs would verify the fact that all were benefitted. All the members confirmed the identification. The GM, appreciating their identification, stressed regular weekly meetings and savings. He also cited examples from Gilgit and Skardu. He further clarified that Haji Ghulam Ali as President, and Haji Mehboob Ali as

Manager, were answerable to the VO while the VO as a whole was answerable to AKRSP. He advised that the well-off should save more and the poor should not be denied membership.

Thereafter, Hussain Wali got the full details on the survey done by Sahib Khan. He was informed by the VO that there was no dispute on the channel. Hussain Wali clarified that maintenance after completion would be the responsibility of the VO. Then he read out the details of the Sildhi irrigation channel:

Length of the channel	18400 feet
Explosives	Rs 23,917
Tools	Rs 6,591
Labour	Rs 131,375
Total	**Rs 161,883**

Besides this, land development tools worth Rs 6,000/- would be given provided they saved Rs 200/- per member within three months of the initiation of their PPI.

Haji Mohammad Hussain apprehended that the grant was insufficient. The GM responded by explaining the LB&RD and NAWO models, adding that AKRSP worked with people. He clarified that the survey was done in their presence and that Hussain Wali now had experience of 450 schemes. He added that AKRSP could not pay for their courage and determination. A first installment cheque amounting to Rs 32,376/- was given to President Haji Ghulam Ali by Haji Mohammad Hussain as desired by the VO members. Thereafter, the GM discussed at length the protection bund of Kashmal VO but they did not change their priority.

High performance standards set by the programme were based on continuous self assessment and reflections. The success of the programme in maintaining these standards was captured in the following conversation between the GM and the chief minister of Punjab.

The Number Game[1] (November 1985)

Chief Minister (Punjab): What is your annual budget for running such an interesting programme?

General Manager: We started with Rs 14 million in 1983 which increased to Rs 22 million in 1984. The current year's budget stands at Rs 42 million which includes whole of Chitral and selected areas in Baltistan district.

Chief Minister: And what is your establishment cost?

General Manager: One seventh of the development cost.

Chief Minister: Have you done a prior assessment of the felt needs of these people or do you have to decide every time when you initiate a new project?

General Manager: The programme's main thrust is on the creation of self-perpetuating Village Organizations. It is left to these organized units of small farmers to determine their own priorities. We only ask them to identify a project that would result in immediate returns to all or most of the households in an organized village. I remember when I first opened dialogues...the villagers demanded schools and dispensaries but we explained that this programme was initially concentrating on the productive sector.

Chief Minister: Who has the ownership of barren land in the villages that these VOs are going to reclaim?

General Manager: Customarily, it belongs to the villagers themselves. The government also recognizes villagers' collective right to barren land if they are able to reclaim it.

Chief Minister: What is your procedure for the disbursement of funds?

General Manager: Once we agree on the terms of partnership with a VO, we immediately release, in public, one-fifth of the total grant for initiating the project and then leave it to the entire VO to work out its allocation. Our field engineers then measure each phase of the physical work and recommend the VO for the subsequent installments. These are released on the basis of a written resolution from the general body of the VO.

Federal Minister: There are elected councillors in the villages; do they participate in your VOs?

General Manager: All councillors are active members of the VOs and in some cases they are even office bearers. The Chairman, District Council Gilgit himself was the president of his VO.

Federal Minister: I would like the elected councillors to be more actively involved in this type of development exercises.

General Manager: We recognize that they can play an activist's role in the village-level activities, therefore, from time to time, we also invite them to our Monthly Managers' Conference.

Federal Minister: How many PPI projects have been completed so far and at what cost?

General Manager: As of the end of September, 1985, 213 projects have been initiated in Gilgit District at a total cost of Rs 28.6 million, of which 142 had been fully completed.

Federal Minister: What is the ratio of irrigation channels?

General Manager: Of the total 213 projects, 137 are irrigation projects which will channel more than 581 cusecs of water to roughly 20,630 acres of new land and increase the watering frequency to 22,412 acres of existing (developed) land. The most distinguishing feature, however, is the comparative cost of these small projects—i.e. Rs 27,237 per cusec as compared to Rs 125,730 in similar irrigation projects undertaken by other agencies through the contractors.

The Counting Game[2] (September 1988)

Straight from the airport, Syed Mutahir Shah and his staff, and Feroz Shah who was visiting Baltistan for the first time, took me on a village visit.

At VO Brakchun there were about 25 persons assembled and Feroze Shah had a dig at SMS about the poor turnout: 'First impression is the last impression'. Poor Syed Mutahir Shah felt a bit crestfallen until we sat down for a dialogue with the VO members and their Manager

Mohammad Ali and President Syed Taqi Shah. The VO had 26 households and 26 members and according to their attendance register, the participation of the VO members in meetings since 1 April 1987 had been almost 100 per cent. Their savings stood at Rs 18,846. Their PPI was a pipe-line irrigation project, in common with two other VOs—Gayul and Khlang Khong. The project had already been completed and land development by way of planting of 3,000 forest trees had commenced. Their livestock and agricultural specialists are active. They had availed both fertilizer and marketing loans.

In the course of the discussion, a lay member Mohammad Hussain said that the formation of the VO has helped in solving many problems. Firstly, the increased water supply has enabled sowing of an additional crop, besides bringing more area under cultivation. He estimated an annual increase of at least Rs 2000–3000 in his income due to this factor. He also commended the 'prevention of losses' programme, as well as the savings and marketing activities initiated by the VO.

Fifteen year old Ihsan Ali, whose father died a year go, said that the VO had helped him in bringing all his land under cultivation and also in arranging fertilizer and in helping to market his dry fruits. With the availability of sufficient irrigation water, he was now producing enough and was not obliged to buy grain from outside to feed the seven member family, of whom he was the eldest, besides his mother.

This was an active VO in which every member seems to understand the importance of organization and collective management. I would categorise it as 'B'.

Stretching the Dollar (March 1989)[3]

On the issue of payment to local professionals, Akhtar Hameed Khan commented that it was vital that snags be identified and removed. The same old problem confronts the programme once again. Functionaries and specialists were needed and they also had to be remunerated for their services but the peasant mentality did not permit payment to them. In fact, now one more functionary was needed at the intermediate level and the subsidy to be provided by AKRSP at this level would be in the form of expertise offered by the programme.

Akhtar Hameed Khan warned that the VO managers had to be remunerated, otherwise a crisis situation would develop. All the good people would leave. He said that his experience was that it was easy to remunerate the activists. The first source was credit. The activist could be remunerated both at the time of disbursement and recovery. The other sources for securing remuneration were additional collective activities. If the villagers were to provide remuneration voluntarily, then the functionaries would become very effective. His suggestion was that additional sources needed to be identified for remunerating the functionaries. The fight was against both peasant and medieval mentalities which yearned for dependency. The conundrum was that the villagers want the functionaries but do not want to pay them while they have no hesitation in paying the traders.

He added that now the stitchers in Orangi [Pilot Project in Karachi] had formed a consumer cooperative to counter this situation. AKRSP was the only teacher accessible to the villagers. The problem of payment to both the village activist and the intermediate functionary could be solved. For example, small charges could be added to the fertilizer cost, to pay the activist who prepared the list at the village level and the person who consolidated it at the cluster. The important thing was that this problem should not be avoided. Shoaib Sultan Khan said that at present it was difficult to envision the villagers paying the functionary directly and explained the current methodology for dealing with the issue of remuneration for the activist. Akhtar Hameed Khan again cautioned those present not to ignore the village level functionary at any cost. Remuneration had to be divided between the village activist and the cluster office bearer. He said that the AKRSP had changed the village mentality to accept justice, in the sense that the functionary had to be present in their organization and he also had to be paid. The villagers would always demand free service but they had to be told about this. Hussain Wali said that, unfortunately, all the functionaries preferred being on the AKRSP payroll rather than be paid by the villagers.

Barkat Ali Khan then explained how the Sherqilla WO had handled the question of remuneration. Nabeel Anjum Malik asked if AKRSP ought to consider and encourage commodity-based clusters along with the geographic clusters being formed to handle inputs. He gave the example of the seed grower's association. Akhtar Hameed Khan said that private enterprise ought to be encouraged and AKRSP should not behave as a 'champion of the villagers'. Nabeel Anjum Malik agreed and explained the programme's position *vis-à-vis* Jaffer Brothers Limited.

Akhtar Hameed Khan then said that when he visited Gilgit the last time, he had discussed the problem of remuneration to functionaries.

He had also touched on the scope of future village development. He explained that the villagers were caught in the 'poverty trap' and that their peasant mentality did not allow them to see all the resources at their disposal. There were two resources in particular which could be managed collectively and income from them distributed among individuals. The first of these was their pasture and the second was their forest. At present everybody was busy exploiting these resources. The forests needed to be adopted practically by the villagers, which might not necessarily mean legally. More trees needed to be planted. The rajas had taken care of the forests in the past but now these forests had been orphaned and required adoption through collective management.

The Case of Village Mango (10 May 1989)[4]

On 10 May 1989, the Ambassador of the Netherlands and his party flew to village Mango in Shigar valley, where they inspected the PPI and irrigation channel, constructed with a grant of Rs 111,685. This PPI, given by AKRSP, has brought 900 *kanals* of new land under irrigation range, entitling each of the 22 members to 40 *kanals* of land holding. The channel was completed in April 1988 and 700 *kanals* have already been developed on which wheat, fruit, forest trees and vegetables have been planted. The members informed the ambassador that each farmer has increased its assets to the extent of Rs 350,000 and they thanked the ambassador for the assistance given by the Dutch people for this project.

Visit of the Federal Minister Anwar Aziz (May 1987)[5]

The minister, in his comments broadcast on Radio Gilgit, said that if the General Manager AKRSP had explained the activities of the VOs in his office and not taken us to the field, we would never have believed what the GM told us.

Ron Pears described the work being done by AKRSP as being without equal anywhere in Pakistan where he had already spent three months. He praised the AKRSP personnel who were most cooperative and forthright in giving information about AKRSP, unlike other places Pears had visited in Pakistan. He observed that, after visiting AKRSP, he had to change his impression that development could not be initiated under the aegis of Islam.

Micro-Macro Comparison (October 1984)[6]

To illustrate the higher payoff of micro-level projects relative to huge undertakings, the GM mentioned the Khaiber Hydel project being constructed by the Northern Areas Administration, at a cost of Rs 25 million. This huge project provides electricity, for lighting purposes to only 500 households. Out of the 131 projects in progress in the AKRSP programme (before the new CIDA funding), 82 are irrigation schemes, at an average cost of Rs 109,000, with a total investment of less than Rs 9 million. More than 10,000 households will benefit from these projects. Discussing the training programme, the GM informed the visitors that as yet 94 organizations have had livestock and plant protection specialists trained by AKRSP.

World Bank's View of the AKRSP Approach[7] (February 1988)

While basically, in concept, an agricultural production approach, the World Bank's rural development strategy required the introduction of new social organizations and institutional arrangements as essential pre-requisites for success. However, it did not allow sufficient time for such fundamental changes to occur and become part of the rural landscape. The Northern Pakistan AKRSP experience (also documented at their request by OED), to be discussed in our third session, highlights the sequential relationship between early institutional and human resource inputs and later production growth, in contrast with the Bank's implicit assumption that these changes would occur virtually concurrently. Furthermore, there is clearly a risk in allowing worthwhile social and welfare components that have come to be associated with rural development, to overshadow those essential human resource and institutional improvements which are necessary precursors to production growth. An overload of 'basic needs' concerns at the expense of production by rural people can clearly undermine the sustainability of the basic needs supply itself. Generally, social or basic needs components will work best in rural environments where production expansion is providing extra income. The reverse order of priorities has often proved damaging to overall project success.

Professor Brigegard on AKRSP (February 1988)

I hope my colleague, Professor Brigegard, will not mind if I quote from his Issues Paper, which you already have, in which he says, 'Development Interventions should be a matter of learning-by-doing, accepting inadequate knowledge, and be characterized by experimentation, learning from errors, adjustment to changing conditions and improvement of activities in a desired direction rather than aiming at definite pre-determined targets. Learning and problem solving should be made in close interaction with the intended project beneficiaries. The learning process should be a growth process'.[8]

The session began with a brief introduction by the coordinator, Mr Sohail Malik, giving the socio-economic profile of Pakistan. I showed the first eighteen minutes of the [film] *First Harvest* and used the overhead transparencies to explain the conceptual package and the progress of the development partnership between AKRSP and the village organizations.

Kathy McPhail explained the different facets of AKRSP, within the parameters of the incentives and economic model, social and institutional model and the technical model developing and identifying suitable production packages. She highlighted the successes of AKRSP and the need for more work in developing production packages. Of the 400 rural development projects the Bank has funded, she quoted FELDA in Malaysia and the Cotton Projects in West Africa, as examples of successful projects like AKRSP.

She also referred to the per capita cost in AKRSP over a 12-year period as half of the World Bank rural development projects over a 6 to 8 years span. She also lauded the great strides made by AKRSP in WID.

In the discussion, issues were raised pertaining to replication, successor institutions, population problems, village activists, dominance by elites, the quality of leadership both at the village and project level and the process approach.

Ten Years/Substantive Issues/Proposals (1992)[9]

As you are well aware, AKRSP will complete its first ten years in a few days' time. This has been a revolutionary decade for the rural people living in the Northern Areas and Chitral, bringing in its wake a new wave of positive change, both in the economic and attitudinal realms. Also, these momentous ten years have been truly rewarding and full of inspiration for those of us who have been fortunate enough to be associated with this epoch-making Programme.

My colleagues and I wish to take this historic opportunity to renew our commitment to keeping AKRSP as the 'market leader' in this field. Knowing the challenges of the coming years, we do not wish to turn this anniversary into any high-profile event. The best way to celebrate this occasion, I think, is to do some soul-searching, and to prepare ourselves for yet another challenging decade. We can do this by identifying and addressing substantive issues concerning AKRSP. But before we take any concrete action, I would like to share my thoughts with you, both with a view to have your guidance in these important matters, and also to avoid possible overlap with the activities and responsibilities of the SDC.

1. Institutional Renewal

Ten years ago, when Shoaib Saheb first came to Gilgit, he summed-up the whole concept of AKRSP in three simple and easy to understand principles: organization, capital and skills. Today, everyone in the project area knows and understands these basic essentials of rural development. The power of these simple and popular conceptual tools is undeniable.

The three cardinal principles of small farmers' development are universally valid and, for AKRSP, they have achieved the intended primary objectives: organization of the majority of rural people, creation of a sizeable capital reserve, and the establishment of a large network of village level specialists and activists. To build further upon this solid groundwork, and to capture the popular development rhetoric in the villages, I feel it is necessary to set higher goals for the next stage. These goals, by definition, must be a natural progression of the primary purposes enshrined in the three basic principles. For instance, the organization leading to capacity-building; investment and enterprise development as the next logical step after accumulation of capital and techno-economic efficiency as a consequence of enhanced knowledge and skills. The articulation of these goals in popular language will take some time, but I think they already give us a clear sense of purpose and continuity, as well as capture the essence of the future direction, no matter how we organize the support structures.

2. Institutional Capacities

As we all know, AKRSP enjoys a considerable degree of recognition in the field of rural development. From the start, the Programme has tried to share its particular approach and field experience with other agencies through formal and informal contact. Needless to say, the Programme has also benefitted conceptually and otherwise through that exchange. After the establishment of the HRDI, AKRSP has been offering formal courses to the staff of other agencies with the basic idea to promote its approach. In addition, AKRSP has tried, with remarkable success, to influence the thinking and development policy at the highest national and international levels.

The launching of SRSC, BRSP and NRSP in the country, as well as Shoaib Saheb's representation at the SAARC Commission for the Alleviation of Poverty, his appointments at the boards of many national bodies, numerous presentations to heads of governments and inter-governmental bodies, including a recent one to the President of the World Bank, the prestigious Magsasay and Sitara-i-Imtiaz awards, and the participation of senior management staff at various seminars and symposia, are all examples of the relevance of a unique development alternative promoted by AKRSP.

Clearly, there is a good demand for the expertise developed at AKRSP, both within Pakistan and outside. This demand can be met to a limited extent by individual staff members who might find it financially more attractive to leave AKRSP. At the institutional level, however, there appears to be a much greater opportunity to take up new and challenging assignments. For instance, AKRSP as an institution could take up consultancy work, ranging from project appraisal and design to start-up operations, project evaluation and revamping tasks. Just short of outright bidding, AKRSP should make its expertise available to potential donors or sponsoring agencies to do a series of tasks through sending appropriately qualified and experienced teams.

There are several advantages in this option. First of all, it would promote the Programme's particular approach for small farmers' development. Second, it would be a good way to utilise expertise currently under-engaged at AKRSP (Social Organization and Engineering, for example) and promote the objective of financial sustainability by introducing a new 'enterprise culture' in the set-up. Third, it would bring outside knowledge and experience to AKRSP, and enhance the professional capability and confidence of the staff. Lastly, it would provide a good and effective way to build a 'talent bank' at AKRSP. The revenue generated in this way could be used to both reward the talent and to cross-subsidise other programmes such as the HRDI.

On the down side, such a programme would give an 'outward' orientation to the professional cadres. Staff members may only concentrate on the outside assignments, thus giving little attention to the original work. The counter argument is that, if this becomes a viable avenue for institutional earnings, AKRSP could easily hire extra help. That way, it would also overcome one of its existing problems, namely, the absence of a second layer of managers. With appropriate training and an effective structure of incentives, the idea of institutional consultancy appears both timely and promising.

EXTRACTS FROM FIRST INTERIM EVALUATION OF AKRSP BY THE OPERATIONS EVALUATION DEPARTMENT OF THE WORLD BANK, MAY 1987—SUMMARY AND RECOMMENDATIONS

Evaluation of the Programme

The achievements are largely attributable to the effectiveness of the institution-building efforts at the village level. Several management principles are critical to this effectiveness. First is the principle of primacy of the VO. The VO is the focal point of all AKRSP activities but its sovereignty is sacrosanct, although AKRSP is firm in keeping to the agreed conditions of the partnership. The VO and AKRSP are seen as contractual partners where activities of the VO are supported but never undercut. Second is the principle of continued attention to innovations. Villagers and AKRSP staff alike are encouraged to innovate, using a trial and error approach that is carefully monitored. This creates a 'learning environment' of active improvisation and innovation.

Implications for the Future

Evaluation of the successful implementation record of AKRSP invites comparison with less successful rural development projects assisted by other agencies. First, the programme is directly implemented by an independent company associated with the sponsoring agency which was also the original donor. This is rare in rural development. AKRSP can conduct its routine affairs without recourse to government authorizations by distant officials or the uncertainty of annual budget approvals. It can react flexibly to problems as they arise. It has staff who are familiar with the area, and who speak the local languages. It can attract high calibre staff. It can spend much more time in the field and less in reporting upwards than any government programme. Some of these characteristics may be attainable in semi-autonomous project entities but few now in operation can compare with the effectiveness of AKRSP. Government agencies cannot function with the same flexibility or single-minded effort.

Second, the order of priorities and phasing of AKRSP is unique. The institutional model is well honed, and the early and almost exclusive emphasis on institution building deserves special attention. In some respects the first four years of AKRSP correspond to the missing years in many 'delayed' rural development schemes. The programme horizon of 10 to 15 years is much longer than the typical five to six-year cut-off of most projects.

Third, village programmes supported by AKRSP are planned from the bottom up. Infrastructure projects are selected by the villagers themselves. Later developments are similarly the village's choice. This is in contrast to most projects where standard packages are prepared and offered to rural communities with little if any prior consultation. Given a little insight into human motivation, it is not surprising that the AKRSP approach has been more successful.

Characteristics of the Model

The model used in the implementation of the AKRSP has been developed carefully and has a distinguished history. The basic concept is drawn *inter alia,* from the experiences with rural cooperatives in nineteenth century Europe. Additional elements have been adapted from versions of village organization and cooperation that were tried successfully in Taiwan and Korea in the post 1945 era and, less successfully, in the Village Development Programme in India in the 1950s. The current model owes much to Akhtar Hameed Khan and his work at the Comilla Academy of Rural Development in Bangladesh during the 1960s and early 1970s. It has been further tried and modified to fit local conditions by Shoaib Sultan Khan (the General Manager of AKRSP) at both Daudzai (near Peshawar, in the North West Frontier

Province, Pakistan) in the early 1970s and subsequently in the Mahaweli Ganga Development Project in Sri Lanka in the late 1970s.

The AKRSP model is one of 'organization and cooperative management' at the village level. This is based on mass participation of villagers with relatively homogeneous resources, private ownership of cultivated land, group management of irrigation water and common grazing land, and cooperation for the purpose of commercial activities, including village level investment in, and management of capital works, group access to credit and organized marketing. Ideologically the model lies between the socialist and capitalist models for agricultural development. It is idealistic in that it pursues economic development with a high degree of equity, and maintains the family farm concept while accepting the growth of non-farm employment and subsequent adjustments as the local economy diversifies.

The invaluable contribution of Shoaib Sultan Khan has been in refining the model and, above all, in making it operational by introducing a mode of implementation. Thus, the AKRSP model is not so much a concept but more a 'working method'. The process is to establish a VO with all families as participating members, partly by insisting that they all attend meetings and contribute to group savings. The VO's prime function initially is the collective implementation of a PPI project financed by a grant but collectively chosen by the VO. The viability of the VO is fostered through the provision of credit and other support services which enable all the members, individually, to exploit their existing resources through the improved infrastructure and various other technological advances that are made accessible to them. Within this process each village is treated as a separate case, with the rate of progress and the individual steps tailored in response to the villager's reactions. Similarly, the infrastructure and technology proposed is put to work on a trial and error basis so as to ensure that it will work effectively.

All villages are eligible to participate and receive the same support provided they agree to enter a contract with the project entity. The conditions of the contract are that:

(1) The VO has to meet as a general body on a regular basis, preferably weekly or bi-weekly, so as to enable all members to review the performance and needs of their organization regularly. Initially at least, these functions cannot and may not be undertaken by individuals or committees.

(2) All members must make savings deposits at their regular meetings. The accumulated funds are recorded in an individual pass book but are banked collectively. This 'equity capital' is essential to the viability of the VO since it is the key that gives access to the formal rural financial system and its various services at a cost to the farm family significantly below that afforded by the informal credit system.

The basic planning tool is a series of diagnostic dialogues carried out with villagers. The General Manager initiates the first dialogue explaining the objectives and methods of AKRSP and invites the villagers to identify a PPI that could be undertaken by the villagers for the benefit the village as a whole.

The second dialogue explores the feasibility of the PPI under the technical supervision of the Programme Senior Engineer or Programme Agriculturalist. Field operations are managed by the Social Organization Unit (SOU) and the products of the second dialogue are blueprints and estimates for a PPI or some other scheme (such as a VO-financed scheme or a livestock sub-project).

The third dialogue starts with discussion of the finalized scheme. The terms of a partnership between AKRSP and the villagers are discussed: AKRSP describes the form and extent of assistance it can provide and villagers explain how they will plan and implement the scheme, develop skills, meet regularly and establish group savings. If successful, the dialogue ends with the formation of a VO and the presentation of the installment of a grant from AKRSP in support of the agreed PPI. The average grant made to VOs is Rs 153,000 (or US$9,100 in 1986 dollars), paid in originally four, but now five, equal progress installments. The grant covers on average about 40 per cent of the imputed cost of PPIs, when taking account of the village's labour contribution.

Planning is, therefore, inductive and location-specific. In practice, the dialogues are a series of open-ended discussions that not only identify a viable entry point for AKRSP but also develop the relationship between villagers and AKRSP personnel. In addition, through frequent meetings of villagers as an assembly of the whole, and through the preparation of written records, the business of the village in relation to AKRSP becomes public and open to all. In this way the rights of less powerful members of the community are protected and opportunities for individual small groups to appropriate the benefits are minimized.

The PPI is implemented by the VO with occasional technical assistance from AKRSP. The grant generates local employment, initiates capital accumulation, as well as enables the construction of infrastructures of long-term value at financial costs well below those of comparable government schemes, largely because the output of self-help village labour greatly exceeds that of contractors hired by government agencies. Only one grant provided to each VO, and all subsequent activities, including maintenance of the PPI, have to be financed by the VO or through credit.

AKRSP's Social Organizers (SOs) provide the programme regular contact with villages, supported by frequent visits from members of the management group of AKRSP, often including the General Manager. The SO's main task is to nurture the organizational and institutional development of the VO and to call upon expertise from AKRSP for technical services as and when required. As the VOs develop, VO managers are encouraged to emerge from the ranks of VO members.

Methods of Implementation

Management Structure and Mode. AKRSP is a private company under Pakistani law, with its own Board of Directors. The Board has ten members with representation from business, government, the Northern Areas, and the Aga Khan Foundation, Geneva. The Board includes Ismailis, non-Ismailis and non-Muslims. The staff of the company is headed by a General Manager who reports to the Board. He is supported by a Deputy-General Manager and eight other senior management staff. Senior staff appointments are the responsibility of the AKRSP Board, but other appointments and the overall management of the programme are handled by the General Manager (GM) from programme headquarters in Gilgit. Senior staff include specialists in engineering, agriculture (crops and livestock), economics, marketing, training, women in development, social organization, finance and accounting. Senior staff includes representatives of all major Islamic sects. All senior staff are well-qualified professionals, most with many years of experience in their area of specialization. Not all senior staff had extensive experience in the Northern Areas prior to joining AKRSP, but they are all recognized within Pakistan and most have had some international experience.

The current structure of management is shown in the Organization Chart attached to this report [not included in the book]. As shown, the management structure of AKRSP seems unremarkable, except perhaps in its flatness, or lack of functional hierarchy. All seven members of the management group in Gilgit, plus the District Programme Officers in Chitral and Baltistan, report directly to the GM. Even the Programme Senior Engineer, who is also designated Deputy-General Manager, appears to have no more formal responsibility than any other member of the management group, except that he acts for the GM in his absence. The field organizations are similarly flat, with District Programme Specialists reporting directly to the District Programme Officers, while looking to programme specialists in Gilgit for technical guidance.

Programme implementation is managed directly by the GM assisted by the core management team of senior staff. Although some functions and responsibilities have been delegated as the programme has expanded, the GM remains in close daily contact with progress and with all major issues that arise. The level of familiarity of the GM and core management team members with individual villages and issues is remarkable given that there are some 526 villages in the programme. This is made possible by a system of regular senior staff meetings, a very high level of documentation of routine business, and an orientation to the field which is rarely if ever achieved elsewhere in projects of this type.

The management group at headquarters meets every week under the chairmanship of the GM. All senior staff are expected to attend and be able to present progress reports and problems encountered, and to respond to questions. Management group meetings appear to be characterized by their frequency, length and level of detail discussed. In addition to weekly meetings of the management group, monthly review workshops are also held at headquarters, to which senior and junior management and technical staff is invited from all three districts. These are day-long meetings with an agenda that not only reinforces operating principles and reviews performance, goes into great detail in the affairs of individual VOs. Every three months managers' meetings are held, to which the managers of VOs are invited. The meetings last for one day and bring the management group, field staff and VO leaders into direct communication at headquarters. Proceedings of the meetings in Urdu are regularly sent for VO office bearers. At these meetings implementation principles and practices are reinforced, progress is reviewed, experiences are shared, training lessons are repeated, and the concerns of villagers on any topic of their choosing are aired publicly. The proceedings of weekly and monthly staff meetings are available on file in English. All major dialogues with VOs are recorded on tape, and transcripts of the points discussed are available on file. The net effect of the meetings, the extensive reporting, is a system of written and oral communication that links managers, field staff and villagers effectively in both directions: from top to bottom, and from bottom to top. As a result, issues can be raised, discussed and resolved quickly.

Even though the number of villages is large, the GM has generally been present at the first dialogue, when initial contact was made, and at the third dialogue, when the check for the first installment of the grant funds, for the PPI was handed over. Such close involvement with routine implementation by the GM was greatly facilitated by using a helicopter, and indeed it was said that the programme in Chitral could not have started without a helicopter. The loss of the use of the helicopter, following an accident in early 1986, is contributing to the relative independence of the Chitral and Baltistan programmes. However, with or without the helicopter, it is clear that the GM by his individual example influences programme implementation considerably. He spends most of his time on frequent field visits, walking and talking with villagers, SOs and field engineers. The GM's example makes it clear to the staff that the practical needs of villagers come first, that the focus of the programme is the field, not the office.

AKRSP's flat management structure contributes to open communications. AKRSP's management style is described as being one of setting clear objectives, establishing well documented and understood procedures and then, provided that the objectives are being met, not being unduly concerned with the details of implementation. This does not mean that management is not fully aware of significant details of how the programme is being implemented in individual villages, nor of problems as they are encountered. But there is a clear policy that project staff should not become involved in the details resolving village-level problems or disputes, especially where these relate to matters such as land and water allocations. AKRSP's role is to build local problem-solving capabilities, permit them to function, and protect them if necessary from forces that would weaken them during their formative stages. AKRSP' s role is not to protect VOs from making mistakes, but encourage them to take decisions and be accountable. Similarly, the management does not concern itself unduly with the minority of villages that have not embraced the project concept nor welcomed AKRSP assistance; most of the project's energies are directed towards the majority of VOs, which with appropriate assistance are making steady progress. The importance of this working principle has been heightened in the period since April 1986 when the helicopter became inoperable and mobility of the management group was reduced.

Management has relied successfully on the demonstration effect to spread support and participation in the programme rather than devoting resources to difficult cases. The appropriateness of this strategy is indicated by there being no shortage of villages seeking AKRSP's assistance. The demonstration effect of the PPIs is considerable, given that the majority are readily visible irrigation channels often providing irrigation water for new land, or link-roads which connect villages for the first time by vehicle with the nearest jeepable road or with the KKH. All PPIs are well signposted at prominent places on roadsides advertising the AKRSP and acknowledging the relevant donor support.

One notable reason why the GM can devote so much of his time to programme management in the project area is that the major responsibility for international fund-raising rests with the Director of Special Programs (DSP) of the Aga Khan Foundation in Geneva. The GM and the DSP who visit the project area frequently appear to complement each other very well by being mutually very supportive but agreeing to an effective division of labor. If the GM had to play a more prominent fund-raising role it would detract considerably from his programme management functions. In this role, he is ably supported by his senior staff. The Monitoring, Evaluation and Research (MER) Section of AKRSP actively supports the DSP in the preparation of proposals for donor support, routine reports to donors and grant evaluations.

Problem Solving Methods

AKRSP has rejected a 'blueprint approach' to rural development, in favour of a 'learning approach'. Whereas blueprints specify detailed plans of action designers, the learning approach recognizes that designing rural development is a social process that must be learned by the beneficiaries themselves and those who assist them, if it is to be sustainable. AKRSP brings to this development an overriding belief that their role is to enable VOs to be sustainable mechanisms for solving problems locally. To that end, AKRSP seeks to create VOs and equip them with the principles, methods and skills they will need to make decisions effectively in the interests of village-level development.

AKRSP's approach combines well-tested principles with trial and error. The principles are described in paragraphs 1.08 *et seq* of this report: the trial and error approach is embodied both in the design of PPIs through rounds of dialogue and in the open communication processes and reporting that characterizes all of AKRSP's actions. Diagnostic dialogues and open reporting are communication mechanisms for linking players in the development process. If the mechanisms transmit information reliably and quickly, AKRSP management learns what the consequences of its actions are and can modify or adjust them quickly. Because AKRSP's senior management goes to the field, frequently in groups including the GM, villagers can learn about AKRSP directly from the senior staff. As time passes, confidence in AKRSP grows and the level of information shared by VOs and AKRSP also grows. Over time, the VO has opportunities to test its collective decision-making skill and the AKRSP management has opportunities to reinforce the principles it believes in and to show its responsiveness to new opportunities or past error. By working incrementally, neither the VO nor AKRSP makes commitments that would prove fatal to their mutual confidence in the event the commitment cannot be fulfilled. The SOs are key players in this communication process, since they spend more time with villagers than all other AKRSP staff and transmit more signals in both directions. The conduct of the GM makes it clear that next to the VOs themselves, SOs are perhaps the most important participants in the village development process.

Evaluation and the Programme

The Institutional Model. Much of AKRSP's achievement is attributable to the effectiveness of the institution building efforts at the village level. This success has been, in turn, assisted by a number of factors. Most important among these is the strength of the institution building model. The approach employed has been carefully conceptualized and refined through many applications. The three-part process of establishing the Village Organization, giving it corporate strength through group savings, and making it work through the implementation of a grant-aided infrastructure project, obviously works. Because it has been well tried and tested, the responsibilities of the respective AKRSP staff are clearly specified, which makes for smooth teamwork. This builds the confidence of both the VOs and the AKRSP team and permits considerable flexibility and use of imagination.

Management Principles

Several of the management principles that are part of the model are critical to its effectiveness. First among these is the principle of primacy of the VO. The VO is the focal point of all activities but its sovereignty is regarded as sacrosanct. The AKRSP team may make suggestions or present options but they do not make decisions for the VO nor make demands of them. Nor do they get involved in their internal problem solving. This builds a partnership between the VO and AKRSP whereby the VO management is supported but never undercut. While this principle of 'sovereignty of the village organization' is logical, sensible, and may even seem obvious, it is ignored in most rural development programmes, invariably to their detriment.

A second management principle is that of continued attention to innovation. This principle fosters a learning environment within AKRSP, within and among the VOs and effectively for the whole programme. When one VO proposed building an irrigation tunnel rather than a much longer open channel, they were given the same support despite the tunnel's inherent difficulties and risks. When another VO from an isolated outlying village used part of its grant funds to buy a shop in the Gilgit bazaar this was watched as an interesting experiment. Similarly, the use of new equipment or new varieties is observed carefully, whether proposed by AKRSP or originating from another source and the experiences discussed in meetings at various levels. Thus, both programme staff and village leaders learn from the experience. The effect is to create a 'learning environment' of active improvisation and innovation.

Flexibility in Operation. Pursuit of these principles is greatly aided by the flexibility and freedom of operation AKRSP enjoys as a small, independent non-government organization. It does not have to adhere to set plans and procedures, nor to institutional controls on its staff as larger entities find it necessary to do. There are virtually no hierarchical clearance procedures, only information sharing. If programme management has to ship in fertilizer or vaccines for onward sale to the VOs in order to ensure availability, there are no institutional prohibitions, procurement procedures or project rules that restrict this. Similarly, if another agency offers support for an activity or can provide an input, it can be welcomed and the programme adjusted to accommodate it. This flexibility, carefully husbanded by AKRSP management, greatly facilitates the 'working method' of experimentation, adaptation and trial and error innovation that is a hallmark of the programme.

Implications for the future

Management. At first glance the effectiveness of AKRSP seems directly attributable to the high quality of leadership and the high calibre of its professional staff. This prompts the question as to whether its success is attributable to personal characteristics of the staff which make it difficult if not impossible to replicate. Broken down into its component characteristics, as above, the management approach of AKRSP seems far from superhuman. Unquestionably, the standard of management skill is very high but the principles could all be pursued by the managers of a similar project, particularly once these principles are documented. In this respect, AKRSP might not only provide a model for replication of rural development programmes, but may have an important future role as a training ground for the management and staff of other projects.

Projects Compared

Much of the success of AKRSP can be attributed to the particular environment and the timing of the programme's initiation just after the area was opened up to the outside world. But even so, evaluation of the successful implementation record invites comparison with less successful rural development projects assisted by the World Bank and other multilateral institutions. Even given the special environment and timing of the programme, why are AKRSP results so impressive? What distinguishing features can be identified that might be replicable elsewhere?

First, the programme is directly implemented by an independent company associated with the sponsoring agency, which was also the original donor. This is very unusual in rural development. AKRSP can conduct its routine affairs in its capacity as a Pakistani NGO without reference and recourse to government but with support from its parent AKF in Geneva and sister foundations in donor countries. Thus, it is not bound by the civil service rules and procedures typically applicable to many implementing agencies and it is not staffed by civil servants who may have little experience of and motivation for this type of work. AKRSP is not subject to the uncertainty of annual budget approvals although it did suffer a shortage of donor funding at one stage. AKRSP can react flexibly to problems as they arise, including providing additional critical resources when needed.

Often the staff of many rural development projects are strangers to the project area and even sometimes to the country, whereas AKRSP has Pakistani staff (almost without exception) and has recruited the first-level contact staff (the Social Organizers) from among qualified local people who speak local languages in addition to the *lingua franca*, Urdu. AKRSP has freedom to hire and fire its staff, since it is not bound by civil service procedures and all staff are on contract. Financial incentives and a professional working environment combine to attract exceptionally good staff from both the public and private sectors; turnover is low. Time spent by AKRSP management and staff in the field on well-structured and fully recorded work programmes is well above that normally found in such rural programmes, despite the sometimes difficult and hazardous conditions. Some of these characteristics may be attainable in semi-autonomous project entities (and indeed these are the main arguments for setting up such project-specific agencies), but few such entities now in operation can compare with AKRSP and its implementation success.

The open management style, free and easy communication along the management chain and comprehensive record-keeping review and exchange, all contribute to a dynamic and responsive problem solving process which is almost the reverse of the typical behaviour of more bureaucratic organizations. In such organizations the tendency is to be wary of disclosure and not seek out problems and failures, but where these are found, to suppress such information. In the typical public sector environment mistakes and problems are often not openly debated until they can no longer be ignored and solutions are more difficult to find. AKRSP is willing, however, to learn from its mistakes and has the self-confidence to discuss them openly on-the-record. Thus, solutions are easier to come by, and at an early stage before real damage is done. AKRSP then has the flexibility to apply a wide range of pragmatic responses to problems.

Secondly, the Northern Areas programme was set up in a small but dynamic way with room to expand and develop year-by-year according to a statement of general objectives (quantitatively the targets were very ambitious at the outset and exceeded initial funding). The main features of the implementation mode had been well tested elsewhere including by the General Manager, such that AKRSP could be characterized almost as the follow-on operation to pilot phases elsewhere. Even so the early implementation objectives were institutional development and infrastructure construction, and not, as in many comparable projects, incremental production from Year 2 or so.

In some respects, the first four years of the AKRSP programme corresponded to the missing years in many 'delayed' rural development plans, where there is often frustration as institutions are established and essential infrastructure is constructed, but production targets are missed. AKRSP's programme horizon, originally around ten years and now stretching out to fifteen years, is much longer than in more traditional rural development projects. Thus the patient pursuit of much longer term institutional and social objectives is possible in AKRSP, compared with the typical five to six year cut-off of secured funding in other projects, which can lead to frenzied pursuit of money-consuming infrastructure construction, with less emphasis on careful introduction of permanent institutional and social changes.

Thirdly, village programs are planned from the bottom up. The infrastructure projects, which act as the catalyst for institution building, are identified by the beneficiaries themselves with assistance from AKRSP. Later developments, for which credit is supplied, are similarly the villages' choice. Nothing is imposed upon the village as part of an externally determined master plan, and since villages have to implement and maintain the PPIs, the projects chosen are likely to be of very high priority. This approach differs from the approach used in many other projects, where a standard package of works and improvements may be offered to rural communities (or even implemented and then offered) with limited prior consultation, on what resembles a take-it-or-leave-it basis. To wit, with any insight into the nature of human motivation, it is not surprising that the AKRSP approach has been successful.

NOTES

1. NFR—1 November 1985.
2. NFR—General Manager's Tour of Baltistan, 15-20 September 1988.
3. NFR—Workshop with Dr Akhtar Hameed Khan at Islamabad Hotel, 19 March 1989.
4. NFR—Visit of the Dutch Ambassador Mr J.J. de Roos and Mrs de Roos along with Mr Tenuissen to AKRSP—10 May 1989.
5. NFR—Visit of Government of Pakistan Delegation to AKRSP—6 May 1987.
6. NFR—Briefing of the CIDA Team and Mr Nazeer Ladhani of AKF Canada, 21 October 1984.
7. NFR—Shoaib Sultan Khan's visit to Geneva, 16-17 February 1988.
8. NFR—Shoaib Sultan Khan's visit to Geneva, 16-17 February 1988.
9. Note from Hussain Wali to Chairman AKRSP BoD. Ten Years/Substantive Issues/Proposals, 1992.

10

Partners in Development

WORKING WITH THE GOVERNMENT

The Northern Areas is a post-feudal enclave. The abolition of the role of the Mir resulted in most of the tenants becoming peasant landholders, the majority owning less than one hectare of land. The fact that almost everyone holds the same amount of land has made it easier to form Village Organizations, although we at AKRSP believe that this relative economic homogeneity does not mean that the approach would not succeed where wider disparities in land holdings exists.[1]

Of course it would not work with medium or large farmers but wherever there are small farmers—and the majority of Pakistani agriculturists fall in this category—the strategy would work. Because the biggest handicap of the small farmer is his subsistence holding and unless he pools his resources, cuts down overheads and achieves economies of scale in cooperation with other small farmers, he cannot be helped to rise above the level of subsistence. The land development component of the small farmer development package benefits the bigger farmers, the small farmers and the landless, and thus proves a great cementing factor and helps in strengthening the village organization.

AKRSP also evolved a women's development package based on labor saving devices, livestock management and poultry training. By 1986, women in 95 villages had organized women's groups (WOs) comprising over 5,000 households. They had accumulated over one million rupees as their equity capital.

The members of the VO are encouraged to keep their leaders under control. The mechanism for this is a regular 'general body' meeting. This is unlike traditional cooperatives which place authority and control in the hands of an executive committee. The general body meeting is also essential for increased savings because it is in their weekly and monthly meetings that each member deposits his or her savings. The government and the elected councillors have looked at VOs with interest.

Under the existing Local Council structure there is no statutory body at the village level. The Union Council comprises on average ten villages with the one member from each village. Whereas, the Council is a viable and effective body for inter-village planning, taxation and political education, it is hopelessly inadequate as a vehicle for economic or agricultural development of individual villages. The VOs fill this vacuum and act as a forum for development out-reach for the Union Council. The District Council of Baltistan has accepted this approach and AKRSP is collaborating with the District Council in implementing the Programme there. We are hopeful that other Councils and the government will emulate this example once it is proved viable.

As to the criticism that the AKRSP strategy would perpetuate the gulf between the haves and have-nots, I have explained that what AKRSP is aiming at is to help subsistence farmers rise above the level of subsistence and become commercial farmers. If it succeeds in doing so, it doesn't matter that the well-to-do farmers of today become rich farmers in the future, because this would not be at the cost of the small farmers. AKRSP is an economic programme and not a political one aiming to bringing everyone to the same level. The VOs are being fostered to develop into small-scale entrepreneurs and thereby ensure social justice and equitable distribution of the fruits of development.

Local Level Institutions. Physical infrastructure cannot be built by government in such extraordinarily difficult terrain. The AKRSP approach to the problem was unconventional. It was our assessment that the task could not be implemented by a centralized organization. Therefore, the social and institutional infrastructure had to be established to shoulder the responsibility of constructing and maintaining the productive physical infrastructure. The history of the area shows that no new land development was undertaken after the decline of feudalism in the region. The absence of improved inputs hampered productivity. AKRSP's approach once again was unconventional: we focused on capital generation and investment.

Terms of Partnership[2]

During his visit in 1986, Dr Heuckroth and Hsan Sing Tse wanted to know if AKRSP counselled the villagers on identifying and choosing a project. I replied that the villagers are in the best position to set their own priorities. AKRSP, however, tells them that the project they choose should have a direct monetary benefit for the village. This rules out drinking water schemes and other social-sector [health and education] interventions. There has not been a single village where AKRSP identified a project for the people. Sonia Plouride wanted to know whether it was easy for AKRSP to go to villages and have its 'terms of partnership' agreed to readily. I replied that during the initial stages, AKRSP was in the 'buyers' market' but is now in the 'sellers' market'. All the villages are very keen for AKRSP to establish a relationship with them even though we have made our terms a lot more stringent than in the past. AKRSP has started the second generation of PPIs, financed by the villagers themselves. I informed Hsan Sing that AKRSP's way of working is entirely in collaboration with the villagers and the responsibility for managing finances rests with the VO. Hsan Sing wanted to know how I saw the future developing for the programme. I replied that AKRSP would nurture the VOs, and in ten years' time the villagers should be in a position to control their own resources and benefit everybody. By then the VOs will be able to take over AKRSP's function. Robert Shaw added that AKRSP wants to leave behind a set of local institutions which will be purely autonomous and self-sustaining.

Responding to another query I said that the Terms of Partnership depend on the objective of a programme. Our objective is to improve the living standards of 98,000 households (that is nearly a million people). Of course, the creation of industries and improving health care are all useful activities. But the immediate question is: what will bring the quickest results in the shortest time? The answer, of course, is to raise rural households' income levels. With greater income, the household can access other services.

Initially, we had just three conditions for partnership between the village and AKRSP: (1) organization of the village into a VO (with at least 75–80 per cent participation); (2) the VO agreeing to raise farmers' skill levels by accepting the AKRSP Human Resource Development packages; and (3) the generation of capital through regular savings. Now that we are in a seller's market, we have over 25 conditions! The village has to meet all conditions and obligations before AKRSP starts to support that village by, for example, giving it a PPI.

Hsan Sing wondered whether the AKRSP methodology was replicable in the rest of the country and elsewhere. Robert Shaw said that tremendous interest has been generated throughout the country. A recent International Fund for Agriculture Development grant for Malakand Division[3] says that the AKRSP methodology is to be utilised there. This decision was made entirely independently by IFAD. The German government is anxious to have their personnel in Baltistan trained by AKRSP as well. Hsan Sing and Ms Plouride wanted to know what made AKRSP work when the fate of cooperatives in the rest of Pakistan has been very discouraging. I responded by saying that most other programmes were not based on the sound and tried principles of rural development. The chief minister of Punjab who was visiting Gilgit, wondered why such a programme could not be started in Punjab. After this session, the visitors left for their field trips to AKRSP villages.

Social Organizers and Technical Work. Social Organizers (SOs) have always been the main pillars of AKRSP's work in organizing communities. The SOs and the technicians had to work together. The background to this maxim was that during the days of 'Village AID' one village worker was given two years' training and was made a 'jack-of-all-trades'. There were absolutely no results generated from this practice and the experiment was a failure. 'Village AID' tried to channel advice through one person but the 'village workers' proved to be inefficient technical teachers. The solution for AKRSP was that the SO would have elementary knowledge about everything. He would not become the specialist but should not be uninformed either. The team had to be present. The PPI teams had two members: the SO and the Engineer. During the village survey, this team grew to three: the SO, the engineer and the resource person from the village (the village manager). Manuals needed to be prepared to help transfer knowledge and this could be done through case studies.[4]

The Social Organizer: Officer or Teacher. During one of his visits Akhtar Hameed Khan clearly described the role of a SO. He said that sometimes the SOs complained. Their role was to groom Activists (village volunteers who understood the AKRSP vision and were willing to commit their time and energies to accomplishing it) and their routine expansion role had ended. He had issued his note titled 'The Evolving Role of SOs' expressly for this purpose. Without Activists, the visits of SOs to villages would not achieve anything. Akhtar Hameed Khan said that the Senior SOs with 4–5 years experience now had to teach both Activists and colleagues. They would face a 'bureaucratic' mentality, especially among their colleagues who felt they were officers and demanded discipline and obedience. Hussain Wali commented that his problem was that the SOs were weak in technical matters. The link between the SOs and the technical sections was very important and it was this link that needed improvements. Akhtar Hameed Khan said that the AKRSP was not a programme of discipline and routine. Even in credit, the routine had ended although trouble shooting was still required. An officer felt that he was enforcing discipline but was actually enforcing routine. The teacher, however, concentrated on improving students.[5]

Implementation of the different packages is the full responsibility of SOs, just as the development of the packages is the responsibility of the specialists. If the SOs do not accept this responsibility, they will have little to do after a VO has been formed and the basic package of savings, loans, PPIs and training of specialists was accepted. [6]

Shoaib Sultan Khan then suggested that AKRSP might initiate inter-district transfers for the SOs, to maintain the interest in their work. Akhtar Hameed Khan noted that this would not be the optimal solution and that the SOs should not be transferred to counter 'burn-out'. Instead, this counter productive feeling should be eliminated through two means: (i) sabbatical leaves and (ii) participation in refresher courses and seminars. In universities these elements helped the professors from getting stale. A roster ought to be prepared for the SOs and they ought to be sent to university for their sabbaticals. Arrangements should also be made to send them to Chandigarh (in Indian Punjab) or to visit the Kulu valley (in Himachal Pradesh). In forestry, they ought to visit the 'Chipko' [forest protection] movement in Uttarakhand; they could also visit the 'Anand' project in Gujarat (India). A list ought to be prepared of all the extraordinary places in India and other parts of the world and the SOs sent to study these projects through a regular programme. Shoaib Sultan Khan said that some lists had been prepared of courses available both locally and in other countries. Akhtar Hameed Khan pointed out that these courses ought to be field based for the SOs to really benefit from them. Shoaib Sultan Khan asked whether visits to places like the Mitchell's fruit farms might also be beneficial. He said that like in Nepal, a cheese industry ought to be developed. Modern large-scale plants were not needed in Gilgit but smaller units were required. If possible, a village Activist should be sent with the SO to visit such places.

There was a need to establish a staff development policy, possibly along the line of the Japanese model which concentrated on nurturing employee loyalty and satisfaction with their work.

Another indicator of organic growth was the fact that the burden of work on SOs was decreasing. The SOs were now working with a group of Activists in each village. Previously the SOs did all the work themselves but they now had less responsibility.

Experts and Others. Akhtar Hameed Khan also guided the programme staff on relationship between experts and others. The expert cannot dictate, but only graft upon traditional knowledge and traditional world-views. If something works we should multiply it. Demonstrations should highlight successes and the demonstrators should be seen as teachers.

Responding to a question about whether to separate or mainstream the role of women, Akhtar Hameed Khan said: 'In Bengal, I came to the conclusion that the Bengali farmer will never be as productive as the Japanese farmer—the Japanese had an intelligent partner, his wife. The Bengali wife, for instance, had no concept of seed treatment and seed selection. I thought that the main problem was the segregation of women. But I never understood the subsequent attempts by donors to promote separate women's programmes.'

'Where you have a family farm, the unit of training is the family. In Gilgit, the real solution is that the women must start attending the VO meetings—there is no other solution. In the intermediate stage, there can be compromises: (1) attendance by elderly women; (2) teaching in the village. The women's programme cannot be another programme of segregation—it has to be a programme of equal partnership.'

He added: 'Don't give advice to those who are not willing to listen to advice. The weaver-birds gave advice to the monkeys, and the monkeys tore down the shelter of the weaver-birds'.

Partners in Human and Social Development. As mentioned in a seminar in Canada on Rural Development in the South[7] the training in AKRSP had to be need-specific initially. AKRSP leaned heavily on Government Departments for formulating and conducting training courses, with AKRSP playing the role of host. The next stage was to introduce innovations. This required the best experts in the field to develop relevant packages. Expatriate experts were considered for help provided they had the relevant expertise suited to AKRSP needs. For disseminating extension education, AKRSP is utilizing written materials: instruction sheets, case studies, village profiles, and an in-house magazine as well as audio visual aids, monthly conferences and seminars on topics useful to farmers and the AKRSP staff.

The Role of a Catalyst.[8] CIDA expert John Martin attributed the success of AKRSP to its emphasis on organization and commented that failure to organize well resulted in community members not participating in developmental effort. It followed that the objectives of development programmes in many parts of the world were not achieved. AKRSP, in his view addressed the fundamental need of organizing people right from the beginning, which proved to be the programme's greatest strength. Some people may ask why this capacity was dormant for so long and how AKRSP had awakened this 'sleeping giant'. Mr Martin observed that the AKRSP experience clearly showed that an external catalyst for change is essential. The great need now is to keep the VOs alive and functioning. He commended the AKRSP method of requiring the VOs to generate their own capital and to pay for services. He cautioned, however, against spreading the programme too thinly in other areas.

Why do we need a catalyst.[9] From 10 am to 11:30 Nazir Ladhani (Aga Khan Foundation Canada) and I met the publisher Roy McGarry and Editor-in-Chief Norman Webster, of Canada's only national newspaper, *The Globe and Mail* in Toronto. Roy enquired about the rationale for an external catalyst and Norman wanted to know the reasons for the local apathy and why the small farmers could not organize themselves on their own. I gave them the example of a vehicle stuck in a swamp: the small farmers are bogged down in the morass of poverty and without a push from outside, it is not possible for them to extricate themselves.

Roy spoke about the dilemma of donors: both in the Chinese and the Korean examples authoritarianism has played a vital role but then he conceded that although AKRSP did not practice authoritarianism, it did not enter into a partnership until certain obligations were accepted by the villagers. He also raised the issue of an individual's charisma and observed that AKRSP would not have been what it is today without

Shoaib Sultan Khan's efforts. He felt that a Programme would flourish with only a few dozen charismatic people, adding that he had been encouraged and impressed to see how much one individual can achieve. I explained that, although the AKRSP strategy is neither difficult to understand nor impossible to learn and practice, its implementation needs long-term commitment by everyone concerned.

The Government. Roy asked whether NGOs or the government should implement development programmes. Nazeer expressed the view that an NGO was the most viable forum for such an initiative. I submitted that rural development programmes cannot be run on a shoe-string budget and that if NGOs did not have financial and technical support, successful programmes such as AKRSP could not be implemented countrywide. Only governments have the requisite resources. The governments of Taiwan and South Korea have shown that it can be done. The other alternative would be to create numerous AKRSP-type NGOs to undertake this type of development. There are no short-cuts.

Roy brought up the importance of social development in terms of health and education and literacy as a *sine qua non* for development. On being challenged he accepted the importance of economic development at grassroots level as pre-requisite for helping small farmers to rise above the level of subsistence. I quoted the examples of Sri Lanka and the Philippines where, despite nearly 100 per cent literacy, the condition of the rural poor is only marginally better than in countries with low literacy rates.

Adaptation of NGO Model by Government[10]

I pointed out that of the four programmes Comilla espoused, only the Thana Training and Development Centres covered the whole country. The Thana irrigation programmes had 36,000 groups covering nearly two million people. The principles of Comilla adopted by the government, was an excellent example of a government acting like an NGO. Samaual Undong in South Korea is another such example. The point I made was that the NGO sector, even Grameen in 12 years, has been able to cover only 0.4 million of the 18 million rural poor in Bangladesh. Khalid Shams from Bangladesh observed that the processes of development enshrined in the Comilla project are of eternal value and the Grameen approach also is based on the same principles.

During a visit in 1987, US AID Director Rocky Staples referred to the politics of doing such a programme and association of such a programme with a particular political party. The Chief Secretary Sahibzada Imtiaz felt that economic schemes such as the proposed SRSC are normally unaffected by political changes. As to Rocky Staples' question about the politics of bureaucracy, the chief secretary felt that there was no categorical answer and criticism of bureaucracy was inherent in doing things better. As regards the reaction of MPAs and councillors, the chief secretary said that elected bodies ought to have a say in the formulation and review of the Programme but not in its day to day implementation and he felt that a Programme which directly benefits the rural poor, would not be opposed by the politicians. Rocky Staples felt that to make an NGO relatively independent of the political change, it should preferably not involve itself in a political organizational format. The chief secretary agreed with the suggestion and suggested a Board of Directors with representatives from all over Pakistan to avoid dictation by local interest groups.[11]

NGOs to innovate; government to replicate. His Highness also favoured the idea of replication of AKRSP by promoting setting up of autonomous Rural Support Programmes without the direct involvement of AKRSP, except in training. AKRSP needs to concentrate fully on development of a viable model in its present area of activity for the time being and can ill-afford to overstretch its existing resources. According to Bob, His Highness appeared fully satisfied with the progress of AKRSP to date.[12]

For Localizing Development, Government should Work like an NGO

Mr Azam Khan (Additional Chief Secretary Development, NWFP) repeated his feelings about the elected office holders. He said that in the methodology of the government, the elected officials cannot be bypassed and he wanted to know how they could be involved in the VO. He added that the union council would be the more appropriate system for implementing government programmes. The GM answered that the union council member is usually part of the VO but is not the sole arbiter in the village. The portfolio of the projects comes in very handy for AKRSP. It becomes difficult for the councillor to over-rule a project chosen by the people. Secondly, the allocation for these projects is very small. Through this system money was not distributed across the board. AKRSP lobbied with the district councillor and the Northern Areas councillors. Some people accepted it and others did not. The GM noted that Mr Sartaj Aziz thought that the VO was a tier below the union council, which should be the identifying and implementing authority. AKRSP's method for support from the elected officials has been to lobby with them. In Baltistan the union councils have pooled their money with AKRSP.

Answering Mr Azam Khan's previous query, the GM said that AKRSP did not 'straitjacket' itself in cooperative law. He added that community pressure was a much greater force than legal force. The VO, even when it is formalized, will not be a traditional cooperative because a general body, rather than a management body, will rule. Mr Azam Khan said that they had tried to organize cooperatives from the top end and had failed. It seemed to him, however, those AKRSP organizations were cooperatives in the true sense. The GM said that the acceptance by the VO of the equity principle is a tremendous step forward. AKRSP will provide a legal cover without compromising the cooperative spirit.

Mr Ijaz Qureshi, Secretary Planning asked a more direct question. He asked that for the IFAD funds, how could the government collaborate with AKRSP? All the elected people want a share in the decision-making and the disbursement of funds. UNICEF had prepared a Five-year Plan but nobody 'owns' the document. There are also personnel problems and most government functionaries are unwilling to stay in the rural areas. The GM said that the tendency is to give NGOs the responsibility for development. Unless the government is involved, there can be no countrywide development. He said he would try and convince the government to behave like an NGO.

The GM noted it that it was not difficult to make plans—the real difficulty lay in operationalising them. In the diagnostic survey, there are no pre-conceived plans. Again the GM noted that he was talking about village-level plans. Robert Shaw commented that there was another incentive with the councillors. The money given to the VO can go much further and produce quicker results. In Taiwan the farmers are an integral part of the government. The performance of the councillors over time determines future elections for them. Regarding the performance of government employees, Shaw said that he had the greatest respect for the people stationed in the rural areas. He said that in his experience, having more government staff in the Line Departments would ensure a good job but they are constrained in resources. AKRSP can offer them a genuine partnership to increase productivity. For example, AKRSP had a training centre but government employees do most of the training. Mr Ijaz Qureshi reiterated his stance that the government could not bypass the elected people. The GM said that in Chitral AKRSP would organize the people. He said that we could offer you that forum in at least 100 villages. Together we have to lobby and explain to the elected officials and we will have to take them to the villagers.

Robert Shaw added that Chitral district is cut off for six months every year and has an enormous set of problems. IFAD money may look large but is not large in comparison to the needs. AKRSP was set up as a private company because it offered the greatest flexibility. AKRSP is also trying to make the best possible use of these sources. There are, however, certain needs, which have to be met by the government. It might be possible to divide the IFAD loan into two parts, one to meet district-wise needs and the other for village level needs. At the village level, if collaboration is possible with the cooperation of the politicians, then the money might be used in a more cost-effective and efficient way through the VO.

People Centered Development by the Government[13]

As a sequel to the meeting at Islamabad, the Adviser to the Prime Minister in the Ministry of Kashmir Affairs and Northern Affairs Mr Qurban Ali came on an exploratory visit to Gilgit on 13 May 1990 and visited VOs along with Shoaib Sultan Khan, Hussain Wali, Noor Mohammad and the Assistant Director General of the Peoples Works Programme in the Ministry of LG&RD.

At Fikar in Nagar area, more than 200 villagers, all members of the VO Fikar, greeted the Adviser. In the welcome address, read by Dr Habibullah, numerous demands were made—for provision of electricity, upgrading the middle school to a high school, upgrading the post office box to a sub-post office, repairing old drinking water pipe lines, upgrading a dispensary to a 10-bed hospital, construction of Tishote-Fikar link road, constructing an irrigation channel and providing education of girls.

The Manager of the VO, Fikar Alhaj Ibadullah, stated that the VO was formed in 1984 with 350 households and identified improvement and expansion of existing irrigation channel as its PPI. AKRSP gave Rs 100, 000 as a grant with which the work was completed. Prior to the completion of this work, each household had to contribute to the completion of the work. Each household had to contribute Rs 180 annually to the maintenance of the channel. With the completion of the channel, the cost per household does not come to more than Rs 30–40 per year. Thus, each household has saved Rs 150 annually. The VO is well satisfied with what it has done but being a very large VO, it did not take advantage of other packages of AKRSP, hence to streamline the VO and make it more effective, the households have now decided to divide themselves in 3 VOs.

The Adviser expressed great satisfaction with the way AKRSP had functioned in the Northern Areas over the last seven years. He stated that even when they were out of the government, they supported AKRSP and now when his party is in power, he would like to support the activities of AKRSP even more. He said that the sincerity of purpose of AKRSP is most impressive. He spoke about the PWP and the minister's proposal to implement the programme through VOs, noting that he had come to Fikar to explore the possibilities of this idea. He stated that he would be willing to offer construction of a school building in Fikar village through the VO under the PWP. The announcement was received with loud clapping.

On being asked by the Adviser to explain the methodology of AKRSP as it applied in the case of PWP projects, Shoaib Sultan Khan recounted the terms of partnership VOs accepted in case of an AKRSP assisted project. The VO responded to this explanation by stating that a school building was not a priority for them: it was an irrigation channel which would bring nearly 4,000 *kanals* of new land under irrigation range and help every household. Hearing this, the Adviser agreed to change the priority from the school building to an irrigation channel. It was agreed that the local SOU would help in the survey and preparation of the cost estimates of the channel, in consultation with the VO representatives. The estimate would be submitted by the ADG of PWP to the Adviser for approval. Thereafter, the ADG PWP would adopt the terms of partnership of AKRSP for implementation of the channel and for supervision of the work the SOU would help the ADG PWP. The cheques would be paid directly by the ADG or the Adviser to the VO. AKRSP would be entitled to charge appropriate fees for the preparation of the cost estimates and supervision of its implementation, but no money would be channelled through AKRSP, nor would it be accountable for rendering any accounts.

The next visit was to village Minapin where, again, more than 250 villagers of VOs Minapin, Pissan and Mianchar had assembled. Mr Muzaffar Hussain, Manager of the Minapin VO recounted the activities of his VO including completion of the PPI and VO banking with Rs 381, 000 through current savings. The manager also emphasized the need for collaboration between the government and the AK Network and welcomed the Adviser's initiative in undertaking PWP projects through VOs.

The Adviser, in his speech, explained the purpose of his visit and asked the VO their priority project for implementation under PWP. A discussion ensued between construction of a link road and a girls' school. A consensus was reached on the construction of the girls' school, provided the Adviser would undertake to provide the teachers and maintain the building through the Education Department. The school will have to be built according to the plan provided by the Education Department. The local SOU, on payment of fees, would prepare cost estimates and supervise the construction. The payment would be made directly by the ADG PWP to the VO on terms and conditions similar to those of AKRSP, and would be between the VO and the ADG PWP.

At Nilt, which is a village comprising 120 households, there are two VOs, Nilt Paeen and Tong Dass, comprising 26 and 21 households respectively. About 45 villagers greeted the Adviser. Mr Alam Sher, Manager of Nilt Paeen VO, explained the activities of the VO, comprising the construction of an irrigation channel at Rs 86,000, and savings of Rs 80,555 accumulated for land development (Rs 42,000) and the initiation of a women's programme.

The Adviser explained the concept of PWP and asked the VO to identify their priority project to be implemented under the PWP. There was considerable discussion and the consensus was that their priority project which was an irrigation channel, was too difficult for them to implement. Therefore, they requested the Adviser to ask the government to do the job. As a second priority, they identified the construction of an addition to the existing girls' school building which already had a total of over 200 students. Since all the households were not members of the 2 VOs, there was discussion as to who would take responsibility for constructing the school. The two VOs offered to do the job on the request of the non-VO members, provided the cost estimates were fair.

The arrangement agreed at Minapin for the construction of the girls' school was explained to the VO members. The VO Manager said very candidly that if the Adviser desired quality work, he would have to ensure reasonable funds. The Adviser reiterated that the building must be constructed according to the Education Department plan and be of a quality acceptable to the NA PWD before it would assume responsibility for its maintenance. The VO accepted the decision provided sufficient funds were made available and agreed to enter into an agreement with the ADG PWP on similar conditions as AKRSP.

Dealing with the Bureaucratic Mindset

Despite the need to work closely with the government, problems arise due to the different style of work. These need to be confronted softly but firmly. One such issue related to the settlement of land reclaimed by AKRSP.

The GM requested an emergency Programme Planning Meeting to discuss with the Management Group the outcome of his meeting with the Acting Commissioner, Mr Zahoor A. Malik on the issue of land resettlement in the Northern Areas. This meeting had been necessitated by a letter from the Legal Advisor, Office of the Commissioner, Northern Areas, Gilgit to the GM. This letter specified that AKRSP should supply the following information regarding the irrigation schemes being sponsored by AKRSP:[14]

(i) A complete list of irrigation schemes;
(ii) The *Hisa Rasidi* shares of each member in the village in case new land is being brought under cultivation by the channel; and
(iii) Desirability of starting work on a channel only after the individual ownership is determined.

The GM had conveyed to the commissioner that (i) would be no problem. AKRSP had a complete list of 79 irrigation channels which it had sponsored at that point. The commissioner seemed visibly surprised by this disclosure and enquired whether work on all these channels was in progress. The GM informed him that not only was work in progress but had, in certain cases, also been completed. Regarding the second issue, AKRSP was in no position to ensure the settlement of land. Its Articles of Association specified its responsibility. Land settlement was an issue between the government and the people, which normally takes up to ten years after the initiation of settlement operations. The only role that AKRSP could undertake in this regard was to give whatever assistance it could.

The GM also explained to the commissioner that land settlement was a time-consuming exercise and if the people were asked to wait to complete the formalities, the programme of irrigation channels and land development would come to a standstill. In that case, the management would have no recourse but to go back to the federal government which had approved its Articles of Association. The commissioner protested that harming AKRSP was not his intention at all. In order to demonstrate his sincerity he would rescind the orders. His only intention was to try and avoid subsequent problems with the revenue authorities such as had occurred in Shirote-Shikote. The GM replied that he was convinced that the commissioner was interested in the development of the area but did not understand the purpose of all these conditions. The commissioner responded that there would be a time when the development of new land could lead to distributional problems. The revenue authorities could, in such cases, exploit the situation. If the commissioner could get an application listing the total amount of new land which would be developed by building a channel and its distribution among the villagers, then he would ensure its settlement to avoid future problems. In fact, the commissioner undertook to process all cases submitted to him within the month of March 1984.

Hussain Wali interjected to state that this exercise would be time consuming and would entail making detailed village plans and demarcating the land and its distribution. Tariq Husain felt that the difficulty would be in trying to specify how much land would go to each farmer in villages for which no plans were available. Mohammad Saleem pointed out that the exercise seemed pointless since ownership of the present land owned by their fathers and forefathers had not even been regularized.

The Powers that Be

The GM was invited by the Martial Law Administrator (MLA) Zone E to receive the president[15] on arrival at the [Gilgit] airport on 7 November 1983 and to attend a dinner in honour of the president on the same day, hosted by the MLA.[16]

In the evening the GM was informed separately by the additional secretary, Ministry of Kashmir Affairs and Northern Affairs, commissioner Northern Areas and deputy commissioner, Gilgit that the president wanted to see him. After the dinner, the MLA walked up to the GM and said the same things. The president asked the GM about the progress of the programme and mentioned that His Highness the Aga Khan had especially mentioned AKRSP and requested him to see the programme. When the GM invited the president to visit AKRSP, the president expressed his inability to do so because of lack of time, but expressed his desire to discuss with the GM any assistance and collaboration that AKRSP might be in need from the Northern Areas Administration. The GM informed the president about the full support and help the programme had been receiving from the MLA and other officials.

On the morning of 9 November 1983, Deputy MLA (Brig. Munir) and Col. Martial Law (Col. Beg) informed the GM that he should accompany the DMLA to Hunza where the president would like to meet him at lunch. At the luncheon meeting (at the Mir of Hunza's home at Karimabad), first the president enquired of the GM if a boys' school in Hunza could be upgraded to college level and a girls' school upgraded to a high school, in a collaboration between the government and the Aga Khan Foundation. The GM informed the president about the mandate of the AKRSP and offered to convey his wishes to the president of the Aga Khan Foundation (Pakistan).

Responding to a query by the president as to what the government could do to help the programme, the GM requested the president's patronage and blessings. On being assured by the president that this was already there, the GM mentioned the adverse and baseless reports being made by intelligence agencies about the programme. On the president's response that the director, Intelligence Bureau met him every week but had not made any such report, the GM drew the president's attention to a recent report (said to be 20 pages long) submitted by the Inter-services Intelligence Agency in which the GM has been dubbed a CIA agent and the whole programme as 'anti-state' in flavour. The commissioner (who was present) informed the president that the AKRSP had made a tremendous impact in a very short time and that everyone had acclaimed its achievements. The president directed the MLA Zone E to tell the agencies concerned that it was not their business to report on AKRSP in this way. The GM offered to explain and show anything connected with AKRSP which the agencies consider suspect.

The GM briefly explained to the president the strategy of AKRSP of organizing small farmers, noting that the strategy was based on the distillation of 150 years' of world experience in this field in countries as diverse as Germany and Japan. Recounting the activities of AKRSP, the GM informed the president that so far 129 out of 216 villages had been contacted and nearly 100 organized around infrastructure works and credit interventions. On the president's query if there were banks, especially the Agricultural Development Bank, in the area, the GM stated that the mere presence of banks would not ensure the availability of credit to small farmers unless they are organized. It is for this reason that in the last three years, despite the availability of interest free credit, not a single loan had been disbursed by the banks. However, with the organization of the small farmers, nearly 4,000 farmers have availed of the facility in less than eight months. The GM also submitted to the president the need and importance of a broad-based VO as an outreach of the union council for undertaking development planning and implementation of projects, without which the union councils cannot be effective.

The president observed that His Highness the Aga Khan had spoken to him about the programme and the president was keenly interested in its progress because if it succeeded in the Northern Areas, he would like to expand and replicate it in the rest of the country. He again enquired of the GM as to what he could do for the programme. The GM requested the opportunity to explain the programme fully (with the help of slides) to the president, adding that thereafter the president could decide for himself what type of assistance he was in a position to provide. The president agreed to do so in Rawalpindi and asked the GM to get in touch with his Military Secretary (Brigadier Durrani).

Before the president left Hunza, the Military Secretary contacted the GM and informed him that the president has asked him to make an appointment for the GM in Rawalpindi. The GM promised to contact the Military Secretary on his next visit to Rawalpindi.

Politicians[17]

Syed Qasim Shah, Minister of State for Kashmir Affairs and Northern Affairs accompanied by Mr Z. A. Temuri, Secretary Incharge of the Ministry, the Administrator Northern Areas and other officials paid a visit to the office of the AKRSP on 10 May 1985 at 1900 hours.

The minister's entourage was joined by the members of the Northern Areas Council for a briefing given by the GM AKRSP which also included showing the video film on AKRSP *Valleys in Transition*. The GM described the programme's progress and the response of the villagers of Gilgit to the programme. He stated that in less than 29 months, 87 per cent of the rural households in Gilgit district had responded positively to AKRSP's terms of partnership by organizing themselves into 302 VOs and by accumulating savings of over Rs 6 million. That amount was an average of Rs 18,700 per VO, compared to Rs 3,870 per agricultural village cooperative in Punjab after 78 years. In addition, the villagers of Gilgit District have embarked on 207 village-level projects at a total cost of Rs 25 million. Of these, 112 have already been completed and are being fully maintained by the VOs. Pointing out the cost-benefit ratio of small projects, the GM cited the example of 107 irrigation channels costing a total of Rs 13 million, benefiting 12,000 families by bringing more than 34,000 acres of land under irrigation range. In Gilgit District, where the average holding under crops is only one and half acres per family, the addition of more than 2 acres to the land holding of each family is a significant measure towards achieving increased incomes.

Summing up, the GM informed the minister that the villagers of Gilgit had responded marvellously to the AKRSP package of organization and collective management, land development, increased productivity and the generation of their own capital. He also made an impassioned appeal to the councillors to allocate at least 15–20 per cent of the ADP (Annual Development Programme) for village-level projects to be identified, implemented and maintained by the VOs. AKRSP's two years of experience has shown that given the resources and responsibility, the villagers can achieve wonders and participate fully in the development process.

Difference between VOs and UCs. It was brought home to the delegation that the VOs are an effective outreach for the Union Councils (UC) because UCs are incapable of organizing economic production. The VOs supplement, but do not replace, the UCs. It was also clarified that VOs cannot be created by merely passing a law unless they are nurtured and fostered by a support mechanism.[18]

Field demonstration and clear description of the fundamental principles of AKRSP played the key role in mainstreaming AKRSP's approach with the government. A record of one conversation with WAPDA officials in given in the following Box.

Briefing of WAPDA Group, 27 June 1988

A briefing meeting for a group of WAPDA officers visiting the Northern Areas was held on 27 June 1988. The meeting started at 12:15. The GM welcomed the group and an introduction of the AKRSP Management Group followed. The visitors were shown a combined edited version of the video films *Valleys in Transition* and *The First Harvest*. A question and answer session followed. The GM and Hussain Wali responded to the questions raised by the visitors.

Question: I have an introductory comment and a question. This movie has shown different development projects but it does not mention anything about a hydel power project. Now the question: How will the programme sustain itself?

Answer: Partnership furnishes the basis of the programme. Managerial skills provided to VO managers ensure results. Villagers' response is the key. 49 per cent of the rural households are covered by our programme in the NA. and $2 million in savings have been generated in an area twice the size of Switzerland. It all depends on the villagers' response. It will take 15 years or more to make it sustainable. The form of this programme will change over time, in response to needs.

Question: What about coverage?

Answer: We might not expand to villages with different needs, perceptions and beliefs.

Question: Why was this area selected?

Answer: The area was selected by His Highness the Aga Khan, one reason being that it is an Ismaili concentration area. Charity always begins at home. But once started, the programme has been for all the area, which is now 70 per cent non-Ismaili.

Question: How do you motivate?

Answer: Hussain Wali: We hold diagnostic dialogues with the villagers to identify their needs and then work on fulfilling those needs.

Question: We failed in a village when we took a scheme for electrification over there.

Answer: Because you went with a readymade scheme. Priority should be determined by the villagers. That will motivate them to work on the scheme.

Question: How is it possible to motivate people in this area with low literacy compared to Tribal Areas?

Answer: Ask the villagers what they want.

Question: How is the ratio of contribution and distribution determined?

Answer: Villagers are not asked to make monetary contribution for the first project. The contribution we require is in the form of (a) organization (b) identification of the project and (c) savings by the villagers.

Question: How are earnings distributed among village families?
Answer: Each village has its own rules, but they have to undertake a project which benefits them collectively.
Question: So it's the commune system under the capitalists?
Answer: It is a commune system with private property.
Question: How do the VOs resolve their disputes?
Answer: We do not interfere with that. The villagers have to resolve that.
Question: What is AKRSP's part after the project is launched?
Answer: Technical assistance and verification. We also check to see if the work has been completed according to the specification. Our interest is in creating a forum.
Question: If money is wasted because of a dispute, what do you do?
Answer: We waste the money because we can't resolve the dispute. There has been only one case in Gilgit out of 290 projects, where this has happened.
Question: In Chitral, a water channel was destroyed after completion, why?
Answer: Afghan bombing.
Question: What have you done about marketing the villagers' products?
Answer: (Nabeel Anjum Malik): Collective marketing provides economy of scale. We provide them training and credit. We train them to improve their product. With agricultural and livestock development, we establish their links with Gilgit and down-country markets.
Question: What about perishables?
Answer: We train them to preserve perishable products such as apricots. If they do not dry and preserve the product, it is lost. If not quickly moved to the market, the same thing happens.
Question: Have you introduced animal-drawn implements?
Answer: No animal-drawn implements yet but other improved instruments have been introduced.
Question: What is the nature of fund provided for PPI?
Answer: It is grant money.
Question: Any limit on the grant money?
Answer: As much as villagers can themselves use for implementation of a project. The maximum we have given is Rs 3 million for the Shimshal road project. The average is Rs 150,000 per project.

NFR—27 June 1988—Briefing of WAPDA Group.

NOTES

1. Seminar on Rural Development in South Asia sponsored by South Asia Partnership of Canadian NGOs (SAP), Ottawa, 5 February 1986.
2. NFR—Briefing of the CIDA Country Programme Mission, 6 November 1985.
3. In Pakistan's North-West Frontier Province.
4. Workshop with Dr Akhtar Hameed Khan 19-20 March 1989 at Islamabad Hotel.
5. Workshop with Dr Akhtar Hameed Khan 19-20 March 1989 at Islamabad Hotel.
6. NFR—General Manager's tour of VOs, 9 November 1988.
7. NFR—Seminar on Rural Development in South Asia sponsored by South Asia Partnership of Canadian NGOs (SAP), Holiday Inn Ottawa, 5 February 1986.
8. NFR—21-24 October 1984—Visit of CIDA Team comprising M/S John Martin (JM), Tom Schatzky (TS) and Nazeer Ladhani (NL).
9. NFR—AKFC—3 February 1986.
10. Asian Seminar on Community Participation organized by EDI, World Bank, IFAD, Asian and Pacific Centre for Development (APCD) and UNCRD in collaboration with UNICEF, ADB and Commonwealth Secretariat, 4 June 1988.
11. NFR—Replication of AKRSP—Setting up the Sarhad Rural Support Corporation (SRSC), 23 June 1987.
12. NFR—National Cooperative Seminar, 20-21 June 1987.
13. Implementation of Peoples Works Programme projects through Village Organizations (VOs). 31 May 1990.
14. NFR—Programme Planning Meeting, 29 February 1984.
15. General Zia ul Haq.
16. NFR—President of Pakistan's Visit to Northern Areas, 7 November 1983.
17. NFR—Visit of Syed Qasim Shah, Minister of State for Kashmir Affairs and Northern Affairs to AKRSP, 10 May 1985.
18. NFR—Visit of Government of Pakistan officials to AKRSP, 6-8 May 1987.

11

Community Mobilization at AKRSP

RURAL DEVELOPMENT IN ACTION: THE PROCESS

During a briefing to Ismaili ladies from the UK in 1984, I pointed out that the Project area in Gilgit covered 27,250 households with a population of 227,000. The number of villages identified in the project area had increased from 216 in 1983 to 291 at present in 1984. I estimated that there are about 350 villages altogether in the Gilgit District. I then recalled the AKRSP strategy that was outlined in the movie shown to the group:[1]

- Formation of a VO and the need for collective management and responsibility
- Identification of PPI (an income generating project)
- Provision of credit and banking facilities
- Extension training and the provision of supplies
- Marketing

The Village Organization. The belief that villagers in remote areas cannot organize themselves was rebuffed by the excellent response of the villagers in forming VOs. Eighty-eight per cent of the population had formed 254 VOs by June 1984. This response to organization is unbelievable and the strength of the VOs can be judged by their savings, the total of which amounts to almost three million rupees. This is quite phenomenal, since it was said that these villagers would not save money regularly. These savings are in the bank, as Mr Saifur Rehman, Zonal Chief of Habib Bank Limited in the Northern Areas, who is present here, will testify.

Identification of PPIs. Once the villagers had formed themselves into an organization, and were meeting and saving regularly, they were asked to collectively identify an income-generating project that would bring maximum benefit to their villages.

AKRSP agreed to provide technical support in assessing the feasibility of a project by making available an agriculturist, economist or engineer. However, it was the responsibility of the VO to identify, implement and maintain the project, which could be anything from the widening of an existing water channel to the construction of a link road. The villagers' response to this has been very rapid. So far 426 projects have been identified in the Gilgit district, of which 138 have already been initiated and 79 completed.

This proves that if the people are involved, given responsibility, and provided with resources, they are highly responsive as well as responsible for the implementation and maintenance of the project.

Credit and Banking. The villagers are asked to save money regularly so that they can have sufficient equity capital against which they will be able to borrow money from the banks. The notion that these people do not know how to save and bank their money has been laid to rest once and for all by their response to saving money. These savings also show clearly that they can generate income from their activities. The VOs have also started saving regularly in areas where a PPI has not yet been initiated as they have realized that the more they save, the greater the credit they will be able to get from the banks.

Savings are linked to the Agricultural Credit Programme. Those VOs that have savings are given credit. So far 162 VOs have borrowed a total of Rs 2.61 million. None of these farmers had previously received the production loans given by the banks. This was the first time they had borrowed money. The amazing thing is that the recovery rate has been almost 100 per cent, with only one VO failing to pay its due loan up to now. The people's response to the project has been very impressive. The strategy consists of:

- Organization and collective management
- Land development
- Increased productivity
- Credit and banking
- Marketing

Extension Training and Supplies

Extension training and the provision of supplies to implement the training are essential to development. Prevention of losses in the first instance is necessary to sustain the income of the farmer. In Shimshal, 200 yaks worth Rs 4,000 each died last year. With the help of preventative measures, all of these could have been saved, if the village had had a trained livestock/veterinary specialist. Then his services could have been utilized at a small cost to prevent a large loss. The specialists have to be carefully chosen for training and paid for their services. The revenue would enable them to replenish their stocks of medicines and equipment. The specialist has to be responsible for the village. Refresher courses will ensure that his knowledge is up to date and fresh. Each village is encouraged to have its own livestock, plant protection, marketing and management specialists so that the affairs of the village can be catered to collectively. This would also create the spirit of cooperation amongst the villagers. AKRSP's strength lies in training specialists as the Management Group of AKRSP is very small itself and cannot possibly look after the affairs of the entire area on its own.

At this point, the discussion moved to the economy in the area and someone enquired whether the barter system still existed. I replied that it is a mixed economy; in one village, three heads of sheep were asked for, in exchange for a loan.

Tariq Husain stated that the barter system is still prevalent in Yasin. I said that this was also a hindrance to the marketing strategy since consumer goods were bought on credit in the off season and paid for in fruits after they had been dried in the summer season. This means that a farmer cannot take his fruits to the Gilgit or Rawalpindi markets where he could get 5 to 10 times more money from the sale of his dried fruits. With the provision of marketing loans, the VO could pay off its debts to the shop-keeper and take the dried fruits to better markets to obtain the maximum price.

Then the discussion moved to the introduction of mechanized farming. I said that the aim was to prevent losses in the first instance, before going on to innovations which would have to be well researched and well selected prior to implementation. The first aim is to bridge the gap for those farmers who have smaller yields. We need to find out why this is so and how we can overcome this before we can introduce mechanization. Moreover, this could be difficult considering the pattern and size of land holdings which average out to about half an acre per farmer. Mechanization can be introduced if the farmers cooperate and the whole village becomes a farm. The technology used should correspond to the needs of the land and the village. Mechanization may be possible in the cooperative development of new lands acquired by villagers through irrigation or land reclamation. It is entirely the responsibility of the VO to pursue whatever policy they consider suitable for their needs.

One person present asked whether the villagers know about crop rotation. I replied that the villagers are already quite knowledgeable about this. If somebody has some better technology, then the farmers are willing to learn and adopt it. An example is the introduction of vetch (a fodder) by the FAO/UNDP (Food & Agricultural Organization/United Nations Development Programme) Agriculturist, Mr Peter Whiteman. New ideas on the agricultural sector from AKRSP may come forth when the new Programme Senior Agriculturist Dr Zahur Alam arrives later this month.

Secret of Organization—the Activist. There is no such thing as 'the people'—the people are created by the Activist and we must accept variations, because we have accepted to work without sanctions.[2]

Take one valley or a collection of VOs and study it well. But wait for an activist to emerge at the supra-village level; give him time. At the moment, we don't know how it will evolve, 'If you want to cook a rabbit, first catch your rabbit'. If a good idea emerges, call a conference and discuss the idea. This is different from planning; it is like planning a spiritual or political movement.

Village organization: In any society there is bound to be a dominant group, an articulate group. But to give an opportunity to others, we have a process of dialogues, We do not talk to committees but to the whole village. If all the villagers don't gather for the dialogue, then we just don't hold the dialogue! This method checks the dominant group. If the weaker groups are helped, they get a forum to articulate their needs and demands.[3]

What about electricity? I exclaimed 'Why should we have it?' Anyway, I will ask Hussain Wali, our Senior Programme Engineer, to answer this. He said 'if the villagers do not identify electricity as their foremost need, then why should we provide it? Anyway the government has a huge electricity programme for the Northern Areas. However, some small and remote VOs have identified electricity as their greatest need. The major reason for this is probably that they don't feel that the government will supply it to their villages.

I added a few comments, noting that the government is installing small hydel (hydro-electricity) units, say 500 KV. These are expensive investment, costing about Rs 25 million and providing power to about 700 households, and that only for lighting!

AKRSP has invested Rs 18 million in 1,966 irrigation channels. Those led to the development of 24,000 acres of new land and increased the water supply to 25,000 acres. 12,000 families have benefitted from this. Now, you tell us: what choice did we have? Government projects are expensive, we cannot emulate them. However, we have set up a few micro-hydel units (20/50 KV) to provide power to 25 to 50 households. In areas where government has plans to supply power, there is no need for us to set up any hydels.

Lack of management or resources:[4] AKRSP makes a distinction between resource constraints and reallocation of resources. Available resources, if rationally reallocated between macro and micro plans, should suffice to meet the objectives of rural development. I explained the 'blue-print' and the 'process' approach and the importance of investment in organization. I also expressed my dismay at the lack of concrete action or allocation by the government for fostering grassroots institutions in rural Pakistan.

The Evolving Role of Social Organizers[5]

The SOs are the sheet-anchors of AKRSP. They are the eyes and ears of the MG. They are the bridge between the VOs and the MG. Their role is evolving and dynamic. This is so because their 'client' is simultaneously a worker and an owner, a producer and a consumer, a buyer and a seller, a manager and a cooperator, a traditionalist and an innovator and God knows what else. The SO can only hope to help the small holder by acquiring some expertise in all the fields that impinge on the well-being of the subsistence farmers.

The SO, as the name indicates, achieves this objective through motivation. However, organization is only a means to achieve the avowed objectives and not an end in itself. Similarly, motivation is not something in the abstract: it manifests itself in at least six different forms:

- VO formation
- generation of capital through savings
- willingness to subscribe to collective management
- identification, implementation and maintenance of PPIs
- upgrading of human skills through VO nominees;
- obtaining credit for different productive purposes

Initially the success of the SO depends on the degree of acceptance of the above-mentioned packages by the VOs. He receives support from the GM and the DPOs generally for all packages but especially for VO formation, capital generation through savings, collective management and credit. The Engineering Section helps him in respect of PPIs and Agriculture, Livestock, Accounts etc., in regard to training. MER helps in monitoring progress. This may be termed as AKRSP's Basic Package for social organization, to which activities under WID and Marketing have also been added. Motivation for the Basic Package is the primary responsibility of the SO in the initial stages.

As the VO becomes stronger, in terms of participation by holding regular meetings of the maximum number of households, savings, collective management, implementation and maintenance of PPI, training of village specialists and their use and remuneration, obtaining of loans, other packages are added to the Basic Package. The acceptance of the new packages by the VOs, is the responsibility of the SO, at exactly the same level as the Basic Package. If the motivational efforts of the SO do not result in VOs going beyond the Basic Package, which with the passage of time becomes a Routine Package needing no special motivational effort, the SO should feel very concerned. It is, therefore, imperative on SOs to ensure acceptance of not only the Basic Package, but all the new packages by the VOs within their charge. Failure to do so is tantamount to failure of the SO's motivational efforts.

To help SOs have a focus and a direction to their motivational effort, I have requested each Section Head in the MG, to prepare a checklist to help SOs monitor the progress of each package. The phase of general motivation is no more relevant to VOs that have accepted and implemented the Basic Package. These VOs now entered the phase of intensive monitoring needing intensive motivation. A very useful document has already been prepared and issued by Hussain Wali and his staff in the shape of a Rural Development Manual, in Urdu, along with a categorisation of VOs *proforma*. These should help SOs in firstly, understanding the true state of affairs of the VOs, within their jurisdiction, and most importantly to channelize their resources and energies productively. In this context, you might recollect Dr Akhtar Hameed Khan's observation on SO's work, in the initial stages, that SO were very busy but were only 10 per cent effective. What he meant was that SOs lacked a sense of direction and focus, consequently their efforts were ineffective. The sense of direction and focus to SOs' work, needed now, should be forthcoming by following the package checklists.

Package checklists: Agriculture, livestock, marketing, accounts and appropriate technology.

Village Dialogues 1982[6]

Case 1. In Sonikot, Tawalludd Shah introduced the AKRSP team to those present. Shoaib Sultan Khan then explained the methods and objectives of AKRSP and outlined the avenues of cooperation between AKRSP and the residents of Sonikot. He invited the village leaders to identify an income-generating project that would benefit most of the villagers.

The village elders nominated the Member Local Council to be their spokesman. He noted that their biggest problem was lack of water for irrigation and drinking. He suggested two complementary solutions: i) The repair and extension of a channel dating back to British days and ii) Installation of lift pumps along with the Gilgit river.

Shoaib Sultan Khan: Once the plans have been made for these projects, who will implement them?

Member: We will make a committee of 3 or 4 people.

Shoaib Sultan Khan: No, Member Sahib, that is not the way we work. Our method has 3 requirements: (i) the villagers should identify the project, (ii) all those benefiting from the project should form an organization and (iii) the organization should undertake to execute, manage and maintain the project, which in your case is a water channel.

Villager No. 1: But the channel will be 9 miles long—it will involve all of Gilgit—at least 10,000 people. We can't take the responsibility for maintaining the channel.

Member: We could consider the lift pump proposal.

Villager No. 2: Lift pumps require 1300 feet of pipe. If you provide us this and a generator, we will happily take care of maintenance and diesel.

Shoaib Sultan Khan: We'll send our engineer to do the survey. Once that is done, we will return with the survey report to meet with all the 100 households which are represented in your village organization.

Member: But the 100 households have put their signatures down and elected me as their representative.

Shoaib Sultan Khan: That we don't accept: I must again remind you of the examples of Germany and Japan. The organization we insist on, must include all the beneficiaries of the irrigation scheme. This organization will then be a conduit for other resources that the AKRSP will bring to this village. Those who do not join the organization will not benefit at all from our programme.

(Several villagers speak up at once and insist that they will form an organization).

Villager No. 4: We had been dreaming about this project for ten years—we have yearned for it. Now, with your presence here, a dream has come true.

It was then agreed that an AKRSP sub-engineer would start his survey at 1000 hours the next day.

Observations and Impressions
IPS (P) had a proposal to install a lift pump at Sonikot. The capital cost would have been Rs 275,000 and the operating cost was estimated at Rs 1,100 per day.

Case 2.[7]
Introduction by Tawallud Shah.

Shoaib Sultan Khan: I am here today to explain the aims and objectives of AKRSP and to indicate how we can cooperate in our efforts to develop your village. The AKRSP is a non-communal programme, established to help reduce poverty in the Northern Areas. I think it is better to explain our method of working at the very outset. One thing we must understand clearly: we have not come here to listen to and accept your demands. Further, we will cooperate only on projects that increase incomes. These projects you will have to identify, keeping in mind that they should benefit as many people as possible, and can be implemented and managed by you with technical, financial and training assistance from us.

All villagers present agreed that lack of irrigation water was their biggest problem. They suggested a channel be dug to bring water from a spring two-and-a-half miles away.

Observations and Impressions. This was the first entirely non-Ismaili village we visited. The reception we got was heart-warming. We had relied so far on Ismaili institutions for organizing the first meeting with villagers. That a successful first meeting took place in a non-Ismaili village augurs well for our hopes of organizing every village in Gilgit around productive activities.

Case 3 1983.[8] The group started at 09.30 hours from Gilgit. Syed Mutahir Shah and Sher Ghazi were in one and the rest of the members of the group were in the GM's jeep. Our jeep went to a filling station in Gilgit for diesel. We had our luggage in the jeep as we were required to establish our office in Aliabad (Hunza). When we reached there, Shoaib Sultan Khan was speaking. The number of persons present was 225. They belonged to 10 villages around Chalt. The main villages represented were (1) Chalt Bala, (2) Chalt Paeen, (3) Sonikot, (4) Rahbat, (5) Mamosh Deding, (6) Chaprot, (7) Shutindas, (8) Bodalus, (9) Bar and (10) Torboto Das.

Shoaib Sultan Khan: We have neither come here to listen to your demands nor we can fulfil them. We can't tell you a lie. When we can't do this, then why we have come here? I have come here along with my colleagues to sit with you and discuss your problems and then see how they can be solved. For example, if poverty is a disease, then who will diagnose it. Experience has shown that the village people can diagnose it. The Chalt people know their problems. If the village people can do the treatment, then why don't they? This is because they don't have the medicine. We will provide the required medicines. We will train you. If you so desire that we should work with you, then both of us have some duties and responsibilities.

Your first duty is to identify such problems of your area which will benefit the majority of the people. To eradicate poverty, income should increase.

Shoaib Sultan Khan enquired from Yahya Shah the number of households, which Shah indicated as 700. To this Shoaib Sultan Khan said that the scheme should be such that would benefit all the 700 households, or at least the majority of them. He further added that schemes like drinking water supply will not increase your income. For such schemes, there are other institutions like UNICEF and LB&RD. When you have identified your problem, our duty begins. The Engineer Sher Ghazi and Social Organization Expert Mutahir Shah are sitting here. In the formulation of a project, the people should participate. We know that the people can't make estimates and blueprints, and here you need experts who will come to you and formulate the project. After formulation, it will be discussed with the people. The people will execute the scheme themselves as there will be no contractor. You should formulate schemes which you can execute yourself. He further added that you cannot construct a bridge on Hunza river. NAWO can do that. This programme is to eradicate poverty. If we ask you for free labour, then it is against our programme. If we do this how can poverty be eradicated? The labourer will get his remuneration.

Your second duty is to form your organization. This is a must because you will execute the project and there will be no contractor. We will provide the financial and technical help.

Your third duty starts after the completion of the project. Maintenance of the project after completion is your responsibility. We cannot do maintenance of 157 schemes. This is our approach: (1) identification of problems by you. (2) Your organization to shoulder the responsibility of executing and completing the project. (3) The maintenance of the completed project.

If you accept these principles, then we will sit with you and hold discussions on your problems. The people said that the chairman will present our problems.

S. Yahya Shah stood up and presented the following 16 problems:

- Kurkundas pipeline. He identified a pipeline of 6' or 8' diameter and said that some 3,000 *kanals* of land would be brought under the plough. Two crops can be grown on this land. Some 500 families would benefit.
- Ghasho Maling Das Channel. Here remodelling of the channel is required. 200 families and land of more than 3,000 *kanals* will be benefitted.
- Chalat drainage: The excess water should be drained from the soil. The whole of Chalat will be benefitted from this scheme.
- Rahbat link road—half mile.
- Sonikot link road—half mile.
- Chalt Payeen link road—1-1/2 miles.
- Link road for Bar village. It is two miles.
- Dad Das Bar link road.
- Chalt road—half mile.
- One thresher for Bar Das. There are 70 households.
- A water channel Broshky Chaprot—about 3 miles.
- Gonar water channel from Rahbat to Chaprote.
- A water channel Kannah Jee. It will irrigate 500 kanals of land.
- A water reservoir for irrigation in Shutindas.
- Thaley Bodalus channel.
- A protection bund for Mamosh Deding.

Shoaib Sultan Khan: The AKRSP will cooperate in all these projects, but gradually. He quoted a Persian proverb which means that 'catch hold of one but firmly'. He further added that if we undertake schemes in Chalt only, the DC Badrul Islam will oust us. This is not a project but a programme and will continue for an indefinite period. All problems will be solved but not at once. Just identify that project which will benefit majority of the people, if not all. There are ten villages in Chalt. The people of each village should consult amongst themselves and identify the most important projects. Ghazi and Mutahir Shah will make a programme with you and will see the scheme. Indicate the names of the ten villages with names of contact men. Projects will be formulated with your cooperation.

S. Yahya Shah asked for one common project but the people did not agree. The names of villages with contact men and schemes as given by the people were as under:

(1) Qorqondas Water Channel: It will benefit about 6,000 *kanals* of land of Chalt Bala, Sonikot and Mamosh Deding. The contact man is Latif Anwar, Chairman, Union Council Chalt.
(2) Ghashmaling water channel: It is about 3 miles. It will benefit 200 families with 3000 to 4000 *kanals* of land. The contact man is Mohammad Shafa, Vice Chairman, UC Chalt.
(3) Link Road Rahbat: It is 2-1/2 miles long. The beneficiaries are 100 houses. The contact men are Sub. Safdar Khan and Aun Ali.
(4) Bar to Dopas pony track: It is 3 miles. The contact man is Amir Haider, Member UC Chalt.
(5) Torboto Das: There are 70 to 100 households. They need a thresher. The contact man is Amir Haider, Member UC Chalt.
(6) Chaprot Utaimaling khul: It will benefit 300 families with 18,000 *kanals* of land. The contact men are Ghulam Rasool and Mohammad Khan. It is 6 miles long but 3 miles has already been constructed.
(7) Dodo Das link road: It is one mile and will benefit 50 households. The contact man is Amir Haider, Member, UC Chalt.
(8) Bodalus Khul: It is about four miles. It will benefit 300 to 4,000 *kanals* of land belonging to 130 families. The contact men are Sarwar Khan and Mirza Ali.
(9) Shutin Das water channel is 4 miles long. It needs widening. It will benefit 130 families. The contact man is Sarwar Khan.
(10) Mamosh Deding Flood Protection Bund: It will benefit 70 families.

The main villages of the Chalt Union Council are:

- Chalt Bala
- Sonikot
- Mamosh Deding
- Shutin Das
- Bar
- Chalt Payeen
- Rahbat
- Chaprot
- Bodalus
- Torboto Das

From Chalt the group travelled to Sikandarabad. Shoaib Sultan Khan thanked the people especially S. Yahya Shah and Latif Anwar, Chairman, Union Council Chalt. At this point, it would be useful to describe the physical setting of the meeting. Villagers and visitors were positioned as above when the Chairman, UC Sikanderabad started reading from a prepared list. The first project he identified was an irrigation scheme that would help develop 5,000 *kanals* of barren land. At this point, some dissenting voices were heard from among the villagers present. A young man from Sikandarabad stepped up, snatched the list from his UC Chairman and stated emphatically that the proposed scheme was the business of Sikandarabad villagers since it benefitted them. An immediate sharp retort was issued by a Tongdas hothead—to the effect that since the channel being proposed would draw water from Tongdas, which is located upstream of Sikandarabad, the scheme was a disputed one and would antagonize Tongdas residents. The Sikandarabad troops told the Tongdas hothead, in no uncertain terms, to mind their own business. A temporarily successful attempt was made by the DC to quieten things down. The advantage of this calm was claimed by a Nilth interceptor: tall and dark, with a beard like Salahuddin Ayubi's, a flowing white robe on his shoulders, a white cap perched at an angle on his head, this member of the House of Nagar stepped into the centre of the gathering and announced to all the world: 'This channel will not be dug.' That did it!

General disorder prevailed as claims and counterclaims were flung across the gathering and insults traded liberally. Appeals for calm from the Pope (Syed Yahya) and the Caesar (Deputy Commissioner) went unheeded. The police Inspector and his men stepped up and positioned themselves around the GM and the DC. Haji Jan started laughing at the absurdity of the spectacle! Somehow, the GM managed to tell the villagers that AKRSP was in no hurry to start any projects and that villagers had to settle their disputes before presenting proposals to AKRSP. The DC advised the contending parties to make a reasonable settlement with each other, to which end he offered his services as mediator.

All of this was in vivid contrast to the orderly proceedings at Chalt earlier in the day. It was an instructive contrast, one that brought home in technicolour the rewards and hazards of life with AKRSP.

Case 4: Address by GM.[9] I am grateful to you all on behalf of my colleagues and myself. As introduced by Tawallud Shah, the purpose of our visit is to exchange views about the objectives of AKRSP and what and how this programme can benefit the villagers. It is necessary to understand each other's obligations. First of all this is a development programme. Many organizations and institutions exist such as His Highness's Social Welfare Institutions, government organizations, Jamat Councils etc. Why did His Highness consider the AKRSP important in the presence of so many other organizations? This is because AKRSP's focus is on eliminating poverty from the rural areas in the shortest possible period. Other inputs such as health, education and water supply etc. have long term perspective. These are important but these cannot help in increasing the income of the people in the short run. Our programme focuses on income generating projects of direct and immediate value. The first thing is to work on income generating projects for the prosperity of the farming community. I don't mean that other types of schemes should not be taken up. I would submit that priority should be given to those projects which can help in improving the income of the people.

As explained by Tawallud Shah, this programme is not meant for one community but for all the people of the Northern Areas. In order to demonstrate this fact, none of the members of the present team appointed by His Highness belongs to the Ismaili community.

In the beginning, I would like to make it clear that neither I nor my colleagues can be of any help to you unless you extend your full cooperation. The aim is not to present demands as is the practice with other officers who come to you. We have not come for this purpose. I have seen many countries of the world whose people were very poor and possessed only little pieces of land. They belonged to different religions. How they got rid of poverty. They are good examples for us. If we take the case of Germany and Japan, in Japan the farmers worked so hard that they not only increased their own income from the small holding of 10-20 kanals but also contributed to the overall gross income of the country. It is now one of the richest countries in the world.

We have two examples: one is that of countries like Japan and Germany and the other is that of the countries which failed to improve their lot. Either we should wait for someone to come to change our way of life or let us work hard to wipe out our poverty once and for all like other countries. According to our experience the residents of the villages can best understand and judge the problems of the village. For example, they know the disease but are unable to cure it because they lack the necessary medicines and instruments. They are living in poverty but do not have the resources for its treatment.

At the moment there are 50/60 families around us. If they point out schemes which could benefit even 75 per cent of them, we can send our engineer to help you in the preparation of the scheme. The AKRSP will arrange financial, technical and training requirements, subject to the condition that the people prepare the scheme with the assistance of the engineer and implement it without contractors. The labourers will be paid due wages according to the decision of all the members of the organization. All beneficiaries will come together and work collectively. The organization of the beneficiaries will be responsible for the maintenance of the completed project. Feroz Shah will explain in detail the principles and procedures of the organization after you agree to form it.

To summarize, you have to point out productive schemes which can benefit the majority of the village and which can be executed and implemented by the villagers and maintained after completion.

Discussion and Problems. Syed Abbas Shah: I heartily thank all members of the team on behalf of my village dignitaries for their visit and desire for the uplift of the village. Next to Gilgit, Nomal is the biggest village, but up till now no one had paid attention to it. We made every effort but no one listened. We are grateful to His Highness who is kind enough to send you here for the uplift of the rural masses. We will sit together and propose the projects for the benefit of all the villagers. The officers pass through Nomal while going to Naltar where the camp is located but they did not bother to look at the difficulties and problems of Nomal. They have provided every facility to Naltar for their own comfort. We consider the following as priority problems for the social and economic benefit of the village:

(i) Metalling of main road from Nomal to Gilgit—about 27 kms. It can help in the improvement of the quality of life.
(ii) Construction of hospital.
Other elders of the village will present the remaining problems.

GM (Shoaib Sultan Khan): You may discuss among yourselves and identify the problems directly related to income-generation. (The MG gave opportunity to the gathering for discussion and went away to the site of the Hydel power station.)

Problems reported by villagers:

(i) Construction of Bridge: The KKH (Karakoram Highways) passes close to the village on the other side of the river but the village is deprived of its benefits. A large number of the villagers work outside the village in offices/army and face great hardships in communication.
(ii) Widening of main *khul* for adequate supply of water.
(iii) Metalling of Nomal road to Gilgit.

GM (Shoaib Sultan Khan): We are not here to receive demands like other officers and disappear. I have already pointed out in the beginning that big schemes such as bridges and road metalling are beyond our capacity as well as of the people. These are the schemes which big organizations like NAWO could take up. We can help only in channelizing these to the concerned department.

As far as the second scheme of *khul* is concerned, this can be considered jointly both by AKRSP and the people. We will send our engineer for conducting detailed feasibility survey and cost estimation in consultation with knowledgeable elders. Once the scheme is prepared, the concerned experts will come again to explain the necessary details and procedure of work and organization.

Once the irrigation water is adequately arranged, farmers will be able to make best use of improved seeds, fertilizer etc. All these inputs and other needs can easily be managed through the village organization. There is a Persian proverb: 'Hold one thing and firmly'. With the irrigation project, we can initiate our relationship as partners.

Villagers: We have presented big problems only. There are several small schemes such as: i) Timely supply of agricultural inputs. ii) Arrangements for preservation of fruit. iii) Construction of link road. iv) Construction of second khul (widening) Hurmai khul. v) Construction of third khul. vi) Flood protection bunds for protection of land. vii) Construction (widening) of Aminabad khul. viii) Link road along with main Nomal khul. ix) Drinking water supply for the village. x) Jala—wire rope pulley for **crossing river** to KKH.

GM (Shoaib Sultan Khan): During the visit of the engineer, all the productive schemes will be surveyed by him. The elders present here, should accompany him during the survey. We will try to cooperate with you in some of these productive projects.

Crossing the Hump: Three Case Studies[10]

Terms of partnership: Case 1. On 2 February after a very cold night at Chitral, the MG picked up SOU Buni at 1000 hours from Buni and landed at Sarghuz with 72 households and 52 members, of which no more than 20-25 were present. The organization was formed in January 1984 and has accumulated Rs 4,000 as savings. It is said to meet regularly on Fridays.

It was bitterly cold and the unrelenting, strong gusts of wind numbed even gloved hands. There was snow all around but not much in this village. President and Manager Bahadur Jan and Gul Murad articulated the VO's priority project of protective bunds. One Nadir Ali and his son vehemently protested against the construction of bunds on their lands. On a suggestion to VO to give it in writing to the protestors that the bund would not be constructed on their land, Farasat Khan, the Headmaster, taking the lead vehemently refused to do any such thing. The MG had no choice but to abort the dialogue and refer the matter to SO and AC Buni.

There were over 100/150 persons present at Chung to greet the MG. The VO has 106 members representing 86 households. President Zarmast Khan, Manager Ghulam Mustafa and Model Farmer Sher Khan informed the MG about the formation of the organization in February 1984 and accumulation of Rs 14,750 as its equity capital. The VO is said to hold its regular meetings on Fridays. The Village Supervisor Akbar Ali (Manager of VO Chappali) verified the statements. The VO confirmed protective bunds measuring 950 feet made of stones and wooden batons as its main priority. A cheque for Rs 19,297 as the first installment of the total cost of Rs 77,179 was handed over to the President of the Organization as desired by the members and after each one of them had signed the AKRSP Terms of Partnership.

Immediately after the handing over of the cheque by Hussain Wali, an application was thrust under the nose of the GM with the applicant shouting at GM that he would personally be responsible for the loss of property and lives caused by the construction of the bunds. On a query as to why he had remained a silent spectator and only chose to raise the issue once the dialogue had concluded, his reply was that he had already given an application to the SO six months ago. In the meanwhile tempers started rising and some people started beating and dragging the protestor dubbing him as a mischief-maker. Another fracas developed in another corner. The whole scene appeared serious and ludicrous. Hussain Wali tried to save the protestor from being lynched while I attended to the faction in the other corner. Thanks to MG's good luck the whole thing subsided otherwise at one point it was showing signs of developing into a free for all brawl and Shoaib Sultan Khan and Hussain Wali could possibly have received a few blows — unintended, one would like to believe. Shoaib Sultan Khan made it very clear to the office bearers of the VO that unless they allay the apprehensions of the protestor and obtain his agreement in writing to this effect, work on the protective bunds would not commence and SO Buni would ensure the implementation of this.

Syed Afsar Ali Shah, President and Akhtar Hasan Shah Manager of the Churu VO which has 26 members representing 31 households and was formed in January 1985 and has since accumulated Rs 1,300 as savings, made a request for a protective bund for their village. As the number of members present was no more than about 15 and also there was some dispute about the survey carried out by the sub-engineer, the MG decided to postpone the dialogue to a later date after a resurvey and lapse of sufficient time to adjudge viability of the organization.

The flight to the next village was through a valley completely covered with snow. The deep blue of the river meandering under the snow was visible only occasionally. Nearly 40 to 50 persons from VO Khuz Payeen, braving the intense cold at the elevation of 8,000 feet, greeted the MG. Amanullah Khan President and Ghazi Beg, Manager, informed that the organization was formed in February 1984 and has 44 members representing all the 44 households of the village. The savings amount to Rs 3,344 and meetings are held on Fridays. The VO had identified an irrigation channel as its priority project. On a query from the union council member Rahim Hasan, it transpired that a reservoir was more useful and feasible for the VO. On the proposition being put to vote the UC member appeared to be in a hopeless minority. Almost everyone favoured the channel. Hussain Wali explained the different components of the estimates:

- Length : 1,600 feet
- Cost of explosives : Rs 37,040
- Implements : 5,656
- Labour : 33,950
   Total : 76,286

On acceptance of the terms of partnership in writing by all the members and on their suggestion, the first installment of Rs 19,071 was handed over to the President of the VO. Work is likely to commence in March. The UC member assured of his support despite his initial reservations.

The return journey to Buni took less than half an hour and it was a welcome change to land on the snow-covered polo ground, for instead of raising clouds of dust, the helicopter raised a beautiful spray of powdery snow. On the Shandur Lake, the right side was covered with snow but the left side was naked. The Mastuj channel appeared like a long white ribbon. The Shandur lakes were frozen solid but a handful of yaks were seen grazing. God knows what they could find in that bleak and desolate place. After a brief stopover at Phander, overlooking the frozen lake, the helicopter headed towards Gilgit. Snow left us beyond Shamaran. The Khalti lake was, however, frozen solid and men and animals were seen crossing it. Hussain Wali showed me the Sharot and Hanzel channels under construction. I had held third dialogues in November. It was amazing to see so much progress achieved since then despite the winter. We waved to the people working on the channels who waved back with obvious glee. The Skarkoi channel was fully functional in sharp contrast to the old channel which was bone dry. The helicopter landed at the Gilgit airport at 1500 hours.

Terms of partnership: Case 2.[11] Reached Ahmedabad at about 1200 hours. After settling down the GM asked the president of the VO about their progress on the project in hand and their future plan. The President Sub. Faraj of the VO said in his reply that their organization was formed on 15 September 1983 with a total number of 75 members representing 62 households of that village. Since then their savings had increased to Rs 110,000. Their first project was the construction of the 7,400 feet long irrigation channel, of which 6200 feet had been completed while work on the remaining portion was underway. They had been given a sum of Rs 214,525 as PPI grant for the scheme.

In answer to another question of the GM, he said that all animals in their village had been vaccinated. He appreciated the work done by the livestock specialist, plant protection/production specialist. With their help the VO had planted 100 fruit trees and 30 wild trees, he remarked. Talking about future plans, he said that they wanted to plant 400 trees more for which help of AKRSP was needed. Along with the plantation of the trees, they wanted to develop 60 *kanals* of land for which he requested a loan of Rs 3,000 for each member. Giving further details of the programme of the project, the President of the VO explained that the 60 *kanals* of land would be divided into various categories depending on the nature of the land and each category would be apportioned for the sowing of alfalfa, fruit trees and firewood. The general manager enquired whether or not these 60 *kanals* of land belonged to all the members equally. The villagers replied in the affirmative.

Further, the GM asked how the loan would be used. The members replied that they would distribute this loan equally among themselves and start the planting. The GM explained to the members that a loan should be utilized in such a manner that the repayment does not become a burden on them. It should be used for productive purposes so that the villagers are able to return it. He appreciated their past performance and encouraged them to continue their work collectively. He suggested that instead of distributing the money first and then working, it would be better if they complete the work first and use this loan as remuneration for the work done. He also asked whether the proposed project had been decided on by all the members of the VO. To which the people present there said that yes, it was a collective decision. The GM urged the villagers to use the loan only on the proposed project instead of spending it on their personal needs so that no problems are faced at the time of repayment.

At this stage one member of the VO clarified that the 60 *kanals* of land under question was not equally owned by 62 households but that it belonged to 49 households with unequal land holding. He suggested that though the land was unequally distributed and 13 households did not even own any of this land, they wanted to distribute the work equally among all the 75 members of the VO. He further stated that this was their collective decision and all of them want to develop the land by sharing the work equally.

In view of the obtaining situation the GM asked about their work plan and emphasized that AKRSP would help only those people who worked collectively, as their programme is not meant for individuals. He suggested that collective work does not mean 75 members working at the same time, they can take turns by making groups of the people according to the size of the land they own. For example, one group can be made of people who each own five *kanals* of land and who can work at one time, he added. By taking these turns, not everybody would be expected to develop the land at one time. However, no part of the land should be left undeveloped as it happened in the past, he remarked. To ensure the presence of each member on his turn, he suggested some penalty on the absentees according to the practice in vogue in that area. He further suggested that AKRSP would send their staff to their area for checking their work plan and for land classification to which the members agreed.

The members of the VO clarified at this stage that they didn't want to use the loan as wages, but would rather work free and keep Rs 3,000 each right from the beginning. This would help them to support their families in a better way, they explained. The GM opposed the idea of straight away distribution of loan and stated that this money should be used as wages and if they want it in lump sum, they may divide it after finishing the work. The loan should be used specifically for development of land and expenditure be made corresponding to the work done which would also help in supporting their families, he said.

The GM told the villagers that if they were ready to do the work collectively and spend the loan productively, then he would give Rs 2,000 to each member as a loan, to which the villagers agreed finally. The GM told Hussain Wali to explain the terms and conditions to villagers.

The following terms and conditions were explained by Hussain Wali:

1. The total amount of the loan was Rs 154,000 on the basis of Rs 2,000 to each member.
2. The loan would be the responsibility of the entire VO.
3. The villagers would work collectively.
4. The VO would continue meeting on weekly basis.
5. The loan was repayable in five years in three installments with the first installment of Rs 51,333 plus Rs 15,400 as service charges at the rate of 5 per cent of the total amount per annum, second

installment of Rs 51,333 plus Rs 5,133 as service charges and third installment of Rs 51,333 plus Rs 2,566 as service charges.
6. Rs 46,200 i.e. 50 per cent of the total loan would be kept in the bank as collateral from the savings of the VO. This would be a joint bank account between AKRSP and Ahmedabad VO for a period of five years. The amount so placed in the bank account will double in five years and would be given back to VO after total refund of the loan.
7. In case of default in the repayment of any installment by the specified time, some penalty would be imposed.

In the end the GM emphasized to the members of the VO that the saving mobilization should be kept going even after taking the loan so that they may be able to get a tractor very soon.

Terms of partnership: Case 3.[12] The GM and Hussain Wali, accompanied by the commissioner Northern Areas and Mr Iqbal Masood, Federal Secretary, Government of Pakistan, took off from Gilgit at 1400 hours. Due to bad weather conditions, the helicopter could not land at Balas as the village was engulfed in clouds and therefore headed towards the next village, Barghin, where about 60 to 70 persons greeted the MG. The president of the organization gave the following details:

- Formation of the VO   April 1984
- Total membership   41 out of 41 households
- Meetings held on   Fridays
- Savings accumulated   Rs 6,000
- Project identified   Widening and improvement of an existing *khul*

Hussain Wali explained the terms of partnership in Shina and Shoaib Sultan Khan clarified the aims and objectives of AKRSP. The project identified had the following components as per estimates prepared by the Engineering Section in consultation with the village representatives:

- Length of the channel   : 18,000 feet
- Dimensions   : 4'x4'x1-1/2'
- Cost of explosives   : 10,691

- Cost of cement : 17,424
- Implements : 3,619
- Cost of labour : to be negotiated

Shoaib Sultan Khan offered them a total amount of Rs 100,000 including the cost of labour. On acceptance of the offer, a cheque for Rs 25,000 representing the first installment was handed over by the commissioner to the president of the organization, as decided by the members present.

Achievements and Irritants[13]

The GM talked of the initial difficulty in ascertaining the number of villages. He said the AKRSP staff estimated that presently the project area encompassed 290 villages and to date it has attempted to organize 245 villages. In response to a question, the GM said that the definition of villages is generally based on interest groups and contiguous areas.

The vision of the programme, the GM stated has been distilled from 150 years of world experience in rural development, organising and motivating the individual farmers by integrating them into the development process. The GM then elaborated on the extension training effort and its remarkable effectiveness. In addition, the savings programme is an integral part of the strategy. AKRSP feels it is imperative that all villagers must save. The benefits of savings are numerous but one is especially striking. Previously loans to individual villages for the purchase of fertilizer were not available, for the villagers could not offer collateral. However, the VO savings now used as collateral enable individual farmers to obtain loans. Referring to the local government, the GM reiterated that the local council is not a proper platform through which rural development can take place. Citing the example of Panchayat Raj and the Mahaweli project, he elucidated how important it is to have a broad based development organization. The GM then explained the responsibilities of the SO and the method utilized in organizing the village.

The deputy commissioner noted, however, that there is some unrest because this programme is run by the Aga Khan Foundation which to some people appears to show sectarian overtones. In addition, the geopolitical sensitivity of the area compounded this problem. Besides, the outstanding programme of AKRSP tended to pale the achievement of other agencies into insignificance and has become a cause for jealousy and hostility. The GM pointed out that it was not possible to get everybody to understand the programme; however, it was important not to aggravate the situation. The GM hoped that eventually the good will and intentions of the AKRSP effort would be appreciated. The adviser agreed to this and advised that when a presentation was made to the president and his key ministers, it should be emphasized that AKRSP needs help on this aspect. The DC noted that AKRSP had become a sore point in this area because it serves as an example to the development planners in Islamabad that the AKRSP approach was better than theirs.

In conclusion, the Adviser congratulated AKRSP for the work it has undertaken and stressed that development is not the prerogative of the government and any initiative by viable organizations complementary to the government effort, is to be commended.

Power of Discourse: Visit to Village Japuka[14]

Venue of general meeting. MYK along with Sher Shah reached the village directly from Singal. He was sitting in the house of Abdul Qamar (*Tehsildar*). The group was first taken to the house of the *Numberdar*. He arranged for seating outside his shop. The group waited there for the people. After some time the group was called to the *tehsildar's* house. There the group was asked to wait. The people had not assembled. The GM said that the group had come to meet other villagers and not those it met last time. The group was then taken to the Jamat Khana where all the villagers were asked to assemble. In all, 35 persons gathered there.

List of problems: After discussion among the villagers in their own language, a list of problems was handed over to the GM. He was told that all the people had jointly identified these problems on priority basis. They included:

(i)   Drinking water supply scheme.
(ii) Nursery development for fruit and forest plants.
(iii) Link road from suspension bridge to village.
(iv) Fruit preservation and processing.
(v)   Agriculture inputs—fertilizer, seed, pesticides/insecticides.
(vi) Agricultural machinery—tractor, thrasher, sprayers.

Address by GM: The objective of AKRSP and comments on the problems. The GM said: The *numberdar* and *tehsildar* may have explained to you the purpose of AKRSP and our visit, but I will explain the highlights of the AKRSP approach again. The AKRSP has been introduced by His Highness with the objective to undertake those income generating activities which would benefit the majority of the farmers in a short time. This programme is not for one community but for the whole of the Northern Areas. In the first instance, Gilgit district, which comprises 157 villages, has been selected. Of these villages, Japuka is the first one to invite us. Now the question is what the people expect from AKRSP within its objectives as envisaged by His Highness and to what extent. The AKRSP has come with specific objectives. There are other programmes such as health and education which His Highness has initiated for the welfare of the people. Why then did His Highness feel the need of rural development programme? The aim is to eliminate poverty. The AKRSP will help the people to undertake schemes which are of direct and immediate benefit to the majority of the villagers i.e. by increasing their incomes in order to improve their standard of living. If the income is increased, poverty can be eliminated.

The other day in Aliabad, one elder rightly said that 'poverty can be removed by the people themselves if they are given the required assistance'. There are in total 110 houses in Japuka out of which representatives of 37 houses are present here. You are required to identify a project benefiting the maximum number of houses/families in a short time. What type of scheme can help to increase the household income and what assistance is required, material, technical and skilled in which the AKRSP can help? This is to be decided by you. You may now decide which one of the proposed schemes, you can do yourself. Expert services will be available to you along with funds from AKRSP. It will be the responsibility of the people, those present here and benefited from the scheme, to plan, execute and maintain the scheme.

Once you form your organization for one work, you can solve all other problems through the organization. The first thing is the readiness for joint deliberations, planning and work.

The GM asked Feroz Shah to explain how they could overcome other needs to increase incomes and what would be the criteria for the organization.

Explanation by Feroz Shah. Feroz Shah explained how the road was to be constructed by the organization and how agriculture inputs were procured. 'The Engineer will come and carry out the survey in consultation with the people and prepare cost estimates. He will also tell you how much land will be affected. About land the organization will decide among itself and fix the compensation. AKRSP will not enter into such disputes. It will not pay the compensation for land. Once the scheme is agreed upon for execution, the organization will make four or five persons responsible for execution and supervision. The villagers working on the road as labourers will be paid. The expenditure on road by the committee, will be presented to all others in weekly/fortnightly meetings of village organizations. After completion of the scheme, the organization will be responsible for its maintenance.

Once the organization is formed, other requirements such as seed, fertilizer, insecticides/pesticides and nursery can be planned and arranged through it with the assistance of AKRSP. It is the people who can properly assess their demand well in time and then seek the assistance of AKRSP in arranging the inputs and developing a nursery of fruit plants and forest trees. These things can be arranged by AKRSP on short term loans to the organization as a whole in which the organization will be responsible. It is difficult for AKRSP to deal with individuals as the experts cannot reach every farmer individually. Therefore, the organization is the basic forum where all the services and facilities can be pooled. Necessary skills can be imparted to selected representatives of the people who in turn will disseminate them to other members of the organization in the village.

Discussion. The people started a discussion among themselves in their own language and decided to take up the link road project. They said that they were ready to organize around it and extend all cooperation from their side. Most of the people said that without a link road, it is difficult to take the produce to the market and use agricultural machinery, therefore, it should be taken up first.

The GM asked the people to decide among themselves and then inform him accordingly. The engineer from AKRSP would come to design the road scheme. Requirements of fertilizer, seed, insecticides/pesticides, sprayers etc., may also be decided and intimated to AKRSP. The Programme Training Specialist would come again on their invitation to explain other necessary details about the organization and its requirements.

Departure. The team left the village leaving the villagers to discuss further details in the light of the preceding instructions. It appeared that of the present assembly, one person was opposed to the construction of a link road because his land was likely to be affected. The other persons were trying to persuade him to agree and offering him different alternatives. The AKRSP group left the resolution of the matter in the hands of the villagers and assured them they would come back as soon as they were ready to start work on the link road.

Buni Cluster: After four years of bickering and internal dissension, the nine VOs of Buni, comprising over 500 households and 4,000 persons, finally came together to construct the Shipushan irrigation channel and the link road leading to the new land. It will irrigate over 1,300 acres of new land and each household will get six *chakarum* (2.6 acres) of land, His Highness being one of them as an owner of a cottage in Buni.

Continuity through change[15]

'Management and Organization' of human and capital resources is key to the development of rural areas, which according to Mr Jaffrey, has been so clearly brought out by AKRSP.

Mr Jaffrey equated AKRSP's village dialogues to the revenue settlement dialogues resorted to by the early British administrators. It was as true then, as it is now, that it is only in the presence of all the villagers, that allotment, transfer or mutation of records of rights to land or formulation of a development programme, could be factually, equitably and productively done.

Sociology of change: moving forward through spiral path.[16] Mr M. Azam Khan, the additional chief secretary, started the round of questions. He inquired if AKRSP had encountered any socio-political or religious problems in organizing the people. The government, he added, had to rely on the participation of the elected people, which added a degree of inflexibility to its efforts to organize. A supplement to the first question was whether a legal cover existed for the VO or was it simply a social code which bound the people together? 'The GM answered that initially the programme was in the Ismaili areas but then it spread to the non-Ismaili areas as well. Baltistan is 100 per cent non-Ismaili. A lot of pressure had been built up from all quarters to move into Baltistan district. It took approximately one and a half years before we made it there. All kinds of allegations were made but we had to confront them.

The religious people are divided about having AKRSP in the area. Chitral has been difficult but the support of the local administration has helped smooth things. The programme started from the lower Chitral area but controversy keeps on resurfacing from time to time. Our District Programme Officer is a member of Tableeghi Jamaat and he has started work in the Arandu area. The GM added that 75 per cent of our money comes from outside donor agencies because of our non-sectarian basis. Collaboration with a government programme would probably increase the acceptability of the programme on a wider basis. He added that he was merely trying to sell the VO to the gathered people as a vehicle for development, the big and the small man is helped through the VO, therefore, everybody is happy. And there is no shortcut to the process and one has to go and explain to the people the merits of organization.

VO categorization: Two Cases

Case 1.[17] The VOs in Gilgit benefitted immensely from the PPI (link road) and fertilizer loans but some of them failed to appreciate the advantages of the other components of the package. Comparing the performance of different VOs, it transpired that the Activist played a critical role in keeping the VO alive. VO Payeen lagged behind because it lacked an activist. There was considerable heat generated as to the cause of indolence of the VOs. The members accused the office bearers for the inactivity whereas Subedar Ayub blamed the members. This was a typical example of a village where office bearers are traditional leaders—the *lumbardar* is the President of Payeen and unless genuine activists emerge, there is little chance for the VO to advance. To test our criteria we developed a VO classification index. Hussain Wali pre-tested the *proforma* he had developed, on categorization of VOs.

Indicators for collective management. The VO in Payeen was rated E because in terms of collective management, they had set up a committee to resolve disputes. The VO was collaborating with the specialists, animals had been vaccinated twice a year and the PPS had set up PAK-81 and vetch trial plots besides spraying fruit trees. They were going to participate in pasture development, feed and breed improvement. They had not taken fertilizer, land development and marketing loans because they were too busy with their PPI.[18]

Classification of VOs.[19] VO were rated A to E, A being the active and E being the dormant. The indicators used for each category is given below:

A   participating in all five packages
B   in all but one
C   in all but two
D   in all but three
E   only PPI and savings or only in organization and savings

Factors for poor VOs.[20] VO members were asked to identify the factor responsible for poor VO and they identified the following factors.

1. Under-estimates of PPI (they could identify only 3 cases which could have been affected by this factor)
2. Traditional leaders/influential persons/bad activists
3. Conflicts: election rivalries
4. Non-identification of a PPI
5. Lack of interest by members
6. Service charge: religious opposition
7. Ethnic and sectarian considerations

I explained to VO members in Payeen that an over-riding consideration in overcoming or countering the factors identified by them was the presence or absence of a good activist in the village. In the absence of such a person they had not even a ghost of a chance to overcome these difficulties. Hence, they must first identify an Activist, before they could hope to organize the VO on genuine lines.

Case 2.[21] Mango is a small village with 20 households and has accumulated a savings of Rs 65,079. Its PPI, an irrigation channel, completed in March, 1988 (8500 feet long with a carrying capacity of 10 cusecs of water, costing Rs 117,000) has brought 909 *kanals* of new land under irrigation range. Each family has got 40 *kanals* of additional land. Because of this additional land, persons like Mahama who were working in Karachi, have now come back and resettled in the village. Some others who did not work on the irrigation channel, paid fines to the VO to lay claim to the additional land. The VO has accumulated Rs 27,500 as fines. Despite these impressive achievements, the members failed to understand the benefits of collective management. They were not willing to get the land developed by pooling resources and efforts. They wanted to leave each member to his own enterprise and resources. The result was apparent. Some members with resources had even started constructing houses and developing all the land, whereas the large majority was not sure what to do. The VO has a critical and positive role to play in such a situation. Unfortunately the activist Manager was away, so we could not discuss how he planned to meet the situation. This is a category 'B' VO.

Dealing with Disputes.[22] Immediately on arrival from Islamabad, Shoaib Sultan Khan along with Hussain Wali and Mutabiat Shah flew off to Aliabad where nearly 500 members of the central Hunza VOs had assembled to meet the MG. The proceedings began with Mr Ghulam Mohammad, Regional President and Wazir Baig, Secretary, introducing the MG. Shoaib Sultan Khan explained the aims and objectives of AKRSP and the vision of His Highness for developing the areas. A question was raised about disputes and obstacles put in the way of development by some people. Shoaib Sultan Khan advised the VO to resolve these disputes through negotiations and goodwill and not to expect or invite outsiders to arbitrate in such matters, because such arbitration would not result in a permanent solution of these disputes. In this regard Shoaib Sultan Khan referred to the apprehensions of the inhabitants of Hasanabad and requested M/S Ghulam Mohammad and Wazir Baig to meet the people of Hassanabad and assure them against any losses or damage by the construction of the proposed channel by the inhabitants of Aliabad. Mr Ghulam Mohammad in his speech agreed with the AKRSP strategy and promised to do everything possible to resolve the disputes and to make the Programme a success. Mr Janan, the President of Aliabad VO thanked the MG and promised to abide by the AKRSP terms of partnership.

Building Local Planning and Use of Resources: Visit of Mr Guy Salter, Assistant Private Secretary to the Prince of Wales

GS's first observation was about the economic effort that people must put in to eke out a living from such a harsh inhospitable physical environment. He admired the remarkable skill that people exhibited in making such fine terraces, literally creating soils from barren mountains. Shoaib Sultan Khan remarked that perhaps these majestic mountains lend some of their strength and greatness to the inhabitants, which is why they are so determined and resourceful. Responding to a query on the irrigation technology, Hussain Wali stated that AKRSP had built on the local knowledge by adding new skills and techniques, such as the use of drilling machines, explosives, instruments for levelling etc.

Successful Model

1. **Village Organization.** The following models have already been built and are spectacularly popular:

a) Meetings are regularly held
b) Good managers and chairmen have been elected
c) Savings are regularly collected from members
d) Excellent infrastructure construction projects have been prepared and in many cases already completed
e) The practice of community discussion and action is beginning to prevail
f) It can now be hoped that the concept of village plans will gradually gain acceptance

2. **PPI Projects.** The second model which is even more spectacularly popular is PPI (Productive Physical Infrastructure) Projects:

- Numerous *khuls* (irrigation channels, across the rocks) have been constructed, are under construction or under planning
- Link roads
- Sedimentation tanks
- Protective spurs

The six most innovative aspects of this model are:

- It is a joint effort by the Village Organization, AKRSP's engineering experts and AKRSP's Social Organizers
- Expert guidance has ensured that the projects are technically sound
- Popular participation has reduced the cost and speeded up the construction
- Village Organizations have assumed the burden and responsibility for maintenance
- The VOs have also assumed the responsibility of management, settlement of dispute and realization of maintenance costs
- The presence of an effective organization further ensures that the subsequent steps for land reclamation may also be organized cooperatively

Village Organizations and their Plans. However, let us first discuss village organizations and their plans. Village organizations are the prime movers. They will fill the institutional vacuum created by the decay of the old social order. They will make plans and execute them. They will husband and control human and material resources. They will be the foundation of a new cooperative and equitable social order. The village groups will be continuously assisted by social organizers and technicians. The village plans will be based on the four factors of development:

- Reconstruction of physical infrastructure—irrigation and land reclamation
- Increased productivity
- Cooperative credit and banking
- Cooperative marketing

AKRSP will assist first in making the plans and subsequently in implementing them. It will promote social organization, provide various kinds of technical guidance and material support. The village organizations will take advantage of whatever facilities may be available from official agencies but the plans will be designed to make the villages self-reliant, as far as possible. In other words, the development will take place mostly in the private sector.

Physical Plans. The first step should be to prepare a topographical map of the village, showing the residential area, cultivated plots, orchards, pastures and woods, irrigation channels, footpaths etc. Then the engineer, in consultation with the group, may prepare a development layout indicating the construction of new channels, the extension of cultivated lands and pastures and the planting of new orchards and wood lots.

On the basis of this comprehensive survey and layout, the village groups should be assisted to make a long range plan which could be implemented incrementally, year after year.

Management. In the development of layout, while the principle of family ownership and family cultivation should be scrupulously observed, the group should be advised to introduce full or partial joint management of certain activities. For instance, there should be a common nursery for fruit and timber trees. The pasture lots should be fenced for rotation. The orchards and woodlots also should be fenced though inside the fence small plots may be allotted to individual families. Similarly, the management of water channels and roads and footpaths must be joint.

Research. Of course much research is needed to ascertain definitely the methods and contents of village physical plans. But this research will not consist in theoretical speculations. It would be action research in the organized villages where the social organizers, the engineers and the village groups will learn by doing, each step being tested in practice and leading smoothly to the next step. Here is the schematic form of the Research, Extension and Supervision approach:

A. A problem is analysed collaboratively by a team consisting of experts, social organizers and village leaders.
B. Based on this research, a package of advice is prepared.
C. It is presented or 'extended' to the village organizations (VOs).
D. If they are willing to participate, they are given technical and material assistance.
E. The guidance is continued through training of VO representatives (managers and specialists), frequent visits by social organizers and regular meetings of VOs.
F. Contact is maintained with the AKRSP Central Office for institutional support and supplies.

A cautious approach would be advisable. Research should be done carefully with a few organizations by the team consisting of an AKRSP expert, Social Organizer and the VO, till a viable model emerges which could be multiplied. Good models will emerge in the best VOs. Therefore, the importance of careful documentation should be realized.

Challenge for MER: Model Building Research. MER should accept the challenge of this model building research for territory of range development in Jalalabad, Morkhun and Chaprot and for a special marketing structure in the Chapurson villages.

The Essence of the AKRSP Extension Approach

In my 'Analytical Review' I have shown how AKRSP programmes differ from departmental programmes. In the first place, no department tries to promote VOs, only AKRSP does it. AKRSP engineers do not build *khuls* or link roads or other physical structure. They teach the VOs to build and maintain them. AKRSP staff does not, like the commercial banks or the Agricultural Development Bank (ADB) select loanees and distribute loans. AKRSP Social Organizers teach VOs to prepare loan plans, distribute and recover loans, collect their own capital and ultimately do their own banking.

AKRSP does not undertake to spray crops or vaccinate cattle. It invites VOs to send members for training as plant or cattle specialists. AKRSP's programmes are directed towards making the VOs independent, not dependent on 'field staff'. They create managerial ability and technical skills inside the village and promote formation of own capital and utilization of own resources.

The essence of the AKRSP approach is training and extension. But the extension agents are the nominees of the VOs: managers, agriculture and livestock specialists, foresters.

Departments want their own extension agents, paid and controlled by them. And they want ever larger numbers of departmental employees—the so-called 'field staff'. The performance of the line departments, with huge numbers of field staff, does not inspire much confidence.

On the other hand AKRSP's performance in engineering, credit, agriculture, forestry—without much field staff, relying mainly on VOs and using their nominees, managers and village specialists as extension agents—has been much more fruitful than the field staff supervised departmental performance.

There is a natural desire to emulate the power and authority of departments and prefer paid subordinate field staff to VO nominees. The temptation should be resisted. AKRSP should certainly strengthen its training capacity where necessary, but in respect of 'field staff' it should not emulate the departments. It should continue to make the VOs self-reliant, not dependent. The nominees of VOs have been the best extension agents and AKRSP experts should continue to rely on them.

Localizing, Planning and Development: Presentation on AKRSP to NWFP Officials

The first question was regarding the absence of social sector interventions in the AKRSP package of activities. The GM explained the difficulty of organizing the small farmer around such interventions. He added, however, that as the VOs become viable institutions, social sector interventions would be introduced. On the importance of involving the people in the identification, implementation and maintenance of village level projects, the GM recalled that Mr V.A. Jaffrey had observed that village level projects were simply not visible to the central planning process.[23]

The low costs of AKRSP projects also prompted a number of queries. The GM assured the audience that all the components of the project, including the labour costs, had been added to the numbers shown. He added that while estimated material costs were given to the villagers, the labour payment was negotiated and it normally worked out to Rs 15-20/day.

On the savings and loan programmes, the GM elaborated that savings were kept in the regular scheduled bank. The loans given to the VO were collective and the actual distribution and collection of loans was the responsibility of the VO. This was for the short production loan. The other, major, loans were the land development loans. These loans were collective as well but in this case AKRSP insists that equal amounts be given to all the members of the VO. This is keeping the idea of social justice in mind.

The GM said that by far the most important change that AKRSP wants to bring about is behavioural. To change the management of the village from an individualistic system to a collective one, RS recollected his experience of visiting all the major valleys before AKRSP started operations. He recalled that a long list of demands would appear inevitably in every village. He added that if one visits the same village today, one can clearly tell the difference AKRSP has managed to bring about. The GM mentioned Akhtar Hameed Khan's analogy of the jeep stuck in mud for the villagers before AKRSP interventions. He said that AKRSP was trying to free the villagers from the mud so they can start moving on their own. While showing the portfolio of projects for Chitral district, the GM admitted that AKRSP had faltered in taking on an abandoned hydel scheme for a village. He said that one cannot expect the villagers to maintain such schemes.

Then the GM made his final submission. He said that the VO is a vehicle for the development of the entire village. Wherever the VO is present in Chitral, the government and AKRSP can collaborate to ensure proper and efficient utilization of funds. AKRSP and the government can especially collaborate in the disbursement of the IFAD funds because the VOs offer an opportunity to involve all the villagers in their development. This also marked the end of the formal presentation and the floor was opened for questions.

Principles of work[24]

Nazeer Ladhani: Perhaps you can try to isolate primary success factors and secondary success factors.

Ans: There does not seem to be any alternative to the method that we follow. If you want to improve the lot of subsistence holders, they have to accept the three principles of organization, skill development and capital formation. The presence of the activist matters in helping people to accept these principles. Other factors, such as the presence of local institutions, appear to be secondary.

Nazeer Ladhani: So the cake mix is the same but you need the yeast.

Ans: No! You need a good cook.

Nazeer Ladhani: That is where charisma matters.

Ans: Yes, but charisma at the village level.

Development, poverty and people. In the historical part, I dwelt on the concept of self-help, the limitations of village aid and other community development programmes. On the theory of rural development, I brought out the micro level and the fallacy of emphasizing only the social sector interventions, which do not prove a viable entry point for organization and collective management, a *sine qua non* for small farmer development. Bringing out the lessons learnt so far from the AKRSP experience, I highlighted the expertise available at local level which only needs a graft of scientific and improved skills, the micro variations from village to village in terms of needs which only respond to a process of diagnostic survey embracing a series of village dialogues and do not lend themselves to a distant planning process, the tremendous response of the small farmers to a partnership involving obligations of organization, collective management, savings, implementation and maintenance of land development projects, upgrading of human skills of village specialists to prevent losses and to introduce innovations.[25]

In the question-answer session, issues were raised pertaining to training and upgrading of human skills and the role of an expatriate expert; dissemination of knowledge and experience through extension; obstacles and problems in organization of small farmers and the role of influential and elites; women's programmes and their participation in the village development process; the danger of village organization being dominated by the influential few in the village; the attitude of government towards this self-governance institution at the grassroots and the danger of the perpetuation of the gulf between the haves and have-nots. One of the participants pointed out the similarity between the Comilla model and AKRSP and observed that Comilla was in fact not a model but an approach and AKRSP brings out very clearly how the approach has been developed and adapted to the Northern Areas situation.

Institution building and service delivery.[26] Ms Poe added that USAID had a major new thrust in the policies of the agency which was to give equal weight to institutional development as to technical packages. It was quite revolutionary for USAID to admit that the institutional package was as important as the technical package. Ms Poe said that now when she had to speak on the subject, she would use the AKRSP and the AKHS programmes as examples. She said that she thought that she would be a great promoter of the programme. Then Mr Hummeler and Mr Chatta introduced themselves and the work of their organizations respectively. Mr Chatta commented that AKRSP was increasing productivity and the AKHS was improving health and in all this while population was increasing. He then wondered if all the AKRSP's efforts would be negated by the increase in population. Shoaib Sultan Khan answered that AKRSP was basically an institution building programme. It was not a service delivery programme. The hope was that the service delivery organizations would be able to be more effective in their delivery by working through the institutions fostered by AKRSP.

The way to learn is paved with...[27]

We took the shortcut from Kachura bridge to Shigar and repented having made this decision. It was a dangerous trail, a half completed road which only our expert precision driver could negotiate. We finally made it to Shigar by 7 p.m. and I was pleasantly surprised to find a well maintained and comfortable NAPWD rest house.

17 March 1986. The day began at 7.30 a.m. and our first stop was Seldhi and Kashinal villages where we successfully negotiated the third dialogues, ably assisted by the member NA council, Chairman District Council and the local District and Union Councillors.

From Seldhi we proceeded to Chutran having skirted round the Askuli valley—the gateway to K2. Chutran is the last but one village of the valley. Here also a third dialogue was scheduled which was successfully concluded. Chutran is also famous for its hot springs which provide naturally heated bathing water to the local population from the surrounding areas. We were told some people spend whole nights in the hot water during winters. The District Council has made concrete enclosures for men and women.

Our next village, Gulapur, had become inaccessible due to an avalanche on the jeep track. However, when we reached the avalanche to cross it on foot, the villagers had already cut a path through the ice for the jeeps to get across. Three village organizations had gathered at Gulapur with whom third dialogues were held. Details of dialogues are being separately circulated by SMS.

We had by now circumvented the whole Shigar valley with the exception of its two extremities, one leading to K2 and the other to Arandu. Shigar is comparatively an open valley with substantial tracts of cultivable land and orchards—mainly apricot. The large thorny tracts in the bed of the Shigar river could be gainfully exploited for rearing wild fowl.

At 5.30 p.m. the Shigar VO was awaiting our arrival and a dialogue was held with them which concluded late in the evening. The local district councillor had organized the VO and was also its president. All the three tiers of the councils represented their viewpoints about AKRSP and resolved to make it a success in the area and assured us of their fullest cooperation. On this optimistic note the day concluded.

18 March 1986. It had started snowing and the Shigar rest-house presented a different picture from the previous day, when we left by jeep at 7.30 a.m. for the Skardu airport with little prospect of getting a flight to Islamabad. It took us an hour to reach Skardu. It snowed throughout. After a futile visit to the airport we took the Gilgit road. Hussain Wali estimated that I should be able to reach Bisham by 6 p.m. and Abbottabad by 8.30 p.m. Instead of wasting another day in the waiting game for the PIA flight I thought it prudent to push ahead to Islamabad, having bid goodbye to Hussain Wali and SMS at the KKH Skardu road junction.

The KKH turned out to be in a terrible mess. Although this was my umpteenth trip on it, I had never found the KKH in such a bad condition. It was literally an obstacle race against falling rock, land slides and mud flow besides falling water. I was not sure if the melting snow or the recent rains were responsible for this carnage. There were over 100 rock falls and landslides. At one point we made it just in time for the road to open after a closure of a few hours. A few miles ahead a truck was sandwiched between two giant boulders which had fallen on the KKH. After some precision maneuverability the truck was able to extricate itself and we breathed a sigh of relief. By 6 p.m. we made it to Bisham as predicted by Hussain Wali and I complimented the driver on having made it in good time. But I said it a bit too soon, for just on the outskirts of Bisham near the PTDC Motel sign was an oven fresh landslide blocking the road.

Very soon all the drivers ganged together and started preparing a passage through the blockage. A Suzuki tried to negotiate the blockade and failed. Mir Ahmed ventured with the jeep and I foolishly kept sitting on it. The jeep got on top of the rubble and its left wheels, the side on which I was sitting, were only a few inches away from the precipice. I thanked my stars after reaching the safety of the other side of the KKH. When we crossed the Thakot bridge I anticipated arrival in Islamabad by 11 p.m. Fate had something more in store and the inevitable happened. Just short of Batagram a big mud flow completely blocked the road making it impassable. I wondered how JP Naz and Salim were able to negotiate the road three days earlier in the car and Nizar only a day earlier.

Mir Ahmed waded across and negotiated a seat for me on a Datsun pick-up, up to Abbottabad, nearly 100 km. away. I sandwiched myself on the front seat with three others. Just before taking off Mir Ahmed brought out a wad of hundred rupee notes which he wanted me to carry for Naib Khan, my car driver. I knew carrying of cash so publicly was inviting trouble and asked Mir Ahmed to bring the money himself next day. As the ancient Datsun started off I knew I was in the dubious company of three Pathans—most likely drug peddlers and I feared the worst on the way. However, in my not so chaste Pushto I was able to put across to them who I was and since they said they came from Swat, I let them know some of the prominent people I knew there. I knew that gave me safe conduct.

At Abbottabad, having failed to make contact with the commissioner (Ejaz Rahim) or some other acquaintance, I hired a Suzuki van to drive me down to Islamabad, reaching there by the early hours of the morning. On reaching the destination I calculated that in the preceding 60 hours I had been on a jeep or Suzuki for over 32 hours. I had developed a nasty cough and I spent the next two days in bed on the doctor's advice to avoid a severe attack of bronchial pneumonia.

Marvels of People's Power. The next stopover was at the site of Mastuj irrigation channel where by coincidence the group also met Shahzada Mohiuddin, Chairman of the Chitral District Council and recently elected member of the national assembly who was visiting the area along with other councillors. Shahzada Mohiuddin informed that attempts were made once before by the Local Government and Rural Development Department to construct the Mastuj channel which is nearly 7 miles long but without success. The Irrigation Department had estimated the cost of the construction of the channel at Rs 7.5 million. However, the VO with the assistance of AKRSP have completed the channel for less than Rs 300,000.

The Ahmadabad VO was formed on 21.10.83 with 75 members and has since accumulated savings of Rs 75,000. The manager of the VO explained their village plan of developing fuel wood, orchards, pastures and potatoes. He also requested a land development loan. The livestock and plant protection specialists explained their activities and the payments received by them for services rendered to the members. The PP specialist suggested extension of the rod of the spray pumps to achieve better results.

This was Shoaib Sultan Khan's fifth visit but with a difference. Besides the Administrator, Northern Areas (formerly designated as commissioner),[28] Mr Khalid M. Ahmad, the helicopter flew with Mir Ghazanfar Ali, Raja Bahadur Khan, Member NAC and Gilgit district council respectively and the chairman, UC to Shimshal. Unlike previous occasions, we had a firm offer to make to the Shimshalis on the issue of their link road to Passu—virtually their lifeline to the outside world.

When in early 1983, Bill Spoelberch had enquired at the instance of His Highness, if AKRSP could do anything to help build the Passu-Shimshal link road, Shoaib Sultan Khan's reply had been negative. AKRSP could never hope to raise the resources to undertake the project. In less than 24 months, it was happening. Thanks to the initiative of the administrator and the willingness of Mir Ghazanfar, the impossible had become possible.

But the credit really belongs to the villagers of Shimshal who refused to budge and tenaciously clung to their most dire need. They accepted AKRSP's call for organization and collective management, started a regular savings programme but politely refused to have anything to do with the increased productivity, prevention of losses, credit or marketing packages unless and until they were helped to construct the link road. In sheer desperation they started construction of the road from Shimshal side and with the help from the Northern Areas Administration in terms of explosives, steel wires and grains, completed 14 miles of the road through the easier terrain. AKRSP had to bow down before such determination and unwavering resolve. The engineering section undertook the survey of the link road and once and for all settled the controversy about the length of the road. It came out to be 30 miles, unlike earlier guess estimates of 45 to 50 miles. The Administrator's visit on 1 May 1985 spurred Hussain Wali to prepare the PC-1 for the link road before the session of the NA Council scheduled on 9 May. With NAWO estimation figures and a generous 15 per cent ESR, the cost totalled up to Rs 8 million. Surely the village organization could do it in much less and it was with this hope that the group was going to Shimshal to have a dialogue with the villagers.

Nearly 100 persons of the 124 households greeted the group. Mir Ghazanfar spoke to them in a forthright and unambiguous manner. He told them that the NA Council with the consent of the district and union councillors was willing to help in construction of the link road provided the villagers were willing to do the work themselves and not through NAWO or contractors. The VO must undertake the responsibility to complete the project. AKRSP would provide them the technical support and advise them in getting compressor and explosives. All the councillors would also help and would moreover make a sum of Rs 2 million, in addition to Rs 1 million of AKRSP, available to the VO for undertaking the project. He said this was being done because of His Highness' interest in the area and because of the initiative taken by the administrator. He explained that this was a very large grant compared to the size and population of the village but he was doing so because he believed that the villagers could do it and no one else could.

Shoaib Sultan Khan followed Mir Ghazanfar by exhorting the villagers to consider the offer carefully and make no mistake about it. The villagers have to complete the link road in Rs 30 lacs, which in terms of their own work represents the cost of material and partial labour wages. It does not include the cost of their determination and resolve because no price could be put on these qualities. The average cost of AKRSP aided village projects in Gilgit district is only Rs 127,000 but the offer of a million rupees is being made in addition to 2 million rupees by the councillors keeping in view the resolve of the villagers. Shoaib Sultan Khan cautioned that they must not accept the offer in the hope that they will be able to get an increase in the future. Under AKRSP methodology there are no revisions. The only allowance AKRSP is prepared to make, is not to insist on the VO accepting the responsibility for maintenance of the road.

They would be at liberty to approach government agencies in this behalf. Shoaib Sultan Khan paid glowing tributes to Khalid M.Ahmad for taking the initiative in getting funds allocated for the road and also thanked Mir Ghazanfar and the councillors responding to the needs of Shimshalis.

One of the villagers expressed some doubt about the capacity of the VO to undertake such a big project and especially underscored the difficulty in maintaining the road even if it was constructed. Mir Ghazanfar and the administrator assured him of government help in maintenance.

The administrator, in his speech, made a reference to his earlier visit and the deputations of Shimshalis who had been calling on him at Gilgit and seeking assistance only to the extent of being provided with material and food grains for them to undertake the construction of the link road. These he had been making available to them even when he had to seek approval of the ministry. He was, therefore, under the impression that the Shimshalis were prepared to construct the road with the barest assistance. He was consequently somewhat surprised at their reluctance to accept the offer of Rs 3 million to construct the road. He warned them that if they did not avail of this offer, they would never get another chance and the funds would immediately be diverted to other areas and projects. He believed in their hardiness and determination to complete the work which would be a marvel to be shown to the outside world. Work which outsiders had refused to do was being undertaken and successfully completed by villagers. He assured the villagers of the administration's fullest support. After the administrator's speech, the villagers unanimously expressed their resolve to undertake the construction of the road and assured its successful completion.

The group flew out of Shimshal, which was chilly and cold, promising to come back as soon as the VO had finalized its work plan for the construction of the road.

Wisdom is the lost treasure of the faithful: Contribution of Rs 500,000 to AKRSP from Northern Areas Council (NAC) Member (1986)[29]

Agha Syed Mohammad Ali Shah, member NAC, from Kharmang sub-division of Baltistan District saw Shoaib Sultan Khan at Gilgit on 5 July and especially requested the initiation of AKRSP in his sub-division on the lines of Shigar sub-division, where another member of the NAC had pooled resources with AKRSP to undertake PPIs. Consequently the MG (Shoaib Sultan Khan and Hussain Wali) along with DPO Baltistan and Nabeel Malik visited Tulti, Baghicha and Gasing in Kharmang sub-division on 10 July 1986.

Agha Syed Mohammad Ali Shah, who is also the most prominent religious leader of the area, in his speeches at Tulti and Baghicha, thanked His Highness for initiating a development programme in the area to assault poverty. He observed that AKRSP was based on true

Islamic principles and anyone who opposed AKRSP was in fact opposing Hazrat Ali because AKRSP was carrying out his principles of welfare and development. Citing the example of Hazrat Ali, the member of the Northern Areas Council exhorted the villagers to work hard and make their projects a success. He said that the message of organization being given by AKRSP was really the function of the *ulema* who had neglected it. The *ulema* should be grateful to AKRSP for discharging their duties.

As a token of his commitment and support to AKRSP, Agha Syed Mohammad Ali Shah handed over a cheque of Rs 500,000 to AKRSP (through the DPO Baltistan) in public, for PPIs in six VOs. The amount was part of the funds placed at his disposal by NAC. He promised to continue with this collaboration and prayed for the success of this joint venture.

Packages: In the discussion, each section gave a progress report and identified the successful package. Kulsum Farman, Acting District Coordinator in the Women-in-Development section, said that 40 VOs were participating in packages developed for women and 50 additional VOs had sent 'Resolutions' expressing their desire to initiate women's activities. The poultry package, for example, comprised home-based chick-rearing, after training in prevention of diseases. 370 units of 6 Fayumi chicks each had been taken by 25 VOs at cost price and the package had apparently been highly successful.

Field Coordinator Asia Karim gave the details of the vegetable package, of which 16 demonstration plots had been made and 70 women trained and 4 VOs marketed their vegetable produce. This package also appeared to have a good potential. Field Coordinator Gulshan Siddiqi described the 'appropriate technology' package under which 34 nut cracking machines, 9 butter churners and 37 apricot drying demonstrations had been done. All these tools were acceptable to women and had not caused problems of maintenance or major breakdowns. The cost was the only inhibiting factor in the propagation of this package. Engineer Hayat had already developed butter churner-cum-nut cracking unit, thereby reducing the cost from Rs 2,200 to 1,100. The manager of Pari VO was determined to bring down the cost further. If he did succeed in reducing the cost, this package should also prove highly effective.

Both Kulsum and Asia have gained tremendous confidence over the years in understanding and extending the women-focused activities.

Gulshan is also becoming well-versed in the appropriate technological package. They need to now focus their attention on extending the proven packages, instead of dissipating their energy and resources in trying new things.

Agriculture: Gari Khan (agriculturalist) explained the details of the activities and the success achieved in preventing losses and crop improvement. The high-yielding PAK-81 variety of wheat was to be planted in 2,900 ha. in Baltistan. Eleven VOs had already accepted the seed and some had even become seed producing villages. The next focus would be on barley, which is grown on 6,400 ha. There is little scope for improvement in seed but the cropping intensity of the land under barley has a potential for increase. Another important and exciting prospect is of increasing cropping intensity by stopping free grazing. The Agriculture Section would do well by concentrating on these packages in addition to development of orchards and vegetable gardening.

Livestock: Dr Mastan Ali explained that the 93 livestock specialists had covered a small percentage of the vaccination programme. In 1988, in the first round, 12,000 animals and 2823 poultry birds were vaccinated. He plans to increase the coverage in the autumn vaccination fourfold. His next emphasis is on feed improvement and the poultry package. For breed improvement, he will wait for advice from the livestock specialist Reyaz Ahmad Khan.

Engineering Section: Darjat explained the progress of the PPI which appeared satisfactory. I commended him on the installation of project signs but to earn the award of Rs 2,000, the engineering section has to get the signs properly fixed by constructing a base for each signboard.

Architect Ghulam Saeed submitted his report on improvement of housing along with three type plans. I requested him to supplement the report with actual plans of the houses under construction and the suggestions he would like to make to improve the sanitation in the existing designs being followed by the villagers.

The windmill installed by Patrick Arnoldi also came under discussion. Arnoldi's letter alleging construction defects, rather than design defect, was considered. I was told that the fans and the mill buckled with the force of the wind and the cost of fibreglass fans is prohibitive. The second windmill prepared by Arnoldi, has not as yet, been installed because the first has not proved successful. Engineer Hayat offered to have another look at the mill and try to repair it. I advised Syed Mutahir Shah to give him all necessary assistance, including funds if needed, for the purpose and submit a detailed report about feasibility or otherwise of the windmill.

Sustainability of AKRSP

Sustainability was inbuilt both in the work of male and female organizations of AKRSP. An observation of most of the guests was on AKRSP's strong emphasis on sustainability, which they said was central in any development initiative, but was missing in the majority of the areas. They particularly liked the idea that AKRSP would eventually phase itself out, once its major functions were taken over by the local institutions. Seeing their interest in this fundamental issue, Shoaib Sultan Khan explained the process of institution building which effectively means investing in organization, combining education with motivation and enhancing the technical and managerial skills of the rural population. As to how one would know if this process would succeed, Shoaib Sultan Khan said that the VOs' savings was a good measure, which now amounted to more than US$4 million. The result of this strong capital base means greater financial autonomy and self reliance in the rural areas, Shoaib Sultan Khan observed.

What is so innovative about the programme?[30]

GM: The most innovative thing about this programme, and the secret behind its success, is the focus not on social sector activities e.g. health, education etc., but on the productive sector.

Question: What about the geographical coverage of the programme area, are all areas covered in the Northern Areas?

GM: The programme is spread over three districts of the Northern Areas and the NWFP. The geographical target area is about twice the size of Switzerland. So far the programme has covered 50 per cent of the target area. In Gilgit district, because the programme has been functioning here for the past five and half years, the coverage is 90 per cent. The Chitral and Baltistan programmes started a few years after the Gilgit programme, therefore, the coverage there is lower. However, we are confident that given another few years, they too would have high coverage.

NOTES

1. NFR—Visit by UK Ismaili ladies to AKRSP, 11 October 1984.
2. NFR—Akhtar Hameed Khan—Meeting, 31 August 1986.
3. Visit of the Information Service Group Probationers to AKRSP, 2 November 1988.
4. NFR—Panel discussion at National Defence College, Rawalpindi, 1 August 1988.
5. NFR—The Evolving Role of Social Organizers, 1988.
6. NFR—Village Dialogue-The Old DJ School, 19 December 1982.
7. NFR—Village Dialogue-House of *Numberdar*, 23 December 1982.
8. NFR—Village Dialogues, 5 January 1983.
9. NFR—Village Dialogues, 30 December 1982.
10. NFR—Chitral Visit—Discussions with Malakand Administration and Third Dialogues at Buni, 1 February 1984.
11. NFR—Land Development Dialogue...Ahmedabad, 17 November 1985.
12. NFR—Third Dialogues, 14 October 1984.
13. NFR—Visit of Dr (Mrs) Attiya Inayatullah, Adviser to the President of Pakistan on Population Welfare to AKRSP offices accompanied with Mr Iqbal Ali Muhammad of UNHCR and Mr S. Faisal Saud, Deputy Commissioner, Gilgit, 29 July 1984.
14. NFR—Tour Diary-Management Group (Shoaib Sultan Khan, TH & FS accompanied by TS) Village Japuka.
15. December 1982. The first of the First Dialogues.
    15 NFR—Visit of the Deputy Chairman/Secretary General, Planning Commission/ Planning Division.
    Mr V.A. Jaffrey to AKRSP—5 June 1986.
16. NFR—Presentation on AKRSP to NWFP officials, 16 June 1986.
17. NFR—Follow-Up Visits, 13 October 1986.
18. NFR—General Manager's tour of VOs, 8 November 1988.
19. NFR—General Manager tour of Baltistan, 15-20 September 1988.
20. NFR—General Manager tour of Baltistan, 15-20 September 1988.
21. NFR—General Manager tour of Baltistan, 15-20 September 1988.
22. NFR—Follow-up Visits, 22 March 1984.
23. NFR—Presentation on AKRSP to NWFP Officials, 16 June 1986.
24. NFR—Briefing and discussion with CIDA Appraisal Mission, 27 October 1989 and Nazeer Ladhani (NL).
25. Seminar on Rural Development in South Asia sponsored by South Asia Partnership of Canadian NGOs (SAP), Holiday Inn Ottawa, 5 February 1986.
26. NFR—The group was shown 'The Changing Valleys', 12 April 1988.
27. NFR—The Aga Khan Rural Support Programme, Gilgit, 16-17 November 1987.
28. NFR—Visit to Shimshal, 30 May 1985.
29. NFR—Contribution of Rs 500,000 to AKRSP from Northern Area Council (NAC Member)—10 July 1986.
30. NFR—Visit of the Information Service Group Probationers to AKRSP, 2 November 1988.

12

Women, Equity and Economic Justice

WOMEN IN DEVELOPMENT

It was the women who made me realize that they were also there. My initial dialogues were all with men. One day I received a letter from the women of Sherqilla saying that they had heard about the terms of partnership with AKRSP and as a consequence had organized themselves into a women's organization, elected a chairperson and manager and started holding weekly meetings at a fixed time on a fixed day. They had also started a savings programme. They very much desired to enter into a partnership with AKRSP like the menfolk. This was the beginning of the women's programme in AKRSP and the search for women staff members. It was quite obvious that the need was not segregation but the emancipation of women. However, without their separate identity, women were unable to find a voice. In places where mixed men's and women's organizations were formed, women soon preferred to form separate organizations. They did not trust their menfolk with their savings and savings became a great source of giving the women a sense of security and importance. Very soon the organization of women became synonymous with empowerment but the main constraint for AKRSP was finding women staff and programme packages for women's organizations (WOs).

Despite the difficulties the women in development programme gradually started picking up pace and soon became a mainstream programme for AKRSP. Hussain Wali encouraged women staff members to drive the jeeps and Rubab Muzaffar overcame religious opposition to her driving in Baltistan, a very conservative area. In 2005, two of the AKRSP women staff, Kulsoom Farman and Yasmin Karim, were nominated in the effort to nominate 1000 women Nobel laureates of the world.

Maliha Hussein, Khalida Nasir, Amneh Azam Ali, Najma Siddiqi, Dr Shahida Jaffrey and Shandana Khan were the feminine face of

AKRSP during my time, with many local girls spreading the message. In Chitral two sisters, Rehana and Humaira Hashmi, laid the foundation of the women's programme assisted by a local girl Sartaj, as Kulsoom Farman had done in Baltistan. Yasmin, Noreen, Uroos, Gulistan and others became the pioneers in Gilgit.

Visit of Ismaili ladies from UK led by Isobel Shaw

The women's programme generated many questions, which led to a vigorous discussion on many issues related to the women's role in the community. The GM raised the issue by stating that it was now time to talk about 'the controversial women's programme'. Many of those present asked why it was controversial. He replied that so far, to their credit, many women's organizations had spontaneously sprung up and were meeting and saving money regularly. However, the women had not yet identified any viable programmes similar to the men's 'PPI' projects. There had been suggestions from several quarters but nothing had been done as yet. Hence, the field was still wide open for suggestions on how best to encourage the women.

One suggestion was to set up income-generating 'cottage industries' such as carpet weaving. The GM replied, 'How do we know these will generate income, especially with the competition from down country?' The government had set up carpet weaving classes for the women but could not find markets for them. This had led to tremendous frustration on the part of the women. They would only take up projects that could bring them income, because they were already busy in productive activities on the farm and in the home, and spent as much time, if not more, as the men on farming. If they had any spare time it was primarily in the winter.

It was suggested that vocational training was not a permanent solution for the women. Rather, their day-to-day problems and activities should be addressed. Animal husbandry, water supply, more effective utilization of wood, walled gardens for fodder, food preservation techniques and marketing were mentioned as areas on which to focus. Proposed solutions should be applicable to other villages too, where similar problems exist.

This is not to say that there is no use for other income-generating activities such as quilt-making, embroidery, weaving and soap-making. In fact, Khalida Nasir (WID Programme Officer) pointed out that quilt-making had been successful in several villages, and had resulted in good profits for the WOs. Mrs Shoaib outlined the specialization by the WOs whose members make beautifully patterned bed sheets, tablecloths, napkins and tea-cozies from cloth obtained cheaply from down country. There are also ready markets for some other things they produce and they fetch a very good price. Beyond these two examples the point was made that different villages could specialize in different activities, thereby avoiding the problems of saturating the market with one product and, in effect, competing to drive prices down.

Decreasing Women's Burdens through Collective Action

Another very important point raised was how to lessen the burden of women's work and how to lessen the drudgery associated with that work. Income generating activities are useful but they do not address the core of the problems affecting women, which, if tackled, would lead to women having more time to spend on profitable activities. The discussion returned to the need for appropriate technology: a nut cracking machine for apricots, almonds and walnuts had already proved its value and could be utilized throughout the programme area. On a similar note, it was stated that if the work could be shared, the burden on individuals would be reduced and the work could be more productive. Collectively there is also greater incentive and motivation to succeed.

In terms of improving animal husbandry practices, winter fodder grown in a collective walled garden would lead to economies of scale, reduce the work of fodder collection and storage and greatly simplify looking after livestock. Growing fodder would also improve soil fertility. Similar principles would apply if several small orchards were merged into a single large one.

The discussion then shifted to the suggestion that the Women's Organizations (WOs) should merge with the men's VOs: this would mean the existence of only one organization, but women would have a voice in it. The women could suggest through the men, the kinds of projects they like to have undertaken. An example could be a PPI that would benefit the women. Hussain Wali (Engineering Specialist) pointed out that PPI projects—such as reclaiming agricultural land—benefit both men and women, although the PPI was undertaken by the VO. Similarly, the link roads eased the path for women bringing wood and fodder from far away places. Tariq Husain (Monitoring, Evaluation and Research Specialist) asked the women to suggest how their labour could be minimized when new lands are developed in Passu.

The discussion then turned to the customs and traditions prevalent in the area, with the acknowledgement that just forming a WO was an achievement in itself. However, these organizations were formed only in areas where the women are less restricted. In other places it is much more difficult to approach the women or guide their activities.

A paper prepared by Khalida Nasir was read aloud and discussed. The discussion focused on reproductive patterns (male preference, high infant mortality and high birth rates); literacy rates (very low overall, although relatively higher in the progressive villages) and the strength and endurance of family relationships.

Other points mentioned during the course of the morning's discussions, were the iodized salt programme (promoted vigorously by IPS and very successful), the high cost of latrines and the production of dairy products especially cheese.

Finally, Isobel Shaw, with loud approval from the ladies in the visiting team, said that she had been very excited by this morning's programme and looked forward to the rest of the programme.

Forward View.[1] The GM indicated that he supported whole-heartedly the principle of targeting training programmes directly to the concerned group in the village and that this principle would be followed. However, he foresaw problems in extending training courses to women who could not, due to customary and/or religious constraints, come to Gilgit for courses. He asked the participants what AKRSP's response should be to demands for village-level training for women, given the present training infrastructure. Both Najma and Quratul Ain stressed that AKRSP should use its leverage to enhance the participation of women in the training programme in Gilgit. They recommended that a training programme be developed based on the tasks in which women have the major responsibility in the Northern Areas.

With regard to the workload of rural women and AKRSP's response to this, the GM indicated that he was in favour of interventions to reduce their present heavy workload, such as nut-cracking machines and drinking water supply. Zahoor Alam (Natural Resource Management Specialist) felt that women's heavy workload would prevent them from being effective extension workers since they would not have the time to go from house to house to spray crops and vaccinate livestock. Most of the other participants felt that AKRSP should not make presumptions about women's ability to carry out these activities. However, training men in tasks that were traditionally done by women would not be effective in raising agricultural productivity. Ultimately, only increased productivity levels could reduce the women's workload.

The issue of how AKRSP could impose conditions on the VOs regarding the active participation of women was discussed. Hussain Wali felt that this would take time but that eventually AKRSP could impose these conditions on the VOs. Moreover, he stressed that before amendments to the Terms of Partnership could be introduced, the training package for women must be developed fully. Both the outside participants reiterated their strong belief that AKRSP presently has enough leverage to enter into partnership with villagers on its own terms. Anis Dani (from ICIMOD) supported this point by stating that if AKRSP was able to convince villagers to meet and save weekly, it could convince them to incorporate women into the AKRSP programme.

The issue of how best to productively invest the WOs' savings of approximately Rs 0.6 million was raised. Because the village women have indicated that they do not know to what end they are saving, this is an issue for the MG. AKRSP needs to examine how the savings rates of women will be affected if a single organization with men and women members is formed. Presently, the savings are in large part the result of men giving money to women to put in the WO accounts, though some savings have been generated by the quilt project. Najma indicated that, during her field visits, she found women who had saved 100 per cent of their earnings from the sale of quilts.

Both the participants underlined the need to engage more women in the various disciplines at AKRSP. They felt that participation of village women could be enhanced substantially by the presence of women social organizers, agricultural officers and engineers. Furthermore, the MG must involve itself intensively in the development and implementation of a programme incorporating this overlooked segment of the rural population into AKRSP's programmes. The participants felt that the very capable AKRSP professional staff should be used effectively in this area and should be supported by additional full-time staff for the women's programme.

The GM stressed that AKRSP was committed to the development of women but had lacked direction in developing a programme. He thanked the participants for their contributions and invited them to visit AKRSP again as soon as possible.

Michael Stuhrenburg also asked some questions; the most interesting concerned the views of the women on the future of their daughters. Their answer was 'Why do you think we work so hard? It is so that we can send our daughters to school. We want them to become teachers and doctors and leave this hard life of *zamindari* (land-based economy) behind, due to which we bear so much trouble and strife.'

Gindai Women's Organization: An Example of Sustainable Change

A visit to Gindai (Ghizer District) demonstrated that it was a successful and mature WO. Both the specialists are working hard: the poultry specialist vaccinates about 1,000 chickens every three months, which she says takes her three days each time, and she is paid regularly by the WO members. The Vegetable PP sprays against pests, and is paid for the cost. Everyone now grows vegetables on their home plots; 15 members work on the collective plot, where they grow potatoes and onions for sale. Women also earn income form the sale of eggs, poultry, ghee, dried fruit and dried tomatoes.

I asked the women what they felt about the WO. They said the most important things for them were savings and skills training. Before, they never used to meet in this way, participate in a training course or save money. They added that the WO was a forum in which they could discuss their activities and problems and help each other. For example, if a woman was alone because her husband was away, or she did not have an adult male at home, others would help her with farm or domestic work when necessary. Before they joined the WO they did not know about each others' problems. They emphasized how important the visits of the Aga Khan Health Services were. They felt that the presence of a trained Community Health Worker had made a major impact on their health and that of their children. They seemed to think that this was also a result of the WO, as the health workers operated through the WO and did not differentiate between AKRSP and AKHS.

The interventions of various specialists have led to lowered mortality of people and their poultry flocks. The cultivation of vegetables has brought them income and they are eating better food: 'Before, we used to have only tea and bread; now we have a variety of vegetables'. Many households are growing and selling potatoes and onions through Pathan traders.

I tried to learn what else they wanted to do through the WO or whether they had any complaints about AKRSP, but they assured me they were very happy with both their WO activities and AKRSP.

Women's participation. Women participate in different ways. In some villages they have formed separate Women's Organizations. In others, women are full members in the VO. In yet other situations women are neither VO or WO members, but AKRSP is providing development inputs to them. There are no WOs in the District of Baltistan but women's programmes are active in 131 VOs.

Of the 54,400 VO members, approximately 2,000 are women. In addition, there are over 270 WOs, with an additional 10,000 members. AKRSP's WID packages have been accepted in over 130 other VOs.

Participation has to be understood as a family affair. There are on average 8.3 people per family, three of them adults. We can estimate that half of the adults are women. AKRSP has mobilized approximately half the households of the programme area. Thus of the nearly half a million people covered by the programme, 50 per cent would be women.

NOTE

1. Management Group meeting with Ms Najma Siddiqui, Quratul Ain and Anis Dani From ICIMOD), 30 March 1985.

13

New Management Paradigm

PARTICIPATION AND OWNERSHIP[1]

The AKRSP was not introducing socialism, but the cooperative spirit. Cooperatives allowed private ownership but some services were collective. Collective management in pastures, however, meant that ownership was collective also, just as in the case of forests. The VO met all the costs and shared in the benefits or losses. The idea of collective ownership was simple for the villagers to understand as in the case of the PPI and their territory.

Collective management did not mean that everybody interfered. The VOs had to appoint a Manager and then let the Manager do his job. The VO should not profit from ownership of capital only. Through the land development loans, the AKRSP did not want to destroy private ownership. However, collective ownership had to be encouraged in cases where individual ownership was not possible, in pastures and forests for example. Sultan Hameed commented that anything that was made clear to the villagers and also had clear benefits was accepted by them. Akhtar Hameed Khan continued and said that we were not purists. Collective ownership was not beneficial for everything and in certain cases private ownership had to be encouraged. If the villagers benefitted from somebody's land then the VO should pay the individual. Heifers should have been kept individually and collective management should never have been pursued. An animal needed individual attention and even in China, pig-keeping was not collectivized.

Javed Hasan inquired whether the AKRSP should encourage private ownership. Akhtar Hameed Khan again explained the difference between private and collective management. The tractor could be owned collectively but required individual management. The experience of pooling land had historically been extremely controversial and the experiences were not good. Services, however, could be pooled and their benefits were very clear. The holdings of pastures and forests, however, should not be broken up. Shoaib Sultan Khan further clarified the point, saying that as far as credit was concerned, we would not give any funds directly to an individual. The credit would be disbursed to the VO and the entire VO would be responsible. Barkat Ali Khan asked what would happen if the VO took out a marketing loan and gave it to an individual to use and then charged a high mark up from him. He was advised not to promote this sort of use of the loan. Noor Mohammad then wanted to know if it was acceptable to use the marketing loan for starting consumer cooperatives. Akhtar Hameed Khan said that because of marketing more and more supply to the markets, ought to be encouraged. Consumer cooperatives too should be formed.

Shoaib Sultan Khan asked if it were acceptable for the VO to engage in trading. Akhtar Hameed Khan explained that the AKRSP was a bank for the VOs and the VOs were the bank for the individual members. The VO ought to have an agreement with the villagers over the use of funds. The VO should use the money to create employment in the village and should present accounts for approval. The Social Organizers also needed to educate the VO officers and to carefully scrutinise loan applications. Credit was the only thing which could be controlled and needed careful attention. The casualties should not bother AKRSP. The programme was fighting a war and casualties would always be present but the SO should be able to pinpoint the weaknesses. The SOs also had to be careful not to interfere in the internal affairs of the VOs and to restrict their input to guiding them. Javed Hasan asked about the way to deal with default. Akhtar Hameed Khan replied that no bank was without any default. This did not, however, mean that the programme should do nothing. There were basically two types of default: (i) natural and (ii) wilful. The SO had to differentiate between the two. The SO also has to organize people to take responsibilities for planning their own development.

Without fostering a framework of grassroots institutions, involvement of the people is not possible. A poverty alleviation programme shall have to first start with institution building. The question is whose responsibility it should be to organize people at grassroots for development to launch an assault on poverty. Governments find it difficult and have found an easy way of shifting this responsibility on to NGOs. The answer to the problem is, as advocated by the *London Economist* a few years ago, not in passing on the responsibility to NGOs, because the NGOs will never have the resources to launch countrywide programmes for alleviation of poverty but for governments to learn to act like NGOs. This might sound contradictory and impractical but over the last ten years I have been trying to demonstrate through AKRSP how this can be done. The fact that the prime minister of Pakistan should have nominated me on the prestigious SAARC Commission for Alleviation of Poverty makes me believe that I am making some headway.

What makes Community Participation (CP) possible? To foster organizations at grassroots level, a support organization is essential. CP should be an integral part of national policy with focus on target groups. The cost of CP is more than offset by the benefits, in terms of sustainable development, efficiency, cohesion, less dependence on external assistance, time saving, political consciousness and awareness and, above all, ensuring equity and social justice through equitable development.

Community Participation (CP) and Social Development[2]

In the discussion questions were asked about participation and sustainable development. In my intervention, I urged the seminar participants not so much to concentrate or discuss what to do in terms of CP, but how to do it, because there seemed little difference of opinion on the efficacy of CP.

In the Nepal case, two case studies were presented as examples of CP: Integrated Rural Development (IRD) and Small Farmer Development Programme (SFDP). Both cases were evaluated in terms of the level of CP by measuring the element of sharing in decision-making process, labour and cash contribution and income generation activities.

In the discussion, the view was expressed that if the benefits revolve around change agents and do not filter down, it is not true CP. A question was asked about integration of Line Department activities with the project operations. At this juncture, I explained the role of Line Departments and the model in which technical experts are not placed in a position of subordination to non-technical personnel but are made effective service agents to beneficiaries by organizing them in groups. On group formation, apprehensions were expressed about damaging national integration if groups are formed on ethnic lines. It was clarified that the formation of interest groups for economic development does not deter national integration. Rather, it facilitates it.

The Thailand case highlighted the impact of CP on institution building, strengthening of sub-district administration, initiating the local level planning process and community control on corruption and accountability towards community.

The Pakistan case study was presented by Minhajuddin Khan of PARD Peshawar, who presented the Integrated Rural Development Project implemented by Dir District Council and AKRSP as examples of CP. Ms Sadiqa Salahuddin of NIPA Karachi, in her comments, contrasted the level of CP in the Dir and Gilgit cases, and highlighted the lack of CP in Dir.

I contrasted the importance of CP in social and productive sector projects. To my mind in social sector schemes, CP helps to bridge the gap between available resources and the desired level of services. However, in case of the productive sector, for example, helping small holders to rise above the level of subsistence, CP plays a critical role and is a *sine qua non* for improving the economic situation of the rural poor. Mr Kirtee Shah came up to me, after the session and said that he had not heard people say the things that I was saying.

Practical Steps for Participatory Planning and Management. Dr Akhtar Hameed Khan provided his guidance on important management practices for AKRSP. He saw the potential of sustainable development through development of non-farm resources in Gilgit. He proposed the following steps in this regard. For streamlining field research and extension in:

a) Forestry and pasture
b) Horticulture
c) Animal husbandry and dairying

Appointment of a consultant: I would suggest that contact be established with the Forest Institute in Peshawar, the Tarnab Farm in Peshawar and Faisalabad Agricultural University to persuade some bright young professors to get involved in the following activities:

Planning for credit and marketing. It must be clearly understood that increased productivity requires, at the initial stage, an infusion of capital:

i) For the construction of infrastructure — mostly grants
ii) For the reclamation of land — mostly long term loans
iii) For larger inputs in agriculture — mostly short term loans

Training. The second step is the adoption of improved methods. This can be achieved by training, with the help of AKRSP, of village specialists, chosen by the village group from among themselves. Foremost among the specialists is the Manager. Then there is the model farmer. An animal 'first-aider' has recently been added and a plant protection man. More specialists should be trained in future according to the need felt for them.

A: Survey. After the foremost comes the survey — a complete mapping and classification of all the resources in the territory: water, soil, trees, bushes, grass, herbs etc. The survey should be done under the guidance of the engineer and the forester. It is necessary to combine local knowledge with scientific knowledge. The survey and the map will make their vision concrete and indicate the directions of the VOs' endeavours.

B: Planning. The resources map of their range or territory should be thoroughly discussed in VO meetings. Having assumed responsible ownership of the territory, the VO should start to plan its development. The grafting of scientific knowledge of experts on traditional skills should continue. In other words the plan should be prepared jointly by the VO and the Engineer/Forester/Social Organizer/Economist team.

The long term nature of the plan should always be kept in view. Two pitfalls should be avoided:

a. The obsession of subsistence farmers for extension of cropland
b. The demand for large grants and loans

The emphasis should be on gradual extension of forestry and pasturing through economical investment of labour and on the scientific utilization of the existing resources and range development.

C: Organization. Survey and planning would not be too difficult if the VO is committed to the concept of responsible ownership and it is blessed with good managers. Much more difficult than the survey and the plan would be the creation of the organization which would be needed for the cooperative management of the vast area.

Fortunately the rudimentary forms of cooperative management are already visible among the advanced VOs in the shape of collective plantings, appointments of *chowkidars*, control of grazing, payment of specialists etc. Intensive efforts should be made in special villages to help them to further develop the model of future organization.

Advanced Planning

Ownership crisis. Traditionally the territory around the village belonged to the Raja and the Mir. The villagers could only beg or steal from it. Feudal authority was exercised with an iron hand and the forests were well preserved. Now that the iron hand has been removed, the territory is ownerless and derelict. Its resources, instead of being developed, are being ruthlessly depleted. The absence of protective ownership on the one hand, and the increased pressure of population on the other, has hastened the destruction of forests and pastures.

Responsible ownership. I tried to explain the vital necessity of protecting the trees, bushes and grass cover of the mountains through responsible ownership. The functions of responsible ownership would be: (1) Protection, (2) Servicing and (3) Investment.

Scientific utilization. For subsistence farmers, a change of attitude would be essential for operating a large range jointly. They would have to learn to exercise two kinds of ownership: the private and personalized ownership of their small farms and the cooperative ownership of a huge range.

Returns on Investment. I pointed out to them the economics of range management—how the returns on their investments in large scale forestry, pastures and animal husbandry would be many times larger. The intensive labour required for the reclamation and cultivation of cropland would not be required for forestry and pasturage. Range development is suitable for cooperative management rather than small farmers. Another important consideration is that while the small family farms will soon be fragmented, the forests and pastures will remain as a most valuable common property.

Improving Extension Methods. The strategy of consolidation demands the improvement of not only research but also of extension. Full advantage should be taken of the fact that most of the Managers and Chairmen of VOs are literate. Leaflets should be written and distributed widely. The SOs should always have a package of leaflets with them. A quarterly magazine should also be widely distributed. Tapes of successful managers and specialists should be played at VO meetings. Conferences of activists should be held frequently. And the best of them should sometimes tour with the Social Organizers.

Five facts about expansion

1. On account of the nature of its design, AKRSP can be duplicated but its area of operation cannot be extended indefinitely. Hence, if AKRSP projects are desired in other districts, each district should have the same central set-up as in Gilgit. Every district project must be autonomous. It will be impossible to organize, train, supervise and supply VOs of other districts from Gilgit. Each district project must have its own supporting institutions, engineering, training, banking, marketing and monitoring. Extending these services from Gilgit to other districts will prove ineffectual. It would also weaken the programme in Gilgit.

2. Plans for new districts should be made separately and resources obtained separately. There should be no mix-up with Gilgit plans and no transfer of resources. The enormous proportions of the demands from other district may jeopardize development in Gilgit itself.

3. It must be clearly understood that AKRSP, as a private company, can restrict its operation, unlike the government, to a selected region. In fact a private organization must be selective because it does not possess the resources available to the government.

4. It must also be clearly understood that AKRSP is concentrating on activities which belong primarily to the private sector:

a) Village organization

b) Land development
c) Increased productivity
d) Credit and banking
e) Marketing

While there is no conflict with the work of government departments, nevertheless, these activities thrive better under autonomous institutions than under bureaucratic control.

5. In other words, the AKRSP model is relevant for the private sector. If the government wants intensive development they should rehabilitate the IRDP which was designed as a decentralized government programme and has all the components for achieving rapid development of a small region, a thana, tehsil or subdivision. These components are:

a. A markaz with a representative officer from each department and a coordinating development officer
b. A local council and a rural works programme
c. A central cooperative association and bank and a credit and marketing programme
d. Primary cooperatives in every village
e. Regular training classes to manager, model farmers, teachers, imams, midwives etc.

The government has the resources for starting an IRDP in every tehsil. But if it is short of funds, it can find many foreign donors. AKRSP cannot become the surrogate of the government.

Planning by the Villagers[3]

Akhtar Hameed Khan started the proceedings by apologizing for meeting with us after a long time. He wanted to know about the progress and mentioned that from the reports he discerned that the formation of clusters seemed very important. Shoaib Sultan Khan asked Hussain Wali to provide the update. Hussain Wali said, with particular reference to cluster formation, that there were a number of activities that were repetitive and that initially the VOs in the Yasin valley got together to form a cluster, after which VOs in other far-flung valleys started forming supra-VO bodies. At this point Akhtar Hameed Khan inquired about the objectives of forming clusters. It was mostly to ensure timely provision of inputs, replied Hussain Wali. Then Akhtar Hameed Khan wanted to know who suggested cluster formation, the VOs or AKRSP. Hussain Wali explained that with the passage of time, the VOs had started becoming dependent on AKRSP. They felt that they (the VOs) were absolved of all responsibility if they simply informed the SO of their requirement and that AKRSP would then respond and provide them with whatever it was that they needed. Akhtar Hameed Khan wanted to know why this dependency of the people had increased, and about AKRSP's response in reversing the trend. It was basically the lack of any planning on the part of the VOs that gave rise to this situation, explained Hussain Wali. Noor Muhammad while clarifying the situation said that the people started to believe that everything was available with AKRSP and that AKRSP did not have to request any other agency for anything. It was basically to counter this situation that clusters were formed so that the villagers themselves could assume the responsibility of input supply.

Akhtar Hameed Khan commended this development and explained that both the Orangi and Gilgit projects were dealing with a medieval mentality. A distinctive feature of this mentality was that there is no concept of prevention of losses or planning for it. He said that he was a theoretician and would explain the theory behind this. He said that in the Punjab the capitalist agricultural pattern was being followed. There was no concept of village plans and only shop-keepers and money lenders would plan and profit from it. In Russia it was the bureaucrats who undertook planning. In Gilgit, Akhtar Hameed Khan hoped that the Punjab pattern would not be established. In the AKRSP programme area the people expected the government to provide everything, whether it was vaccines, seeds or anything else. Under the socialist model, everything would indeed have to be provided to the village by the government. We, however, were working with the cooperative model and through the development of the clusters, AKRSP had shifted the responsibility for planning back to the villagers. This was a very good development and the private profiteer would be pushed out because of it.

Combining traditional and modern knowledge.[4] Mr Wilkinson noted that our success had been impressive and wondered whether we had had any failures. I replied firstly, that the failure rate in the case of specific projects had been very low, because we had tried to combine traditional knowledge and practice with modern scientific knowledge. Secondly, there was a gray area in the case of management decisions, where a VO's decision not to follow our suggestion may be a VO's 'success' even if it is AKRSP's 'failure'. For example, the evolving nature of the village management of the heifer cattle is clearly a learning process for both AKRSP and the VOs in which, so far, 'success' and 'failure' remain ambiguous terms. Similarly, our initial attempts at assisting VOs with land-use planning were rejected by many VOs. This may be AKRSP's failure, but it was the VO's success, in that it was not overcome by inappropriate advice!

Participation or patronage.[5] Mr Spielman very much appreciated the cooperation extended to him by the entire staff. He spoke very highly of the Village Organizations he had visited and was particularly impressed by the fact that the members of the AKRSP Village Organizations view AKRSP personnel as a resource, not as a patron, and were willing to raise difficult issues.

Flexibility of working through an NGO.[6] The feasibility of replication featured prominently in the discussions. Mr Eqbal Ahmed's query about Shoaib Sultan Khan's experience in varied situations as (1) government servant, (2) an international bureaucrat and now (3) as an international NGO bureaucrat was followed with much interest.

Shoaib Sultan Khan replied that he never had it so good as now. However, bureaucrats in whatever capacity and status have tremendous opportunity and power when in government but require the support of colleagues from other departments, and superiors. His good fortune had been that this support had been forthcoming during his various tenures and fortunately continues to be so even when outside the government.

The fundamental need was to develop a consistent philosophy and to implement the same without regard to personal status and with genuine concern for the intended beneficiaries. The greater dispersal of such a policy could lead to more rapid development of other areas and in general an equally successful replication of the programme content. After the briefing, the team was taken to Hanuchal and Shahtote.

Transformation from traditional to modern management.[7] Masoot VO represents an excellent example of the transformation from the traditional system of management to the modern one. The VO has 40 households and 32 members. The eight households are reported to have walked out of the organization including the previous President Ghulam Raza because they did not want to abide by the decision of the VO about banning free grazing. They refused to pay fines of Rs 3 for small animals and Rs 5 for large animals and lodged a report in the local tehsil against the VO. The tehsil authorities directed the VOs not to impose any fines. However, in case of damage to any individual members' plants or crops, the offending animal could be brought to the tehsil for impounding. The VO members followed the direction and the non-members found that whereas the VO was only fining Rs 3–5, they had to pay more than Rs 10 to retrieve the animal from the tehsil. This compelled the non-members to abide by the rules made by the VO on cattle grazing. According to the VO members, the non-members have realized how beneficial the ban on cattle grazing has been for developing orchards and in cultivating vegetables and although they have still not become members of the VO, they are following its dictates.

Another example of collective management from Masoot is the way they have organized the development of their nursery. The land has been donated to the VO by a member for a period of 20 years and their 5-*kanal* nursery has been divided in 5 parts. Each part has been assigned to a group of 6 members, who will be responsible for developing the nursery in their portion. The VO as a body decided which group will grow what and the income will be distributed once the whole nursery has been fully developed.

Comparing AKRSP Pakistan with AKRSP India[8]

We do not go to the villagers with a preconceived and predetermined portfolio of productive projects. We ask the villagers to identify the projects and we make them solely responsible for the implementation including procurement of material, payment of wages for labour and so on, and its maintenance, through their village organization. Our engineering section only provides technical assistance and supervision. It does not undertake any of the implementation functions. Involvement of the programme staff in procurement of material, keeping or checking of muster rolls, distribution of wages *etc.*, would have not enabled us to undertake over 500 projects in less than five years. These functions have to be performed by the VOs. The Social Organizers ensure that the VOs adhere to the Terms of Partnerships in regard to equitable development and the unit engineer verifies the quality of work and that it is done according to the agreed specifications. The grant money is disbursed in five instalments subject to these checks and verifications, done jointly by the Social Organizer and the unit engineer. Each request for installment is presented in the shape of a VO resolution (in a prescribed format) duly signed by all members, preferably in a meeting attended by the Social Organizer.

This brings us to the characteristics of the Gram Vikas Mandal (GVM) [in India] and the VO. I met members of Pingkot, Mandala, Kuntalpur, Chanderliya and Thoriyali GVMs and held discussions with them. I even held the first dialogue with Pingkot and Kuntelpur GVMs. Unlike VOs, the GVMs were formed subsequent to the initiation of the productive projects and there are no clear-cut terms spelling out the obligations on both sides, forming the basis of partnership between the programme and the GVM. The VOs are formed only after the villagers agree to organization and collective management, the generation of capital through savings and upgrading of human skills by fully participating in the programme's human resource development scheme. The GVMs have not fully grasped the importance of organization and collective management and their regular meetings have not been fully established. Unlike VOs, where a PPI is now only started if the VO comes up with an average saving of Rs 300 per household, the GVM savings are directly linked with the wages earned during implementation of a scheme, with the result that after the completion of the project, the process of savings stops. In some cases the savings have been returned and in others, it has been used for purchase of agricultural inputs thus progressively eating into their equity capital, unlike the VOs which do not touch their savings except by putting in more and more savings. Any withdrawals have to be authorized by the general manager personally, in view of a VO resolution to this effect. In practice, the VOs have never, with the exception of a very few cases, withdrawn from their savings but on the other hand, they have used savings as collateral for getting medium term loans in addition to production or input loans. This has resulted in an accumulation of over Rs 26 million as VO savings, making the setting up of a financial institution owned, operated and managed by VOs, a distinct possibility.

In respect of upgrading of human skills, the GVMs can learn quite a lot from the VO experience which have by now nominated and got trained over 1,500 village level specialists in the fields of agriculture, livestock, marketing, poultry, accounting etc., besides nearly 1,400 managers and presidents of VOs, who attend the monthly managers' conference once in three months at programme headquarters.

Finally this brings me to the important role played by the Social Organization Units (SOUs) in organization and development of the VOs. Without SOUs it would not be an exaggeration to say that the MG and DPOs would not have succeeded in involving the rural populace in the development process. The SOUs are the sheet anchor and eyes and ears of the programme. As the World Bank Report observed, the role and importance of the SOUs is only second to that of the VOs, which is brought home to everyone in AKRSP by the GM's personal conduct and treatment of SOUs.

Let us agree to disagree.[9] I spoke to the GVM at length about the principles of development. One person said that unity was not possible, while others did not seem to agree. One promised that they would do it. This was a strife-ridden village and we should not really have cooperated with them without their cooperation. However, there seemed clear prospects of organizing not one but may be more than one GVM in this village. One member advocated open management as the Pramukh seemed to be doing things without taking them into confidence. There was a great uproar because an ordinary member had objected to malpractice, which the office bearers thought was only their prerogative. I sat in the jeep while the matter was resolved by the Programme Coordinator. In Gilgit another golden principle followed by AKRSP staff is to never get involved in resolving VO disputes. In some VOs disputes dragged on for years but finally got resolved permanently. Decisions forced by outsiders would have been very short lived, besides wasting a lot of the programme staff's time and energy.

Two Years After.[10] The GM then gave some information on the statistics relating to the project area: At present 254 VOs have been formed in the Gilgit District. This covers 88 per cent of the population of the area and comprises 21,241 households. The main indicator of a VO's viability is its saving. By June this year, the VOs had total savings of about Rs 3 million and the latest figure would be much higher.

In reply to a question from the visitors, the GM stated that the VOs deposit their savings in the bank, from where AKRSP gets its figures.

The VOs have so far identified 436 projects. The GM stated that since April this year, new project initiation had been completely halted due to lack of funds. Within 20 days of the good news from CIDA, the number of projects initiated jumped from 131 to 151.

The stoppage since April did have positive aspects, since it tested the durability of the VOs. They remained organized and participated in training programmes and marketing etc. In fact, between April and September the VOs' savings doubled. A question was asked as to why this had occurred. The GM felt that this was an indication that the other components of the programme were as attractive to the VOs as PPIs.

A question was asked whether AKRSP looked at its package components as separate inputs or as an integrated programme to raise the standard of living. The GM replied that although the implementation of the components may be phased, they were part of a unified package.

From Grants to Loans[11]

Highlighting AKRSP's strategy in the second phase of development, Akhtar Hameed Khan observed that the programme should go ahead with PPI projects already planned. At the same time, the second generation of projects should be commenced in villages where PPIs have already been undertaken. The important point to note in this connection was that these post-PPI projects would be pursued entirely on the basis of loans. Akhtar Hameed Khan continued that it was important to explain fully the nature of this new approach, *i.e.* that AKRSP would pursue its second generation of projects through extending short/long term loans to the VOs which had already benefited from a PPI project.

Akhtar Hameed Khan noted that SOs should be briefed on this new policy shift. They could certainly publicize AKRSP's 'One funded PPI for each VO policy'. But at the same time they should make it clear that AKRSP encourages, and will assist their post-PPI projects in a different way—through loans for pastures and forestry development.

Regarding the villagers' apprehension about loans, Akhtar Hameed Khan noted that initially this would be a serious problem. People may not agree to undertake projects on loan basis, but would have to be convinced, just as a physician convinces his patient to agree to surgery so as to remove the cause of his illness. Besides, it should be explained to them that the money which they take as a loan does not go anywhere else. Except for a small portion on explosives it would remain with them since they exchange their labour for it. The loan would be paid back with the money they had earned through their labour, plus with the increased income which will result from the new project undertaken. Moreover, the loan would be serviced through easy installments and over a longer period.

Hussain Wali then reported on the successful experiment of implements which had been gifted to the VO on the basis of savings performance. He appreciated the idea and remarked: 'This was a very good step which helped to concentrate labour and equity capital'. Akhtar Hameed Khan called it 'The working capital' of the villages. Akhtar Hameed Khan suggested transportation as one such tool, which can also help integrate the rural labour and its nascent economy.

The GM noted that five VOs had submitted loan applications in this regard but the bank had declined to entertain their request or was dragging its feet. Akhtar Hameed Khan commented that this was a basic weakness. He said that we needed to set up an institution which would serve as a bank for our village cooperatives. Citing the example of the Comilla project, Akhtar Hameed Khan observed, 'In Comilla the system was very simple. The United Bank served as the banker for our Central Cooperative Bank. We did the loaning ourselves at a service charge of 5 per cent and earned Rs 7.5 *lakh* within a year and a half.' With regard to the AKRSP's loan and credit system, Akhtar Hameed Khan advised that records should be kept at all three levels: loans to individuals, to the VOs and project accounts, so that full information about any defaults would be easily available.

The GM asked Sultan Shahabuddin to devise such a system as the first step towards establishing an independent bank. Akhtar Hameed Khan said that the SOs should not be burdened with these details. They should be provided with ready-made charts so that they can easily collect information about loans/credits in their units, since the managers are managers and not accountants. Akhtar Hameed Khan suggested appointing village accountants like village supervisors in every SOU to avoid gradual deterioration in the credit system.

Cost Effectiveness of Community Participation[12]

Mr Jaffrey was greatly struck by the unit cost of land development projects and considered the package as highly attractive for IDA funding, which, according to him, was as good as a grant. He expressed his willingness to take up the matter with the World Bank as part of a regional development project for the area, once the unit costs were worked out more thoroughly and the cost benefit projections made.

Mr Jaffrey expressed an interest in the forthcoming mid-term evaluation of AKRSP by the World Bank Operations Evaluation Department and did not consider the association of a Planning Division nominee necessary for purposes of lending authenticity and weight to the evaluation. He considered the OED's association good enough for government purposes.

Mr Jaffrey was unhappy at the way his proposal for utilization of funds at the micro level by AKRSP-type VOs had been 'hijacked' and the funds placed at the disposal of the whims of individual MNAs, leaving it absolutely to chance and *'ad hocism'*. He considered AKRSP's most positive feature to be its ability to reach the grassroots, which is so glaringly absent in most government development programmes for the rural areas.

The 'management and organization' of human and capital resources is key to the development of rural areas, which, according to Mr Jaffrey, has been so clearly brought out by AKRSP.

Mr Jaffrey perceived some difficulties in replicating the AKRSP strategy in the provinces of Punjab and Sindh owing to skewed land holdings and presence of powerful vested interests, but considered it well suited for the provinces of Balochistan and NWFP.

On a direct request by Shoaib Sultan Khan to the deputy chairman for helping AKRSP raise Rs 40 crores for the next five years' work in the Northern Areas and the district of Chitral, Mr Jaffrey said that he considered the amount very reasonable in view of the cost effectiveness and high payoff of the AKRSP package. On the way to Baltistan, Mr Jaffrey enquired that if he were to suggest diverting to AKRSP the Rs 110 million allocated for the Satpara Dam, projected to irrigate 10,000 acres, would AKRSP be able to bring more than twice that area of land under irrigation range? Shoaib Sultan Khan responded with a vehement affirmative.

Heroic performance of collective will[13]

The president of Aliabad VO welcomed the administrator and other guests and described the history of the Aliabad channel. He said that there had been an acute shortage of irrigation water in the area comprising 6 villages, which were served by only one *khul*. As a result, there was severe competition for water and at times people even fought over the distribution. When AKRSP arrived in Hunza in 1982, Aliabad and the surrounding villages formed VOs and decided to construct a new channel to increase their water supply.

However, the AKRSP engineers discouraged them, pointing to the immense technical and physical difficulties and the history of failed attempts: in 1925, the then Mir of Hunza had twice tried to have a *khul* constructed and there had been further attempts in 1945, 1947 and 1972, all of them failures. But the people were determined to go ahead and convinced AKRSP to assist them. They raised money to buy a compressor machine, which was taken to the construction site with great difficulty. The project began in January 1984 and took over four years to complete. In the process, three people died. The VO's president described how the channel had been carved through rock and steep mountain sides, and said that everyone, from orphan children to widowed women, had been determined to contribute whatever they could to its construction. Now 200 *kanals* of new land would be irrigated, and increased water supply to existing irrigated land generated.

Clearly, the people of these VOs had decided that their future survival in this area depended on the construction of the channel and had overcome both physical difficulties and social difference in order to make it possible. It seems the 6 VOs had the enthusiastic support of the villagers; there are also 6 active WOs in the area. Given the access to the KKH and the rapidly growing importance of the Hunza valley as a tourist attraction, it seems that production on the new land will find ready markets.

After the president had spoken, the VO leaders accompanied the Administrator and other guests up the steep mountain slope to the site of the *khul*, for the inauguration. The traditional ritual of pouring milk, *ghee* and flour into the flowing waters of the *khul*, symbolizing the hoped-for production, was performed by the Administrator. Looking down at the newly demarcated, yet still barren new land, which would be fed by the waters of the *khul* next year, one could appreciate what immense determination and faith the villagers had displayed and join them in their vision of the future.

NOTES

1. Third visit to AKRSP by Akhtar Hameed Khan—17-30 April 1984, Eleventh visit to AKRSP by Dr Akhtar Hameed Khan, 16-25 September 1989, Ninth visit to AKRSP by Dr Akhtar Hameed Khan, 25 July to 6 August 1987.
2. NFR, 4-9 June 1988 Asian Seminar on Community Participation organized by EDI, World Bank, IFAD, Asian and Pacific Centre for Development (APCD) and UNCRD in collaboration with UNICEF, ADB and Commonwealth Secretariat.
3. NFR—Workshop with Dr Akhtar Hameed Khan at Islamabad Hotel, 19 March 1989.
4. NFR—Visit of Foreign Journalist, 18 November 1987.
5. NFR—Visit of Mr Stephen J. Spielman, Regional Legal Adviser USAID, Islamabad, 5 July 1987.
6. NFR—Visit of Pakistan Administrative Staff College Team, 18 June 1987.
7. NFR—Follow-up Visits, 13 October 1986.
8. NFR—Visit to AKRSP (India), 28 November–10 December 1987.
9. NFR—Visit to AKRSP (India), 28 November–10 December 1987.
10. NFR—Briefing of the CIDA Team and Mr Nazeer Ladhani of AKF Canada, 21 October 1984.
11. NFR—Dr Akhtar Hameed Khan's briefing with Engineering, MER, Accounts, Women's Section, Extension and Training and the Management, 19 September 1984.
12. Visit of the Deputy Chairman/Secretary General, Planning Commission/Planning Division Mr V.A. Jaffrey to AKRSP, 5 June 1986.
13. NFR—Opening of Aliabad Channel by the Administrator, Northern Areas, 8 October 1988.

14

Dr Akhtar Hameed Khan

MEMORIAL ADDRESS BY SHOAIB SULTAN KHAN

I wonder how I can truly do justice to the memory of a person of the stature of Akhtar Hameed Khan, who passed away in 1999. Since I met him I had always looked upon him as my mentor and teacher. I was his disciple. His presence was overpowering, commanding respect not out of fear but out of intellectual superiority which belies description. I feel rather like a pygmy trying to describe a giant. My relationship with Akhtar Hameed Khan was like that of Boswell's with Dr Johnson. I can at best be a biographer or a historian recounting my association with him. I am unable to capture his innate qualities, his intellect, his vision, his depth of knowledge and scholarship, his understanding of the religions of the world—his Sufi streak, his Buddhist way of life, his understanding of Islam and the Quran—his academic work and his poetic abilities. Nor can I fully convey his love for his family and above all his mission of helping suffering humanity and his passion to benefit his countrymen by his experience. I have captured only a few facets of a personality which was so versatile and complete that in the words of Shakespeare 'that nature might stand up and say to all the world: This was a man'. Akhtar Hameed Khan was a complete human being, who lived by the precept of simple living and high thinking.

I once asked him why he resigned from the ICS.[1] It was generally assumed that he had resigned in protest against the policies of the colonial regime. His answer, however, was typical of his personality and his approach to life. He said that he had learnt a great deal from the British and had realized that they had nothing more to offer him. The British were masters of good administration centred on establishing *Pax Britannica* but they had little to offer when it came to alleviating the suffering of impoverished humanity. He did, however, praise the British for respecting his views and his way of living and for never interfering with his personal life.

In order to understand the problems of the poor, Akhtar Hameed Khan decided to quit the prestigious civil service. He became a labourer, apprenticing himself to a blacksmith. However, he realized one day that God had not created him to be a labourer. He decided to join the Jamia Miilia in Delhi, headed at that time by Dr Zakir Hussain, who would eventually become the President of India. Akhtar Hameed Khan became disillusioned with the Jamia Miilia, as he had previously been disillusioned with Allama Mashriqi. He was a pacifist and a follower of the Buddha's teachings. He despaired at the hero worship prevalent in Pakistan. Sometimes he used to compare Pakistan to Maharaja Ranjeet Singh's regime, when the Khalsa Army boasted that they would fly their flag on the Red Fort. The maharaja used to beg his generals to desist from adventurism and never to take on the British army. Immediately on Ranjeet Singh's death, the chauvinistic Khalsa engaged the British and lost the Sikh kingdom.

I first heard of Akhtar Hameed Khan from the younger brother of a Bengali colleague of mine, while I was working as an assistant magistrate and collector (under training) in 1956. The young man very proudly announced that the principal of his College at Comilla had resigned from the prestigious ICS. He added that the principal was a man of very simple habits and was always dressed in homespun cloth. I paid no attention, assuming he was exaggerating the man's qualities. Three years later, however, I came face to face with Akhtar Hameed Khan. He had chosen my sub-division (Brahaman Baria) in which to conduct the field-orientation training of the faculty members of the Comilla Academy. I knew that whatever the Academy's instructional staff had seen at Brahaman Baria had come under microscopic inspection, as I had read the faculty meeting reports. I was, therefore, pleased when Akhtar Hameed Khan remarked when we were introduced that, 'You were put under close scrutiny and came out with flying colours.' At the Brahaman Baria railway station he disappeared quietly and without ceremony, refusing my offer of a lift in my borrowed jeep.

This initial meeting in 1959 was followed by many visits to the Academy and more than a year later, at the request of Akhtar Hameed Khan, the chief secretary of East Pakistan assigned me to help organize a course for additional deputy commissioners (Development), for the Academy. I was overwhelmed and somewhat embarrassed when Akhtar Hameed Khan came to the railway station to receive me and personally escorted me to the Abhoy Ashram, the abode of the Comilla Academy at that time. I was shown into the guesthouse cottage, only to be told that the previous occupant had died there of T.B., having been ill for 15 years. Perhaps Akhtar Hameed Khan read my worried thoughts on my face because he assured me that the event had taken place many years ago and the cottage had since been fully disinfected. Although I did help in organizing and drawing up the course outline, I was unfortunately unable to join the course. Thereafter, I ran into Akhtar Hameed Khan in Lahore a couple of times and was always accused of having 'run away'.

In 1971, I visited Comilla again as a member of a 3-person group that had been put together to study the Comilla Project. The idea was to undertake a similar project in West Pakistan, preferably in Peshawar District, under the aegis of the Pakistan Academy for Rural Development (PARD). The director, another PARD faculty member and myself, as deputy commissioner of Peshawar, made up the group. We met Akhtar Hameed Khan, who was busy writing a monograph on his recent tour of 20 thanas.

I was keen to visit my own previous sub-division and Akhtar Hameed Khan encouraged me to do so. I thus revisited, after ten years, Sarial, Brahaman Baria and Quasba Thanas, I found it a different world altogether. The whole countryside had been transformed in the intervening ten years. There was an excellent network of roads and thriving markets all along the way. The produce was in abundance and the Thana centres were pulsating with energy and activity. Even the Brahaman Baria Thana (which had the Tehsil Offices also) Development Centre was so crowded with people trying to learn new techniques or obtain services that one could only marvel at the effectiveness and utility of the Thana Centres. When I asked Akhtar Hameed Khan's advice about replicating the project in West Pakistan, he was very candid and suggested that I take a Thana in Peshawar District and develop it as a model for replication in the rest of the country. Unfortunately, our return to West Pakistan in the wake of the March 1971 events and my subsequent posting from Peshawar, brought the whole plan to naught.

In October 1972, I learnt from my friend Tariq Siddiqi, whose intellectual depth even Akhtar Hameed Khan used to praise, that Akhtar Hameed Khan was visiting Punjab at the invitation of the then chief minister of Punjab. I suggested that Akhtar Hameed Khan might also pay us a visit. A few days later he arrived in Peshawar. He was very discouraged by his experience in Punjab and indicated his pessimism.

I showed him around the Daudzai Markaz. He felt happy with what he saw but was still doubtful whether the policy-makers in the province wanted or would allow this type of work to continue. I tried to assure him in every possible way that this was feasible, adding that I was convinced that both in the bureaucratic and the political circles there was support for this project. I arranged for him to meet with the chief secretary and with the governor. It so happened that when he called on the Governor there was a cabinet meeting in session, which gave Akhtar Hameed Khan the opportunity to meet the Chief Minister and some provincial ministers also. After the meeting Akhtar Hameed Khan was still not so sure and his response was definitely not positive.

He was of the view that the policy-makers did not understand the programme. On my rejoinder that we should not worry about their understanding so long as we continued getting their support, Akhtar Hameed Khan remained unconvinced. I could see the wisdom of his remark when, a few days later, at a function of the academy, the governor publicly had a dig at me and said that a few years ago a project had been started at Sardar Garhi and everybody was taken there and now one found nothing there. He added 'Similarly Shoaib Sultan Khan has set up a Daudzai and everybody is being taken there'.

IRDP, with AKH as its chairman, had been formulated in 1972 by a committee established by the government. However, in implementing the IRDP Committee's report, Akhtar Hameed Khan regretted that he had presented an architect's plan but the government had only committed to building the dome without taking note of the foundation and the walls. He used to put great emphasis on the theory of development which, he maintained, was as precise as the law of gravity and any attempt to go against the principles of development was like building crooked walls.

Akhtar Hameed Khan left with a half-hearted promise to return. I finally persuaded him to visit us before taking up his assignment abroad. By March 1973, the Markaz had been well established but we were almost in a blind alley. The mere appointment and placement of Markaz functionaries at Daudzai was not showing any tangible results; nor was it creating any impact on the public. In fact, every time I went to the Markaz, my heart sank when I saw how deserted it was. Although visitors praised us and encouraged us, I knew in my heart that we were literally doing nothing to solve the people's problems. Akhtar Hameed Khan came, looked at the situation and drew up a blueprint of work for us for the upcoming year. He also encouraged us greatly, assuring us that we were working on the right lines and that the difficulties we were encountering were a sure indication of our making headway.

After his departure from Peshawar and before going abroad to Michigan University, he wrote me a letter in which he said 'My stay at Peshawar was delightful for me, physically and intellectually, except that sometimes I feel that your hospitality to me was excessive. I have told my friends here how you picked me up from the dustbin and used me. I shall remain deeply interested in the Daudzai Project. It is like an island of sincerity in a sea of hypocrisy'.

A year later, true to his promise, he did return from America. At Peshawar Akhtar Hameed Khan was in his element again after the trauma of East Pakistan. Reading monthly progress reports of the Daudzai Project had made him leave the comforts of Michigan University and, at my invitation, to participate in an International Seminar the Academy was arranging. He offered to come back permanently on the condition that he would not accept more than Rs 1,500 per month. When I insisted that he would have to accept a salary equivalent to my emoluments as joint secretary to the federal government, he agreed to accept Rs 2,100/-. In Peshawar he found his old friends, especially Professor Durrani of the Engineering College. Khan Sahib used to argue with him, debunking his spiritual claims, and Durrani Sahib would always laugh these arguments away. Once I asked Durrani Sahib why he didn't respond to Akhtar Hameed Khan's criticism. He laughed and confided that when he saw Akhtar Hameed Khan angry he felt the love and affection for him that he would feel for a small child and it brought out in him the desire to pick up Akhtar Hameed Khan and caress him as he would an innocent child.

My wife Musarrat persuaded him to publish a diary, written in Urdu, of his stay in America. She wrote the preface which Khan Sahib greatly enjoyed as she wrote that to some people Akhtar Hameed Khan appears a fraud and to many others a saint. The reality is that he is a perfect human being.

Daudzai attained widespread acclaim, especially from foreigners and foreign aid-giving agencies. After his visit to Daudzai, Edgar Owens wrote to me 'Thanks to you, there is at least one good rural project in Pakistan. How do we persuade presidents and prime ministers to make Daudzai the basis for nation-wide rural development? When someone can answer that question, one can begin to believe again in a better future for all of us'.

The success and fame of the Daudzai project aroused jealousy and hostility in certain quarters. The Pakistan Academy for Rural Development became the target of a whispering campaign and sometimes of open propaganda that it was becoming a provincialised Academy and was only providing services to the NWFP. The factual position supported by relevant data proved these allegations false and baseless, and yet attempts to subvert the academy's work and the Daudzai project continued. The academy made it abundantly clear to the rural development wing of the federal government that the principles on the basis of which the Daudzai Model had been developed were as relevant in Daudzai as anywhere else in the country. In fact, Professor Guy Hunter, commenting on *Daudzai, a Case Study* pointed out 'the important points of principle which have been applied in Daudzai...are relevant to the Rural Development projects in almost any context'. Guy Hunter circulated over 100 copies of the case study, later published in the Journal *Agricultural Administration* from Reading, England. The provinces, especially Sindh and Punjab at the policy level (the chief minister and chief Secretary) did express interest in Daudzai and the possibilities of starting projects in those provinces on these lines. The academy always endeavoured to be of service to other provinces. In fact, the director made many visits to Lahore and Karachi to canvass for the acceptance of the academy's approach to rural development. But it must be appreciated that the academy could only canvass, and had no authority to force any province to accept its approach. Belatedly the federal rural development wing realized the need for giving encouragement to the academy in its IRD work. But alas! it was too late.

On the basis of an invective submitted by a disgruntled trainee (a Tehsil level officer) who was sent back by the academy in the fifth week of the course for indifference and lack of interest in training, the new Chief Secretary NWFP and *ex-officio* chairman of the Academy Board of Governors commented on the allegation that Akhtar Hameed Khan was fanning a Sindhudesh Movement at the Academy:

> I am enclosing a copy of the explanation of Dr Iftikhar Ali Khilji (Assistant District Health Officer) for your prompt consideration and comments. As you would notice he has made some telling observations and asked some leading questions as regards what the Academy is doing and what some of its staff members are saying. From the way he has questioned certain loyalties, disputed certain *bona fides*, mentioned certain names and

criticized certain views, one would seriously wonder whether the Academy was serving its true purpose. You are indeed the right person to tell'.

I did try to convince the chief secretary that the allegations were baseless. My initial explanation was followed by another attempt during an interview, at Akhtar Hameed Khan's request, which was followed by Akhtar Hameed Khan's written explanation—all making the point that the allegations were baseless. But the Chief Secretary was probably not convinced of our *bona fides* or maybe he was? However, on 8 August 1975 while opening the 'fresh receipts', the following words stared me in the face:

Notification No. 812/75-AI dated 7 August 1975:

Mr SHOAIB SULTAN KHAN, Director, Pakistan Academy for Rural Development, Peshawar, in Grade 20, is appointed as Officer on Special Duty, Establishment Division, Rawalpindi in his own grade with immediate effect and until further orders.

My exit from PARD resulted in Akhtar Hameed Khan's immediate resignation from the advisorship of the academy. He joked to his wife that he was going to go back to Karachi to work as a labourer on his brother's house which was under-construction. Khan Sahib would let pass no opportunity to tease her. Many a time she and I used to gang up against him. She always used to reassure me 'you were his most coveted disciple and behind your back he expresses great concern and solicitude for you'.

I wrote to the chief secretary that posterity would ask 'who were the people responsible for this debacle, for having deprived the poor of this province to get out of poverty'. The greatest social scientist Pakistan had produced was at the disposal of the province but no one cared. Akhtar Hameed Khan went back to Michigan and I felt great anguish to have subjected him to the whims and mercy of people who had no idea what a great person he was. I was subjected to an investigation by the FIA for indulging in subversion through the Daudzai project approach and when cleared of these baseless charges, decided to seek protection of the UN umbrella and left the country.

My new pastures first took me to Japan and then to Sri Lanka. By now Akhtar Hameed Khan had come back to Pakistan and initiated the now world famous Orangi Pilot Project (OPP) supported by the late Agha Hasan Abedi. Akhtar Hameed Khan described his first meeting with Abedi, in which he asked Akhtar Hameed Khan to come up with a grandiose project befitting the image of the now defunct BCCI. In his next meeting Akhtar Hameed Khan presented OPP's plan asking for a few *lakhs* of rupees as against the millions which Abedi wanted him to take. At one time, once a reluctant Abedi had agreed to his plans, Akhtar Hameed Khan wanted me to come and work with him at OPP. I was invited for an interview accompanied by Akhtar Hameed Khan who briefed me that Abedi was like a tsar. In the meanwhile Robert Shaw of the Aga Khan Foundation (AKF) approached Akhtar Hameed Khan to suggest a suitable person for initiating the Aga Khan Rural Support Programme (AKRSP) in the Northern Areas of Pakistan. On my invitation Akhtar Hameed Khan came to Sri Lanka and advised me to return to Pakistan. Having been bitten once I told both my well wishers—the BCCI and the AKF—to secure my services on deputation from UNICEF, my employer in Sri Lanka. Agha Hasan Abedi and His Highness the Aga Khan wrote to the Executive Director of UNICEF Mr James Grant. Since UNICEF had collaborated with the Aga Khan Foundation my deputation to AKF was agreed to for five years. Akhtar Hameed Khan was quite pleased. The only reason he had wanted me to come to OPP was to deal with the local officialdom as, according to him, the people of his generation in government had now given way to a new generation whom he called *ghatia* (petty) and considered me to be better equipped to deal with them. Later on in Tasneem Siddiqi, Arif Hasan and Parveen Rehman he found an excellent team who are still keeping Akhtar Hameed Khan's flag flying, not only in Karachi but in many towns of Pakistan, and abroad.

During my stay in the Northern Areas, Akhtar Hameed Khan made twelve visits and the twelve reports[2] serve as the best text book on poverty reduction programmes that I have read or seen anywhere in the world. I was shocked when, on his first visit to Gilgit, he advised me to forget about Comilla and Daudzai. Whereas the earlier two programmes were implemented and supported by the government, AKRSP had no such advantage or disadvantage. Comilla and Daudzai both showed the fickleness of dependency on government. Although the conceptual package embracing organization, upgrading of human skills and the generation of capital through savings remained unchanged, the government was supplemented by an independent and autonomous support organization endowed with adequate human, technical and monetary resources. He compared AKRSP to the Joint Commission for Relief and Reconstruction (JCRR) set up by the

Americans in Taiwan in the wake of the Kuomintang defeat at the hands of the Communists. In a more expansive mood he compared me to Montgomery—the way he amassed massive resources before launching the assault. He always decried high salaries and extravagance. I would always accuse him of being an exploiter and insensitive to others who could not live on Rs 5,000 per month as he used to do. He would relent in the case of others but never in his own.

He used to immensely enjoy his visits to the Northern Areas despite physical hardships. Besides travelling on tortuous and dangerous roads in the programme area, many a time, due to inclement weather resulting in cancellation of PIA flights, he wouldn't hesitate for a moment to embark on the 600 plus km journey on the Karakoram Highway (KKH). He would endorse Guy Hunter's comment when he came to visit AKRSP that this was not a rural development programme; it was a heroic programme.

Despite Akhtar Hameed Khan's full involvement in OPP, his heart was still in rural development. He used to say *Chor chori say jata hai heera pheri say nahin jata*' ('A thief may give up theft but will not desist from fraud'.). In fact, he persuaded me to give a small grant from the National Rural Support Programme (NRSP) in the early 1990s to initiate a rural development project in the villages surrounding Karachi and persuaded his son Akbar to come back from Canada and take charge of the rural component of OPP.

During his visits to AKRSP, he used to spend hours with the field staff and the activists and get to the bottom of the rural situation. Every time I accompanied him, I used to learn something new. He was a walking encyclopedia. His knowledge was fathomless. When on his visit to Sri Lanka, he asked me to take him to a Buddhist monastery to meet a monk he surprised everyone there by reciting the *Dhammapadda* in the original Pali which even the monks could not understand because they had learnt only the Sinhalese translation. He used to caution me never to go to the original sources in matters of religion. He would say 'You will be in for a shock [when you see] what interpreters have made of the original and any challenge to their interpretation would be fought tooth and nail, forcing you to retreat for the sake of your own skin'. He was greatly influenced by Buddha's teachings and often used to call himself a Buddhist Muslim. He would have chosen Buddha's way and desisted of worldly desires but he said I love my family too much. I can't leave them. But in adversity he would always seek solace in Buddha's saying 'This world is full of *dukha* (suffering)'.

If AKRSP had the Aga Khan as its founder and inspiration, Akhtar Hameed Khan was indeed the mentor and guide of the programme. AKRSP was initiated at a time when Akhtar Hameed Khan had reached the conclusion that any programme which depends on foreign aid and assistance will not be sustainable. He used to contrast Comilla with the Chinese Commune and the difference between the two he clearly saw, was of outside dependence and self-reliance. In OPP he finally succeeded in mobilizing local resources from the community to undertake development. When he first came to Gilgit, he chided me for offering a development partnership which nobody would refuse because of the element of subsidy. He insisted that the people themselves should raise the resources for whatever they want to do or if they don't have the capital, they should take loans but no grants. However, when I took him to some of the villages and he clearly saw that unlike Karachi or Orangi, the poor villagers of the Northern Areas had no regular income or employment opportunities, he relented and agreed to the AKRSP policy of a one-time grant for a productive activity not only for their economic empowerment but also as an investment in their institution building at the grassroots. Through the holistic approach under the guidance of Akhtar Hameed Khan, AKRSP succeeded in doubling the income of the people in ten years according to the two evaluations undertaken by the World Bank in the first decade.

Unfortunately, when the stage came to put Akhtar Hameed Khan's vision of self-reliance in its comprehensive form into practice through AKRSP, the experts in Geneva felt AKRSP had reached '*terra incognita*' and started strategizing a new direction. Akhtar Hameed Khan's advice was considered redundant and dismissed as more of the same and a golden opportunity to develop a self-reliant, self-sustaining rural development programme for poverty reduction was lost. Akhtar Hameed Khan felt very dejected and I felt helpless before the superior wisdom of Geneva-based AKF experts and accepted UNDP's offer to take lessons from AKRSP to South Asia.

I tried getting Akhtar Hameed Khan interested in the National Rural Support Programme (NRSP). Initially, he was very sceptical of my having accepted an endowment of Rs 500 million from the government for NRSP. He had reached the conclusion that in Pakistan there was no government and no governance. He used to quote Dante's hell as the equivalent of the Pakistan government which had these words inscribed on the gate 'All ye who enter, give up hope'. With some reluctance he agreed to visit NRSP regularly and encouraged us by saying 'NRSP is a great national asset. It is our last hope. I also tell you, yours is no easy job'. His apprehensions about the danger of supping with the government came to the fore when the government of the day wanted NRSP to return the five hundred million rupees given to it. Fortunately, on Akhtar Hameed Khan's advice, the money had already been converted into an endowment, and when the government demanded that all the directors resign and liquidate the company, Akhtar Hameed Khan being one of the directors, reminded the Board of its moral responsibility to NRSP's clientele, the 100,000 (at that time, now the number has risen to over 500,000) rural households and the staff of NRSP, and carried the day with him against the liquidation of NRSP.

Once when I asked him if I would have to wear *khaddar* (homespun cloth) like him to do the work he was doing, he retorted 'You don't have to become a *behropia*' (masquerade). Don't insult the intelligence of the people. They will recognize your true worth in any garb.' In the Northern Areas he used to remind me that 'Your western dress or hat or travel by helicopter has made no difference to poor people in recognizing your real worth'.

My leaving AKRSP greatly saddened him for he felt that another opportunity to develop a self-reliant model for Pakistan was lost. I missed terribly the regular contact I used to have with him in AKRSP. He concentrated more and more on urban development and when I would complain to him supported by his wife, about not giving me enough time, he chided me for not concentrating on developing and replicating models at home, and instead, running abroad all the time. He was most solicitous about my health and sometimes would innocently ask me 'Do you really need to earn so much money?' He would never understand that I did not need the money for myself but like him I also loved my family and wanted to give them everything in the world. He had already seen me living in a small room without modern amenities in the elephant country of the Mahaweli forests in Sri Lanka, or in the small apartment in Gilgit for fifteen years. Anyway, I was happy that he had started finding new disciples and the complaint he made in 1983 in the following speech was true no more:

'Nowadays there is a curious reluctance, especially among the younger generation to understand and learn. Everyone seems to think he is a master. It is strange because Masters are not born. What my sneering friends dismissed as my *charisma* was an acquired skill, a skill acquired after a long period of apprenticeship under British, Gandhian and American masters, a skill further sharpened by the study of many successful models in other countries—Japan, Taiwan, Yugoslavia, China, India and Israel. I never felt ashamed of my long and multiple discipleship. I never pretended to be an original thinker. I thought I could teach after I had devoted much time and labour to learning from many sources. When I was young I accepted the wise precepts of Khwaja Hafiz: *'Nasihat gosh kun janan ki as jan dost tar darand javanan-i-saadatmand pindi-piri-dana ra'.*

'As I grew old I began to think, perhaps wrongly, that I have not grown old in vain, that throughout my long life I have been a good student; therefore, in my old age I could be a good teacher. In my delusion I thought that at last I too had become a *pir-i-dana* (a wise old man) and I could give guidance to *jawanan-i-saadatmand* (enlightened young men). Alas, in twenty years, only one enlightened young man Shoaib Sultan Khan cherished me as a worthy teacher. He applied my methods, of course with necessary modifications, first in Daudzai and then in Mahaweli. And now he is applying them with further refinement and thoroughness in Gilgit. He has definitely disproved the obscurantist charisma theory. Is it my fault that I found only one enlightened young man?'

Despite his modesty, the fact is that more than four of his disciples received the Magsaysay Award, which is perhaps a record in the history of the Magsaysay Award Foundation. Akhtar Hameed Khan got the award in 1963. I was fortunate to be given the award in 1992. (See Appendix 14.1 for my acceptance speech).

He used to tell with great glee that his contemporaries in the ICS, after his resignation from the service, used to call him a fool but a good fool. I found him most gullible. He would accept everyone at his or her face value and many a time he was disappointed. He could not think ill of anyone because his heart was so pure and so full of innocence. One of my relatives who had retired as a marine chief engineer and had also been the Managing Director of the Pakistan Automobile Corporation was introduced by me to him. Very soon he won over Akhtar Hameed Khan's heart, so much so that he started grooming him as his successor. Very soon Akhtar Hameed Khan realized his folly and for the sake of OPP had to get rid of him. In this unjust and crooked world, the dismissed employee easily succeeded in concocting false allegations against Akhtar Hameed Khan and blasphemy cases were instituted against Akhtar Hameed Khan at Multan and in Karachi. We all knew these were false allegations. Dr Tariq Siddiqi even got written statements from religious scholars in defence of Akhtar Hameed Khan but his persecution continued. Dr Inayatullah mobilized public opinion in Islamabad against this injustice and Fayyaz Baqir approached all his contacts in Multan.

When I had the opportunity at a dinner hosted by the prime minister, I spoke to him about the injustice to Akhtar Hameed Khan. He agreed to see him and Qazi Alimullah arranged the meeting. The prime minister listened to Akhtar Hameed Khan for nearly an hour but I knew from his expression he was not listening because Akhtar Hameed Khan only spoke of development and did not realize he had gone to him to talk about his blasphemy cases. After the meeting Akhtar Hameed Khan observed the PM did not understand what he was saying. When I asked him 'why didn't you speak about your blasphemy case', he replied, 'Do you know, when Monim Khan, Governor of East Pakistan used to complain against me to President Ayub, the latter used to brush away all complaints by retorting Akhtar Hameed Khan is the only person in Pakistan who never comes to me for any personal favour'. Anyway, the prime minister ordered the withdrawal of the cases against Akhtar Hameed Khan. The request of the Government of Sindh in Karachi was accepted by the presiding judge and the case was allowed to be withdrawn. However, the case registered in Multan was not allowed to be withdrawn by the court despite the Punjab government's request and remained pending till Akhtar Hameed Khan's death.

OPP gave him great satisfaction. I often used to visit him in Karachi. He would show me the new OPP premises designed by Arif Hasan and quote Shakespeare's jester who used to point to his rather not too beautiful beloved, exclaiming 'She is not much but she is mine'. OPP may not be too grandiose in the eyes of Mr Abedi but Akhtar Hameed Khan was very happy with it. He would advise me against grandeur and too fast an expansion. His greatest qualities were flexibility and an open mind. He used to preach an 'organic pragmatic sociological' approach. I saw how in AKRSP he adapted the Comilla and Daudzai experience and could immediately discern the differences between the situation obtaining in Karachi for OPP and the conditions in the Northern Areas for AKRSP.

At one time he vehemently argued against setting up support organizations and advocated using existing NGOs as support mechanisms. He felt I was unnecessarily wasting resources in replicating AKRSP-type structures all over the country in the shape of rural support programmes. However, when he found out after collaborating with more than 60 existing NGOs that only two or three were honest and the others cheated OPP, he had no hesitation in making a public admission that he was wrong and declared publicly that RSPs are lucky that they are not like the traditional NGOs. His organic pragmatic, sociological approach often used to confuse people. They would declare that Akhtar Hameed Khan had changed. They would not realize that he had the vision and foresight to adapt strategies to evolving situations. In the lanes of Orangi organizing people on the lines of village organizations in the Northern Areas was not only difficult but also useless; and when there were no organizations, basing OPP's credit programme on savings was futile. He crafted new structures and new designs suitable for the evolving situation, keeping organic, pragmatic and sociological dimensions in view. He had become a strong believer in self-reliance. In a talk at NRSP, he described the situation:

> As I look back, I realize that there is one main feature in Pakistan which is very disturbing; the failure of governance. Things, which were done competently in the colonial past, are neglected. Let me give you an example. In the Punjab, the world's largest irrigation network was built by Indian experts, the chief engineer might have been an Englishman but he had worked in India for 20 to 30 years. He was not a London-based consultant but an Indian officer and all his assistants were Indians.
>
> Now take, for instance, the sewerage system in Karachi. Its last expansion took place in Ayub Khan's time. Since then it has been grossly neglected and is all silted up and choked. We are sitting on a time bomb. Now what has been done to rectify Karachi sewerage? The Government of Pakistan and the Karachi Water and Sewerage Board (KWSB) has rushed to the World Bank and the Asian Development Bank and asked for loans. The first condition of loans is that the banks call in foreign consultants. So, foreign consultants came and they recommended the most modern system, which was not only ten times more expensive than the old system we had, but was also inoperable in Karachi. It was too deep and sophisticated. It needed robots to clean it. In the old system, the *nalas* could be cleaned by scavengers, as they only had to go down 8 feet instead of 30 feet.

We have been researching this problem in Karachi for the last 8-9 years and we are lucky that we have won our fight with the Asian Bank and the World Bank who are willing to accept our alternative model (the local design) which is much cheaper, functional and already connected to thousands of sewers. But our problem is the Sewerage Board's Foreign Aid Section, which is as willing to give up the foreign loan as a heroin addict is willing to give up heroin. They are not willing to forego the thrills and the highs that they get from dollar loans.

Akhtar Hameed Khan had no complaint against the World Bank, ADB or IMF but he used to describe them as bad bankers who unlike good bankers keep on giving loans and increasing the debt burden of their clients.

Despite the gloom enveloping the country, Akhtar Hameed Khan could always see the brighter side. He spoke of the resilience and success of the informal sector. He used to challenge anyone to find a beggar in Orangi. He had great faith in the people—in their willingness to do things themselves to improve their situation. All they needed, according to him, were support organizations and level playing fields. He used to say, 'In Pakistan development will not come from the top. It will come from the bottom and it shall happen in pockets—one island formed here and one island there and one island will be made by you'.

On his last visit to Islamabad when I mentioned Jahangir Tareen's request to visit Lodhran to initiate a sewerage and sanitation model for small townships, he readily agreed to go to Lodhran despite his earlier disappointment at nothing coming out of the chief minister's visit to OPP. He took a keen interest in supervising the development of the model in Lodhran. In fact, his last email to me from the United States was about Lodhran.

Akhtar Hameed Khan was the very epitome of the principle of simple living and high thinking. In his non-rural development garb his humility and generosity as a man, was amazing. His rapport with the rustic, the non-genteel, the labour, the lower government functionaries and the like was inimitable. He was absolutely at ease with them as much as he was uncomfortable with the pseudo intellectuals and experts. He neither knew evil nor could perceive evil and thus was very gullible in judging people. He was often deceived by unscrupulous persons, the experience leaving him hurt and confused. He had no cunning and accepted everything on its face value. Why such an open, forthright, honest and simple person should have ever been misunderstood was something beyond my comprehension.

Akhtar Hameed Khan passed away in the United States where he was visiting his beloved daughter, three days before the change in government in Pakistan. Tariq Aziz persuaded a willing General Pervez Musharraf to posthumously honour Akhtar Hameed Khan by conferring on him a *Nishan-i-Imtiaz*.

In conclusion I will repeat what I have often said. 'In all my travels throughout the world, I have never come across a person of the stature of Akhtar Hameed Khan. I sometimes wonder if Pakistan really made the best use of the unique experience with which he was so willing and keen to benefit his countrymen and women. But now it is too late even to ask this question. The country has missed the opportunity of a century'.

NOTES

1. Indian Civil Service.
2. *Twelve Reports on AKRSP*. The Aga Khan Rural Support Programme. Gilgit: Northern Areas, 1994.

Section III
Scaling Up and Replication

15

Scaling Up by the Government

PROGRAMME EXPANSION

The founding fathers of AKRSP had envisaged two objectives for AKRSP: doubling the income of the households in the Northern Areas and Chitral and developing a replicable model of rural development.

The first indication that AKRSP was demonstrating a potential for replication was voiced by the Director of USAID, Rocky Staples, on his visit to the NAs in 1987. Rocky asked me if any other province in Pakistan would be interested in initiating a programme like AKRSP. NWFP came to my mind immediately because the Chief Secretary Sahibzada Imtiaz, in every meeting with him, would ask me to initiate a programme in the Sarhad. However, his condition was that such programmes could not be implemented by government departments and hence must be done by AKRSP. Akhtar Hameed Khan had strictly forbidden me from making any attempt at expansion of AKRSP beyond its current geographical limits. The only viable route was to replicate by facilitating the setup of an AKRSP-type independent and autonomous not for profit joint stock company with its own Board of Directors and Chief Executive. Rocky offered US$5 million if NWFP would be willing to replicate AKRSP. The NWFP was indeed the pioneer in initiating AKRSP-type development in 1972 through the Daudzai Project which, within three years, had not only spread to 30 of 110 Thanas but the Development Commissioner, the late Masoodur Rauf, had even got a plan approved by ECNEC at a development outlay of Rs 500 million to cover the entire province. Why it did not happen I have already described in the earlier chapter relating to my first visit to the Northern Areas.

The Chief Minister Arbab Jahangir, who knew me well, expressed keen interest in the USAID proposal. In the meantime, however, the national government changed. Sartaj Aziz and Chaudhry Anwar Aziz, both federal ministers who were trying their utmost to incorporate AKRSP into the local government structure, much to my serious reservation, also left the scene, as did Arbab Jahangir. When the new government threw out the local government structure of the previous regime, lock, stock and barrel, Sartaj Aziz understood the reasons for my reservations. Chaudhry Anwar Aziz does not give up easily. One day I was pleasantly surprised to be invited to make a presentation before the new prime minister, arranged at the behest of Chaudhry Anwar Aziz.

The prime minister listened to my presentation and even viewed the film *Valleys in Transition* but commented that it was a revolutionary programme which would be very difficult to implement, especially in her province where there was so much dissension and discord at the grassroots. Anwar Aziz stood up and remarked 'Prime Minister! You have been elected to implement difficult programmes'. She retorted 'Don't give me a sales pitch'. A few days later Salman Faruqui showed me two letters which had been written at the behest of the PM to the Chief Ministers Aftab Sherpao and Qaim Ali Shah, both belonging to her party, commending AKRSP. A couple of months later when I met the PM at Shandur Polo ground, she complained about my not starting the programme in Larkana. On my submission that she had never asked me to do so, she commented that she had been given the impression that I was after the Peoples Works Programme funds. I was invited by Chief Minister Sindh to give a briefing on AKRSP, which I did, but nothing much happened.

In NWFP, a number of meetings were held with USAID, AKF and provincial government representatives participating, but finally it was Aftab Sherpao who approved it, despite strong departmental opposition. He told me that he only did it because he had come to know that I was behind it. I knew Aftab very well on account of my friendship with his elder brother, the late Hayat Sherpao.

The Sarhad Rural Support Corporation (SRSC) was set up in 1989 and within a couple of years, due to the Pressler Amendment, faced a financial crisis. It goes to the credit of the first CEO of SRSC Javed Majid, fully supported by Chairman Azam Khan that he kept the organization alive by agreeing to implement government development projects on terms and conditions laid down by the government. This greatly diluted and changed the AKRSP approach but kept the organization alive. Later on, the support to SRSC by the Dutch NGO NOVIB, enabled SRSC to get back on the rails. Feroz Shah, as CEO, worked extremely hard to revive and reinstate the AKRSP approach in SRSC.

The setting up of the Pakistan Poverty Alleviation Fund (PPAF) and their funding to SRSC greatly supported social mobilization. With Masoodul Mulk as CEO, SRSC (now SRSP, the Sarhad Rural Support Programme) is indeed in very safe hands. Despite its chequered progress, SRSP did not lose its autonomy and independence and weathered even the worst onslaught. Today SRSP has an independent Board of Directors with a most conscientious, dedicated and true volunteer as Chairperson, Mrs Munawar Humayun. Even Azam Khan, as the first Chairman of SRSC, though a civil servant, acted only in his personal capacity and always upheld the independence and autonomy of the organization. His contribution to the development of SRSC from 1989 to the end of 1996 was critical to the survival of the programme. SRSP now has a presence in 14 out of 24 districts of NWFP.

The most important replication was Prime Minister Nawaz Sharif's allocation of Rupees five hundred million to the National Rural Support Programme (NRSP). One night in Gilgit in 1992, I received a telephone call at the Chinar Inn from my erstwhile probationer at the Civil Service Academy Reyaz Khokhar. In those days we used to have joint training for Civil Service of Pakistan (CSP) and Foreign Service of Pakistan (PFS) probationers at the Academy at Lahore. Reyaz was a PFS probationer. Now he was Additional Secretary in the Prime Minister's Secretariat. Reyaz began by telling me that the PM had heard about my getting the Magsaysay Award from the President of the Philippines and desired to meet me immediately. Fortunately, the PIA flight operated next morning and I presented myself in Reyaz's office in the afternoon. Reyaz advised me that I should have some concrete proposals for the PM for the replication of AKRSP countrywide so I drafted a one page summary which Reyaz got typed.

In the meeting the PM asked me if what I was doing in the NAs could be replicated countrywide. He also mentioned that on his last visit to the NAs everyone had told him that if Shoaib Sultan Khan stood for election, he would be elected unopposed. I presented the one-page summary to the PM who read it and thereafter picked up the telephone and asked his Finance Minister Sartaj Aziz, to join us. On Sartaj's arrival, he read out the summary to him. Sartaj had been a great supporter of AKRSP since his first visit in 1984 along with the late Jamil Nishtar. The summary envisaged an outlay of ten billion rupees over a period of seven years to replicate AKRSP countrywide. The PM and the finance minister, in principle, approved the summary.

On 2 August 1991, the finance minister called a meeting which I could not attend as a day earlier my elder brother Marine Captain Sohail Sultan's eldest son, Major Khalid Sultan, an aviation helicopter pilot, had been killed in action on the Siachin front. However, a few days later I was invited to make a presentation to an inter-provincial conference presided over by the PM and attended by all the chief ministers of the four provinces and AJK and their officials, as well as federal ministers and officials. When I was called in, the PM vacated his chair and asked me to make a presentation from there. He himself moved to where all the others were sitting. After my presentation, the Chief Minister of Punjab, Wyne, spoke of the work he was doing in his native village. Sardar Abdul Qayyum, Prime Minister Azad Jammu and Kashmir (AJK) wanted a clarification on the relationship between the local government structure and the institutional structure at the grassroots that AKRSP had been fostering.

However, I was completely taken aback by a comment from Khalid Aziz, Additional Chief Secretary (Development) NWFP, who severely warned me against working with the government which, he said, was like supping with the devil. He then expressed great concern about the success of the AKRSP approach if it was replicated through government.

Of course, I had no intention of replication through the government. When in my first meeting the PM had asked me to join his government and implement the programme I had respectfully submitted that for the last ten years I had implemented AKRSP by remaining outside the government, adding that if the PM wanted the replication of AKRSP, the only credible, tried and tested route was to set up organizations and structures like AKRSP—not 'for profit' joint stock companies under the Companies Ordinance with independent autonomous Boards of Directors.

The Federal Government's Social Action Programme (SAP) was on the anvil with a projected outlay of about eight billion dollars. Sartaj Aziz made a strong case to the provinces for community participation in SAP through organized communities and simultaneously allocated the first tranche of Rs 1,000 million to replicate AKRSP in 16 out of 114 Districts. When he asked to whom the first installment of Rs 500 million should be transferred, I mentioned the National Rural Support Programme (NRSP).

SCALING UP BY THE GOVERNMENT

Commander A. A. Naseem, Federal Secretary, Ministry of Local Government and Rural Development, was a great admirer of Akhtar Hameed Khan and most appreciative of AKRSP and the Orangi Pilot Project (OPP). I had known Naseem since my days as Deputy Commissioner, Kohat in 1963. He is the personification of gentleness, integrity and humility. In the wake of the government's *Tameer-e-Watan* programme, Naseem discussed his idea with me. I had suggested setting up an AKRSP-type structure, which he did. He even got the PM's approval for the membership of the Board which included Akhtar Hameed Khan and myself, with Naseem as Chairman of the Board and Federal Secretaries Finance, Planning and Local Government as *ex-officio* members plus nine other members from civil society. NRSP initiated its activities from four villages in the Islamabad Capital Territory under the direct supervision of Naseem.

Sartaj Aziz accepted my suggestion that instead of setting up another organization, NRSP was eminently suited to replicate AKRSP and facilitate setting up similar organizations when needed. The first tranche of Rs 500 million was received within three weeks of the Interprovincial Conference with Mian Tayyab, Additional Secretary, Ministry of Finance facilitating the approval process in record time. My main concern was finding a CEO for NRSP and I requested Najma Siddiqi, who had worked in AKRSP, if she would be willing to take up the challenge. The Board, however, insisted on my becoming the CEO and Najma kindly agreed to become the first GM of NRSP. In due course, the Board accepted my recommendation to make Najma the CEO. Najma's contribution in laying the foundation of NRSP was tremendous. Her emphasis on human resource development and selecting and training staff gave NRSP an excellent start.

The Board, with the benefit of the wisdom of Akhtar Hameed Khan, decided in its first meeting to convert the first tranche of a grant of Rs 500 million from the government into an endowment. With earnings of 18 per cent interest, the Board instructed the staff to keep the recurrent expenditure within the income of the endowment. As luck would have it the change in national government resulted in no more funding for NRSP. The Board's decision to create an endowment and to initiate the programme in only eight districts proved to be sound and very prudent.

Unfortunately, the new national government felt that NRSP was a handmaiden of the previous government. Why else did it get such a large sum of government funds? No one could believe that the former

PM and finance minister did not control NRSP. One day I received a decision of the Federal Cabinet saying that it be suggested to Mr Shoaib Sultan that he return the Rs 500 million given to NRSP. The legal adviser of NRSP, Azam Chaudhry, opined that the grant money, once given, could not be taken back, especially if it was held in trust. The Board took its decision in accordance with the legal advice. We came to know that on receiving our response, the government asked the Chairman of the Corporate Law Authority, Shamim Ahmad, to liquidate NRSP. However, he refused, citing the lack of grounds to justify the action. Thereupon, the Cabinet decided to ask the Prime Minister's Inspection Commission to look into the affairs of NRSP. Initially, suggestions were made in the Cabinet to refer the matter to the Federal Investigation Agency, but on the intervention of Ahmad Sadik and Shahnaz Wazir Ali, the idea was dropped. The Inspection Commission's report was presented by its Chairman, Syed Khalid Mahmood, before the Cabinet, who said that NRSP was a good programme. He was supported by Finance Secretary Qazi Alimullah who stated that there was no irregularity committed by the previous government in allocating funds for NRSP and cited similar actions taken by the present government in many cases. I made an impassioned appeal to the PM along with Naseem, outlining the real objective of NRSP for poverty reduction.

Najma got so frustrated that she offered to resign. I took my own and her resignation to the principal secretary to the PM, Ahmad Sadik, to convey to the PM if she felt anything personal against us, she should let NRSP continue. I never heard from him but while I was in Bangladesh, I got an urgent phone call from Najma asking me to accept her resignation as she did not want to continue any more and to make immediate arrangements for someone to take over from her. She left me no option but to ring up Naseem to come to my rescue and take over as CEO in an honorary capacity. Naseem complied with my request without hesitation.

One day, Shamsh Lakha rang me up from Karachi to enquire if he could see me on his next visit to Islamabad. It transpired that on one of her visits to the AKU Hospital, the PM had complained to Shamsh that I was not returning the money given to me by the previous government in a most irregular manner. I was simply shocked at the disinformation campaign launched by vested interests to poison the PM's mind. I would have certainly returned the money if it was with me or if I could.

When an instruction of the government was conveyed to me through the Cabinet Division, that all the directors should resign, everyone sent in their resignation except Zafar Altaf. However, Azam Chaudhry advised the Board against it because this would lead to liquidation of the NRSP and the Directors had a moral duty to over 100,000 rural households organized by the NRSP as VOs/WOs and over 200 staff members. The directors would have to be answerable in the High Court and give cogent reasons for their action resulting in the winding up of the organization. We faithfully conveyed the legal opinion expressing our helplessness in complying with the wishes of the government.

During this period, as senior adviser to the UNDP sponsored the South Asia Poverty Alleviation Programme (SAPAP), I had to travel extensively in Asia. While I was on one of my visits to Myanmar, my residential office in Islamabad was broken into and the files and documents were rummaged through. Nothing was taken, including some cash kept in one of the locked drawers by Rauf. For the protection of my family, who were alone during my absence, I had to employ a security guard for night duty.

One day Shahnaz Wazir Ali, Adviser to the PM, conveyed the PM's wish to give an appointment to Mrs Pervez Saleh, although having been persuaded by Shahnaz not to insist on her appointment as the CEO of NRSP. I complied by creating a post of Adviser on Social Sector, as that seemed to be her area of expertise. A fortnight later the government changed and Mrs Pervez Saleh rang me up to ask if she should go to the office. I asked her if anyone had asked her not to. She continued for a few months before leaving NRSP.

The NRSP episode taught us a lot of things. It also demonstrated the protection and security available to NGOs under the Companies Ordinance if you have a competent, courageous and upright legal adviser and a government which, despite unforgivable irritants in its view, was not willing to flout the law of the land. The legal structure of AKRSP, adopted by NRSP, stood the test of time, demonstrating its resilience in safeguarding the independence and autonomy of the RSPs. Even other organizations sponsored by the government, like the Pakistan Poverty Alleviation Fund, whose independence and autonomy were to be protected, adopted the AKRSP legal structure.

With the change in government, an interim government under Mairaj Khalid took over. President Farooq Leghari and his Principal Secretary Shamsher Ali Khan, both of whom had been probationers at the Civil Service Academy during my tenure there as deputy director, arranged for me to make a presentation on NRSP at the presidency for the prime minister and the Cabinet. As a result of that presentation, the Ministry of Local Government and Rural Development was asked to send a summary to the Cabinet allowing NRSP to retain the endowment grant. However, the decision taken on the summary restricted NRSP from using the interest income of the endowment on its administrative expenditure. When Additional Secretary, Local Government Ministry Zafarullah Khan conveyed the decision to me, I again ran to Shamsher. The interim government had only two more days to last and their final Cabinet meeting was scheduled for the next day. Shamsher rang up the Minister Local Government Shafqat Mahmood who very kindly got an amendment to the Cabinet decision approved, deleting the restriction on the use of endowment income imposed in the previous decision.

NRSP weathered a big storm in which the Board and the staff played the roles expected of them. After Najma's resignation, the search for a full time CEO became imperative. Dr Rashid Bajwa, a DMG officer, who had served as Assistant Commissioner and Additional Deputy Commissioner in the NAs during the implementation of AKRSP, came to me and expressed a desire to work for NRSP. I referred him to Najma who appointed him as a Social Organizer to learn and to prove that he was genuinely committed to working in NRSP. Rashid put his heart and soul into it and by sheer dint of his hard work, dedication and commitment to the strategy of development being followed by NRSP, and having tremendous qualities of leadership, demonstrated to me and Naseem that there was no better candidate for the position of CEO, NRSP. When Bob Shaw succeeded in securing my services as GM AKRSP, Akhtar Hameed Khan had told Bob that he had won a million dollar lottery. For me to have found Rashid has been no less, if not more. Rashid, with support from Agha Javad—first in finance and later on in everything—and Roomi Hayat in human resource development (HRD) has taken NRSP to unimaginable heights. With the endowment grant currently more than rupees one billion, despite a sharp dip in interest rates adversely impacting the income from endowment, NRSP currently has its presence in 40 districts in all four provinces and AJK.

Shamsul Mulk, Chairman Water and Power Development Authority (WAPDA) approached me in 1994 and requested help in setting up a project NGO to mitigate the suffering of the affectees of the Ghazi Brotha Hydro Power (GBHP) project and to undertake sustainable development in all 18 Union Councils affected by GHBP. For the sustainability, independence and autonomy of the project NGO, I requested Shams to set up a not-for-profit joint stock company on the pattern of AKRSP with an endowment grant of Rs 100 million. An agreement was accordingly signed between NRSP and WAPDA and countersigned by me, accepting the two requirements. The organization was named Ghazi Brotha Taraqiati Idara (GBTI) at the suggestion of WAPDA. The World Bank insisted on the affectees' representation on the Board, hence the composition of the Board included seven technical directors and eight directors chosen by the affectees with Member, Water and Power Development Authority (WAPDA) and CEO NRSP as *ex-officio* members.

The fact that GBTI's requirements and needs were totally different from a Rural Support Programme (RSP), dawned on me on my first field visit. We had wasted a year in exhorting and motivating people to enter into a development partnership with GBTI. The interest of the affectees was first and foremost to receive compensation for the land which GBHP had either acquired or was planning to acquire. The project area fell in both the provinces of Punjab and NWFP. The criteria adopted by one province for acquisition of land had repercussions in the other province. GBTI, as a neutral mediator between WAPDA and the affectees, was, as somebody described it, between the devil and the deep blue sea. GBTI was WAPDA's creation and it expected total loyalty. The affectees were GBTI's moral responsibility and their expectations were high for just or unjust demands.

The land compensation issue reached a deadlock with cases filed in the court both by WAPDA and the affectees, resulting in stoppage of work, with the foreign contractor demanding thousands of dollars daily as compensation from WAPDA. GBTI had a number of meetings with WAPDA which ultimately authorized GBTI to negotiate fair and just land compensation according to the market rate instead of the yearly average. The Board constituted a committee with the late Omar Asghar Khan as technical director, Ahsan Khan as local director, WAPDA representative and the CEO GBTI Riaz Ahmad Khan and a few others. An agreed package of land compensation was presented before Shams, which stipulated immediate disbursement of the entire compensation money and the simultaneous withdrawal of all court cases filed by both WAPDA and the affectees. The agreement was implemented and WAPDA saved millions of dollars it was paying as compensation to the foreign contractors.

With the retirement of Shamsul Mulk, the new Chairman of WAPDA, who probably thought that he was the only honest man in the world, unilaterally rescinded the agreement signed by his predecessor and referred the land compensation cases, above a certain amount given under the agreement, to NAB for enquiry and action, irrespective of the area of land acquired in each case for which land compensation was given. The NAB rounded up hundreds of affectees and kept them in solitary confinement, asking them to admit their crime of taking exorbitant land compensation. The affectees felt let down by GBTI. We knocked at the doors of the World Bank, which had observed how the agreement was signed. I and some Directors of the Board called on NAB and requested the Federal Minister for Water and Power to intercede on behalf of the affectees. The first CEO of GBTI was also arrested and a case was registered against some of the GBTI staff.

For two years the cases dragged on and hundreds of poor affectees suffered. One of them, I was told, even died in prison. Ultimately NAB closed the case. Ninety-five per cent of the affectees have been paid compensation but the cases of 7,000 affectees were kept pending because no revenue officer was willing to serve as Land Acquisition Collector in the GBHP area for fear of NAB. Ultimately, Ejaz Rahim, Cabinet Secretary happened to attend one of the GBTI Board meetings and took up the matter with the Punjab Chief Secretary. Hopefully the chapter of land compensation would soon be closed to the satisfaction of the affectees.

No sooner had GBTI embarked on sustainable development in the 18 Union Councils, than WAPDA decided to wind up GBTI because, in their books, GBHP had been completed. Despite Azam Chaudhry's comprehensive explanation of the legal position and the status of GBTI, WAPDA kept on repeating their stand. GBTI was the first experiment anywhere in the world of a project NGO for a Hydro Power or Big Dam Project. The progress of GBTI was keenly observed by the World Bank and the role played by it greatly appreciated. Even an evaluation commissioned by WAPDA was very positive in favour of GBTI. But the WAPDA authorities persisted in asking the Board to return the endowment of Rs 100 million given to GBTI. Finally I wrote a letter to the new Chairman WAPDA.

We had heard nothing from WAPDA for months. Suddenly in June 2007, we heard about filing a civil suit by GM GBHP asking for the return of Rs 100 million from GBTI. I spoke to Shamsul Mulk who wrote a letter to Chairman WAPDA reinforcing our stand. At a subsequent meeting with Chairman WAPDA, through the courtesy of the Federal Secretary, Water and Power, Ismail Qureshi, Mr Tariq Hameed promised to withdraw the case. Ambassador Amir Usman as Vice Chairman of the Board has been a tremendous support to me in steering GBTI. GBTI is finally now fully focused on RSP type development.

The most important landmark in replicating AKRSP countrywide was the setting up of the Pakistan Poverty Alleviation Fund (PPAF). The initial sponsors of the Fund, under the Companies Ordinance on the pattern of AKRSP, were all government officials with Deputy Chairman Planning Commission Hafiz Pasha as its chairman. The government of Pakistan (GoP) made a request to the World Bank for a 91 million dollar loan to be channelled to PPAF in the ratio of 45 per cent as a loan for micro credit and 55 per cent as a grant for physical infrastructure and capacity building of partner organizations (POs).

I received a call from the Vice President of the World Bank Ms Meiko Nishimizu asking me to come to Washington to plead the PPAF case, as most of her sector managers were sceptical about its success. Meiko was an ardent supporter of AKRSP. She had even initiated a Village Immersion Programme (VIP) for the management staff in her division after seeing AKRSP. On my request, she had spent a week in Andhra Pradesh visiting SAPAP and had sanctioned Bank funding for Andhra Pradesh for replication of SAPAP state-wide. She called SAPAP 'UNDP's miracle'. In Washington DC, with Azmat Isa, I gave presentations on AKRSP, SAPAP and the RSPs in workshops attended by all Sector Managers in Meiko's division. I tried to dispel their apprehensions about lack of capacity in Pakistan to effectively utilize PPAF funds. This discussion was all taking place in the shadow of Pakistan's nuclear explosions. Ultimately, Meiko won the day and the Executive Board of the Bank approved the GoP's request for US$91 million for PPAF.

Sartaj Aziz was back in the new government ushered in after the elections. Sartaj was very keen that there should be an institutional arrangement for replication of AKRSP instead of *ad hoc* grants depending on the whims and wishes of individuals. He ensured that PPAF had a Board of independent persons with *ex-officio* representation only from the ministry of finance and a professional CEO. With Hussain Dawood as Chairman and Kamal Hyat as CEO, we have a perfect team in PPAF to ensure its independence and autonomy. PPAF has since received another tranche of US$335 million. During the earthquake, PPAF, in addition to emergency relief, also helped in the reconstruction and rehabilitation of 120,000 earthquake affected households. 106,000 of these households were reached by PPAF through NRSP and SRSP. Seventy-nine per cent of the PPAF resources have flowed through RSPs.

Recently, the prime minister has specifically sanctioned US$120 million for PPAF, to be channelled to the RSPs for the social mobilization of an additional two million households. PPAF is preparing its request for the third tranche of funding with greater emphasis on social mobilization. Hopefully, within the next 5–7 years, through PPAF support, RSPs should be able to replicate AKRSP countrywide.

There is a saying that 'history repeats itself'. In 1997, I experienced a repeat of what had happened in 1991. I was in Kathmandu in Nepal, which was my headquarters for SAPAP, when I received a telephone call from Tariq Sultan, Chairman, Planning and Development Board, Government of the Punjab, informing me that the chief minister of Punjab would like to meet me on my return to Pakistan. I made a presentation to Shahbaz Sharif. I began by noting that a few years ago his elder brother had called me and I emerged from the meeting richer by Rs 500 million. The chief minister smiled, saying it would be the other way round this time. After the presentation a committee was established, which met three times within a month and submitted the proposal to set up the Punjab Rural Support Programme (PRSP), with an endowment grant of Rs 500 million to the provincial Cabinet. At the Cabinet meeting, the senior minister enquired 'How can there be a non-political programme in a political environment?' The chief minister responded by saying that for the last fifty years we had tried political programmes for rural poverty reduction; let us try a non-political programme, with a track record of success, to achieve the objective. Tariq Sultan took care not to have problems like those faced by NRSP and had a PC-I prepared and cleared by the Provincial Development Working Party (PDWP) and sent to CDWP for approval. The Federal Planning Division raised certain routine objections which Tariq spoke to me about and I took it up with Fazlullah Qureshi, Federal Secretary Planning, who very kindly cleared the PC-I through CDWP. PRSP gained strength from day to day and is now present in twenty districts of Punjab. PRSP has a very close relationship with the provincial government and its endowment has increased to Rs 750 million with the provincial government giving an annual subsidy of Rs 50 million to offset the reduction in interest income.

My introduction to Punjab brought me in contact with Jahangir Tareen who was adviser to the chief minister. Jahangir urged me to initiate a micro-credit programme in the cotton belt of southern Punjab. Despite my reservations about a pre-conceived package approach, I had to give in when Jahangir arranged a luncheon meeting at which Shaukat Tareen, President of Habib Bank Limited, not only agreed to give NRSP a line of credit of six hundred million Rupees at 14 per cent but also a grant of twenty million Rupees to defray the social mobilization cost of the operations in Vehari district. I could not believe my ears and to make doubly sure I reiterated to Shaukat that I had no collateral to offer. His spontaneous response was 'Your track record is good enough collateral for the bank'. I had never come across such a dynamic banker with such foresight. The credit line, in due course, was increased to over two and a half billion rupees with Shaukat's successor Zakir Mahmud following in his footsteps. NRSP paid millions of Rupees as the cost of capital to the Bank, along with 100 per cent return of the capital. Jahangir put NRSP in a different league. He is one of the most dynamic persons I have met. Too dynamic at times for me but he is one person with influence and wealth who went with me to dozens of dialogues and spent hour after hour absorbing what I had to say and what the rural poor had to say. I have often heard him say publicly that, through these dialogues, he learnt to have rapport with poor villagers instead of only having a condescending attitude towards them.

Jahangir also persuaded me to experiment with the revival and revamping of basic health units (BHUs) and persuaded Ismail Qureshi, Provincial Secretary Health, to transfer three BHUs in Lodhran District to NRSP. The experiment produced excellent results. However, I had always maintained that there was a need for a specialized organization to take up this kind of activity as in the case of AKRSP where the AKHS and AKES had implemented the social sector programmes. Still, by using the RSPs' umbrella, Jahangir has launched the President's Primary Healthcare Initiative in all the provinces, after he had persuaded PRSP to replicate an improved Lodhran initiative in 104 BHUs of Rahim Yar Khan (RYK) and the RYK model in 1200 BHUs of Punjab. In Farooq Haroon he found the ideal person to implement this programme.

In 2003, I was most pleasantly surprised to have been invited by the Provincial Government of Sindh to chair the Board of Directors of the newly established Sindh Rural Support Organization (SRSO) with an endowment grant of Rupees five hundred million. In Brigadier Zamin, Secretary to Governor and a Director of SRSO, I found tremendous support. Of course, the approval for setting up SRSO was accorded by Governor Mohammad Mian Soomro. In Additional Chief Secretary Ghulam Sarwar Khero and Finance Secretary Malik Israr, there was so much support that within its first year, the endowment grant of SRSO was doubled to Rupees one billion. My main challenge was to find a CEO and Dr Sulaiman Shaikh very kindly came to my rescue until we found a full time CEO in Nazar Memon. Although most of the Board members were based in Karachi, they agreed to have the SRSO headquarters at Sukkur. SRSO operates in nine districts of upper Sindh. I succeeded in persuading Fazlullah Qureshi, Aazar Ayaz, Arif Hasan and Tasneem Siddiqi to join the SRSO Board.

The Rural Support Programmes Network (RSPN) has played a major role in the replication of AKRSP. In the case of PRSP and SRSO, initially from the umbrella of NRSP and subsequently as an independent organization, RSPN has been ensuring the integrity of the RSP approach as espoused by AKRSP. RSPN has also acted as an experience-sharing forum, besides helping the RSPs both technically and with funds to launch innovations and technological packages. In Shandana Khan as CEO, RSPN found a most dedicated and peerless professional for the job.

In the case of the Balochistan Rural Support Programme (BRSP), RSPN has been most active. BRSP started as a Pak-German Project in the early eighties and in the early nineties, after many visits to AKRSP and my visits to Balochistan, the German donors decided to convert the project into a not-for-profit joint stock company like AKRSP. Unfortunately, due to internal squabbles and a lack of interest on the part of the government of Balochistan, the donors lost interest and walked out of BRSP. For years BRSP remained in limbo, until PPAF agreed to revive it. Dr Shahida Jaffrey, who had worked in AKRSP, offered to work *gratis* as the CEO of BRSP. BRSP was confined only to District Mastung. I gave many presentations to different governors and chief ministers to elicit the provincial government's interest in expanding BRSP but without much success. Hopefully, with the Prime Minister's Livestock Programme and the PPAF Social Mobilization Project, BRSP may achieve the desired expansion.

AKRSP Replication beyond Pakistan

The opportunity to take lessons learnt at AKRSP beyond Pakistan came up at the Annapolis Workshop, organized by the World Bank in 1993 to discuss the report of the Independent South Asia Commission on Poverty Alleviation (ISACPA) which had received endorsement at the highest political level by the SAARC Summit in April 1993 at Dhaka. One of the participants of the workshop was Dr Henning Karcher, representing UNDP. Henning had been in Pakistan in the early seventies and knew the Daudzai Project well. After my presentation at the workshop, he came up to me and commented that the enthusiasm he had noticed nearly two decades ago seemed to have changed from a spark to a full-fledged fire. A few months later I received an invitation from the UNDP Regional Bureau for Asia and the Pacific (RBAP) to participate in the cluster meeting of the UNDP Resident Representatives at Kathmandu. Henning asked me to make a presentation on AKRSP and to describe how it could be replicated in South Asia. He also introduced me to the acting Director of RBAP, Elena Martinez from Cuba. On my return, I received a phone call from Henning from New York, asking if I would be willing to go on a mission to SAARC countries to ascertain if they would be agreeable to UNDP helping them in operationalising the recommendation of the Poverty Commission, namely that 'Social Mobilization should be the centerpiece of all poverty alleviation strategies of South Asian governments'. As I had now contacts in all the countries as a member of the Commission, I had no hesitation in responding positively to Henning's offer.

Foreign Secretary Shehryar Khan rang me up one night in Gilgit to inform me that the prime minister had appointed me to the Commission. The Commission was the idea of the late Premadasa, Prime Minister of Sri Lanka. According to the Foreign Secretary, Premadasa had personally spoken to the PM about a suitable nomination on the Commission and the PM had approved my nomination. I found Abed of BRAC, Shri Krishna Uppadhya of Nepal, Venugopal, the prime minister of India's secretary, Poona Wignarajah of Sri Lanka, Safdar Kazmi and myself from Pakistan amongst others on the Commission. The Commission held its deliberations over a year and visited most of the countries to look at projects and programmes which had succeeded in reducing poverty. In India, in our meeting with the Prime Minister Narsimha Rao, when a member tried to define poverty, the PM interjected that he was not interested in definitions—he knew there was poverty and wanted to know from the Commission how it could be reduced. That set the tone of the Commission and it was for this reason that the Commission made feasible and operational recommendations with one overarching recommendation pertaining to Social Mobilization.

I sent Henning a draft Terms of Reference (ToR) for my Mission under the title 'Institutional Development at the Grassroots for Poverty Alleviation'. The ToRs were approved and my suggestion to include Dr Anis Dani, who had worked with me at AKRSP, to be the other member of the Mission, was also accepted. From February to May 1994, the Mission travelled to Bangladesh, Nepal, Sri Lanka and India. We not only obtained the willingness of the governments for UNDP to launch a Regional Programme to implement the Commission's recommendations, we also identified the demonstration pilot area and likely team members to implement the programme.

In Bangladesh, my old UNICEF colleague Dr Eimi Watanabe was the UNDP Resident Representative. Eimi had appreciated and supported my work in the Mahaweli Ganga Project beyond my wildest expectations. She was a true believer in the development approach I was implementing, and greatly publicized it in the development circle in Sri Lanka. In the government, Dr Kamal Siddiqi, Principal Secretary to the Prime Minister, gave his full backing and suggested Badiur Rahman's name for the post of National Project Coordinator (NPC). He also selected Kishoregunj Thana for the proposed SAPAP pilot demonstration. Similarly, in Nepal, Shri Krishna Uppadhya, Member of the Nepal Planning Commission, suggested the name of Dr Jaysingh Sah for the post of NPC and selected Syangja District for the project area. Carrol Long, UNDP Resident Representative came fully on board. In India, Venugopal personally took matters in hand and even got the PM's approval for a Pakistani to work as an adviser on a project in India. Three districts of Andhra Pradesh—Mahboobnagar, Kurnool and Anantpur—were chosen for purposes of demonstration. In the Maldives, the Ministry of Atoll Development chose Noonu Atoll for the demonstration and Minister Sobir, who was member of the Commission, fully supported the idea. In Sri Lanka, in view of the Janasaviya political programme, the government was not too sure what value addition SAPAP could bring; however, they agreed to try the project in Nuwara Eliya and UNDP selected Dayaratne to be the NPC. In Pakistan, UNDP Resident Representative Von Sponeck readily agreed to use 40 per cent of my time in Pakistan to replicate AKRSP through RSPs. He also provided technical assistance worth US$8.5 million, on the GoP's request, to NRSP. Subsequently, on UNDP Resident Representative Robert England's insistence, a SAPAP demonstration was initiated in the Lachi area of Kohat district with Azam Khan as NPC.

My Mission had two objectives. The first was to secure the agreement of the Governments of Bangladesh, the Maldives, Nepal, India and Sri Lanka to initiate SAPAP and the second was to identify an NPC to lead the project team. I knew that if I could find the right NPC, who believed in the development approach espoused by AKRSP, SAPAP would be a success. In all six countries, I was lucky to find the kind of professionals I was looking for. In India, after the initial hitch, SAPAP found the right leader in K. Raju who took SAPAP to unbelievable heights.

SAPAP was launched on 1 August 1994, and in Nepal over 800 VDCs in 60 of the 75 Districts in the country are following the approach. In the Maldives from the initial Atoll the SAPAP approach was replicated in six of the twenty Atolls in the country thanks to the commitment and dedication of NPCs Abdulla Rasheed and Zahid. There are plans to cover the entire country. However, it is in India that SAPAP has really blossomed: from a demonstration in twenty Mandals in three districts covering 1,000 villages, the replication has reached more than 900 of the 1,100 Mandals in the state with presence in over 30,000 villages.

The methodology adopted for replication of AKRSP beyond Pakistan was to have a two-week orientation training of the NPC and his team from each country in the Northern Areas at AKRSP. Raju told me that if he had not visited AKRSP, he would never have believed that villagers had the potential to do all the things they have achieved in AKRSP.

Henning was very keen that the country offices of UNDP should own SAPAP because normally the UNDP Regional Programmes were looked upon by the Country Offices as an imposition from above. In addition to the Resident Representatives (RRs), UNDP Programme Officers Rini Raza from Bangladesh, Manoj Basnyat from Nepal, Neera Burra and Radhakrishnan from India, Asoka Kasturichchi from Sri Lanka, Shaheem from the Maldives and Samina Kamal from Pakistan literally owned SAPAP as their programme. Henning was the prime mover and sometimes I heard complaints that, instead of the Chief of Section covering 33 countries, he was only concentrating on

SAPAP. Henning was attached to SAPAP not only professionally but also emotionally and at his own request got himself transferred to Nepal as RR to personally support the implementation of SAPAP. He selected a team of dedicated and competent professionals to help him, led by Mohammad Pournik who was later joined by Dr Alain Jacquemin and Dr Subrahmanyam Ponthagunta.

SAPAP, though funded by UNDP, was technically being implemented by UNOPS. Ingunde Fuehlau would approve our proposals by return fax and solved all SAPAP financial problems in a way that I have never seen happening before. Under UNDP rules, where national professionals had no financial powers, she got the administrator to delegate powers for incurring and authorizing expenditure up to US$50,000. Ingunde's successor, Richard Snellen, was in a class by himself. His sole objective used to be to facilitate the implementation of SAPAP in the most expeditious way.

In 2002 SAPAP phased out, but in India, Nepal, Maldives and Pakistan its replication was taken up by newly-created national institutions like the Society for Elimination of Rural Poverty (SERP) in Andhra, the Local Governance Programme in Nepal, the Atoll Development Programme in the Maldives and the RSPs in Pakistan. An allocation of US$11 million by UNDP for SAPAP between 1994 and 2002 catalysed programmes worth billions of dollars. Except for Nepal and the Maldives, UNDP phased out in favour of the World Bank in India. In Pakistan, DFID, at the behest of Steve Jones, supported the Lachi component of SAPAP and Dr Inayatullah, as UNDP Programme Incharge, did his utmost to keep UNDP interest alive. However, UNDP has a tendency to walk away when the time comes for programmes to mature and replicate. Fortunately, there are other development agencies that take full advantage of UNDP's work and build their name and reputation on it. No wonder, when UNDP is asked to show what it has done, there is not much to show as someone else has stepped in their shoes.

For me SAPAP was a unique experience. An opportunity to interact with communities at the grassroots in six countries of South Asia was a dream come true. I learnt a great deal from the field and above all it reinforced my conviction and faith in the strategy of development I had learnt from Akhtar Hameed Khan and implemented in AKRSP. I can never thank Henning Karcher enough for this opportunity.

The Politics of Non-Partisan Development

People often wonder how RSPs have been able to survive political changes in federal and provincial governments despite being recipients of funds from an outgoing prime minister, chief minister, governor and governments.

I have scrupulously tried to keep RSPs non-partisan, neutral, non-agitational and fully focused on development—especially, economic development—at the grassroots level. Initially, there were a great many misconceptions in the minds of the NGOs and civil society organizations, especially Rights-based NGOs, about the objective of RSPs. No one would believe that the RSPs could maintain their independence and autonomy if the financial sponsorship had been provided by Federal or Provincial governments. I have the greatest regard and respect for Rights-based NGOs and admire the courage and commitment of their leaders. I always used to explain that the RSPs are not NGOs in the traditional sense but they are also not GoNGOs because the Boards of the RSPs are independent of any government control, direction or supervision. In 1997, I even convened a seminar on the subject. AKRSP, having been sponsored by AKF, is probably the only RSP where the selection of Directors, *de facto*, vests in AKF and not the Board of AKRSP. In all the other RSPs, it is the founding sponsoring Directors and the General Body who, in accordance with the provisions of their Articles and Memorandum of Association, formulated under Section 42 of the Companies Ordinance, elect their respective Board every three years.

I have tried to keep the neutrality of RSPs paramount while keeping a cordial and polite relationship with all tiers of government and elected representatives irrespective of their party affiliations. Anyone and everyone who supported the RSP approach was welcome and the RSPs courted them. This policy paid dividends and the RSPs were seldom brought under pressure by the politicians or the administration. Whichever community in a village within an RSP area of operation was willing to accept the RSP terms of partnership, RSP was willing to forge a development partnership with them.

I was often advised to publicise RSPs, but the RSPs seldom sought any publicity through newspaper advertisements or TV clips. The RSPs always believed in others publicizing the RSPs if they found it worth appreciation. The RSPs do ensure that regular reports of their activities and achievements are issued, and welcome visitors from within the country and abroad to give exposure to the work being done by VOs/WOs and their organizations.

I often used to feel embarrassed at all the awards and recognitions being given to me personally for the tremendous achievements of the VOs/WOs and the AKRSP staff without whose commitment and dedication, nothing would have been achieved. All that I could do was to recognize this fact in my acceptance speeches.

16

A Case Study of Advocacy with the Government[1]

THE WORKING GROUP ON RURAL DEVELOPMENT AND FUNDING FOR SOCIAL MOBILIZATION

In 2004, at the behest of the then chief economist, the then secretary planning agreed to make me the chairman of the Working Group on Rural Development and Devolution as an input in the forthcoming Mid Term Development Framework (MTDF). The chief economist also persuaded the authorities to allow me to have a say in the composition of the Working Group. Amongst others I persuaded three Members of the National Assembly (MNA) from both sides of the House to join the Group. The deputy chairman, planning commission suggested an additional two names who he felt had some insight into rural development.

In the first meeting of the Group, I showed them the video prepared by Rural Support Programmes Network (RSPN) based on the dialogues held in 49 districts with 121 men and women organizations comprising over 5,000 persons. The video had the most salutary effect on the members and in a short period of three months, a consensus report of the Group was finalized after detailed discussions including field visits. The draft report prepared by Zafar Ahmad of RSPN was approved unanimously by the Group members and submitted to the Planning Commission in October 2004, meeting the deadline set up by the Commission. The Deputy Chairman appreciated the efforts of the Group.

I was pleased to see the Group Report incorporated in the Draft of the MTDF. However, I was shocked to see the chapter containing the Group Report missing from the final document of the MTDF. I felt most disappointed and crestfallen and rang up the chief economist to convey my dismay and anger. He advised me to write to the deputy chairman, as he had no input in the final document which had been prepared by a consultant commissioned by the planning division. I wrote a letter of protest to the deputy chairman.

The deputy chairman took serious notice of my protest and convened a meeting of the consultant, the chief economist and myself in his office and decided that a supplement to the MTDF should be issued containing the recommendations of the Working Group. The Chief Economist took the lead role in getting the Supplement issued in September 2005, entitled 'Poverty Reduction through Social Mobilization'.

On the basis of the Supplement, the chief economist successfully piloted through the Central Development Working Party (CDWP) the concept clearance authorizing Economic Affairs Division (EAD) to negotiate with the World Bank and other donors their interest in funding the Social Mobilization Programme.

In February 2006, the chief economist persuaded the secretary planning division to initiate a consultative process with stakeholders for preparation of a PC-I on the basis of the Supplement 'Poverty Reduction through Social Mobilization'.

The consultative process continued till April 2006, comprising consultations and field visits by the planning commission team, often joined by the secretary himself, with government of Azad Jammu and Kashmir and the ministry of Kashmir Affairs and Northern Areas and Islamabad administration and the ministry of Interior at Islamabad, government of NWFP at Peshawar, Northern Areas administration at Gilgit, government of Punjab at Lahore, government of Sindh at Karachi and government of Balochistan at Quetta. The consultative process was finalized with a field visit to the Northern Areas by the deputy chairman along with two members of the commission.

In May 2006, PC-I for mobilizing communities in 5,375 Rural Union Councils was submitted to CDWP by the planning division. The CDWP decided to split the PC-I into two phases and the deputy chairman directed that the First Phase, comprising about 2,000 Rural Union Councils, should be taken with the balance forming part of Phase II to be submitted in 2008.

It was at this stage that secretary planning was transferred and a new secretary took over. However, the chief economist, undeterred, put up the revised PC-I before the CDWP which recommended to ECNEC in May 2006 for approval at an estimated cost of Rs 9,800 million including foreign exchange component (FEC) of Rs 7,200 million with the proviso:

- The project should be renamed Social Mobilization for Participatory Development.
- In the meantime the ministry of Local Government and Rural Development should engage the provinces and area administrations for evolving a consensus on implementation mechanism/strategy of the programme that catered to the distinct social requirements of each area.

A meeting was held in July 2006 attended by the secretary planning, secretary local government and rural development, representatives of the government of Punjab and two newly inducted members of the recently reconstituted planning commission who not only opposed the project but desired to override the decision of the CDWP recommending the project to ECNEC for approval.

Since CDWP had given the directive to secretary, ministry of local government and rural development who had recently moved from the planning division to the local government, he accepted the proposal of the Punjab government to hold a workshop at Lahore to evolve a consensus as desired by CDWP. The secretary expanded the scope of the workshop and invited representatives of all the provinces and areas at Lahore.

At the end of July 2006, a workshop of all the stakeholders comprising 72 participants was sponsored by the ministry of local government & rural development and hosted by the planning and development department of the government of Punjab. Soon after the workshop, the chief economist was also transferred.

No action was taken after the stakeholders' workshop, despite strong endorsement of the PC-I 'Participatory Development through Social Mobilization' and consensus on implementation mechanism which was incorporated in the revised PC-I for submission to ECNEC.

It was at this stage in October 2006, that the country director World Bank met the deputy chairman and secretary planning division and proposed the programme mode for World Bank funding of the project instead of PC-I mode.

The then cabinet secretary, being *ex-officio* Secretary of ECNEC, accompanied me to see the deputy chairman to request acceptance of the proposal made by the country director as contained in my letter addressed to the deputy Chairman. The deputy chairman, having ascertained from the member concerned the consensus reached by the stakeholders on PC-I, issued instructions on my letter for conveying planning division consent to the ministry of finance for the programme mode for the project as proposed by the World Bank.

I requested my batchmate Dr Humayun Khan, with whom the secretary planning had served in the High Commission at London, to intercede on our behalf with the secretary. We both met him in secretary's office and he promised to send the requisite letter. The secretary even rang me up to clarify that he was not the one standing in the way of the approval of the project.

In the meanwhile, the Secretary Planning was transferred to EAD and a new secretary took over as planning secretary. However, the serving secretary planning promised to send the letter to the ministry of finance before he handed over charge.

A few days earlier, at a dinner hosted by the prime minister, I met the secretary general finance and secretary EAD and solicited their support for the project. Both promised to help and SG Finance even encouraged me to speak to the PM, which I did, and he asked the SG to speak to the deputy chairman. The SG rang me up a few days later to enquire what action had been taken as he had conveyed the PM's wishes to the secretary planning.

The secretary planning did keep his promise and sent the letter to the ministry of finance on the day he handed over charge and moved to the economic affairs division.

A week later, the PM hosted a dinner in honour of Prince Charles and I was also invited to the PM House. While taking leave at the end of the dinner, I reminded the PM of my request and he said it had already been done. I said this would be my dream come true. A couple of days later, the secretary Agriculture just mentioned in passing to me that the livestock project to be implemented by Rural Support Programmes was opposed by many at the ECNEC meeting but the PM had approved it after reaffirming from the secretary Agriculture that this was Shoaib Sultan's Project. I felt crestfallen at this confusion. John Wall had still not received the request from EAD for the funding of social mobilization by the World Bank.

Mr Ejaz Rahim was to hand over charge of the Cabinet Division on retirement, as he had declined to accept an extension, on 1 November 2006. I explained the whole turn of events to Ejaz who assured me that once the PM came to know of the facts, he would immediately take action. To help me out, Ejaz submitted a *suo motu* Summary for the prime minister seeking his orders on the Social Mobilization Project which had already reached the ECNEC stage.

The Summary, instead of being submitted to the PM for orders, was sent by the PM's Secretariat to the planning division, asking them to send their views through he ministry of finance, despite the fact that planning division had already recommended to the ministry of finance to adopt the programme mode as proposed by the World Bank.

I met the new secretary planning to explain the whole background of the case and to request an immediate response to the PM Secretariat on the Summary. Later I came to know that the secretary planning had referred the Summary to all the provinces for their views on the matter: whether the World Bank funds should go to the RSPs through the Pakistan Poverty Alleviation Fund (PPAF) instead of the government channels. It was quite obvious what the provinces would say in the matter. John Wall's point of view was that PPAF was the quickest channel for securing resources, otherwise it may take up to two years to get approval for channelling funds through any other conduit.

In desperation, I sought a meeting with Dr Akram Sheikh, Deputy Chairman, Planning Commission. He genuinely went out of his way to help me out. As the secretary planning was busy in a meeting, he kept me in his office for nearly an hour and personally took me to the office of the secretary. He explained that a decision had already been taken by him in the matter, after due consideration, and there was no justification for reopening the case. He asked the secretary that his decision, already conveyed to Ministry of Finance, should be re-conveyed to the ministry for onward transmission to the PM's Secretariat. He desired this to be done immediately and the Secretary Planning did comply with the deputy chairman's instructions the same day.

In the ministry of finance, another drama was unfolding. I was keeping the SG informed of the developments. However, since he was not directly concerned and the matter was being dealt with by secretary finance directly with the adviser finance, he promised to find out the status of the case. Soon he rang me up to inform me that the adviser had ordered that the planning division be asked to channel the Social Mobilization Project funds through Khushhal Pakistan Fund (KPF). I explained John Wall's point of view in the matter. The SG said he had withheld the response of the ministry of finance, and in the meanwhile John and I should try to convince the adviser to change his mind.

I sought an immediate interview with the adviser and also rang up the minister of state for finance for his support in the matter. Omar Ayub promised his full support. The adviser very kindly agreed to see me but made it very clear that the Bank had no business to tell the government which channel it should use for expending funds. In any case he felt that PPAF was already overloaded and lacked the capacity to implement even their normal work.

John spoke to SG Nawid Ahsan and met the adviser with the finance secretary. John [Wall] felt that he had been able to convince the Adviser that the current request for Social Mobilization Funds should channel through PPAF and a request for funds for KPF should be submitted, which would be dealt with as per the laid down procedure.

I was attending the PRSP Board of Directors meeting at Lahore when my mobile rang. Nawid was on the phone informing me that on the Summary to the PM, it had been minuted that John had agreed to channel the Social Mobilization funds through KPF. I tracked down John between Sahiwal and Renala Khurd and relayed to him what Nawid had said and requested him to talk to Nawid which he did.

A couple of days later I met John at a World Bank sponsored workshop at LUMS and he confided that he had explained to the adviser that he must have misunderstood him and reiterated the World Bank position in the matter.

Now the whole thing was in a flux. Suddenly, out of the blue, Jahangir Tareen called me and I went to see him. After suitable admonishment for abandoning him and not seeking his support, Jahangir offered to speak to the PM. Earlier, the Chairman PPAF had asked me to see Humayun Gauhar to seek his assistance in the matter. I had rung up Humayun to meet him the next day. I had already spoken to him on the phone. Now I wanted to change the date of the meeting, as Jahangir hoped to arrange the meeting with the PM on that day.

My heart sank when Humayun Gauhar told me that he had raised the issue with the PM and the curt response was that it was loan money and the government would use it in the most effective way it considered suitable. I felt as if someone had pulled the carpet from under my feet.

I knew that my meeting with the PM was my only chance to retrieve the situation. Jahangir had already, in the meanwhile, got time from the PM to hold a meeting on Microfinance, to which the RSPs and, on my suggestion, PPAF were invited. But I knew that in this meeting I would not get an opportunity to speak to the PM about the Social Mobilization Project.

Zamir Akram is in the PM Secretariat. His wife Saadia is the late Air Commodore Allahdad's daughter. I have known her since her childhood when I was Deputy Commissioner Kohat in 1963 and her father was the president of the Inter Services Selection Board (ISSB). I asked Zamir to get me time with the PM, and when the Military Secretary to PM rang me up about the Microfinance meeting, I requested him to get me time separately also. Zamir had already spoken to him. I was given time a day prior to the Microfinance meeting. Ejaz had advised me to take a copy of the views of the Planning Commission on the Summary to the PM. On my request Dr Akram Sheikh readily made a copy available to me.

On the afternoon of 21 December 2006, I met the PM. He was his usual warm and courteous self in welcoming me and remarked 'So many important people have spoken to me and I know all about what you have come for. Why don't you accept US$60 million to begin with now and start the work', and he asked on the phone to be connected to the adviser. I thanked him and commended the speech which he had given at the Microfinance Conference in Halifax, Canada. In that meeting the PM had, along with credit, underscored the importance of Social Mobilization and a holistic approach to poverty reduction. Rashid Bajwa, who had attended the Conference, had made a copy of the speech available to me. I showed the speech to him and read out the piece he had said about Social Mobilization. PM looked at it and called his Public Relations Officer and asked him to give publicity to the speech in Pakistan. I was glad to make my copy available for the purpose.

In the meanwhile, the adviser came on the phone and the PM spoke to him about his decision to make half the amount of the Social Mobilization Project available through PPAF. I also gave the PM my Note for the Record of a five-day visit to the earthquake-affected areas of NWFP. He glanced through the NFR and observed that he was happy to learn that PPAF was doing very well, as otherwise he had been getting adverse reports on PPAF performance in earthquake areas. I explained to the PM that without PPAF support, NRSP and SRSP would never have been able to help 106,000 households in reconstruction and rehabilitation.

While I was with the PM, he desired to speak to the president of the World Bank and was connected to him in a few minutes. The conversation, which I could not help overhearing, related to the successor of John Wall. The PM said he didn't mind whether the new incumbent was African Muslim or of any religion, so long as he or she was competent and efficient. The PM again rang the adviser to tell him about his conversation with the president of the World Bank, about who would succeed John when he retired on 1 March 2007.

After the telephone conversation with the adviser and the World Bank President, the PM sent for his principal secretary and conveyed to him his decision on the Summary which Ejaz Rahim had submitted. I had the copy along with the planning division's views. The principal secretary enquired about the views of the ministry of finance. I told him to obtain those from them because they had been pending with them.

I thanked the PM and took leave of him. He enquired about my visit to his favourite village, Ezz, in France where I go every year to meet my daughter who lives in Monaco (next to Ezz) with her husband. I spent a few minutes with the principal secretary, requesting him to convey the orders as soon as possible. Next day, at the Microfinance meeting with the PM, the principal secretary, who was sitting next to me, whispered to me that the orders had been conveyed in less than twelve hours.

I left for London on 24 December 2006 literally sailing on clouds. For days I heard nothing except that the Bank had as yet not received the request from EAD. I rang up Shandana [CEO of RSPN] and Rashid [CEO of NRSP] to go and check the status of the case in EAD. They met the additional secretary who seemed very sympathetic but the section officer had raised all kinds of objections. I was shocked to hear that orders issued by the PM were being reexamined by the section officer. I rang up Zamir from London to find out what was happening. He promised to speak to the principal secretary.

As luck would have it, out of the blue, I got a request from the CEO of PPAF to participate in the World Bank sponsored workshop in Islamabad on 15 January 2007 in which the Andhra Pradesh Case Study was being presented. I had been associated with the Andhra Project since 1995 under South Asia Poverty Alleviation Programme (SAPAP). Kamal Hyat wanted me to make a presentation on Social Mobilization in Pakistan.

I rang up the Secretary EAD from London requesting him to send the letter to the Bank as decided by the PM. He assured me it would be done. He was only waiting for the return of the adviser who was in Lahore in connection with the marriage of his daughter. He explained that the letter had to be shown to him before issue.

At the workshop, the additional secretary EAD told me that the letter had been approved and John told me he said the same thing to him.

The same evening at a dinner hosted by John, the Secretary EAD told me that the letter had been issued.

We waited, yet the letter did not arrive at the Bank. Instead, John told me that the section officer had sent a letter to John's newly arrived deputy, asking him the World Bank's views on the Social Mobilization Project funding through PPAF. John was surprised and intrigued and rang up the Secretary EAD who reassured him and asked him to ignore the section officer's letter. It transpired that the section officer had appeared for a job in RSPN and Shandana had not selected her. God knows what the truth was, but I could not believe that orders issued by the PM could be handled with such nonchalance when his principal secretary had conveyed them in less than twelve hours.

In the backdrop of these happenings, at a lunch I happened to meet the Finance Secretary Tanwir Ali Agha, who evinced keen interest in visiting the field to see what the RSPs were doing. I asked NRSP to arrange a field visit on 24 January 2007 as the PM was going to Davos and the finance secretary could take time off from routine work and meetings. Tanwir spent nine hours visiting Thoa Muhram Khan Union Council in Talagang Tehsil.

The letter for US$120 million for Social Mobilization through PPAF was received by the Bank from EAD on 25 January 2007.

Advocates of the RSP Approach

Despite all the goodwill I assumed officials had for me, only those genuinely supported the Project who had personally been to the field and had seen Social Mobilization in action. Dr Akram Sheikh, Ejaz Rahim, Humayun Farshori, Pervez Tahir, Tanwir Ali Agha were the most prominent in this category. Nawid and Zamir believed in me and gave personal support to me.

John Wall proved the greatest advocate of Social Mobilization and made public statements in the Pakistan Forum. Not only this, he followed it up with concrete action to secure funding despite internal opposition. He stood firm like a rock in the face of tremendous pressure. Without John, there would have been no World Bank funding for Social Mobilization.

Pervez Tahir was the catalyst who put the RSPs on the path of mainstreaming Social Mobilization in Pakistan's development planning process. He had been responsible for involving the RSPs in the Poverty Reduction Strategy Paper (PRSP) consultative process; offering me the chairmanship of the Working Group for MTDF; including the Group's report in the Draft MTDF and issuing the Supplement to MTDF based on Group reports. He had also had significant involvement in securing concept clearance by CDWP of Social Mobilization, leading to the EAD request to the Bank and other donors for funding, as well as the preparation of the PC-I. He also guided the consultation by the planning commission team, including the secretary planning, with all the provinces and areas, and was instrumental in the inclusion of the PC-I on Social Mobilization in successive CDWP meetings and the correct recording of minutes.

Pervez Tahir's contribution in mainstreaming Social Mobilization is unmatched, which was also probably one of the reasons for his exit from the planning division despite being on its permanent cadre. I cannot thank Pervez enough for what he did for the Social Mobilization movement in Pakistan.

One of the most important challenges was how to carry the entire RSP family with the concept, as some of them were quite sceptical about undertaking social mobilization without a guaranteed allocation of funds for a community infrastructure package. One of the CEOs was totally opposed to the holistic concept of social mobilization. The Rural Support Programmes Network (RSPN) was the key to taking the process forward which made tremendous demands in terms of drafting PC-Is, organizing meetings and field visits all over Pakistan and the final workshop at Lahore and maintaining constant contact with Federal and Provincial officials. Despite frustration and disappointments, RSPN, under Shandana's helmsmanship, never gave up. She always strove to do the best and did so in every aspect of the exercise. Without RSPN, I could never have imagined embarking on this path. Once the CEOs of the RSPs understood what I was striving for, they gave unreserved and unqualified support. The Chairman PRSP despite CEO PRSP's reservations, did all he could do whenever I requested his help. The Chairperson SRSP never wavered in her support and inspired others to follow her example.

Without Kamal Hyat of PPAF agreeing to act only as a conduit for channelling of Social Mobilization Project funds to the RSPs, the objective of comprehensive, district-wise coverage could not have been achieved. I am grateful to Kamal for his full support once the *raison d'etre* of the Project was understood by him.

Above all it was the prime minister who made it happen. The investments I made in him when he was finance minister, by taking him to villages to see Social Mobilization in action for himself, finally paid off.

Post Script

On a chance participation in a workshop organized by the World Bank, the Bank official confided, on my query about the progress of the Social Mobilization Project, that the economic affairs division (EAD) did not want the case to be pursued and taken to the Executive Board of the Bank for approval. I was stunned. Six months had passed since the Prime Minister's instructions on the subject.

I sought an interview with the PM and apprised him of the situation. The reason for non-compliance was shortage of IDA funds. The PM kindly instructed use of hard IDA funds for the project. A letter was promptly issued to the Bank saying that soft and hard IDA be used for the project.

Nothing happened for another month because the Bank was not being informed of the exact amounts to be taken from each head.

I had to run to the PM again. This time he sent for the official concerned and told him in no uncertain terms to clarify the position to the Bank.

Accordingly, this enabled the country office to get the approval of the Executive Board of the Bank on 11 October 2007. It took another two months and another visit to now the ex-PM for the agreement to be signed between the Bank and the Government of Pakistan (GoP) on 7 December 2007.

I called on the Secretary Finance Ahmad Waqar to expedite the signing of the subsidiary loan agreement (SLA) between the ministry of finance and the Pakistan Poverty Alleviation Fund (PPAF) so that the funds became available to PPAF for the initiation of the project. Fortunately like his predecessor, Ahmad Waqar, strongly urged by the Additional Secretary Asif Bajwa, also agreed to go on a field visit on the 25 December 2007 and was so moved by what he saw that he publicly announced the provision of funds for Social Mobilization through PPAF.

NOTE

1. Shoaib Sultan Khan, 15 February 2007.

17

SAPAP and Andhra Pradesh[1]

I am of the firm conviction that countrywide programmes to eradicate poverty can only be launched by governments of the Third World taking the lead role; and if NGOs and voluntary agencies have demonstrated in many countries how poverty can be alleviated, then there is a strong case for persuading governments to act like NGOs. The Aga Khan Rural Support Programme is such a demonstration and has had its impact both within Pakistan and abroad. The National Rural Support Programme, the Sarhad Rural Support Corporation and the Balochistan Rural Support Programme are national examples of such initiatives and the UNDP project RAS/94/500 is an attempt in the same direction in the countries of the SAARC region.

My five days in Andhra Pradesh brought me closest to witnessing the phenomenon of government departments and functionaries imbibing and emulating a corporate culture like that of NGOs. I was accompanied by Mr S.P. Tucker (SPT), National Project Coordinator, Mr Manohar Prashad (MP), Dr Fatima Ali Khan, (FAK), Mr Paul Diwakar, Mr Murali and UNDP Programme Officer Mr B. Radhakrishnan. We travelled by road nearly 1,000 km through the districts of Anantpur, Kurnool and Mahboobnagar and interacted with over twelve village groups, held detailed discussions with eleven NGOs, visited 18 projects, met district officials under the chairmanship of the respective Collectors and attended a meeting of over 150 government officials and NGOs. Throughout our tour, the Collector of the District or the Joint Collector accompanied us with a horde of officials from other departments. Some of them had even come from adjoining and far off districts of the tribal belt to learn about the UNDP initiative. Although UNDP has, as yet, not provided a single vehicle to the project, there were more than half a dozen government vehicles at our disposal throughout my visit of the area. As a final demonstration of the keen interest and support of the government of Andhra Pradesh for RAS/94/500, on arrival at Hyderabad, I was invited to an official dinner attended by the principal secretary to the chief minister, secretary to the chief minister, principal secretary Rural Development, Panchayat Raj and Relief, secretary Rural Development, commissioner Rural Development and joint secretary, General Administration Department. Considering the pressures on these high officials, in view of the recent induction of the new state government, it was indeed a great honour for me and each one of them assured me of the state government's fullest support to the programme and of their utmost endeavour to make it a success. On my observation that continuity would be an important factor in undertaking institutional development at the grassroots, Mr C. S. Rao, the principal secretary to the chief minister, assured me that the team of officials deputed to the programme would not be disturbed at least for the next five years during the tenure of the current state government.

To my mind, India offers UNDP a unique and a rare opportunity to demonstrate in the State of Andhra Pradesh how to undertake institutional development at the grassroots, the key to eradicating poverty by convergence of services and harnessing of local resources, especially human resources. Most of the inputs required from UNDP would be in the shape of software: catalysts and facilitators at all levels of policymaking and implementation, lobbyist, advocates and intermediaries for the poor with Government and donor agencies. The World Bank is contemplating a US$500 million programme entitled District Poverty Initiatives Project (DPIP) in three states, which includes nine of Andhra's 23 districts. The state offers the UNDP a canvas on which to operate, which can have substantial impact on national policy pertaining to poverty eradication. Besides the software inputs for meeting the cost of a small but highly dynamic, motivated, talented and effective management group and district teams, funding would be required for human resource development and strengthening of partner NGOs, by way of modest investments in organizations and assistance to communities.

If I were Von Sponeck [Resident Representative UNDP] I would not let this opportunity slip by at any cost. This is an opportunity for UNDP to have a very high profile in Andhra Pradesh with a modest investment and thereafter to create an impact on the national scene in assaulting poverty, the biggest scourge of South Asia.

Andhra Really Shining (24 to 31 March 2007)[2]

Subakurtama (alias Subama) belongs to a nomadic tribe and twelve years ago she used to survive by begging and selling broomsticks. Her husband had deserted her and left her with a daughter to look after. Her father and sister were dead so she had to take care of her sister's two children. Some of the members of the Self Help Group (SHG) in the village, formed under South Asia Poverty Alleviation Programme (SAPAP) supported by UNDP, asked her to join the SHG. She could not afford to save the one rupee a day required for SHG membership. By now the SHGs formed in village Seva comprising 1,271 households, had also federated into a Village Organization (VO). In 1997, the VO offered to pay savings of one rupee a day for the next five months for all those who could not afford to save, to be repaid in due course.

Subama's abode was under a tree, and whenever it rained she would either make a shelter with a tarpaulin or shift to a common shelter for destitutes in the village. She joined this pre-SHG group of ten scheduled tribe members. The VO also arranged to get them daily wage labour. Subama went to Hasanapuram and Kalva for training under SAPAP. She never believed that, by becoming a member of an SHG, she could come out of poverty, but training built up her confidence.

As she had no roof over her head, Subama persuaded her SHG to make housing an agenda item for securing shelter for all destitutes in the village. The VO, on the demand of the SHGs, carried out a survey and identified 25 shelterless families and made a demand for housing on their behalf to the *sarpanch* of the *panchayat,* and persuaded the *sarpanch* to allocate housing funds received by the *panchayat* as housing grants from the state government to the deserving destitutes. The *gram panchayat* sanctioned 24 housing grants. Subama was one of the recipients.

However, Subama could only access the housing grant of Rs 16,000 if she could show that she had laid the foundations of the house. Her SHG came to her rescue and lent her Rs 5,000. With the housing subsidy money she could build only up to ceiling level; her SHG again came to her rescue and lent her Rs 10,000 and recommended her candidature to the Panchayat for appointment as *Aganwadi* (Day Care Centre) caretaker at Rs 200 p.m. She was also sanctioned a loan of Rs 20,000 for income generating activities with which she bought two milch animals and paid back Rs 35,000 from the income she generated. She then borrowed Rs 60,000 to buy six buffaloes which produced 40 litres of milk every day. She proudly showed the buffaloes to us and also the milk collection vehicle which took away the milk from her doorstep, after she had measured the density of the milk.

Being a daycare centre caretaker, she offered to be trained as a para-health worker. After completing the training she arranged medical health camps and helped build HIV AIDs awareness besides dealing with immunization and nutrition needs of pregnant women. Once, while traveling in a bus, she helped deliver a baby to a woman passenger in distress.

After joining the SHG Subama understood the importance of education and is now in the forefront of the plan of the VO for construction of an English medium school. She is confident that the school will make more than 5,000 villagers proficient in English in the next ten years, even enabling them to acquire education abroad.

Although she had to marry her daughter off at a young age because there was no male member in her household, she was fully conscious of the evils of child marriage. However, her son-in-law agreed to her daughter continuing her education after marriage and the girl is now a qualified practising nurse.

Subama calls the SHG her life, because it enabled her to access Rs 200,000 over ten years, when not long ago she was a beggar and a shelterless woman. Now she has not only one house, she has even bought a plot of land for Rs 27,000 and is building on it a spacious house for her daughter and her sister's children. In the past the government did allocate funds for the rural poor but the money never reached the intended recipients. With the support of the VO not only does the money reach the poor; they now have access even to the Collector and the superintendent of Police. SHG has given the destitutes and the poor a status and equal rights.

Subama was most grateful to the SHG Council members who reached her, and despite her reluctance, did not give up persuading her to join the group. Now Subama is acting as community resource person (CRP), persuading destitutes and poor people to organize and has herself organized 50 SHGs. She is also undertaking pension distribution under a government programme. She proudly publicizes her example and what she has made of herself by joining the SHG/VO/Mahila Mandal Samakhya.

Subama's life story is the story of hundreds of thousands of rural poor families of Andhra Pradesh (AP) who decided to join the SHG. Beginning with 20 Mandals in three districts covering no more than

100,000 families in 1996 under SAPAP, now the coverage with World Bank assistance has been taken by the state government through the Society for Elimination of Rural Poverty (SERP) to 884 Mandals in 22 districts of AP covering eight million families.

The centrepiece of the programme, now being called Indira Kranti Patham (IKP), is social mobilization motivating rural poor women to organize in groups of 10–15 and, when a sufficient number of SHGs are formed, to federate them in a Village Organization (VO). Subsequently, the VOs federate at the Mandal level in a Mahila Mandal Samakhya representing around 30 VOs which in turn represent about 350–500 SHGs comprising 4,500 to 6,000 women, each representing a family of on average five members. SERP is the support organization which fosters SHGs/VOs and MMSs. In 2000 it subsumed SAPAP when the World Bank stepped into the shoes of UNDP.

The grassroots institutional framework of SHGs/VOs/MMSs is, unlike NGOs, a sensitive support organization of the poor for the poor. It is financially self-managed. In the year 2000, they had accessed Rs 700 crores (Rs 7000 million) from the commercial banks, beginning with a seed capital of five million rupees provided by UNDP to each of the 20 Mandals. By 2004 this had increased to Rs 1,100 crores.

However, in 2004 the newly elected state government redeemed its promise made in the election manifesto and provided an interest subsidy to SHGs of 75 per cent of the interest paid by them to the bank. By early 2007 the credit uptake had shot up to 2,500 crores and next year the SHGs hope to cross the 3,500 crores figure, coupled with the state government's directive to the banks for priority banking for the poor.

Another important initiative by the state government has been the housing subsidy for destitute and shelterless people identified by the VOs. This, coupled with the union governments' launch of the 100-days employment guarantee scheme to the rural jobless, has accelerated poverty reduction.

Andhra has demonstrated a poverty reduction model unparalleled anywhere in South Asia. It has already impacted the livelihood of 8 million families and targets to reach another three million in the next two years. SERP has not stopped only at alleviating poverty, as most micro-credit programmes do: it has facilitated millions of poor and destitute families to come out of poverty.

SERP's most effective strategy in scaling up its operations from coverage of 100,000 households to eight million households has been the use of Community Resource Persons (CRPs) from the SAPAP Mandals. Each of these Mandals has a pool of Social Capital comprising 250–300 CRPs. These CRPs form themselves in groups of five and normally two groups take up a Mandal for fostering SHGs spending a fortnight a month for the next six months in the Mandal. The end result is 100 per cent coverage of the destitutes and the poor, comprising Backward Classes and the minorities and also the upper caste poor. The SHGs so formed federate in VOs and subsequently in MMS. The engagement of CRPs for social mobilization to achieve an institutional framework at the grassroots of SHGs/VOs/MMSs has given phenomenal results at very low cost.

The Orvakal Mandal in Kurnool District has 489 SHGs and 27 VOs with 5,562 households as members represented by women. They have 978 leaders trained in different descriptions. SAPAP gave them seed capital of three million rupees and SERP has given them Rs 2.9 million as a Community Investment Fund (CIF) since 1996. They accessed Rs 11 crores 65 lacs (Rs 116.5 million) in loans from banks. Thus, during the last 12 years, by turnover of their savings, seed capital, CIF grants and bank loans, the SHGs/VOs and MMSs gave 33,226 loans amounting to Rs 18 crores (Rs 180 million) to the 5,562 members.

The Orvakal MMS linked with 23 development programmes of government and also forged partnership with seven donors and constructed their own building at a cost of two crores (Rs 20 million) called Social Mobilization and Experimentation Learning Centre (SMELC). It has so far trained 18,000 women from all over the state.

The Orvakal MMS designed its own programme for the landless with a grant received from the Turner Foundation through UNDP SAPAP. It has acquired 182 hectares of land and settled 98 landless families.

Under the Jeevna Joyti (Life Saving) programme, the MMS supports 292 families suffering from malaria and TB.

Twenty-three VOs have their own Mahila banks with a capital of 2 crores 11 lacs (Rs 21.1 million) of 1,149 members.

Under the Bhavita programme, the MMS has provided 1,050 child labourers with residential schooling, leading to their admission in educational institutions including centres of higher education. The Mandal has been rid of bonded child labour. SMELC also runs a computer training center.

Empowerment has persuaded the government to link up with MMS at the Mandal level. MMS has been given a role in ensuring delivery of government services such as health, education, peace committees for policing, and other government programmes. The *sarpanch* of the *panchayat* also heeds the suggestions of the MMS and acts on their complaints.

The activities of women as demonstrated through SHGs/VOs/MMS had a salutary effect on the menfolk, and their criticism and scepticism have now turned into admiration as many of them had got capital through their wives and are doing thriving businesses.

The Orvakal Mahila Mandal Samakhaya's vision is elimination of poverty by 2008 and their slogan is 'women need development and development needs women'.

The spirit behind Orvakal Mandal's spectacular achievements is Vijayabharti who joined SAPAP in 1995 as a Social Organizer and has now dedicated herself to the cause of empowering women for poverty reduction. Under her guidance and patronage, the Orvakal MMS plans to build a residential school to which the erstwhile child labourers, now grown-up and fully qualified nurses, contributed a substantial sum of money saved from their earnings. This was their contribution to the future generations. It was a most touching gesture.

Gradually the women are also making inroads into the political set-up and have succeeded in winning many of the seats in the *panchayat*. A few of them have also been elected as *sarpanch*. However, their effort in winning a seat against a 300-acre landowner did not succeed. As against 600 votes the woman candidate got only 300 votes. But she had the satisfaction of knowing that she had not paid a penny for the votes, unlike her opponent.

The *Adarsh Mahila Mandal Somakhya* in Anantpur District was formed in March 1998 and is now nine years old. It comprises 438 SHGs, 38 VOs and 4,373 families represented by women. The total savings of SHGs/VOs and MMS is Rs 1 crore 28 lacs (Rs 12.8 million) and a loan turnover of Rs 15 crores 6 lacs (Rs 150.6 million). They have employed 155 bookkeepers for SHGs and 38 animators for the VOs. Their salaries are paid by the SHGs and VOs. The MMS has an income of Rs 70,831 and expenditure of Rs 38,000 monthly. The MMS is paying professional staff. The VOs bear the cost of participation of their representatives in monthly MMS meetings. Like Orvakal they also have close links with Mandal government departments.

The Collector of Anantpur, Mr Kadmiel, described some of the pro-poor programmes being implemented in the district, which is the biggest in area in the state, and a rain shadow region. He described the

SHGs as formidable groups along with VOs and MMS. These are now helping the district administration in distributing Rs 200 per month old age pensions to 160,000 persons; a housing subsidy of Rs 25,000 to 150,000 shelterless destitutes; and a minimum of 100 days' work to the jobless. According to the Collector, 7,000 people were provided more than 100 days' work under the employment guarantee scheme.

The SHGs have accessed more than 95 crores (950 million) in loans from commercial banks under a priority banking scheme for the rural poor. Rs 2 crores 79 lacs (Rs 27.9 million) was paid back to the SHGs as interest subsidy.

The VOs have been given responsibility for selecting engineers for the housing scheme and the distribution of wages under National Employment Guarantee Scheme, which was launched by the Prime Minister of India from the district of Anantpur. Rs 73 crores (Rs 730 million) has so far been disbursed under this scheme in the district through the SHGs/VOs/MMSs.

The 7 UNDP/SAPAP Mandals in Anantpur District have formed a *Maha Mahila Mandal Samakhya* (MMMS) and this meeting was being held in their newly constructed building. The objectives of the MMMS were described as follows:

- documentation of case studies of the thousands of poor who came out of poverty, and putting it on the website
- facilitating the MMS
- making SHGs/VOs/MMSs self managed
- training of MMSs
- mobilizing support for the poorest of the poor (PoP) and the poorest families (PF)

MMMS is the only facilitator to MMSs and will perform only those functions which are beyond the purview and capacity of MMS. Three representatives from each of the 7 MMSs sit on the MMMS. There are 1,000 CRPs fostered by 7 SAPAP Mandals.

To identify gaps MMMS requires each MMS to report on the following:

- Whether SHGs are self managed in terms of paying Book Keepers
- Do VOs have trained and paid animators?
- Do VOs have their own office?

- Do VOs pay travel expenses for participation in MMS meetings to their representatives?
- Number of meetings of MMS and the percentage of the attendance
- Percentage of recovery of loans taken by SHGs
- Percentage of recovery of loan money taken by VO from MMS
- Percentage of recovery of loan money disbursed by MMS to VOs
- Rotation of capital by SHGs/VOs/MMSs
- Demand collection sheets preparation
- Identification of training needs
- Volume of bank support

The functioning of MMS is to be evaluated on the following criteria:

- How many girls have been sponsored for higher education? In one Mandal we were told the MMS had sponsored 30 girls for higher education in engineering, medical and computer science colleges
- Identification and stoppage of child labour
- Support to pregnant women
- Support to *Balika Sanghas* (Youth Groups)

One of the important areas of focus of the MMMS would be strengthening of not only financial but management audit. The auditors of one MMS would be asked to audit and rate an MMS other than their own. The auditors will seek explanations for amounts of money sitting idle and not in circulation. An intensive training of auditors would be arranged by MMMS.

MMMS would also encourage sharing of experiences between Mandals both good and bad to learn from each other. It is also planning to encourage MMSs to establish family counseling centers.

On my query as to why the need for MMMS was felt in the presence of a *Zila Mahila Mandal Samakhya* the response was that the seven SAPAP Mandals are the resource group for providing CRPs and manual of good practices to the remaining 56 Mandals in the district. It was critical that the SAPAP Mandals not only be centres of excellence for others to follow, but keep on preserving the integrity of the social mobilization approach.

About the weaknesses in non-SAPAP Mandals, it was pointed out that it is only the leaders of the SHGs who are participating, and not the entire group. In SAPAP Mandals, to ensure participation by every member of the SHG, weekly meetings are held by rotation in the house of each of the 10–15 members, who presides at the meeting. The Council of the SHG, comprising three to five members, changes every three years.

The weekly meetings of non-SAPAP SHGs were irregular, without fixed days and time, so their training was reduced from 20 days to 10 days. SAPAP SHGs always meet during the day while non-SAPAP SHGs were mostly meeting at night. The ratio of Book Keepers in SAPAP Mandals is one to three, while in non-SAPAP Mandals it was one to eight/ten SHGs.

The Collector of Anantpur was also present in the meeting. MMMS has been given the responsibility of rectifying the defects and their CRPs are working in 20 Mandals.

When the UNDP SAPAP Mandal women representatives expressed their thanks for my contribution towards their development, I protested that it was all due to their determination and hard work. They responded that if UNDP had not planted the seedling, it would never have grown into the tree you see today.

Warangal District initiated the social mobilization approach only three years ago.

We were received by the Collector of the District Ms Damayanthi, who had earlier worked with UNDP SAPAP. We visited a village where non-pesticide management (NPM) is being practiced in growing cotton and chillies. More than 40 surrounding villages have taken note of the success and demonstrations of NPM and are gradually adopting it.

Our next visit was to a village where physically challenged individuals have been organized into groups of seven by the MMS comprising 790 members who have accessed credit worth Rs 23 lacs (Rs 2.3 million), residing in 24 villages. These included beggars, people with severe disabilities and the disabled. It was most heartwarming to see what each one of them had achieved in a short period of less than three years with the help of the Disability Project. It was something new for me too as also for other members of the Rural Support Programmes Network (RSPN) group. It was most moving.

After a sumptuous lunch hosted by the Collector at the Circuit House, Warangal, which was at one time the capital of the Kakutiya dynasty and is the second largest town after Hyderabad in AP, we proceeded to Preegeeta Mahila Mandal Samakhya, accompanied by the

Joint Collector Mr Jaleel, who was speaking chaste Hyderabadi Urdu.

Two years ago 500 SHGs were formed, which met monthly and irregularly till two groups of CRPs comprising ten members arrived from Anantpur. Now, according to the President of the MMS, 98 per cent of the 8,719 poor have been organized in SHGs living in 53 villages and 53 VOs have been formed. The SHGs have appointed and are paying 224 Book Keepers. 40 VOs have their offices on rent. In addition:

- 25 VOs are distributing government pensions to 2,072 persons amounting to Rs 533,000. 599 members have insured themselves at a premium of Rs 100 per year against accidental and natural death. The insurance policy covers a family of five.
- 38 VOs have registered themselves as Cooperatives under AP Mutual Cooperative Societies Act.
- 633 SHGs have received Rs 942,000 as interest subsidy.
- The MMS has an income of Rs 36,607 per month and an expenditure of only Rs 1,500 monthly.

The Anantpur CRPs have motivated and trained SHGs to hold weekly meetings and savings and group training. CRPs gave training on preparing Micro Investment Plans (MIPs). They also trained office bearers of the SHGs and trained book keepers and community animators.

The Anantpur CRPs gave such excellent training that the MMS has now a pool of their own CRPs who are going to adjoining Districts Maidak, Rangareddy and Adilabad to train SHG office bearers.

Mr Jaleel proudly told us that the VOs were assigned by the district administration the procurement of maize and paddy, which they did to the entire satisfaction of the Collector. The system saved the administration not only a lot of botheration but also prevented leakages and corruption. On an average the VOs made a profit of Rs 100,000 each as commission. The VOs procured 40,000 tons, worth Rs 9 million, and got 1 per cent commission.

Our visit to the 'training for jobs' programme, an innovation of Collector Damayanthi, was another heartwarming experience. We met three distinct groups who had rural backgrounds and who had obtained degrees and educational qualifications but were not employable. In collaboration with industry leaders, the Trade Training Development

Centre has designed special three-month courses for men, boys and girls to equip them with the skills needed by commercial and industrial firms. These courses focused on communication skills and confidence building. Many trainees came to the stage and spoke with confidence. When one girl felt a bit nervous and someone suggested she take a pause, she confidently responded 'It is OK' and gathered herself up and spoke with full confidence. Many of them who had graduated from training for job courses spoke what kind of jobs they had secured and how pleased they were with themselves. Damayanthi should rightly feel proud of this wonderful initiative she has espoused.

The dinner at the Collector's 120-year old house for the Pakistani group was an expression of hospitality and warmth of welcome coming straight from the heart of the hostess who ten years ago had visited Pakistan, including the Northern Areas. We were simply overwhelmed.

At Hyderabad, the Minister for Rural Development, Rural Water Supply and Employment Generation, Mr D. Srinivas, hosted a banquet for the group in the regal surroundings of the Nizam of Hyderabad's Jubilee Manzil. He made a speech which was full of generous praise for the UNDP SAPAP strategy. In an aside, he said to me, 'Raju must have mentioned your name a hundred times to me'. The interest and enthusiastic support that the minister was giving to SERP is rarely found in politicians. His concern for the poor seemed to override all other considerations.

Our meeting with the Chief Minister Dr Rajsekhar Reddy was like meeting the ideologue of the state government's policies for poverty reduction. It was his brainchild to provide an interest subsidy complemented with priority banking for the poor and a housing subsidy for the shelterless destitutes. These two initiatives have made all the difference to the poor, pulling them out of abject poverty to a prosperous and comfortable existence.

In 1995, when UNDP initiated SAPAP, my job as senior adviser was to identify one person in Andhra Pradesh who would understand the potential of people and how it can be unleashed through the process of Social Mobilization. I was lucky that my friend K.R. Venugopal identified K. Raju for me. I had to do nothing except interact with Raju. He found his team and implemented SAPAP. Raju was lucky in finding Vijay Kumar. My mentor and teacher Akhtar Hameed Khan used to say 'You don't replicate programmes, you replicate people.'

Conclusion

This is the 54th year of my working life. I have spent the last 29 years holding dialogues with rural poor communities in Pakistan and the preceding 12 years in South Asia including Andhra Pradesh from 1995–2002. I have since been visiting Andhra once in a year on the invitation of the Society for Elimination of Rural Poverty (SERP) set up by the State government.

My week-long visit to Andhra at the end of the last month and seeing the achievements of the State government in the last three years has encouraged me to conclude that Andhra has been able to demonstrate an approach of poverty reduction encompassing 8 million rural poor families which has no parallel anywhere in South Asia, including the Grameen Bank. Andhra has found the solution to rural poverty comprising:

i) a three-tier institutional grassroots framework of Self Help Groups (SHGs), Village Organizations (VOs) and Mahila Mandal Samakhyas (MMSs);
ii) an independent and autonomous sensitive support organization like SERP for fostering a statewide 3-tier grassroots institutional framework;
iii) an interest-subsidy policy for the poor matched with priority banking by scheduled banks for the poor;
iv) a state-wide housing subsidy for the destitutes and shelterless identified by VOs:
v) full and active support by the State and district administrations under the direction of the Honourable Chief Minister and the Minister for Rural Development; and
vi) pro-poor Union Government policies such as the employment guarantee scheme and other pro-poor initiatives.

We should not look anywhere else for rural poverty reduction in South Asia although the saying that the neighbour's grass always looks greener makes one do so. India has now a home-grown model for poverty elimination. It would be a tragedy and injustice to the rural poor of India, if the rest of India does not take advantage of the Andhra demonstration.

In Delhi, I had the privilege of being received by Mr Jairam Ramesh, Union Minister, to whom I conveyed my thoughts and my pleas.

NOTES

1. Shoaib Sultan Khan, Back To Office Report—India, 7–14 January 1995.
2. Shoaib Sultan Khan, 3 April 2007.

List of Appendices

1. A Man Named Khan by Varindra Tarzie Vittachi, *Newsweek*—5 January 1981 — 415
2. My daughter—Falaknaz — 418
3. His Highness the Aga Khan's address to the VOs of Garam Chashma and Karimabad, Chitral 1987 — 422
4. Conversation with His Highness the Aga Khan on working with Government — 423
5. Meeting with His Highness the Aga Khan—24 March 1983 — 427
6. Ah! Hussain Wali—A Tribute — 433
7. The Helicopter Crash — 436
8. Visit of Her Highness Princess Zahra Aga Khan — 440
9. Note by an Intern — 442
10. Shimshal—Exile to a Haven — 444
11. The Shadows of Violence and Shelley's Anguish — 449
12. Akhtar Hameed Khan's Summary of the AKRSP approach to Sustainable Development — 452
13. Two Days with Mr Rahul Gandhi, MP—22 July 2008 — 457
14. Activists turned CRPs of Andhra Pradesh—24 July 2008 — 466

Appendix 1
A Man Named Khan

In a remote Asian Village, an unusual 'International Expert' keeps his feet on the ground and sows the seeds of real progress

Newsweek/5 January 1981

Varindra Tarzie Vittachi

OPINION

A MAN NAMED KHAN

I met a rare man the other day. His name is Khan and what gives him distinction is the fact that he is one 'International Expert' on village development programmes who actually lives in a village. I have been in that village, a place miles from what city folk call Anywhere. There is no piped water in the village, nor air conditioning, no electrification, not even a toe-powered pankah batting the hot breeze this way and that as was done in the days of the British raj.

    Mr Khan's speciality is that he is a generalist. He knows how to tie together the activities of the irrigation department, the education department, the health department and the public works department so that they help the people for whose benefit, presumably, such departments were established. Since he shares the lifestyle of the villagers and knows their local idiom, he has become credible. When he explains why kitchen refuse turns the rain drains outside their houses into breeding places for the malaria mosquito, or how nursing mothers should-and can-have a balanced diet even if they are poor, and why it is better for their babies to be breast-fed despite the blandishments of 'fashion', they believe him.

    One result of all this is that the people of the village have begun to be involved and to understand the development process going on around them. The buzzword for it in the operational planning centres is 'community participation'. Where Mr Khan lives, that phrase is no longer a piece of pious humbug mouthed by professional bureaucrats and alleged experts in made-to-major safari jackets, but a meaningful response to an understood need.

There are other men and women like Mr Khan working in other villages on human development programmes, but there are still far too few. In the two remaining decades of this century, many more of these people will be needed if the grand goals of the world community, such as 'health for all by 2000' and 'literacy for all by 2000' are going to be more than hollow slogans. Even to achieve the less ambitious goals of reducing hunger and eliminating the worst aspects of poverty, the elitist approach to development will have to change. It took two decades for people to realize that the system that was initially established was expensive and irrelevant. It often served as a sinecure for colonial officers left by the receding tide of imperialism. Often these ex-colonials marched towards what they called modernism. They built dams and highways and hospitals in which the doctors practiced on people when they were already sick, instead of preventing illness through effective health programmes. The foreign experts—as well as their local counterparts—lived in the city and believed that what was good for urban residents was good for those who lived in the villages.

The second set of 'experts' came from a wider pool of technicians working for United Nations agencies. They too were mostly city gents bent on 'transferring technology' from Europe and America to the developing world. The era of high dams and hydropower plants that loomed like indifferent giants over the heads of the villagers was followed by the era of overpasses and underpasses that became the new symbols of modern development. And still the Third World's foreign debts grew while opportunities for a tolerable life for the rural people dwindled. The people trekked to the cities to find jobs. But the pilgrimage was too late; there were too few jobs to go around.

At the great development planning centre-all in metropolitan cities of the Industrial democracies-some belated lessons were being learned. The benefits of the transfer of technical assistance and money were not trickling down to the villages. As the experts had expected, social and economic distinctions separating the cities elite and the country gentry from the rural poor were powerful bearers, against an equitable distribution of development gains. 'Top down' development strategies—one of those bureaucratic phrases that means less than meets the eye or ear—was found to be ineffective because without the willing and active participation of the people whose lives would be affected, no true social change could occur. At long last it had also become evident that if technical expertise was to be useful, it had to be directly relevant to the village.

This year's 'World Development Report' of the World Bank enshrines these lessons. It says that efforts to improve people's lives must begin where the people are, that human being are what development is all about, that the village community is the building block of national growth. That is indeed a *tour de force* from a body that has spent thirty years supplying money and experts to finance top-down development programmes. It is a document that has given legitimacy to the notion that villagers are bankable even if they cannot yet sign a check.

They tell a story about the visit by Robert McNamara the World Bank President to a village in Asia. The area has been developing rapidly because now it has access to water that can be used for irrigating the crop lands. McNamara remarked to a farmer: 'I hear you are becoming prosperous'. The farmer replied yes, things were improving. 'And what is your annual income now?' asked McNamara. 'None of your business', replied the farmer and walked away. That is the most heartening human-development story I have heard in many a year. But perhaps the best thing about it is that the person who tells the story is Robert McNamara himself. And this Asian village is the village in which Mr Khan lives.

Appendix 2

My daughter—Falaknaz

On that fateful day, Tuesday, 20 December 1988 our Balti houseboy, Ishaq, picked up the phone and asked me to return to the house immediately saying 'Manchu Bibi's children have been affected by gas and Begum Sahiba has taken them to the hospital'. This being an emergency I reasoned that they must have gone to the Polyclinic. As I opened the door of the Polyclinic, I was relieved, for a fleeting moment, to see Musarrat sitting there. But just as she saw me she cried out in anguish and simultaneously Dr (Mrs) Kazmi, wife of my senior service colleague Mr M.A. Kazmi (Federal Secretary), got up and took me outside. She mumbled something and I asked 'Bhabhi, are you telling me they are dead?' She said 'Yes'. I went numb and simply asked 'Could I see them?' She took me to a room where Manchu lay covered by a white sheet. Shan and Pareesa lay in their own clothes. They all appeared sound asleep. I could not believe that she was no more. I went to Shan and Pareesa and found the same expression.

I was in a daze. Everything went numb. It seemed a walking nightmare. I had no tears in my eyes. I could not face Musarrat who did not know that they were no more and was still clinging to hope. Musarrat was told that they were all in intensive care and nobody was allowed to see them. We both sat there. The silence was more expressive than any number of words.

I went back to the Emergency Block and wanted to have another look at my sleeping children. A hospital staff came and hustled me out. By now Tariq Siddiqi had come followed by Hasan Zaheer (the Cabinet Secretary) and others. The police also appeared and started asking questions about the tragedy. The police recorded my statement and took my signatures. In the meanwhile doctors confirmed the gas suffocation verdict.

I listened to everyone and did whatever they wanted me to do. They wanted to know about burial arrangements. I could not decide anything without consulting Jamshed. Musarrat didn't know what had happened and everyone was trying to take her away from the Polyclinic. Finally, Qumri (Musarrat's nephew) succeeded in persuading her to go to his house. Tariq and Kazimbhai had in the meantime flashed the news of the tragedy to Jamshed in Peshawar and to Manchu's sisters in London and all other near and dear ones in Pakistan.

It was nearing three o'clock when someone whispered to me that Manchu, Shaan and Pareesa were in two ambulances, ready to go home.

APPENDICES

Shireen, Tariq and Bhabhi had made all the arrangements to receive Manchu, Shaan and Pareesa. They were taken to the Pink Room—Shelley's room. Everything seemed normal except that my three darlings were sleeping on stretchers and camp cots. My relatives, friends and well-wishers started pouring. Jamshed had arrived. I took him to the Pink Room and he looked at each face and cried his heart out. The stream of visitors to the Pink Room was unending. It was now getting dark. I had to break the news to Musarrat. I broke the news and she went into a state of shock.

* * *

Extract from a letter from Falaknaz dated 2 June 1979, addressed to me:

My very Dearest and Darling and Beautiful and my Love from the core of my heart I love you very much and I miss you immensely. I wonder if you get time off your work to even give me a second thought (of course Ammi first) I miss her so much that it seems my boarding school stone-heart has melted into a human one again.

* * *

Someone sent me the following poem to console me:

Do Not Stand at my Grave and Cry

Do not stand at my grave and weep;
I am not there.
I do not sleep.
I am a thousand winds that blow.
I am the diamond glints on snow.
I am the sunlight on ripened grain.
I am the gentle autumn's rain.
When you awaken in the morning's hush,
I am the swift uplifting rush of quiet birds in circled flight.
I am the soft stars that shine at night. Do not stand at my grave and cry;
I am not there.
I did not die.

* * *

In Memory of Falaknaz

My tears are dry
But my soul still cries
Is it in vain
To rid the pain?

I see you lie
Under a quilt of narcissi
A bed of roses
Reflect your poses

Thy frozen beauty
Invokes tears bloody
That shed in vain
To rid the pain

Shelley Shoaib
20 December 1988

* * *

FALAKNAZ HAS FORSAKEN US

The beauty of the Earth Falaknaz has forsaken us,
The most good natured and the most pleasant mannered has forsaken us:
We don't know with whom she was annoyed but she left us,
We don't know with whom she was unhappy that she forsook us:
She is calling us from the heights of the skies,
But our capacity to fly has forsaken us:
That story did not reach its end,
That story forsook us at the very beginning:
The minds are numb and the hearts are at a standstill,
Because every voice of life has forsaken us:
Had she waited, we would have won her back,
But with haste and hundreds of coquettish gestures she forsook us:
Shoaib is heartbroken and Musarrat has her life on her lips,
The one who used to breathe life in everyone has forsaken us:
There is neither budlike Pareesa nor flowerlike Zeeshan,
The one who used to spread spring in the home has forsaken us:
In the darkness of the night she called us many a time,
When no door opened she forsook us:
Words failed the pen and I had to drip blood,
Faraz even the wealth of words has forsaken me.

Ahmad Faraz

فلک ناز ہم سے روٹھ گئی

زمین کا حسن فلک ناز ہم سے روٹھ گئی
نہ جانے کس سے خفا تھی، جدا ہوئی ہم سے
وہ آسمانوں سے ہم کو پکارتی ہے مگر
دماغ سن ہیں دلوں پر سکوت طاری ہے
وہ قصہ پایۂ تکمیل تک نہیں پہنچا
وہ انتظار جو کرتی تو ہم منا لیتے
شعیب زخم بہ دل جان بلب مسرت ہے
نہ وہ کلی سی پریسا نہ پھول سا ذیشان
شب سیاہ میں اس نے بہت پکارا ہمیں

وہ خوش مزاج و خوش انداز ہم سے روٹھ گئی
نہ جانے کس سے تھی ناراض ہم سے روٹھ گئی
ہماری طاقت پرواز ہم سے روٹھ گئی
کہ زندگی کی ہر آواز ہم سے روٹھ گئی
وہ داستاں سر آغاز ہم سے روٹھ گئی
وہ جلد باز بصد ناز ہم سے روٹھ گئی
وہی جو سب کی تھی دمساز ہم سے روٹھ گئی
بہار خانہ بر انداز ہم سے روٹھ گئی
جو در ہوا نہ کوئی باز ہم سے روٹھ گئی

ملے نہ حرف قلم کو تو خون ٹپکایا!
فراز دولت الفاظ ہم سے روٹھ گئی

Appendix 3

His Highness the Aga Khan's Address to the VOs of Garam Chashma and Karimabad, Chitral 1987

I am deeply honoured and happy to be amongst you today. For many years, I have been concerned about the quality of life of people in the Northern Areas, Chitral and other parts of North West Pakistan. The programmes that you are participating in represent to me a beginning. A vision of the future which, *Inshallah*, will be better, happier, healthier and more united. It is my conviction that the Village Organizations, run successfully, as you have been running yours, will be capable of extending their activities into new areas of endeavour in the years ahead. And it is my hope that as your Village Organization become stronger, they will address themselves to new and more challenging problems in addition to improving the quality of agriculture in your area. I would like to congratulate you on the excellent work that has been achieved and on laying the foundations of organization, of hard work, discipline and integrity which, *Inshallah*, will enable you to make good progress in the years ahead. I wish to emphasize, however, that this progress is dependent on unity; on seeking to achieve together results which are impossible to achieve where individuals work alone. In the years ahead, *Inshallah*, you will create wealth for the villagers. Creating wealth is one problem that we seek to share in addressing. Managing wealth after it has been created is the second problem. I hope that the second phase will be administered by the Village Organization with the same integrity and the same wisdom as the first phase of the Rural Support Programme. In that second phase, we will continue to assist you so that the labour of one generation produces better and more fruit for the successive generation. It is my hope to extend their knowledge, their wisdom, and their understanding of the area, to domains of endeavour, which are also important to the quality of life in the Northern Areas. I am referring to health, to education and to housing. These are all areas where, *Inshallah*, as the Village Organizations get stronger, they will be capable of assisting you to improve the quality of health, the quality of education and the quality of housing in the Northern Areas, so that future generations can benefit from a total improvement in the quality of their life.

Appendix 4
Conversation with His Highness the Aga Khan on working with Government (May 1983)

GM: Sir, I must mention that without the support of government institutions, the programme would not have made such progress. It was possible only under the patronage of the Martial Law Administrator, the Commissioner and Deputy Commissioner Badrul Islam, who is here. The administration has been extremely supportive of our effort. We work in close collaboration with them, with the Commissioner and with the Additional Commissioner (Development). We exchange plans with them. We tell them where we are, what we are doing and of course when we are putting together a portfolio of micro-level projects we hope that working with the LB&RD Department would provide an excellent ground for collaboration. I feel that each of these projects can be jointly implemented because we can provide them with both technical and implementation expertise. The Deputy Commissioner (DC) might like to say something because he has been associated with our work and he has been going to these places.

DC: I think we have, Your Highness, been probably unduly flattered. We do try to help but it's Mr Shoaib Sultan's charismatic personality itself which has done the trick. As far as the administration is concerned, I think that AKRSP is a great asset for the district. We try to sort out the small issues and conflicts that arise on account of diametrically opposed rural development programme operating in this area. So far we have successfully handled the issues.

His Highness: So you don't have any questions you would like to raise now.... I think that at the beginning of a programme it is very useful that one benefits from everybody's comments and views and people's perceptions on what is being done and how it is being done. [It is also good to note] what might be done better or differently. Bill and the others in the Foundation and I like listening to what people have to say—they have the greatest contributions to make.

GM: When there are major projects we refer them to agencies like Northern Areas Works Organization (NAWO).

His Highness: It would be interesting to know about them.

DG NAWO: Our projects have a slightly bigger size, there are schools, and the other major projects are in the field of power, electricity generation and roads.

His Highness: And now the Directors of the company perhaps want to comment. I see one or two around the table. Any comments?

His Highness: I think it has been a very, very useful exercise for me to see some of the projects and to understand the way they are put together. I have a feeling that there are two areas which need attention. The first is the direction of the programme. The sense I had today (and perhaps it's unwise as it is on the basis of the sense of one day) but, nevertheless, I think that [it is] these micro-projects which have a direct impact on village life and perhaps that is something we all ought to think more about. I think the other area is perhaps economic development where there is a lot to do.

AKRSP tends to generate…a lot of activity. And to do that one has to define the natural outlet in terms of the economic benefits to the area. The last point really would be the coordination with other programmes like those of the Aga Khan Central Health and Education Boards. We can discuss that in Karachi, but coordinating the activities of these groups is important, so that we understand what they are doing and so that their programmes would be mutually supportive. The last comment, which has nothing to do with AKRSP but, nonetheless, affects everybody's efficiency is that I dearly desire that that piece of equipment (the helicopter) should be flying. I think that the decision to use a helicopter was rather unilateral and I am more than happy to be proven wrong if that equipment is being used. If it is sitting on the ground, then it is of no use. It has to help people to get to the remoter areas, to see for themselves what is going on.

Talk to the people. It is not possible to run these programmes on the strength of capital-intensive equipment alone. I have a lot of difficulty explaining to people that the cost is there in any event, whether the equipment flies or not. The additional cost is not much and so I would ask that this equipment be used. Not irrationally, not improperly, but used continuously for the purpose of the programme. I feel very strongly about this. I think so much can be achieved in this programme if good communication is assured. That is the basic premise of the programme and if you want to keep the Head Office team small, they have got to be efficient. They have to be able to move around. I know that people are cost conscious and they come to me and say, on one side you have this very expensive piece of equipment and on the other side you are cost conscious. I say we can achieve both objectives. I know there are people who will challenge that and I am willing to be proven wrong but I am not going to be proven wrong if the equipment is not used. The Directors of the Company are here…you have something to do with it. Let us try and ensure it is used.

GM: It would be very unfortunate if it were to be withdrawn from the programme. Many people were initially sceptical about the helicopter, including myself. I am the one who has used it the most. I think it is really very useful in determining the cost estimates and cost benefits to see how much the pace of development has been accelerated through its use. One problem, Sir, is that it has to be based in Gilgit.

His Highness: I mentioned to the General that maybe there was some area where we could look together at having fuel and maybe keeping sufficient spare parts in Gilgit. [We could keep] simple pieces of equipment so when it is out of operation, we don't have to fly to Islamabad. When it is here it can fly consistently. The other thing I would say is that if we can combine the visits with those of other institutions, so that all the people working in the area can use it together, we could add up the costs and compare them with what they would be if those people went by road. The helicopter has got to be well used. I think it is an exercise we ought to try and make a success. If it is a failure we can say it's a failure. I'm quite happy to hear that but not any comments before having done what was really needed to be done.

GM: As an example, Sir, what took me three days before we had the helicopter now takes five hours. Without the helicopter, reaching Chitral is impossible. Without the helicopter I would not have been able to go to Chitral before June. Nor could I have involved the government functionaries in the programme. What we achieved in three days would have taken weeks.

His Highness: I hear that people in the Foundation feel that it is a bee in my bonnet. They might even say it is a helicopter in my bonnet. In any case it is an issue to which I attach importance, whether rightly or wrongly.

GM: The Management Group is behind you Sir. (Laughter).

Guillaume de Spoelberch: Sir, I speak from the position of somebody who has seen maybe several hundred development projects start in different countries around the world, but I think there are few I have seen that have achieved this degree of rapid implementation with results coming in very shortly after the team is established in the field. I think it is a tribute to the members of the team and the leadership of that team and I think that we are very fortunate to have that team (applause).

His Highness: I would like to subscribe wholeheartedly to that and to thank everybody for organizing my visit today. It has been a most exciting and most inspiring visit and I hope that it will encourage people to feel that there is, all the way to the highest decision makers, full support to them. I think that is something you should feel confident of, both in the implementation and the policy thinking behind it. I feel that is something to depend on and I think the government departments should know that and the people working with the programme should know that, because it is a source of great satisfaction to me.

Appendix 5
Meeting with His Highness—24 March 1983, Rawalpindi

NOTE FOR THE RECORD

Subject: <u>MEETING WITH HIS HIGHNESS</u>

Date, time and venue: 24 March 1983—8.30 a.m. State Guest House, Rawalpindi.

<u>Participants</u>:

– His Highness The Aga Khan
– Mr Ramzan Merchant, Chairman BOD AKRSP
– Mr Shoaib Sultan Khan, General Manager AKRSP

The meeting with His Highness was arranged through the courtesy and good offices of Mr Ramzan Merchant who informed the GM on arrival (at 3.00 a.m. after 16 hours road journey) in Islamabad on 23.3.1983 morning that His Highness was desirous of meeting the GM. The meeting was planned for 10'O clock at night after the state banquet given by the President of Pakistan in honour of His Highness. However at 9.30 p.m., GM was informed that His Highness has desired to meet the GM at breakfast at 8.30 a.m. on the following day. Thanks to UNICEF (Ms Marta Mauras and Nasimur Rehman), GM was able to get an overhead projector by 9.30 p.m. for giving a briefing on AKRSP activities to His Highness.

His Highness came to the breakfast room in the State Guest House punctually at 8.30 a.m., and enquired from the GM if it was necessary for the Chairman to be present at the briefing. The GM responded that the Chairman was most welcome to stay on. The GM had been wondering if he was going to eat breakfast with His Highness, how could he be able to simultaneously give a presentation, hence His Highness's query from the GM if he had eaten the breakfast, gave GM the opportunity to excuse himself from eating breakfast and straight away seek permission from His Highness to make the presentation to which His Highness readily consented.

GM made the presentation with the prologue about the importance of the theory and principles on which AKRSP's strategy is based and expressed the view that over the years—to be exact nearly 150 years—a body of knowledge has evolved in the world on the basis of which the theory of agriculture and rural development could be articulated in as precise terms as, for example, the theory of gravity. (His Highness had not caught the word precise and asked the GM to repeat it). With this introduction, the transparencies depicting the essentials of agricultural and rural development were projected and GM briefly explained the importance of productive physical infrastructure realised through the experience gained in implementation of the community development programme in India and Village-AID programme in Pakistan in the 1950s. A programme in which billions of dollars were invested by the Americans and which extended to 44 countries, failed to produce results due to the lack of understanding by the planners and implementers about the importance of productive physical infrastructure in agricultural and rural development. Both the importance of physical and administrative infrastructure is now understood and in most of the countries, development plans give due emphasis to these essentials of agricultural and rural development but the dimension of a social and economic infrastructure is still not appreciated, especially in Pakistan. There are three available world models of agricultural and rural development namely; private capitalist agriculturist approach; communist approach of collectivisation and cooperative approach of the Japanese, Taiwanese etc., which was originally fostered by Raiffeisen in Germany 150 years ago to help small farmers. The small farmers, like those of Northern Areas whose average holding per household is only 20 *kanals*, suffer from many handicaps and unless they are helped to overcome these handicaps by giving them economies of scale, through group action, they would be unable to rise above the level of subsistence. Unfortunately in many developing countries including Pakistan, the approach being advocated is the private capitalist agriculturist approach of USA which only succeeds if land holdings are large.

With this background the AKRSP has devised its programming cycle based on diagnostic survey. GM referred to His Highness's recent speech at the Seminar in Karachi where His Highness had underlined the importance of urban-rural dialogue in the context of housing and considered it as important as the North-South Dialogue. GM submitted that in his view an urban-rural dialogue was necessary in all aspects of development and His Highness indicated his complete agreement. GM briefly explained the different components of the village dialogues and gave examples of the reactions of the villagers in these dialogues. In regard to acceptability of the AKRSP, GM pointed out the attitude he sensed in his initial visits to non-Ismaili villages in whose eyes the bonafides of AKRSP appeared to be suspect: In one village, after clear explanation of AKRSP objectives and methods, namely, identification of village level projects with focus on income-generation, village elders demanded of 'Sir Aga Khan' a multi-million rupee bridge over the River

Hunza. Thereupon an Ismaili sitting next to the GM, whispered, 'Why don't they ask Imam Khomeni to give them the Bridge', His Highness had a hearty laugh at this—but was very pleased to learn that a couple of months later, the same village specially asked the GM to help in doing a village level project namely an irrigation channel to irrigate 1,000 *kanals*. His Highness also enjoyed the dialogue between the GM and one of the Sunni leaders who demanded of the GM as to why only Ismailis had been appointed in the Management Group and when informed that out of seven members of the group, five are non-Ismailis, the leader could not believe his ears. The GM informed His Highness that in regard to Ismaili villages, he did not face any problem because he exploited His Highness's name to the fullest and whenever he found that the community people were not responsive, he brow-beat them by telling them that His Highness had specially selected him to implement this programme. His Highness smiled at this.

His Highness took keen interest in the monitoring and evaluation chart and specially noted the requirement of submission of reports on a regular basis. His Highness also enquired about the arrangements for follow-up action. GM again projected programming cycle transparency and pointed out the activities under implementation and completion including long term evaluation of persistence of results. His Highness enquired about the time lag between execution and evaluation of benefits. GM stated that on the basis of experience, the MG has gained so far, the time lag between first dialogue and the third dialogue of the project is roughly 8 to 12 weeks. The evaluation of benefits could be after 6 to 9 months, depending on the type of project implemented. The GM informed His Highness about the MG's commitment to rigorous internal evaluation and the role of the Programme Economist as a watchdog. His Highness agreed with the approach regarding rigorous monitoring.

GM showed the helicopter grid as the last transparency and submitted that he had been sceptical about the utility of the helicopter before coming to Northern Areas, but having been in the area for three months, GM had come to realize that the helicopter could be of great help in accelerating the pace of development and thereby in terms of cost benefit paying for itself, in due course of time.

His Highness observed that he always believed that this was the situation with the Northern Areas. However when GM informed him that the helicopter was not as yet available for the development work in the Northern Areas, His Highness turned to the Chairman and told him in very clear terms that he would take away the helicopter if it was not used. He observed that if due to technical reasons or operating troubles, one machine was not enough, he was prepared to give another one. He quoted the saying 'One is an aeroplane and two are an airline'.

By now 40 minutes had elapsed and GM thought that he had already taken ten minutes more than his allotted time and apologized to His Highness for having been so long-winded. His Highness observed that this was not the case and the briefing had been very well timed and invited GM to sit down with him at the breakfast table. While the presentation was being made, His Highness confined his breakfast only to coffee. He asked GM to have something and ordered an egg for himself. His Highness observed how distressed he was for not being able to visit the Northern Areas and said it was for this reason that he was coming again on 11th of May, and expressed his personal thanks and happiness on GM's acceptance of the job and hoped very much to see him in Gilgit during his visit in May. He further observed that he was greatly impressed at the intellectual change that had occurred in the people of Northern Areas as evident in his discussions with them the previous evening. He was also impressed at the speed AKRSP was moving and observed that he, nor probably the GM, had expected that so much progress would be made in such a short time. His Highness said that he agreed with and supported everything that GM was doing with regard to AKRSP. His Highness observed that he was excited about the programme and considered it unique in many ways and was of the belief that it would provide answers to poverty in the deprived and undeveloped areas. GM responded that with His Highness' blessings, this might come true.

His Highness further observed that he was thinking of setting up a Coordination Body, if GM agreed, for the Northern Areas to ensure an integrated and synergistic approach to development by bringing the different agencies of development set up by His Highness in the Northern Areas under one umbrella. He explained that this was necessary in view of the concerns expressed by community members and although he thought there was no problem with AKRSP because there was a clearly articulated strategy in place, it was not so with all the agencies. His Highness further observed that he had made it clear to the community that development has to be for everyone and could not be restricted or confined. His Highness also referred to his concern regarding economic imbalances and in this context mentioned the case of Chitral where he was greatly distressed by people killing each other and expressed the hope that with initiation of programmes of economic benefit, the situation might improve.

His Highness also referred to his meeting with the Finance Minister and the Deputy Chairman, Planning Commission, Government of Pakistan and said that he was struck by GM's comment about the power of capital and the need for the rural people to acquire capital through savings and building up of equity. His Highness observed that substantial savings would not be forthcoming without increased incomes. In this regard he mentioned the availability of capital to the rural populace through cooperatives in the Northern Areas. He was sorry to note that there was no such institution nor there were apex banks which could make capital available and he advocated a programme to ascertain the need for loans required by the rural people and to provide them access to management and cooperative organization. He was discouraged to note that both the Finance Minister and the Deputy Chairman seemed to have a mental block in relation to the development of cooperatives in the Northern Areas. His Highness quoted the example of India where cooperatives have been very successful in some areas. However in the Northern Areas, government seems to be unwilling to take concrete steps in this direction as there were not even facilities available for registration of cooperatives. However, His Highness indicated that the Finance Minister has agreed to allocate more capital for cooperatives for Northern Areas, if necessary. He quoted the Finance Minister as saying that 'Government is an ass' and one can get round anything if one has the will.

His Highness also observed that only economic upsurge is not enough. The construction of KKH does not necessarily mean prosperity to everyone. The situation could be exploited by unscrupulous businessmen.

He spoke on conceptualisation of bigger projects in the Northern Areas through agricultural cooperatives in the field of food processing etc. He referred to the Venture Capital Company set up for assisting local entrepreneurs. He referred to the institutionalization of enterprises. He asked GM to give thought to these issues and said that he would like to discuss these in greater detail during his visit in May with GM and the MG of AKRSP.

GM mentioned that he used the term 'social and economic infrastructure', instead of cooperatives, because of the observations made by His Highness about the mental block in the minds of the policy makers of Pakistan regarding cooperatives. The GM also brought to the notice of His Highness the interest taken by one of the Intelligence Agencies in the activities of AKRSP, GM's dismay at the paranoia exhibited by the agency's representative and GM's action in contacting the head of the agency to counter the move to present AKRSP in an adverse light. GM also informed His Highness about the excellent rapport AKRSP has with the local administration. He also informed His Highness about his action in writing to the President of Pakistan with a copy of His Highness's letter written to Mr Grant regarding AKRSP, with the request to seek an interview from the President to inform him about the AKRSP activities. GM explained that he had to take these steps to keep the policy makers and people who matter, well informed about the AKRSP activities.

At this stage it was already 9.30 a.m., and the Chief of Protocol came to enquire of His Highness what time His Highness would be free to receive the President who was going to see His Highness off at the airport. His Highness asked for another five minutes and before leaving, expressed his great pleasure and satisfaction at whatever was being done by AKRSP and asked GM to bring any matter or problem which the GM faced, to His Highness's notice. His Highness bid goodbye to GM and went away to see the President who was due to arrive any moment. The GM was, therefore, surprised when a few minutes later while GM was collecting the transparencies, His Highness reappeared with the Chief of Protocol and introduced GM to the Chief of Protocol and requested Brig. Zamir to give help and assistance to GM if he was ever in need of such assistance. The GM could not resist telling Brig. Zamir that the people of Gilgit really cursed him when they came to know that it was the Protocol that stopped His Highness from coming to Gilgit. Before Brig. Zamir could say anything, His Highness interjected that it was not Brig. Zamir's fault. He could not help it.

GM presented a copy of the AKRSP briefing papers at which His Highness observed that he very much wanted something like that.

The meeting with His Highness ended at 9.45 a.m.

Appendix 6
Ah! Hussain Wali — A Tribute

When Shandana broke the sad news of Hussain Wali's demise on the morning of 11 February 2002, followed by a tearful call from his daughter, it was not totally unexpected. I had gone to see him a few days earlier at his flat in Islamabad. He was a pale shadow of his earlier self, yet he was cheerful in reassuring me that there was nothing wrong with him. I thought my eyes were deceiving me and that Hussain Wali would pull through this. Hence, when the news came I did not want to believe it. I went to his flat with a heavy heart and saw many old faces, some of whom Hussain Wali himself had introduced to me. There was a fathomless sense of loss in the air. Nobody had to say anything. Everyone felt it and left it there. When Zahoor, whose sister was married to Hussain Wali, asked me if I would like to meet the family, I very much wanted to share my grief with them and theirs with me. I had seen little Erum grow up and could not believe the beautiful little girl who used to visit the AKRSP office would grow up before my eyes into an elegant and professional working woman.

Hussain Wali, like my wife Musarrat, was a dreamer and a planner. Every time they got together, there was always some project in the making. The last time Musarrat came with me to Gilgit, we visited Hussain Wali's beautiful new house on the Kargah Nallah and Musarrat fell in love with it. Hussain Wali offered to build her a cottage in the compound of the house. Bhabhi, Hussain Wali's wife, and the children would welcome us with such warmth and affection that we always felt fully at home visiting Hussain Wali.

As I went up the stairs of the flat and Zahoor led me to the room where Hussain Wali was in eternal sleep, I lost my courage and turned back. I had always seen him full of life, living it intensely, bubbling with energy and ideas, raring to do things. He hated being idle and had to be doing something all the time. I could not bring myself to see that man devoid of everything that I had known him with. I wanted to remember him alive. I wanted to remember him full of gusto and energy. I didn't want to believe that he was dead. I refused to see him dead and retraced my steps from the room where he lay, without entering it. But the truth dawned on me very soon. Hussain Wali was put in a wooden box for his last journey on the Karakoram Highway, the same KKH which we had traversed together so many times. For Hussain Wali, the KKH was like his back garden. How many hundreds of times had he driven on it. But his last journey had to be in a box — lifeless. What an irony.

I could not accompany Hussain Wali because I had to fly to Delhi. Throughout my flight from Islamabad to Karachi to Dubai to Delhi, I could not take my mind away from the thought that while I was flying in the air, there was somebody making his last journey by road. When the Emirates flight landed at Delhi, I knew that Hussain Wali must also have reached his destination. This is the stuff life is made of and yet we strive so hard for worldly things.

I still remember my first meeting with Hussain Wali in Gilgit in January 1983. When I told him what AKRSP was all about he turned around and asked me why did I want an engineer and that too a chief engineer? He said there was no engineering involved in what AKRSP was planning to do. I assured him I did need an engineer, but of course not a traditional one. An engineer who would respect the expertise of people; who would believe that local people can do many things even better than qualified engineers and that, in most cases, what engineers need to do is only to graft modern engineering technology onto local indigenous practices. I urged him to train a cadre of rural engineers who would seek to foster partnerships with people instead of looking down on local expertise and working only in the engineer-contractor mode. It was amazing how the engineer in Hussain Wali gave way to the Social Organizer. He soon became the most accomplished social engineer and the biggest supporter of villagers and their expertise.

When he introduced micro-hydels, he groomed an illiterate village manager as the most competent micro-hydel expert, so much so that he used to call him the micro-hydel chief engineer. All new micro-hydels were installed in Gilgit District under the guidance of this village manager. Hussain Wali also had the courage and wisdom to admit when he was wrong, as in the case of the Sust Channel-tunnel. He initially considered this beyond the expertise or capability of the villagers but once they had demonstrated even on a small scale that they could do it, he not only withdrew his objection but gave his whole hearted support and ensured the successful completion of the project.

I very soon discovered in Hussain Wali not only an engineering professional and a person with immense local knowledge but a person with vision, dedication and a burning desire to do something for the area to which he belonged. I nurtured him as my successor but he was humble enough to admit that he would never work as hard as I do. Even when I came away from Gilgit, he used to chide me for working so hard. I was very happy when Hussain Wali took over from me but kept my office with my nameplate intact. When I asked him why he was doing so, he said it was a ruse: when he wanted to do some work he used to disappear into my office.

He was an honest and upright person and when he felt that he could not meet the local demands both of the staff and the people, he chose the honourable course of resigning. He was getting a fabulous salary in his hometown but he rejected it all when he felt he could not do justice to his people or his area.

I often wonder how I worked and survived for twelve years in the Northern Areas. It would not have been possible without the guidance of Akhtar Hameed Khan and the patronage of His Highness the Aga Khan. But the real glory I got was from the people of the Northern Areas and Chitral and the staff of AKRSP. Without their affection, support and total confidence in me, I would have achieved nothing. Amongst them Hussain Wali's contribution in my diary will be written in letters of gold.

Shoaib Sultan Khan

Appendix 7
The Helicopter Crash

In July 1984 I had accompanied Nick Gardner of OXFAM to Phander by road. Just 15 miles short of our destination, we saw a jeep plunge in the river below. We later learned that eight persons had been killed on the spot and the rest badly injured. I had looked meaningfully at Nick, who adamantly refuses to undertake journeys by helicopters because of the dangers involved. Nick had stated categorically that the AKRSP helicopter would crash one day—to him it was the most dangerous mode of transportation. Despite the horrendous sight we had just witnessed, I was unconvinced by Nick's statement but it certainly left me a bit uneasy.

On 12 March 1986 we were making one of our now too common crossings by helicopter to Chitral via the Shandur Pass. There were only five passengers making the journey: myself, Hussain Wali, Feroze Shah, Alnasir Babul and Nabeel Anjum Malik. On the seats in front of us were two sacks of imported fruit plants destined for the Garam Chashma nursery. In the two luggage compartments there were other items such as pipes for a compressor, vegetable packets, VOs' passbooks, the most recent Managers' Conference proceedings and our lunch and brief-cases. Some packages had to be stacked next to the seats, because nothing could be stored under occupied seats. Since my usual seat was a bit cluttered, I decided to sit on the extreme right hand seat, just behind the pilot. The weather was not too good but it never is in these valleys, and most of the time we have to adopt the policy of pushing ahead until we reach our destination or wait on the way for weather to clear up.

Today also we were quite prepared for such an eventuality. As we flew past Khalti Lake, I could not take my eyes off the enchanting sight of the azure blue of the frozen top, with crisscross lines of cracking ice. Now snow could be seen on the mountainsides and by the time we crossed over Pingle, the site of our road accident, I could see the weather changing. Pilot Iqbal started flying along the river instead of making his usual beeline over the Phander lake corner and coming out in the open valley. I knew we could go no further—it was a white mist of darkness. Iqbal started descending with the intention of landing on the wide, snow-covered valley which in summer looks like a big park. Hussain Wali spoke into my ear about the dangers of landing on snow because of disorientation about the depth of the snow. We often talked about such risks while flying. No sooner had Hussain Wali said this than the helicopter made a landing but it whipped up so much snow that the machine took off again.

Immediately, we noticed a vibration which started to intensify. I thought that Iqbal was trying to find another landing spot because I had noticed the right ski making a faint impression on the snow at the first place. In seconds the vibration increased to such an extent that Hussain Wali asked me to open the door. I did so, but remained belted. My mind started racing, considering the feasibility of jumping out. By now the helicopter was back-tracking on the river. Any thoughts of jumping were quickly extinguished by the sight of the icy water and my inability to swim. The helicopter was back on the snow, skimming just a few feet from the surface but giving the feeling of a machine out of control. The vibration had by now turned into ugly jolts. I thought that now was the time to jump out but by the time I had undone my seat belt the helicopter, with a final giant jolt, toppled and came to rest on its left side. This made me slide on top of the other four. If I had been in my usual seat, the others would have been on top of me. I soon found myself on my feet on the floor of the cabin: it seemed so commodious and high.

By now Hussain Wali and Feroze Shah had climbed to the top of the cabin and thrown themselves out on the snow. I neither noticed nor was I aware of Alnasir Babul and Nabeel in the cabin. With a single-minded approach, I wondered how to get out. I found to my great amazement and relief that all I had to do was to climb the ladder which, by some miracle had been placed there, to climb to the top. The safety features of this helicopter are amazing. None of the glass windows had shattered and nothing malfunctioned. The thought uppermost in my mind was that the helicopter might blow up and to escape before it did so.

Having reached the top of the cabin, I leaned on the ski and threw myself onto the snow nearly ten feet below. Fortunately the snow cushion was magnificent. Once I had collected myself I found Babul crouching in the snow and crawling away from the helicopter. Some villagers were standing nearby. I thought that Babul was injured but he later said that he was only taking precautionary measures against a possible explosion. He obviously had been seeing too many movies. I found Nabeel still in the cabin, trying to retrieve my spectacles case. He had been assured by the engineer Bob Dunfort that there was no danger of the helicopter blowing up. This advice was given only after Bob had shattered his front windscreen with his left hand. But for this self-inflicted injury, no one even got a scratch.

My heart bled to see the helicopter lying in this sorry condition. I had often admired its sleek looks and had been wonder-struck with what it could perform. To see it lying there in a helpless condition, like a beautiful swan with its wings broken, made me feel as if I had lost someone very near and dear to me. But thank God everybody was safe.

Bob Dunfort assured me that he had seen much worse accidents and that our helicopter should be flying no more than three months from the time its dismantled body reached the workshop. The snow was covered with debris, shrapnel and splinters. I thanked God I had not jumped out earlier. The rotors really presented a sad spectacle. Two were completely wrenched away and broken and lying stuck in the snow—sad reminders of once magnificent beings. We took some photographs.

By now a number of villagers had collected. After all, this particular helicopter had become a familiar sight to them. They all felt sad about the crash but happy that we were safe. All the baggage retrieved from the helicopter was soon stored in a house nearby, where we were forced to have a cup of tea. We then proceeded to Gulukh, two and a half miles away, where the local public call office (PCO) was situated. We crossed the river over two wooden beam bridges and reached the PCO by 12:45. We walked on a jeep track which was covered with two to three feet of snow. The yaks lay browsing in the snow as if they had no care in the world but the other animals were in a sad condition. Babul felt one of them and he could count its ribs. The lack of fodder probably kills more animals than disease in this area.

The PCO was manned by our friend Mastaan Ali, who is the President of Sarabal VO and the Chairman of the Union Council. Through the Gupis exchange operator, we were able to make contact with the office in Gilgit, informing them about the incident and our need for jeeps to be sent to Pingle, 15 miles from Gulukh. This was the closest that jeeps could travel, because of the snow. We later learned that the message had been given in such low key terms that the office did not realise that a major catastrophe had befallen us. We plodded back in the snow to the Phander Rest House. Babul had already been given gum boots by the villagers but Feroz Shah insisted that his fur-lined slippers would be adequate. On the way we encountered men and horses on their way to Gilgit to be in time for the polo season beginning April 15. The trek to Phander Rest House had exhausted us. The helicopter used to take us to and fro in the valley without our ever realising the effort involved. Once at the Rest House I decided to rest for the night against the advice of some to continue the journey as far as the next village. I knew I could not make it and thought it prudent to have a fresh start the next morning.

At the Rest House, villagers kept visiting us, especially the office bearers of the Village Organizations. They brought the news that emergency meetings of the surrounding VOs had been convened, 'resolutions' passed that all necessary help should be provided and the services of the VOs were at our disposal. It was all very touching and heartening.

Sometimes my thoughts drifted to the machine, which had given us such faithful service over the last three years, now lying helpless out in the cold and covered with only a tarpaulin. We had already appointed the occupants of the house closest to the scene of the accident as custodians of the helicopter. At night we saw a light blinking in the distance. We were told the custodians had put a lantern next to the helicopter.

I knew that if General Safdar Ali Khan learned of our plight he would immediately send his helicopter to rescue us. Although we did not inform him, and could not even if we had wanted to, our local office in Gupis informed the local assistant commissioner, who informed the DC. Through him, Ijaz Hussain Malik came to know that, although we had played down the incident, something serious had happened. In the meanwhile two jeeps started out from Gupis and I was pleasantly surprised to see our two drivers at the Phander Rest House at 21:00 hours. They had left their jeeps at Pingle and walked the 12 miles through the snow to meet us. It was reassuring to see them. They told us that it should take us six hours to walk to Pingle.

The next morning we set out at 07:30 hours but by the time we had reached the first village, we saw an Army Puma helicopter coming in our direction. The weather was bad and we had had little hope of the helicopter coming in this weather. After some anxiety about whether the helicopter had seen us, the Puma landed in a field and IHM came bounding out to embrace us. The general had canceled his own programme to enable the helicopter to rescue us. What would have been a 16-20 hour journey on foot and by jeep on perilous roads was covered in less than an hour. We landed at the army helipad by 09:30 hours.

I drove straight to the general's office to thank him for his kindness. At the office, everyone came to greet me as if I had got a new life, saying how happy they were that we were safe. When J.P. Naz looked in to see if everything was all right, the cumulative effect was too much. Such moments are one's cherished treasure. How could one ever repay such concern, solicitude and affection?

Appendix 8
Visit of Her Highness Princess Zahra Aga Khan

Her Highness Princess Zahra visited AKRSP on Saturday, 15 June 1991. Mr Asif Fancy, Chairman AKES and member AKRSP BoD accompanied her. Prince Rahim was unwell and did not attend the briefing.

Mr Shoaib Sultan Khan, General Manager of AKRSP conducted the briefing. He warmly welcomed Princess Zahra to AKRSP and introduced the Management Group to her. Princess Zahra had already seen 'First Harvest' and had been provided with literature on AKRSP. A briefing note with an update on AKRSP and profiles of the villages to be visited over the next few days, was provided to the guests.

The general manager provided a brief overview of AKRSP's objectives and principles and a few examples of what AKRSP has achieved. GM then invited Princess Zahra to ask questions about the programme.

Princess Zahra: Will AKRSP withdraw completely in the next five years?

GM: The VOs are moving toward financial independence but will need continued technical support. We are trying to bring the VOs to a stage where they would be able to pay AKRSP for technical services. AKRSP's role is that of a trainer and a teacher. The VOs are like students. Some are good students, others are not. This explains why the performance of VOs is variable.

Princess Zahra: What will happen if AKRSP disappears?

GM: This is not envisaged in the immediate future. The VOs need continued support for the time being, although the nature of the support they need is changing over time.

Princess Zahra: What is the breakdown of investment in the villages, in terms of development grants vs management cost?

GM: We no longer, provide grants to the VOs. Training is our responsibility but functional activities are financed by the VOs. We recommend that the VOs charge a markup of 5 per cent over and above the normal markup to meet management costs of the credit programme.

Asif Fancy added to the list of questions:

AF: How well are the VOs now willing and able to participate in the social sectors?

GM: On his last visit to the Northern Areas in 1987, His Highness the Aga Khan said that if people of the Northern Areas are able 25 years down the road, to pay as much for social sectors as the rest of the country, he would be satisfied. In fact, people in the Northern Areas are already paying more for social sector activities than their counterparts in the plains.

AF: Can the VOs not be used in educating the villagers of their responsibility in the social sector?

GM: This is already happening. The major obstacle is the competition from soft government programmes running in parallel, which undermine our efforts to develop self-reliance.

With a word of thanks, Princess Zahra moved on to the airport for the field visits.

Appendix 9

Note by an Intern (Shandana Khan, Gilgit AKRSP, 21 September 1990)

I arrived in Gilgit on 17 September 1990. Gilgit is a valley surrounded by awesome stretches of rock, stretching barren towards the sky and the loftiest, most spectacular mountains on the face of the earth. These Northern Areas of Pakistan, dotted with little villages strewn across the rock, a test of survival for people who, at times, have to walk three days to fetch water, who die in hope for lack of medical facilities.

Seven years ago something new appeared. It was a machine with a big fan on top. What is this, the villages thought? It descended slowly throwing the wheat field into a flurry of waves, raising dust in huge dry curtains from the ground, sending animals helter skelter and the children into their mothers' laps. What was this monster?

'What is it that you need most for your village?' asked the man in the hat.

What does he want? Who is he? they wondered. Slowly, cautiously they spoke. Water, medicines, schools. The list was unending. 'OK, we will help you build your irrigation channel but you yourselves will have to build it. We will tell you how to do it', said Shoaib Sultan Khan. 'But this is impossible. What does this mean? How can we do it?'

The man who brought this message was Shoaib Sultan Khan. The machine he stepped out of was a helicopter belonging to the Aga Khan Foundation and its message was basically — nothing is impossible (for people to do).

The philosophy behind the programme is one of self-help. The face of the mountains is being changed. All over the Northern Areas the life-blood of the people — water — is now winding its way through the barren rock, blasted by dynamite, into land, creating stretches of green, of crop, providing food, providing life. But what is it that makes this so different from any other development programme? The answer lies with the man who builds the channel, the road, the bridge — the villager himself, when he said proudly 'We made this ourselves.' This is true development.

The basic tenet of AKRSP is to develop (and work according to) this philosophy, and this conceptual package can only be self-realized by the villagers through economic need (being met). Alongside this need is developing a powerful sense of ability, an immense confidence, a self-reliance. The dictates of nature are no longer the fate of men and women. If mountains have to be moved, they can be moved, they will be moved and they are moved.

This confidence arises out of challenging fate. It is not something that is easily admitted—as a women in Hanuchal said 'First it was God, now it is AKRSP!' But surely it is these villagers themselves. The problem today is not so much the self realisation of ability, it is a step ahead—channelling their abilities, directing them into productive work. An area where self-sufficiency was once the problem is now talking about surplus, about marketing. In short, the integration of the NAs is being made possible into the national economy.

I used to be sceptical about 'development.' To me it was a snobbish word. Yes, at times I thought—why disturb their lives if one is not even sure what repercussions it will have. Shoaib Sahib dismissed this as a 'romantic notion' when I asked him this question in his PTDC house in Gilgit. Bit by bit it all began to make sense, I began to realise what he meant when he said 'We are not missionaries, we are mercenaries!.' This was only realised when I asked the villagers themselves about what they thought of AKRSP and what it had done for them.

Perhaps one of the greatest developments in the social sphere has been the creation of the social organization unit. Unity means productivity but unity also means a sense of community.

The self-sufficient family unit is now looking outside its four walls. Concepts like collective loans are important for economic reasons (progress) for example buying a tractor, chicks, threshers but are a social glue as well. This in essence represents the opening up of the mind. It is an experiment which is irreversible as far as learning, curiosity, progress are concerned. It is a long, long path but it is wide open, untouched and exciting.

Reflections: 10 October 1990

The leaves turn yellow, the trees are bare, the green sprouts appear and once more the leaves rustle green in the wind. Time is cyclical, the only sign of age is the individual, the wrinkles on his face, the birth of his sons, of his grandsons. But life is a cycle of seasons for men, different men. Such is the measurement of Time.

People see themselves in an ongoing process. The modern man's life is his only life, the humility and acceptance of death is absent—it is the end before all must be accomplished. The man in the village also accomplishes but he does so to fill in slots of his life, to fit into the community, to see the seasons change, inconspicuous, not talked about and then dead. Only those who do the uncommon, the unacceptable, descend into the tales of their sons, their grandsons. In this way is created the harmony of society. So natural are their beliefs, it makes one wonder why we must remove ourselves from them and, in the process, remove them.

Appendix 10
Shimshal—Exile to a Haven (Maliha H. Hussein; Programme Officer)

Spring comes late to this valley locked away in the mountains of upper Hunza. Situated at an altitude of 10,000 feet, there are two ways to get to Shimshal from Gujal. One is from Passu and the other is through the high pasturelands of Morkhon at Paryar. Both these journeys involve three days of walking through deep gorges, under loose rocks, over glaciers and across the icy waters of the Shimshal river numerous times. The path through Morkhon is no longer used as it involved crossing the treacherous Qarun Pass which in Wakhi means bad tempered and is indicative of the rigours of the journey. The path presently used is the one through Passu called 'Tung' (narrow). The villagers have helped to sparsely furnish two huts along the way in Dut and Ziarat. These provide some shelter for weary travellers to Shimshal. The only other access to the valley is over the Pamirs from the Chinese side.

The history of Shimshal, like that of most villages in the Northern Areas, does not distinguish between fact and fiction. The mythology which the mountains have helped create is as towering and potent as the mountains themselves. Perhaps these myths contribute to the endurance of the inhabitants. Shimshal is no exception. Its founding father Mahmud Shah, popularly known as Mamusing, lived about 1,200 years ago and was a famous hunter of the wild life of the mountains. His passion for hunting made him a constant wanderer. He moved from Chaprote to Baltit and then to Kamaris. The unstable environment of the Kamaris glacier forced him to move on to Sarikul. He married a woman from there. Some suggest that he eloped with her and had to seek refuge. This took him to Morkhon and from there on to Ufgarch. He crossed the Mulanguti glacier and stumbled on to the wide valley of Shimshal. He had his wife Khadija and some livestock with him and decided to settle there. Khadija was so dismayed at the prospect of living in this isolated valley that she took to calling her husband 'Shuinsing' (stubborn) when she failed to dissuade him to leave Shimshal.

The couple found traces of an earlier settlement in the valley. A covered water channel was accidentally discovered by Mamusing and they found some evidence of the fields having been cultivated previously. Some village elders like Mohammad Nayab believe that the Shugnani were the first to settle in Shimshal. These people had travelled across the Pamirs from a place near Ruskum which presently forms part of China. It is believed that the Shungnani were driven out as a result of an attack by villagers from Nagat. Mamusing and Khadija did not have any offspring. This fact was a source of great distress to them. One day, while she was working indoors, Khadija had an unusual visitor, Shah Shams Tabriz! Khadija was so overcome by this unexpected visit that, in a spontaneous gesture, she spread her headscarf at his feet. She warmed some goat's milk and poured it in a cracked pan—the only utensil, in the house and the milk held in the pot. Overwhelmed as she witnessed this little miracle, Khadija decided to confess her worries to the saintly visitor. She told him how much she wanted a child but that she and her husband were too old to bear children. Shah Shams dispelled her fears and promised that she would soon bear a son. Having said this he disappeared. The old couple had a son whom they named Sher. In turn Sher bore five sons. Two of them were childless. The people of Shimshal trace their ancestry to the other three sons of Sher: Baki, Bakhti and Wali.

There are 125 households in Shimshal. The estimated average of 8.33 members per household in the district indicates that its population is just over a thousand. All the families are Shia Imami Ismaili. The Ismaili faith was first introduced to the village at the end of the Fatimid Caliphate in the ninth century. An Ismaili preacher, Khawaja Shahdat, passed through Shimshal after crossing the Pamirs on his way to Hunza. He was chiefly responsible for organising the spread of Ismailism to this area. This was the height of the Ismaili Dawa—the mission to invite people to convert to the Ismaili faith.

Right up to 1960, Shimshal was virtually secluded from the rest of Gilgit. As such, it was a favourite of the Mirs as an exile for offenders. The miscreants, unable to escape, would wander around aimlessly until they served their term and returned home. None of these exiles ever settled permanently in Shimshal. The Mir had a *Numberdar* or Arbab, a local person, who was his executive, administrative and judicial representative. He helped in collecting the taxes which the Mirs imposed on the valley. Shimshal was heavily taxed. The taxes were paid mostly in the form of livestock, dairy produce and rock salt which they extracted from beyond the Pamirs. The most difficult aspect of the taxation was the delivery of the *malia* to the Mir's doorstep. Most of these taxes were removed only in 1967 when the Mir visited the valley in an army Puma. The valley survived the burden of the taxation due to its relative prosperity. Its wealth was attributed to the free and generous grazing its animals were provided in the Pamirs. It is popularly believed that Mahmud Shah's son Sher won for his people grazing rights in the Pamirs by defeating a polo team of the Tajiks he met there on a hunting trip. Even today, it is one of the few villages which is in a position to raise livestock. This measure of self-sufficiency of the village did not make it urgent for it to establish contact with the outside world.

The first major exposure that the valley had to outside influences was in the early 1960s when the government decided to have a military outpost at Kuz. The only way to Kuz was through Shimshal and the army established a base camp there. This exerted a decisive influence on the perceptions, ambitions and dietary habits of the Shimshalis. Tea, sugar and kerosene were dropped by parachute for the troops for the first time in the valley. This was Shimshal's first encounter with these commodities. Although they reluctantly took these in exchange for meat and fuel wood, they were unable to decide what to do with them. At first they sold these items in Passu and when the journey proved too much they began consuming these themselves. Today, sweetened tea is the most cherished part of a Shimshali's diet.

The contact with the army officers and troops made the Shimshalis aware of another option they had not contemplated before; the army as a profession. The army post was removed in 1972 but its pervasive effect is indicated by the fact that, at present, fifty Shimshalis are with the army. This outside exposure, shared with the young men of Shimshal, is making them very restless. For most, joining the army still provides the only avenue to leaving the village.

The Shimshal of today is almost half its original size. The village elders claim that the Gurdapin glacier blocked the Verjerab *nalla* and caused a flood every twenty years. The last flood in the 1960's was so severe that it lasted for several years and caused massive erosion. It persuaded the people to scatter their dwellings all over the valley. A visitor to Shimshal can see the ruins of the homes on the edge of the river where all the villagers lived huddled together until the great floods. The loss of precious land has made the people move away to marginal lands in the valley. These new lands were equally distributed among all the households according to the norms of land distribution which have traditionally been followed in these mountains. As a consequence, all households have land in two places, in the main area known as central Shimshal and in the surrounding areas of Salaluksh and Chokurt.

The valley is in the single crop region and its two main crops are wheat and barley. Poplar trees and a thorn bush for fuel are generally grown in the marginal lands. This manner of using the marginal lands does away with the need to develop them. However, in answer to the expanding population the villagers have developed segments of these marginal lands to grow wheat and barley in them. Chemical fertiliser has been used only once, by a farmer who carried the sacks for three days on his back in order to bring it to the village. He reported excellent yields. Although most farmers want to use chemical fertiliser on their fields, they are unable to do so due to the difficulty in transporting it. It appears that the average yields of wheat in the valley range between 16 and 24 *maunds* (40 Kg) per acre, which is roughly the same as reported elsewhere in Gilgit.

There are some apricot, apple and mulberry trees in the valley and there are plans to plant more fruit trees. However, the most popular tree is the poplar. The poplar was first introduced to the valley by an enterprising villager who brought a sample from Passu. Almost all households grow the tree. It provides good construction material and its utility was first demonstrated when the

Shimshalis started moving away from the river and building new houses. The quick growing poplar is also sold to local villagers.

Livestock-rearing is by far the most important economic activity in the village. The ample grazing provided to the animals in the Pamirs enables each household to afford some livestock. The yaks and the stronger goats are kept in the Pamirs throughout the year. A group of men is chosen from the village to shepherd the animals. In the middle of May each year, women and children and at least one male from each household migrate to the Pamirs for the summer. The women busy themselves making cheese, *qurut* (dried cheese), butter oil and other dairy products. They return to Shimshal in September or October, well stocked for the frugal winter months. In November, the Shimshalis either bring their animals to Passu and Gilgit for sale or sell them to contractors from Hunza who travel to Shimshal for the purpose. Taking advantage of the difficult journey, the outside contractors are able to secure very low prices for the livestock they purchase. The Shimshalis report that they sell about 700 animals each year before Nisalo — a festival at which the people of the district slaughter animals and store the meat for use throughout the winter. This number includes yaks, goats and sheep. Apart from the income that the village earns by selling livestock, Shimshal is famous for the traditional rugs made from yak hair. These *sharmas* are reputed to last for several generations.

The people of Shimshal form a very closely-knit community and they are quick to introduce themselves as members of the same family. They form a cohesive group and have considerable experience in undertaking collective ventures. People have perfect freedom to enter each other's homes without announcing themselves and make themselves comfortable. They are an extremely hospitable people and take great pride in the fact that no one has ever left Shimshal displeased with the treatment they were accorded in the village. Members of a household contribute grain, butter oil and livestock to pay for the labour costs of constructing a public utility. The gift is made to honour a respected member of the household, usually a grandfather. The local school and the *Jamat Khana* in Shimshal received generous aid from a handful of village families who wanted to honour a family member.

The isolation of the village is most evident among the women. They do not leave the village unless they are married out in one of the Gujal villages. The Shimshalis marry only in Gujal villages which share the Wakhi language with them. The only women with some measure of exposure are those women from Passu and Gulmit who have married into Shimshali households. These women have tried to introduce new things into the family. They have persuaded some women to have variety in their diets and grow more vegetables. Although these women share the same responsibilities in the field as the women of Hunza, they are far less aware. Very few of them believe that they will ever leave their village. Their standard of hygiene is appalling. This is in spite of the fact that there is plenty of fresh spring water in the valley. There is only one Matriculate woman in the village and, although she aspires to be a doctor, there is considerable pressure on her to train as a teacher. This pressure is exerted by other women hoping to educate their girls with the presence of a lady teacher in the village.

The economy of the village is caught in a transitional phase. The people feel as comfortable with money as with barter. The part-monetization of the economy has been affected chiefly by the sale of livestock and employment within the army. In answering questions about the cost of a house, a Shimshali is apt to reply, 'Eight *maunds* of wheat, four *seers* of butteroil, one yak and two goats'. When a family starts building a house in the village, locals come to them and offer assistance. They do not ask any payment for their services but it is customary to provide their meals as long as they work on the house. The carpenter is usually offered a yak for his specialised services.

Very few innovations have reached the village. The people have had to count on their own resourcefulness and enterprise. In some ways the introduction of the sewing machine is typical of the manner in which Shimshal has received innovations. The machine was introduced in the village as late as 1964 when an enterprising local carried one to Shimshal. The villagers would line up and wait their turn to see the machine. Today, it sits inside a beautiful handmade wooden case; its crippled owner is too old to use it. Despite its introduction to the village only one or two families have bought the machine due to the difficult journey to the village. The problem of Shimshal is not so much lack of awareness as the absence of a link with the outside world.

The older generation claims self-sufficiency for the village. This proud state of 'sufficiency', which very few would publicly disavow, is born more out of compulsion than a genuine ability to meet the needs of the village. This declaration has been encouraged by visitors who repeatedly commend Shimshal for its ability to survive on its own. The Shimshalis have grasped this theme and refuse to admit to any dependence on the outside. A couple of the younger men will take you aside and confess that they do import some wheat. Moreover, the village's need for sugar, kerosene, soap, tea and salt is wholly met from outside. Shimshal is also becoming increasingly dependent on the Gilgit market for sale of its livestock.

Reactions to the outside world are mixed. Most members of the older generation have only heard about the Karakoram Highway. They express an indifference towards it. The women will only talk of it in hushed tones as if it was something fearsome and beyond their reach. It is mostly the younger men and a handful of educated women who get a wistful look as they talk of what lies outside their secluded haven and the possibility of linking it with the outside by a road. As one woman confided, 'I would not have had to marry an illiterate man in the village if we had a road.'

Appendix 11
The Shadows of Violence and Shelley's Anguish (NFR dated 9.6.1988—Meeting with the President of Pakistan, Rawalpindi)

An informal telephone call to my friend, Mr Hasan Zaheer, the Cabinet Secretary resulted in this meeting. On hearing what I had to say about the Gilgit disturbances, the Cabinet Secretary felt that I must see the president and arranged the interview himself.

The president, despite a long and busy day, was his usual gracious self and apologized for the late hour of the evening for the meeting and added he had no choice, as he was told that I was due to leave for Gilgit. On the president's query as to how the development programme was progressing, I poured out to my heart's content the anguish, frustration and sorrow I had been harbouring since the unfortunate events. I informed the president that during my 55 years of life, I had lived through many difficult situations, including the days of the Indian attack, as Commissioner, Karachi in 1971, but I had never seen such fear and panic as I witnessed in Gilgit, when even women and children came out on the street to run for their lives, irrespective of the sect they belonged to.

I was inundated with requests from Shias, Sunnis and Ismailis alike for transport to evacuate families. This was like medieval times, when invaders used to terrorize and subjugate populations. I handed to the president our preliminary estimates of losses, indicating how nothing was spared—human beings, houses and property, animals and trees, which came in the way of the *Lashkar* (group of armed men; tribal army). I mentioned the contingent headed by an absconder, which descended on Punyal and ransacked two villages and only went back after transport had been provided to them by the administration. I showed him my NFR and requested him to read the last page containing the big question marks in the minds of the people as to why the *Lashkar* was allowed to come to Gilgit and once it had arrived, why the administration had failed to repulse it. I submitted to the president the acute lack of confidence of the people in the government to protect their lives and properties, which I found not only in the areas visited by the *Lashkar* but even 40 odd far flung villages which I had visited since these unfortunate happenings.

I also gave to the president 'Proceedings of the Village Managers' Conference' addressed by His Highness, in November last, at Gilgit in which more than 500 villages of Gilgit and Baltistan districts sent their representatives and addresses of welcome were presented to His Highness by a Shia and a Sunni delegate. I informed the president of His Highness' great pleasure and satisfaction at this development and now how our six years' work was being destroyed by outside incursions and interventions. The president asked if he could keep the different documents I had shown him, to which I most willingly acquiesced.

The president said he was most distressed by these happenings and had already appointed a Supreme Court judge to hold an enquiry and had also ordered action against the local administration. I submitted to the president that there was little the local administration could do with 200 policemen against 20,000 armed persons. It is the people who allowed the *Lashkar* to reach Gilgit who should really be answerable. I added that, according to my information, for 36 hours the police tried to keep the attackers at bay, but because there were not sufficient troops, the police was overwhelmed. The president said that he had personally spoken to the chief minister of NWFP, who had assured him that no one would be allowed to cross over to the Gilgit area, and yet he did nothing. The federal minister went there and further compounded the issue. I submitted to the president that unless measures are taken to instil confidence in the local population that such a *Lashkar* would not attack again, the credibility of the government would not be redeemed. The president said that he was planning to visit the Northern Areas soon. To my request that in the meanwhile, he might consider sending his emissary to have a dialogue with different sects, with a view to helping them sink their differences, the president agreed, and said that he would ask the new minister to do so, and made a note to this effect in his notebook.

The president asked if he could do anything for the programme and on my observation that the president's greatest contribution was asking the intelligence agencies to leave us alone, he smiled, and then on a serious note referred with great regret to the campaign started by some periodicals against His Highness and observed that some people in the country do not allow any good work to be done and if someone succeeds in doing it, they gang up in decrying it. He considered this attitude very unfortunate. He asked me to approach him anytime I needed his help in any matter.

I presented to the president a copy of *Ujala*, edited by my wife Musarrat, in which his photographs and reference to his briefing on AKRSP had appeared. He greatly appreciated the get-up of the magazine and enquired if it came out regularly, to which I replied in the affirmative.

While taking leave I said to the president that my sole purpose in seeing him was to convey the anguish of the people of the Northern Areas. The president gave the impression that he was determined to see to it that this wound was healed. Despite my protests, the president graciously saw me off to the car.

This poem is an expression of the anguish felt by my daughter, Shelley, on the barbaric attack by the *Lashkar* on the helpless people of Gilgit in 1988, in the name of religion.

For Daddy, whom I respect and admire and love and will go on doing so for the rest of my life.

>The melancholic mountains
>Stand stained red
>A woman weepingly staggers
>to shelter,
>Her child clenched to her bosom.
>The fear flows through her eyes,
>While the infant squeaks with fright
>Touching its protector's heart with pain.
>
>The air drenched with death
>Allows no hope or happiness
>To come to the aid of these
>Pathetic souls of the world.
>
>Simple mind trapped in fanaticism
>Obey unquestionably
>Destroying universe
>Replaced by despair

With love from
your loving daughter

Shelley

17 June 1988

Appendix 12
Akhtar Hameed Khan's Summary of the AKRSP Approach to Sustainable Development

Present Condition. You have created a social and institutional infrastructure, which is developing and maintaining the necessary physical infrastructure of *kuhls* and roads, the economic infrastructure of credit and marketing, and the technical infrastructure of plant protection and animal husbandry. In my opinion these are now permanent institutions, which have taken root when they perform necessary functions — when they deliver, so to speak

The VOs have built and maintained *kuhls* and roads; they have disbursed and recovered loans; they have collected savings, organized marketing, and trained and remunerated their own specialists. This new tradition of cooperative action and skill will not be forgotten easily or quickly. Rather, it will spread.

Compare the poor condition of villages that have no trained specialists or whose managers have not learnt management, with the well-organized villages. Inevitably the former will, sooner or later, follow the example of the latter. By teaching the village to become autonomous you are actually reviving an old tradition. If you read the history of India or China, you find that conquerors came and disappeared but the civilization continued because its basis was the autonomous village looking after its own affairs. The new and foolish expectation is that a lot of things would be done for the village by the government or outsiders. This is a dream, a mirage. You should not encourage it.

Inadequacies. Your Programme — Social Organization, PPIs, Credit and Marketing and Agricultural Extension — are in a healthy condition as proved by statistical indicators. But let us carefully examine some inadequacies.

Let us begin with our first inadequacy, which is the mountain ecology. We understand the priority of *kuhls* and roads but I think we have not yet fully understood that this area depends for its climate, its rainfall, its agriculture and livestock on the preservation of forests. This [lack of understanding] is the greatest danger and the biggest challenge faced by this area. The forests were well protected in the Raja's time, in the first place because the people were tightly controlled and secondly, because a small population was controlled by high mortality. Now there is anarchy and the population is doubling every fifteen or twenty years. The forests are practically ownerless. They are being raped as a country is raped by invaders or a village by robbers.

The forests are without any protector. They are being distributed as loot or plunder. Foolishly, suicidally, the villagers themselves have joined in the plundering of forests, instead of protecting them as the very support of their lives. Everything that is being done—building social or physical infrastructure, agriculture or horticulture—will fade and disappear if the forests disappear. Without protection and further development and loving maintenance of forests, there is no future for rural Gilgit. Why are the forests being destroyed? On account of anarchy and the absence of responsible ownership. No property is safe unless it has an owner and protector.

It is embarrassing for me, a generalist, to speak of inadequacy in a specialist programme. But I crave your indulgence [while I make a second point]. I want to point out that it is a temptation for experts to hope for quick results by introducing improved breeds. In my view we should pay more attention to the improvement of traditional methods of feeding and housing. I know from personal experience in Bengal that the Union Council member's cow gave five *seers* of milk while the small farmer's cow gave two *seers*. The breed was the same but the feeding and housing were different. Without improved feeding and housing, the 'improved' breeds will soon fall to the level of local breeds. Why not first upgrade the feeding, housing and health of the local breeds? Let us concentrate at least some of our research and extension effort on upgrading traditional methods and local breeds.

[On a third point] there were some inadequacies in our women's programme. One reason was that health, child care, nutrition and family planning were excluded. The other reason was the misunderstanding that there can be in Gilgit villages separate economic programmes for women. As a matter of fact, the family farms are very much of a joint business in which the whole family is inextricably bound in partnership. You have now redesigned the programme. In the future strategy, this inadequacy has been remedied by recognizing the fact of partnership and integration. My analysis on women's programme and its future strategy has been summarized separately by Ameneh.

Future Strategy—Investment in Woodland. We do not have to bother about the VOs: they are by now firmly rooted. Neither need we worry about the physical infrastructure of kuhls and roads. Much has been completed and the remainder will also be completed in course of time. There is no need here for changes in approach, stance or organization.

A new factor which we should introduce in our future strategy is to convince the VOs that the most profitable investments can be made inside the village itself. The VOs put their savings in a bank or post office, they get a mere 7 per cent from which 2.5 per cent *zakat* is deducted. Instead they can make local investments which would bring much higher gain.

Some VOs have already discovered one spectacular avenue of investment, tree plantation—a woodlot. When I first went to Oshikandas, I was amazed at what I saw. Oshikandas had thousands of trees, every family had a woodlot, which was their main source of income. In a recent visit to Mohammadabad, I saw that it is becoming another Oshikandas. The duplication of a model is the real proof of its success. Oshikandas is a model which can be duplicated in many villages.

We can divide land development into two categories: cropland and woodland or woodlots. Levelling for cropland requires much investment and gives poor returns compared to tree plantation for woodland which requires less investment and labour and gives much higher returns. Your forestry experts can recommend excellent varieties of timber, fuel and fodder trees for the woodlots. AKRSP should propagate this concept and help the VOs to make this investment both with loans and savings. Films of villages like Oshikandas and Mohammadabad should be shown to other VOs and their managers should be encouraged to make personal visits.

Digression on the Rural Economy of Gilgit. Fifty years ago this area was importing perhaps 10 per cent of its requirements. Neither the Raja nor the people needed any subsidies or foreign aid. Both were self supporting. But what is the present position? Most consumer goods are imported from outside, very little is exported and small tax revenue is generated while large subsidies are consumed. Watch the trucks on the KKH and notice the proportion of imports and exports. Even timber and animals are imported. What is the future of such an economy? It must change. There must be more exports and fewer subsidies.

Can Gilgit export wheat? No. It can export only fruits, timber, animals and other wealth hidden in the mountains, herbs, minerals, precious stones. Your assignment is to make Gilgit prosperous. How can you make an area prosperous which is importing 90 per cent and exporting 10 per cent? For Gilgit the mountains are the real source of development and the only true hope of prosperity.

You have built the VOs, you have built the social and physical infrastructures, you have built the credit structure. You have popularized the concept of savings and investment. You have started the process of development. Now you should make the VOs see that their real objective should be to produce a big exportable surplus of fruits, timber, animals and other wealth from the mountains.

For this purpose, the VOs should reconstruct the third infrastructure—the mountain—with its forests and pastures, nurturing large herds of cattle and producing vast quantities of timber, meat, skins, butter and cheese.

Future Strategy: Features of Developed Village. Let us paint a picture of the future 'developed' villages. A 'developed' village will have two new features:

1. Protection and improvement of its territory

2. Cooperative services and supplies

By territory I mean all the land in and around the village, with all its resources, water, soil, forest and pastures. A developed village will have a clear concept of responsible ownership of its territory, and its protection and improvement, instead of the present suicidal concept of plunder.

A developed village will organize cooperative services and supplies for credit, marketing, plant protection and animal husbandry. Numerous VOs have acquired the second feature (cooperative services) while only a few have acquired the first feature (protection of territory).

We should remember that if we have a developed model, it is easy to duplicate it. There already are a few villages which have acquired or are in the process of acquiring both of these two features. What should be the new priority in promoting this model of a developed village? [It should be] the creation of a conviction that their territory belongs to them: it is their future resource, it is their legacy to their children. On the growth of this conviction will depend the protection and improvement of territory, afforestation and range development.

As in the case of irrigation, so in the case of forestry and pastures 'grafting' of scientific material must be done by traditional methods. This may be more difficult in forestry than in irrigation. Much initial research about trees, grasses, soils, elevation and so on has to be done and many experiments and demonstrations have to be conducted. Research, experiment and demonstration require time and should not be hurried too much.

Your full package of advice for territorial or land development will emerge slowly from your research and demonstration, which in my opinion, is being very well done by Consultant Michael Junkov.

When you are introducing innovations you may be introducing either something simple or complicated. A simple innovation can be multiplied fairly fast. Credit was a simple innovation and you have multiplied quickly. Marketing was more complicated and it has spread slowly.

Protection and improvement of territory is a complicated innovation. You must proceed stage by stage, not omitting any link. You should first concentrate on only five or six already existing model villages adopting territorial protection and improvement with forestation, pastures, collective herds of cattle and so on. As these villages go further forward, they may be turned into training and demonstration centres. Let the Managers and Chairmen of other VOs come there and see with their own eyes and hear with their own ears. Thus next year you will have 25 new models.

There is a part of the advanced model which can be introduced quickly and widely: the village [forest] nursery. The village nursery, like other programmes, reduces dependence on outside sources. I would advise you not to insist on the nursery being a collective enterprise of the VO. It would be better managed by a private entrepreneur. Forests and pastures should be collectively managed though with specialized and paid gangs. But nurseries require individual attention.

Your programmes have created a favourable climate for the emergence of private entrepreneurs in the village. We need not encourage exploitative middlemen like the traditional merchant moneylender or privileged (with the help of ADB loans) tractor or thresher *waderas*. But there is room for commercial farmers, commercial dairymen, commercial poultry farmers, commercial nursery owners and other private entrepreneurs.

They are not exploiters. They promote production and employment. And it is their presence in sufficient numbers that will turn the present subsistence economy into a commercial economy which will produce the surplus for export. The favourable climate for private entrepreneurs has been created because your programmes: PPIs, credit, marketing and agricultural extension have created new opportunities as well as an urge for profitable investment through increased production. They have also created the means—*i.e.* easily available credit and the habit of saving. You may remember that when we first went to the village, we found that the farmers did not think that their land had a great profitable potential. Now the potential is visible.

Future Strategy—Increasing Family Production. Taking full advantage of this favourable climate in our future strategy, we should make an important addition. We should start a special programme for increasing production of family units. What is the difference between the family unit and the commercial entrepreneur? The commercial entrepreneur operates full time and on a larger scale, as nursery owner, dairyman, poultry farmer and processor. For the family unit, however, the work is part time, supplementary and on small scale. It is done by members of the family themselves. The families will plant trees, cultivate kitchen gardens, keep poultry and milk cows to supplement their farm income.

You may exclaim 'But they are already doing this' and this is quite true. They are doing it in the traditional manner. Now you are going to teach them 'grafting' of scientific methods, onto traditional methods. This will create a synthesis which will increase productivity and reduce losses.

Take for instance, chickens or milch cows: you should give scientific advice about housing and feeding or teach them to plant woodlots and kitchen gardens in their compounds. By modernizing family production, you can bring about considerable increase in the family income. I am sure that as the families increase their produce, there will be no difficulty in organizing marketing of their wood, milk, eggs or vegetables.

Appendix 13
Two Days with Mr Rahul Gandhi, MP—22 July 2008

Note for Record

By: Shoaib Sultan Khan
22 July 2008

Subject: Two Days with Mr Rahul Gandhi, MP

I received an invitation (see box) from Rajiv Gandhi Charitable Trust.

We drove into Munshigunj (Amethi) Rest House late in the evening of 14 July and the place was bristling with security personnel. Mr Rahul Gandhi had already arrived. We were received by the Project Manager of Rajiv Gandhi Mahila Vikas Preyojana (RGMVP), Mr Y.S. Yadav. The Rest House is the camp of Shrimati Sonia Gandhi and Rahul Gandhi as both of them have been elected MPs to the Indian parliament from adjoining constituencies Amethi in Sultanpur district and Rae Bareli. It seemed that the suite under use of Rahul's associate next to his suite was given to me.

I briefly met Rahul in the morning as there were hundreds of people sitting in the lawn under an elegant *shamiana* waiting to meet him. It was at 8.00 p.m. when I had been taken for a village dialogue by Sampath Kumar, CEO RGMVP that Rahul joined us. Under gas lights the deliberations started with the Project Manager Y.S. Yadav doing the introductions. All the households in Teri village had organized into Self Help Groups (SHGs) and the SHGs had federated in a Village Organization called Cluster Level Association (CLA).

At this juncture Rahul, along with his secretary Kanishka Singh being guided by a torch light, came and sat down on the floor by my side. At our back, there were a few goats sitting and munching quite disinterested in the proceedings.

Rahul asked Kumar if I had been introduced to the gathering and then asked if he could speak for a minute and again introduced me to the VO and asked me to address the villagers. I thanked Rahul for inviting me and expressed great pleasure in meeting him especially as I had met his great-grandfather Pandit Jawahar Lal Nehru as a young student, when, as head of the Interim Government, Panditji had come to visit Ghazipur, where my grandfather was Collector in 1947. I explained to the gathering the three principles of social mobilisation based on the conviction that even the poorest man or woman has the potential to improve their economic and social condition if helped to unleash the potential within them. I illustrated the effectiveness of the principles of organization, human resource development and generation of capital through savings by describing my experience of working with a million people of the Northern Areas of Pakistan and thereafter, especially in Andhra Pradesh, where 100,000 families organized by the South Asia Poverty Alleviation Programme (SAPAP) initiated by the UNDP has now blossomed to cover over nine million organized households and how they have improved their economic and social status beyond recognition.

Thus, I explained that the success of this approach is dependent on i) peoples willingness to get organized to enable them to unleash their potential; ii) presence of an honest and committed leader within the group willing to acquire through human resource development training human skills to lead the group, and iii) presence of a sensitive support organization of dedicated and committed staff to be the catalyst in organizing the poor in SHGs and facilitating removal of obstacles in the way of the SHGs to achieve the full potential of what they are willing and capable of doing.

I emphasized that the Social Mobilisation approach demands of the poor in the beginning to fulfil their obligations of organization comprising SHG meetings and participation of all on a fixed day (initially weekly), fixed time and a place in full knowledge of everyone and initiating a capital generation programme through weekly savings and finally willing to fully participate in human resource development training. It is only when SHG fulfils these obligations that the support organization can enter into a partnership with them. Being a Development Partnership both partners: communities (SGHs/CLA/BLA and support organization (RGMVP) have to discharge their obligations on equal terms.

I asked Teri CLA how RGMVP is different from scores of government departments and other development agencies. It is only RGMVP which focuses on unleashing the potential of the people by organizing them. Secondly, RGMVP has no pre-conceived package of interventions to reduce poverty. It is SHGs which identify the interventions which could facilitate unleashing of their potential. And thirdly, RGMVP, by organizing SHGs reaches the household level, most of the government programmes and projects only reach the village or gram level. Poverty prevails at household and family level and unless a programme helps and facilitates the family to rise above the level of subsistence, poverty from the village would not go away. I congratulated the women of Teri because they had fulfilled their obligations of the Development Partnership they have entered in with RGMVP.

The SHGs members of Teri who had now federated in Cluster Level Association (CLA) at village level narrated their experiences since getting organized.

After formation of SHGs and CLA, the women said that many of their problems have been solved. Many narrated how they were indebted borrowing money at 10 per cent per month, now the SHG offers credit at only 2 per cent per month, thus saving them Rs 8 per month per Rs 100/-. One member described how she was able to redeem her plot of land by paying off her debt through acquisition of cheap credit from her SHG. Another one described how an initial loan of Rs 2000 from SHG for a sewing machine helped her build her credibility and subsequently enabled her to borrow money for buffalo and even a tractor. Another case study was of a member who started borrowing small sums from SHG and repaying in time graduated borrowing large sums for buffaloes which has enabled her to send her children to school for education. Another story was of starting with a Rs 5000 loan from SHG going upto Rs 30,000 and now she possessed cows and buffaloes and repaid every penny of the loan. Another heartwarming story was of a woman whose husband was out of job when their son fell ill. With SHG support, she got her son treated in hospital. Even her house fell down due to heavy rains but the SHG did not give up on her and helped her in every adversity to get on her feet. Today she was in a position to send her child to a good school paying Rs 2600 fees per term quarterly.

When asked how many of the 104 households of Teri were destitutes and what the SHGs or the CLA has done for them, a couple of the destitutes came forward and described how they have been helped by SHG/CLA. In one case the villager sold his land to build a house for himself and had nothing now for livelihood. The SHG was debating how to help the family for livelihood.

The women claimed to have been empowered since they got organized in SHGs and formed the CLA. One of their members complained against her husband for maltreatment and beatings. The SHG/CLA decided to act and confronted the man about his cruel behaviour towards his wife. The man threatened to beat the SHG women and shouted at them saying it was a domestic matter and none of their business. A group of thirty women went to the local police station and complained against the culprit. The Police Officer came immediately and took the man away and locked him up. The next day the women asked the Police Officer to release him without registering a case against him because they only wanted to teach him a lesson. The man has been on his best behaviour since then towards his wife and towards all the women of the village. The women stated but for their SHG/CLA, they would have suffered in silence as they used to do prior to RGMVP. Now even the *Pradhan* (Chairman) of the *panchayat* takes them seriously if they go with any request.

In his address Rahul Gandhi said that six years ago people said what was achieved in Andhra Pradesh can't work here in UP. People are divided because of caste. RGMVP was begun in 2002 and it is now the biggest programme of poverty reduction and women's empowerment in UP. It all happened because you stood together. If you unite, people are not divided. Wrongdoings can be stopped if you are united. Today you are united at the village level. Hopefully soon you would unite at Block, District and the national level and maybe one day at the regional level. United, you are our strength.

The dialogue ended with a song and we all headed towards our vehicles. Rahul invited me to sit in his vehicle along with Singh and Kumar. On the way he discussed how social mobilisation can be scaled up and whether it really can be? Recounting my experience of last 55 years and especially of the last 30 years the including 12 years in the Northern Areas, organizing one million people, there are three pre-requisites for the success of the social mobilisation approach. Firstly, willingness of the community, secondly, presence of an honest and committed activist as community resource person (CRP) within the SHG, and thirdly, a sensitive support organization like RGMVP. If these three ingredients are there, all you need are resources to scale up. From what I have seen in Sultanpur Amethi, I have no doubt that all the three pre-requisites are present in UP. The main constraint is resources.

For resource mobilisation, I described to Rahul the Pakistan Poverty Alleviation Fund (PPAF) structure and proposed a similar organization to be set up by the Union Government. In the case of India, unlike PPAF, the Fund needs only two windows to fund sensitive support organizations like RGMVP, namely the Social Mobilisation window supplemented by a Community Investment Fund (CIF) window. The RGMVP experience shows a requirement per Block of roughly ten million rupees for social mobilisation through CRPs and CIF. I suggested to Rahul to set up a US$500 million Fund to mobilise each and every poor household in nearly 1000 Blocks of UP. Rahul and Singh seemed most interested in the proposal.

By now we had reached Amethi Rest House and Rahul asked me if I could wait for a little while for dinner as he had asked for food to be brought from Lucknow including the famous *tundaywaley kabab*. I was simply overwhelmed at Rahul's humility, kindness and hospitality. It was indeed a feast to remember.

The next morning Rahul wanted me to see the eye hospital he had set up at Amethi. Singh took me there. It was a state-of-the-art establishment comparable to any hospital anywhere in the world being run in a most professional manner. The beauty of the arrangement is that 30 per cent of the paying patients cross-subsidise 70 per cent of the poor patients. The eye hospital, named after Rahul's grandmother, is indeed a blessing for the people of Sultanpur and adjoining districts.

Rahul joined us at the hospital and we drove together to the Jaisi Training Centre of RGMVP to attend the final session of the RGMVP Vision Building Workshop. On the way Rahul would stop even if a lone person would signal him to stop and listen to him or take his application. At one place, the man offered a hot mug of tea to Rahul who was nonplussed how to drink such hot tea in one gulp in order to save time. However, his problem was solved when the man asked Rahul to take the mug with him. Rahul's sensitivity towards his constituents and his behaviour towards them left me most impressed. For his young age, he displays remarkable patience, empathy and compassion. A tribute to his parents upbringing.

The workshop participants included Kumar's management staff and field level Block Coordinators, Community Volunteers and field workers besides CRPs. Some of the CRPs had come from Andhra Pradesh along with Vijayabharti. I had a session the previous day in the workshop and had emphasized the niche of RGMVP. An activity which neither the government departments nor the development agencies address. Because if the RGMVP tries to do the same things which the government departments are mandated to do RGMVP will get nowhere for the simple reason that what the government departments could not do in over sixty years with massive resources, how could RGMVP claim to achieve these activities with scarce resources. Thus, RGMVP's vision should be focused on harnessing people's, especially the poor's, potential to come out of poverty. If RGMVP deviates from this vision, it would not achieve its ultimate goal of elimination of poverty. RGMVP has to have a very focused vision and a clear mission like the Persian proverb 'catch hold of one and hold it firmly instead trying to catch many and succeed in catching none'. I quoted the incident when the Poverty Commission called on Prime Minister Narsimha Rao and the vice chairman of the Commission began by defining poverty. The prime minister cut him short by observing we all know there is poverty. Tell us how the Commission is going to eliminate it.

In his presentation before Rahul on how RGMVP is going to achieve its ultimate objectives of *Gharibi Hattao* (eliminate poverty), Kumar made an excellent and focused Vision and Mission statement, namely, harnessing the potential of people through organization and reaching 500,000 households in the nine districts of the programme area by the year 2015. He further elucidated the non-negotiable values, poverty reduction strategy, and implementation strategy with the strength of RGMVP currently—especially a sensitive support organization and a pool of CRPs which has reached 130,000 households in 9 districts, 43 Blocks, 1224 Garam Panchayats, 4287 villages comprising 11312 SHGs covering 13,7200 families with over 40 million rupees savings, accessing bank credit amounting to Rs 16.20 crores.

Some of the CRPs, after Kumar's presentation, narrated their experiences after getting organized as SHGs. They described how SHG gave them confidence and recognition. Prior to SHG, they were only busy in domestic chores with no savings. Now they were tasting the power of capital from Rs 850 of personal savings to Rs 15,000 of SHG savings to Rs 400,000 of village savings to Rs 5 million of Block savings. Rekha said she now did not feel alone. She had the support of our own institutions which were well endowed with capital to at least come to their help in emergencies instead of them having to run from pillar to post.

CRP Gita described how her status was raised. In the beginning, when the RGMVP staff took her to a high caste family's house and she sat on the cot, she was ordered by the house mistress not to forget her status and sit on the ground. She apologized and sat on the ground. A few months later, the house mistress needed money for the marriage of her son. She asked the RGMVP staff for a loan and he directed her to Gita as the competent authority to sanction a loan on behalf of the SHG. The mistress now invited Gita to sit on the cot.

CRP Urmilla thought that the poor were a burden on society and can do nothing except to beg. The SHG gave her confidence and when as CRP she was required to go outside the village, she was most apprehensive. However, when she went to one village she got such a pleasure in helping her other sisters that she started going to many villages.' When her family members complained about who was going to look after her children, she replied God will look after them.' Some outsiders made sarcastic comments, such as, she must be getting a good salary that she is roaming around all the time'. One day, she received a message that her house has been damaged due to rains. However, as she had given time and women were waiting, she did not tell anybody and went to the village where the women were waiting. She said, 'When I reached home, my family reprimanded me but I retorted all of you were there and I had to go because the women were waiting for me.' 'If we take care and think of others, they will also take care of us'.

CRP Gita Panday described how helpless they were before formation of SHGs. After SHGs when the landlord refused to pay two of us our wages, we went to our SHG and described our plight. Two SHG members, numbering 30, volunteered to help us and came with us to the landlord's house. Seeing so many women coming to his house, the landlord immediately paid us our wages. We have no fear now. We now have power. We can fight for our rights.

CRP Mahbooba Begum was kept in *purdah* like a prisoner by her husband. When he died, she came back to her village with her children and after getting introduced to RGMVP and becoming a CRP, she made 17 SHGs and opened their bank accounts. 'My children were out of school, however, after joining SHG, I have got them admitted in the English medium school. At Aganbari, I did work but the madam refused to pay my three weeks wages on the plea that she had not received resources from her superiors. I put the matter to the SHG and they accompanied me but madam had gone. The next day the SHG members went again and demanded from madam to show the registers that she had not received resources. She started sweating and was forced to give my dues.'

CRP Rubina Bano described how, before SHG, as her husband is working in Mumbai, a demagogue came to the house and in her absence, frightened her little girl. No one came to her help. 'Now that is history. With the formation of SHGs, CLAs and BLA, no one dare harass us. In Jagdishpur Block, the entire households have been organized. There is peace in the Block and we are forging linkages with government departments.'

When I was asked to address the Workshop, I complimented Kumar on his presentation of a very clear Vision and Mission of RGMVP. However, I submitted to Rahul that reaching 5 lakh poor households by 2015 would hardly make a dent on the poverty profile of UP where over 50 million need RGMVP support. I urged him to scale up the RGMVP operations to cover entire UP as the three pre-requisites, described earlier by me, for harnessing the potential of the people to come out of poverty, are there. All that is needed to scale up the operations are the resources.

Rahul, in summing up, said that he was reminded of a story when he saw some people cutting iron with a machine but it was not visible how the machine was cutting the iron. When Rahul asked the person operating the machine, how it was being done, Rahul was surprised to see that it was through a water jet that the iron was being cut. Listening to the CRPs and looking at the work done by RGMVP, the potential of the people is like the jet of water cutting the iron. Like the water, the potential of the people is also not visible. People have potential but it is lying dormant. SHG is like the water jet. Rahul posed the question why not harness the potential of every poor instead of targeting numbers. Rahul admitted that since yesterday his thinking has changed. He would like RGMVP to reach every poor in UP.

Some time ago when Raju and Vijay, my friends in Andhra Pradesh, had mentioned the possibility of my visit to UP on the invitation of the Rajiv Gandhi Charitable Trust to look at their social mobilisation project being implemented by RGMVP, it was not in my wildest dreams that the visit would turn out the way it did.

From the moment I stepped out of the train at Sultanpur station, Kumar took care of me in a way I have no words to thank him. But what really was the most pleasant surprise to me was the way RGMVP is being implemented. The Project Manager Y.S. Yadav who initiated the project in 2002, laid a very good foundation on which Kumar, in a short period of nine months, has done wonders. I could only encourage them to do what they were already doing. I agreed with Rahul that finding the right person to implement the programme is like winning the battle. In finding Kumar as CEO of RGMVP is the best thing that could have happened to the programme. I mentioned the case of SAPAP to Rahul. How, for one year, we got nowhere till my friend Venugopal identified K. Raju for the job. Thereafter, I had to do nothing—Raju did all even finding his team of persons like Vijay Kumar.

Above all, it was Rahul who left a deep impression on me and the people who are around him, like Kanishka Singh. Rahul's perception and grasp of the problems of the poor and the understanding of the strategy of social mobilisation to harness the potential of the poor left me in a state of euphoria. Here is a champion of the poor who will leave no stone unturned to reach each and every poor person in UP and hopefully in India to pull them out of poverty. That will be the day India will be really shining.

<u>Annex</u>

- copy -

SEAL

P. Sampath Kumar, IAS
CEO, Rajiv Gandhi Mahila Vikas Pariyojana

RGMVP/PFD/104/2008-09/104, Dated 21st July 2008, Raebareli

Respected Sir,

Subject: Vision building workshop of Rajiv Gandhi Mahila Vikas Pariyojana—Mission for Poverty Reduction & Women's Empowerment in Uttar Pradesh, India

I have the honour to inform you that Rajiv Gandhi Charitable Trust is implementing a special project for poverty reduction in the name of Rajiv Gandhi Mahila Vikas Pariyojana in Uttar Pradesh, in collaboration with National Bank for Agriculture and Rural Development and Society for Elimination of Rural Poverty, Hyderabad. The project aims at eradicating poverty with particular emphasis on empowering women through the proven SHG institutional model as demonstrated under UNDP's South Asian Poverty Alleviation Programme.

The project, as on date, reached 37 backward blocks of Central and Eastern Uttar Pradesh and has succeeded in mobilizing 10,500 women Self Help Groups under the institutional building process, covering about 1.3 lakh rural poor households. The project has been implementing the Community Resource Person Strategy in which the social mobilization process is initially induced by the Community Resource Persons who were nurtured and developed under the South Asian Poverty Alleviation Project implemented in Andhra Pradesh. Deriving inspiration from the enthusiastic response and active participation of the community, it is proposed to extend the project activities to other parts of the Uttar Pradesh covering a total 100 backward Blocks in the next 7 years.

In this connection, we propose to organize a 'vision building workshop' in the month of July 2008 and we would like to seek your advise and guidance to build up the project into a dedicated Mission for Poverty Reduction and Women Empowerment in Uttar Pradesh.

Sir, we are aware about your immense contribution to the successful demonstration of institutional model of poverty reduction under South Asian Poverty Alleviation Programme, the model which we would like to bring in under our project. We will be very grateful if you could accept this invitation to kindly participate in the Vision Building Workshop of Rajiv Gandhi Mahila Vikas Pariyojana proposed to be held w.e.f. 14th July to 16th July, 2008.

Many thanks.

With kind regards.

Very truly yours,

P. Sampath Kumar

To

Shri Shoib Sultan Khan,
Chairman, National Rural Support Programme Network
Pakistan

SEAL

Project Management Unit, Rajiv Gandhi Mahila Vikas Priyojana—Special SHG Initiative Project,
Rajiv Gandhi Charitable Trust, Raebareli, Utter Pradesh, India—229001
+91-535-2204484 (O) 2203300 (FAX) 2204566 ®

Postscript: Email from Sampath Kumar, CEO, Rajiv Gandhi Women Empowerment Project in response to NFR

Dear Sir

I feel extremely grateful to you for taking pains to visit our project and for giving us most valuable advice and vision for the project. Truly, your visit has brought a renewed energy into the project. We are extremely delighted for having shared this note (NFR)—a masterpiece with us. We shall always look forward to you for guidance.

Many thanks and warm regards

Sampath. 27 July 2008

Appendix 14
Activists turned CRPs of Andhra Pradesh— 24 July 2008

Note for Record

By: Shoaib Sultan Khan
July 24, 2008

Subject: Activists turned CRPs of Andhra Pradesh

Principal Secretary to Government of Andhra Pradesh K. Raju and Chief Executive Officer (CEO), Society for Elimination of Rural Poverty (SERP) Vijay Kumar insisted that I should pay a visit to Andhra after my visit to the Rajiv Gandhi Charitable Trust project in Sultanpur—Amethi in UP.

As always they had drawn up a most inspiring and exhilarating programme for me. My courtesy call on the Chief Minister Mr Jayasekhra Reddy indicated the immense personal interest the chief minister was taking in the activities of the self help groups (SHGs) and SERP. He was all praise the way Raju was implementing the Prime Minister's Employment Guarantee Scheme through SHGs and higher organizations. He was also full of praise for Vijay the way SERP was fostering institutions of the people. I have yet to see a chief minister taking this level of interest in the welfare of the poor. Mr Reddy is a real ideologue whose initiative of performance-based loan interest subsidy has ushered in a real revolution in making capital available to the poorest of the poor.

The Minister for Rural Development and SHGs, Dr Chinna Reddy spent five hours with us in the Zilla Samakhyas Workshop, mostly listening instead of making long speeches which is the normal habit of ministers in our countries. Dr Reddy, though he looks very young, has been in politics from his student days, and is now in his thirtieth year in politics. His sensitivity towards the problems of the poor was only matched by his chief minister.

There was some kind of a *Bandh* so my field visit was hastily shifted from Nizamabad to Ranga Reddy district. However, when I reached village Nomula, one would have thought this was all prearranged. Of course it was just at an hour's notice. Nomula has the distinction where all SHGs have achieved Total

Financial Inclusion (TFI) meaning every member has accessed a loan from the banks in addition to CIF, internal savings loaning and Mahila Banks.

We had an interesting discussion about the differences between the earlier programmes and SERP. Earlier, there were no regular meetings of the group and no horizontal meetings like the VO under SERP. The revolving fund given to the group used to be so small that it would suffice the needs of no more than two or three members at a time with long gaps in the availability of capital to others resulting in their losing interest. The officials, after initial organization, would only keep contact with one person of the organization and instead of coming to the field, would call the representatives of the groups to their offices. Since 2001, with the arrival of SERP and its community coordinator Sunanda, things are totally changed. SHGs have become a vibrant organization with 470 households and two VOs in view of the large number of SHGs. SERP's great strength is effective follow-up and monitoring instead of the earlier projects only emphasizing savings of Re 1 a day in a campaign mode which meant collection of Rs 365 per year per household and had little significance by itself. Under the TFI initiative, each SHG has now accessed Rs 500,000 from the banks.

Another most interesting programme being implemented by the VO is the Non-Pesticide Management (NPM). Under this programme, technical support has been provided by an NGO and an NPM CRP has been trained who first demonstrated the efficacy of NPM in her own field two years ago and has now covered half of the village and hopes to convert the entire village to NPM within the next two years. NPM would not only usher in organic agriculture, it would also rejuvenate the soil. This is an important initiative for small farmers owning even less than two acres. Some of the Mandal Samakhyas have now acquired the technical expertise of NPM and are spreading the programme without waiting for NGO technical support.

The Rural Support Programmes Network (RSPN) in Pakistan may consider sending some farmers along with an NRM professional to learn NPM techniques adopted by SERP for adoption by RSPs.

The formation of Disabled SHGs of 7-10 members is another critical intervention to help a sizeable group of impoverished people. In this Mandal alone, there were over 300 disabled persons.

However, the most impressive phenomenon I noticed this time, was the emergence of the Activists turned Community Resource Persons (CRPs) movement. The Institution Building (IB) CRPs are now being complemented by what Vijay calls them Thematic CRPs. I interacted with a group of these CRPs at the Andhra Pradesh Human Resource Development Institute where SERP was holding its Zilla Samakhya Workshop. This is an incredible cadre of CRPs addressing:

1. Institution Building
2. Marketing

3. Dairy
4. Health and Nutrition
5. Non-Pesticide Management
6. Village Construction
7. Registration
8. Gender
9. Land
10. Job Creation & Employment
11. Total Financial Inclusion
12. Urban Development

One had only to listen to these CRPs to realize what they are capable of achieving. Their initiative, dynamism and dedication is amazing. When the Marketing CRP could not access capital from the bank, she asked SHGs to provide her funds promising to give them 18 per cent on the loans to offset 12 per cent SHGs will have to pay to the bank. On top of it when she had sold their produce, she gave them a profit of Rs 180,000. A group of 4–5 VOs have set up procurement centres under each Marketing CRP whom SERP has trained. The Marketing CRP is a new breed of middlemen or women who plow back profits to producers after taking a fixed amount for their services. There are now more than 600 Marketing CRPs trained by SERP, of which 100 have already become master trainers multiplying number of Marketing CRPs.

The Dairy CRP has learnt how to use Milk Testers to judge the quality of milk which determines the price. The Mandal level Milk Cooling Centre accepts the Dairy CRPs readings and this has resulted in milk producers getting Rs 18 instead of Rs 10 paid to them by local buyers per litre. Dairy is a big business and is now institutionalized through Village Dairy Development Committee, Mandal level committee and Zilla Samakhya level committee. 85 per cent of the SHG members survive on agriculture or dairy. The Dairy CRPs have ensured proper return for their produce.

The Gender CRPs have been most effective in reduction of violence against women in increasing women's negotiating power. The CRP is helped by Village Social Action Committee comprising ten members to help resolve issues and do family counseling. Even police cooperates in getting summons of the committee complied with and the magistrates refer family disputes first to be resolved by the Committee before admitting the petition.

Each category of CRP be it Health or Nutrition or NPM or Land or Job etc., have a clear cut role which they are trying to perform in a most effective way. Their confidence and determination in performing their duties is incredible.

The ZS comprise the presidents of Mandal Mahila Samakhyas (MMSs) and has an Executive of 5 selected members with 7 sub-committees for different subjects comprising five members each. The General Body of ZS meets once in six months and EC every month. The need for ZS was felt for resource mobilization, registration, accounting and bookkeeping, training MMSs, monitoring MMSs, linking MMSs with government and NGOs, undertaking direct activities like insurance, acting as mother organization of MMSs, undertaking large scale district level activities and ensuring sustainability of the institutions of the poor.

Raju raised the issue of the niche of ZS and its relationship with SERP and the effectiveness of the committees.

On the issue of niche of ZS, I reinforced Raju's concern and gave the example of the Cooperatives in the sub-continent. In the fifties, the All India Congress in its annual meetings from 1952 onwards applauded Cooperative movement as the panacea for the poverty of India. Prime Minister Pandit Jawahar Lal Nehru was euphoric about the potential of cooperatives. He got extremely dejected when this did not happen and constituted a Cooperative Commission to look into the causes of the failure of Cooperatives. The Commission came to the conclusion that the Executive Committees of the Cooperatives proved the bane of the movement. The General Body used to meet only once in a year and the Executive Members became all powerful and corrupt. I cautioned the ZS to be conscious of this factor. The social mobilisation movement fostered by SERP is based on SHGs as the foundation, the Village Organizations are the walls and Mandal Samakhyas the roof and ZS is the dome. The dome needs the support of the foundation, the walls and the roof to remain in tact. If the dome undermines the foundation, the walls or the roof, it would disintegrate. ZS will only survive and be effective if SHGs are viable along with VOs and MMSs. The only way this can be ensured if the institutions do not trespass on each others functions. I am glad that ZS is conscious of that but they have to remain so for ever, if ZS is going to ensure sustainability of the SHGs, VOs and MMSs.

Dr Reddy supported my argument by quoting his personal example that as President of a Cooperative, no one used to come to the General Body meeting and perforce he had to fill up the hall with his own party workers. The minister underscored the importance of the democratic process of SHGs and the review and monitoring functions of ZS. It has to ensure that every poor household has access to loans and there should be equality and no one should be left out. He plans to reach all the ten million households in Andhra. SERP has already organized more than nine million. He also warned against political bribes when some unscrupulous politicians may try to buy whole groups. He urged the ZS, MMS, VOs and SHGs to be vigilant about government programmes and how these are being implemented.

The minister paid rich tributes to Raju and Vijay and observed we rarely find the likes of them in bureaucracy. It is for this reason that on his visit to Washington DC, the World Bank complained that the District Poverty Initiatives Project (DRIP) has not been as successful in other states as Andhra.

The ZS representatives assured the minister that no one can buy them. They would only support those who are good to them.

When the minister asked me to speak, I pointed out my dilemma because the CRPs, the ZS office bearers, the SERP professionals from the field to the CEO and the Principal Secretary are like the Sharapovas, Serenas, Venuses, Sonia Mirzas and Federers of the game of Tennis. These women and men are as proficient in their jobs as those are in their games. How can one tell them to improve anything? They are already on the top. What I can do is only to reemphasize the basics. This whole edifice is built on the willingness of the communities, the CRPs and the support organization. Any weakness in any of the three would damage the edifice.

This edifice has been nurtured by the state government, personally by the chief minister and the minister for Rural Development. This is the most critical support. Without this support, the edifice would not have been able to achieve much. I only wish in every state and in every country could we find such champions of the poor as the CM and the minister as in Andhra Pradesh, it will only be then that poverty will become history which I am confident it will be in Andhra. I also mentioned about my visit to Rajiv Gandhi Mahila Vikas Preyojana in Sultanpur-Amethi and my interaction with Mr Rahul Gandhi and how impressed I have been by his perception and understanding of the process of social mobilization harnessing the potential of the people and his empathy and compassion for the poor and the down trodden and how he is determined to reach each and every poor household not only in UP but the whole of India. With such champions of poverty elimination, the goal of a poverty free country is certainly attainable.

I mentioned how in implementing South Asia Poverty Alleviation Programme (SAPAP), my friend Venugopal found K. Raju for me which was the best thing that could have happened to SAPAP and to me. I had to do nothing, thereafter, Raju did all, even finding Vijay Kumar. And now I see another Raju and Vijay emerging in Sampath. This trio will indeed set a shining example for the rest of India.

I concluded by quoting my mentor Akhtar Hameed Khan how he used to call the CRPs the diamonds and jewels of the communities. If they remain honest and selfless, the organizations will go very far. As he used to say, the problem of our countries is not economic but moral. The SHGs, VOs, MMSs, ZSs of Andhra have shown that at the grassroots there is both honesty and selflessness. They are the real social capital.

Vijay compared my visit to a festival and how I encourage and inspire them and spur them to go higher and higher. He said I may not be physically with them but my presence is always with them. I could not have asked for a more endearing compliment.

The CRPs said you called us diamonds but to us your words are diamonds.

Minister Reddy hosted a dinner for me in one of the Nizam of Hyderabad's houses called Lake House where I met my old friend former Chief Secretary Madhav Rao, who cut short his stay in Pune to come and see me. I was most touched by his kind gesture. He was SAPAP's great supporter. My old colleague from SAPAP days Subra, who is now principal secretary to the CM, also came and so did Satya Prakash Tucker who brought two fine books for me. I was happy to see Murali who was a member of the first SAPAP team and is now working with Raju.

At the minister's dinner, the Minister for Cooperatives from the State of Punjab and his secretary of the department also came straight from the airport. They had come to see the Andhra SHG model first hand. The secretary came upto me and said, 'we hear you are the founder of this model.' I said, yes, to the extent that I found Raju. It was he who made it happen and later found people like Vijay who took it to its present level. The minister was very keen that I should visit Punjab and extended a warm invitation to come to Chandigarh. Although, Punjab is governed by the Akali Dal but their minister had no hesitation to come and see something being done by the Congress and he was heartily welcomed. This indeed is political maturity.

Andhra has achieved the most magnificent model of elimination of rural poverty that I know of anywhere in the world. The CRP initiative is fully homegrown and a powerful tool to take the programme to scale. The thematic CRPs have added many dimensions to the core function of institution building. The CRPs of Andhra can stand their ground in any situation against any professional. This could not have happened without the full support and the tireless efforts of the SERP professionals who are fully convinced that without CRPs the programme would never have gone to scale. The SERP professionals have made CRP approach their primary function.

I would never tire of saying that since 1996, Raju has nurtured and guided the programme and his cloning Vijay has paid the greatest dividends. Without these two, we would not have the SHG movement that we have in Andhra.

The boost that the Programme got from Chief Minister Reddy with the introduction of interest subsidy and overall support to SERP made it possible to scale up the programme from three million households to over nine million and bank loans to SHGs from 700 crores to 6,500 crores. In Minister Dr Chinna Reddy, SERP has found a most supportive and knowledgeable person who has all the time to address the issues affecting the rural poor. With these two political champions for elimination of rural poverty from Andhra Pradesh, it is no wonder what SERP has achieved. If this support from the State Government continues for SERP, that day is not far away when rural poverty would be history in Andhra Pradesh.

At Delhi, Sampath arranged for me to meet Mr Jairam Ramesh, Union Minister of State for Commerce and an important voice in the Congress Party. I had met him in April 2007 also when I had urged him to look at their homegrown model in Andhra instead of outside India, although the neighbours grass always looks greener. Minister Jairam produced a speech which he had given and quoted me. I could sense he seemed more convinced that Andhra Model indeed has the answer for India's rural poverty. He mentioned about

Rahul Gandhi's impressions of my visit to Amethi but felt a Union Poverty Elimination Fund may not be the way to take the SHG movement to scale. He felt without the support of the state government, this may not be possible. I agreed that with state government support, the process can be accelerated but the process of social mobilisation is more dependent on willingness of the communities to organize, presence of CRPs and a sensitive support organization. If these three elements are present, the movement can be taken to scale if resources are made available either by state government or by the Union government like AKRSP where the Aga Khan Foundation and donors provided the resources. In the case of UP, the Rahul Gandhi Trust has demonstrated the presence of all the three requisites including a CEO in the person of Sampath. We have seen how important this factor is in the case of Andhra.

Minister Jairam conceded that in UP all the 800 Blocks must be covered which according to Sampath can be done in less Rs 1000 crores. The minister asked Sampath to prepare a plan for scaling up SHGs from the current 50 Blocks to 800 Blocks in the next five years. That can then become the basis of how to mobilise the resources.

Index

A

Abbas, Waseem (uncle), 3
Abbottabad, 89, 180, 316-7
Abdullah, Mrs, 135
Abed, 383
Abedi, Agha Hasan, 160, 356-7, 362
Abeygunawardena, Dr, 114, 126, 128, 136, 140, 144, 157
Abhoy Ashram, 351
Abrysthwithe, 110
Achutta, 49, 57
Adarsh Mahila Mandal Somakhya, 406
Addleton, Mr, 230
Adilabad (India), 410
ADP (Annual Development Programme), 274
Afghanistan, 55, 134; border, 97; Counsellor, 54; diplomatic service, 55; Foreign Office, 55; refugees, 6
Africa, 38, 81
African Muslim, 396
Afshan (daughter), 64, 110, 123, 139, 143, 149
Afzal, Dr, 166
Aga Khan Education Services (AKES), 172, 210, 381
Aga Khan Foundation (AKF) Geneva, 68-9, 159, 160, 167, 172, 173-5, 203-4, 210-12, 247, 250, 254, 272, 300, 357, 359, 387; Team of Experts, 212, 213, 217
Aga Khan Foundation (AKF) Pakistan, 176-8, 185, 213, 272
Aga Khan Foundation Canada, 203, 263
Aga Khan Foundation's rural development programme–AKRSP, 68-9, 77, 81, 160, 171, 210, 230, 239, 302, 357-8
Aga Khan Health Services (AKHS), 172, 201, 210, 314-5, 330, 381
Aga Khan Network, 172, 211-12, 269
Aga Khan Rural Support Programme (AKRSP), 167, 172, 173-7, 179, 184-192, 193-202, 203-8, 211-12, 214-15, 217, 222, 226-7, 229-30, 232, 237, 239-42, 243, 245-7, 249-52, 253-62, 263-72, 273, 276, 278-82, 285, 288, 290-2, 293, 297, 299, 301, 303, 305, 308, 311-12, 313-21, 323, 325-6, 328-31, 332, 333-6, 338-42, 344-5, 347-8, 358-60, 362, 370-3, 375, 376, 379-85, 386-7, 400; Strategic Development Committee, 69, 70, 76; Strategy Paper, 211-12; Conceptual Package, 196, 212, 240, 357; as a not-for-profit joint stock Company, 210, 213, 377; Articles and Memorandum of Association, 210, 387; objectives, 213-16, 221, 227, 249, 284, 286, 291, 299, 302, 307; economic programme, 216, 225, 258; methodology, 222, 223-4, 227, 230, 260, 266, 268, 284, 319, 385; Diagnostic Survey, 219, 222, 225-8, 275, 314; Feasibility Survey, 227; Implementation functions, 228, 243, 245, 247-9, 252, 253, 261, 265, 280, 309, 314, 329, 342, 343, 345, 376; payroll, 236-7; management principles, 252; learning environment, 243, 250, 252; working method, 245, 253; a new enterprise culture, 242; Institutional model, 251, 314; Articles of Association, 210, 270-1; loan and credit system, 346; founding fathers, 369; legal structure of, 375
Aga Khan University Hospital (AKUH), 171, 374
Aganwadi (Day Care Centre), 402-3
Agartala, 13
Agha, Tanwir Ali, 397
Agrarian Research and Training Institute, 125
Agricultural Administration, 355

INDEX

Agricultural Credit Programme, 208, 220, 279
Agricultural Development Bank (ADB), 273, 311
Agricultural farming, 67
Agricultural machinery, 301, 303
Agricultural Research and Training Institute (ARTI), 125-6, 141
Agricultural Research Farm (Sri Lanka), 112
Agriculture assistant (Daudzai Markaz Project), 27-8, 30
Agriculture Development Authority (Sri Lanka), 130
Agriculture inputs, 293, 302, 303, 340, 343
Agriculture sector, 208, 221, 281
Agriculture Training Centre (Bulnewa), 100 see also Bulnewa Community Training Centre
Agriculture, Department of, 24, 27, 32, 35; experts, 31; extension programme, 32, 35; plant protection, 35
Agriculture, Ministry of (Sri Lanka), 131
Agriculture, 59, 60, 66, 113, 186, 216-17, 230, 247, 276, 283, 322, 336, 343; Secretary, 392
Agriculturists, 208-9, 227, 257, 279, 281
Agro-chemicals, 220
Agronomist, 38
Ahmad, Khalid M., 189, 318-9
Ahmad, Mir (car driver), 182, 316-7
Ahmad, Mohammad, 41, 68
Ahmad, Rasheed, 11
Ahmad, Shamim, 374
Ahmad, Sir Iqbal, 7
Ahmad, Zafar, 389
Ahmed, Eqbal, 341
Ahmed, Jamil, 16
Ahmedabad, 296
Ahsan, SG Nawid, 394, 397
Aichi, 66
AID, 145
Aiglemont, 69, 174
Ain, Quratul, 328
Aisalaby tea estate, 104-5
Akbar, 123
AKF (UK), 204
AKF (USA), 204
AKF Board, 166, 217

AKF Farm Information Centre, 182
AKF Islamabad office, 176-180, 370
Akhora, 14-5
Akisan, 78, 82
Akram, Zamir, 395, 396-7
AKRSP Agriculture Section, 322
AKRSP Board of Directors, 69, 70, 171-2, 210-12, 247, 369, 387
AKRSP Engineering section, 184-5, 198-9, 206, 242, 247, 249, 279, 283, 293, 299, 303, 309, 311, 318, 322, 342, 343, 348
AKRSP Finance section, 184-5, 206, 247, 283
AKRSP Gilgit head office, 182, 183-4, 247-8, 310, 344, 360; at Babar Road, 184; Visitors Centre, 184; Library, 184
AKRSP Helicopter, 195, 249-50, 296, 299, 318, 360
AKRSP India, 204
AKRSP Management Group (MG), 182, 184-6, 192, 193, 196, 205, 211-12, 226-30, 247, 240-51, 253-4, 270-1, 275, 280, 282, 283, 292, 294-5, 299, 307, 312, 320, 329, 344; structure of, 248; meetings, 248
AKRSP Pakistan, 204
AKRSP Programming Cycle (APC), 225, 227; Programme Activity Status Table, 225-6
AKRSP staff member, 192, 193, 203, 227, 230, 238, 242, 243, 247, 249, 251-2, 253-4, 263, 298, 300, 304, 329, 342, 344, 388; Activist, 196, 200, 205, 260-2, 281, 305-6, 313, 358; field staff, 186, 189, 196, 248-9, 311-12, 358; support staff, 185-6; Pakistani, 254; women staff, 325; precision drivers, 182, 183, 186, 193
AKRSP visitors' centre, 78
AKRSP's Basic Package, 283, 312, 321, 345, 347; checklist, 283-4; agriculture, 284, 311; livestock, 284, 311; marketing, 284; accounts, 284; appropriate technology, 284, 311, 321; poultry, 321-2; vegetable, 321
Alahdad, Air Commodore, 152
Alam, Dr Zahur, 281; Natural Resource Management specialist, 328

INDEX

Alexandra Place, 111
Alfalfa, 297
Ali, Akbar (Manager of VO Chappali), 294
Ali, Amneh Azam, 325
Ali, Ashiq, 201
Ali, Aun, 289
Ali, Dr Farman, 203
Ali, Dr Mastan, 322
Ali, Haji Ghulam, 232
Ali, Haji Mehboob, 232
Ali, Hazrat (RA), 321
Ali, Ihsan, 236
Ali, Iqbal Noor, 204
Ali, Mir Ghazanfar, 318-9
Ali, Mirza, 289
Ali, Mohammad (Manager), 236
Ali, Nadir, 294
Ali, Qurban, 267
Ali, Safdar, 203
Ali, Shahnaz Wazir, 374-5
Ali, Sher (car driver), 182
Ali, Shoukat (Mirpur), 57
Ali, Taffuzal, 13
Aliabad, 183, 286, 302, 307, 348
Alimullah, Qazi, 362, 374
Allahabad High Court, 7
Allahdad, Air Commodore, 395
Allaidiwa, Pat, 120
Allauddin (Chacha), 123
Allauddin Bhai, 179
Allauddin, Mr, 114, 123
Altaf, Dr Zafar, 179, 375
Alwis, Sam, 87, 116-7, 130; as DRPM Agriculture, 95, 130; as Director of Training, 130
Amanullah, King, 23n.1
American Presbyterian Mission High School, 6
American, 57, 75, 77-8, 98, 106, 113, 124, 163-4, 358; society, 82
Amika, Queen, 136
Amil (grandson), 149
Aminabad khul, 293
Anand project, 261
Anantpur, 384, 400, 406-7, 410; Collector of, 406, 409; CRPs, 410
Andhra Pradesh (AP), 379, 384, 386, 400-4, 409-12
Andhra Pradesh Case Study, 396

Animal husbandry, 186, 326-7, 335, 337
Animal husbandry, Department of, 27, 35
Animateur system, 39
Animators, 406-7
Anis, 75-6
Annapolis Workshop, 383
Annual General Meeting (AGM), 210
Anthony, 92
Anuradhapura Rest House, 115
Anuradhapura, 86, 92, 97, 115, 125, 135
Anwar, Latif, 289-90
AP Mutual Cooperative Societies Act, 410
Appropriate Rural Technology Institute (ARTI), 135
Appropriate technology package, 321-2; nut cracking machines, 321, 327-8; butter churners, 321; apricot drying, 321
Apricot, 193, 200, 276, 315, 327
APWA (All Pakistan Women's Association), 100
Arandu area, 305, 315
Arayama, Prof, 75
Ariana Afghan Airlines, 164
Arizona University, 3
Army Puma, 183
Arnoldi, Patrick, 322, 323
Arundale, Hugh, 117, 119
Ashden Award, 199
Ashraf, 143
Ashraf, Mr (of Pakistan Planning Commission), 42
Asia, 75, 156
Asian Development Bank (ADB), 41, 363-4
Asian Institute of Technology (AIT), 125, 135
Askuli valley, 315
Astor subdivision, 190
Astore Programme (AKRSP), 204
Athula, 137
Atoll Development Programme, 386
Atoll Development, Ministry of, 384
Atoll, 133, 385
Attapattu, Dr, 146
Aukana, 92
Aurangzeb, Emperor, 191
Australia, 77, 80, 107, 155
Australian, 54, 67, 127

INDEX

Authoritarianism, 263
Awami League, 13
Ayaz, Aazar, 382
Ayub, Omar, 394
Ayubi, Salahuddin, 290
Azad (cousin), 182
Azad Jammu and Kashmir (AJK), 372, 376, 390
Azad Kashmir, 57, 207
Azam, Zaki, 41
Azamgarh, 8
Azfar, M., 17, 178
Azhar, K.M., 21
Aziz, Chaudhry Anwar, 238, 369-70
Aziz, Khalid, 372
Aziz, Sartaj, 187, 208-9, 265, 369-70, 371-3, 379
Aziz, Subedar, 198
Aziz, Tariq, 364

B

Babic, Drajon, 146
Babusar Pass, 161
Backward Classes, 405
Badran, Dr (Mrs) Hoda, 148-9, 151-2, 154-5, 159, 160, 167
Baghicha, 320
Bagrote valley, 199
Baig, G.M., 186-7
Baig, Wazir, 307
Baig's Bookshop, 186
Bajwa, Asif, 399
Bajwa, Rashid, 203, 376, 395, 396; as CEO NRSP, 376
Baker, Stan, 124, 158, 160n.2
Balas, 299
Balika Sanghas (Youth Groups), 408
Balochistan Rural Support Programme (BRSP), 242, 382, 400
Balochistan, 26, 207, 347
Balti (language), 194
Baltistan, 172, 190, 194-5, 202, 204, 214, 234-5, 248-9, 258, 260, 266, 305, 320-2, 323, 325-6, 331, 347
Banda, 146
Bandara, Siva, 128
Banderwela, 104-5
Bandranaike Memorial International Conference Hall, 122

Bangash, Afzal, 19
Bangkok, 47, 52, 56, 125, 135, 141-2; airport, 56
Bangladesh, 30, 36, 38, 56, 58, 60, 119, 120, 143, 244, 264, 374, 384-5
Banking (VOs), 200, 210, 269, 278-9, 309, 311, 339 *see also* Savings programme; Credit programmes; Loans
Baotenire, 107
Baqi, 195
Baqir, Fayyaz, 199, 362
Bar Das, 288
Bar valley, 188, 201, 286, 289
Barghin, 299
Bari, Abdul, 13
Barkulti, 172
Barrington, Sir Nicholas, 204; as British High Commissioner in Pakistan, 204
Barter system, 280
Barth, Frederick, 119
Base-Line Survey, 228-9
Basic Democracies, 15-6, 23n.2, 25
Basic Democrats, 16
Basic health units (BHUs), 381
Basnyat, Manoj, 385
Battagram, 162, 180, 317
Bayer, Martin, 134
BCCI (Bank of Credit and Commerce International), 159, 160, 357
Beadley, (MP) Mrs, 117
Beef-cattle, 67
Beg, Col., 272
Beg, General Aslam, 189
Beg, Ghazi, 295
Beg, Sultan Ahmad, 6
Begaar (free, involuntary labour), 191
Beirut, 154
Beldars (ploughmen), 32
Bengal, 12, 101, 262
Bengali, 262, 351
Bentuta Beach Hotel, 115
Berkeley University, 204
Berne, 150
Besham, 181
Bhalla, 58
Bhavita programme, 405
Bhutto (Zulfiqar Ali), 97, 154; execution of, 104
Bhutto, Mumtaz, 22
Big Dam Project, 378

INDEX

Bio-chemistry, 45
Biron, Paul, 134
Bisham, 316
Block Development Officers (India), 38
Block/Mandal, 35, 38, 385, 404, 405, 408-9; government departments, 406
Bodalus, 286, 289
Bokhari, 195
Bonsai (miniature trees), 61
Book Keepers, 406-7, 409-10
Bostak, 105
Boswell, 350
Botanical Gardens, 107
BRAC, 383
Brahaman Baria Thana Development Centre, 352
Brahmanbaria, 13-5, 101, 351-2
Brazil, 80
Brazilian village, 83
Bridge on the River Kwai, The, 88
Bridle, Clare, 139
Bridle, Richard, 134, 139
Brigegard, Professor, 240
British army, 351
British Civil Service, 64
British government, 124-5, 173; colonial administration, 25, 36; law-and-order based, 25, 35; revenue collection based, 25, 35
British, 23n.1, 25, 35, 45, 63, 71, 86, 89, 106, 109, 119, 284, 350, 360; motorway, 57; administrator, 304
Broghil, 173
Broiker, Ms, 127
Broilers, 67
Broshal, 173
Broshky Chaprot, 288
Broyd, Richard, 110
Brushaski (language), 194
Buddha, 57, 86, 92, 96-7, 107, 112, 351, 358; Reswelira, 97; Aukana, 97, 146
Buddhism, 57
Buddhist temples, 97; monastery, 358
Buddhists, 55, 62, 86, 89, 90, 94, 101, 350
Buffalo, 403
Bulandshahr, 6
Bulnewa Community Training Centre, 117, 123, 137, 146
Bulnewa, 100, 117, 124

Buni valley, 199, 294-6, 304
Burewala, 15
Burgess, Mr, 11, 22
Burma, 120
Burmese, 74
Burra, Neera, 385
Butalia, Colonel, 13

C

Cabinet Division (Pakistan), 164, 166, 375, 392
Cairo, 149
Calgary, 203
Cambridge, 10, 12, 86, 88, 96, 107, 113, 119
Canada, 203, 207, 262, 358, 395
Canadian Development Counsellor, 199
Canadian International Development Agency (CIDA), 157, 203-4, 206, 239, 263, 345
Canadian, 97, 106, 124, 138, 157, 206
Capitalist model, 245
Carlson, Mrs Margaret Catley, 155-6, 167, 203-4
Carpet weaving, 326
Central Asia, 162
Central Board of Revenue (CBR), 177-8
Central Cooperative Bank, 346
Central Development Working Party (CDWP), 380, 390-1, 398
Ceramics, 66, 68
Ceylon Administrative Service, 86, 98
Ceylon Tobacco Company, 139
Chakarum (2.6 acres) land, 304
Chalat drainage, 288
Chalt Bala, 286, 289
Chalt Paeen, 286, 288-9
Chalt, 187-8, 286, 288-90
Chanderliya GVM, 343
Chandigarh, 261
Chandrakirti, Dr, 114
Chaprot Utaimaling khul, 289 *see also Khuls*
Chaprot, 286, 288-9, 311
Chapursan valley, 194, 311
Charles, Prince, 392
Charsadda, 165
Chatta, Mr, 315
Chattorkhand, 188

Chaudhry, Azam, 374-5, 378
Chicago, 71, 75, 179
Chief Economist, 389-90
Chilas, 161
Child labour, 405, 408
China, 55, 63, 103, 130, 187, 332, 35
Chinar Inn, 75, 167, 181-2, 198, 360, 371
Chinese 'Bare-Foot Doctors' programme, 32
Chinese Commune, 359
Chinese cuisine, 44; restaurant, 48, 50, 52
Chinese Nobel Laureate, 82
Chinese, 30, 54, 64, 161, 191, 193-4, 263
Chipko [forest protection] movement, 261
Chitral Programme (AKRSP), 204
Chitral Scouts Mess, 173, 193
Chitral, 171, 173-4, 180, 190, 193-4, 199, 201, 203, 212, 214, 234, 240, 248-9, 267, 276, 294, 305, 313, 323, 326, 347, 369
Chittagong, 14-5
Choe, Professor, 58
Chowk Yadgar, 19
Chung, 49, 57, 294
Churchill College, 86
Chutran, 315
CIA, 163-4, 272
Civil Service Academy, 11, 17, 54, 98, 154, 166, 179, 193, 371, 375
Civil Service of Pakistan (CSP), 10-1, 56, 161, 165, 371; probationer, 123; rules and procedures, 254
Civil service of Sri Lanka, 86
Cliff, 98, 103
Coimbatore, 131
Collective management, 209-10, 215-16, 222, 236, 238, 274, 278-9, 283, 305, 307, 314, 318, 332, 342, 343; indicators of, 306
Colombo, 15, 84-5, 87, 92, 94, 97-8, 100-2, 104, 107-9, 110-2, 115, 118-9, 120-5, 128-9, 130-1, 135-6, 140-3, 145-8, 152, 154-5, 158, 167, 181
Colonel Brown's School, 6
Comilla Academy of Rural Development, 244, 351

Comilla Combined Military Hospital, 14-5
Comilla Project, 23, 30, 39, 120, 142, 153, 264, 314, 346, 352, 357, 359, 362
Comilla Thana Training and Development Centre (TTDC), 35-6, 264
Comilla, 143, 209, 351-2
Commercial banks, 40
Communications, 28
Communists, 46, 358
Community Health Worker, 330
Community Investment Fund (CIF), 405
Community participation (CP), 135, 334-5, 372; Training, 336; Survey, 336; Planning, 336; Organization, 337
Community Resource Persons (CRPs), 405, 408-10
Companies Ordinance 1984, 210, 372, 375, 379, 387
Consumer cooperatives, 333
Consumer goods, 27
Continents in Collision, 186
Coomaraswamy, Priya, 136
Cooperative management, 337
Co-operative Unit (Daudzai Markaz), 28; organizers, 28-9, 33, 35; project managers, 33-5
Cooperatives, 35, 39, 40, 60, 238, 260, 266, 332, 340, 410
Cooperatives, Department of, 24, 27, 35, 60
Cornelius, Justice, 182
Corporate Law Authority, 374
Cottage industries, 326
Cotton Projects, 240
Credit programme, 40, 209, 216, 223, 236, 245, 247, 261, 273, 278-9, 283, 309, 333, 336, 339, 346, 363
Credit union model, 221 *see also* Raiffeisen model
Criminal Procedure Code, 13
Cromer, Russ, 111
Cropping intensity, 59, 60, 322
Crops, 59, 80, 202, 219, 236, 247, 281, 288, 322, 328; rice, 59, 67, 80, 85, 95; vegetables, 59; mushrooms, 59, 65; strawberry, 59; lettuce, 59; potatoes, 59, 317, 330-1; sweet potatoes, 81; maize, 209; millet, 209; buckwheat,

209; wheat, 238, 322; barley, 322; onions, 330-1; tomatoes, 330; cotton, 409; chillies, 409
Croydon, 95
CSP officer, 12, 20-1
Cuba, 383
Cultivation Committee, 99
Curzon, Lord, 187

D

Dacca (Dhaka), 14, 37, 56, 383
Dad Das Bar, 288
Dad, Ali, 182, 184, 186
Dairy products, 328; cheese, 328
Dairying, 335
Damayanthi, Ms, 409-11
Dambulla, 92, 96
Dani, Anis, 329, 384
Dante, 359
Dantonaryan, Mr, 100; Assistant General Manager of Mahaweli Development Board, 100
Danyore, 162, 188
Darel, 191
Darjat, 203, 322
Darkut, 187
Dassu (Comilla), 181
Daudzai area, 18, 28-9, 30, 32-3, 163-5, 353
Daudzai Markaz Pilot Project, 23-4, 32, 34-5, 37, 58, 120, 129, 132, 136, 142, 154, 159, 161-2, 165-7, 186, 192, 244, 356-7, 361-2, 369, 383; development units, 29
Daudzai police station (*thana*), 26-7
Daudzai, a Case Study, 355
Davos, 397
Dawood, Hussain, 379
Dayaratne, 384
De Silva, Mr, 91, 94-6
De Silva, Rohini, 98, 14
Dehra Doon, 4, 6
Deosai brown bear, 201
Department for International Development (DFID), 204, 386
Deputy Resident Project Manager (Operations and Maintenance), 86
Dera Ismail Khan, 10

Development Administration (DA), 24-6, 35; principles of, 24-5; rural, 33; three infrastructure, 36; administrative infrastructure, 36; political infrastructure, 36; socio-economic infrastructure, 36
Devolution Plan of 2001, 36
Dhammapadda, 358
Dhattusana, King, 92, 105
Diamir, 190-1
Diary of Anne Frank, 146
Diaz, Ralph, 44, 61-2, 66, 68, 166
Dir district, 335
Director of Special Programs (DSP), 250
Disability Project, 409
Dispensary, 26, 32, 223, 234, 267; compounder (para-pharmacist), 32
Dissanayake, Miss, 127
Dissanayake, Mr Dudley (School of Social Work), 130, 138
Dissanayeke, Gamini, 91
District Council, 25, 36, 93, 172, 184, 188, 190, 200, 258, 315; Gilgit, 190, 318; Baltistan, 258; Chitral, 317; Dir, 335
District Poverty Initiatives Project (DPIP), 401
District Programme Officer (DPO), 209, 248, 283, 305, 320-1, 344
Diwakar, Paul, 400
Dodo Das, 289
Dollars, 41
Donaldson, Dr Graham, 199, 205, 230
Dong (pronounced Yong), NguYen Tri, 45-6, 52, 54, 65, 68, 76-7
Dong, Mrs Yen, 77
Doon School, The, 6
Dopas pony track, 289
Douglas, Mike, 65
Drinking water schemes, 259, 267, 284, 287, 293, 301, 328
Drought, 30
DRPM Agriculture Extension (Mahaweli project), 87, 95, 111-2, 126, 130
DRPM Community Development (Mahaweli project), 87, 95, 111-2, 126, 140
DRPM Engineering (Mahaweli project), 87-8, 95, 111, 126
DRPM Water Management units (Mahaweli project), 112-3, 126, 137
Dufferin, 8

480 INDEX

Duncan, Brian, 118
Dunhill, ODM Coordinator Frank, 118, 130, 138, 150
Durrani, Military Secretary Brigadier, 273
Durrani, Professor, 354
Durrani, Shakil, 189
Dushanbe, 203
Dutch, 89, 109, 204, 238; NGO, 370

E

East Anglia University, 65
East Pakistan Rifles, 14
East Pakistan, 11-2, 20-1, 178, 351, 354
East Pakistan, Governor of, 362
East Pakistanis, 12
ECNEC, 369, 390-1
Economic Affairs Division (EAD), 189-190, 195, 199, 204, 390, 392, 396-9
Economics (course), 179
Education programme, 33, 35, 203
Education, 172, 219-20, 258-9, 267, 291, 302, 323, 405; engineering, 408; medical, 408; computer science, 408
Education, Department of, 12, 18, 20, 27, 35, 163, 269-70
Education, 28, 33, 35
Egger, Charles, 156
Egypt, 149, 151
Eiffel tower, 54
Ejaz, Colonel, 195
Elam, 101
Electricity, 85, 182, 267, 281-2
Elephants, 84-5, 92, 98, 104, 112, 131, 360
Ena multipurpose Cooperative Federation, 67
Ena, 67
Engibrigsten, Mr, 127
Engineering College, 354
Engineering Unit (Daudzai Markaz), 28-9
England, 52, 59, 64, 74, 110, 178, 355
England, Robert, 385
English language, 41, 44, 46, 48, 72, 82, 94-5, 105, 107, 128, 160n.1, 249, 403; medium school, 403
English Literature, 8-9
Englishman, 98, 112, 164

Entrepreneurs, 208, 213, 258
Epstein, Professor Scarlet, 122-3
ESCAP (UN Economic and Social Commission for Asia and the Pacific), 47, 56; Agriculture division, 56
Establishment Division, 11, 17, 20, 162-6, 179, 356
Ethiopia, 39
Europe, 43, 117, 221, 244; motorway, 57
Ewing, Dr, 6
Ezaki, Professor, 76
Ezz, 396

F

Faisalabad Agricultural University, 335
Falaknaz (daughter), 176
Family Planning (UN), 108
Family Planning Association of Pakistan, 47, 88
Family Planning Association of Sri Lanka, 88, 90
FAO women's programme, 129
FAO/UNDP (Food & Agricultural Organisation/United Nations Development Programme, 281
FAO/WHO team, 122
Faraj, Sub., 296
Fareed, Shoukat, 154
Farm management course (Japan), 67
Farman, Kulsum, 321, 325-6
Farmers leaders' training session (Sri Lanka), 111, 113-4, 116, 120, 125-8, 133, 138, 150-1, 157
Farmland Development Agency, 67
Farooqi, Nasreen, 154
Farooqi, Tariq, 134, 149, 153-4
Farshori, Humayun, 397
Faruqui, Salman, 370
Fayumi chicks, 321
FCNA Headquarters, 189
Federal Cabinet, 374, 376
Federal Government, 178, 205, 271, 354-5, 372, 387
Federal Investigation Agency (FIA), 163, 356, 374; DG, 165
Federal Public Service Commission, 9, 10
Feerasta, Hakim, 176
FELDA, 240

INDEX

Felicia (Mahzent's secretary), 148
Fernando, Denis, 120
Fertilizers, 28-9, 218-20, 236-7, 253, 293, 300, 301, 303, 305-6
Feudalism, 258
Field Officers Project Regions III and IV, 99, 100
Finance, Ministry of, 379, 392-3, 399; Secretary General, 392
First Harvest (documentary), 206, 240, 275
Fisheries, Ministry of (Maldives), 134
Flood protection bunds, 289, 293-5
Fodder, 200, 209, 219, 326-8
Fonseka, Cecil, 130
Force Commander Northern Areas (FCNA), 188-9
Ford Foundation, 160, 164
Foreign Affairs, Ministry of (Maldives), 134
Foreign exchange component (FEC), 391
Forest Institute of Peshawar, 335
Forest, 209, 238, 332, 337-8
Forestry, 81, 174, 186, 200, 202, 204, 261, 311, 335, 337, 345
Forestry, Department of, 27, 35
France, 118, 186, 396
Francophone Africa, 40
Franklin, Sir Eric, 167
Freidman, 58
French, 118
Friendship Bridge, 162
Fruits preservation, 280, 293, 326; dried fruits, 280, 330
Fruits processing, 83, 280
Fuehlau, Ingunde, 386

G

Gable, Clark, 15
Gakuch, 188, 190, 198
Galbraith, Professor, 71, 75
Galnewa, 85, 87, 89, 91, 94-5, 97, 101, 105-8, 111-2, 114, 119, 122-3, 127-8, 131, 134, 136, 139, 146, 149, 150, 181
Galoya irrigation scheme, 111, 122
Ganawatte, Sena, 115-6
Gandhi, 83
Ganesh, 187-8

Ganges-Kobadak Project, 12
Gardner, Nick, 194
Gauhar, Humayun, 394
GBP(currency), 172
Geen, Ambassador Von, 204
General administration department, 24
General Manager AKRSP, 167, 171, 173, 176, 197, 199, 205, 211-12, 227, 230, 232, 233-5, 238-9, 246-51, 265-6, 270-2, 273-5, 283, 286, 290, 294, 296-302, 304, 312, 313, 323, 326, 328, 344-5
Geneva, 173, 176, 203, 250
George V, King, 4
German, 104, 123, 204, 382
Germany, 273, 285, 291; government, 260
Ghasho Maling Das Channel, 288-9
Ghassami, H., 155; as Chief Advisor on Nutrition at UNICEF, 155
Ghazi Brotha Hydro Power (GBHP) project, 376-8; General Manager of, 378
Ghazi Brotha Taraqiati Idara (GBTI), 377-9; Board of Directors, 377-9; endowment fund, 377-8; affectees, 377-8
Ghazi, Sher, 286-9
Ghizer district, 330
Ghonssey, Sadullah, 54
Ghulkin, 183
Gifu Agricultural College, 67
Gifu Livestock Prefectural Corporation, 67
Gifu, 66
Gilgit river, 284
Gilgit, 15, 68-9, 78, 160, 162, 167, 171, 174-6, 178-9, 181-2, 183, 185, 187, 190, 194-5, 198, 202, 205, 209, 212, 214, 217-20, 226-7, 228-9, 235, 237, 241, 247, 252, 260, 262, 267, 270, 272, 274, 276, 278-9, 285-6, 292, 293, 296, 299, 302, 305, 316, 319-20, 323-4, 325-6, 328, 335, 338, 340, 344, 357, 359, 361, 371, 383, 390; airport, 167, 179, 271, 296
Gilgit-Ghizar road, 183
Gindai, 330
Global Development Network Award, 199

482 INDEX

Global Water Partnership, 204
Globe and Mail, The, 263
Gojali (language), 194
Gonar water channel, 288
GoNGOs, 387
Gotosan, 78, 81, 82-3
Government House, 104
Government Line Departments, 267, 334
Government of Balochistan, 382, 390
Government of Bangladesh, 385
Government of India, 385
Government of Indonesia, 166
Government of Maldives, 139, 385
Government of Nepal, 385
Government of NWFP, 20, 24, 33, 161, 180, 205, 282, 312, 390; Chief Secretary, 355-6
Government of Pakistan (GoP), 11, 17, 37, 111, 167, 174, 178, 264, 266, 269, 299, 359-60, 363-4, 379, 385, 399
Government of Punjab, 362, 380, 390-1; Chief Secretary, 378
Government of Sindh, 161, 362, 381, 390
Government of Sri Lanka, 94, 99, 385; Additional General Manager of, 94; Additional Secretary of, 94
Government of West Pakistan, 17
Graduate School of International Development (GSID), 69, 70-2, 74, 76, 78, 166 staff, 73
Gram panchayat, 402
Gram Sahayaks, 39
Gram Vikas Mandal (GVM), 343-4
Grameen Bank, 264, 412
Grant, James, 357
Griffins, Keith, 58
Griffith, Martin, 98, 103, 147-8
Grindarkotte, 130, 138, 141
GTZ, 204
Gudamunne, Lalit, 144-5, 147-9, 157, 159
Gujal valley, 183, 188
Gujarat, 261
Gulapur, 315
Gulistan (woman pioneer), 326
Gulmit plant, 199
Gulmit, 162, 187, 199
Gunnawardena, DRPM Culson, 151
Gupis, 183, 188, 194, 226

H

Habarana, 134-5
Habarana-Anuradhapura Road, 135
Habib Bank (Male), 134
Habib Bank Limited, 209, 278, 381
Habib, Ghulam (SO), 186
Habibullah, Dr, 267
Habrana, 118
Hafiz, Khawaja, 361
Haider, Amir, 289
Haiku, 55
Halifax, 395
Hamaran, 199
Hambantota integrated project, 127, 152
Hameed, Sultan, 332
Hameed, Tariq, 379
Hamirpur, 6-7
Hamlet, 4
Handungama Circuit Bungalow, 85-8, 91-7, 99, 100-1, 105, 107, 114, 119, 181
Hanneda, 42
Hanuchal, 188, 190, 198, 341
Hanzel channels, 296
Haq, Ziaul, 185, 195
Haramosh, 188, 195
Haroon, Farooq, 381
Harrow College, 64
Hart, Dame Judith, 117
Harvard University, 204
Hasan, Arif, 357, 362, 382
Hasan, Javed, 332, 333
Hasan, Rahim, 295
Hasanabad, 307
Hasanabdal, 180
Hasanapuram, 402
Hasegewa, 68
Hashiguchi, Mr, 78-9, 81, 83
Hashmi, Humaira (pioneer), 326
Hashmi, Rehana (pioneer), 326
Hashtnagar area, 19
Haxton, Davé, 152
Hayat, Engineer, 321, 323
Hayat, Roomi, 376
Hazara, 15
HBFC, 66
Health care, 172, 259, 287, 291, 302, 323
Health Education Bureau (Sri Lanka), 125

Health programme (Daudzai Markaz), 32, 35
Health, Department of, 12, 18, 20, 27, 35, 163
Heart of a Continent, The, 187
Heifer cattle project, 201, 332, 341
Henderson, Julia, 135
Heuckroth, Dr, 258
Heyward (English explorer), 187
Heyward, Elizabeth, 155
Heyward, Mr, 153-6
Higashiyama Park, 73
Higgins, Benjamin, 58
Hillary, Lady, 194
Hillary, Sir Edmund, 194
Himachal Pradesh, 261
Himalayan Wildlife Foundation, 201
Hindi (language), 99
Hindus, 89, 90, 101
Hirano, 68
Hisa Rasidi shares, 270
Hispar, 188
Hog-raising, 67
Holiday Inn, 179
Hollesteiner, Mary, 153
Hong Kong, 47-8, 181
Honjo (Director of the Centre), 52, 62-3, 68
Hopper, Mr, 127
Horticulture, 67, 335
Hosaka, 49, 68
House Building Finance Corporation of Japan, 66
Housey, 143
HRDI, 242, 243
Human capital, 219, 230, 241, 283, 304, 314
Human Resource Development (HRD), 182, 204, 206, 222, 239, 259, 304, 343, 347, 373, 376, 401
Humayun, Mrs Munawar, 371
Hummeler, Mr, 314
Hungarian, 188
Hunter, Mrs Guy, 131
Hunter, Professor Guy, 37, 58-9, 61, 131, 188, 355, 358; his ten propositions, 37-8; Administration, 38; Survey and Diagnosis, 38; Investment, 38; Farmers groupings, 39; Training, 39; Financing and Credit, 40

Huntings Technical Services of UK, 117-9, 123, 130; Block 409, 124, 129
Hunza Council, 189
Hunza Rest House, 162
Hunza river, 187, 197, 287
Hunza, 162, 183, 188, 194, 203, 218, 226, 272, 273, 286, 348
Hunza, Mir of, 272, 348
Hunzai, Izhar Ali, 203
Hurd, Douglas, 204
Hurmai khul, 293 *see also Khuls*
Husain, Dr Ishrat, 166
Husain, Haji Mohammad, 233
Husain, Tariq, 179-188, 185, 206, 271, 280, 328; as Programme Economist, 179, 228
Hussain, Dr Mushtaq, 104, 114
Hussain, Dr Zakir, 351; as the President of India, 351
Hussain, Manzoor, 203
Hussain, Meraj, 47-8
Hussain, Minhaj, 47
Hussain, Mohammad, 236
Hussain, Muzaffar, 269
Hussain, Shafqat, 180
Hussein, Maliha, 185, 325
Hyat, Kamal, 379, 396, 399
Hyde Park, 188
Hyderabad, 400, 409, 411
Hyderabad, Nizam of, 411
Hyderabadi Urdu, 410
Hydro power generations, 195, 378

I

Ibahullah, Alhaj, 267
Ibex, 201
Ibrahim (car driver), 182
Ibrahim, 179
ICIMOD, 329
ICS (Indian Civil Service), 350-1, 361
IDA, 346, 399
Idgah (mosque), 190-1
Idris, Kunwar, 16, 21-2, 178-9
Ignatieff, Catherine, 97, 135, 154
Ignatieff, Paul, 96, 103-5, 115, 117-9, 120, 124, 127, 131-3, 135-7, 139, 141, 143-9, 150-1, 154; as Head of UNICEF in Colombo, 97
Ikram (SO), 186

Imaike hospital, 44
Imam Bargah, 188
IMF, 364
Imtiaz, Sahibzada, 265, 369
Inayatullah, Dr, 362; as UNDP Programme Incharge, 386
Inbal, 78-9, 80-1, 83
Independence, 25, 27
Independent South Asia Commission on Poverty Alleviation (ISACPA), 36, 383
India, 4, 13, 21, 35-6, 38-9, 49, 57-8, 74, 86, 89, 93, 107, 114, 244, 261, 343, 361, 363, 383-5, 386, 401, 412
India, Prime Minister of, 407
Indian Institute of Agricultural Research (IIAR), 205
Indian(s), 13-4, 54, 63, 77, 114, 363; bombers, 21; Counsellor, 54; food restaurant, 65
Indira Kranti Patham (IKP), 404
Indonesia, 166
Indo-Pak War of 1971, 21
Indus river, 162
Insead, 175
Inspection Commission, 374
Institute of Management, 144
Institutional Development at the Grassroots for Poverty Alleviation, 384
Integrated Rural Development (IRD), 26, 27, 34-5, 334, 355
Integrated Rural Development Programme (IRDP), 24, 26, 161, 165, 186, 335, 339, 350; Pilot projects, 24; project area, 26
Integration of Community Participation Approaches in Country Programmes (seminar), 151, 154
Intelligence Bureau, 272
Inter Services Selection Board (ISSB), 395
Interior, Ministry of, 22, 390
International Fund for Agriculture Development (IFAD), 260, 266-7, 313
International Planned Parenthood Federation (IPPF), 47, 135
Inter-Provincial Conference, 373
Inter-services Intelligence Agency (ISI), 18, 272

Iodized salt programme, 328
IRDP area (Daudzai Markaz), 27
Irrigala, Gamini, 126
Irrigation channel, 29, 174, 202, 209, 232, 235, 238, 250, 267-71, 274, 279, 282, 284-5, 295, 306-8, 310 *see also Khuls*
Irrigation projects/schemes, 195, 239, 270, 285, 290, 293
Irrigation system, 27, 30, 220, 232, 236, 284, 347, 363
Irrigation, Department of, 24, 27, 317
Isa, Azmat, 379
Ishkoman Rest House, 194
Ishkoman, 188, 194, 218, 226
Islam, 238, 350
Islam, DC Badrul, 288
Islamabad Airport, 70
Islamabad, 22, 43, 53, 69, 72, 78, 95, 106, 160, 164, 167-9, 175-7, 185, 267, 301, 307, 316-7, 362, 364, 373-5, 390, 396
Islamic economics, 75
Ismaili area, 172, 173, 275, 305
Ismaili *Jamaat*, 188
Ismaili Regional Councils, 227
Ismaili(s), 188, 190, 197, 247, 275, 278, 286, 291, 328
Israel, 79, 361
Israeli *kibbutz*, 61, 79, 80-1, 83-4
Israr, Malik, 382
Issues Paper (Professor Brigegard), 240
Italian, 110
Italy, 61, 130
IUCN, 204

J

Jacquemin, Dr Alain, 386
Jaffer Brothers Limited, 237
Jaffna, 101
Jaffrey, Dr Shahida, 184, 325, 382
Jaffrey, V.A., 304, 312, 346-7
Jaffrey, Tariq, 68
Jaglote, 162
Jahangir, Arbab, 369-70
Jahanzeb College, 10, 111
Jalalabad, 311
Jala—wire rope pulley, 293
Jaleel, Mr, 410
Jalil (car driver), 182
Jamaat Khana, 188, 301

INDEX

Jamaats, 204
Jamat Councils, 291
Jamia Miilia, 351
Jan, Bahadur, 294
Jan, Dil, 164
Jan, Haji, 290
Jan, Karim, 206
Janan, Mr, 307
Janasaviya political programme, 384
Janata Corporation (Sri Lanka), 115
Japan Airlines, 47
Japan, 23, 41-9, 50-2, 55, 57, 59, 60, 62-3, 66-7, 68-9, 70-2, 74-8, 80, 82, 88, 94, 115, 157, 166, 179, 273, 285, 291, 356, 361
Japanese tea-ceremony, 49, 50
Japanese, 41-5, 50, 58, 65-6, 68, 72, 82, 262; farmers, 59, 95; agriculture, 67; architecture and history, 55; bath, 82; cake, 49; cuisine, 44, 72; culture, 55; expressway, 57; agricultural income, 59; language, 42, 45, 55, 72, 78; male/men, 54, 66, 68; maples (tree), 58; poetry, 55; police, 46; steel, 54; traffic, 46; women/girls, 42-4, 52, 54, 65-6, 68, 71-2, 77, 82
Japanising, 55
Japuka, 191-2, 301-2
Javad, Agha, 376
Jayantha, Christine, 181
Jayawardene, Mr, 125
Jayawardne, Mr (of MDA), 147-8
Jayawickrama, Mr, 87, 96
Jayweardena, Jayantha, 129, 131, 139, 147, 150-2, 155, 157, 181
Jayweardena, Torry, 159
Jeevna Jyoti (Life Saving) programme, 405
Jerry, 123
Jilani, General, 18
Jilani, Salim Abbas, 16
Jinnah, Fatima, 16
John Hopkins University, 204
Johnson, Dr, 350
Joint Commisssion for Relief and Reconstruction (JCRR), 357
Jolly, Dr Richard (UNICEF's Deputy Executive Director), 156
Jones, Brian, 119
Jones, Steve, 204, 386

Jubilee Manzil, 411
Judaism, 81
Juglote, 188
Jumna river, 7
Jurko, 68
Jutal, 199

K

K2 (mountain), 188, 315
Kabul, 134, 164, 203
Kachura bridge, 315
Kadmiel, Mr, 406
Kaghan, 161
Kahut, Afzal, 189
Kakutiya dynasty, 409
Kalabagh, Nawab of, 16-7
Kalawewa Circuit Bungalow, 108, 111, 113, 117, 121, 130-1, 135, 137, 147
Kalawewa Rest House, 98
Kalawewa tank, 89, 92, 98, 105
Kalawewa, 84, 121-2, 125, 127, 131, 132, 134, 140, 145-7, 150-1, 160n.2
Kallankuttiya, 138
Kalva, 402
Kamal, Samina, 385
Kamarasky, Mr, 54
Kamura, Mr, 57
Kanals, 217-19, 232, 238, 268, 288-90, 297-8, 306, 342, 348
Kandalama Scheme, 96
Kando, 68
Kandy, 88, 97, 107-8, 112-4, 116, 122, 131
Kannah Jee, 288
Kanno, 66
Karachi Water and Sewerage Board (KWSB), 363; Foreign Aid Section, 363
Karachi, 12, 15, 21-3, 63, 76, 95, 131, 142, 148, 152, 154, 159, 160-1, 167, 171, 174, 176, 180, 184-5, 212, 221, 237, 307, 335, 355-7, 359, 361-2, 363, 374, 382, 390; sewerage system of, 363
Karachi-ites, 174
Karakoram Highway (KKH), 161, 167, 180-2, 183-4, 191, 193-4, 197, 230, 250, 293, 316-7, 348, 358
Karcher, Dr Henning, 383-5, 386
Kardar, A.H., 179

Karim, Asia, 321
Karim, General Bachhu, 21
Karim, Yasmin, 325
Karimabad, 183, 272
Karunaratne, RPM, 129
Karunatillake, Mr, 86, 125, 129, 132, 150
Karvi, 6
Kashinal, 315
Kashmir Affairs and Northern Affairs, Ministry of, 267, 271, 273, 390
Kashmir, Maharaja of, 187
Kassyapa, King, 105
Kasturichchi, Asoka, 385
Kathmandu, 380, 37
Kato, 74
Katusan, 63
Kawahara, Dr, 45
Kawashima, Mr, 41-3, 68
Kazi, Abida Ashraf, 54-5
Kazi, Ashraf, 42, 54-6, 61, 63-4, 179
Kazmi, Safdar, 383
Kazuhiko, Terao, 65
KDD (international telephone and telegraph office), 46, 48
Keats, 69
Kekirawa, 101
Kelly, Roy, 45, 68
Kensan, 79, 80-3
Kentucky Fried Chicken, 44, 46, 52
Kenya, 38
Kernim, George, 116-7
Kew gardens, 107
KGB, 163
Khaddar (homespun cloth), 360
Khaiber Hydel project, 239
Khalid, 179
Khalid, Mairaj, 375
Khalsa Army, 351
Khalti lake, 296
Khan, His Highness (The) Aga, 69, 171-2, 173-5, 186, 195, 197-8, 203, 210-11, 265, 272, 273, 275, 291-2, 302, 304, 307, 319-20, 357, 359
Khan, Abdul Ali, 20
Khan, Abdul Qayum, 181
Khan, Ahsan, 377
Khan, Akbar, 358
Khan, Akhtar Hameed, 23, 36, 41, 75, 102, 136, 142, 153-5, 157, 159, 160-1, 163-7, 186, 191-2, 197-8, 207, 211, 232, 236-7, 244, 260-2, 284, 313, 332, 333, 335, 339-40, 345-6, 350-2, 350, 355-7, 359-62, 363-6, 373, 376, 386, 411; Sufi streak, 350; as a blacksmith, 351; a Buddhist Muslim, 358; develop his skill under Gandhian and American master, 360; received the Magsaysay Award, 361; blasphemy case against, 361-2; awarded *Nishan-i-Imtiaz*, 364
Khan, Amanullah, 295
Khan, Ayub, 16, 23n.2, 362, 363
Khan, Azam (Chairman SRSC), 370-1, 385
Khan, Barkat Ali, 237, 333
Khan, Baz Muhammad, 134
Khan, Commissioner Shamsher Ali, 193
Khan, Dr Dilawar Ali, 57
Khan, Dr Fatima Ali (FAK), 400
Khan, Dr Humayun, 16, 20, 392
Khan, Farasat, 294
Khan, Gari (agriculturist), 322
Khan, Her Highness Begum Aga, 186-7
Khan, Jamilur Rehman (Pedro), 179
Khan, Khan Abdul Qayyum, 19
Khan, Khan Abdul Wali, 19
Khan, M. Azam (Additional Chief Secretary), 265-6, 304
Khan, M.R., 119
Khan, Mahmood, 189
Khan, Major General Safdar Ali, 189
Khan, Masroor Hasan, 16, 171
Khan, Minhajuddin, 335
Khan, Model Farmer Sher, 294
Khan, Mohammad (chaprot), 289
Khan, Monim, 362
Khan, Musarrat (wife), 9, 10-2, 14-7, 20-1, 61, 64, 69, 70, 78, 130-1, 146, 149, 165, 171, 174-7, 185-7, 327, 354
Khan, Naib (car driver), 182, 317
Khan, Nawab Saeed, 123
Khan, Nighat Rasheed, 56
Khan, Nusrat Fateh Ali, 77
Khan, Omar Asghar, 377
Khan, Prince Amyn Aga, 175
Khan, Prof. Mahmood Hasan, 207
Khan, Raja Bahadur, 199, 318
Khan, Rasheed, 41, 56
Khan, Reyaz Ahmed, 10; livestock specialist, 322
Khan, Riaz Ahmad, 377

Khan, Roedad, 164, 166
Khan, Safdar, 289
Khan, Sahib, 233
Khan, Salim, 181
Khan, Sarwar, 289
Khan, Shamsher Ali (Principal Secretary), 375, 376
Khan, Shandana, 203, 325, 382, 396-7
Khan, Shehryar, 383
Khan, Shoaib Sultan, 94, 109, 111, 117, 124, 128, 144, 153, 156, 165, 237, 241-2, 244-5, 261, 264, 267-8, 284-7, 290, 295, 299-300, 307-8, 315, 318-20, 323, 333, 339, 341, 347, 350, 350, 356, 361, 371, 374, 392; appointed as UNICEF Social Development Consultant, 84; as Senior Project Officer (Social Development), 152, 166; nominated to Office Management group, 152; as Officer-on-special duty (OSD), 163-4, 356; as General Manager AKRSP, 167, 171, 173, 176, 197, 199, 205, 211-12, 227, 230, 232, 236-8, 244, 292, 293, 300, 360, 376; chairman of Working Group on Rural Development and Devolution, 389
Khan, Zafarullah, 52, 376
Khan, Zarmast, 294
Khaplu, 194
Kharif (summer crop), 30
Kharmang sub-division, 320
Khattak, Ajmal, 19
Kheri, 6
Khero, Ghulam Sarwar, 382
Khilji, Dr Iftikhar Ali, 355
Khokhar, Reyaz, 371
Khomeini, Imam, 173, 188, 197
Khuls (irrigation channel), 198-9, 289, 293, 299, 308, 311, 347-8
Khunjerab Pass, 194
Khushhal Pakistan Fund (KPF), 393-4
Khustia, 12
Khwar (language), 194
Khyber agency, 16
Kimonos, 49, 52, 71
King Leopold Development Prize, 205
Kings College, 112-3
Kishoregunk Thana, 384
Kitachai, 143
Kitamura, 58, 68

Kitchener, Lord, 187
Koda, Professor Takao, 74
Kohat, 12, 15-6, 18, 92, 163, 373, 385, 395; circuit bungalow, 16
Kohistan Development Authority, 185
Kohistan, 181, 190
Koirala, Mr, 154
Konrad Adenauer Foundation's Halbach, 204
Korea, 49, 57, 244
Korean, 263
Kotmale settlers, 120-2
Kotmale, 120
Kotwali Thana Central Co-operative Association (KTCCA), 60; dairy farming, 60; cold storage, 60; processing industries, 60
Kruegar, Mr, 149
Kulu valley, 261
Kumar, Vijay, 411
Kuntalpur GVM, 343
Kuomingtang, 358
Kurkundas pipeline, 288
Kurnool, 384, 400, 405
Kutcha (mud-brick), 218
Kyoto University, 45
Kyoto, 48, 57-8

L

Lachi area, 385, 386
Ladduwehetty, Mr, 127
Ladhani, Nazeer, 203, 263-4, 313
Lahore, 11, 98, 162, 182, 352, 355, 371, 390-1, 394, 396-8
Lakha, Shamsh, 374
Lakhimpur Kheri, 7
Land Acquisition Collector, 378
Land and Lands Development (Sri Lanka), Ministry of, 91, 94
Land and Lands Settlement (Sri Lanka), Ministry of, 91, 122
Land development, 28-9, 30-1, 35, 38, 200, 217-20, 233, 236, 257-8, 269, 271, 274, 279, 297-8, 306-7, 312, 314, 317, 332, 339, 346
Land protection works, 29
Landlord-tenant committees, 19
Landlord-tenant dispute, 19, 165
Landowners, 27, 59, 162, 223, 245, 271

488 INDEX

Larkana, 370
Latif, Mr, 190; as Hanuchal District Council Chairman, 198
Latif, Shahid, 58
Latin America, 134
Laxmipur, 13-5
LB&RD, 233, 287
Le Breton, Tim (son-in-law), 175
Lee, Park, 143
Leghari, Farooq, 198
Leghari, Farooq, 375
Lilongwe Land Development Programme, 40n.4
Lilongwe Project (Malawi), 40n.4
Ling, Jack, 153; as Chief of Information Section UNICEF, 153
Ling, Mr, 146
Ling, Mrs, 146
Lingua franca, 254
Link road, 267, 279, 288-9, 293, 301, 303-5, 308, 311, 318-20, 327; Rahbat, 289
Literacy rate, 86, 264, 328
Livestock, 67, 201-2, 209, 216, 219, 230, 236, 239, 247, 257, 276, 283, 322, 327, 329, 344, 392; census, 218; cows, 218; bullocks, 218; sheep, 218; goats, 218; poultry birds, 218, 257, 322, 330, 344
Livestock/veterinary specialist, 280, 297, 306, 311, 317, 322, 330
Loans, 40, 193, 216, 219, 261, 273, 280, 297-300, 303, 305-6, 311-12, 333, 343, 345-6, 359, 363, 379, 407-8
Local Administration Training Institute (LATI), 142
Local Governance Programme (Nepal), 283
Local Government and Rural Development (LG&RD), Ministry of, 166, 267, 373, 376, 391
Local Government and Rural Development Department (Pakistan), 162, 200, 317, 355
Local government, 35, 162, 200, 370, 372
Local Support Organisations (LSOs), 201
Lodhran, 364, 381
London Economist, 333

London, 17, 41, 46, 48, 53, 61, 63-4, 78, 92, 110, 123, 148-9, 155, 160, 164, 172, 176, 180, 363, 396
London, High Commission at, 392
Long, Carrol, 384
Long, Congressman Clarence, 116
Long-term evaluation, 228
Loquian, Dr, 139
Los Angeles, 204
Lowari Pass, 180
Lucknow University, 8-9
Lumbardar, 305
LUMS, 394
Lwin, Dr Maung Maung, 74
Lyallpur, 17
Lyvers, Ken, 106

M

Magsaysay: Award Foundation, 3, 361; award, 3, 242, 361, 371
Maha Illuppallama Circuit Bungalow, 112
Maha Mahila Mandal Samakhya (MMMS), 407-9
Maha paddy crop, 87, 89, 93, 96
Maha, 54, 56
Mahailluppallama, 158
Mahama, 307
Mahaweli community development officers, 125, 131
Mahaweli Development (Sri Lanka), Ministry of, 91, 92, 120, 129, 131
Mahaweli Development Authority (MDA), 84, 90, 117, 127-8, 131, 137, 143-4, 147, 151, 156
Mahaweli Development Board (MDB), 86, 91, 103, 106, 108, 116-7, 121, 127-8, 131-2, 144; Agricultural Engineering Unit, 118; Settlement Division, 122
Mahaweli Ganga Development Project, 84-5, 89, 90, 98, 103, 109, 112, 114, 120, 126-8, 139, 143, 145, 147, 149, 151-3, 155, 166, 206, 245, 300, 361, 384; Area 'H' Project, 103, 108, 111, 113, 117-9, 120-2, 125-9, 130-1, 132; H1 area, 129, 151, 157; H2 area, 129, 151, 157; H4 area, 120-2, 130, 132-3, 140, 150-1, 157; H5 area, 128-9, 130, 132, 140, 145, 150, 157; H7 area, 129,

151, 157; H9 area, 129, 131, 139, 151, 157; System 'C', 130-2, 138, 140-2, 145, 147-8, 150; System 'H', 135, 145, 151, 155-6, 158, 181; Block 404, 124, 129
Mahaweli Ganga river, 89
Mahaweli women's programme, 124
Mahaweli, 85-7, 89, 91-2, 97, 103, 108-9, 110, 116, 120, 123, 130, 134, 142, 149, 160, 181-2, 360
Mahazent, 139, 143
Mahboobnagar, 384, 400
Mahila Bank, 405
Mahila Mandal Samakhya (MMSs), 403-4, 405-10, 412; meetings, 406; staff, 406
Mahiyangana, 147
Mahmood, Shafqat, 376
Mahmood, Syed Khalid, 374
Mahmood, Zakir, 381
Maidak District, 410
Majid, Javed, 370
Malakand Division, 260
Malang, Abdullah, 198
Malaria, 405
Malaysia, 240
Maldives islands, 97, 133, 139, 147-8, 152, 155, 181, 384-5, 386
Male (island city), 133-5, 139, 181
Malik, Dr Shaukat, 177
Malik, Nabeel Anjum, 237, 276, 320
Malik, Sohail, 240
Malik, Zahoor A., 270
Mamosh Deding Flood Protection Bunds, 289
Mamosh Deding, 286, 288-9
Man Named Khan, A, 84, 152
Management specialist, 280
Manchester Guardian, 163-4
Manchu (daughter; alias of Falaknaz), 64, 72, 95, 104, 107, 109, 110, 114-5, 118, 123, 149, 178
Mandala GVM, 343
Mandi towns, 36
Mangla lake, 89
Mango village, 238, 306
Manila, 41, 56, 61, 68, 130, 143
Maratha, 7
Mardan, 16
Margalla Road, 177

Markaz Council, 34-5
Markaz engineers, 29, 31, 35
Markaz functionaries, 28-9, 30, 34, 350; survey research, 27-8, 35
Markaz level, 26-9, 30-5, 60, 339; as training centre, 35; as development centre, 35; its development, 350 *see also* IRDP area
Marker, Aban, 204
Marketing specialist, 280
Marketing, 27, 60, 202, 216, 219-20, 223, 230, 236, 245, 276, 278-9, 283, 306, 309, 311, 318, 326, 333, 336, 339, 344-5
Marshall, Alex, 103, 139; as UNFPA Coordinator, 103
Martial Law Administrator (MLA) Zone E, 271-2
Martin, John, 203, 263
Martinez, Elena, 383
Masako, 68
Mashriqi, Allama, 351
MASL, 159
Masood, Iqbal, 299
Master Farmers (Daudzai Markaz), 39
Mastuj channel, 296, 317
Mastung, 382
Matale district town, 90
Mathur, Mrs, 63
Mathur, O.M., 63
Matsuura, 70
Matsuzaka beef country, 59, 60; beer, 60
Matsuzaka railway station, 61
Matthew, Mr (Deputy Minister), 120
McDonalds, 44
McGarry, Roy, 263-4
McKay, Dr Colin, 128
Mechanization, 280-1
Medagama, 151, 158
Medical attendance, 27-8
Meiko's division, 379; Sector Managers, 379
Members of Provincial Assembly (MPAs), 21, 265
Members of the National Assembly (MNAs), 21, 347, 389
Memon, Nazar, 382
Merchant, Ramzan, 171, 173, 176; Chairman of the AKF Board, 211
Mianchar, 269

Michigan State University, 161, 166, 354, 356
Micro credit programme, 379, 381
Micro hydel units, 199, 282, 292, 313
Micro Investment Plans (MIPs), 410
Microfinance Conference, 395
Microfinance, 211, 395
Mid Term Development Framework (MTDF), 389-90, 398
Middle East, 153
Mid-Term Development Framework (2005-2010), 37
Midwives, 339
Milk, 67, 403
Minallah, Nasrum, 17, 165
Minapin, 269-70
Mintaka Pass, 194
Mintaka valley, 187
Mir (ruler), 257, 337 *see also* Swat, Wali of; Hunza, Mir of
Mira, 101
Mirpur (Azad Kashmir), 57
Mirral, Professor, 118
Misgar, 188, 194
Misra, 58; as Director of Institute of Development Studies University of Mysore, 58
Mithchell's fruit farm, 261
Model Farmers, 33, 39, 294, 336, 339
Mohallah, 182
Mohammad, Allama Ghulam, 172
Mohammad, Fida, 19
Mohammad, Ghulam (mountaineer), 197
Mohammad, Ghulam, 189, 307
Mohammad, Noor, 267, 333, 340
Mohiuddin, Shahzada, 190, 317
Mohmand agency, 16
Mohsin (Director FIA), 163
Mohsin [Police Service of Pakistan officer], 115
Monaco, 396
Monitoring, evaluation and research (MER) section, 206, 211, 216, 224, 229-30, 250, 283, 311, 328
Montgomery, 358
Moradabad Government Intermediate College, 8
Moradabad, 5, 8-9; Municipality, 5
Morkhun, 311
Motoyama, 72

Mozzam, 152
Mughals, 191
Mulaqat (open meeting) days, 20
Mulk, Masood ul, 199, 203; as CEO SRSC, 371
Mulk, Shamsul, 376, 378
Multan, 361-2
Munir, DMLA Brig., 272
Murad, Gul, 294
Murali, Mr, 400
Musharraf, Pervez, 198, 364
Muslim League, 13, 15-6, 19
Muslim Patti, 5
Muslim, The, 153
Muslims, 49, 90; Sri Lankan, 88-9, 115; Tamils, 101
Mustafa, Col., 195
Mustafa, Ghulam, 294
Mutahir (SO), 186
Muto, 68
Muzaffar, Rubab, 325
Myanmar, 375
MYK, 301
Mysterious Mr Khan of *Newsweek*, The, 153

N

NAB, 378
Nagamine, Haruo, 44, 47-9, 50, 65, 68-9, 70-4, 76, 78, 166
Nagamine, Mrs, 50
Nagar, 173, 188, 201, 226, 267, 290
Nagoya Plaza Hotel, 42-3
Nagoya University, 69, 70, 74, 76; Hashigayama campus, 70-1; School of Economics, 70-4; Toyota auditorium, 71; International Residence, 70, 72-4, 77
Nagoya, 41-8, 52-3, 56-7, 59, 61, 63, 66-7, 69, 70, 74-5, 77, 85, 110, 143, 146, 166; train station, 59; botanical gardens, 45-6; Festival, 52; shrine, 46; underground (subway), 44-5; Kimono Girl, 52
Naib-Tehsildar (assistant revenue officer), 27
Naik, Ejaz, 20-1, 164-6, 211; as Secretary General of Economic Affairs Division, 189-190, 199, 204

Naini Tal, 107
Naltar, 292
Nandasiri, 95
Nanga Parbat, 162, 167, 179, 188
NAP-PPP alliance, 19
Naqvi, Prof, 75
Naqvi, Reyaz, 178
Naqvi, M.H. (AKRSP Programme Specialist), 182
Narita International Airport, 41-2, 63-4, 70
Naseem, Commander A.A., 373-4, 376
Naseer, 90
Nashad, 172; as Chairman Baltistan District Council, 190
Nasim (Pakistan Embassy), 65
Nasir, Khalida, 325, 328; WID Programme Officer, 326
Nathiagali, 104
National and Grindlays Bank, 98
National Assembly, 16, 20, 36, 389
National Awami Party (NAP), 19, 163
National Employment Guarantee Scheme, 407
National Planning Agency (Maldives), 134
National Project Coordinator (NPC), 384-5, 400
National Rural Support Programme (NRSP), 37, 175, 203, 242, 358-60, 363, 371-5, 376-7, 380-2, 385, 395, 397, 400; endowment fund, 37, 359-60, 371, 373-4, 376; Board of Directors, 360, 373-5, 376; staff, 373, 375, 376; government action against, 373-5, 376; agreement with WAPDA, 377
National Steering Committee, 110
Nationalization, 105, 115
Natural Resource Management (NRM), 182, 201, 204, 206, 211
Nature (newly broken land) Rules of Government, 200
Nawarelliya hill station, 108, 114-5
NAWO model, 233, 287, 293, 318-9
Naz, J.P., 203, 317
Nazrab, Deputy Superintendent of Police, 183; awarded *Tamgha-e-Shujaat*, 183
NBC TV, 128

Nelliyagama, 88-9, 90; mosque committee, 90
Nepal Planning Commission, 384
Nepal, 143, 261, 334, 380, 383-5, 386
Nepal, Prime Minister of, 154
Nepalese development officers, 135
Netherland, 118, 204; Ambassador of, 195, 238
Nethersole, Mr, 8
New Delhi, 46, 73, 135, 152, 351, 413
New Plaza Hotel, 42-3, 70
New York, 134, 136, 139, 142, 147, 149, 150-5, 167, 383
Newsweek, 84, 109, 152
NGO(s), 36, 164-5, 199, 201, 204, 221, 253-4, 264-5, 333-4, 341, 362, 363, 375, 376-8, 387, 400-1; Dutch, 370
Niaz, Kamran, 114
Nicky, 104
Nigerian, 82
Nilt Paeen, 269
Nilt, 269, 290
Nilufer, 54
NIPA, 335
Nishimizu, Meiko, 379
Nishtar, Jamil, 371
Nizar (car driver), 317
Noaga power station, 107
Nochiyagama (H5), 151
Nomal, 292, 293
Nomani, Allama Shibli, 8
Non-agricultural occupation, 217
Non-Ismaili, 190, 201, 247, 275, 286, 305
Non-Muslims, 247
Non-pesticide management (NPM), 409
Non-SAPAP Mandals, 408
Non-SAPAP SHGs, 409
Noonu Atoll, 384
NORAGRIC, 204
Noreen (pioneer), 326
North American Agricultural Development Model, 208
North American capitalist model, 221
North West Frontier Province, 89, 111, 194, 244 *see also* NWFP
Northern Areas (NAs), 10, 159, 161-2, 167-9, 173-5, 181, 183, 185-6, 189, 194-5, 200-2, 203, 205, 212, 213, 216, 221, 240, 247, 255, 257, 268, 270, 273,

275, 278, 282, 286, 291, 299, 302, 314, 323, 328, 347, 357-60, 362, 363, 369, 371, 376, 385, 390, 411; post-feudal enclave, 257
Northern Areas Administration, 188-9, 239, 272, 273, 318, 390
Northern Areas Council (NAC), 188, 190, 200, 227, 265, 274, 315, 318-21
Northern Areas Public Works Department, 185
Northern Areas PWD, 191, 194, 197, 270
Northern Areas Transport Company (NATCO), 184-5
Norway, 146, 203
Norwegian Agency for Development (NORAD), 127, 152, 204
Norwegian, 98, 118-9, 204
Note for the Record (NFR), 196, 395
NOVIB (Dutch NGO), 370
Numberdar, 301-2
Nursery development, 301, 303, 342
Nuwara Eliya, 384
NWFP, Chief Minister of, 163
NWFP, Governor of, 23, 350
NWFP, 10-2, 16, 18, 24, 26, 89, 163, 165, 186, 265, 323, 347, 355, 369-72, 377, 395

O

Odille, 118
Ohara temples, 57
Ohio State University, 75
Okada, Hirako, 49, 68
Orangi Pilot Project (OPP), 142, 154, 160, 237, 340, 356-9, 361-2, 363-4, 373
Orchards, 200, 209, 217, 310, 315, 317, 322, 327, 342; fruits 280; Almonds, 327; California apples, 201; cherries, 201; orange, 83; Walnuts, 327
Orvakal Mahila Mandal Samakhaya, 405-6
Osada, Professor, 76
Osaka University, 74
Osaka, 48, 54, 82
Ottawa, 203
Overseas Development Agency (ODA), 150, 204
Overseas Development Institute (ODI), 37-8; research, 37

Overseas Development Minister, 117 *see also* Hart, Dame Judith
Owens, Edgar, 354
Oxfam, 172, 194, 204
Oya, 49, 66, 68; Research Associate, 59

P

Paddy cultivation, 85, 87, 89, 96, 152
Paddy Lands Act 1958, 99
Paire, Dr, 130
PAK-81, 306, 322
Pak-German Project, 382
Pakistan Academy for Rural Development (PARD), 12, 18, 23-4, 26-9, 33, 118, 161, 163-4, 182, 185-6, 206, 335, 352, 350-3; researchers, 24-6, 28, 30, 34
Pakistan Air Force, 176
Pakistan army, 180, 189
Pakistan Automobile Corporation, 361
Pakistan Day, 19
Pakistan Embassy (Japan), 42
Pakistan Foreign Service (PFS), 154, 185, 371
Pakistan Forum, 397
Pakistan Institute of Medical Sciences (PIMS), 177
Pakistan International Airline (PIA), 70, 177, 316, 358, 371
Pakistan Planning Commission, 43, 70, 379, 389, 391-3
Pakistan Poverty Alleviation Fund (PPAF), 371, 375, 379-80, 393-4, 396-7, 399
Pakistan Tourism Development Corporation (PTDC) Motel, 167, 181, 316
Pakistan, President of, 15-6, 183, 271-2, 273
Pakistan, Prime Minister of (PM), 24, 37, 69, 70, 163-5, 175, 267, 334, 362, 370-5, 380, 392-8, 399
Pakistan, 9, 10, 13, 21, 33, 35, 37-8, 45, 47, 52, 56-8, 60, 62-3, 66, 68, 71, 74-7, 81, 86, 88-9, 94-5, 97, 101, 104, 107, 109, 111, 117, 120, 129, 132, 134, 153-4, 159, 160-1, 164, 166-7, 186, 194, 202, 203, 207-9, 213, 219, 238-40, 242, 245, 248, 260, 265, 282, 351, 354, 356-7, 359, 362, 363-6, 379-80, 383-5, 386, 396, 398, 400, 411-12;

nuclear programme, 204, 379; law, 247; Missions, 185
Pakistani(s), 44, 52, 54, 104, 115, 161, 213, 254, 257, 384, 411; golf team, 123
Pali (language), 358
Palpulla, 95
Pamir Steppes, 187
Pan (Canadian), 157-8
Panchayat Raj, 300, 401-2, 405
Panditratne, Mr, 90-1, 137, 140-1, 159
Parahera, 92
Paris, 123, 175
Parliament, House of (Sri Lanka), 153
Participatory Development through Social Mobilization, 391
Participatory Development, 391
Partner organizations (POs), 379
Pasha, Hafiz, 379
Pashto, 12
Passu, 184, 188, 197, 318, 328
Passu-Shimshal link road, 318
Pasture land, 209, 219, 310, 317, 332, 335, 337-8; development, 306, 345
Pathan, 331
Patrick, Dr Walter, 125
Pattan valley, 162
Patwari, 18, 23n.3
Pax Britannica, 25, 350
Payne, Dr, 122
PC-1, 380, 390-2, 398
Pearl Harbour, 55
Pears, Ron, 238
Peerzada, Hafeez, 22
Peerzada, PSO General, 21
Peking, 63
Penguins, 46
People's Works Programme (PWP), 31, 267-8, 370; ADG of, 268-70; projects, 269
Per capita income, 214, 240
Peradeniya University, 107, 130
Perahera, 112
Perera, Austin, 132
Perera, Dr, 125
Personal Staff Officer (PSO), 21
Peshawar, 10, 12, 16, 18-9, 20-1, 23-4, 41, 53, 58, 89, 118, 134, 154, 161-4, 176, 178, 244, 335, 352, 354, 356, 390; subdivision, 25-6; cantonment area, 20
Pesh-Imam (religious leader), 32, 90, 190-1, 339; as compounder, 33
Pesticides/insecticides, 28, 301, 303
Phander Valley, 174, 182, 183, 188, 296
Pharia, 5
Philippines, 49, 61, 264; President of, 371
Phiti (bread), 188
Physical capital, 217-18
Physical infrastructure, 258, 309, 311, 335, 379
PIDE, 75
Pig-keeping, 332
Pingkot GVM, 343
Pirith (religious ceremony, 121
Pissan, 269
Pitambar, 143
Plan Implementation (Sri Lanka), Ministry of, 103, 107-9, 114, 131, 135
Planning and Finance (Sri Lanka), Ministry of, 120
Planning Division, 347, 380
Plant protection/production specialist (PPS), 280, 297, 306, 311, 318, 330, 336
Plouride, Sonia, 259-60
PM Secretariat, 393, 395
Poe, Ms, 314
Polgolla, 107
Police department, 25, 27, 35-6, 403
Pollunurwa, 97
Ponthagunta, Dr Subrahmanyam, 386
Population, 25-6, 172, 217, 221, 278, 315, 319, 337; Daudzai, 32; Gilgit, 344
Portuguese, 89
Post-Project Survey, 228-9
Pournik, Mohammad, 386
Poverty alleviation/reduction, 37, 81, 94, 172, 213, 216, 287, 291, 302, 320, 333, 357, 359, 374, 380, 395, 400-2, 406, 411-12
Poverty Commission, 383-5
Poverty Reduction Strategy Paper (PRSP), 37, 398
Poverty Reduction through Social Mobilization (supplement), 390
Poyaday (the full moon day), 92
PPP, 22; government, 21

Pradillo, Dr, 122
Pramukh, 344
Prasad, Manohar (MP), 400
Prawvak Chitral, 199
Preble, Elizabeth, 142
Preegeeta Mahila Mandal Samakhya, 409
Premadasa, 383
President's Primary Healthcare Initiative, 381
Presidential Elections 1964-65, 15-7
Pressler Amendment, 370
Presswood, John, 125
Prime Minister's Livestock Programme, 382
Princeton University, 204
Productive Physical Infrastructure (PPI), 191, 193, 199-202, 211, 215-16, 230, 233, 235-6, 238, 245-7, 249-51, 255, 258-61, 269, 272, 276, 278-9, 283, 296, 305-6, 308, 320-22, 326-7, 332, 343, 345
Programme Economist (AKRSP), 179, 228-9, 279
Programme Planning meetings (PPMs), 186, 270
Programme Senior Agriculturist, 227, 246, 281
Programme Senior Engineer, 227, 246, 248
Programme Training Specialist, 227, 280, 303, 311
Progressive Farmers, 39
Project committees (village organizations), 31
Proposal for a Rural Development Programme in the Northern Areas of Pakistan, 213
Provincial Development Working Party (PDWP), 380
PTDC Hotel Falettis, 182
Public sector (Japan), 67
Public sector (Pakistan), 67
Public Works Department (Irrigation Branch), 28
Punjab Rural Support Programme (PRSP), 380-2, 394; endowment fund, 380; Board of Directors, 394
Punjab University, 164
Punjab, 11, 15-6, 260, 274, 340, 347, 355, 363, 377, 380-1; cotton belt of, 381

Punjab, Chief Minister of, 233-5, 260, 352, 355, 372, 380
Punyal valley, 188, 191, 194, 226
Purana (old) villages, 89
Pushto language, 317
PWD (Sri Lanka), 91
PWD Rest House, 180, 187, 315

Q

Qamar, Abdul (*Tehsildar*), 301
Qayyum, Captain Abdul, 189
Qayyum, Colonel, 18
Qayyum, Sardar Abdul, 372
Qorqondas water channel, 289
Quaid-e-Azam University, 166; Public Administration course, 166
Quandt, Anna, 127
Quasba, 13; thana, 352
Quddus, 143
Quetta, 390; Stoves, 63
Quilt-making, 326, 329
Quran, 350
Qureshi, Fazlullah, 380, 382
Qureshi, Ijaz, 266-7
Qureshi, Ismail, 379, 381

R

Rabi (winter crop), 30, 87
Radhakrishnan, 385
Radhakrishnan, B., 400
Radio Gilgit, 238
Radio Sri Lanka, 145
Radosavich, Dr, 122
Rahbat, 286, 288-9
Rahim Yar Khan (RYK), 381
Rahim, Ejaz, 317, 378, 392-3, 397
Rahman, Badiur, 384
Rahman, Dr Anisur, 201
Raiffeisen model, 221
Raiffesen's principles, 30
Raja (ruler), 337
Rajendran, Mrs Marty, 98, 103, 143
Raju, K., 385, 411
Ram, Mrs, 54
Rama, Miss, 45-6
Ramesh, Jairam, 413
Rangareddy District, 410
Range management, 337

INDEX

Rao, C.S., 401
Rao, Narsimha, 383
Rasheed, Abdulla, 385
Rasmussen, Steve, 201
Rasool, Ghulam, 289
Rauf, 75, 186, 375
Rauf, Masoodur, 162, 369
Rawalpindi, 164, 273, 280, 356
Raza, Ghulam, 342
Raza, Rini, 385
Raziq, Abdul, 163
Reading University, 37
Reading, 355
Red Fort, 351
Red Horse Club, 52
Reddy, Dr Rajsekhar, 411
Regional Bureau for Asia and the Pacific (RBAP), 383
Rehman, Ataur, 13
Rehman, Fazlur, 177-8
Rehman, Parveen, 357
Rehman, Saifur, 278
Renala Khurd, 394
Report of the Experts Group, The, 213
Resident Project Manager (RPM) (Mahaweli Project), 86-8, 91, 93-6, 100, 106, 108, 111, 113, 117-8, 121, 124-6, 128-9, 132-3, 135, 137-9, 140-2, 144-5, 151, 158-9
Reswelira, 97
Revenue, Department of, 25, 27, 35-6, 271; officer, 378
Ritigala, 135
Riza, Iqbal, 154
Rock Temple, 92
Role of SOs, The (note), 260
Romanian, 77
Roohi (daughter), 47, 64, 123, 149
Rose, Jun, 155
Rose, Mrs Jun, 155
Roy, Dr Ashwani Kumar, 77
Royal Institute of Public Administration, 17
Rupert, 98, 103
Rural Academy (Comilla project), 39
Rural areas, 24, 26, 29, 220, 266, 304, 323, 347; of Japan, 78
Rural cadres, 33-5, 39, 40, 223; model farmers, 33, 39; co-operative managers, 33; Imam-compounders, 33; training of, 40
Rural Development Manual, 284
Rural Development Projects, 193, 214, 240, 243, 253, 284-6, 347, 355, 358
Rural Development, Rural Water Supply and Employment Generation, Minister of (India), 411-12
Rural development, 24, 29, 41, 75, 175, 209, 212, 213, 220-22, 223, 239, 241-2, 243, 250, 253-4, 260, 262, 264, 300, 314, 355, 358-9, 389, 401
Rural population, 24, 26-9, 33-4, 37-8, 329
Rural Support Programmes (RSPs), 203, 265, 362, 363, 375, 377, 379-81, 385, 386-7, 392-3, 398; movement, 207
Rural Support Programmes Network (RSPN), 186, 203-4, 382, 389, 397-8, 409
Rural works programme, 339
Rural Works Resthouse, 180-1
Rushbrook, Professor, 3
Russia, 55, 340; Counsellor, 54-5; Embassy, 55
Russians, 55, 114, 163-4
Rust, Hammond, 111
Ryoko, 73

S

Saadia, 395
Saaltink, Mr, 124, 138, 157
SAARC Commission for the Alleviation of Poverty, 242, 334
SAARC summit (Dhaka), 37, 383
SAARC, 36, 242, 383, 400
Sadik, Ahmad (Principal Secretary), 374
Sadiq, Dr (Mrs) Nafis, 117
Sadiq, Mohammad, 206
Saeed, Ghulam, 322
Sah, Dr Jaysingh, 384
Sahib, Dr Khan, 11
Sahiwal, 394
Saidu Sharif, 111
Saif, 195
Sakae shopping centre, 45-6, 52, 66, 71
Salahuddin, Sadiqa, 335
Salam, Prof, 74
Saleem, Mohammad, 271

Saleh, Mrs Pervez, 375; as Advisor on Social Sector NRSP, 375
Salim (car driver), 317
Salinity, 27, 30
Salter, Guy, 308
Samarsinghe, 157
Sanskrit, 99
SAPAP Mandals, 408
Sarah (granddaughter), 64, 149
Sardar Garhi, 350
Sarghuz, 294
Sarhad Rural Support Corporation (SRSC), 242, 265, 370-1, 400
Sarhad Rural Support Programme (SRSP), 371, 380, 395; Board of Directors, 371
Sarhad Rural Support Programme, 203
Sarhad, 369 see also NWFP
Sarial thana, 352
Sarpanch, 402, 406
Sartaj (local girl), 326
Sartaj (SO), 186
Sarwar, Subedar Major, 14; awarded *Sitara-e-Jurat*, 15
Satpara Dam, 347
Savings programme, 30-1, 40, 193, 196, 200, 209, 216, 222, 232, 236, 246, 252, 257, 259, 261, 269, 274, 278-9, 283, 294, 299-300, 312, 314, 325-6, 329-30, 343-4, 346, 357, 406, 410; equity capital, 246, 279, 294, 343, 346
Scala, 123
School of Social Work, 130, 138, 141, 144
School, 26, 267-9, 272, 330; Teachers, 330, 339; Primary school teachers, 186
Scot, 97
Scudder, Ted, 145, 150
Seager, Andrew, 124-5
Seaweeds, 65
Second World War, 57
Seed grower's association, 237
Seeds, 29, 218, 293, 301, 303, 322; treatment, 262; selection, 262
Seldhi, 315
Self Help Group (SHG), 402-4, 405-10, 412; Council members, 403, 409; weekly meetings, 409
Self-help, 29, 247, 312, 314, 323

Selwyn College, 86, 96
Seminar on Community Participation: Expertise of Mr Khan, 156
Sena, 98, 103
Senewaratne, Brian, 107
Serano, Lea, 49
Services and General Administration Department, 17
Seto, 66
Shabu shabu, 44, 57, 60, 65
Shafa, Mohammad, 289
Shafi, Brigadier, 176
Shah, Agha Syed Mohammad Ali, 320-1
Shah, Akhtar Hussain, 295
Shah, Feroz, 182, 235, 292, 302, 303, 370; as AKRSP Programme Specialist, 182
Shah, Jamil Haider, 167, 172, 184, 189
Shah, Kirtee, 335
Shah, Mutabiat, 185, 307
Shah, Qaim Ali, 370
Shah, S. Yahya, 287-90
Shah, Sher, 301
Shah, Syed Abbad, 292
Shah, Syed Afsar Ali, 295
Shah, Syed Mutahir (DPO), 209, 235, 286-9, 323
Shah, Syed Qasim, 273
Shah, Syed Taqi, 236
Shah, Tawallud, 182, 186, 284-5, 290-1
Shahabuddin, Sultan, 346
Shaheem, 385
Shahibagh, 19
Shahjehan, Mughal Emperor, 4
Shahjehanpur, 4
Shahtote, 195, 199, 341
Shakespeare, 9, 350, 362
Shakoor, 186
Shamaran, 296
Shams, 377
Shams, Khalid (of Bangladesh), 264
Shandur lake, 296
Shandur Pass, 182
Shandur Polo Ground, 370
Sharda, 123
Sharif, Admiral, 55
Sharif, Nawaz, 175, 371
Sharif, Shahbaz, 380
Sharkoi channels, 296
Sharot channels, 296
Shaw, Isobel, 327-8

INDEX

Shaw, Robert d'Arcy, 160, 167, 174, 179, 182, 203, 205-6, 259-60, 265-7, 357, 376
Sheikh, Dr Akram, 393, 395
Sheikh, Dr Sulaiman, 382
Shelley (daughter), 17, 64, 91, 110, 114-5, 118, 149, 175, 204
Shelley, 9
Sher, Alam, 269
Sher, Molvi Gul, 190
Sherazi, 178
Sherpao, Aftab, 370
Sherpao, Hayat Muhammad Khan, 19, 23, 165, 370
Sherqilla, 237, 325
Shia, 172, 188-190, 197
Shia-Ismaili dispute, 188
Shigar river, 316
Shigar valley, 194, 238, 315-6
Shikarpur, 180
Shimshal road project, 276, 318-20 *see also* Passu-Shimshal link road
Shimshal valley, 194, 280, 318, 320
Shimshalis, 319-20
Shina (language), 194, 299
Shinkansen (Japanese bullet train), 48, 54, 64; Nagoya-Tokyo distance, 48
Shinto shrines, 55
Shintu (religion), 57; temples, 57
Shipusan valley, 199
Shipushan irrigation channel, 304
Shirote-Shikote dispute, 271
Shishkat, 184
Shoaib (Finance Minister of Pakistan), 117
Shutindas, 286, 290-1
Siachin front, 372
Siddiqi, Bilal, 179
Siddiqi, Dr Kamal, 384
Siddiqi, Dr Tariq, 129, 145, 156, 161-5, 352, 361
Siddiqi, Gulshan, 321-2
Siddiqi, Najma, 325, 328-9, 374; as GM NRSP, 373; resignation, 374, 376
Siddiqi, Nigar, 179
Siddiqi, Tariq (Additional Secretary, O&M Division), 177-9
Siddiqi, Tasneem, 357, 382
Sigriya fortress, 104-5
Sigriya Rock, 115
Sikandarabad, 290
Sikh kingdom, 351
Sildhi irrigation channel, 233
Sildhi, 232
Silk route, 194
Simon Fraser University, 207
Sindh Rural Support Organization (SRSO), 382; endowment fund, 382; Board of Directors, 381-2; headquarter at Sukkur, 382
Sindh, 22, 180, 347, 355, 382
Sindh, Chief Minister of, 370
Sindhis, 97, 163
Sindhudesh Movement, 164, 355
Singal, 301
Singaporian, 74
Singh, Brahm Pal, 77
Singh, Dr (UNDP Dacca), 125
Singh, Maharaja Ranjeet, 351
Sinhala New Year, 101, 106, 136
Sinhalese, 88-9, 94, 96, 99, 101, 115, 358
Sino-Japanese treaty, 55
Siphon irrigation project, 199
Sirajganj, 120
Sitalpati type, 49
Sitara-e-Jurat, 15
Sitara-i-Imtiaz, 242
Sivananam, Mr, 124, 129
Skardu, 194, 232, 316; airport, 316
Skill development, 27-8, 31, 33-4, 213, 221-2, 227-8, 241, 246, 283, 313, 343, 357
Small Farmer Development Programme (SFDP), 334
Small farmers development, 211; administrative Infrastructure, 211, 221; Productive Physical Infrastructure (PPI); socio-economic infrastructure, 211
Small industries, Department of, 35
Smithsonian Foundation, 57
Snellen, Richard, 386
Soap-making, 326
Sober, Minister, 384
Social Action Programme (SAP), 70, 372
Social capital, 200, 405
Social Mobilization and Experimentation Learning Centre (SMELC), 405
Social Mobilization Funds, 394

Social Mobilization Project (PPAF), 382, 390, 393, 395, 398-9; funding from World Bank, 392, 397
Social mobilization, 162, 214, 371, 380-1, 383-4, 389, 391, 395, 396-9, 404, 405, 409, 411
Social Organization Units (SOUs), 186, 212, 227-8, 242, 246-7, 268-9, 283, 294, 344, 346
Social organizers (SOs), 186, 193, 196, 200, 206, 227, 232, 247, 249, 251, 254, 260-2, 282, 283-4, 294-5, 300, 310-11, 329, 333, 336, 338, 340, 342, 343, 346, 376, 406
Social Welfare Institution, 291
Social welfare, Department of, 12, 18, 20, 163; programmes, 223
Socialism, 81, 332
Socialist model, 208, 221, 245, 340
Society for Elimination of Rural Poverty (SERP), 386, 404, 405, 411-12
Socio-economic infrastructure (SEI), 36-7, 211, 217
Sogreah (French firm), 103-4
Soleman, Dr Ali, 134
Sonikot Gilgit, 199, 284, 285, 288-9
Soomro, Mohammad Mian, 382
SORADEP (French-aided), 39
South Asia Poverty Alleviation Programme (SAPAP), 175, 375, 379-80, 384-5, 386, 396, 402, 404, 405-6, 408-9, 411
South Asia, 37, 82, 143, 175, 359, 383, 386, 401, 404, 412
South India, 101
South Indian, 46
South Korea, 140, 142, 166, 264; government of, 264
South Korean, 58
Special Rural Development Programme (Kenya), 38
Spielman, Mr, 341
Spoelberch, Bill, 174, 203, 318
Sponeck, Von, 384, 401
Sri Lanka Freedom Party, 86
Sri Lanka Mahila Samity, 100
Sri Lanka, Prime Minister of, 383
Sri Lanka, 15, 47, 49, 68, 84-5, 87, 91, 93-7, 101, 104-7, 109, 110-2, 114, 119, 120, 122, 125, 131, 135, 143, 149, 151-6, 159, 160, 177-8, 181, 206, 245, 264, 356-8, 360, 383-5; population of, 86, 89
Sri Lankan rupees, 103
Sri Lankans, 86, 88-9, 93-5, 98, 103, 113, 130, 154-5, 160n.1; MPs, 120, 123
Srikul Lake, 187
Srinivas, D., 411
Standard Bank, 20
Staples, Rocky, 265, 369
State Corporation (Sri Lanka), 115
State Plantation Corporation, 114
Steni, Dr Herman, 155
Stuhrenburg, Michael, 330
Subakurtama (alias Subama), 402-3
Subhasingha, Dr, 126
Subsidiary loan agreement (SLA), 399
Sudarshan, 56
Suhrawardy, Huseyn Shaheed, 12
Sukiyaki, 65
Sukkur, 382
Sulaiman, 186
Sultan, Major Khalid (nephew), 372
Sultan, Marine Captain Mahmood (cousin), 6
Sultan, Marine Captain Sohail (brother), 3, 6, 372
Sultan, Rafat (uncle), 3
Sultan, Shoukat (uncle), 6
Sultan, Tariq, 380
Sunni, 173, 188, 190-1
Supra-VO bodies, 339
Sussex Institute of Development Studies, 141
Sust Channel tunnel, 189, 198
Sust, 198
Sustainable development, 376, 378
Suwan, Governor of, 143
Suzuki, Kanako, 71
Suzukisan, 56
Swat, 10-1, 111, 119, 317
Swat, Wali of, 10, 111
Sweden, 103
Swiss, 81
Switzerland, 80, 171, 275, 323; government, 149
Syangja District, 384
Sylhet, 14, 143

INDEX

T

Tableeghi Jamaat, 305
Tahir, Pervez, 397-8
Taiwan, 244, 266, 358, 361; government of, 264
Tajikistan, 186, 203
Tajimi, 67
Takayama, 68
Talagang Tehsil, 397
Taluka, 36
Tambutegama, RPM, 129
Tambuttegama areas, 131; H4 area, 151
Tamer-e-Watan programme, 373
Tamil New Year, 101
Tamils, 88-9, 101, 114
Tangir, 191
Tank irrigation system (Sri Lanka), 89
Tannekoon, 96
Tarbela lake, 89
Tareen, Jahangir, 364, 381, 394
Tareen, Shaukat, 381
Tariq, 123
Tarnab Farm, 335
Taunton, 112
Tayyab, Mian, 373
TB, 405
Teak forest, 85
Tehsil (subdivision) level, 25-6, 36, 227, 339, 342, 351-2, 355; headquarters, 27
Tehsildar, 301-2
Telecommunications system (Japan), 48
Temuri, Z.A., 273
Teramura, 68
Terms of Partnership (AKRSP), 222, 227-8, 258-9, 268, 274, 294, 296, 299, 307, 325, 329, 343, 387
Terms of Reference (ToR), 384
Tetlay, Khalil, 203
Thailand, 143, 335
Thakot bridge, 317
Thaley Bodalus channel, 288
Thana Irrigation Programme, 209, 264
Thana level organization, 25-6, 35-6, 38, 40
Thana(s) (Police station), 25-6, 35-6, 38, 40, 161, 339, 352, 369; jurisdiction, 26-7, 35; as a symbol of development, 26

Thar desert, 207
Thoa Muhram Khan Union Council, 397
Thoriyali GVM, 343
Tishote-Fikar link road, 267
Tokai Bank, 52
Tokaya, Ms, 78, 80
Tokyo Hilton, 64
Tokyo tower, 54
Tokyo University, 45, 74
Tokyo, 42, 54-5, 63-5, 70, 73
Tolstoy, 83
Tong Dass, 269
Tongdas, 290
Tono Dairy Farm Cooperative Federation, 67
Torboto Das, 286, 289
Torie, 68
Toronto, 203, 263
Toyota company, 44
Tractors, 116-7, 173, 218, 301, 332
Trade Training Development Centre, 410
Training and Supervision, 228
Training Research and Evaluation Committee, 88
Trial and error approach, 243, 251, 253
Tribal areas, 89, 275
Truth About Mahaweli, The, 126
Tse, Hsan Sing, 258-60
Tucker, S.P. (SPT), 400
Tufail House, 15
Tufail Memorial Football Tournament, 15
Tufail Memorial Health Dispensary, 15
Tufail, Major Mohammad, 14-5; awarded *Nishan-e-Haider*, 15; commandant of Scouts, 15
Tulti, 320
Turner Foundation, 405
Tutsumi, 68
Tweeten, Dr, 75

U

UC Chalt, 289-90
UC Sikandarabad, 290
UK, 17, 65, 88, 117-8, 203-4, 278, 327; Labour Government, 117
Ulema, 321
Ullmann, Liv, 145-6
Umemoto, Steve, 142-3
UN Day, 122

UN Social Development Institute, 130
UNCRD Project MPCRD, 166
Undong, Samaual, 264
UNDP Colombo, 127
UNDP Dhaka, 42, 125
UNDP, 103, 122, 144, 174-5, 186, 359, 375, 379, 382, 384-5, 386, 401-2, 404, 405, 409, 411; Administrative Officer, 45; Resident Representative (RRs), 383-5, 386, 401; Regional Programmes, 385, 400; Programme Officer, 400
UNDP/FAO Project, 202
UNFPA (population people), 103, 108, 117, 129, 135, 139, 143
UNICEF Health Programme (Sri Lanka), 98
UNICEF Korea, 142
UNICEF News Bulletin, 153
UNICEF NY headquarters, 134, 136, 139, 142, 147, 149, 150, 160; Asia Section, 156
UNICEF Project, 143, 147
UNICEF Sri Lanka, 84, 96-7, 110, 114, 130, 143, 166; Programme Officers, 98, 103, 139; Assistant Programme Officers, 98, 103; water section (drinking water), 98; Finance section, 98
UNICEF, 47, 74, 84, 110, 112, 115 117-9, 127-9, 131, 133-7, 139, 141-2, 144, 146, 147-9, 152-6, 158-9, 160, 166-7, 174, 178, 186, 203, 206, 266, 287, 357, 384; Annual Report, 152
Union Council (UC), 36, 190, 200, 227, 258, 265, 273-4, 295-6, 318, 376, 378, 390
Union Councillors, 315, 319
Union Government (India), 412
United Bank, 346
United National Party (Sri Lanka), 86
United Nations (UN), 104, 108, 111, 130-1, 156, 160, 174, 176, 178, 184, 356; staff system, 136
United Nations aid agencies, 109
United Nations Centre for Regional Development (UNCRD), 41-3, 45, 57-9, 61-3, 65, 68, 77, 84, 166; advisory council, 57-8; Expert Group meeting, 58-9, 61; New Year's staff party, 62; training course, 66

United States of America, 16, 41, 43, 46, 74-5, 82, 130, 146, 182, 207, 354, 364
University of Colombo, 118; Geography Department of, 118
University of London, 64, 123
University of Mysore, 58
University of Oxford, 113, 179
University of Peshawar, 118
UNOPS, 386
UNP (ruling party), 117
UP (Uttar Pradesh), 4, 39
Uppadhya, Shri Krishna, 383-4
Urbanization, 36, 209
Urdu, 5, 194, 249, 254, 284, 354
Uroos (woman pioneer), 326
US Senate Foreign Aid Sub-Committee, 116
USAID, 91, 106, 111, 122, 164, 265, 314, 369-70; water management farm, 116
Usman, Amir, 379
Utopia, 84
Uttarakhand, 261

V

Valleys in Transition (documentary), 206, 274-5, 370
Vancouver, 203
Vanessa, 104
Varma, Amarnath, 56
Vaseth, Bjorn, 98, 118-9
VDCs (Nepal), 385
Vegetable gardening, 322, 330, 342
Vehari district, 381
Venugopal, K.R., 383-4, 411
Vestring, Ambassador, 204
Vetch (a fodder), 281; trial plots, 306
Veterinary dispensary, 26
Vietnam, 77; government, 77
Vietnamese, 45-6, 54, 68, 76-7; trainee, 77; schools, 77
Vijayabharti, 406
Village accountants, 346
Village AID, 260
Village Development Programme (India), 244
Village Immersion Programme (VIP), 379
Village Level Worker (*Gram Sewak*), 39

Village Organizations (VOs), 31-3, 173-4, 186, 190-2, 193, 199-205, 205, 208-10, 212, 215-16, 220-22, 223-4, 228, 230, 233-6, 238, 243, 245-52, 253, 257-9, 261-2, 263, 265-9, 274, 276, 279-82, 283, 285, 293-4, 296, 298-9, 304-5, 307-9, 311-12, 313, 315, 317-9, 321-2, 323, 327, 329, 331-2, 333, 336-42, 343-8, 375, 388, 402-4, 405-8, 410; formation of, 246, 278, 283, 294, 299; office bearers, 249, 295, 305; *proforma*, 284, 305; classification of, 305-7; factors for poor, 306; their plans for development, 309-10

Village specialists, 311, 314, 330, 336, 338, 343

Vittachi, V. Tarzie, 109, 152-3, 155

VO Ahmedabad, 299

VO Aliabad, 307, 347; President of, 348

VO Brakchun, 235

VO Chappali, 294

VO Churo, 295

VO Fikar, 267-8

VO Gayul, 236

VO Hamaran, 199

VO Kashmal, 233

VO Khlang Khong, 236

VO Khuz Payeen, 295

VO Masoot, 341-2

VO Minapin, 269-70

VO Nilt Paeen, 269

VO Pari, 321

VO Passu, 197, 318

VO Payeen, 305-6

VO Sherqilla, 237

VO Shigar, 316

VO Sildhi, 232

VO Terru, 174

VOs Hunza, 307

VOs/WOs managers, 186, 192, 196, 236, 247, 275, 310, 338, 344, 346; meetings, 248; appointment, 332

VOs/WOs presidents, 186, 192, 196, 294-6, 338, 344

VOs/WOs weekly meetings, 30-1, 192, 196, 232, 249, 257, 283, 310, 325-6, 329

W

Wakhi (language), 194

Waki, Kunio, 156

Wales, 110

Wales, Prince of, 308 *see also* Charles, Prince

Wali, Husain, 75, 174, 182, 184-5, 187, 191, 194, 198-9, 203, 232, 233, 237, 261, 267, 271, 275, 281, 284, 294-5, 298-9, 305, 307-8, 316, 318, 320, 325, 327, 339-40, 346; as Project Engineer, 185

Wall, John, 392-4, 396-7

Waqar, Ahmad, 399

Warangal Circuit House, 409, 411

Warangal, 409; Collector of, 409

Washington, 145, 379

Watanabe, 74

Watanabe, Eimi, 74, 103, 109, 119, 120, 139, 384; as Programme officer Planning of UNICEF Colombo, 97-8;

Watanabe, Keiko, 74

Water and Power Development Authority (WAPDA), 35, 274, 376-8; briefing, 275; Chairman, 377-8

Water and Power, Ministry of, 378-9

Water channel, 279, 284-6, 288-9, 295-6, 306; Aliabad, 347-8

Water logging, 27, 30

Water management, 28, 111, 113, 122, 249, 347; Mahaweli Ganga Development Project, 106; British expert of, 109

Water supply development, 38, 282, 284, 291, 293, 326, 348

Watt, Mrs, 123

Weaving, 326

Weber, Prof., 125

Webster, Norman, 263

Weerakoddy, Mr, 140, 150-1

Weerasooriya, Dr Wikrama, 103-4, 114

Weerasooriya, Mr, 88, 103

Weerawardena, I.K., 130, 132, 141, 145, 147, 150

Welikela, Mr, 141-2, 150

Welshman, 98, 110

West Africa, 240

West Germany, 61

West Pakistan, 12, 15-6, 18, 352

West Pakistanis, 12
Whiteman, Peter, 281
Wickramaratne, Mr, 128-9, 130-1, 137
WID Programme Officer, 326
Wignarajah, Poona, 383
Wijemanne, Dr (Mrs) Hiranthi, 98, 103, 125, 144, 155
Wijenaike, Rohan, 121-2, 125-6, 129, 131, 132, 137, 139, 140, 142-3, 145, 147-9, 150-2, 155-7, 181
Wikramaratne, Mahe, 138, 141, 143-5, 148, 156-9
Wildlife Department, 201
Wilkinson, Mr, 340
Wilpattu National Park, 115
Wimaladharma, Mr, 133
Wimladharma, Kapila, 106, 108, 113-4, 122, 144-5
Windmill, 323
Wolfson College, 86, 96
Women in Development (WID) section, 185, 216, 240, 247, 283, 314, 321, 325-6, 331
Women Organization (WOs), 173, 186, 192, 193, 196-7, 200-1, 205, 212, 257, 325-31, 375, 388; Aliabad, 348
Women training programme, 328-31
Working Group on Rural Development and Devolution, 389-90; Report, 389
World Bank Evaluation Team, 198-9, 347
World Bank Operations Evaluation Department (OED), 205, 239, 347, 359
World Bank Report, 344
World Bank, 102, 106, 127-8, 133-4, 138, 150, 157, 184, 193, 199, 204-5, 209, 230, 239, 242, 253, 347, 363-4, 377-9, 383, 386, 390-93, 396-7, 399, 401, 404; Team, 123-5; Review Mission, 157-8; rural development projects, 193, 239, 240, 347
Wyne (CM), 372

Y

Yahya, Agha, 188-9
Yahya, President, 20
Yaks, 280, 296
Yala crop, 89, 93, 96, 99

Yamagashi (YG), 78-9, 80-4; corporate structure of, 83; village reception centre, 78; Academy, 82-3; workshop, 79
Yamagishi, Mr, 80
Yamagishisan's farm, 80
Yar, Ali, 186
Yar, Mohammad, 182, 186
Yasin Valley, 187-8, 194, 226, 280, 339
Yasmin (woman pioneer), 326
Yen, 41, 43-4, 56, 67
Yogo, 59, 66, 68; Agricultural and Rural Development expert, 59, 66
Younghusband, Francis, 187
Yugoslavia, 146, 361

Z

Zahid, 385
Zahira College mosque, 115
Zaidi, Ijlal Haider, 16, 18, 165, 178
Zaki, Mrs, 154
Zaman, Sultanuz, 56
Zamin, Brigadier, 382
Zamindari (land-based economy), 330
Zeeshan, 149
Zila Mahila Mandal Samakhya, 408